Prayer Book Parallels

ANGLICAN LITURGY IN AMERICA

Volume Two

Prayer Book Parallels

The public services of the Church arranged for comparative study

Paul V. Marshall

THE CHURCH HYMNAL CORPORATION, NEW YORK

Contents

The Type: An attempt has been made to match the CAPITALS, SMALL CAPITALS, *italics* and **bold** as used in the original editions of the Prayer Books. Word spacing and letterspacing were limited by the capabilities of the computer used.

Introduction

This volume brings to a close *Prayer Book Parallels,* the first part of *Anglican Liturgy in America.* In it the reader will find a good deal more and somewhat less than was promised in the early days of the project.

What is not delivered here is a reduction of the lectionary to tables. The patterns of development in this country, particularly the present-day shift to a two-year daily office lectionary and a three-year Eucharistic lectionary, combined with a recasting of the liturgical year and a wholly new approach to the Psalter, would have required an entire volume for meaningful presentation. Such a volume would have limited utility at best, and its pages would have been four-fifths blank paper.

On the other hand, this volume has gone beyond expectations in a number of ways. The reader will find that earlier sources and better texts for the ancient collects are supplied than were available to Brightman when *The English Rite* was prepared. Modern sources for the newer collects have also been located and presented here with their authors identified. Some collects can be seen to have textual sources not previously identified by commentators. Finally, the preparation of the Psalter has proven to be a fascinating study: the text itself, like its versification and visual presentation, has gone through more evolution than we sometimes suppose when we imagine that the Coverdale version continued unmodified until 1979.

Since the appearance of the first volume, readers have expressed curiosity as to how these volumes were produced since it was apparent to them that typesetting such a book would have put the per-copy cost at many times the price of the present edition. Another way had to be found if students were to have these volumes available for their work on the liturgy. Each of the double pages you see in these volumes represents a single page on the computer screen, using the side-by-side paragraph feature of Microsoft Word. Thus, while your compiler may not have written this book in the strictest sense, he most assuredly did type it. The typeface used here and in the parallels themselves is the very compact Goudy Old Style modified from outlines made for laser printers by the Bitstream Corporation. The long introduction to the first volume is set in an easier-on-the-eye font, named for and based on one designed by John Baskerville, the important 18th century Cambridge printer of Bibles and prayer books. Nelson Gruppo, designer of the 1979 prayer book, laid out the resulting legal size sheets into the deeper pages you encounter here.

From 1659 on, all such books as this have contained textual errors, and some mistakes have indeed been discovered in the first volume, and the blame is wholly mine. Readers' observations have been and remain most welcome in establishing a clean text. In preparing the second volume I have employed four rather than two proofreaders in the hopes of producing a more accurate work. I am grateful to Ms. Anna Williams for overseeing this part of the work and doing the lion's share of it herself. The historical study which will form the third volume of this series will also contain a list of corrigenda for *Prayer Book Parallels.*

Through a slip in the publication process, the first volume does not bear the dedication page that appeared in the page proofs. I thus extend the publisher's apologies and note in this more public space that *Prayer Book Parallels* is dedicated upon his retirement to my friend and great teacher, The Reverend Thomas Julian Talley. He taught me the preeminence of structural questions in the study of liturgy, and is in that and many other ways the progenitor of this work.

New Haven
Holy Cross Day, 1990

The Collects, Part One

The collects of the 1979 American book are presented here together with their sources and parallels. Readers who have access to Brightman's *The English Rite*, will note that familiar sources are worded or spelled differently here. This results from the fact that today much better editions exist of many texts. In addition, preference is here given to the oldest source for the collects when known, rather than intermediate developments of the texts, so the reader will occasionally find sources given that are not cited in Brightman or in the commentaries written on the 1928 and 1979 American books. This rule is departed from when a particular text in its evolved form had special influence on the English wording, or, more rarely, when a particular English translation of an ancient text was the basis for a prayer book collect.

Abbreviations.

The Book of Common Prayer in English and American editions is simply indicated by year: 1549, 1552, 1662 in England, and 1789, 1871, 1928, and 1979 in America. The editions from other national and regional bodies are indicated by the church and the year, e.g., Scottish 1637.

CSI. Church of South India, *The Book of Common Worship,* London and Madras, 1963.

Eng. 1928, The unsucessfully proposed book for England.

Gel. *Liber Sacramentorum Romanae Aeclesiae Ordinis Anni Circuli.* Vatican Codex Reginensis latinus 316. Edited by L. C. Mohlberg (Rome, 1968). The "Gelasian" Sacramentary.

Greg. *Le Sacramentaire Grégorien. Ses principales formes d'après les plus anciens manuscrits.* Edited by Jean Deschusses (Fribourg, 1971). The "Gregorian" Sacramentary. In addition, "**Greg. supp.**" indicates the supplemental material once thought to be the work of Alcuin, and now attributed to Benedict of Aniane.

The Collects of the Church Year

Sources	1662-1871	1892-1928

The First Sunday in Advent.

ALmightie God, geue vs grace, that we maye caste away the workes of darkenes, and put vpon vs the armour of light, now in the time of this mortal lyfe, (in the which thy sonne Iesus Christe came to visite vs in great humilitie) that in the last daye, when he shall come again in his gloryous maiestie, to iudge both the quicke and the dead: we maye ryse to the lyfe immortall, through him, who liueth and reigneth with thee and the holy gost, nowe and euer. Amen. [1549, The first Sonday in Aduente.]

ALMIGHTY God, give us grace that we may cast away the works of darkness, and put upon us the armour of light, now in the time of this mortal life, in which thy Son Jesus Christ came to visit us in great humility; that in the last day, when he shall come again in his glorious Majesty to judge both the quick and the dead,[1] we may rise to the life immortal, through him who liveth and reigneth with thee and the Holy Ghost, now and ever. *Amen.*

O LORD Jesus Christ, who at thy first coming didst send thy messenger to prepare thy way before thee: Grant that we, paying urgent heed to the message of repentance, may with hearts prepared await thy final coming to judge the world; who with the Father and the Holy Spirit ever livest and reignest, one God, world without end. **Amen.** [CSI, Second {Sunday} Before Christmas, Third in Advent.]

The Fourth Sunday in Advent.

Excita, domine, potenciam tuam et magna nobis uirtute succurre, ut per auxilium gloriae tuae quod nostra peccata praepediunt indulgenciae tuae propiciacionis acceleret: per. [Gel., 1121.]

O LORD, raise up, we pray thee, thy power, and come among us, and with great might succour us; that whereas, through our sins and wickedness, we are sore let and hindered in running the race that is set before us, thy bountiful grace and mercy may speedily help and deliver us; through Jesus Christ our Lord;[2] to whom, with thee and the Holy Ghost, be honour and glory, world without end. *Amen.*

Consciencias nostras, quaesumus, omnipotens deus, cotidie uisitando purifica, ut ueniente domino filio tuo paratam sibi in nobis inueniat mansionem: per. [Gel., 1127.]

[1]"quick and dead" [1662].

[2]until 1928, "through the satisfaction of thy Son our Lord; to whom," etc.

Miss. Goth. *Missale Gothicum* Edited by L. C. Mohlberg (Rome, 1961).

Sarum. *The Sarum Missale.* Edited by J. Wickham Legg (Oxford, 1916, repr., 1969).

Ver. *Sacramentarium Veronense.* Verona Capitular Library LXXXV[80]. Edited by L.C. Mohlberg (Rome, 1978). The "Leonine" Sacramentary.

1979-I	1979-II
First Sunday of Advent	**First Sunday of Advent**
Almighty God, give us grace that we may cast away the works of darkness, and put upon us the armor of light, now in the time of this mortal life in which thy Son Jesus Christ came to visit us in great humility; that in the last day, when he shall come again in his glorious majesty to judge both the quick and the dead, we may rise to the life immortal; through him who liveth and reigneth with thee and the Holy Ghost, one God, now and for ever. *Amen.*	Almighty God, give us grace to cast away the works of darkness, and put on the armor of light, now in the time of this mortal life in which your Son Jesus Christ came to visit us in great humility; that in the last day, when he shall come again in his glorious majesty to judge both the living and the dead, we may rise to the life immortal; through him who lives and reigns with you and the Holy Spirit, one God, now and for ever. *Amen.*
Second Sunday of Advent	**Second Sunday of Advent**
Merciful God, who sent thy messengers the prophets to preach repentance and prepare the way for our salvation: Give us grace to heed their warnings and forsake our sins, that we may greet with joy the coming of Jesus Christ our Redeemer; who liveth and reigneth with thee and the Holy Spirit, one God now and for ever. *Amen.*	Merciful God, who sent your messengers the prophets to preach repentance and prepare the way for our salvation: Give us grace to heed their warnings and forsake our sins, that we may greet with joy the coming of Jesus Christ our Redeemer; who lives and reigns with you and the Holy Spirit, one God, now and for ever. *Amen.*
Third Sunday of Advent	**Third Sunday of Advent**
Stir up thy power, O Lord, and with great might come among us; and, because we are sorely hindered by our sins, let thy bountiful grace and mercy speedily help and deliver us; through Jesus Christ our Lord, to whom, with thee and the Holy Ghost, be honor and glory, world without end. *Amen.*	Stir up your power, O Lord, and with great might come among us; and, because we are sorely hindered by our sins, let your bountiful grace and mercy speedily help and deliver us; through Jesus Christ our Lord, to whom, with you and the Holy Spirit, be honor and glory, now and for ever. *Amen.*
Fourth Sunday of Advent	**Fourth Sunday of Advent**
We beseech thee, Almighty God, to purify our consciences by thy daily visitation, that when thy Son our Lord cometh he may find in us a mansion prepared for himself; through the same Jesus Christ our Lord, who liveth and reigneth with thee in the unity of the Holy Spirit, one God, now and for ever. *Amen.*	Purify our conscience, Almighty God, by your daily visitation, that your Son Jesus Christ, at his coming, may find in us a mansion prepared for himself; who lives and reigns with you in the unity of the Holy Spirit, one God, now and for ever. *Amen.*

The Nativity of Our Lord, or the Birthday of Christ, Commonly called Christmas Day.

Deus, qui nos redempcionis nostrae annua expectacione laetificas, praesta, ut unigenitum filium tuum quem redemptorem laeti suscipimus, uenientem quoque iudicem securi uideamus: per. [Gel., 1156.]

GOd, which makest vs gladde with the yerely remembraunce of the birth of thy onely sonne Iesus Christe: graunt that as we ioyfully receiue him for our redemer, so we may with sure confidence beholde hym, when he shall come to be our iudge, who liueth and reigneth. &c. [1549, Christmas Day.][3]

O GOD, who makest us glad with the yearly remembrance of the birth of thine only Son Jesus Christ; Grant that as we joyfully receive him for our Redeemer, so we may with sure confidence behold him when he shall come to be our Judge, who liveth and reigneth with thee and the Holy Ghost, one God, world without end. *Amen.* [1928, Second Communion.]

Deus, qui hanc sacratissimam noctem ueri luminis fecisti inlustratione clariscere, da, quaesumus, ut cuius lucis mysterium in terra cognouimus, eius quoque gaudiis in caelo perfruamur: per. [Gel., 5.]

Omnipotens sempiterne deus, qui hunc diem per incarnationem uerbi tui et per partum beatae uirginis Mariae consecrasti, da populis tuis in hanc caelebritate iustitiae, ut et qui tua gratia sunt redempti tua adoptione sint filii: per dominum. [Gel., 17.]

ALMYGHTIE God, whiche haste geuen vs thy only begotten sonne to take our nature vpon him, and this daye to be borne of a pure virgin: Graunt that we being regenerate and made thy children by adopcion and grace, maye dayly be renued by thy holy spirite, through thesame[4] oure Lorde Iesus Christe, who lyueth and reigneth, &c. [1549 "At the seconde Communion"]

ALMIGHTY God, who hast given us thy only begotten Son to take our nature upon him, and as at this time to be born of a pure virgin;[5] Grant that we being regenerate, and made thy children by adoption and grace, may daily be renewed by thy Holy Spirit;[6] through the same our Lord Jesus Christ, who liveth and reigneth with thee and the same Spirit ever, one God, world without end. *Amen.*

The Second Sunday after Christmas Day.

Da quaesumus omnipotens deus, ut qui noua incarnatione uerbi tui luce perfundimur, hoc in nostro resplendeat opere quod per fidem fulget in mente. Per. [Greg., 42.]

ALMIGHTY God, who hast poured upon us the new light of thine incarnate Word; Grant that the same light enkindled in our hearts may shine

[3]The collect was dropped in 1552, and did not reappear until its use in the American book of 1928.

[4]*sic.*

[5]"Virgin" until 1832.

[6]"holy Spirit," until 1928.

1979-I

The Nativity of Our Lord: Christmas Day

O God, who makest us glad with the yearly remembrance of the birth of thy only Son Jesus Christ: Grant that as we joyfully receive him as for our Redeemer, so we may with sure confidence behold him when he shall come to be our Judge; who liveth and reigneth with thee and the Holy Ghost, one God, world without end. *Amen.*

or the following

O God, who hast caused this holy night to shine with the illumination of the true Light: Grant us, we beseech thee, that as we have known the mystery of that Light upon earth, so may we also perfectly enjoy him in heaven; where with thee and the Holy Spirit he liveth and reigneth, one God, in glory everlasting. *Amen.*

or this

Almighty God, who hast given us thy only-begotten Son to take our nature upon him, and as at this time to be born of a pure virgin: Grant that we, being regenerate and made thy children by adoption and grace, may daily be renewed by thy Holy Spirit; through the same our Lord Jesus Christ, who liveth and reigneth with thee and the same Spirit ever, one God, world without end. *Amen.*

First Sunday after Christmas Day

Almighty God, who hast poured upon us the new light of thine incarnate Word: Grant that the same light, enkindled in our hearts, may shine forth in our lives; through the same Jesus Christ our Lord, who liveth and reigneth with thee, in the unity of the Holy Spirit, one God, now and for ever. *Amen.*

1979-II

The Nativity of Our Lord: Christmas Day

O God, you make us glad by the yearly festival of the birth of your only Son Jesus Christ: Grant that we, who joyfully receive him as our Redeemer, may with sure confidence behold him when he comes to be our Judge; who lives and reigns with you and the Holy Spirit, one God, now and for ever. *Amen.*

or this

O God, you have caused this holy night to shine with the brightness of the true Light: Grant that we, who have known the mystery of that Light on earth, may also enjoy him perfectly in heaven; where with you and the Holy Spirit he lives and reigns, one God, in glory everlasting. *Amen.*

or this

Almighty God, you have given your only-begotten Son to take our nature upon him, and to be born [this day] of a pure virgin: Grant that we, who have been born again and made your children by adoption and grace, may daily be renewed by your Holy Spirit; through our Lord Jesus Christ, to whom with you and the same Spirit be honor and glory, now and for ever. *Amen.*

First Sunday after Christmas Day

Almighty God, you have poured upon us the new light of your incarnate Word: Grant that this light, enkindled in our hearts, may shine forth in our lives; through Jesus Christ our Lord, who lives and reigns with you, in the unity of the Holy Spirit, one God, now and for ever. *Amen.*

forth in our lives; through Jesus Christ our Lord. *Amen.* [1928]

ETERNAL Father, who didst give thine only Son the Name most dear to thee and needful for mankind, betokening not his majesty, but our salvation: We pray thee to set the Name of Jesus high above every name, and to plant in every heart the love of the only Saviour; who liveth and reigneth with thee and the Holy Ghost, one God, world without end. Amen. [Eric Milner-White, *A Cambridge Bede Book*, "The Holy Name."]

Deus, qui in humanae substantiae dignitate et mirabiliter condedisti et mirabilius reformasti: da, quaesumus, nobis Iesu Christi filii tui eius diuinitatis esse consortes, qui humanitatis nostrae fieri dignatus est particeps: per. [Ver., 1239.]

ALMIGHTY God, who didst wonderfully create man in thine own image, and didst yet more wonderfully restore him: Grant, we beseech thee, that as thy Son our Lord Jesus Christ was made in the likeness of men, so we may be made partakers of the divine nature; through the same thy Son, who with thee and the Holy Ghost liveth and reigneth, one God, world without end. *Amen.* [Eng. 1928, The Second Sunday after Christmas.]

The Epiphany, or the Manifestation of Christ to the Gentiles.

Deus qui hodierna die unigenitum tuum gentibus stella duce reuelasti, concede propitius ut qui iam te ex fide cognouimus, usque ad contemplandam speciem tuae celsitudinis perducamur. Per. [Greg., 87.]

O GOD, who by the leading of a Star didst manifest thy only-begotten Son to the Gentiles; Mercifully grant that we, who[7] know thee now by faith, may after this life have the fruition of thy glorious Godhead; through the same thy Son[8] Jesus Christ our Lord. *Amen.*

[new]

ALMIGHTY God, who hast manifested thy Son Jesus Christ to be a light to mankind: Grant that we thy people, being nourished by thy word and sacraments, may be strengthened to show forth to all men the unsearchable riches of Christ, so that he may be known, adored, and obeyed, to the ends of the earth; who liveth and reigneth with thee and the Holy Spirit, one God, world without end. **Amen.** [CSI, Twentieth {Sunday} after Pentecost, "The Church in the World."]

[7]"which" [1662].

[8]Prior to 1928, "through Jesus Christ our Lord."

The Holy Name *January 1*

Eternal Father, who didst give to thine incarnate Son the holy name of Jesus to be the sign of our salvation: Plant in every heart, we beseech thee, the love of him who is the Savior of the world, even our Lord Jesus Christ; who liveth and reigneth with thee and the Holy Spirit, one God, in glory everlasting. *Amen.*

Second Sunday after Christmas Day

O God, who didst wonderfully create, and yet more wonderfully restore, the dignity of human nature: Grant that we may share the divine life of him who humbled himself to share our humanity, thy Son Jesus Christ; who liveth and reigneth with thee, in the unity of the Holy Spirit, one God, for ever and ever. *Amen.*

The Epiphany *January 6*

O God, who by the leading of a star didst manifest thine only begotten Son to the peoples of the earth: Lead us, who know thee now by faith, to thy presence, where we may behold thy glory face to face; through the same Jesus Christ our Lord, who liveth and reigneth with thee and the Holy Spirit, one God, now and for ever. *Amen.*

First Sunday after the Epiphany:
The Baptism of our Lord

Father in heaven, who at the baptism of Jesus in the River Jordan didst proclaim him thy beloved Son and anoint him with the Holy Spirit: Grant that all who are baptized into his Name may keep the covenant they have made, and boldly confess him as Lord and Savior; who with thee and the same Spirit liveth and reigneth, one God, in glory everlasting. *Amen.*

Second Sunday after the Epiphany

Almighty God, whose Son our Savior Jesus Christ is the light of the world: Grant that thy people, illumined by thy Word and Sacraments, may shine with the radiance of Christ's glory, that he may be known, worshiped, and obeyed to the ends of the earth; through the same Jesus Christ our Lord, who with thee and the Holy Spirit liveth and reigneth, one God, now and for ever. *Amen.*

The Holy Name *January 1*

Eternal Father, you gave your incarnate Son the holy name of Jesus to be the sign of our salvation: Plant in every heart, we pray, the love of him who is the Savior of the world, our Lord Jesus Christ; who lives and reigns with you and the Holy Spirit, one God, in glory everlasting. *Amen.*

Second Sunday after Christmas Day

O God, who wonderfully created, and yet more wonderfully restored, the dignity of human nature: Grant that we may share the divine life of him who humbled himself to share our humanity, your Son Jesus Christ; who lives and reigns with you, in the unity of the Holy Spirit, one God, for ever and ever. *Amen.*

The Epiphany *January 6*

O God, by the leading of a star you manifested your only Son to the peoples of the earth: Lead us, who know you now by faith, to your presence, where we may see your glory face to face; through Jesus Christ our Lord, who lives and reigns with you and the Holy Spirit, one God, now and for ever. *Amen.*

First Sunday after the Epiphany:
The Baptism of our Lord

Father in heaven, who at the baptism of Jesus in the River Jordan proclaimed him your beloved Son and anointed him with the Holy Spirit: Grant that all who are baptized into his Name may keep the covenant they have made, and boldly confess him as Lord and Savior; who with you and the Holy Spirit lives and reigns, one God, in glory everlasting. *Amen.*

Second Sunday after the Epiphany

Almighty God, whose Son our Savior Jesus Christ is the light of the world: Grant that your people, illumined by your Word and Sacraments, may shine with the radiance of Christ's glory, that he may be known, worshiped, and obeyed to the ends of the earth; through Jesus Christ our Lord, who with you and the Holy Spirit lives and reigns, one God, now and for ever. *Amen.*

[new]

The Second Sunday after the Epiphany.

Omnipotens sempiternae deus, qui caelestia simul et terrena moderaris supplicationes populi tui clementer exaudi, et pacem tuam nostris concede temporibus. Per dominum. [Greg., 922]

ALMIGHTY and everlasting God, who dost govern all things in heaven and earth; Mercifully hear the supplications of thy people, and grant us thy peace all the days of our life; through Jesus Christ our Lord. *Amen.*

[new]

The First Sunday after Trinity.

Deus, in te sperantium fortitudo, adesto propitius inuocationibus nostris, et quia sine te nihil potest mortalis infirmitas, praesta auxilium gratiae tuae, ut in exequendis mandatis tuis et uoluntate tibi et actione placeamus: per dominum. [Gel., 566.]

O GOD, the strength of all those who put their trust in thee; Mercifully accept our prayers; and because, through the weakness of our mortal nature, we can do no good thing without thee, grant us the help of thy grace, that in keeping thy commandments we may please thee, both in will and deed; through Jesus Christ our Lord. *Amen.*

The Sunday called Quinqagesima, or the Sunday next before Lent.[9]

O Lord, which dost teache vs, that all our doinges without charitie are nothyng worthe; sende thy holy gost and powre into oure heartes that moste excellent gyfte of charitie, the very bonde of peace and all vertues, without the whiche, whosoeuer lyueth is counted dead before thee: Graunt this for thy onely sonne Iesus Christes sake. [1549, The Sonday called Quinquagesima.]

O LORD, who hast taught us that all our doings without charity are nothing worth; Send thy Holy Ghost, and pour into our hearts that most excellent gift of charity, the very bond of peace and of all virtues, without which whosoever liveth is counted dead before thee. Grant this for thine only Son Jesus Christ's sake. *Amen.*

O most loving Father, Who willest us to give thanks for all things, to dread nothing but the loss of Thee, and to cast all our care on Thee Who carest for us; preserve us from faithless fears and worldly anxieties, and grant that no clouds of this mortal life may hide from us the light of that Love which is immortal, and which Thou hast manifested unto us in Thy Son, Jesus Christ our Lord. [Wm Bright, *Ancient Collects*, "For Cheerfulness."][10]

O MOST loving Father, who willest us to give thanks for all things, to dread nothing but the loss of thee, and to cast all our care on thee, who carest for us; Preserve us from faithless fears and worldly anxieties, and

[9]"the next Sunday before" thru 1892.

[10]Bright appended to his translations of ancient prayers, collects of his own composition, of which those quoted here are examples, except as noted.

1979-I

Third Sunday after the Epiphany

Give us grace, O Lord, to answer readily the call of our Savior Jesus Christ and proclaim to all people the Good News of his salvation, that we and all the whole world may perceive the glory of his marvelous works; who liveth and reigneth with thee and the Holy Spirit, one God, for ever and ever. *Amen.*

Fourth Sunday after the Epiphany

Almighty and everlasting God, who dost govern all things in heaven and earth: Mercifully hear the supplications of thy people, and in our time grant us thy peace; through Jesus Christ our Lord, who liveth and reigneth with thee and the Holy Spirit, one God, for ever and ever. *Amen.*

Fifth Sunday after the Epiphany

Set us free, O God, from the bondage of our sins and give us, we beseech thee, the liberty of that abundant life which thou hast manifested to us in thy Son our Savior Jesus Christ; who liveth and reigneth with thee, in the unity of the Holy Spirit, one God, now and for ever. *Amen.*

Sixth Sunday after the Epiphany

O God, the strength of all those who put their trust in thee: Mercifully accept our prayers; and because, through the weakness of our mortal nature, we can do no good thing without thee, grant us the help of thy grace, that in keeping thy commandments we may please thee both in will and deed; through Jesus Christ our Lord, who liveth and reigneth with thee and the Holy Spirit, one God, for ever and ever. *Amen.*

Seventh Sunday after the Epiphany

O Lord, who hast taught us that all our doings without charity are nothing worth: Send thy Holy Ghost and pour into our hearts that most excellent gift of charity, the very bond of peace and of all virtues, without which whosoever liveth is counted dead before thee. Grant this for thine only Son Jesus Christ's sake, who liveth and reigneth with thee and the same Holy Ghost, one God, now and for ever. *Amen.*

Eighth Sunday after the Epiphany

O most loving Father, who willest us to give thanks for all things, to dread nothing but the loss of thee, and to cast all our care on thee who carest for us: Preserve us from faithless fears and worldly anxieties, and grant that no clouds of this mortal life may hide from us the light of that love which is immortal, and which thou hast manifested unto us in thy Son Jesus Christ our Lord; who liveth and reigneth with thee, in the unity of the Holy Spirit, one God, now and for ever. *Amen.*

1979-II

Third Sunday after the Epiphany

Give us grace, O Lord, to answer readily the call of our Savior Jesus Christ and proclaim to all people the Good News of his salvation, that we and the whole world may perceive the glory of his marvelous works; who lives and reigns with you and the Holy Spirit, one God, for ever and ever. *Amen.*

Fourth Sunday after the Epiphany

Almighty and everlasting God, you govern all things both in heaven and on earth: Mercifully hear the supplications of your people, and in our time grant us your peace; through Jesus Christ our Lord, who lives and reigns with you and the Holy Spirit, one God, for ever and ever. *Amen.*

Fifth Sunday after the Epiphany

Set us free, O God, from the bondage of our sins, and give us the liberty of that abundant life which you have made known to us in your Son our Savior Jesus Christ; who lives and reigns with you, in the unity of the Holy Spirit, one God, now and for ever. *Amen.*

Sixth Sunday after the Epiphany

O God, the strength of all who put their trust in you: Mercifully accept our prayers; and because in our weakness we can do nothing good without you, give us the help of your grace, that in keeping your commandments we may please you both in will and deed; through Jesus Christ our Lord, who lives and reigns with you and the Holy Spirit, one God, for ever and ever. *Amen.*

Seventh Sunday after the Epiphany

O Lord, you have taught us that without love whatever we do is worth nothing: Send your Holy Spirit and pour into our hearts your greatest gift, which is love, the true bond of peace and of all virtue, without which whoever lives is accounted dead before you. Grant this for the sake of your only Son Jesus Christ, who lives and reigns with you and the Holy Spirit, one God, now and for ever. *Amen.*

Eighth Sunday after the Epiphany

Most loving Father, whose will it is for us to give thanks for all things, to fear nothing but the loss of you, and to cast all our care on you who care for us: Preserve us from faithless fears and worldly anxieties, that no clouds of this mortal life may hide from us the light of that love which is immortal, and which you have manifested to us in your Son Jesus Christ our Lord; who lives and reigns with you, in the unity of the Holy Spirit, one God, now and for ever. *Amen.*

grant that no clouds of this mortal life may hide from us the light of that love which is immortal, and which thou hast manifested unto us in thy Son, Jesus Christ our Lord. *Amen.* [1928,Family Prayer: *For Trustfulness*]

O GOD, who before the passion of thine only-begotten Son didst reveal his glory upon the holy mount: Grant unto us thy servants, that in faith beholding the light of his countenance, we may be strengthened to bear the cross, and be changed into his likeness from glory to glory; through the same Jesus Christ our Lord. *Amen.* [Eng. 1928, The Transfiguration.]

ALmightie and euerlastyng god,[12] which hatest nothing that thou haste made, and doest forgeue the synnes of al them that be penitent: Create and make in vs new and contrite heartes, that we worthily lamentyng our synnes, and knowlegyng our wretchednesse, may obtayne of thee, the God of all mercy, perfecte remission and forgeuenesse, through Iesus Christe. [1549, The first day of Lent, commonly called Ashwednesday.[13]]

The first day of Lent, commonly called Ash Wednesday.[11]

ALMIGHTY and everlasting God, who hatest nothing that thou hast made, and dost forgive the sins of all those who[14] are penitent; Create and make in us new and contrite hearts, that we, worthily lamenting our sins and acknowledging our wretchedness, may obtain of thee, the God of all mercy, perfect remission and forgiveness; through Jesus Christ our Lord. *Amen.*

Merciful and faithful High Priest, Who didst deign for us to be tempted of Satan; make speed to aid Thy servants who are assaulted by manifold temptations; and as Thou knowest their several infirmities, let each one find Thee mighty to save, Who livest, &c. [Wm. Bright, *Ancient Collects,* "For the Tempted."]

[Omnipotens sempiterne deus, qui omnes saluas et niminem uis perire, respice ad animas diabolica fraude deceptas, ut omni heredica perueristate depulsa errancium corda resipiscant et ad ueritatis tuae redeant firmitatem: per dominum. {Gel., 413.}]

[11]"Ash-Wednesday" thru 1892.

[12]*sic.*

[13]*sic.*

[14]"them that" [1662].

1979-I

Last Sunday after the Epiphany

O God, who before the passion of thy only-begotten Son didst reveal his glory upon the holy mount: Grant unto us that we, beholding by faith the light of his countenance, may be strengthened to bear our cross, and be changed into his likeness from glory to glory; through the same Jesus Christ our Lord, who liveth and reigneth with thee and the Holy Spirit, one God, for ever and ever. *Amen.*

Ash Wednesday

Almighty and everlasting God, who hatest nothing thou hast made and dost forgive the sins of all those who are penitent: Create and make in us new and contrite hearts, that we, worthily lamenting our sins and acknowledging our wretchedness, may obtain of thee, the God of all mercy, perfect remission and forgiveness; through Jesus Christ our Lord, who liveth and reigneth with thee and the Holy Spirit, one God, for ever and ever. *Amen.*

First Sunday in Lent

Almighty God, whose blessed Son was led by the Spirit to be tempted of Satan: Make speed to help thy servants who are assaulted by manifold temptations; and, as thou knowest their several infirmities, let each one find thee mighty to save; through Jesus Christ thy Son our Lord, who liveth and reigneth with thee and the Holy Spirit, one God, now and for ever. *Amen.*

Second Sunday in Lent

O God, whose glory it is always to have mercy: Be gracious to all who have gone astray from thy ways, and bring them again with penitent hearts and steadfast faith to embrace and hold fast the unchangeable truth of thy Word, Jesus Christ thy Son; who with thee and the Holy Spirit liveth and reigneth, one God, for ever and ever. *Amen.*

1979-II

Last Sunday after the Epiphany

O God, who before the passion of your only-begotten Son revealed his glory upon the holy mountain: Grant to us that we, beholding by faith the light of his countenance, may be strengthened to bear our cross, and be changed into his likeness from glory to glory; through Jesus Christ our Lord, who lives and reigns with you and the Holy Spirit, one God, for ever and ever. *Amen.*

Ash Wednesday

Almighty and everlasting God, you hate nothing you have made and forgive the sins of all who are penitent: Create and make in us new and contrite hearts, that we, worthily lamenting our sins and acknowledging our wretchedness, may obtain of you, the God of all mercy, perfect remission and forgiveness; through Jesus Christ our Lord, who lives and reigns with you and the Holy Spirit, one God, for ever and ever. *Amen.*

First Sunday in Lent

Almighty God, whose blessed Son was led by the Spirit to be tempted by Satan: Come quickly to help us who are assaulted by many temptations; and, as you know the weaknesses of each of us, let each one find you mighty to save; through Jesus Christ your Son our Lord, who lives and reigns with you and the Holy Spirit, one God, now and for ever. *Amen.*

Second Sunday in Lent

O God, whose glory it is always to have mercy: Be gracious to all who have gone astray from your ways, and bring them again with penitent hearts and steadfast faith to embrace and hold fast the unchangeable truth of your Word, Jesus Christ your Son; who with you and the Holy Spirit lives and reigns, one God, for ever and ever. *Amen.*

The Second Sunday in Lent.

Deus qui conspicis omni nos uirtute destitui interius exteriusque custodi, ut et ab omnibus aduersitatibus muniamur in corpore et a prauis cogitationibus mundemur in mente. Per dominum. [Greg., 202.]

ALMIGHTY God, who seest that we have no power of ourselves to help ourselves; Keep us both outwardly in our bodies, and inwardly in our souls; that we may be defended from all adversities which may happen to the body, and from all evil thoughts which may assault and hurt the soul; through Jesus Christ our Lord. *Amen.*

O LORD and heavenly Father, Who hast given unto us Thy people the true Bread that cometh down from heaven, even Thy Son Jesus Christ: grant that our souls may so be fed by Him Who giveth life unto the world, that we may abide in Him and He in us, and Thy Church be filled with the power of His unending life; through Jesus Christ our Lord. [F. B. McNutt, *The Prayer Manual* (1952), #488.][15]

The Fourth Sunday after Easter.

Deus, qui fidelium mentes unius efficis uoluntati, da populis tuis id amare quod praecipis, id desiderare quo promittis, ut inter mundanas uarietates ibi nostra fixa sint corda ubi uera sunt gaudia. per. [Gel., 551.]

O ALMIGHTY God, who alone canst order the unruly wills and affections of sinful men; Grant unto thy people, that they may love the thing which thou commandest, and desire that which thou dost promise; that so, among the sundry and manifold changes of the world, our hearts may surely there be fixed, where true joys are to be found, through Jesus Christ our Lord. *Amen.*

The Sunday next before Easter. [through 1982]

The Sunday next before Easter, commonly called Palm Sunday. [1928]

Deus, qui humano genere ad imitandum humilitatis exemplum saluatorem nostrum et carnem sumere et crucem subire fecisti, concede propitius, ut et pacientiae eius habere documentum et resurrectionis eius consortia mereamur, Christi domini nostri: qui tecum uiuit et regnat deus in unitate spiritus sancti: per. [Gel., 329.]

ALMIGHTY and everlasting God, who, of thy tender love towards mankind, hast sent thy Son, our Saviour Jesus Christ, to take upon him our flesh, and to suffer death upon the cross, that all mankind should follow the example of his great humility; Mercifully grant, that we may both follow the example of his patience, and also be made partakers of his resurrection; through the same Jesus Christ our Lord. *Amen.*

Monday before Easter.

ALMIGHTY God, whose most dear Son went not up to joy but first he suffered pain, and entered not into glory before he was crucified; Mercifully grant that we, walking in the way of the cross, may find it none other than the way of life and peace; through the same Jesus Christ our Lord. *Amen.* [Wm. Reed Huntington, "For the Monday Before Easter," *Materia Ritualis*. He adds, "Compiled from the Visitation Office."]

ALMIGHTY God, whose most dear Son went not up to joy but first he suffered pain, and entered not into glory before he was crucified; Mercifully grant that we, walking in the

[15]McNutt's was an adaptation from *A New Prayer Book* (Oxford, 1923), but his was the text from which the American revisers worked.

Third Sunday in Lent

Almighty God, who seest that we have no power of ourselves to help ourselves: Keep us both outwardly in our bodies and inwardly in our souls, that we may be defended from all adversities which may happen to the body, and from all evil thoughts which may assault and hurt the soul; through Jesus Christ our Lord, who liveth and reigneth with thee and the Holy Spirit, one God, for ever and ever. *Amen.*

Fourth Sunday in Lent

Gracious Father, whose blessed Son Jesus Christ came down from heaven to be the true bread which giveth life to the world: Evermore give us this bread, that he may live in us, and we in him; who liveth and reigneth with thee and the Holy Spirit, one God, now and for ever. *Amen.*

Fifth Sunday in Lent

O Almighty God, who alone canst order the unruly wills and affections of sinful men: Grant unto thy people that they may love the thing which thou commandest, and desire that which thou dost promise; that so, among the sundry and manifold changes of the world, our hearts may surely there be fixed where true joys are to be found; through Jesus Christ our Lord, who liveth and reigneth with thee and the Holy Spirit, one God, now and for ever. *Amen.*

Sunday of the Passion: Palm Sunday

The Proper Liturgy for this day is on page 270.

Almighty and everlasting God, who, of thy tender love towards mankind, hast sent thy Son our Savior Jesus Christ to take upon him our flesh, and to suffer death upon the cross, that all mankind should follow the example of his great humility: Mercifully grant that we may both follow the example of his patience, and also be made partakers of his resurrection; through the same Jesus Christ our Lord, who liveth and reigneth with thee and the Holy Spirit, one God, for ever and ever. *Amen.*

Monday in Holy Week

Almighty God, whose most dear Son went not up to joy but first he suffered pain, and entered not into glory before he was crucified: Mercifully grant that we, walking in the way of the cross, may find it none other than the way of life and peace; through the same thy son Jesus Christ our Lord, who liveth and reigneth with thee and the Holy Spirit, one God, for ever and ever. *Amen.*

Third Sunday in Lent

Almighty God, you know that we have no power in ourselves to help ourselves: Keep us both outwardly in our bodies and inwardly in our souls, that we may be defended from all adversities which may happen to the body, and from all evil thoughts which may assault and hurt the soul; through Jesus Christ our Lord, who lives and reigns with you and the Holy Spirit, one God, for ever and ever. *Amen.*

Fourth Sunday in Lent

Gracious Father, whose blessed Son Jesus Christ came down from heaven to be the true bread which gives life to the world: Evermore give us this bread, that he may live in us, and we in him; who lives and reigns with you and the Holy Spirit, one God, now and for ever. *Amen.*

Fifth Sunday in Lent

Almighty God, you alone can bring into order the unruly wills and affections of sinners: Grant your people grace to love what you command and desire what you promise; that, among the swift and varied changes of the world, our hearts may surely there be fixed where true joys are to be found; through Jesus Christ our Lord, who lives and reigns with you and the Holy Spirit, one God, now and for ever. *Amen.*

Sunday of the Passion: Palm Sunday

The Proper Liturgy for this day is on page 270.

Almighty and everliving God, in your tender love for the human race you sent your Son our Savior Jesus Christ to take upon him our nature, and to suffer death upon the cross, giving us the example of his great humility: Mercifully grant that we may walk in the way of his suffering, and also share in his resurrection; through Jesus Christ our Lord, who lives and reigns with you and the Holy Spirit, one God, for ever and ever. *Amen.*

Monday in Holy Week

Almighty God, whose most dear Son went not up to joy but first he suffered pain, and entered not into glory before he was crucified: Mercifully grant that we, walking in the way of the cross, may find it none other than the way of life and peace; through Jesus Christ your Son our Lord, who lives and reigns with you and the Holy Spirit, one God, for ever and ever. *Amen.*

way of the cross, may find it none other than the way of life and peace; through the same thy Son Jesus Christ our Lord. *Amen.* [1928]

O God, who by the passion of thy blessed Son hast made the instrument of shameful death to be unto us the means of life and peace: Grant us so to glory in the Cross of Christ, that we may gladly suffer shame and loss; for the sake of the same thy Son our Lord. *Amen.* [Eng. 1928, Holy Cross Day.]

Tuesday before Easter.

O LORD God, whose blessed Son, our Saviour, gave his back to the smiters and hid not his face from shame; Grant us grace to take joyfully the sufferings of the present time, in full assurance of the glory that shall be revealed; through the same thy Son Jesus Christ our Lord. *Amen.* [1928]

Thursday before Easter, commonly called Maundy Thursday

ALMIGHTY Father, whose dear Son, on the night before he suffered, did institute the Sacrament of his Body and Blood; Mercifully grant that we may thankfully receive the same in remembrance of him, who in these holy mysteries giveth us a pledge of life eternal; the same thy Son Jesus Christ our Lord, who now liveth and reigneth with thee and the Holy Spirit ever, one God, world without end. *Amen.* [1928]

Good Friday.

Respice domine quaesumus super hanc familiam tuam, pro qua dominus noster iesus christus, non dubitauit manibus tradi nocentium et crucis subire tormentum. Per. [Greg., 327.]

ALMIGHTY God, we beseech thee graciously to behold this thy family, for which our Lord Jesus Christ was contented to be betrayed, and given up into the hands of wicked men, and to suffer death upon the cross; who now liveth and reigneth with thee and the Holy Ghost ever, one God, world without end. *Amen.*

Tuesday in Holy Week

O God, who by the passion of thy blessed Son didst make an instrument of shameful death to be unto us the means of life: Grant us so to glory in the cross of Christ, that we may gladly suffer shame and loss for the sake of thy Son our Savior Jesus Christ; who liveth and reigneth with thee and the Holy Spirit, one God, for ever and ever. *Amen.*

Wednesday in Holy Week

Lord God, whose blessed Son our Savior gave his back to the smiters and hid not his face from shame: Grant us grace to take joyfully the sufferings of the present time, in full assurance of the glory that shall be revealed; through the same thy Son Jesus Christ our Lord, who liveth and reigneth with thee and the Holy Spirit, one God, for ever and ever. *Amen.*

Maundy Thursday

Almighty Father, whose dear Son, on the night before he suffered, did institute the Sacrament of his Body and Blood: Mercifully grant that we may thankfully receive the same in remembrance of him who in these holy mysteries giveth us a pledge of life eternal, the same thy Son Jesus Christ our Lord; who now liveth and reigneth with thee and the Holy Spirit ever, one God, world without end. *Amen.*

Good Friday

Almighty God, we beseech thee graciously to behold this thy family, for which our Lord Jesus Christ was contented to be betrayed, and given up into the hands of sinners, and to suffer death upon the cross; who now liveth and reigneth with thee and the Holy Ghost ever, one God, world without end. *Amen.*

Tuesday in Holy Week

O God, by the passion of your blessed Son you made an instrument of shameful death to be for us the means of life: Grant us so to glory in the cross of Christ, that we may gladly suffer shame and loss for the sake of your Son our Savior Jesus Christ; who lives and reigns with you and the Holy Spirit, one God, for ever and ever. *Amen.*

Wednesday in Holy Week

Lord God, whose blessed Son our Savior gave his body to be whipped and his face to spit upon: Give us grace to accept joyfully the sufferings of the present time, confident of the glory that shall be revealed; through Jesus Christ your Son our Lord, who lives and reigns with you and the Holy Spirit, one God, for ever and ever. *Amen.*

Maundy Thursday

Almighty Father, whose dear Son, on the night before he suffered, instituted the Sacrament of his Body and Blood: Mercifully grant that we may receive it thankfully in remembrance of Jesus Christ our Lord, who in these holy mysteries gives us a pledge of eternal life; and who now lives and reigns with you and the Holy Spirit, one God, for ever and ever. *Amen.*

Good Friday

Almighty God, we pray you graciously to behold this your family, for whom our Lord Jesus Christ was willing to be betrayed, and given into the hands of sinners, and to suffer death upon the cross; who now lives and reigns with you and the Holy Spirit, one God, for ever and ever. *Amen.*

Easter-Day.

Deus qui pro nobis filium tuum crucis patibulum subire uoluisti, ut inimici, a nobis expelleres potestatem, concede nobis famulis tuis, ut resurrectionis gratiam consequamur. Per dominum. [Greg., 324.]

O God, who for our redempcion diddest geue thine onely begotten sonne to the death of the crosse: & by hys gloryous resurreccion hast delyuered vs from the power of our enemye: Graunte vs so to dye dayly from sinne, that we maye euermore liue with him in the ioye of his resurreccion: through the same Christ our Lord. Amen. [1549, Matins of Easter day.][16]

O GOD, who for our redemption didst give thine only-begotten Son to the death of the Cross, and by his glorious resurrection hast delivered us from the power of our enemy; Grant us so to die daily from sin, that we may evermore live with him in the joy of his resurrection; through the same thy Son Christ our Lord. *Amen.* [Second Communion Service.]

Deus, qui hanc sacratissimam noctem gloriosae dominicae resurrectionis inlustras, conserua, in noua familiae tuae progeniem adoptionis spiritum quem dedisti, ut corpore et mente renouati puram tibi exhibeant seruitutem: per dominum. [Gel., 454.]

Deus qui hodierna die per unigenitum tuum aeternitatis nobis aditum deuicta morte reserasti, uota nostra quae praeueniendo adspiras, etiam adiuuando prosequere. Per eundum dominum nostrum. [Greg., 383.]

ALMIGHTY God, who through thine only-begotten Son Jesus Christ hast overcome death, and opened unto us the gate of everlasting life; We humbly beseech thee that, as by thy special grace preventing us thou dost put into our minds good desires, so by thy continual help we may bring the same to good effect; through the same[17] Jesus Christ our Lord, who liveth and reigneth with thee and the Holy Ghost ever, one God, world without end. *Amen.*

Tuesday in Easter Week.[18]

Concede qüaesumus omnipotens deus, ut qui festa paschalia uenerando egimus, per haec contingere ad gaudia aeterna mereamur. Per. [Greg., 429.]

GRANT, we beseech thee, Almighty God, that we who celebrate with reverence the Paschal feast, may be found worthy to attain to everlasting joys; through Jesus Christ our Lord. *Amen.* [1928]

---

[16]Dropped in 1552; restored in 1892.

[17]"the same" added in 1928.

[18]"Easter-Week" [1892].

1979-I

Holy Saturday

O God, Creator of heaven and earth: Grant that, as the crucified body of thy dear Son was laid in the tomb and rested on this holy Sabbath, so we may await with him the coming of the third day, and rise with him to newness of life; who now liveth and reigneth with thee and the Holy Spirit, one God, for ever and ever. *Amen.*

Easter Day

O God, who for our redemption didst give thine only-begotten Son to the death of the cross, and by his glorious resurrection hast delivered us from the power of our enemy: Grant us so to die daily to sin, that we may evermore live with him in the joy of his resurrection; through the same thy Son Christ our Lord, who liveth and reigneth with thee and the Holy Spirit, one God, now and for ever. *Amen.*

or this

O God, who didst make this most holy night to shine with the glory of the Lord's resurrection: Stir up in thy Church that Spirit of adoption which is given to us in Baptism, that we, being renewed both in body and mind, may worship thee in sincerity and truth; through the same Jesus Christ our Lord, who liveth and reigneth with thee in the unity of the same Spirit, one God, now and for ever. *Amen.*

or this

Almighty God, who through thine only-begotten Son Jesus Christ hast overcome death and opened unto us the gate of everlasting life: Grant that we, who celebrate with joy the day of the Lord's resurrection, may be raised from the death of sin by thy life-giving Spirit; through the same Jesus Christ our Lord, who liveth and reigneth with thee and the same Spirit ever, one God, world without end. *Amen.*

Monday in Easter Week

Grant, we beseech thee, Almighty God, that we who celebrate with reverence the Paschal feast may be found worthy to attain to everlasting joys; through Jesus Christ our Lord, who liveth and reigneth with thee and the Holy Spirit, one God, now and for ever. *Amen.*

1979-II

Holy Saturday

O God, Creator of heaven and earth: Grant that, as the crucified body of your dear Son was laid in the tomb and rested on this holy Sabbath, so we may await with him the coming of the third day, and rise with him to newness of life; who now lives and reigns with you and the Holy Spirit, one God, for ever and ever. *Amen.*

Easter Day

O God, who for our redemption gave your only-begotten Son to the death of the cross, and by his glorious resurrection delivered us from the power of the enemy: Grant us so to die daily to sin, that we may evermore live with him in the joy of his resurrection; through Jesus Christ your Son our Lord, who lives and reigns with you and the Holy Spirit, one God, now and for ever. *Amen.*

or this

O God, who made this most holy night to shine with the glory of the Lord's resurrection: Stir up in your Church that Spirit of adoption which is given to us in Baptism, that we, being renewed both in body and mind, may worship you in sincerity and truth; through Jesus Christ our Lord, who lives and reigns with you, in the unity of the Holy Spirit, one God, now and for ever. *Amen.*

or this

Almighty God, who through your only-begotten Son Jesus Christ overcame death and opened to us the gate of everlasting life: Grant that we, who celebrate with joy the day the Lord's resurrection, may be raised from the death of sin by your life-giving Spirit; through Jesus Christ our Lord, who lives and reigns with you and the Holy Spirit, one God, now and for ever. *Amen.*

Monday in Easter Week

Grant, we pray, Almighty God, that we who celebrate with awe the Paschal feast may be found worthy to attain to everlasting joys; through Jesus Christ our Lord, who lives and reigns with you and the Holy Spirit, one God, now and for ever. *Amen.*

O God, who by the glorious resurrection of thy Son our Saviour Jesus Christ hast destroyed death, and brought life and immortality to light: Grant that we, being raised together with him, may know the comfort and strength of his presence, and rejoice in hope of thy everlasting glory; through the same Jesus Christ our Lord, to whom be dominion and praise for ever and ever. [Frank Colquhoun, *Parish Prayers,* 302.]

Monday in Easter Week.

O GOD, whose blessed Son did manifest himself to his disciples in the breaking of bread; Open, we pray thee, the eyes of our faith, that we may behold thee in all thy works; through the same thy Son Jesus Christ our Lord. *Amen.*

Omnipotens sempiternae deus qui paschale sacramentum in reconciliationis humanae foedere contulisti da mentibus nostris, ut quod professione caelebramus imitemur affectu. Per dominum. [Greg., 423.]

The First Sunday after Easter.

ALmightie father, whiche hast geuen thy onely sonne to dye for our synnes and to ryse agayne for oure iustification: Graunt vs so to put away the leauen of malice and wickednesse, that we may alway serue the[19] in purenesse of liuyng and trueth, through Iesus Christ our Lord. [1549, Easter Day, "At the second communion."]

ALMIGHTY Father who hast given thine only Son to die for our sins, and to rise again for our justification; Grant us so to put away the leaven of malice and wickedness, that we may always[20] serve thee in pureness of living and truth; through the merits of the same thy Son Jesus Christ our Lord. *Amen.*

We give Thee thanks, O God the Father, Who hast delivered us from the power of darkness, and translated us into the kingdom of Thy Son; grant therefore, we pray Thee, that as by His death He has recalled us to life, He may raise us up in His love to joys eternal. [Wm. Bright, *Ancient Collects,* "Prayers for the Sacred Seasons," based on a Mozarabic text.]

Omnipotens sempiternae deus qui paschale sacramentum in reconciliationis humanae foedere contulisti da mentibus nostris, ut quod professione caelebramus imitemur affectu. Per dominum. [Greg., 423.]

[19]*sic.*

[20]"alway" until 1928.

Tuesday in Easter Week

O God, who by the glorious resurrection of thy Son Jesus Christ destroyed death and brought life and immortality to light: Grant that we, who have been raised with him, may abide in his presence and rejoice in the hope of eternal glory; through the same Jesus Christ our Lord, to whom, with thee and the Holy Spirit, be dominion and praise for ever and ever. *Amen.*

Tuesday in Easter Week

O God, who by the glorious resurrection of your Son Jesus Christ destroyed death and brought life and immortality to light: Grant that we, who have been raised with him, may abide in his presence and rejoice in the hope of eternal glory; through Jesus Christ our Lord, to whom, with you and the Holy Spirit, be dominion and praise for ever and ever. *Amen.*

Wednesday in Easter Week

O God, whose blessed Son did manifest himself to his disciples in the breaking of bread; Open, we pray thee, the eyes of our faith, that we may behold him in all his redeeming work; through the same thy Son Jesus Christ our Lord, who liveth and reigneth with thee, in the unity of the Holy Spirit, one God, now and for ever. *Amen.*

Wednesday in Easter Week

O God, whose blessed Son made himself known to his disciples in the breaking of bread; Open the eyes of our faith, that we may behold him in all his redeeming work; who lives and reigns with you, in the unity of the Holy Spirit, one God, now and for ever. *Amen.*

Thursday in Easter Week

Almighty and everlasting God, who in the Paschal mystery hast established the new covenant of reconciliation: Grant that all who have been reborn into the fellowship of Christ's Body may show forth in their lives what they profess by their faith; through the same Jesus Christ our Lord, who liveth and reigneth with thee and the Holy Spirit, one God, for ever and ever. *Amen.*

Thursday in Easter Week

Almighty and everlasting God, who in the Paschal mystery established the new covenant of reconciliation: Grant that all who have been reborn into the fellowship of Christ's Body may show forth in their lives what they profess by their faith; through Jesus Christ our Lord, who lives and reigns with you and the Holy Spirit, one God, for ever and ever. *Amen.*

Friday in Easter Week

Almighty Father, who hast given thine only Son to die for our sins and to rise again for our justification: Grant us so to put away the leaven of malice and wickedness, that we may always serve thee in pureness of living and truth; through the same thy Son Jesus Christ our Lord, who liveth and reigneth with thee and the Holy Spirit, one God, now and for ever. *Amen.*

Friday in Easter Week

Almighty Father, who gave your only Son to die for our sins and to rise for our justification: Give us grace so to put away the leaven of malice and wickedness, that we may always serve you in pureness of living and truth; through Jesus Christ your Son our Lord, who lives and reigns with you and the Holy Spirit, one God, now and for ever. *Amen.*

Saturday in Easter Week

We thank thee, heavenly Father, for that thou hast delivered us from the dominion of sin and death and hast brought us into the kingdom of thy Son; and we pray thee that, as by his death he hath recalled us to life, so by his love he may raise us to joys eternal; who liveth and reigneth with thee, in the unity of the Holy Spirit, one God, now and for ever. *Amen.*

Saturday in Easter Week

We thank you, heavenly Father, that you have delivered us from the dominion of sin and death and brought us into the kingdom of your Son; and we pray that, as by his death he has recalled us to life, so by his love he may raise us to eternal joys; who lives and reigns with you, in the unity of the Holy Spirit, one God, now and for ever. *Amen.*

Second Sunday of Easter

Almighty and everlasting God, who in the Paschal mystery hast established the new covenant of reconciliation: Grant that all who have been reborn into the fellowship of Christ's Body may show forth in their lives what they profess by their faith; through the same Jesus Christ our Lord, who liveth and reigneth with thee and the Holy Spirit, one God, for ever and ever. *Amen.*

Second Sunday of Easter

Almighty and everlasting God, who in the Paschal mystery established the new covenant of reconciliation: Grant that all who have been reborn into the fellowship of Christ's Body may show forth in their lives what they profess by their faith; through Jesus Christ our Lord, who lives and reigns with you and the Holy Spirit, one God, for ever and ever. *Amen.*

Monday in Easter Week.

O GOD, whose blessed Son did manifest himself to his disciples in the breaking of bread; Open, we pray thee, the eyes of our faith, that we may behold thee in all thy works; through the same thy Son Jesus Christ our Lord. *Amen.*

ALmightie God, whome truely to knowe is euerlasting lyfe: Graunte vs perfectelye to knowe thy sonne Iesus Christe, to be the waye, the trueth, and the life, as thou haste taught saint Philip, and other the Apostles: Through Iesus Christe our Lorde.[21] [1549, Sainct Philip and James.]

The Sixth Sunday after Trinity.

Deus, qui diligentibus te bona inuisibilia praeparasti, infunde cordibus nostris tui amoris affectum, ut te in omnibus et super omnia dilgentes promissiones tuas quae omni disiderio superant consequamur: per dominum nostrum. [Gel., 1178]

O GOD, who hast prepared for those who[22] love thee such good things as pass man's understanding; Pour into our hearts such love toward thee, that we, loving thee above all things, may obtain thy promises, which exceed all that we can desire, through Jesus Christ our Lord. *Amen.*

The Ascension Day.

Adesto, domine, supplicationibus nostris, ut sicut humani generis saluatorum consedere tecum in tua maiestate confidimus, ita usque ad consummationem saeculi manere nobiscum, quemadmodum es pollicitus, sentiamus: per. [Ver., 169.]

Concede quaesumus omnipotens deus, ut qui hodierna die unigenitum tuum redemptorem nostrum ad caelos ascendisse credimus, ipsi quoque mente in caelestibus habitemus. Per dominum. [Greg., 497.]

GRANT, we beseech thee, Almighty God, that like as we do believe thy only-begotten Son our Lord Jesus Christ to have ascended into the heavens; so we may also in heart and mind thither ascend, and with him continually dwell, who liveth and reigneth with thee and the Holy Ghost, one God, world without end. *Amen.*

[21]St. James is not named in the text of the prayer until 1662, which also adds the result clause.

[22]"them that" [1662].

Third Sunday of Easter (1979-I)

O God, whose blessed Son did manifest himself to his disciples in the breaking of bread: Open, we pray thee, the eyes of our faith, that we may behold him in all his redeeming work; through the same thy Son Jesus Christ our Lord, who liveth and reigneth with thee, in the unity of the Holy Spirit, one God, now and for ever. *Amen.*

Third Sunday of Easter (1979-II)

O God, whose blessed Son made himself known to his disciples in the breaking of bread: Open the eyes of our faith, that we may behold him in all his redeeming work; who lives and reigns with you, in the unity of the Holy Spirit, one God, now and for ever. *Amen.*

Fourth Sunday of Easter (1979-I)

O God, whose Son Jesus is the good shepherd of thy people: Grant that when we hear his voice we may know him who calleth us each by name, and follow where he doth lead; who, with thee and the Holy Spirit, liveth and reigneth, one God, for ever and ever. *Amen.*

Fourth Sunday of Easter (1979-II)

O God, whose Son Jesus is the good shepherd of your people: Grant that when we hear his voice we may know him who calls us each by name, and follow where he leads; who, with you and the Holy Spirit, lives and reigns, one God, for ever and ever. *Amen.*

Fifth Sunday of Easter (1979-I)

Almighty God, whom truly to know is everlasting life: Grant us so perfectly to know thy Son Jesus Christ to be the way, the truth, and the life, that we may steadfastly follow his steps in the way that leadeth to eternal life; through the same thy Son Jesus Christ our Lord, who liveth and reigneth with thee, in the unity of the Holy Spirit, one God, for ever and ever. *Amen.*

Fifth Sunday of Easter (1979-II)

Almighty God, whom truly to know is everlasting life: Grant us so perfectly to know your Son Jesus Christ to be the way, the truth, and the life, that we may steadfastly follow his steps in the way that leads to eternal life; through Jesus Christ your Son our Lord, who lives and reigns with you, in the unity of the Holy Spirit, one God, for ever and ever. *Amen.*

Sixth Sunday of Easter (1979-I)

O God, who hast prepared for those who love thee such good things as pass man's understanding: Pour into our hearts such love toward thee, that we, loving thee in all things and above all things, may obtain thy promises, which exceed all that we can desire; through Jesus Christ our Lord, who liveth and reigneth with thee and the Holy Spirit, one God, for ever and ever. *Amen.*

Sixth Sunday of Easter (1979-II)

O God, you have prepared for those who love you such good things as surpass our understanding: Pour into our hearts such love towards you, that we, loving you in all things and above all things, may obtain your promises, which exceed all that we can desire; through Jesus Christ our Lord, who lives and reigns with you and the Holy Spirit, one God, for ever and ever. *Amen.*

Ascension Day (1979-I)

O Almighty God, whose blessed Son our Savior Jesus Christ ascended far above all heavens that he might fill all things: Mercifully give us faith to perceive that, according to his promise, he abideth with his Church on earth, even unto the end of the ages; through the same Jesus Christ our Lord, who liveth and reigneth with thee and the Holy Spirit, one God, in glory everlasting. *Amen.*

or this

Grant, we beseech thee, Almighty God, that like as we do believe thine only-begotten Son our Lord Jesus Christ to have ascended into the heavens, so we may also in heart and mind thither ascend, and with him continually dwell; who liveth and reigneth with thee and the Holy Ghost, one God, world without end. *Amen.*

Ascension Day (1979-II)

Almighty God, whose blessed Son our Savior Jesus Christ ascended far above all heavens that he might fill all things: Mercifully give us faith to perceive that, according to his promise, he abides with his Church on earth, even to the end of the ages; through Jesus Christ our Lord, who lives and reigns with you and the Holy Spirit, one God, in glory everlasting. *Amen.*

or this

Grant, we pray, Almighty God, that as we believe your only-begotten Son our Lord Jesus Christ to have ascended into heaven, so we may also in heart and mind there ascend, and with him continually dwell; who lives and reigns with you and the Holy Spirit, one God, for ever and ever. *Amen.*

Sunday after Ascension Day.[23]

O God, the kyng of glory, whiche haste exalted thine only sonne Iesus Christe, wyth greate triumphe ynto thy kingdom in heauen: we beseche thee leaue vs not comfortles, but sende to vs thine holy gost to comforte vs, and exalte vs vnto the same place, whyther our sauioure Christe is gone before: who lyueth and reigneth. &c. [1549, The Sondaye after the Ascencion.]

O GOD, the King[24] of glory, who hast exalted thine only Son Jesus Christ with great triumph unto thy kingdom in heaven; We beseech thee, leave us not comfortless; but send to us thine Holy Ghost to comfort us, and exalt us unto the same place whither our Saviour Christ is gone before; who liveth and reigneth with thee and the Holy Ghost, one God, world without end. *Amen.*

Whitsunday.[25] | Pentecost, commonly called Whitsunday.

Deus, qui sacramentum festiuitatis hodiernae uniuersam aecclesiam tuam in omni gente et natione sanctificas, in totam mundi latitudinem spiritus tui sancti dona defunde, ut quod inter ipsa euangelicae praedicationis exordia operata est diuina dignatio, nunc quoque per credentium corda defunde: per. [Gel., 638.]

Deus qui hodierna die corda fidelium sancti spiritus inlustratione docuisti, da nobis in eodem spiritu recta sapere, et de eius consolatione gaudere. Per. [Greg., 526]

O GOD,[26] who as at this time didst teach the hearts of thy faithful people, by sending[27] to them the light of thy Holy Spirit; Grant us by the same Spirit to have a right judgment in all things, and evermore to rejoice in his holy comfort; through the merits of Christ Jesus our Saviour, who liveth and reigneth with thee, in the unity of the same Spirit, one God, world without end. *Amen.*

Trinity Sunday.

Omnipotens sempiterne deus qui dedisti famulis tuis in confessione uere fidei eterne trinitatis gloriam agnoscere. et in potencia maiestatis adorare unitatem. quesumus ut eiusdem fidei firmitate ab omnibus semper muniamur aduersis. Qui uiuis. [Sarum, In die sancte trinitatis.]

ALMIGHTY and everlasting God, who hast given unto us thy servants grace, by the confession of a true faith, to acknowledge the glory of the eternal Trinity, and in the power of the Divine Majesty to worship the Unity; We beseech thee that thou wouldest keep us stedfast in this faith, and evermore defend us from all adversities, who livest and reignest, one God, world without end. *Amen.*

Memento, domine, quod es operatus in nobis, et non quid mereamur, sed conlati gratiam tui muneris intuere; ut sicut me sacris altaribus tua dignatio pontificali seruire praecipit officio, ita dignum prestet et merito: per. [Ver., 976.]

[23]"Ascension-Day" through 1892.

[24]"king" until 1928.

[25]Thus through 1892.

[26]"O" not present in 1662 and 1786.

[27]"by the sending" [1662 & 1786].

Seventh Sunday of Easter: The Sunday after Ascension Day

O God, the King of glory, who hast exalted thine only Son Jesus Christ with great triumph into thy kingdom in heaven: We beseech thee, leave us not comfortless, but send to us thine Holy Ghost to comfort us, and exalt us unto the same place whither our Savior Christ is gone before; who liveth and reigneth with thee and the same Holy Ghost, one God, world without end. *Amen.*

The Day of Pentecost: Whitsunday

Almighty God, who on this day didst open the way of eternal life to every race and nation by the promised gift of thy Holy Spirit: Shed abroad this gift throughout the world by the preaching of the Gospel, that it may reach to the ends of the earth; through Jesus Christ our Lord, who liveth and reigneth with thee, in the unity of the same Spirit, one God, for ever and ever. *Amen.*

or this

O God, who on this day didst teach the hearts of thy faithful people by sending to them the light of thy Holy Spirit: Grant us by the same Spirit to have a right judgment in all things, and evermore to rejoice in his holy comfort; through the merits of Christ Jesus our Savior, who liveth and reigneth with thee, in the unity of the same Spirit, one God, world without end. *Amen.*

First Sunday after Pentecost: Trinity Sunday

Almighty and everlasting God, who hast given unto us thy servants grace, by the confession of a true faith, to acknowledge the glory of the eternal Trinity, and in the power of the divine Majesty to worship the Unity: We beseech thee that thou wouldst keep us steadfast in this faith and worship, and bring us at last to see thee in thy one and eternal glory, O Father; who with the Son and Holy Spirit livest and reignest, one God, for ever and ever. *Amen.*

The Season after Pentecost

Proper 1 *The Sunday closest to May 11*

Remember, O Lord, what thou hast wrought in us and not what we deserve; and, as thou hast called us to thy service, make us worthy of our calling; through Jesus Christ our Lord, who liveth and reigneth with thee and the Holy Spirit, one God, now and for ever. *Amen*

Seventh Sunday of Easter: The Sunday after Ascension Day

O God, the King of glory, you have exalted your only Son Jesus Christ with great triumph to your kingdom in heaven: Do not leave us comfortless, but send us your Holy Spirit to strengthen us, and exalt us to that place where our Savior Christ has gone before; who lives and reigns with you and the Holy Spirit, one God, in glory everlasting. *Amen.*

The Day of Pentecost: Whitsunday

Almighty God, on this day you opened the way of eternal life to every race and nation by the promised gift of your Holy Spirit: Shed abroad this gift throughout the world by the preaching of the Gospel, that it may reach to the ends of the earth; through Jesus Christ our Lord, who lives and reigns with you, in the unity of the Holy Spirit, one God, for ever and ever. *Amen.*

or this

O God, who on this day taught the hearts of your faithful people by sending to them the light of your Holy Spirit: Grant us by the same Spirit to have a right judgment in all things, and evermore to rejoice in his holy comfort; through Jesus Christ your Son our Lord, who lives and reigns with you, in the unity of the Holy Spirit, one God, for ever and ever. *Amen.*

First Sunday after Pentecost: Trinity Sunday

Almighty and everlasting God, you have given to us your servants grace, by the confession of a true faith, to acknowledge the glory of the eternal Trinity, and in the power of your divine Majesty to worship the Unity: Keep us steadfast in this faith and worship, and bring us at last to see you in your one and eternal glory, O Father; who with the Son and Holy Spirit live and reign, one God, for ever and ever. *Amen.*

The Season after Pentecost

Proper 1 *The Sunday closest to May 11*

Remember, O Lord, what you have wrought in us and not what we deserve; and, as you have called us to your service, make us worthy of our calling; through Jesus Christ our Lord, who lives and reigns with you and the Holy Spirit, one God, now and for ever. *Amen*

The Twentieth Sunday after Trinity.

Omnipotens et misericors deus, uniuersa nobis aduersantia propitiationis exclude, ut mente et corpore pariter expediti quae tua sunt liberis mentibus exequamur: per. [Gel., 1234.]

O ALMIGHTY and most merciful God, of thy bountiful goodness keep us, we beseech thee, from all things that may hurt us; that we, being ready both in body and soul, may cheerfully accomplish those things which thou commandest; through Jesus Christ our Lord. *Amen.*

The Fifth Sunday after Trinity.

Da nobis, domine deus noster, ut et mundi cursus pacifico nobis tuo ordine dirigatur, et aeclesia tua tranquilla deuotine laetetur: per. [Ver., 633.]

GRANT, O Lord, we beseech thee, that the course of this world may be so peaceably ordered by thy governance, that thy Church may joyfully serve thee in all godly quietness; through Jesus Christ our Lord. *Amen.*

The Eighth Sunday after Trinity.

Deus, cuius prouidencia in sui disposicione non fallitur, te supplices exoramus, ut noxia cuncta submoueas et omnia nobis profutura conceas: per. [Gel., 1186.]

O GOD, whose never-failing providence ordereth all things both in heaven and earth; We humbly beseech thee to put away from us all hurtful things, and to give us those things which are profitable for us, through Jesus Christ our Lord. *Amen.*

The Fifth Sunday after Easter.[28] (1662-1871)

The Fifth Sunday after Easter, commonly called Rogation Sunday. (1892-1928)

Deus, a quo bona cuncta procedunt, largire supplicibus, ut cogitemus te inspirante quae recta sunt et te gubernante eadem faciamus: per. [Gel., 556.]

O LORD, from whom all good things do come; Grant to us thy humble servants, that by thy holy inspiration we may think those things that are good,[29] and by thy merciful guiding may perform the same through our Lord Jesus Christ. *Amen.*

The Second Sunday after Trinity.

Sanctae nominis tui, domine, timorem pariter et amorem fac nos habere perpetuum, quia nunquam tuam gubernationem distitues, quos in solidatate tuae dilectionis instituēs: per. [Gel., 586.]

O LORD, who never failest to help and govern those[30] whom thou dost bring up in thy stedfast fear and love; Keep us, we beseech thee, under the protection of thy good providence, and make us to have a perpetual fear and love of thy holy Name; through Jesus Christ our Lord. *Amen.*

[28]Thus through 1892.

[29]"which be good," [1662].

[30]"them" [1662 & 1786].

1979-I

Proper 2 *The Sunday closest to May 18*

O Almighty and merciful God, of thy bountiful goodness keep us, we beseech thee, from all things that may hurt us, that we, being ready both in body and soul, may with free hearts accomplish those things which belong to thy purpose; through Jesus Christ our Lord, who liveth and reigneth with thee and the Holy Spirit, one God, now and for ever. *Amen.*t

Proper 3 *The Sunday closest to May 25*

Grant, O Lord, we beseech thee, that the course of this world may be peaceably governed by thy providence, and that thy Church may joyfully serve thee in confidence and serenity; through Jesus Christ our Lord, who liveth and reigneth with thee and the Holy Spirit, one God, for ever and ever. *Amen.*

Proper 4 *The Sunday closest to June 1*

O God, whose never-failing providence ordereth all things both in heaven and earth: We humbly beseech thee to put away from us all hurtful things, and to give us those things which are profitable for us; through Jesus Christ our Lord, who liveth and reigneth with thee and the Holy Spirit, one God, for ever and ever. *Amen.*

Proper 5 *The Sunday closest to June 8*

O God, from whom all good doth come: Grant that by thy inspiration we may think those things that are right, and by thy merciful guiding may perform the same; through Jesus Christ our Lord, who liveth and reigneth with thee and the Holy Spirit, one God, for ever and ever. *Amen.*

Proper 6 *The Sunday closest to June 15*

Keep, O Lord, we beseech thee, thy household the Church in thy steadfast faith and love, that by the help of thy grace we may proclaim thy truth with boldness, and minister thy justice with compassion; for the sake of our Savior Jesus Christ, who liveth and reigneth with thee and the Holy Spirit, one God, now and for ever. *Amen.*

Proper 7 *The Sunday closest to June 22*

O Lord, we beseech thee, make us to have perpetual fear and love of thy holy Name, for thou never failest to help and govern those whom who hast set upon the sure foundation of thy loving-kindness; through Jesus Christ our Lord, who liveth and reigneth with thee and the Holy Spirit, one God, for ever and ever. *Amen.*

1979-II

Proper 2 *The Sunday closest to May 18*

Almighty and merciful God, in your goodness keep us, we pray, from all things that may hurt us, that we, being ready both in mind and body, may accomplish with free hearts those things which belong to your purpose; through Jesus Christ our Lord, who lives and reigns with you and the Holy Spirit, one God, now and for ever. *Amen.*

Proper 3 *The Sunday closest to May 25*

Grant, O Lord, that the course of this world may be peaceably governed by your providence; and that your Church may joyfully serve you in confidence and serenity; through Jesus Christ our Lord, who lives and reigns with you and the Holy Spirit, one God, for ever and ever. *Amen.*

Proper 4 *The Sunday closest to June 1*

O God, your never-failing providence sets in order all things both in heaven and earth: Put away from us, we entreat you, all hurtful things, and give us those things which are profitable for us; through Jesus Christ our Lord, who lives and reigns with you and the Holy Spirit, one God, for ever and ever. *Amen.*

Proper 5 *The Sunday closest to June 8*

O God, from whom all good proceeds: Grant that by your inspiration we may think those things that are right, and by your merciful guiding may do them; through Jesus Christ our Lord, who lives and reigns with you and the Holy Spirit, one God, for ever and ever. *Amen.*

Proper 6 *The Sunday closest to June 15*

Keep, O Lord, your household the Church in your steadfast faith and love, that through your grace we may proclaim your truth with boldness, and minister your justice with compassion; for the sake of our Savior Jesus Christ, who lives and reigns with you and the Holy Spirit, one God, now and for ever. *Amen.*

Proper 7 *The Sunday closest to June 22*

O Lord, make us have perpetual love and reverence for your holy Name, for you never fail to help and govern those whom you have set upon the sure foundation of your loving-kindness; through Jesus Christ our Lord, who lives and reigns with you and the Holy Spirit, one God, for ever and ever. *Amen.*

ALmightie God, whiche hast builded the congregacion vpon the foundacion of the Apostles and prophetes, Iesu Christ hymselfe beyng the head corner stone: graunte vs so to bee ioyned together in vnitie of spirite by theyr doctrine, that we may be made an holye temple acceptable to thee: throughe Iesus Christe our Lorde. [1549, Symon and Iude Apostles.]

Deus, qui aeclesiam tuam in dilectione[m] tuae diuinitatis et proximi cuncta seruare caeles[t]ia mandata docuisti: da nobis spiritum pacis et gratiae, ut uniuersa familia tua et toto tibi sit corde deuota, et pura sibi uoluntate concordet: per. [Ver., 971.]

Vota quaesumus domine supplicantis populi caelesti pietate prosequere, ut et quae agenda sunt uideant, et ad implenda quae uiderint conualescant. Per dominum nostrum iesum. [Greg., 86.]

The First Sunday after the Epiphany.

O LORD, we beseech thee mercifully to receive the prayers of thy people who[31] call upon thee; and grant that they may both perceive and know what things they ought to do, and also may have grace and power faithfully to fulfil the same; through Jesus Christ our Lord. *Amen.*

ALmightie God, the fountaine of all wisdome, whiche knoweste our necessities before we aske, and our ignoraunce in asking: we beseche thee to haue compassion vpon our infirmities, and those thinges whiche for our vnwoorthines we dare not, and for our blyndnes we cannot aske, vouchsaue to geue vs for the woorthines of thy sonne Iesus Christe our Lorde. Amen. [1549, "Collectes to be sayed after the Offertory, when there is no Communion, euery suche day one."]

ALMIGHTY God, the fountain of all wisdom, who knowest our necessities before we ask, and our ignorance in asking; We beseech thee to have compassion upon our infirmities; and those things, which for our unworthiness we dare not, and for our blindness we cannot ask, vouchsafe to give us, for the worthiness of thy Son Jesus Christ our Lord. *Amen.* [1789-1892, appointed as in 1549; 1928, "*to be used after the Collects of Morning or Evening Prayer, or Communion, at the discretion of the Minister.*"]

Protector in te sperantium deus, sine quo nihil est ualidum, nihil sanctum, multiplica super nos misericordiam tuam, ut te rectore te duce, sic transeamus per bona temporalia, ut non amittamus aeterna. Per. [Greg., supp, 1138]

The Fourth Sunday after Trinity.

O GOD, the protector of all that trust in thee, without whom nothing is strong, nothing is holy; Increase and multiply upon us thy mercy; that, thou being our ruler and guide, we may so pass through things temporal, that we finally lose not the things eternal. Grant this, O heavenly Father, for the sake of Jesus Christ our Lord.[32] *Amen.*

Ecclesiam tuam, domine, miseracio continuata mundet et muniat, et quia sine te non potest salua consistere, tuo semper munere gubernetur: per. [Gel., 1218.]

The Sixteenth Sunday after Trinity.

O LORD, we beseech thee, let thy continual pity cleanse and defend thy Church; and, because it cannot continue in safety without thy succour, preserve it evermore by thy help and goodness; through Jesus Christ our Lord. *Amen.*

[31]"which" [1662].

[32]Prior to 1928, "for Jesus Christ's sake our Lord."

Proper 8 *The Sunday closest to June 29*

O Almighty God, who hast built thy Church upon the foundation of the apostles and prophets, Jesus Christ himself being the chief cornerstone: Grant us so to be joined together in unity of spirit by their doctrine, that we may be made an holy temple acceptable unto thee; through the same Jesus Christ our Lord, who liveth and reigneth with thee and the Holy Spirit, one God, for ever and ever. *Amen.*

Proper 9 *The Sunday closest to July 6*

O God, who hast taught us to keep all thy commandments by loving thee and our neighbor: Grant us the grace of thy Holy Spirit, that we may be devoted to thee with our whole heart, and united to one another with pure affection; through Jesus Christ our Lord, who liveth and reigneth with thee and the same Spirit, one God, for ever and ever. *Amen.*

Proper 10 *The Sunday closest to July 13*

O Lord, we beseech mercifully to receive the prayers of thy people who call upon thee, and grant that they may both perceive and know what things they ought to do, and also may have grace and power faithfully to fulfill the same; through Jesus Christ our Lord, who liveth and reigneth with thee and the Holy Spirit, one God, now and for ever. *Amen.*

Proper 11 *The Sunday closest to July 20*

Almighty God, the fountain of all wisdom, who knowest our necessities before we ask and our ignorance in asking: Have compassion, we beseech thee, upon our infirmities, and those things which for our unworthiness we dare not, and for our blindness we cannot ask, mercifully give us for the worthiness of thy Son Jesus Christ our Lord; who liveth and reigneth with thee and the Holy Spirit, one God, now and for ever. *Amen.*

Proper 12 *The Sunday closest to July 27*

O God, the protector of all who trust in thee, without whom nothing is strong, nothing is holy: Increase and multiply upon us thy mercy, that, thou being our ruler and guide, we may so pass through things temporal, that we finally lose not the things eternal; through Jesus Christ our Lord, who liveth and reigneth with thee and the Holy Spirit, one God, for ever and ever. *Amen.*

Proper 13 *The Sunday closest to August 3*

O Lord, we beseech thee, let thy continual pity cleanse and defend thy Church, and, because it cannot continue in safety without thy succor, preserve it evermore by thy help and goodness; through Jesus Christ our Lord, who liveth and reigneth with thee and the Holy Spirit, one God, for ever and ever. *Amen.*

Proper 8 *The Sunday closest to June 29*

Almighty God, you have built your Church upon the foundation of the apostles and prophets, Jesus Christ himself being the chief cornerstone: Grant us so to be joined together in unity of spirit by their teaching, that we may be made a holy temple acceptable to you; through Jesus Christ our Lord, who lives and reigns with you and the Holy Spirit, one God, for ever and ever. *Amen.*

Proper 9 *The Sunday closest to July 6*

O God, you have taught us to keep all your commandments by loving you and our neighbor: Grant us the grace of your Holy Spirit, that we may be devoted to you with our whole heart, and united to one another with pure affection; through Jesus Christ our Lord, who lives and reigns with you and the Holy Spirit, one God, for ever and ever. *Amen.*

Proper 10 *The Sunday closest to July 13*

O Lord, mercifully receive the prayers of your people who call upon you, and grant that they may know and understand what things they ought to do, and also may have grace and power faithfully to accomplish them; through Jesus Christ our Lord, who lives and reigns with you and the Holy Spirit, one God, now and for ever. *Amen.*

Proper 11 *The Sunday closest to July 20*

Almighty God, the fountain of all wisdom, you know our necessities before we ask and our ignorance in asking: Have compassion on our weakness, and mercifully give us those things which for our unworthiness we dare not, and for our blindness we cannot ask; through the worthiness of your Son Jesus Christ our Lord, who lives and reigns with you and the Holy Spirit, one God, now and for ever. *Amen.*

Proper 12 *The Sunday closest to July 27*

O God, the protector of all who trust in you, without whom nothing is strong, nothing is holy: Increase and multiply upon us your mercy; that, with you as our ruler and guide, we may so pass through things temporal, that we lose not the things eternal; through Jesus Christ our Lord, who lives and reigns with you and the Holy Spirit, one God, for ever and ever. *Amen.*

Proper 13 *The Sunday closest to August 3*

Let your continual mercy, O Lord, cleanse and defend your Church; and, because it cannot continue in safety without your help, protect and govern it always by your goodness; through Jesus Christ our Lord, who lives and reigns with you and the Holy Spirit, one God, for ever and ever. *Amen.*

The Ninth Sunday after Trinity.

Largire nobis, domine, quaesumus, spiritum cogitandi quae bona sunt promptius et agendi, ut qui sine te esse non possumus, secundum te uiuiere ualeamus: per. [Ver., 1015.]

GRANT to us, Lord, we beseech thee, the spirit to think and do always such things as are right;[33] that we who cannot do any thing that is good without thee, may by thee be enabled to live according to thy will; through Jesus Christ our Lord. *Amen.*

The Second Sunday after Easter.

ALmightie God, whiche haste geuen thy holy sonne to be vnto vs, bothe a sacrifice for synne, and also an example of Godly lyfe: Geue vs the grace that we may alwayes moste thankfully receiue that his inestimable benefite, and also dayly indeuour our selfes, to folowe the blessed steppes of his moste holy lyfe. [1549, The second Sondaye after Easter.]

ALMIGHTY God, who hast given thine only Son to be unto us both a sacrifice for sin, and also an ensample of godly life; Give us grace that we may always most thankfully receive that his inestimable benefit, and also daily endeavour ourselves to follow the blessed steps of his most holy life; through the same Jesus Christ our Lord. *Amen.*

Tuesday in Whitsun Week.

Da quaesumus ecclesiae tuae misericors deus, ut sancto spiritu congregata hostili nullatenus incursione turbetur. Per. [Greg., 542.]

GRANT, we beseech thee, merciful God, that thy Church, being gathered together in unity by thy Holy Spirit, may manifest thy power among all peoples, to the glory of thy Name; through Jesus Christ our Lord, who liveth and reigneth with thee and the same Spirit, one God, world without end. *Amen.* [1928]

The Seventh Sunday after Trinity.

Deus uirtutum, cuius est totum quod est optimum, insere pectoribus nostris amorem tui nominis et praesta, ut et nobis relegionis augmentum quae sunt bona nutrias ac uigilantia studium quaesomus nutrita custodias: per. [Gel, 1182.]

LORD of all power and might, who art the author and giver of all good things; Graft in our hearts the love of thy Name, increase in us true religion, nourish us with all goodness, and of thy great mercy keep us in the same; through Jesus Christ our Lord. *Amen.*

Da nobis, domine, quaesumus, in te tota mente confidere: quoniam sicut superbis in sua uirtute praesumentibus semper obsistis, ita non deseris in tua misericordia gloriantes: per. [Ver., 540.]

The Nineteenth Sunday after Trinity.

Dirigat corda nostra, domine, quaesumus, tuae miserationes operatio, quia tibi sine te placere non possimus: per. [Gel., 1230.]

O GOD, forasmuch as without thee we are not able to please thee; Mercifully grant that thy Holy Spirit may in all things direct and rule our hearts; through Jesus Christ our Lord. *Amen.*

[33] "are rightful" [1786]; "be rightful" [1662].

1979-I

Proper 14 *The Sunday closest to August 10*

Grant to us, Lord, we beseech thee, the spirit to think and do always such things as are right, that we, who cannot exist without thee, may by thee be enabled to live according to thy will; through Jesus Christ our Lord, who liveth and reigneth with thee and the Holy Spirit, one God, for ever and ever. *Amen.*

Proper 15 *The Sunday closest to August 17*

Almighty God, who hast given thy only Son to be unto us both a sacrifice for sin and also an example of godly life; Give us grace that we may always most thankfully receive that his inestimable benefit, and also daily endeavor ourselves to follow the blessed steps of his most holy life; through the same thy Son Jesus Christ our Lord, who liveth and reigneth with thee and the Holy Spirit, one God, now and for ever. *Amen.*

Proper 16 *The Sunday closest to August 24*

Grant, we beseech thee, merciful God, that thy Church, being gathered together in unity by thy Holy Spirit, may manifest thy power among all peoples, to the glory of thy Name; through Jesus Christ our Lord, who liveth and reigneth with thee and the same Spirit, one God, world without end. *Amen.*

1979-II

Proper 14 *The Sunday closest to August 10*

Grant to us, Lord, we pray, the spirit to think and do always those things that are right, that we, who cannot exist without you, may by you be enabled to live according to your will; through Jesus Christ our Lord, who lives and reigns with you and the Holy Spirit, one God, for ever and ever. *Amen.*

Proper 15 *The Sunday closest to August 17*

Almighty God, you have given your only Son to be for us a sacrifice for sin, and also an example of godly life: Give us grace to receive thankfully the fruits of his redeeming work, and to follow daily in the blessed steps of his most holy life; through Jesus Christ your Son our Lord, who lives and reigns with you and the Holy Spirit, one God, now and for ever. *Amen.*

Proper 16 *The Sunday closest to August 24*

Grant, O merciful God, that your Church, being gathered together in unity by your Holy Spirit, may show forth your power among all peoples, to the glory of your Name; through Jesus Christ our Lord, who lives and reigns with you and the Holy Spirit, one God, for ever and ever. *Amen.*

1979-I

Proper 17 *The Sunday closest to August 31*

Lord of all power and might, who art the author and giver of all good things: Graft in our hearts the love of thy Name, increase in us true religion, nourish us with all goodness, and bring forth in us the fruit of good works; through Jesus Christ our Lord, who liveth and reigneth with thee and the Holy Spirit, one God, for ever and ever. *Amen.*

Proper 18 *The Sunday closest to September 7*

Grant us, O Lord, we pray thee, to trust in thee with all our heart; seeing that, as thou dost alway resist the proud who confide in their own strength, so thou dost not forsake those who make their boast of thy mercy; through Jesus Christ our Lord, who liveth and reigneth with thee and the Holy Spirit, one God, now and for ever. *Amen.*

Proper 19 *The Sunday closest to September 14*

O God, forasmuch as without thee we are not able to please thee, mercifully grant that thy Holy Spirit may in all things direct and rule our hearts; through Jesus Christ our Lord, who with thee and the same Spirit liveth and reigneth, one God, now and for ever. *Amen.*

1979-II

Proper 17 *The Sunday closest to August 31*

Lord of all power and might, the author and giver of all good things: Graft in our hearts the love of your Name; increase in us true religion; nourish us with all goodness; and bring forth in us the fruit of good works; through Jesus Christ our Lord, who lives and reigns with you and the Holy Spirit, one God, for ever and ever. *Amen.*

Proper 18 *The Sunday closest to September 7*

Grant us, O Lord, to trust in you with all our hearts; for, as you always resist the proud who confide in their own strength, so you never forsake those who make their boast of your mercy; through Jesus Christ our Lord, who lives and reigns with you and the Holy Spirit, one God, now and for ever. *Amen.*

Proper 19 *The Sunday closest to September 14*

O God, because without you we are not able to please you, mercifully grant that your Holy Spirit may in all things direct and rule our hearts; through Jesus Christ our Lord, who lives and reigns with you and the Holy Spirit, one God, now and for ever. *Amen.*

Da nobis, domine, non terrena sapere, sed amare caelestia, et inter praetereuntia constitutos iam nunc inherere mansuris: per. [Ver., 173.]

The Eleventh Sunday after Trinity.

Deus, qui omnipotenciam tuam parcendo maximae et miserando manifestas, multiplica super nos graciam tuam, ut a tua promissa currentes caelestium bonorum facis esse consortes: per. [Gel., 1198.]

O GOD, who declarest thy almighty power chiefly[34] in showing mercy and pity; Mercifully grant unto us such a measure of thy grace, that we, running the way of thy commandments, may obtain thy gracious promises, and be made partakers of thy heavenly treasure; through Jesus Christ our Lord. *Amen.*

The Twelfth Sunday after Trinity.

Uirtutum caelestium deus, qui plura prestas, quam petimus aut meremur: tribue, quaesumus, ut tua nobis misericordia conferatur, quod nostrorum non habet fiducia meritorum: per. [Ver., 917.]

Omnipotens sempiterne deus qui habu[n]dancia pietatis tuae et merita supplicum excedis et uota. effunde super nos misericordiam tuam. ut dimittas que consciencia metuit. et adicias quod oracio non presumit. per. [Sarum, Dominica xii. {post festum sancte trinitatis}]

ALMIGHTY and everlasting God, who art always more ready to hear than we to pray, and art wont to give more than either we desire or deserve; Pour down upon us the abundance of thy mercy; forgiving us those things whereof our conscience is afraid, and giving us those good things which we are not worthy to ask, but through the merits and mediation of Jesus Christ, thy Son, our Lord. *Amen.*

The Seventeenth Sunday after Trinity

Tua nos domine quaesumus gratia semper et praeueniat et sequatur, ac bonis operibus iugiter prestet esse intentos. Per. [Greg., 966]

LORD, we pray thee that thy grace may always prevent and follow us, and make us continually to be given to all good works; through Jesus Christ our Lord. *Amen.*

Omnipotens sempiterne deus, qui gloriam tuam in omnibus in Christo gentibus reuelasti, custodi opera misericordiae tuae, ut aecclesia tua toto orbe diffusa stabili fide in confessionem tui nominis perseueret: per dominum. [Gel., 401.]

The Fourteenth Sunday after Trinity.

Omnipotens sempiterne deus, da nobis fidei spei et caritatis aumentum; et ut mereamur adsequi quod promittis, fac nos amare quod praecipis: per. [Ver., 598]

ALMIGHTY and everlasting God, give unto us the increase of faith, hope, and charity; and, that we may obtain that which thou dost promise, make us to love that which thou dost command; through Jesus Christ our Lord. *Amen.*

[34]"most chiefly" [1662 & 1786].

Proper 20 *The Sunday closest to September 21*

Grant us, O Lord, not to mind earthly things, but to love things heavenly; and even now, while we are placed among things that are passing away, to cleave to those that shall abide; through Jesus Christ our Lord, who liveth and reigneth with thee and the Holy Spirit, one God, for ever and ever. *Amen.*

Proper 21 *The Sunday closest to September 28*

O God, who declarest thy almighty power chiefly in showing mercy and pity: Mercifully grant unto us such a measure of thy grace, that we, running to obtain thy promises, may be made partakers of thy heavenly treasure; through Jesus Christ our Lord, who liveth and reigneth with thee and the Holy Spirit, one God, for ever and ever. *Amen.*

Proper 22 The Sunday closest to October 5

Almighty and everlasting God, who art always more ready to hear than we to pray, and art wont to give more than either we desire or deserve: Pour down upon us the abundance of thy mercy, forgiving us those things whereof our conscience is afraid, and giving us those good things which we are not worthy to ask, but through the merits and mediation of Jesus Christ thy Son our Lord; who liveth and reigneth with thee and the Holy Spirit, one God, for ever and ever. *Amen.*

Proper 23 *The Sunday closest to October 12*

Lord, we pray thee that thy grace may always precede and follow us, and make us continually to be given to all good works; through Jesus Christ our Lord, who liveth and reigneth with thee and the Holy Spirit, one God, now and for ever. *Amen.*

Proper 24 *The Sunday closest to October 19*

Almighty and everlasting God, who in Christ hast revealed thy glory among the nations: Preserve the works of thy mercy, that thy Church throughout the world may persevere with steadfast faith in the confession of thy Name; through the same Jesus Christ our Lord, who liveth and reigneth with thee and the Holy Spirit, one God, for ever and ever. *Amen.*

Proper 25 *The Sunday closest to October 26*

Almighty and everlasting God, give unto us the increase of faith, hope, and charity; and, that we may obtain that which thou dost promise, make us to love that which thou dost command; through Jesus Christ our Lord, who liveth and reigneth with thee and the Holy Spirit, one God, for ever and ever. *Amen.*

Proper 20 *The Sunday closest to September 21*

Grant us, Lord, not to be anxious about earthly things, but to love things heavenly; and even now, while we are placed among things that are passing away, to hold fast to those that shall endure; through Jesus Christ our Lord, who lives and reigns with you and the Holy Spirit, one God, for ever and ever. *Amen.*

Proper 21 *The Sunday closest to September 28*

O God, you declare your almighty power chiefly in showing mercy and pity: Grant us the fullness of your grace, that we, running to obtain your promises, may become partakers of your heavenly treasure; through Jesus Christ our Lord, who lives and reigns with you and the Holy Spirit, one God, for ever and ever. *Amen.*

Proper 22 *The Sunday closest to October 5*

Almighty and everlasting God, you are always more ready to hear than we to pray, and to give more than we either desire or deserve: Pour upon us the abundance of your mercy, forgiving us those things of which our conscience is afraid, and giving us those good things for which we are not worthy to ask, except through the merits and mediation of Jesus Christ our Savior; who lives and reigns with you and the Holy Spirit, one God, for ever and ever. *Amen.*

Proper 23 *The Sunday closest to October 12*

Lord, we pray that your grace may always precede and follow us, that we may continually be given to good works; through Jesus Christ our Lord, who lives and reigns with you and the Holy Spirit, one God, now and for ever. *Amen.*

Proper 24 *The Sunday closest to October 19*

Almighty and everlasting God, in Christ you have revealed your glory among the nations: Preserve the works of your mercy, that your Church throughout the world may persevere with steadfast faith in the confession of your Name; through Jesus Christ our Lord, who lives and reigns with you and the Holy Spirit, one God, for ever and ever. *Amen.*

Proper 25 *The Sunday closest to October 26*

Almighty and everlasting God, increase in us the gifts of faith, hope, and charity; and, that we may obtain what you promise, make us love what you command; through Jesus Christ our Lord, who lives and reigns with you and the Holy Spirit, one God, for ever and ever. *Amen.*

The Thirteenth Sunday after Trinity.

Omnipotens et misericors deus, de cuius munere uenit, ut tibi a fidelibus tuis dignae et laudabiliter seruiatur: tribue, ut ad promissiones tuas sine offensione curramus: per. [Ver., 574.]

ALMIGHTY and merciful God, of whose only gift it cometh that thy faithful people do unto thee true and laudable service; Grant, we beseech thee, that we may so faithfully serve thee in this life, that we fail not finally to attain thy heavenly promises; through the merits of Jesus Christ our Lord. *Amen.*

The Sixth Sunday after the Epiphany.

O God, whose blessed Sonne was manifested, yt he might destroy the works of the divel, & make us the Sons of God and heyres of eternall life; Grant we beseech thee that having this hope in us, wee may purifie our selves even as he is pure: that when he shall appeare againe with power & great glory, we may be made like unto him in his eternall & glorious kingdome where with Thee ô Father & ye Holy Ghost he liveth & reigneth one God world without end. Amen. [John Cosin.]

O GOD, whose blessed Son was manifested that he mighty destroy the works of the devil, and make us the sons of God, and heirs of eternal life; Grant us, we beseech thee, that, having this hope, we may purify ourselves, even as he is pure; that, when he shall appear again with power and great glory, we may be made like unto him in his eternal and glorious kingdom; where with thee, O Father, and thee, O Holy Ghost, he liveth and reigneth ever, one God, world without end. *Amen.*

The Second Sunday in Advent.

BLessed Lorde, whiche haste caused all holy scriptures to be written for our learning; graunt vs that we maye in suche wyse heare them, reade, marke, learne, and inwardly digeste them: that by pacience and coumforte of thy holy worde, we maye embrace and euer holde fast the blessed hope of euerlastyng lyfe, whiche thou haste geuen vs in our sauiour Iesus Christe. [1549, "The seconde Sonday" {in Advent}]

BLESSED Lord, who hast caused all holy Scriptures to be written for our learning; Grant that we may in such wise hear them, read, mark, learn, and inwardly digest them, that by patience and comfort of thy holy Word, we may embrace, and ever hold fast, the blessed hope of everlasting life, which thou hast given us in our Saviour Jesus Christ. *Amen.*

Omnipotens sempiterne Deus, qui in dilecto Filio tuo, universorum Rege, omnia instaurare voluisti, concede propitius, ut tota creatura, a servitute liberata, tuae maiestati deserviat ac te sine fine collaudet. Per dominum. [*Missale Romanum* of Paul VI, collect for Christ the King.]

Holy Days

Saint Andrew's Day.[35]

Saint Andrew the Apostle. [November 30.]

ALmightie god which didst geue such grace vnto thy holy Apostle Saincte Andrewe, that he redily obeyed the callyng of thy sone Iesus Christ, and followed hym without delaye: Graunte vnto vs all, that we being called by the holy worde, maye furthwith geue ouer our selfes, obediently to folow thy holy commaudements: through thesame[36] Iesus Chryste our Lorde. [1552, Sainct Andrewes daye.]

ALMIGHTY God, who didst give such grace unto thy holy Apostle Saint Andrew, that he readily obeyed the calling of thy Son Jesus Christ, and followed him without delay; Grant unto us all, that we, being called by thy holy Word, may forthwith give up ourselves obediently to fulfil thy holy commandments, through the same Jesus Christ our Lord. *Amen.*

[35]Thus through 1892. [36]*sic.*

Proper 26 *The Sunday closest to November 2*

Almighty and merciful God, of whose only gift it cometh that thy faithful people do unto thee true and laudable service: Grant, we beseech thee, that we may run without stumbling to obtain thy heavenly promises; through Jesus Christ our Lord, who liveth and reigneth with thee and the Holy Spirit, one God, now and for ever. *Amen.*

Proper 27 *The Sunday closest to November 9*

O God, whose blessed Son was manifested that he might destroy the works of the devil and make us the children of God and heirs of eternal life: Grant us, we beseech thee, that, having this hope, we may purify ourselves even as he is pure; that, when he shall appear again with power and great glory, we may be made like unto him in his eternal and glorious kingdom; where with thee, O Father, and thee, O Holy Ghost, he liveth and reigneth ever, one God, world without end. *Amen.*

Proper 28 *The Sunday closest to November 16*

Blessed Lord, who hast caused all holy Scriptures to be written for our learning: Grant that we may in such wise hear them, read, mark, learn, and inwardly digest them; that by patience and comfort of thy holy Word, we may embrace and ever hold fast the blessed hope of everlasting life, which thou hast given us in our Savior Jesus Christ; who liveth and reigneth with thee and the Holy Spirit, one God, for ever and ever. *Amen.*

Proper 29 *The Sunday closest to November 23*

Almighty and everlasting God, whose will it is to restore all things in thy well-beloved Son, the King of kings and Lord of lords: Mercifully grant that the peoples of the earth, divided and enslaved by sin, may be freed and brought together under his most gracious rule; who liveth and reigneth with thee and the Holy Spirit, one God, now and for ever. *Amen.*

Proper 26 *The Sunday closest to November 2*

Almighty and merciful God, it is only by your gift that your faithful people offer you true and laudable service: Grant that we may run without stumbling to obtain your heavenly promises; through Jesus Ch~~rist our~~ Lord, who lives and reigns with you and the Holy Spirit, one God, now and for ever. *Amen.*

Proper 27 *The Sunday closest to November 9*

O God, whose blessed Son came into the world that he might destroy the works of the devil and make us children of God and heirs of eternal life: Grant that, having this hope, we may purify ourselves as he is pure; that, when he comes again with power and great glory, we may be made like him in his eternal and glorious kingdom; where he lives and reigns with you and the Holy Spirit, one God, for ever and ever. *Amen.*

Proper 28 *The Sunday closest to November 16*

Blessed Lord, who caused all holy Scriptures to be written for our learning: Grant us so to hear them, read, mark, learn, and inwardly digest them, that we may embrace and ever hold fast the blessed hope of everlasting life, which you have given us in our Savior Jesus Christ; who lives and reigns with you and the Holy Spirit, one God, for ever and ever. *Amen.*

Proper 29 *The Sunday closest to November 23*

Almighty and everlasting God, whose will it is to restore all things in your well-beloved Son, the King of kings and Lord of lords: Mercifully grant that the peoples of the earth, divided and enslaved by sin, may be freed and brought together under his most gracious rule; who lives and reigns with you and the Holy Spirit, one God, now and for ever. *Amen.*

Saint Andrew *November 30*

Almighty God, who didst give such grace to thine apostle Andrew that he readily obeyed the call of thy Son Jesus Christ, and brought his brother with him: Give unto us, who are called by thy Word, grace to follow him without delay, and to bring those near to us into his gracious presence; who liveth and reigneth with thee and the Holy Spirit, one God, now and for ever. *Amen.*

Saint Andrew *November 30*

Almighty God, who gave such grace to your apostle Andrew that he readily obeyed the call of your Son Jesus Christ, and brought his brother with him: Give us, who are called by your holy Word, grace to follow him without delay, and to bring those near to us into his gracious presence; who lives and reigns with you and the Holy Spirit, one God, now and for ever. *Amen.*

Saint Thomas the Apostle.[37]

Saint Thomas the Apostle. [December 21.]

ALmightie euerlyuing God, whiche for the more confirmacion of the fayth, didst suffer thy holy Apostle Thomas, to be doubtfull in thy sonnes resurreccion: graunte vs so perfectly, and without al doubt to beleue in thy sone Iesus Christe, that our faith in thy sight neuer be reproued: heare vs, O Lorde, through thesame Iesus Christe: to with thee and the holy gost be all honour. &c. [1549, Saincte Thomas the Apostle.]

ALMIGHTY and everliving God, who, for the greater confirmation[38] of the faith, didst suffer thy holy Apostle Thomas to be doubtful in thy Son's resurrection; Grant us so perfectly, and without all doubt, to believe in thy Son Jesus Christ, that our faith in thy sight may never be reproved. Hear us, O Lord, through the same Jesus Christ, to whom, with thee and the Holy Ghost, be all honour and glory, now and for evermore. *Amen.*

Saint Stephen's Day.[39]

Saint Stephen, Deacon and Martyr. [December 26.]

[Da nobis quaesumus domine imitari quod colimus, ut discamus et inimicos diligere, quia eius natalicia caelebramus qui nouit etiam pro persecutoribus exorare. Per. {Greg., 62.}]

[GRANT, O Lord, that, in all our sufferings here upon earth for the testimony of thy truth, we may stedfastly look up to heaven, and by faith behold the glory that shall be revealed; and, being filled with the Holy Ghost, may learn to love and bless our persecutors by the example of thy first Martyr Saint Stephen, who prayed for his murderers to thee, O blessed Jesus, who standest at the right hand of God to succour all those who[40] suffer for thee, our only Mediator and Advocate. *Amen.*]

St. John the Evangelist's Day.[41]

Saint John, Apostle and Evangelist. [December 27.]

Aeclesiam tuam, domine, benignus inlustra, ut apostolicis beati Iohannis euangelistae inluminate doctrinis ad dona perueniat, quae de tua fidelibus retributione promisit: per. [Ver., 1283.]

MERCIFUL Lord, we beseech thee to cast thy bright beams of light upon thy Church, that it, being illumined[42] by the doctrine of thy blessed Apostle and Evangelist Saint John, may so walk in the light of thy truth, that it may at length attain to life everlasting;[43] through Jesus Christ our Lord. *Amen.*

37Thus through 1892.

38"more confirmation" [1662 & 1786].

39Thus through 1892.

40"that" [1662].

41Thus through 1892.

42"enlightened" [1662 & 1786]; "instructed" [1789-1892].

43"the light of everlasting life" [1662 & 1786]; "life everlasting" [1789-1892].

Saint Thomas *December 21*

Everliving God, who didst strengthen thine apostle Thomas with sure and certain faith in thy Son's resurrection: Grant us so perfectly and without doubt to believe in Jesus Christ, our Lord and our God, that our faith may never be found wanting in thy sight; through him who liveth and reigneth with thee and the Holy Spirit, one God, now and for ever. *Amen.*

Saint Stephen *December 26*

We give thee thanks, O Lord of glory, for the example of the first martyr Stephen, who looked up to heaven and prayed for his persecutors to thy Son Jesus Christ, who standeth at thy right hand; where he liveth and reigneth with thee and the Holy Spirit, one God, in glory everlasting. *Amen.*

Saint John *December 27*

Shed upon thy Church, we beseech thee, O Lord, the brightness of thy light; that we, being illumined by the teaching of thine apostle and evangelist John, may so walk in the light of thy truth, that we may at length attain to the fullness of life everlasting; through Jesus Christ our Lord, who liveth and reigneth with thee and the Holy Spirit, one God, for ever and ever. *Amen.*

The Holy Innocents *December 28*

We remember this day, O God, the slaughter of the holy innocents of Bethlehem by the order of King Herod. Receive, we beseech thee, into the arms of thy mercy all innocent victims; and by thy great might frustrate the designs of evil tyrants and establish thy rule of justice, love, and peace; through Jesus Christ our Lord, who liveth and reigneth with thee, in the unity of the Holy Spirit, one God, for ever and ever. *Amen.*

Confession of Saint Peter *January 18*

Almighty Father, who didst inspire Simon Peter, first among the apostles, to confess Jesus as Messiah and Son of the living God: Keep thy Church steadfast upon the rock of this faith, that in unity and peace we may proclaim the one truth and follow the one Lord, our Savior Jesus Christ; who liveth and reigneth with thee and the Holy Spirit, one God, now and for ever. *Amen.*

Saint Thomas *December 21*

Everliving God, who strengthened your apostle Thomas with firm and certain faith in your Son's resurrection: Grant us so perfectly and without doubt to believe in Jesus Christ, our Lord and our God, that our faith may never be found wanting in your sight; through him who lives and reigns with you and the Holy Spirit, one God, now and for ever. *Amen.*

Saint Stephen *December 26*

We give you thanks, O Lord of glory, for the example of the first martyr Stephen, who looked up to heaven and prayed for his persecutors to your Son Jesus Christ, who stands at your right hand; where he lives and reigns with you and the Holy Spirit, one God, in glory everlasting. *Amen.*

Saint John *December 27*

Shed upon your Church, O Lord, the brightness of your light, that we, being illumined by the teaching of your apostle and evangelist John, may so walk in the light of your truth, that at length we may attain to the fullness of eternal life; through Jesus Christ our Lord, who lives and reigns with you and the Holy Spirit, one God, for ever and ever. *Amen.*

The Holy Innocents *December 28*

We remember today, O God, the slaughter of the holy innocents of Bethlehem by King Herod. Receive, we pray, into the arms of your mercy all innocent victims; and by your great might frustrate the designs of evil tyrants and establish your rule of justice, love, and peace; through Jesus Christ our Lord, who lives and reigns with you, in the unity of the Holy Spirit, one God, for ever and ever. *Amen.*

Confession of Saint Peter *January 18*

Almighty Father, who inspired Simon Peter, first among the apostles, to confess Jesus as Messiah and Son of the living God: Keep your Church steadfast upon the rock of this faith, so that in unity and peace we may proclaim the one truth and follow the one Lord, our Savior Jesus Christ; who lives and reigns with you and the Holy Spirit, one God, now and for ever. *Amen*

The Conversion of Saint Paul.[44]

The Conversion of Saint Paul. [January 25.]

Deus qui uniuersum mundum beati pauli apostoli tui predicacione docuisti. da nobis quesumus ut qui eius hodie conuersionem colimus. per eius ad te exempla gradiamur. per. [Sarum, In conuersione sancti pauli.]

O GOD, who through the preaching of the blessed Apostle Saint Paul, hast caused the light of the Gospel to shine throughout the world; Grant, we beseech thee, that we, having his wonderful conversion in remembrance, may show forth our thankfulness unto thee for the same, by following the holy doctrine which he taught; through Jesus Christ our Lord. *Amen.*

The Presentation of Christ in the Temple, commonly called the Purification of Saint Mary the Virgin. [February 2.][45]

Omnipotens sempiterne deus, maiestatem tuam supplices exoramus, ut sicut unigenitus filius tuus hodierna die cum nostrae carnis substantia in templo est praesentatus, ita nos facias purificatis tibi mentibus praesentari. Per dominum nostrum. [Greg., 124.]

ALMIGHTY and everliving God, we humbly beseech thy Majesty, that, as thy only-begotten Son was this day presented in the Temple in substance of our flesh, so we may be presented unto thee with pure and clean hearts, by the same thy Son Jesus Christ our Lord. *Amen.*

Saint Matthias's Day.[46]

Saint Matthias the Apostle. [February 24.]

ALmyghtie God, whiche in the place of the traytor Iudas, didst chose thy faythfull seruaunte Mathie, to bee the noumber of thy twelue Apostles: graunte that thy church being alway preserued from false Apostles, may be ordred and guided by faythfull and true pastors: Through Iesus Christ our Lorde. [1549, Sainct Mathies daie.]

O ALMIGHTY God, who into the place of the traitor Judas didst choose thy faithful servant Matthias to be of the number of the twelve Apostles; Grant that thy Church, being alway preserved from false Apostles, may be ordered and guided by faithful and true pastors, through Jesus Christ our Lord. *Amen.*

O GOD, who didst choose thy servant Joseph to be the guardian of thine only-begotten Son, and the spouse of his Virgin Mother: Grant, we beseech thee, that in the family of thy holy church we may ever be united with the same thy Son Jesus Christ our Lord, who liveth and reigneth with thee and the Holy Ghost, ever one God, world without end. *Amen.* [South Africa, 1954]

The Annunciation of the blessed Virgin Mary.[47]

The Annunciation of the blessed Virgin Mary. [March 25.]

Gratiam tuam domine, mentibus nostris infunde, ut qui angelo nuntiante christi filii tui incarnationem cognouimus, per passionem eius et crucem ad resurrectionis gloriam perducamur. Per. [Greg., 143.]

WE beseech thee, O Lord, pour thy grace into our hearts; that, as we have known the incarnation of thy Son Jesus Christ by the message of an angel, so by his cross and passion we may be brought unto the glory of his resurrection; through the same Jesus Christ our Lord. *Amen.*

[44]Thus through 1892.

[45]Date given in 1928 only.

[46]Thus through 1892.

[47]Thus through 1892.

Conversion of Saint Paul *January 25*

O God, who, by the preaching of thine apostle Paul, hast caused the light of the Gospel to shine throughout the world: Grant, we beseech thee, that we, having his wonderful conversion in remembrance, may show forth our thankfulness unto thee for the same by following the holy doctrine which he taught; through Jesus Christ our Lord, who liveth and reigneth with thee, in the unity of the Holy Spirit, one God, now and for ever. *Amen.*

The Presentation *February 2*

Almighty and everliving God, we humbly beseech thee that, as thy only-begotten Son was this day presented in the temple, so we may be presented unto thee with pure and clean hearts by the same thy Son Jesus Christ our Lord; who liveth and reigneth with thee and the Holy Spirit, one God, now and for ever. *Amen.*

Saint Matthias *February 24*

O Almighty God, who into the place of Judas didst choose thy faithful servant Matthias to be of the number of the Twelve: Grant that thy Church, being delivered from false apostles, may always be ordered and guided by faithful and true pastors; through Jesus Christ our Lord, who liveth and reigneth with thee, in the unity of the Holy Spirit, one God, now and for ever. *Amen.*

Saint Joseph *March 19*

O God, who from the family of thy servant David didst raise up Joseph to be the guardian of thine incarnate Son and the spouse of his virgin mother: Give us grace to imitate his uprightness of life and his obedience to thy commands; through the same they Son Jesus Christ our Lord, who liveth and reigneth with thee and the Holy Spirit, one God, for ever and ever. *Amen.*

The Annunciation *March 25*

We beseech thee, O Lord, pour thy grace into our hearts, that we who have known the incarnation of thy Son Jesus Christ, announced by an angel to the Virgin Mary, may by his cross and passion be brought unto the glory of his resurrection; who liveth and reigneth with thee, in the unity of the Holy Spirit, one God, now and for ever. *Amen.*

Saint Mark *April 25*

Almighty God, who by the hand of Mark the evangelist hast given to thy Church the Gospel of Jesus Christ the Son of God: We thank thee for this witness, and pray that we may be firmly grounded in its truth; through the same Jesus Christ our Lord, who liveth and

Conversion of Saint Paul *January 25*

O God, by the preaching of your apostle Paul you have caused the light of the Gospel to shine throughout the world: Grant, we pray, that we, having his wonderful conversion in remembrance, may show ourselves thankful to you by following his holy teaching; through Jesus Christ our Lord, who lives and reigns with you, in the unity of the Holy Spirit, one God, now and for ever. *Amen.*

The Presentation *February 2*

Almighty and everliving God, we humbly pray that, as your only-begotten Son was this day presented in the temple, so we may be presented to you with pure and clean hearts by Jesus Christ our Lord; who lives and reigns with you and the Holy Spirit, one God, now and for ever. *Amen.*

Saint Matthias *February 24*

Almighty God, who in the place of Judas chose your faithful servant Matthias to be numbered among the Twelve: Grant that your Church, being delivered from false apostles, may always be guided and governed by faithful and true pastors; through Jesus Christ our Lord, who lives and reigns with you, in the unity of the Holy Spirit, one God, now and for ever. *Amen.*

Saint Joseph *March 19*

O God, who from the family of your servant David raised up Joseph to be the guardian of your incarnate Son and the spouse of his virgin mother: Give us grace to imitate his uprightness of life and his obedience to your commands; through Jesus Christ our Lord, who lives and reigns with you and the Holy Spirit, one God, for ever and ever. *Amen.*

The Annunciation *March 25*

Pour your grace into our hearts, O Lord, that we who have known the incarnation of your Son Jesus Christ, announced by an angel to the Virgin Mary, may by his cross and passion be brought to the glory of his resurrection; who lives and reigns with you, in the unity of the Holy Spirit, one God, now and for ever. *Amen.*

Saint Mark *April 25*

Almighty God, by the hand of Mark the evangelist you have given to your church the Gospel of Jesus Christ the Son of God: We thank you for this witness, and pray that we may be firmly grounded in its truth; through Jesus Christ our Lord, who lives and reigns

O Christ our God Incarnate, Whose Virgin Mother was blessed in bearing Thee, but still more blessed in keeping Thy word; grant us, who honour the exaltation of her lowliness, to follow the example of her devotion to Thy will, Who livest &c. Wm. Bright, *Ancient Collects*, "On the Example of the Blessed Virgin.]

ALmyghtie God, by whose prouidence thy seruaunte Iohn Baptiste was wonderfully borne, and sente to prepare the waye of thy sonne our sauioure, by preachinge of penaunce: make vs so to folowe hys doctrine and holy lyfe, that we may truly repent according to his preachyng, and after his example constantly speake the trueth, boldly rebuke vice, and paciently suffer for the truethes sake: through Iesus Christe our lorde. [1549, Saynct Iohn Baptist.]

Saint John Baptist's Day.[48]

Saint John Baptist's Day. [June 24.]

ALMIGHTY God, by whose providence thy servant John Baptist was wonderfully born, and sent to prepare the way of thy Son our Saviour by preaching repentance;[49] Make us so to follow his doctrine and holy life, that we may truly repent according to his preaching; and after his example constantly speak the truth, boldly rebuke vice, and patiently suffer for the truth's sake; through the same thy Son Jesus Christ our Lord.[50] *Amen.*

Deus, qui hunc diem beatorum apostolorum Petri et Pauli martyrio consecrasti: da aeclesiae [tuae] toto terrarum orbe diffusae eorum semper magisterio gubernari, per quos sumpsit religionis exordium: per. [Ver 280.]

Independence Day. [July 4.]

O ETERNAL God, through whose mighty power our fathers won their liberties of old; Grant, we beseech thee, that we and all the peo-

[48]Thus through 1892.

[49]"by the preaching of repentance" [1786]; "by preaching of repentance" [1662].

[50]Prior to 1928, "through Jesus Christ our Lord."

reigneth with thee and the Holy Spirit, one God, for ever and ever. *Amen.*

Saint Philip and Saint James *May 1*

Almighty God, who didst give to thine apostles Philip and James grace and strength to bear witness to the truth: Grant that we, being mindful of their victory of faith, may glorify in life and death the Name of our Lord Jesus Christ; who liveth and reigneth with thee and the Holy Spirit, one God, now and for ever. *Amen.*

The Visitation *May 31*

Father in heaven, by whose grace the virgin mother of thy incarnate Son was blessed in bearing him, but still more blessed in keeping thy word: Grant us who honor the exaltation of her lowliness to follow the example of her devotion to thy will; through the same Jesus Christ our Lord, who liveth and reigneth with thee and the Holy Spirit, one God, for ever and ever. *Amen.*

Saint Barnabas *June 11*

Grant, O God, that we may follow the example of thy faithful servant Barnabas, who, seeking not his own renown but the well-being of thy Church, gave generously of his life and substance for the relief of the poor and the spread of the Gospel; through Jesus Christ our Lord, who liveth and reigneth with thee and the Holy Spirit, one God, for ever and ever. *Amen.*

The Nativity of Saint John the Baptist *June 24*

Almighty God, by whose providence thy servant John the Baptist was wonderfully born, and sent to prepare the way of thy Son our Savior by preaching repentance: Make us so to follow his doctrine and holy life, that we may truly repent according to his preaching; and, after his example constantly speak the truth, boldly rebuke vice, and patiently suffer for the truth's sake; through the same thy Son Jesus Christ our Lord, who liveth and reigneth with thee and the Holy Spirit, one God, for ever and ever. *Amen.*

Saint Peter and Saint Paul *June 29*

Almighty God, whose blessed apostles Peter and Paul glorified thee by their martyrdom: Grant that thy Church, instructed by their teaching and example, and knit together in unity by thy Spirit, may ever stand firm upon the one foundation, which is Jesus Christ our Lord; who liveth and reigneth with thee, in the unity of the same Spirit, one God, for ever and ever. *Amen.*

Independence Day *July 4*

Lord God Almighty, in whose Name the founders of this country won liberty for themselves and for us, and lit the torch of freedom for nations then unborn: Grant, we beseech thee, that we and all the people of this land may have grace to maintain these liberties in righteousness and peace; through Jesus Christ our Lord,

with you and the Holy Spirit, one God, for ever and ever. *Amen.*

Saint Philip and Saint James *May 1*

Almighty God, who gave to your apostles Philip and James grace and strength to bear witness to the truth: Grant that we, being mindful of their victory of faith, may glorify in life and death the Name of our Lord Jesus Christ; who lives and reigns with you and the Holy Spirit, one God, now and for ever. *Amen.*

The Visitation *May 31*

Father in heaven, by your grace the virgin mother of your incarnate Son was blessed in bearing him, but still more blessed in keeping your word: Grant us who honor the exaltation of her lowliness to follow the example of her devotion to your will; through Jesus Christ our Lord, who lives and reigns with you and the Holy Spirit, one God, for ever and ever. *Amen.*

Saint Barnabas *June 11*

Grant, O God, that we may follow the example of your faithful servant Barnabas, who, seeking not his own renown but the well-being of your Church, gave generously of his life and substance for the relief of the poor and the spread of the Gospel; through Jesus Christ our Lord, who lives and reigns with you and the Holy Spirit, one God, for ever and ever. *Amen.*

The Nativity of Saint John the Baptist *June 24*

Almighty God, by whose providence your servant John the Baptist was wonderfully born, and sent to prepare the way of your Son our Savior by preaching repentance: Make us so to follow his teaching and holy life, that we may truly repent according to his preaching; and, following his example, constantly speak the truth, boldly rebuke vice, and patiently suffer for the truth's sake; through Jesus Christ your Son our Lord, who lives and reigns with you and the Holy Spirit, one God, for ever and ever. *Amen.*

Saint Peter and Saint Paul *June 29*

Almighty God, whose blessed apostles Peter and Paul glorified you by their martyrdom: Grant that your Church, instructed by their teaching and example, and knit together in unity by your Spirit, may ever stand firm upon the one foundation, which is Jesus Christ our Lord; who lives and reigns with you, in the unity of the Holy Spirit, one God, now and for ever. *Amen.*

Independence Day *July 4*

Lord God Almighty, in whose Name the founders of this country won liberty for themselves and for us, and lit the torch of freedom for nations then unborn: Grant that we and all the people of this land may have grace to maintain our liberties in righteousness and peace; through Jesus Christ our Lord, who lives and reigns

ple of this land may have grace to maintain these liberties in righteousness and peace; through Jesus Christ our Lord. *Amen.* [1928]

O ALMIGHTY God, whose blessed Son did call and sanctify Mary Magdalen to be a witness to his resurrection: Mercifully grant that by thy grace we may be healed of all our infirmities, and alway serve thee in the power of his endless life, who with thee and the Holy Ghost liveth and reigneth, one God, world without end. *Amen.* [Eng. 1928, Saint Mary Magdalen.]

The Transfiguration of Christ.
[August 6.][51]

O GOD, who on the mount didst reveal to chosen witnesses thine only-begotten Son wonderfully transfigured, in raiment white and glistening; Mercifully grant that we also, being delivered from the disquietude of this world, may be permitted to behold the King in his beauty, who with thee O Father and thee O Holy Ghost, liveth and reigneth one God, world without end. *Amen.* [Wm. Reed Huntington, "For the Transfiguration," in *Materia Ritualis.* Huntington notes, "Cento of Collect and Secret for the Day. Sarum."]

O GOD, who on the mount didst reveal to chosen witnesses thine only-begotten Son wonderfully transfigured, in raiment white and glistering; Mercifully grant that we, being delivered from the disquietude of this world, may be permitted to behold the King in his beauty, who with thee, O Father, and thee, O Holy Ghost, liveth and reigneth one God, world without end. *Amen.*

O GOD, who as on this day didst take to thyself the Blessed Virgin Mary, mother of thine only Son: Grant that we who have been redeemed by his blood may share her glory in thine eternal kingdom, through the same thy Son Jesus Christ our Lord, who liveth and reigneth with thee and the Holy Ghost, ever one God, world without end. *Amen.* [South Africa 1954, The Falling Asleep of the Blessed Virgin Mary.]

[51]Date given in 1928 only.

who liveth and reigneth with thee and the Holy Spirit, one God, for ever and ever. *Amen.*

Saint Mary Magdalene *July 22*

Almighty God, whose blessed Son restored Mary Magdalene to health of body and of mind, and called her to be a witness of his resurrection: Mercifully grant that by thy grace we may be healed of all our infirmities and know thee in the power of his endless life; who with thee and the Holy Spirit liveth and reigneth, one God, now and for ever. *Amen.*

Saint James *July 25*

O gracious God, we remember before thee this day thy servant and apostle James, first among the Twelve to suffer martyrdom for the Name of Jesus Christ; and we pray that thou wilt pour out upon the leaders of thy Church that spirit of self-denying service by which alone they may have true authority among thy people; through the same Jesus Christ our Lord, who liveth and reigneth with thee and the Holy Spirit, one God, now and for ever. *Amen.*

The Transfiguration *August 6*

O God, who on the holy mount didst reveal to chosen witnesses thy well-beloved Son, wonderfully transfigured, in raiment white and glistening: Mercifully grant that we, being delivered from the disquietude of this world, may by faith behold the King in his beauty; who with thee, O Father, and thee, O Holy Ghost, liveth and reigneth, one God, world without end. *Amen.*

Saint Mary the Virgin *August 15*

O God, who hast taken to thyself the blessed Virgin Mary, mother of thy incarnate Son: Grant that we, who have been redeemed by his blood, may share with her the glory of thine eternal kingdom; through the same thy Son Jesus Christ our Lord, who liveth and reigneth with thee, in the unity of the Holy Spirit, one God, now and for ever. *Amen.*

with you and the Holy Spirit, one God, for ever and ever. *Amen.*

Saint Mary Magdalene *July 22*

Almighty God, whose blessed Son restored Mary Magdalene to health of body and of mind, and called her to be a witness of his resurrection: Mercifully grant that by your grace we may be healed from all our infirmities and know you in the power of his unending life; who with you and the Holy Spirit lives and reigns, one God, now and for ever. *Amen.*

Saint James *July 25*

O gracious God, we remember before you today your servant and apostle James, first among the Twelve to suffer martyrdom for the Name of Jesus Christ; and we pray that you will pour out upon the leaders of your Church that spirit of self-denying service by which alone they may have true authority among your people; through Jesus Christ our Lord, who lives and reigns with you and the Holy Spirit, one God, now and for ever. *Amen.*

The Transfiguration *August 6*

O God, who on the holy mount revealed to chosen witnesses your well-beloved Son, wonderfully transfigured, in raiment white and glistening: Mercifully grant that we, being delivered from the disquietude of this world, may by faith behold the King in his beauty; who with you, O Father, and you, O Holy Spirit, lives and reigns, one God, for ever and ever. *Amen.*

Saint Mary the Virgin *August 15*

O God, you have taken to yourself the blessed Virgin Mary, mother of your incarnate Son: Grant that we, who have been redeemed by his blood, may share with her the glory of your eternal kingdom; through Jesus Christ our Lord, who lives and reigns with you, in the unity of the Holy Spirit, one God, now and for ever. *Amen.*

Sources	1662-1871	1892-1928
	Saint Bartholomew the Apostle.[52]	Saint Bartholomew the Apostle. [August 24.]
Omnipotens sempiterne deus, qui huius diei uenerandam sanctamque laetitiam beati apostoli tui Iohannis euangelistae festiuitate tribuisti: da aeclesiae tua, quaesumus, et amare quod credit, et praedicare quod docuit: per. [Ver., 1273.]	O ALMIGHTY and everlasting God, who didst give to thine Apostle Bartholomew grace truly to believe and to preach thy Word; Grant, we beseech thee, unto thy Church, to love that Word which he believed, and both to preach and receive the same; through[53] Jesus Christ our Lord. *Amen.*	
	Saint Michael and All Angels.[54]	Saint Michael and All Angels. [September 29.]
Deus qui miro ordine angelorum ministeria hominumque dispensas, concede propitius ut quibus tibi ministrantibus in caelo semper adsistitur, ab his in terra nostra uita muniatur. Per. [Greg., 726.]	O EVERLASTING God, who hast ordained and constituted the services of Angels and men in a wonderful order; Mercifully grant that, as thy holy Angels always do thee service in heaven, so by thy appointment, they may succour and defend us on earth; through Jesus Christ our Lord. *Amen*.	
		Saint Luke the Evangelist. [October 18.]
		ALMIGHTY God, who didst inspire thy servant Saint Luke the Physician, to set forth in the Gospel the love and healing power of thy Son; Manifest in thy church the like power and love, to the healing of our bodies and our souls; through the same thy Son Jesus Christ our Lord. *Amen.* [1928]

[52]Thus through 1892.

[53]Standard of 1793 has "thro'."

[54]Thus through 1892.

Saint Bartholomew *August 24*

Almighty and everlasting God, who didst give to thine apostle Bartholomew grace truly to believe and to preach thy Word: Grant, we beseech thee, unto thy Church to love what he believed and to preach what he taught; through Jesus Christ our Lord, who liveth and reigneth with thee and the Holy Spirit, one God, for ever and ever. *Amen.*

Holy Cross Day *September 14*

Almighty God, whose Son our Savior Jesus Christ was lifted high upon the cross that he might draw the whole world unto himself: Mercifully grant that we, who glory in the mystery of our redemption, may have grace to take up our cross and follow him; who liveth and reigneth with thee and the Holy Spirit, one God, in glory everlasting. *Amen.*

Saint Matthew *September 21*

We thank thee, heavenly Father, for the witness of thine apostle and evangelist Matthew to the Gospel of thy Son our Savior; and we pray that, after his example, we may with ready wills and hearts obey the calling of our Lord to follow him; through Jesus Christ our Lord, who liveth and reigneth with thee and the Holy Spirit, one God, now and for ever. *Amen.*

Saint Michael and All Angels *September 29*

O everlasting God, who hast ordained and constituted the ministries of angels and men in a wonderful order: Mercifully grant that, as thy holy angels always serve and worship thee in heaven, so by thy appointment they may help and defend us on earth; through Jesus Christ our Lord, who liveth and reigneth with thee and the Holy Spirit, one God, for ever and ever. *Amen.*

Saint Luke *October 18*

Almighty God, who didst inspire thy servant Luke the physician to set forth in the Gospel the love and healing power of thy Son: Graciously continue in thy Church the like love and power to heal, to the praise and glory of thy Name; through the same thy Son Jesus Christ our Lord, who liveth and reigneth with thee, in the unity of the Holy Spirit, one God, now and for ever. *Amen.*

Saint James of Jerusalem *October 23*

Grant, we beseech thee, O God, that, after the example of thy servant James the Just, brother of our Lord, thy Church may give itself continually to prayer and to the reconciliation of all who are at variance and

Saint Bartholomew *August 24*

Almighty and everlasting God, who gave to your apostle Bartholomew grace truly to believe and to preach your Word: Grant that your Church may love what he believed and preach what he taught; through Jesus Christ our Lord, who lives and reigns with you and the Holy Spirit, one God, for ever and ever. *Amen.*

Holy Cross Day *September 14*

Almighty God, whose Son our Savior Jesus Christ was lifted high upon the cross that he might draw the whole world to himself: Mercifully grant that we, who glory in the mystery of our redemption, may have grace to take up our cross and follow him; who lives and reigns with you and the Holy Spirit, one God, in glory everlasting. *Amen.*

Saint Matthew *September 21*

We thank you, heavenly Father, for the witness of your apostle and evangelist Matthew to the Gospel of your Son our Savior; and we pray that, after his example, we may with ready wills and hearts obey the calling of our Lord to follow him; through Jesus Christ our Lord, who lives and reigns with you and the Holy Spirit, one God, now and for ever. *Amen.*

Saint Michael and All Angels *September 29*

Everlasting God, you have ordained and constituted in a wonderful order the ministries of angels and mortals: Mercifully grant that, as your holy angels always serve and worship you in heaven, so by your appointment they may help and defend us here on earth; through Jesus Christ our Lord, who lives and reigns with you and the Holy Spirit, one God, for ever and ever. *Amen.*

Saint Luke *October 18*

Almighty God, who inspired your servant Luke the physician to set forth in the Gospel the love and healing power of your Son: Graciously continue in your Church this love and power to heal, to the praise and glory of your Name; through Jesus Christ our Lord, who lives and reigns with you, in the unity of the Holy Spirit, one God, now and for ever. *Amen.*

Saint James of Jerusalem *October 23*

Grant, O God, that, following the example of your servant James the Just, brother of our Lord, your Church may give itself continually to prayer and to the reconciliation of all who are at variance and enmity; through

ALmightie GOD, whiche haste knitte together thy electe in one Comunion and felowship in the misticall body of thy sonne Christe our Lorde: graunt vs grace so to folow thy holy Saynctes in all vertues, and godly lyuyng, that we maye come to those vnspeakeable ioyes, whiche thou hast prepared for all them that vnfaynedly loue thee: through Iesus Christe. [1549, All Sainctes.]

All Saints' Day.[55]

All Saints' Day.
[November 1.]

O ALMIGHTY God, who hast knit together thine elect in one communion and fellowship, in the mystical body of thy Son Christ our Lord; Grant us grace so to follow thy blessed Saints in all virtuous and godly living, that we may come to those unspeakable joys which thou hast prepared for those who[56] unfeignedly love thee; through the same thy Son Jesus Christ our Lord.[57] *Amen.*

The Common of Saints

ALMIGHTY God, who didst give thy servant Polycarp boldness to confess the Name of our Saviour Jesus Christ before the rulers of this world, and courage to die for this faith: Grant that we likewise may ever be ready to give a reason for the hope that is in us, and to suffer gladly for his sake; through the same Jesus Christ our Lord. *Amen.* [*Prayer Book Studies*, XII, Polycarp, Bishop of Smyrna, and Martyr.]

[55]Thus through 1892.

[56]"them that" [1662].

[57]Prior to 1928, "through Jesus Christ our Lord."

enmity; through the same our Lord Jesus Christ, who liveth and reigneth with thee and the Holy Spirit, one God, now and for ever. *Amen.*

Jesus Christ our Lord, who lives and reigns with you and the Holy Spirit, one God, now and for ever. *Amen.*

Saint Simon and Saint Jude *October 28*

O God, we thank thee for the glorious company of the apostles, and especially on this day for Simon and Jude; and we pray that, as they were faithful and zealous in their mission, so we may with ardent devotion make known the love and mercy of our Lord and Savior Jesus Christ; who liveth and reigneth with thee and the Holy Spirit, one God, for ever and ever. *Amen.*

Saint Simon and Saint Jude *October 28*

O God, we thank you for the glorious company of the apostles, and especially on this day for Simon and Jude; and we pray that, as they were faithful and zealous in their mission, so we may with ardent devotion make known the love and mercy of our Lord and Savior Jesus Christ; who lives and reigns with you and the Holy Spirit, one God, for ever and ever. *Amen.*

All Saints' Day *November 1*

Almighty God, who hast knit together thine elect in one communion and fellowship in the mystical body of thy Son Christ our Lord: Grant us grace so to follow thy blessed saints in all virtuous and godly living, that we may come to those ineffable joys which thou hast prepared for those who unfeignedly love thee; through the same Jesus Christ our Lord, who with thee and the Holy Spirit liveth and reigneth, one God, in glory everlasting. *Amen.*

All Saints' Day *November 1*

Almighty God, you have knit together your elect in one communion and fellowship in the mystical body of your Son Christ our Lord: Give us grace so to follow your blessed saints in all virtuous and godly living, that we may come to those ineffable joys that you have prepared for those who truly love you; through Jesus Christ our Lord, who with you and the Holy Spirit lives and reigns, one God, in glory everlasting. *Amen.*

Thanksgiving Day

Almighty and gracious Father, we give thee thanks for the fruits of the earth in their season and for the labors of those who harvest them. Make us, we beseech thee, faithful stewards of thy great bounty, for the provision of our necessities and the relief of all who are in need, to the glory of thy Name; through Jesus Christ our Lord, who liveth and reigneth with thee and the Holy Spirit, one God, now and for ever. *Amen.*

Thanksgiving Day

Almighty and gracious Father, we give you thanks for the fruits of the earth in their season and for the labors of those who harvest them. Make us, we pray, faithful stewards of your great bounty, for the provision of our necessities and the relief of all who are in need, to the glory of your Name; through Jesus Christ our Lord, who lives and reigns with you and the Holy Spirit, one God, now and for ever. *Amen.*

Of a Martyr

O Almighty God, who didst give to thy servant *N.* boldness to confess the Name of our Savior Jesus Christ before the rulers of this world, and courage to die for this faith: Grant that we may always be ready to give a reason for the hope that is in us, and to suffer gladly for the sake of our Lord Jesus Christ; who liveth and reigneth with thee and the Holy Spirit, one God, for ever and ever. *Amen.*

or this

Of a Martyr

Almighty God, who gave to your servant *N.* boldness to confess the Name of our Savior Jesus Christ before the rulers of this world, and courage to die for this faith: Grant that we may always be ready to give a reason for the hope that is in us, and to suffer gladly for the sake of our Lord Jesus Christ; who lives and reigns with you and the Holy Spirit, one God, for ever and ever. *Amen.*

or this

ALMIGHTY God, by whose grace and power thy Martyr *N.* was enabled to witness to the truth and to be faithful unto death: Grant that we, who now remember *him* before thee, may likewise so bear witness unto thee in this world, that we may receive with *him* the crown of glory that fadeth not away; through Jesus Christ our Lord, who with thee and the Holy Spirit liveth and reigneth, one God, for ever and ever. *Amen.* [Canada 1959, *Of a Martyr.*]

Omnipotens sempiterne deus, qui in sanctorum cordibus flammam tuae dilectionis accendis, da mentibus eandem fidem caritatisque uirtutem, ut quorum gaudemus triumphis, proficiamur exemplis: per. [Miss. Goth., 455.]

A Saint's Day.

ALMIGHTY and everlasting God, who dost enkindle the flame of thy love in the hearts of the Saints; Grant to us, thy humble servants, the same faith and power of love; that, as we rejoice in their triumphs, we may profit by their examples; through Jesus Christ our Lord. *Amen.* [1928]

O Lord Jesus Christ, who callest to thee whom thou willest and sendest them whither thou dost choose: We thank thee for calling thy servant *N.* to preach thy Gospel to the nations; and we humbly pray thee to raise up among those who shall be heralds and evangelists of thy kingdom, and shall build up thy Church in every land; who livest and reignest with the Father and the Holy Spirit, one God, world without end. *Amen.* [Eng. 1928, Of Missionaries.]

O Almighty God, who willest to be glorified in thy Saints and didst raise up thy servant *N.* to shine as a light in the world: Shine, we pray thee, in our hearts, that we also in our generation may show forth thy praises, who hast called us out of darkness into thy marvellous light; through Jesus Christ our Lord. *Amen.* [Eng. 1928, Of Any Saint]

Remembering this day *N,* let us pray for all bishops and pastors.

O GOD, who art the Light of thy faithful people and Shepherd of our souls, and didst choose thy blessed servant *N* to be a faithful steward of thy mysteries: We beseech thee so to work in us that we, being instructed by his words and godly life, may grow up to the fullness of Jesus Christ our Lord, who with thee, O Father, and the Holy Spirit, liveth and reigneth, ever one God, world without end. **Amen.** [CSI, Common Forms, 5, Pastors.]

O GOD, our heavenly Father, who didst raise up thy faithful servant *N.* to be a Bishop in thy Church and to feed thy flock: We beseech thee to send down upon all

1979-I

O Almighty God, by whose grace and power thy holy martyr *N.* triumphed over suffering and was faithful even unto death: Grant us, who now remember *him* with thanksgiving, to be so faithful in our witness to thee in this world, that we may receive with *him* the crown of life; through Jesus Christ our Lord, who liveth and reigneth with thee and the Holy Spirit, one God, for ever and ever. *Amen.*

or the following

Almighty and everlasting God, who didst enkindle the flame of thy love in the heart of thy holy martyr N.: Grant to us, thy humble servants, a like faith and power of love, that we who rejoice in *her* triumph may profit by *her* example; through Jesus Christ our Lord, who liveth and reigneth with thee and the Holy Spirit, one God, for ever and ever. *Amen.*

1979-II

Almighty God, by whose grace and power your holy martyr *N.* triumphed over suffering and was faithful even to death: Grant us, who now remember *him* in thanksgiving, to be so faithful in our witness to you in this world, that we may receive with *him* the crown of life; through Jesus Christ our Lord, who lives and reigns with you and the Holy Spirit, one God, for ever and ever. *Amen.*

or this

Almighty and everlasting God, who kindled the flame of your love in the heart of your holy martyr *N.*: Grant to us, your humble servants, a like faith and power of love, that we who rejoice in *her* triumph may profit by *her* example; through Jesus Christ our Lord, who lives and reigns with you and the Holy Spirit, one God, for ever and ever. *Amen.*

1979-I

Of a Missionary

Almighty and everlasting God, we thank thee for thy servant *N.*, whom thou didst call to preach the Gospel to the people of —— (*or* to the —— people). Raise up, we beseech thee, in this and every land evangelists and heralds of thy kingdom, that thy Church may proclaim the unsearchable riches of our Savior Jesus Christ; who liveth and reigneth with thee and the Holy Spirit, one God, now and for ever. *Amen.*

or this

Almighty God, who willest to be glorified in thy saints, and who didst raise up thy servant *N.* to be a light in the world: Shine, we pray thee, in our hearts, that we also in our generation may show forth thy praise, who hast called us out of darkness into thy marvelous light; through Jesus Christ our Lord, who liveth and reigneth with thee and the Holy Spirit, one God, now and for ever. *Amen.*

Of a Pastor

O heavenly Father, Shepherd of thy people, we give thee thanks for thy servant *N.*, who was faithful in the care and nurture of thy flock; and we pray that, following his example and the teaching of his holy life, we may by thy grace grow into the stature of the fullness of our Lord and Savior Jesus Christ; who liveth and reigneth with thee and the Holy Spirit, one God, for ever and ever. *Amen.*

or this

O God, our heavenly Father, who didst raise up thy faithful servant *N.*, to be a [bishop and] pastor in thy Church and to feed thy flock: Give abundantly to all

1979-II

Of a Missionary

Almighty and everlasting God, we thank you for your servant N., whom you called to preach the Gospel to the people of —— (*or* to the —— people). Raise up in this and every land evangelists and heralds of your kingdom, that your Church may proclaim the unsearchable riches of our Savior Jesus Christ; who lives and reigns with you and the Holy Spirit, one God, now and for ever. *Amen.*

or the following

Almighty God, whose will it is to be glorified in your saints, and who raised up your servant *N.* to be a light in the world: Shine, we pray, in our hearts, that we also in our generation may show forth your praise, who called us out of darkness into your marvelous light; through Jesus Christ our Lord, who lives and reigns with you and the Holy Spirit, one God, now and for ever. *Amen.*

Of a Pastor

Heavenly Father, Shepherd of your people, we thank you for your servant *N.*, who was faithful in the care and nurture of your flock; and we pray that, following his example and the teaching of his holy life, we may by your grace grow into the stature of the fullness of our Lord and Savior Jesus Christ; who lives and reigns with you and the Holy Spirit, one God, for ever and ever. *Amen.*

or this

O God, our heavenly Father, who raised up your faithful servant *N.*, to be a [bishop and] pastor in your Church and to feed your flock: Give abundantly to all

thy Bishops, the Pastors of thy Church, the abundant gift of thy Holy Spirit, that they, being endued with power from on high, and ever walking in the footsteps of thy holy Apostles, may minister before thee in thy household as true servants of Christ and stewards of thy divine mysteries; through the same Jesus Christ our Lord, who liveth and reigneth with thee in the unity of the same Spirit, one God, world without end. *Amen.* [Canada 1959, *Of a Bishop or Archbishop.*]

O GOD, who by thy Holy Spirit hast given unto one man a word of wisdom, and to another a word of knowledge, and to another the gift of tongues: We praise thy Name for the gifts of grace manifested in thy servant *N.*, and we pray that thy Church may never be destitute of the same; through Jesus Christ our Lord. *Amen.* [Canada 1959, *Of a Doctor of the Church, Poet, or Scholar.*]

GRANT, we beseech thee, almighty God, that following the teaching of *N,* we may know thee the only true God and Jesus Christ whom thou hast sent, that we may be counted worthy ever to be numbered among the sheep who hear his voice; through the same Jesus Christ our Lord. **Amen.** [CSI, Common Forms, 7, Doctors of the Church.]

O GOD, whose blessed Son became poor that we through his poverty might be rich: Deliver us, we pray thee, from an inordinate love of this world, that, inspired by the devotion of thy servant *N.*, we may serve thee with singleness of heart, and attain to the riches of the age to come; through the same thy Son Jesus Christ our Lord, who liveth and reigneth with thee, in the unity of the Holy Spirit, one God, now and for ever. *Amen.* [Indian Prayer Book *Supplement,* 1960, "Of a Religious."]

O God, by whose grace the blessed Abbot [Abbess] *N.*, enkindled with the fire of thy love, became a burning and a shining light in thy Church: Grant that we may be inflamed with the same spirit of discipline and love, and ever walk before thee as children of light; through Jesus Christ our Lord. *Amen.* [Eng. 1928, Of an Abbot or Abbess.][58]

A Saint's Day.

O ALMIGHTY God, who hast called us to faith in thee, and hast compassed us about with so great a cloud of witnesses; Grant that we, encouraged by the good examples of thy Saints,

[58]This collect has been attributed to the 1954 South African book in other places, but the 1928 English proposed book seems to be the earliest example.

1979-I

pastors the gifts of thy Holy Spirit, that they may minister in thy household as true servants of Christ and stewards of thy divine mysteries; through the same Jesus Christ our Lord, who liveth and reigneth with thee and the same Spirit, one God, for ever and ever. *Amen.*

Of a Theologian and Teacher

O God, who by thy Holy Spirit dost give to some the word of wisdom, to others the word of knowledge, and to others the word of faith: We praise thy Name for the gifts of grace manifested in thy servant *N.*, and we pray that thy Church may never be destitute of such gifts; through Jesus Christ our Lord, who with thee and the same Spirit liveth and reigneth, one God, for ever and ever. *Amen.*

or this

O Almighty God, who didst give to thy servant *N.* special gifts of grace to understand and teach the truth as it is in Christ Jesus: Grant, we beseech thee, that by this teaching we may know thee, the one true God, and Jesus Christ whom thou hast sent; who liveth and reigneth with thee and the Holy Spirit, one God, for ever and ever. *Amen.*

Of a Monastic

O God, whose blessed Son became poor that we through his poverty might be rich: Deliver us, we pray thee, from an inordinate love of this world, that, inspired by the devotion of thy servant *N.*, we may serve thee with singleness of heart, and attain to the riches of the age to come; through the same thy Son Jesus Christ our Lord, who liveth and reigneth with thee, in the unity of the Holy Spirit, one God, now and for ever. *Amen.*

or this

O God, by whose grace thy servant *N.*, enkindled with the fire of thy love, became a burning and shining light in thy Church: Grant that we also may be aflame with the spirit of love and discipline, and may ever walk before thee as children of light; through Jesus Christ our Lord, who with thee, in the unity of the Holy Spirit, liveth and reigneth one God, now and for ever. *Amen.*

Of a Saint

O almighty God, who hast compassed us about with so great a cloud of witnesses: Grant that we, encouraged by the good example of thy servant *N.*, may persevere in running the race that is set before us, until at length, through thy mercy, we may with *him* attain to thine eternal joy; through Jesus Christ, the author and perfecter of our faith, who liveth and reigneth with thee and the Holy Spirit, one God, for ever and ever. *Amen.*

1979-II

pastors the gifts of your Holy Spirit, that they may minister in your household as true servants of Christ and stewards of your divine mysteries; through Jesus Christ our Lord, who lives and reigns with you and the Holy Spirit, one God, for ever and ever. *Amen.*

Of a Theologian and Teacher

O God, by your Holy Spirit you give to some the word of wisdom, to others the word of knowledge, and to others the word of faith: We praise your Name for the gifts of grace manifested in your servant *N.*, and we pray that your Church may never be destitute of such gifts; through Jesus Christ our Lord, who with you and the Holy Spirit lives and reigns, one God, for ever and ever. *Amen.*

or this

Almighty God, you gave to your servant N. special gifts of grace to understand and teach the truth as it is in Christ Jesus: Grant that by this teaching we may know you, the one true God, and Jesus Christ whom you have sent; who lives and reigns with you and the Holy Spirit, one God, for ever and ever. *Amen.*

Of a Monastic

O God, whose blessed Son became poor that we through his poverty might be rich: Deliver us from an inordinate love of this world, that we, inspired by the devotion of your servant *N.*, may serve you with singleness of heart, and attain to the riches of the age to come; through Jesus Christ our Lord, who lives and reigns with you, in the unity of the Holy Spirit, one God, now and for ever. *Amen.*

or this

O God, by whose grace your servant *N.*, kindled with the flame of your love, became a burning and shining light in your Church: Grant that we also may be aflame with the spirit of love and discipline, and walk before you as children of light; through Jesus Christ our Lord, who lives and reigns with you, in the unity of the Holy Spirit, one God, now and for ever. *Amen.*

Of a Saint

Almighty God, you have surrounded us with a great cloud of witnesses: Grant that we, encouraged by the good example of your servant *N.*, may persevere in running the race that is set before us, until at last we may with *him* attain to your eternal joy; through Jesus Christ, the pioneer and perfecter of our faith, who lives and reigns with you and the Holy Spirit, one God, for ever and ever. *Amen.*

and especially of thy servant [Saint ——], may persevere in running the race that is set before us, until at length, through thy mercy, we, with them, attain to thine eternal joy; through him who is the author and finisher of our faith, thy Son Jesus Christ our Lord. *Amen.* [1928]

O God, Who hast brought us near to an innumerable company of Angels, and to the spirits of just men made perfect; grant us during our pilgrimage to abide in their fellowship, and in our Country to become partakers of their joy; through Jesus Christ our Lord. [Wm. Bright, *Ancient Collects,* "On the Communion of Saints."]

Various Occasions

Pentecost, commonly called Whitsunday.[59]

ALMIGHTY and most merciful God, grant, we beseech thee, that by the indwelling of thy Holy Spirit, we may be enlightened and strengthened for thy service; through Jesus Christ our Lord, who liveth and reigneth with thee in the

[59]"Whitsunday" only [1892].

or this

O God, who hast brought us near to an innumerable company of angels and to the spirits of just men made perfect: Grant us during our earthly pilgrimage to abide in their fellowship, and in our heavenly country to become partakers of their joy; through Jesus Christ our Lord, who liveth and reigneth with thee and the Holy Spirit, one God, now and for ever. *Amen.*

or this

O Almighty God, who by thy Holy Spirit hast made us one with thy saints in heaven and on earth: Grant that in our earthly pilgrimage we may ever be supported by this fellowship of love and prayer, and may know ourselves to be surrounded by their witness to thy power and mercy. We ask this for the sake of Jesus Christ, in whom all our intercessions are acceptable through the Spirit, and who liveth and reigneth for ever and ever. *Amen.*

or this

O God, you have brought us near to an innumerable company of angels, and to the spirits of just men made perfect: Grant us during our earthly pilgrimage to abide in their fellowship, and in our heavenly country to become partakers of their joy; through Jesus Christ our Lord, who lives and reigns with you and the Holy Spirit, one God, now and for ever. *Amen.*

or this

Almighty God, by your Holy Spirit you have made us one with your saints in heaven and on earth: Grant that in our earthly pilgrimage we may always be supported by this fellowship of love and prayer, and know ourselves to be surrounded by their witness to your power and mercy. We ask this for the sake of Jesus Christ, in whom all our intercessions are acceptable through the Spirit, who lives and reigns for ever and ever. *Amen.*

---

1. Of the Holy Trinity

Almighty God, who hast revealed to thy Church thine eternal Being of glorious majesty and perfect love as one God in Trinity of Persons: Give us grace to continue steadfast in the confession of this faith, and constant in our worship of thee, Father, Son, and Holy Spirit; who livest and reignest, one God, now and for ever. *Amen.*

2. Of the Holy Spirit

Almighty and most merciful God, grant, we beseech thee, that by the indwelling of thy Holy Spirit we may be enlightened and strengthened for thy service; through Jesus Christ our Lord, who liveth and reigneth with thee, in the unity of the same Spirit ever, one God, world without end. *Amen.*

1. Of the Holy Trinity

Almighty God, you have revealed to your Church your eternal Being of glorious majesty and perfect love as one God in Trinity of Persons: Give us grace to continue steadfast in the confession of this faith, and constant in our worship of you, Father, Son, and Holy Spirit; for you live and reign, one God, now and for ever. *Amen.*

2. Of the Holy Spirit

Almighty and most merciful God, grant that by the indwelling of your Holy Spirit we may be enlightened and strengthened for your service; through Jesus Christ our Lord, who lives and reigns with you, in the unity of the Holy Spirit, one God, now and for ever. *Amen.*

unity of the same Spirit ever, one God, world without end. *Amen.* [1928]

DEUS, qui nobis sub Sacramento mirabili passionis tuae memoriam reliquisti: tribue, quaesumus, ita nos Corporis et Sanguinis tui sacra mysteria venerari; ut redemptionis tuae fructum in nobis jugiter sentiamus: Qui vivis et regnas cum Deo Patre in unitate Spiritus Sancti Deus: per omnia saecula saeculorum. [Thomas Aquinas, Corpus Christi Collect in *Missale Romanum.*]

O LORD Jesus Christ, who in a wonderful Sacrament hast left unto us a memorial of thy passion: Grant us, we beseech thee, so to venerate the Sacred Mysteries of thy Body and Blood, that we may ever perceive within ourselves the fruit of thy redemption; who livest and reignest with the Father in the Unity of the Holy Spirit, one God, for ever and ever. *Amen.* [Scottish, 1929, "At a Thanksgiving for the Institution of the Holy Communion.]

ALMIGHTY God, whose beloved Son, for our sake, willingly offered himself to endure the Cross, its agony and its shame: Remove from us all coldness and cowardice of heart, and give us courage to take up our cross and follow him; through the same Jesus Christ our Lord. [Eric Milner-White and G. W. Briggs, "Taking up the Cross," *Daily Prayer.*]

[60]See St. Michael and All Angels.

[61]See the Second Sunday after Christmas.

3. Of the Holy Angels[60]

O everlasting God, who hast ordained and constituted the ministries of angels and men in a wonderful order: Mercifully grant that, as thy holy angels always serve and worship thee in heaven, so by thy appointment they may help and defend us on earth; through Jesus Christ our Lord, who liveth and reigneth with thee and the Holy Spirit, one God, for ever and ever. *Amen.*

3. Of the Holy Angels

Everlasting God, you have ordained and constituted in a wonderful order the ministries of angels and mortals: Mercifully grant that, as your holy angels always serve and worship you in heaven, so by your appointment they may help and defend us here on earth; through Jesus Christ our Lord, who lives and reigns with you and the Holy Spirit, one God, for ever and ever. *Amen.*

4. Of the Incarnation[61]

O God, who didst wonderfully create, and yet more wonderfully restore, the dignity of human nature: Grant that we may share the divine life of him who humbled himself to share our humanity, thy Son Jesus Christ; who liveth and reigneth with thee, in the unity of the Holy Spirit, one God, for ever and ever. *Amen.*

4. Of the Incarnation

O God, who wonderfully created, and yet more wonderfully restored, the dignity of human nature: Grant that we may share the divine life of him who humbled himself to share our humanity, your Son Jesus Christ; who lives and reigns with you, in the unity of the Holy Spirit, one God, for ever and ever. *Amen.*

5. Of the Holy Eucharist

God our Father, whose Son our Lord Jesus Christ in a wonderful Sacrament hath left unto us a memorial of his passion: Grant us so to venerate the sacred mysteries of his Body and Blood, that we may ever perceive within ourselves the fruit of his redemption; who liveth and reigneth with thee and the Holy Spirit, one God, for ever and ever. *Amen.*

5. Of the Holy Eucharist

God our Father, whose Son our Lord Jesus Christ in a wonderful Sacrament has left us a memorial of his passion: Grant us so to venerate the sacred mysteries of his Body and Blood, that we may ever perceive within ourselves the fruit of his redemption; who lives and reigns with you and the Holy Spirit, one God, for ever and ever. *Amen.*

6. Of the Holy Cross

Almighty God, whose beloved Son willingly endured the agony and shame of the cross for our redemption: Give us courage, we beseech thee, to take up our cross and follow him; who liveth and reigneth with thee and the Holy Spirit, one God, now and for ever. *Amen.*

6. Of the Holy Cross

Almighty God, whose beloved Son willingly endured the agony and shame of the cross for our redemption: Give us courage to take up our cross and follow him; who lives and reigns with you and the Holy Spirit, one God, now and for ever. *Amen.*

7. For All Baptized Christians

Grant, O Lord God, to all who have been baptized into the death and resurrection of thy Son Jesus Christ, that, as we have put away the old life of sin, so we may be renewed in the spirit of our minds, and live in righteousness and true holiness; through the same Jesus Christ our Lord, who liveth and reigneth with thee, in the unity of the Holy Spirit, one God, now and for ever. *Amen.*

7. For All Baptized Christians

Grant, Lord God, to all who have been baptized into the death and resurrection of your Son Jesus Christ, that, as we have put away the old life of sin, so we may be renewed in the spirit of our minds, and live in righteousness and true holiness; through Jesus Christ our Lord, who lives and reigns with you, in the unity of the Holy Spirit, one God, now and for ever. *Amen.*

At the Burial of the Dead.

O ETERNAL Lord God, who holdest all souls in life; Vouchsafe, we beseech thee, to thy whole church in paradise and on earth, thy light and thy peace; and grant that we, following the good examples of those who have served thee here and are now at rest, may at the last enter with them into thine unending joy; through Jesus Christ our Lord. *Amen.* [1928][62]

O GOD, whose mercies cannot be numbered; Accept our prayers on behalf of the soul of thy servant departed, and grant *him* an entrance into the land of light and joy, in the fellowship of thy saints; through Jesus Christ our Lord. *Amen.* [1928]

Omnipotens sempiterne Deus, qui in dilecto Filio tuo, universorum Rege, omnia instaurare voluisti, concede propitius, ut tota creatura, a servitute liberata, tuae maiestati deserviat ac te sine fine collaudet. Per dominum. [*Missale Romanum* of Paul VI, collect for Christ the King.]

[62]Attributed to W. E. Scudmore.

8. For the Departed

O eternal Lord God, who holdest all souls in life: Give, we beseech thee, to thy whole Church in paradise and on earth thy light and thy peace; and grant that we, following the good examples of those who have served thee here and are now at rest, may at the last enter with them into thine unending joy; through Jesus Christ our Lord, who liveth and reigneth with thee, in the unity of the Holy Spirit, one God, now and for ever. *Amen.*

or this

Almighty God, we remember before thee today thy faithful servant *N.*; and we pray that, having opened to *him* the gates of larger life, thou wilt receive *him* more and more into thy joyful service, that, with all who have faithfully served thee in the past, *he* may share in the eternal victory of Jesus Christ our Lord; who liveth and reigneth with thee, in the unity of the Holy Spirit, one God, for ever and ever. *Amen.*

9. Of the Reign of Christ

Almighty and everlasting God, whose will it is to restore all things in thy well-beloved Son, the King of kings and Lord of lords: Mercifully grant that the peoples of the earth, divided and enslaved by sin, may be freed and brought together under his most gracious rule; who liveth and reigneth with thee and the Holy Spirit, one God, now and for ever. *Amen.*

10. At Baptism

Almighty God, who by our baptism into the death and resurrection of thy Son Jesus Christ, dost turn us from the old life of sin: Grant that we, being reborn to new life in him, may live in righteousness and holiness all our days; through the same thy Son Jesus Christ our Lord, who liveth and reigneth with thee and the Holy Spirit, one God, now and for ever. *Amen.*

11. At Confirmation

Grant, Almighty God, that we, who have been redeemed from the old life of sin by our baptism into the death and resurrection of thy Son Jesus Christ, may be renewed in thy Holy Spirit, and live in righteousness and true holiness; through the same Jesus Christ our Lord, who liveth and reigneth with thee and the same Spirit, one God, now and for ever. *Amen.*

8. For the Departed

Eternal Lord God, you hold all souls in life: Give to your whole Church in paradise and on earth your light and your peace; and grant that we, following the good examples of those who have served you here and are now at rest, may at the last enter with them into your unending joy; through Jesus Christ our Lord, who lives and reigns with you, in the unity of the Holy Spirit, one God, now and for ever. *Amen.*

or this

Almighty God, we remember before you today your faithful servant *N.*; and we pray that, having opened to *him* the gates of larger life, you will receive *him* more and more into your joyful service, that, with all who have faithfully served you in the past, *he* may share in the eternal victory of Jesus Christ our Lord; who lives and reigns with you, in the unity of the Holy Spirit, one God, for ever and ever. *Amen.*

9. Of the Reign of Christ

Almighty and everlasting God, whose will it is to restore all things in your well-beloved Son, the King of kings and Lord of lords: Mercifully grant that the peoples of the earth, divided and enslaved by sin, may be freed and brought together under his most gracious rule; who lives and reigns with you and the Holy Spirit, one God, now and for ever. *Amen.*

10. At Baptism

Almighty God, by our baptism into the death and resurrection of your Son Jesus Christ, you turn us from the old life of sin: Grant that we, being reborn to new life in him, may live in righteousness and holiness all our days; through Jesus Christ our Lord, who lives and reigns with you and the Holy Spirit, one God, now and for ever. *Amen.*

11. At Confirmation

Grant, Almighty God, that we, who have been redeemed from the old life of sin by our baptism into the death and resurrection of your Son Jesus Christ, may be renewed in your Holy Spirit, and live in righteousness and true holiness; through Jesus Christ our Lord, who lives and reigns with you and the Holy Spirit, one God, now and for ever. *Amen.*

O Lord Jesus Christ, who didst pray for thy disciples that they might be one, even as thou art one with the Father: Draw us to thyself, that in common love and obedience to thee we may be united to one another, in the fellowship of the one Spirit, that the world may believe that thou art Lord, to the glory of God the Father. [Wm. Temple, in Frank Colquhoun, *Parish Prayers,* 494.]

Almighty God, the giver of all good gifts, who of thy divine providence hast appointed divers Orders in thy Church: give thy grace, we humbly beseech thee, to all those who are to be called to any office and administration in the same: And so replenish them with the truth of thy doctrine, and endue them with innocency of life, that they may faithfully serve before thee, to the glory of thy great Name, and the benefit of thy holy church; through Jesus Christ our Lord. *Amen.* [Scottish, 1637; 1662, In the Ember Weeks.]

12. On the Anniversary of the Dedication of a Church

O Almighty God, to whose glory we celebrate the dedication of this house of prayer: We give thee thanks for the fellowship of those who have worshiped in this place, and we pray that all who seek thee here may find thee, and be filled with thy joy and peace; through Jesus Christ our Lord, who liveth and reigneth with thee, in the unity of the Holy Spirit, one God, now and for ever. *Amen.*

13. For a Church Convention

Almighty and everlasting Father, who hast given the Holy Spirit to abide with us for ever: Bless, we beseech thee, with his grace and presence, the bishops and the other clergy and the laity here (*or* now, *or* soon to be) assembled in thy Name, that thy Church, being preserved in true faith and godly discipline, may fulfill all the mind of him who loved it and gave himself for it, thy Son Jesus Christ our Savior; who liveth and reigneth with thee, in the unity of the same Spirit, one God, now and for ever. *Amen.*

14. For the Unity of the Church

Almighty Father, whose blessed Son before his passion prayed for his disciples that they might be one, even as thou and he are one: Grant that thy Church, being bound together in love and obedience to thee, may be united in one body by the one Spirit, that the world may believe in him whom thou didst send, the same thy Son Jesus Christ our Lord; who liveth and reigneth with thee, in the unity of the same Spirit, one God, now and for ever. *Amen.*

15. For the Ministry (Ember Days)

I. For those to be ordained

Almighty God, the giver of all good gifts, who of thy divine providence hast appointed various orders in thy Church: Give thy grace, we humbly beseech thee, to all who are [now] called to any office and ministry for thy people; and so fill them with the truth of thy doctrine and clothe them with holiness of life, that they may faithfully serve before thee, to the glory of thy great Name and for the benefit of thy holy Church; through Jesus Christ our Lord, who liveth and reigneth with thee, in the unity of the Holy Spirit, one God, now and for ever. *Amen.*

12. On the Anniversary of the Dedication of a Church

Almighty God, to whose glory we celebrate the dedication of this house of prayer: We give you thanks for the fellowship of those who have worshiped in this place, and we pray that all who seek you here may find you, and be filled with your joy and peace; through Jesus Christ our Lord, who lives and reigns with you, in the unity of the Holy Spirit, one God, now and for ever. *Amen.*

13. For a Church Convention

Almighty and everlasting Father, you have given the Holy Spirit to abide with us for ever: Bless, we pray, with his grace and presence, the bishops and the other clergy and the laity here (*or* now, *or* soon to be) assembled in your Name, that your Church, being preserved in true faith and godly discipline, may fulfill all the mind of him who loved it and gave himself for it, your Son Jesus Christ our Savior; who lives and reigns with you, in the unity of the Holy Spirit, one God, now and for ever. *Amen.*

14. For the Unity of the Church

Almighty Father, whose blessed Son before his passion prayed for his disciples that they might be one, as you and he are one: Grant that your Church, being bound together in love and obedience to you, may be united in one body by the one Spirit, that the world may believe in him whom you have sent, your Son Jesus Christ our Lord; who lives and reigns with you, in the unity of the Holy Spirit, one God, now and for ever. Amen.

15. For the Ministry (Ember Days)

I. For those to be ordained

Almighty God, the giver of all good gifts, in your divine providence you have appointed various orders in your Church: Give your grace, we humbly pray, to all who are [now] called to any office and ministry for your people; and so fill them with the truth of your doctrine and clothe them with holiness of life, that they may faithfully serve before you, to the glory of your great Name and for the benefit of your holy Church; through Jesus Christ our Lord, who lives and reigns with you, in the unity of the Holy Spirit, one God, now and for ever. *Amen.*

Good Friday.

Omnipotens sempiterne deus, cuius spiritu totum corpus ecclesiae sanctificatur et regitur, exaudi nos pro uniuersis ordinibus supplicantes, ut gratiae tuae munere ab omnibus fideliter seruiatur: per. [Gel., 405.]

ALMIGHTY and everlasting God, by whose Spirit the whole body of the Church is governed and sanctified; receive our supplications and prayers, which we offer before thee for all estates of men in thy holy Church, that every member of the same, in his vocation and ministry, may truly and godly serve thee, through our Lord and Saviour Jesus Christ. *Amen.*

O God, who hast made of one blood all nations of men for to dwell on all the face of the earth, and didst send thy blessed Son to preach peace to them that are afar off and to them that are nigh: Grant that all the people of this land may feel after thee and find thee. And hasten, O heavenly Father, the fulfillment of thy promise to pour out thy Spirit upon all flesh; through Jesus Christ, our Saviour. [G. E. Lynch Cotton.]

O GOD, who hast made of one blood all nations of men for to dwell on the face of the whole earth, and didst send thy blessed Son to preach peace to them that are far off and to them that are nigh; Grant that all men everywhere may seek after thee and find thee. Bring the nations into thy fold, and add the heathen to thine inheritance. And we pray thee shortly to accomplish the number of thine elect, and to hasten thy kingdom; through the same Jesus Christ our Lord. *Amen.* [1892, Occasional Prayers, "For Missions."]

O GOD of all the nations of the earth, remember the mulitudes of those, who, though created in thine image, have not known thee, nor the redemption wrought by thy Son Jesus Christ; and grant that by the prayers and labours of thy holy Church they may be delivered from all superstition and unbelief, and brought to worship thee; through him whom thou hast sent to be the Resurrection and Life of all men, the same thy Son Jesus Christ our Lord. Amen. [Indian Prayer Book *Supplement,* 1960, "For the Spread of the Gospel."]

O Lord God Almighty, who hast made for thy glory all nations over the face of the earth, that they may do thee service in the joy of freedom; give to this people of

II. For the choice of fit persons for the ministry

O God, who didst lead thy holy apostles to ordain ministers in every place: Grant that thy Church, under the guidance of the Holy Spirit, may choose suitable persons for the ministry of Word and Sacrament, and may uphold them in their work for the extension of thy kingdom; through him who is the Shepherd and Bishop of our souls, Jesus Christ our Lord, who liveth and reigneth with thee and the same Spirit, one God, for ever and ever. Amen.

III. For all Christians in their vocation

Almighty and everlasting God, by whose Spirit the whole body of thy faithful people is governed and sanctified: Receive our supplications and prayers, which we offer before thee for all members of thy holy Church, that in their vocation and ministry they may truly and godly serve thee; through our Lord and Savior Jesus Christ, who liveth and reigneth with thee, in the unity of the same Spirit, one God, now and for ever. *Amen.*

16. For the Mission of the Church

O God, who hast made of one blood all the peoples of the earth, and didst send thy blessed Son to preach peace to those who are far off and to those who are near: Grant that people everywhere may seek after thee and find thee, bring the nations into thy fold, pour out thy Spirit upon all flesh, and hasten the coming of thy kingdom; through the same thy Son Jesus Christ our Lord, who liveth and reigneth with thee and the same Spirit, one God, now and for ever. *Amen.*

or this

O God of all the nations of the earth: Remember the multitudes who have been created in thine image but have not known the redeeming work of our Savior Jesus Christ; and grant that, by the prayers and labors of thy holy Church, they may be brought to know and worship thee as who hast been revealed in thy Son; who liveth and reigneth with thee and the Holy Spirit, one God, for ever and ever. *Amen.*

17. For the Nation

Lord God Almighty, who hast made all the peoples of the earth for thy glory, to serve thee in freedom and peace: Grant to the people of our country a zeal for jus-

II. For the choice of fit persons for the ministry

O God, you led your holy apostles to ordain ministers in every place: Grant that your Church, under the guidance of the Holy Spirit, may choose suitable persons for the ministry of Word and Sacrament, and may uphold them in their work for the extension of your kingdom; through him who is the Shepherd and Bishop of our souls, Jesus Christ our Lord, who lives and reigns with you and the Holy Spirit, one God, for ever and ever. *Amen.*

III. For all Christians in their vocation

Almighty and everlasting God, by whose Spirit the whole body of your faithful people is governed and sanctified: Receive our supplications and prayers, which we offer before you for all members of your holy Church, that in their vocation and ministry they may truly and devoutly serve you; through our Lord and Savior Jesus Christ, who lives and reigns with you, in the unity of the Holy Spirit, one God, now and for ever. *Amen.*

16. For the Mission of the Church

O God, you have made of one blood all the peoples of the earth, and sent your blessed Son to preach peace to those who are far off and to those who are near: Grant that people everywhere may seek after you and find you, bring the nations into your fold, pour out your Spirit upon all flesh, and hasten the coming of your kingdom; through Jesus Christ our Lord, who lives and reigns with you and the Holy Spirit, one God, now and for ever. *Amen.*

or this

O God of all the nations of the earth: Remember the multitudes who have been created in your image but have not known the redeeming work of our Savior Jesus Christ; and grant that, by the prayers and labors of your holy Church, they may be brought to know and worship you as you have been revealed in your Son; who lives and reigns with you and the Holy Spirit, one God, for ever and ever. *Amen.*

17. For the Nation

Lord God Almighty, you have made all the peoples of the earth for your glory, to serve you in freedom and in peace: Give to the people of our country a zeal for jus-

England the passion of righteousness, and the strength of self-control, that they may exercise their liberty with a serious and single desire to fulfill thy gracious will; through Jesus Christ, our Master, Redeemer, and King. [H. S. Holland, in Frank Colqhoun, *Parish Prayers,* 1114.]

ALMIGHTY God, from whom all thoughts of truth and peace proceed: Kindle, we pray thee, in the hearts of all men the true love of peace; and guide with thy pure and peaceable wisdom those who take counsel for the nations of the earth; that in tranquility thy kingdom may go forward, till the earth is filled with the knowledge of thy love; through Jesus Christ our Lord. *Amen.* [Eng. 1928, Occasional Prayers, 20. For the Peace of the World.]

The Rogations Day, Being Three Days before Ascension Day.

ALMIGHTY God, Lord of heaven and earth; We beseech thee to pour forth thy blessing upon this land, and to give us a fruitful season; that we, constantly receiving thy bounty, may evermore give thanks unto thee in thy holy Church; through Jesus Christ our Lord. *Amen.* [1928]

Almighty God, Lord of Heaven & Earth, in whom we live, & move, & have our Being; who dost good unto all men, making thy Sunne to rise on ye evill & on ye good, & sending Raine on ye just & on ye unjust; Favourably behold us thy people, who call upon thy Name, & send us thy Blessing from Heaven in Giving us fruitful Seasons, & filling our Hearts with food & gladnes, that both our hearts & mouths may be continually filled with thy praises, giving thanks to thee in thy holy Church through Jesus Christ our Lord. Amen. [John Cosin.]

Almighty Father, Lord of heaven and earth: Of thy great goodness, we beseech thee to give and preserve to our use the fruits of the earth, the treasures of the mines, and the harvest of the sea, so as in due time we may enjoy them with thanksgiving; through Jesus Christ our Lord. [E. W. Benson, in Frank Colquhoun, *Parish Prayers,* 348.]

O LORD Jesus Christ, who in thy earthly life didst share man's toil, and thereby hallow the labour of his hands: Prosper all those who maintain the industries of this land; and give them pride in their work, a just reward for their labour, and joy both in supplying the needs of others and in serving thee their Saviour; who with the Father and the Holy Spirit livest and reignest, ever one God, world without end. *Amen.* [Canada 1959, The Autumn Ember Days—for Labour and Industry.]

For Faithfulness in the Use of this World's Goods.

ALMIGHTY God, whose loving hands hath given us all that we possess; Grant us grace that

tice and the strength of forbearance, that we may use our liberty in accordance with thy gracious will; through Jesus Christ our Lord, who liveth and reigneth with thee and the Holy Spirit, one God, for ever and ever. *Amen.*

18. For Peace

O Almighty God, kindle, we beseech thee, in every heart the true love of peace, and guide with thy wisdom those who take counsel for the nations of the earth, that in tranquility thy dominion may increase till the earth is filled with the knowledge of thy love; through Jesus Christ our Lord, who liveth and reigneth with thee, in the unity of the Holy Spirit, one God, now and for ever. *Amen.*

19. For Rogation Days

I. For fruitful seasons

Almighty God, Lord of heaven and earth: We humbly pray that thy gracious providence may give and preserve to our use the harvests of the land and of the seas, and may prosper all who labor to gather them, that we, who constantly receive good things from thy hand, may always give thee thanks; through Jesus Christ our Lord, who liveth and reigneth with thee and the Holy Spirit, one God, for ever and ever. *Amen.*

II. For commerce and industry

Almighty God, whose Son Jesus Christ in his earthly life shared our toil and hallowed our labor: Be present with thy people where they work; make those who carry on the industries and commerce of this land responsive to thy will; and give to us all a pride in what we do, and a just return for our labor; through Jesus Christ our Lord, who liveth and reigneth with thee, in the unity of the Holy Spirit, one God, now and for ever. *Amen.*

III. For stewardship of creation

O merciful Creator, whose hand is open wide to satisfy the needs of every living creature: Make us, we beseech thee, ever thankful for thy loving providence; and grant that we, remembering the account that we

tice and the strength of forbearance, that we may use our liberty in accordance with your gracious will; through Jesus Christ our Lord, who lives and reigns with you and the Holy Spirit, one God, for ever and ever. *Amen.*

18. For Peace

Almighty God, kindle, we pray, in every heart the true love of peace, and guide with your wisdom those who take counsel for the nations of the earth, that in tranquility your dominion may increase until the earth is filled with the knowledge of your love; through Jesus Christ our Lord, who lives and reigns with you, in the unity of the Holy Spirit, one God, now and for ever. *Amen.*

19. For Rogation Days

I. For fruitful seasons

Almighty God, Lord of heaven and earth: We humbly pray that your gracious providence may give and preserve to our use the harvests of the land and of the seas, and may prosper all who labor to gather them, that we, who are constantly receiving good things from your hand, may always give you thanks; through Jesus Christ our Lord, who lives and reigns with you and the Holy Spirit, one God, for ever and ever. *Amen.*

II. For commerce and industry

Almighty God, whose Son Jesus Christ in his earthly life shared our toil and hallowed our labor: Be present with your people where they work; make those who carry on the industries and commerce of this land responsive to your will; and give to us all a pride in what we do, and a just return for our labor; through Jesus Christ our Lord, who lives and reigns with you, in the unity of the Holy Spirit, one God, now and for ever. *Amen.*

III. For stewardship of creation

O merciful Creator, your hand is open wide to satisfy the needs of every living creature: Make us always thankful for your loving providence; and grant that we, remembering the account that we must one day give,

we may honour thee with our substance, and remembering the account which we must one day give, may be faithful stewards of thy bounty; through Jesus Christ our Lord. *Amen.* [1928; proposed in 1889 with the title, "For the Rich."]

For a Sick Person.

O FATHER of mercies and God of all comfort, our only help in time of need; We humbly beseech thee to behold, visit, and relieve thy sick *servant* [*N.*] for whom our prayers are desired. Look upon *him* with the eyes of thy mercy; comfort *him* with a sense of thy goodness; preserve *him* from the temptations of the enemy; and give *him* patience under *his* affliction. In thy good time, restore *him* to health, and enable *him* to lead the residue of *his* life in thy fear, and to thy glory; and grant that finally *he* may dwell with thee in life everlasting; through Jesus Christ our Lord. *Amen.* [1928]

For Social Justice.

ALMIGHTY God, who hast created man in thine own image; Grant us grace fearlessly to contend against evil, and to make no peace with oppression; and, that we may reverently use our freedom, help us to employ it in the maintenance of justice among men and nations, to the glory of thy holy Name; through Jesus Christ our Lord. *Amen.* [1928]

For Christian Service.

O LORD, our heavenly Father, whose blessed Son came not to be ministered unto, but to minister; We beseech

must one day give, may be faithful stewards of thy bounty; through Jesus Christ our Lord, who with thee and the Holy Spirit liveth and reigneth, one God, for ever and ever. *Amen.*

may be faithful stewards of your good gifts; through Jesus Christ our Lord, who with you and the Holy Spirit lives and reigns, one God, for ever and ever. *Amen.*

20. For the Sick

Heavenly Father, giver of life and health: Comfort and relieve thy sick servants, and give thy power of healing to those who minister to their needs, that those (or *N.*, or *NN.*) for whom our prayers are offered may be strengthened in *their* weakness and have confidence in thy loving care; through Jesus Christ our Lord, who liveth and reigneth with thee and the Holy Spirit, one God, now and for ever. *Amen.*

20. For the Sick

Heavenly Father, giver of life and health: Comfort and relieve your sick servants, and give your power of healing to those who minister to their needs, that those (or *N.*, or *NN.*) for whom our prayers are offered may be strengthened in *their* weakness and have confidence in your loving care; through Jesus Christ our Lord, who lives and reigns with you and the Holy Spirit, one God, now and for ever. *Amen.*

21. For Social Justice

Almighty God, who hast created us in thine own image: Grant us grace fearlessly to contend against evil and to make no peace with oppression; and, that we may reverently use our freedom, help us to employ it in the maintenance of justice in our communities and among the nations, to the glory of thy holy Name; through Jesus Christ our Lord, who liveth and reigneth with thee and the Holy Spirit, one God, now and for ever. *Amen.*

21. For Social Justice

Almighty God, who created us in your own image: Grant us grace fearlessly to contend against evil and to make no peace with oppression; and, that we may reverently use our freedom, help us to employ it in the maintenance of justice in our communities and among the nations, to the glory of your holy Name; through Jesus Christ our Lord, who lives and reigns with you and the Holy Spirit, one God, now and for ever. *Amen.*

22. For Social Service

O Lord our heavenly Father, whose blessed Son came not to be ministered unto but to minister: Bless, we beseech thee, all who, following in his steps, give themselves to the service of others; that with wisdom, patience, and courage, they may minister in his name

22. For Social Service

Heavenly Father, whose blessed Son came not to be served but to serve: Bless all who, following in his steps, give themselves to the service of others; that with wisdom, patience, and courage, they may minister in his Name to the suffering, the friendless, and the needy;

thee to bless all who, following in his steps, give themselves to the service of their fellow men. Endue them with wisdom, patience, and courage to strengthen the weak and raise up those who fall; that, being inspired by thy love, they may worthily minister in thy Name to the suffering, the friendless, and the needy; for the sake of him who laid down his life for us, the same thy Son, our Saviour Jesus Christ. *Amen.* [1928]

For Religious Education.

ALMIGHTY God, our heavenly Father, who hast committed to thy holy Church the care and nurture of thy children; Enlighten with thy wisdom those who teach and those who learn, that, rejoicing in the knowledge of thy truth, they may worship thee and serve thee from generation to generation; through Jesus Christ our Lord. *Amen.* [1928]

For Every Man in his Work.

ALMIGHTY God, our heavenly Father, who declarest thy glory and showest forth thy handiwork in the heavens and in the earth; Deliver us, we beseech thee, in our several callings, from the service of mammon, that we may do the work which thou givest us to do, in truth, in beauty, and in righteousness, with singleness of heart as thy servants, and to the benefit of our fellow men; for the sake of him who came among us as one that serveth, thy Son Jesus Christ our Lord. *Amen.* [1928][63]

[63]"This is a revised and very much abridged form of a prayer entitled 'For the Emancipation of Workers.' It is attributed to the Rt. Rev. Frederick Dan Huntington, first Bishop of Central New York (1869-1904)." Massey Shepherd, *The Oxford American Prayer Book Commentary*, p. 44.

to the suffering, the friendless, and the needy; for the love of him who laid down his life for us, the same thy Son our Savior Jesus Christ, who liveth and reigneth with thee and the Holy Spirit, one God, for ever and ever. *Amen.*

for the love of him who laid down his life for us, your Son our Savior Jesus Christ, who lives and reigns with you and the Holy Spirit, one God, for ever and ever. *Amen.*

23. For Education

Almighty God, the fountain of all wisdom: Enlighten by thy Holy Spirit those who teach and those who learn, that, rejoicing in the knowledge of thy truth, they may worship thee and serve thee from generation to generation; through Jesus Christ our Lord, who liveth and reigneth with thee and the same Spirit, one God, for ever and ever. *Amen.*

23. For Education

Almighty God, the fountain of all wisdom: Enlighten by your Holy Spirit those who teach and those who learn, that, rejoicing in the knowledge of your truth, they may worship you and serve you from generation to generation; through Jesus Christ our Lord, who lives and reigns with you and the Holy Spirit, one God, for ever and ever. *Amen.*

24. For Vocation in Daily Work

Almighty God our heavenly Father, who declarest thy glory and showest forth thy handiwork in the heavens and in the earth: Deliver us, we beseech thee, in our several occupations from the service of self alone, that we may do the work which thou givest us to do in truth and beauty and for the common good; for the sake of him who came among us as one that serveth, thy Son Jesus Christ our Lord, who liveth and reigneth with thee and the Holy Spirit, one God, for ever and ever. *Amen.*

24. For Vocation in Daily Work

Almighty God our heavenly Father, you declare your glory and show forth your handiwork in the heavens and in the earth: Deliver us in our various occupations from the service of self alone, that we may do the work you give us to do in truth and beauty and for the common good; for the sake of him who came among us as one who serves, your Son Jesus Christ our Lord, who lives and reigns with you and the Holy Spirit, one God, for ever and ever. *Amen.*

Sources	1662-1871	1892-1928

25. For Labor Day

Almighty God, who hast so linked our lives one with another that all we do affects, for good or ill, all other lives: So guide us in the work we do, that we may do it not for self alone, but for the common good; and, as we seek a proper return for our own labor, make us mindful of the rightful aspirations of other workers, and arouse our concern for those who are out of work; through Jesus Christ our Lord, who liveth and reigneth with thee and the Holy Spirit, one God, for ever and ever. *Amen.*

25. For Labor Day

Almighty God, you have so linked our lives one with another that all we do affects, for good or ill, all other lives: So guide us in the work we do, that we may do it not for self alone, but for the common good; and, as we seek a proper return for our own labor, make us mindful of the rightful aspirations of other workers, and arouse our concern for those who are out of work; through Jesus Christ our Lord, who lives and reigns with you and the Holy Spirit, one God, for ever and ever. *Amen.*

The Collects, Part Two

In this section, the collects of the 1789-1928 American books are presented together with their sources and parallels. Also indicated is their continued use, if any, in the 1979 book. While many of the collects are had in common with 1662 and could be examined in

Advent Season

Sources	1662-1871	1892

The First Sunday in Advent.

ALmightie God, geue vs grace, that we maye caste away the workes of darkenes, and put vpon vs the armour of light, now in the time of this mortal lyfe, (in the which thy sonne Iesus Christe came to visite vs in great humilitie) that in the last daye, when he shall come again in his gloryous maiestie, to iudge both the quicke and the dead: we maye ryse to the lyfe immortall, through him, who liueth and reigneth with thee and the holy ghost, nowe and euer. Amen. [1549, The first Sonday in Aduente.]

ALMIGHTY God, give us grace that we may cast away the works of darkness, and put upon us the armour of light, now in the time of this mortal life, in which thy Son Jesus Christ came to visit us in great humility; that in the last day, when he shall come again in his glorious Majesty to judge both the quick and the dead,[1] we may rise to the life immortal, through him who liveth and reigneth with thee and the Holy Ghost, now and ever. *Amen.*

[1]"quick and dead" [1662].

Brightman's *The English Rite,* the situation here is as in Part One. Sources are presented that were not available or were unknown to Brightman, and ancient texts are presented from sources superior to those available close to a century ago.

1928	1979-II
The First Sunday in Advent.	**First Sunday in Advent**
ALMIGHTY God, give us grace that we may cast away the works of darkness, and put upon us the armour of light, now in the time of this mortal life, in which thy Son Jesus Christ came to visit us in great humility; that in the last day, when he shall come again in his glorious majesty to judge both the quick and the dead, we may rise to the life immortal, through him who liveth and reigneth with thee and the Holy Ghost, now and ever. *Amen.*	Almighty God, give us grace to cast away the works of darkness, and put on the armor of light, now in the time of this mortal life in which your Son Jesus Christ came to visit us in great humility; that in the last day, when he shall come again in his glorious majesty to judge both the living and the dead, we may rise to the life immortal; through him who lives and reigns with you and the Holy Spirit, one God, now and for ever. Amen.

The Second Sunday in Advent.

BLessed Lorde, whiche haste caused all holy scriptures to be written for our learning; graunt vs that we maye in suche wyse heare them, reade, marke, learne, and inwardly digeste them: that by pacience and coumforte of thy holy worde, we maye embrace and euer holde fast the blessed hope of euerlastyng lyfe, whiche thou haste geuen vs in our sauiour Iesus Christe. [1549, "The seconde Sonday" {in Advent}.]

BLESSED Lord, who hast caused all holy Scriptures to be written for our learning; grant that we may in such wise hear them, read, mark, learn, and inwardly digest them, that by patience and comfort of thy holy Word, we may embrace, and ever hold fast, the blessed hope of everlasting life, which thou hast given us in our Saviour Jesus Christ. *Amen.*

The Third Sunday in Advent.

O LORD Jesus[2] Christ, who at thy first coming didst send thy messenger to prepare thy way before thee; grant that the Ministers and stewards of thy mysteries may likewise so prepare and make ready thy way, by turning the hearts of the disobedient to the wisdom of the just, that at thy second coming to judge the world we may be found an acceptable people in thy sight, who livest and reignest with the Father and the Holy Spirit, ever[3] one God, world without end. *Amen.*

The Fourth Sunday in Advent.

Excita, domine, potenciam tuam et magna nobis uirtute succurre, ut per auxilium gloriae tuae quod nostra peccata praepediunt indulgenciae tuae propiciacionis acceleret: per. [Gel., 1121.]

O LORD, raise up, we pray thee, thy power, and come among us, and with great might succour us; that whereas, through our sins and wickedness, we are sore let and hindered in running the race that is set before us, thy bountiful grace and mercy may speedily help and deliver us; through the satisfaction of thy Son our Lord; to whom, with thee and the Holy Ghost, be honour and glory, world without end. *Amen.*

Christmastide

The Nativity of our Lord, or the birthday of Christ, commonly called Christmas-day.

Omnipotens sempiterne deus, qui hunc diem per incarnationem uerbi tui et per partum beatae uirginis Mariae consecrasti, da populis tuis in hanc caelebritate iustitiae, ut et qui tua gratia sunt redempti tua adoptione sint filii: per dominum. [Gel., 17.]

ALMYGHTIE God, whiche haste geuen vs thy only begotten sonne to take our nature vpon him, and this daye to be borne of a pure virgin: Graunt that we being regenerate and made thy children by adopcion and grace, maye dayly be renued by thy holy spirite, through thesame[4] oure Lorde Iesus Christe,

ALMIGHTY God, who hast given us thy only begotten Son to take our nature upon him, and as at this time to be born of a pure virgin;[5] Grant that we being regenerate, and made thy children by adoption and grace, may daily be renewed by thy holy Spirit, through the same our Lord Jesus Christ, who liveth and reigneth with thee and the same Spirit, ever one God, world without end. *Amen.*

[2]"Jesu" [1662].

[3]Comma moved to this place in 1892.

[4]*sic.*

[5]"Virgin" until 1832.

The Second Sunday in Advent.

BLESSED Lord, who hast caused all holy Scriptures to be written for our learning; Grant that we may in such wise hear them, read, mark, learn, and inwardly digest them, that by patience and comfort of thy holy Word, we may embrace, and ever hold fast, the blessed hope of everlasting life, which thou hast given us in our Savior Jesus Christ. *Amen.*

Proper 28 *The Sunday closest to November 16*

Blessed Lord, who caused all holy Scriptures to be written for our learning: Grant us so to hear them, read, mark, learn, and inwardly digest them, that we may embrace and ever hold fast the blessed hope of everlasting life, which you have given us in our Savior Jesus Christ; who lives and reigns with you and the Holy Spirit, one God, for ever and ever. *Amen.*

The Third Sunday in Advent.

O LORD Jesus Christ, who at thy first coming didst send thy messenger to prepare thy way before thee; Grant that the ministers and stewards of thy mysteries may likewise so prepare and make ready thy way, by turning the hearts of the disobedient to the wisdom of the just, that at thy second coming to judge the world we may be found an acceptable people in thy sight, who livest and reignest with the Father and the Holy Spirit ever, one God, world without end. *Amen.*

The Fourth Sunday in Advent.

O LORD, raise up, we pray thee, thy power, and come among us, and with great might succour us; that whereas, through our sins and wickedness, we are sore let and hindered in running the race that is set before us, thy bountiful grace and mercy may speedily help and deliver us; through Jesus Christ our Lord, to whom, with thee and the Holy Ghost, be honour and glory, world without end. *Amen.*

Third Sunday of Advent

Stir up your power, O Lord, and with great might come among us; and, because we are sorely hindered by our sins, let your bountiful grace and mercy speedily help and deliver us; through Jesus Christ our Lord, to whom, with you and the Holy Spirit, be honor and glory, now and for ever. *Amen.*

The Nativity of our Lord, or the Birthday of Christ, commonly called Christmas Day. [December 25.]

ALMIGHTY God, who hast given us thy only-begotten Son to take our nature upon him, and as at this time to be born of a pure virgin; Grant that we being regenerate, and made thy children by adoption and grace, may daily be renewed by thy Holy Spirit; through the same our Lord Jesus Christ, who liveth and reigneth with thee and the same Spirit ever, one God, world without end. *Amen.*

The Nativity of our Lord: Christmas Day
December 25

Almighty God, you have given your only-begotten Son to take our nature upon him, and to be born [this day] of a pure virgin: Grant that we, who have been born again and made your children by adoption and grace, may daily be renewed by your Holy Spirit; through our Lord Jesus Christ, to whom with you and the same Spirit be honor and glory, now and for ever. *Amen.*

who lyueth and reigneth. &c. [1549 "At the seconde Communion".]

Deus, qui nos redempcionis nostrae annua expectacione laetificas, praesta, ut unigenitum filium tuum quem redemptorem laeti suscipimus, uenientem quoque iudicem securi uideamus: per. [Gel., 1156.]

GOd, which makest vs gladde with the yerely remembraunce of the birth of thy onely sonne Iesus Christe: graunt that as we joyfully receiue him for our redemer, so we may with sure confidence beholde hym, when he shall come to be our judge, who liueth and reigneth. &c. [1549, Christmas Day.][6]

O GOD, who makest us glad with the yearly remembrance of the birth of thine only Son Jesus Christ; Grant that as we joyfully receive him for our Redeemer, so we may with sure confidence behold him when he shall come to be our Judge, who liveth and reigneth with thee and the Holy Ghost, one God, world without end. *Amen.*

Saint Stephen's Day[7]

[Da nobis quaesumus domine imitari quod colimus, ut discamus et inimicos diligere, quia eius natalicia caelebramus qui nouit etiam pro persecutoribus exorare. Per. {Greg., 62.}.]

GRANT, O Lord, that, in all our sufferings here upon earth for the testimony of thy truth, we may stedfastly look up to heaven, and by faith behold the glory that shall be revealed; and, being filled with the Holy Ghost, may learn to love and bless our persecutors, by the example of thy first Martyr Saint Stephen, who prayed for his murderers to thee, O blessed Jesus, who standest at the right hand of God to succour all those who[8] suffer for thee, our only Mediator and Advocate. *Amen.*

Saint John the Evangelist's Day.

Aeclesiam tuam, domine, benignus inlustra, ut apostolicis beati Iohannis euangelistae inluminata doctrinis ad dona perueniat, quae de tua fidelibus retributione promisit: per. [Ver., 1283.]

MERCIFUL Lord, we beseech thee to cast thy bright beams of light upon thy Church, that it, being instructed[9] by the doctrine of thy blessed Apostle and Evangelist Saint John, may so walk in the light of thy truth, that it may at length attain to everlasting life;[10] through Jesus Christ our Lord. *Amen.*

The Innocents' Day.

[ALmightie God, whose prayse this day the young innocentes thy witnesses hath confessed, and shewed foorth, not in speakyng, but in dying: mortifye and kyll al lvyces in vs, that in our conuersacion, our lyfe may expresse thy fayth, whiche with oure tongues we doe confesse: through Iesus Christe our Lorde. {1549, The Innocentes Daye.}]

O ALMIGHTY God, who out of the mouths of babes and sucklings hast ordained strength, and madest infants to glorify thee by their deaths: mortify and kill all vices in us, and so strengthen us by thy grace, that by the innocency of our lives, and constancy of our faith even unto death, we may glorify thy holy Name, through Jesus Christ our Lord. *Amen.*

[6]The collect was dropped in 1552, and did not reappear until its use in the American book of 1928.

[7]Until 1892-1928, the propers for St. Stephen, St. John, and Holy Innocents were placed with other commemorations, after the Sunday propers.

[8]"that" [1662].

[9]"enlightened" [1662 & 1786].

[10]"the light of everlasting life" [1662 & 1786].

O GOD, who makest us glad with the yearly remembrance of the birth of thine only Son Jesus Christ; Grant that as we joyfully receive him for our Redeemer, so we may with sure confidence behold him with he shall come to be our Judge, who liveth and reigneth with thee and the Holy Ghost, one God, world without end. *Amen.*

O God, you make us glad by the yearly festival of the birth of your only Son Jesus Christ: Grant that we, who joyfully receive him as our Redeemer, may with sure confidence behold him when he comes to be our Judge; who lives and reigns with you and the Holy Spirit, one God, now and for ever. *Amen.*

Saint Stephen Deacon and Martyr. [December 26.]

GRANT, O Lord, that, in all our sufferings here upon earth for the testimony of thy truth, we may stedfastly look up to heaven, and by faith behold the glory that shall be revealed; and, being filled with the Holy Ghost, may learn to love and bless our persecutors, by the example of thy first Martyr Saint Stephen, who prayed for his murderers to thee, O blessed Jesus, who standest at the right hand of God to succour all those who suffer for thee, our only Mediator and Advocate. *Amen.*

Saint Stephen *December 26*

[We give you thanks, O Lord of glory, for the example of the first martyr Stephen, who looked up to heaven and prayed for his persecutors to your Son Jesus Christ, who stands at your right hand; where he lives and reigns with you and the Holy Spirit, one God, in glory everlasting. *Amen.*]

Saint John, Apostle and Evangelist. [December 27.]

MERCIFUL Lord, we beseech thee to cast thy bright beams of light upon thy Church, that it, being illumined by the doctrine of thy blessed Apostle and Evangelist Saint John, may so walk in the light of thy truth, that it may at length attain to life everlasting; through Jesus Christ our Lord. *Amen.*

Saint John *December 27*

Shed upon your Church, O Lord, the brightness of your light, that we, being illumined by the teaching of your apostle and evangelist John, may so walk in the light of your truth, that at length we may attain to the fullness of eternal life; through Jesus Christ our Lord, who lives and reigns with you and the Holy Spirit, one God, for ever and ever. *Amen.*

The Holy Innocents. [December 28.]

O ALMIGHTY God, who out of the mouths of babes and sucklings hast ordained strength, and madest infants to glorify thee by their deaths; Mortify and kill all vices in us, and so strengthen us by thy grace, that by the innocency of our lives, and constancy of our faith even unto death, we may glorify thy holy Name; through Jesus Christ our Lord. *Amen.*

The Sunday after Christmas-Day

Omnipotens sempiterne deus, qui hunc diem per incarnationem uerbi tui et per partum beatae uirginis Mariae consecrasti, da populis tuis in hanc caelebritate iustitiae, ut et qui tua gratia sunt redempti tua adoptione sint filii: per dominum. [Gel., 17.]

ALMYGHTIE God, whiche haste geuen vs thy only begotten sonne to take our nature vpon him, and this daye to be borne of a pure virgin: Graunt that we being regenerate and made thy children by adopcion and grace, maye dayly be renued by thy holy spirite, through thesame[11] oure Lorde Iesus Christe, who lyueth and reigneth. &c. [1549 "At the seconde Communion".]

ALMIGHTY God, who hast given us thy only begotten Son to take our nature upon him, and as at this time to be born of a pure virgin;[12] Grant that we being regenerate, and made thy children by adoption and grace, may daily be renewed by thy holy Spirit, through the same our Lord Jesus Christ, who liveth and reigneth with thee and the same Spirit, ever one God, world without end. *Amen.*

The Circumcision of Christ.

ALmightie God, whiche madest thy blessed sonne to be circumcised and obedient to the lawe for man; graunte vs the true circumcision of thy spirite, that our heartes and all our members being mortifyed from al worldly and carnal lustes, may in all thinges obey thy blessed will: through thesame thy sonne Iesus Christe our Lorde. [1549, The Circumcision of Christe.]

ALMIGHTY God, who madest thy blessed Son to be circumcised, and obedient to the law for man; grant us the true circumcision of the Spirit, that, our hearts, and all our members, being mortified from all worldly and carnal lusts, we may in all things obey thy blessed will, through the same thy Son Jesus Christ our Lord. *Amen.*

Da quaesumus omnipotens deus, ut qui noua incarnatione uerbi tui luce perfundimur, hoc in nostro resplendeat opere quod per fidem fulget in mente. Per. [Greg., 42.]

ALMIGHTY God, who hast poured upon us anew the bright light of thine incarnate word: grant that the same light may shine forth in our lives, which now by faith is enkindled in our hearts. Through the same. [Atwell Baylay, *A Century of Collects,* 10.]

Epiphany Season

The Epiphany, or the Manifestation of Christ to the Gentiles.

Deus qui hodierna die unigenitum tuum gentibus stella duce reuelasti, concede propitius ut qui iam te ex fide cognouimus, usque ad contemplandam speciem

O GOD, who by the leading of a Star didst manifest thy only begotten Son to the Gentiles; mercifully grant that we, who[13] know thee now by faith, may after this

[11] *sic.*

[12] "Virgin" until 1832.

[13] "which" [1662].

The First Sunday after Christmas Day.

ALMIGHTY God, who hast given us thy only-begotten Son to take our nature upon him, and as at this time to be born of a pure virgin; Grant that we being regenerate, and made thy children by adoption and grace, may daily be renewed by thy Holy Spirit; through the same our Lord Jesus Christ, who liveth and reigneth with thee and the same Spirit ever, one God, world without end. *Amen.*

Almighty God, you have given your only-begotten Son to take our nature upon him, and to be born [this day] of a pure virgin: Grant that we, who have been born again and made your children by adoption and grace, may daily be renewed by your Holy Spirit; through our Lord Jesus Christ, to whom with you and the same Spirit be honor and glory, now and for ever. *Amen.* [Christmas, III.]

The Circumcision of Christ [January 1.]

ALMIGHTY God, who madest thy blessed Son to be circumcised, and obedient to the law for man; Grant us the true circumcision of the Spirit; that, our hearts, and all our members, being mortified from all worldly and carnal lusts, we may in all things obey thy blessed will; through the same thy Son Jesus Christ our Lord. *Amen.*

The Second Sunday after Christmas Day.

ALMIGHTY God, who hast poured upon us the new light of thine incarnate Word; Grant that the same light enkindled in our hearts may shine forth in our lives; through Jesus Christ our Lord. *Amen.*

First Sunday after Christmas Day

Almighty God, you have poured upon us the new light of your incarnate Word: Grant that this light, enkindled in our hearts, may shine forth in our lives; through Jesus Christ our Lord, who lives and reigns with you, in the unity of the Holy Spirit, one God, now and for ever. *Amen.*

The Epiphany, or the Manifestation of Christ to the Gentiles. [January 6.]

O GOD, who by the leading of a star didst manifest thy only-begotten Son to the Gentiles; Mercifully grant that we, who know thee now by faith, may after this life

The Epiphany *January* 6

O God, by the leading of a star you manifested your only Son to the peoples of the earth: Lead us, who know you now by faith, to your presence, where we

tuae celsitudinis perducamur. Per. [Greg., 87.]

life have the fruition of thy glorious Godhead, through Jesus Christ our Lord. *Amen.*

The First Sunday after the Epiphany.

Vota quaesumus domine supplicantis populi caelesti pietate prosequere, ut et quae agenda sunt uideant, et ad implenda quae uiderint conualescant. Per dominum nostrum iesum. [Greg., 86.]

O LORD, we beseech thee mercifully to receive the prayers of thy people who[14] call upon thee; and grant that thy may both perceive and know what things they ought to do, and also may have grace and power faithfully to fulfil the same, through Jesus Christ our Lord. *Amen.*

The Second Sunday after the Epiphany.

Omnipotens sempiterne deus, qui caelestia simul et terrena moderaris supplicationes populi tui clementer exaudi, et pacem tuam nostris concede temporibus. Per dominum. [Greg., 922.]

ALMIGHTY and everlasting God, who dost govern all things in heaven and earth; mercifully hear the supplications of thy people, and grant us thy peace all the days of our life, through Jesus Christ our Lord. *Amen.*

The Third Sunday after the Epiphany.

Omnipotens sempiterne deus infirmitatem nostram propitius respice, atque ad protegendum nos dexteram tuae maiestatis extende. Per. [Greg., 1102.]

ALMIGHTY and everlasting God, mercifully look upon our infirmities, and in all our dangers and necessities stretch forth thy right hand to help and defend us, through Jesus Christ our Lord. *Amen.*

The Fourth Sunday after the Epiphany.

Deus qui nos in tantis periculis constitutos, pro humana scis fragilitate non posse subsistere, da nobis salutem mentis et corporis, ut ea quae pro peccatis nostris patimur, te adiuuante uincams. Per. [Greg., 193.]

O GOD, who knowest us to be set in the midst of so many and great dangers, that by reason of the frailty of our nature we cannot always stand upright; grant to us such strength and protection, as may support us in all dangers, and carry us through all temptations; through Jesus Christ our Lord. *Amen.*

The Fifth Sunday after the Epiphany.

Familiam tuam quaesumus domine continua pietate custodi ut qui in sola spe gratiae caelestis innititur, caelesti etiam protectione muniatur. Per dominum. [Greg., 228.]

O LORD, we beseech thee to keep thy Church and household continually in thy true religion, that they who do lean only upon the hope of thy heavenly grace, may evermore be defended by thy mighty power, through Jesus Christ our Lord. *Amen.*

The Sixth Sunday after the Epiphany.

O God, whose blessed Sonne was manifested, yt he might destroy the works of the divel, & make us the Sons of God and heyres of eternall life; Grant we beseech thee that having this hope in us, wee may purifie our selves even as he is pure: that when he shall appeare againe with power & great glory, we may be made like unto him in his eternall & glorious kingdome where with Thee ô Father & ye Holy Ghost he liveth & reigneth one God world without end. Amen. [John Cosin.]

O GOD, whose blessed Son was manifested that he might destroy the works of the devil, and make us the sons of God, and heirs of eternal life; grant us, we beseech thee, that, having this hope, we may purify ourselves, even as he is pure; that, when he shall appear again with power and great glory, we may be made like unto him in his eternal and glorious kingdom; where with thee, O Father, and thee, O Holy Ghost, he liveth and reigneth, ever one God, world without end. *Amen.*

[14]"which" [1662].

have the fruition of thy glorious Godhead; through the same thy Son Jesus Christ our Lord. *Amen.*

may see your glory face to face; through Jesus Christ our Lord, who lives and reigns with you and the Holy Spirit, one God, now and for ever. *Amen.*

The First Sunday after the Epiphany.

O LORD, we beseech thee mercifully to receive the prayers of thy people who call upon thee; and grant that they may both perceive and know what things they ought to do, and also may have grace and power faithfully to fulfil the same; through Jesus Christ our Lord. *Amen.*

Proper 10 *The Sunday closest to July 13*

O Lord, mercifully receive the prayers of your people who call upon you, and grant that they may know and understand what things they ought to do, and also may have grace and power faithfully to accomplish them; through Jesus Christ our Lord, who lives and reigns with you and the Holy Spirit, one God, now and for ever. *Amen.*

The Second Sunday after the Epiphany.

ALMIGHTY and everlasting God, who dost govern all things in heaven and earth; Mercifully hear the supplications of thy people, and grant us thy peace all the days of our life; through Jesus Christ our Lord. *Amen.*

Fourth Sunday after the Epiphany

Almighty and everlasting God, you govern all things both in heaven and on earth: Mercifully hear the supplications of your people, and in our time grant us your peace; through Jesus Christ our Lord, who lives and reigns with you and the Holy Spirit, one God, for ever and ever. *Amen.*

The Third sunday after the Epiphany.

ALMIGHTY and everlasting God, mercifully look upon our infirmities, and in all our dangers and necessities stretch forth thy right hand to help and defend us; through Jesus Christ our Lord. *Amen.*

The Fourth Sunday after the Epiphany.

O GOD, who knowest us to be set in the midst of so many and great dangers, that by reason of the frailty of our nature we cannot always stand upright; Grant to us such strength and protection, as may support us in all dangers, and carry us through all temptations; through Jesus Christ our Lord. *Amen.*

The Fifth Sunday after the Epiphany.

O LORD, we beseech thee to keep thy Church and household continually in thy true religion; that they who do lean only upon the hope of thy heavenly grace may evermore be defended by thy mighty power; through Jesus Christ our Lord. *Amen.*

The Sixth Sunday after the Epiphany.

O GOD, whose blessed Son was manifested that he might destroy the works of the devil, and make us the sons of God, and heirs of eternal life; Grant us, we beseech thee, that, having this hope, we may purify ourselves, even as he is pure; that, when he shall appear again with power and great glory, we may be made like unto him in his eternal and glorious kingdom; where with thee, O Father, and thee, O Holy Ghost, he liveth and reigneth ever, one God, world without end. *Amen.*

Proper 27 *The Sunday closest to November 9*

O God, whose blessed Son came into the world that he might destroy the works of the devil and make us children of God and heirs of eternal life: Grant that, having this hope, we may purify ourselves as he is pure; that, when he comes again with power and great glory, we may be made like him in his eternal and glorious kingdom; where he lives and reigns with you and the Holy Spirit, one God, for ever and ever. *Amen.*

Pre-Lenten Season

Sources	1662-1871	1892
	The Sunday called Septuagesima, or the third Sunday before Lent.	
Preces populi tui quaesumus domine clementer exaudi, ut qui iuste pro peccatis nostris affligimur pietatis tuae uisitatione consolemur. Per. [Greg., 801.]	O LORD, we beseech thee favourably to hear the prayers of thy people; that we, who are justly punished for our offenses, may be mercifully delivered by thy goodness, for the glory of thy Name, through Jesus Christ our Saviour, who liveth and reigneth with thee and the Holy Ghost, ever one God, world without end. *Amen.*	
	The Sunday called Sexagesima, or the second Sunday before Lent.	
Deus qui conspicis quia ex nulla nostra actione confidimus, concede propitius ut contra aduersa omnia doctoris gentium proctectione muniamur. Per. [Greg., 147, In Sexagesima ad Sanctum Paulum.]	O LORD God, who seest that we put not our trust in any thing that we do; mercifully grant that by thy power we may be defended against all adversity, through Jesus Christ our Lord. *Amen.*	
	The Sunday called Quinquagesima, or the next Sunday before Lent.	
O Lord, which dost teache vs, that all our doings without charitie are nothyng worthe; sende thy holy gost and powre into oure heartes that moste excellent gyfte of charitie, the very bond of peace and all vertues, without the whiche, whosoeuer lyueth is counted dead before thee: Graunt this for thy onely sonne Iesus Christes sake. [1549, The Sonday called Quinquagesima.]	O LORD, who hast taught us that all our doings without charity are nothing worth; send thy Holy Ghost, and pour into our hearts that most excellent gift of charity, the very bond of peace and of all virtues; without which whosoever liveth is counted dead before thee: Grant this for thine only Son Jesus Christ's sake. *Amen.*	

Lenten Season

Sources	1662-1871	1892
	The first day of Lent, commonly called Ash-Wednesday.	
ALmightie and euerlastyng god,[15] which hatest nothing that thou haste made, and doest forgeue the synnes of al them that be penitent: Create and make in vs new and contrite heartes, that we worthily lamentyng our synnes, and knowlegyng our wretchednesse, may obtayne of thee, the God of all mercy, perfecte remission and forgeueness, through Iesus Christe. [1549, The first day of Lent, commonly called Ashwednesday.[16]]	ALMIGHTY and everlasting God, who hatest nothing that thou hast made, and dost forgive the sins of all those who[17] are penitent; create and make in us new and contrite hearts, that we, worthily lamenting our sins and acknowledging our wretchedness, may obtain of thee, the God of all mercy, perfect remission and forgiveness; through Jesus Christ our Lord. *Amen.*	

[15]*sic.* [16]*sic.* [17]"them that" [1662].

1928

The Sunday called Septuagesima, or the third Sunday before Lent.

O LORD, we beseech thee favourably to hear the prayers of thy people; that we, who are justly punished for our offenses, may be mercifully delivered by thy goodness, for the glory of thy Name; through Jesus Christ our Saviour, who liveth and reigneth with thee and the Holy Ghost ever, one God, world without end. *Amen.*

The Sunday called Sexagesima, or the second Sunday before Lent.

O LORD God, who seest that we put not our trust in any thing that we do; Mercifully grant that by thy power we may be defended against all adversity; through Jesus Christ our Lord. *Amen.*

The Sunday called Quinquagesima, or the Sunday next before Lent.

O LORD, who hast taught us that all our doings without charity are nothing worth; Send thy Holy Ghost, and pour into our hearts that most excellent gift of charity, the very bond of peace and of all virtues, without which whosoever liveth is counted dead before thee. Grant this for thine only Son Jesus Christ's sake. *Amen.*

1979-II

Seventh Sunday after the Epiphany

O Lord, you have taught us that without love whatever we do is worth nothing: Send your Holy Spirit and pour into our hearts your greatest gift, which is love, the true bond of peace and of all virtue, without which whoever lives is accounted dead before you. Grant this for the sake of your only Son Jesus Christ, who lives and reigns with you and the Holy Spirit, one God, now and for ever. *Amen.*

The first day of Lent, commonly called Ash Wednesday.

ALMIGHTY and everlasting God, who hatest nothing that thou hast made, and dost forgive the sins of all those who are penitent; Create and make in us new and contrite hearts, that we, worthily lamenting our sins and acknowledging our wretchedness, may obtain of thee, the God of all mercy, perfect remission and forgiveness; through Jesus Christ our Lord. *Amen.*

Ash Wednesday

Almighty and everlasting God, you hate nothing you have made and forgive the sins of all who are penitent: Create and make in us new and contrite hearts, that we, worthily lamenting our sins and acknowledging our wretchedness, may obtain of you, the God of all mercy, perfect remission and forgiveness; through Jesus Christ our Lord, who lives and reigns with you and the Holy Spirit, one God, for ever and ever. *Amen.*

The First Sunday in Lent.

O Lorde, whiche for our sake, diddest fast fortye dayes and fortie nightes: Geue vs grace to vse such abstinence that our fleshe beyng subdewed to the spirite, we may euer obey thy godly monicions, in righteousnes and true holynes, to thy honour and glory: whiche liuest and reignest. &c. [1549, The first Sonday in Lent.]

O LORD, who for our sake didst fast forty days and forty nights; give us grace to use such abstinence, that, our flesh being subdued to the Spirit, we may ever obey thy godly motions in righteousness and true holiness, to thy honour and glory, who livest and reignest with the Father and the Holy Ghost, one God, world without end. *Amen.*

The Second Sunday in Lent.

Deus qui conspicis omni nos uirtute destitui interius exteriusque custodi, ut et ab omnibus aduersitatibus muniamur in corpore et a prauis cogitationibus mundemur in mente. Per dominum. [Greg., 202.]

ALMIGHTY God, who seest that we have no power of ourselves to help ourselves; keep us both outwardly in our bodies, and inwardly in our souls; that we may be defended from all adversities which may happen to the body, and from all evil thoughts which may assault and hurt the soul; through Jesus Christ our Lord. *Amen.*

The Third Sunday in Lent.

Quaesumus omnipotens deus, uota humilium respice, atque ad defensionem nostram dexteram tuae maiestatis extende. Per. [Greg., 197.]

WE beseech thee, Almighty God, look upon the hearty desires of thy humble servants, and stretch forth the right hand of thy Majesty, to be our defence against all our enemies, through Jesus Christ our Lord. *Amen.*

The Fourth Sunday in Lent.

Concede quaesumus omnipotens deus ut qui ex merito nostrae actionis affligimur, tuae gratiae consolatione respiremus. Per. [Greg., 256.]

GRANT, we beseech thee, Almighty God, that we, who for our evil deeds do worthily deserve to be punished, by the comfort of thy grace may mercifully be relieved; through our Lord and Saviour Jesus Christ. *Amen.*

Passiontide

The Fifth Sunday in Lent.

Quaesumus omnipotens deus familiam tuam propitius respice, ut te largiante regatur in corpore et te seruante custodiatur in mente. Per. [Greg., 285.]

WE beseech thee, Almighty God, mercifully to look upon thy people; that by thy great goodness they may be governed and preserved evermore, both in body and soul, through Jesus Christ our Lord. *Amen.*

The Sunday next Before Easter.

Deus, qui humano generi ad imitandum humilitatis exemplum saluatorem nostrum et carnem sumere et crucem subire fecisti, concede propitius, ut et patientiae eius habere documentum et resurrectionis eius consortia mereamur, Christi domini nostri: qui tecum uiuit et regnat deus in unitate spiritus sancti: per. [Gel., 329.]

ALMIGHTY and everlasting God, who, of thy tender love towards mankind, hast sent thy Son, our Saviour Jesus Christ, to take upon him our flesh, and to suffer death upon the cross, that all mankind should follow the example of his great humility; mercifully grant, that we may both follow the example of his patience, and also be made partakers of his resurrection, through the same Jesus Christ our Lord. *Amen.*

The First Sunday in Lent.

O LORD, who for our sake didst fast forty days and forty nights; Give us grace to use such abstinence, that, our flesh being subdued to the Spirit, we may ever obey thy godly motions in righteousness, and true holiness, to thy honour and glory, who livest and reignest with the Father and the Holy Ghost, one God, world without end. *Amen.*

The Second Sunday in Lent.

ALMIGHTY God, who seest that we have no power of ourselves to help ourselves; Keep us both outwardly in our bodies, and inwardly in our souls; that we may be defended from all adversities which may happen to the body, and from all evil thoughts which may assault and hurt the soul; through Jesus Christ our Lord. *Amen.*

Third Sunday in Lent

Almighty God, you know that we have no power in ourselves to help ourselves: Keep us both outwardly in our bodies and inwardly in our souls, that we may be defended from all adversities which may happen to the body, and from all evil thoughts which may assault and hurt the soul; through Jesus Christ our Lord, who lives and reigns with you and the Holy Spirit, one God, for ever and ever. *Amen.*

The Third Sunday in Lent.

WE beseech thee, Almighty God, look upon the hearty desires of thy humble servants, and stretch forth the right hand of thy Majesty, to be our defence against all our enemies, through Jesus Christ our Lord. *Amen.*

The Fourth Sunday in Lent.

GRANT, we beseech thee, Almighty God, that we, who for our evil deeds do worthily deserve to be punished, by the comfort of thy grace may mercifully be relieved; through our Lord and Saviour Jesus Christ. *Amen.*

The Fifth Sunday in Lent, commonly called Passion Sunday.

WE beseech thee, Almighty God, mercifully to look upon thy people; that by thy great goodness they may be governed and preserved evermore, both in body and soul; through Jesus Christ our Lord. *Amen.*

The Sunday next before Easter, commonly called Palm Sunday.

ALMIGHTY and everlasting God, who, of thy tender love towards mankind, hast sent thy Son, our Saviour Jesus Christ, to take upon him our flesh, and to suffer death upon the cross, that all mankind should follow the example of his great humility; Mercifully grant, that we may both follow the example of his patience, and also be made partakers of his resurrection; through the same Jesus Christ our Lord. *Amen.*

Sunday of the Passion: Palm Sunday

Almighty and everliving God, in your tender love for the human race you sent your Son our Savior Jesus Christ to take upon him our nature, and to suffer death upon the cross, giving us the example of his great humility: Mercifully grant that we may walk in the way of his suffering, and also share in his resurrection; through Jesus Christ our Lord, who lives and reigns with you and the Holy Spirit, one God, for ever and ever. *Amen.*

ALMIGHTY God, whose most dear Son went not up to joy but first he suffered pain, and entered not into glory before he was crucified; Mercifully grant that we, walking in the way of the cross, may find it none other than the way of life and peace; through the same Jesus Christ our Lord. *Amen.* [Wm. Reed Huntington, "For the Monday Before Easter," *Materia Ritualis*. He adds, "Compiled from the Visitation Office."]

Adiuua nos, deus salutaris noster, et ad beneficia recolenda, quibus nos instaurare dignatus es, tribue uenire gaudentes: <per.> [Gel., 74.]

Good Friday.

Respice domine quaesumus super hanc familiam tuam, pro qua dominus noster iesus christus, non dubitauit manibus tradi nocentium et crucis subire tormentum. Per. [Greg., 327.]

ALMIGHTY God, we beseech thee graciously to behold this thy family, for which our Lord Jesus Christ was contented to be betrayed, and given up into the hands of wicked men, and to suffer death upon the cross, who now liveth and reigneth with thee and the Holy Ghost, ever one God, world without end. *Amen.*

Omnipotens sempiterne deus, cuius spiritu totum corpus ecclesiae sanctificatur et regitur, exaudi nos pro uniuersis ordinibus supplicantes, ut gratiae tuae munere ab omnibus fideliter seruiatur: per. [Gel., 405.]

ALMIGHTY and everlasting God, by whose Spirit the whole body of the church is governed and sanctified: receive our supplications and prayers, which we offer before thee for all estates of men in thy holy Church, that every member of the same, in his vocation and ministry, may truly and godly serve thee, through our Lord and Saviour Jesus Christ. *Amen.*

O MERCIFUL God, who hast made all men, and hatest nothing that thou hast made, nor desirest[18] the death of a sinner, but rather that he should be converted and live; Have mercy upon all Jews, Turks, Infidels, and Hereticks; and take from them all ignorance, hardness of heart, and contempt of thy Word; and so fetch them home, blessed Lord, to thy flock, that they may be saved among the remnant of the true Israelites,

18"wouldest" [1662].

Monday before Easter.

ALMIGHTY God, whose most dear Son went not up to joy but first he suffered pain, and entered not into glory before he was crucified; Mercifully grant that we, walking in the way of the cross, may find it none other than the way of life and peace; through the same thy Son Jesus Christ our Lord. *Amen.*

Monday in Holy Week

Almighty God, whose most dear Son went not up to joy but first he suffered pain, and entered not into glory before he was crucified: Mercifully grant that we, walking in the way of the cross, may find it none other than the way of life and peace; through Jesus Christ your Son our Lord, who lives and reigns with you and the Holy Spirit, one God, for ever and ever. *Amen.*

Tuesday before Easter.

O LORD God, whose blessed Son, our Saviour, gave his back to the smiters and hid not his face from shame; Grant us grace to take joyfully the sufferings of the present time, in full assurance of the glory that shall be revealed; through the same thy Son Jesus Christ our Lord. *Amen.*

Wednesday in Holy Week

Lord God, whose blessed Son our Savior gave his body to be whipped and his face to spit upon: Give us grace to accept joyfully the sufferings of the present time, confident of the glory that shall be revealed; through Jesus Christ your Son our Lord, who lives and reigns with you and the Holy Spirit, one God, for ever and ever. *Amen.*

Wednesday before Easter.

ASSIST us mercifully with thy help, O Lord God of our salvation; that we may enter with joy upon the meditation of those mighty acts, whereby thou hast given unto us life and immortality; through Jesus Christ our Lord. *Amen.*

Assist us mercifully with your help, O Lord God of our salvation, that we may enter with joy upon the contemplation of those mighty acts, whereby you have given us life and immortality; through Jesus Christ our Lord. *Amen.* [from the Liturgy of the Palms.]

Thursday before Easter, commonly called Maundy Thursday.

ALMIGHTY Father, whose dear Son, on the night before he suffered, did institute the Sacrament of his Body and Blood; Mercifully grant that we may thankfully receive the same in remembrance of him, who in these holy mysteries giveth us a pledge of life eternal; the same thy Son Jesus Christ our Lord, who now liveth and reigneth with thee and the Holy Spirit ever, one God, world without end. *Amen.*

Maundy Thursday

Almighty Father, whose dear Son, on the night before he suffered, instituted the Sacrament of his Body and Blood: Mercifully grant that we may receive it thankfully in remembrance of Jesus Christ our Lord, who in these holy mysteries gives us a pledge of eternal life; and who now lives and reigns with you and the Holy Spirit, one God, for ever and ever. *Amen.*

Good Friday.

ALMIGHTY God, we beseech thee graciously to behold this thy family, for which our Lord Jesus Christ was contented to be betrayed, and given up into the hands of wicked men, and to suffer death upon the cross; who now liveth and reigneth with thee and the Holy Ghost ever, one God, world without end. *Amen.*

Good Friday

Almighty God, we pray you graciously to behold this your family, for whom our Lord Jesus Christ was willing to be betrayed, and given into the hands of sinners, and to suffer death upon the cross; who now lives and reigns with you and the Holy Spirit, one God, for ever and ever. *Amen.*

ALMIGHTY and everlasting God, by whose Spirit the whole body of the Church is governed and sanctified; Receive our supplications and prayers, which we offer before thee for all estates of men in thy holy Church, that every member of the same, in his vocation and ministry, may truly and godly serve thee; through our Lord and Saviour Jesus Christ. *Amen.*

Almighty and everlasting God, by whose Spirit the whole body of your faithful people is governed and sanctified: Receive our supplications and prayers, which we offer before you for all members of your holy Church, that in their vocation and ministry they may truly and devoutly serve you; through our Lord and Savior Jesus Christ, who lives and reigns with you, in the unity of the Holy Spirit, one God, now and for ever. *Amen.* [For all Christians in their vocation.]

O MERCIFUL God, who hast made all men, and hatest nothing that thou hast made, nor desirest the death of a sinner, but rather that he should be converted and live; Have mercy upon all who know thee not as thou art revealed in the Gospel of thy Son. Take from them all ignorance, hardness of heart, and contempt of thy Word; and so fetch them home, blessed Lord, to thy fold, that they may be made one

and be made one fold under one Shepherd, Jesus Christ our Lord, who liveth and reigneth with thee and the Holy Spirit, one God, world without end. *Amen.*

O MOST gracious God, look upon us in mercy, and grant that as we are baptized into the death of thy Son our Saviour Jesus Christ, so by our true and hearty repentance all our sins may be buried with him, and we not fear the grave: that as Christ was raised up from the dead by the glory of thee, O Father, so we also may walk in newness of life, but our sins never be able to rise in judgment against us; and that for the merit of Jesus Christ that died, was buried, and rose again for us. *Amen.* [Scottish, 1637, Easter Even.]

Grant ô Lord, that as wee are baptized into the death of thy blessed Sonne, our Saviour Jesus Christ, so by continuall mortifying our corrupt affections, our Sins may be buried with him; & that through the grave & gate of death wee may pass to our joyfull Resurrection, for his merits who dyed & was buried, & rose again for us, ye same Jesus Christ our Lorde. Amen. [John Cosin.]

Easter-Even.

GRANT, O Lord, that as we are baptized into the death of thy blessed Son, our Saviour Jesus Christ, so by continual mortifying[19] our corrupt affections we may be buried with him; and that through the grave, and gate of death, we may pass to our joyful resurrection, for his merits, who died, and was buried, and rose again for us, the same thy Son Jesus Christ our Lord. *Amen.*

Eastertide

Deus qui hodierna die per unigenitum tuum aeternitatis nobis aditum deuicta morte reserasti, uota nostra quae praeueniendo adspiras, etiam adiuuando prosequere. Per eundum dominum nostrum. [Greg., 383.]

Easter-Day.

ALMIGHTY God, who through thine only begotten Son Jesus Christ hast overcome death, and opened unto us the gate of everlasting life; we humbly beseech thee, that, as by thy special grace preventing us thou dost put into our minds good desires, so by thy continual help we may bring the same to good effect, through the same Jesus Christ our Lord, who liveth and reigneth with thee and the Holy Ghost, ever one God, world without end. *Amen.*

Deus qui pro nobis filium tuum crucis patibulum subire uoluisti, ut inimici, a nobis expelleres potestatem, concede nobis famulis tuis, ut resurrectionis gratiam consequamur. Per dominum. [Greg., 324.]

O God, who for our redempcion diddest geue thine onely begotten sonne to the death of the crosse: & by hys gloryous resurreccion hast delyuered vs from the power of our enemye: Graunte vs so to dye

O GOD, who for our redemption didst give thine only-begotten Son to the death of the Cross, and by his glorious resurrection hast delivered us from the power of our enemy; Grant us so to die daily from sin,

[19]"by the continual mortifying of" [1786].

flock under one shepherd, Jesus Christ our Lord, who liveth and reigneth with thee and the Holy Spirit, one God, world without end. *Amen.*

Easter Even.

GRANT, O Lord, that as we are baptized into the death of thy blessed Son, our Saviour Jesus Christ, so by continual mortifying our corrupt affections we may be buried with him; and that through the grave, and gate of death, we may pass to our joyful resurrection; for his merits, who died, and was buried, and rose again for us, the same thy Son Jesus Christ our Lord. *Amen.*

Grant that all who have have been baptized into Christ's death and resurrection may die to sin and rise to newness of life, and that through the grave and gate of death we may pass with him to our joyful resurrection. *Amen.* [2d petition of the Prayers of the People, Burial I.]

Easter Day.

ALMIGHTY God, who through thine only-begotten Son Jesus Christ hast overcome death, and opened unto us the gate of everlasting life; We humbly beseech thee that, as by thy special grace preventing us thou dost put into our minds good desires, so by thy continual help we may bring the same to good effect; through the same Jesus Christ our Lord, who liveth and reigneth with thee and the Holy Ghost ever, one God, world without end. *Amen.*

O GOD, who for our redemption didst give thine only-begotten Son to the death of the Cross, and by his glorious resurrection hast delivered us from the power of our enemy; Grant us so to die daily from sin, that we may evermore live with him in the joy of his resurrection; through the same thy Son Christ our Lord. *Amen.*

Easter Day

Almighty God, who through your only-begotten Son Jesus Christ overcame death and opened to us the gate of everlasting life: Grant that we, who celebrate with joy the day the Lord's resurrection, may be raised from the death of sin by your life-giving Spirit; through Jesus Christ our Lord, who lives and reigns with you and the Holy Spirit, one God, now and for ever. *Amen.*

O God, who for our redemption gave your only begotten Son to the death of the cross, and by his glorious resurrection delivered us from the power of our enemy: Grant us so to die daily to sin, that we may evermore live with him in the joy of his resurrection; through Jesus Christ your Son our Lord, who lives and reigns with you and the Holy Spirit, one God, now and for ever. *Amen.*

dayly from sinne, that we maye euermore liue with him in the ioye of his resurreccion: through the same Christ our Lorde. Amen. [1549, Matins of Easter day.][20]

that we may evermore live with him in the joy of his resurrection; through the same Christ our Lord. *Amen.*

Monday in Easter Week.

ALMIGHTY God, who through thine only-begotten....

Tuesday in Easter Week.

ALMIGHTY God, who through thine only-begotten....

Concede quaesumus omnipotens deus, ut qui festa paschalia uenerando egimus, per haec contingere ad gaudia aeterna mereamur. Per. [Greg., 429.]

The First Sunday after Easter.

ALmightie father, whiche hast geuen thy onely sonne to dye for our synnes and to ryse agayne for oure iustification: Graunt vs so to put away the leauen of malice and wickednesse, that we may alway serue the[21] in purenesse of liuyng and trueth, through Iesus Christ our Lord. [1549, Easter Day, "At the second communion."]

ALMIGHTY Father, who hast given thine only Son to die for our sins, and to rise again for our justification; gGrant us so to put away the leaven of malice and wickedness, that we may alway serve thee in pureness of living and truth, through the merits of the same thy Son Jesus Christ our Lord. *Amen.*

The Second Sunday after Easter.

ALmightie God, whiche haste geuen thy holy sonne to be vnto vs, bothe a sacrifice for synne, and also an example of Godly lyfe: Geue vs the grace that we may alwayes moste thankfully receiue that his inestimable benefite, and also dayly indeuour our selfes, to folowe the blessed steppes of his moste holy lyfe. [1549, The second Sondaye after Easter.]

ALMIGHTY God, who hast given thine only Son to be unto us both a sacrifice for sin, and also an ensample of godly life; give us grace that we may always most thankfully receive that his inestimable benefit, and also daily endeavour ourselves to follow the blessed steps of his most holy life, through the same Jesus Christ our Lord. *Amen.*

The Third Sunday after Easter.

Deus, <qui> errantes in uia posse redire ueritatis lumen ostendis: da cunctis qui christiana professiones consentur, et illi respuere qui huic inimica sunt nomini, et ea quae sunt apta sectari: per. [Ver., 75.]

ALMIGHTY God, who showest to them that are in error the light of thy truth, to the intent that they may return into the way of righteousness; grant unto all those[22] who are admitted into the fellowship of Christ's Religion, that they may avoid[23] those things that are contrary to their profession, and follow all such things as are agreeable to the same, through our Lord Jesus Christ. *Amen.*

[20]Dropped in 1552; restored in 1892.

[21]*sic.*

[22]"them that" [1662].

[23]"eschew" [1662 & 1786].

Monday in Easter Week.

O GOD, whose blessed Son did manifest himself to his disciples in the breaking of bread; Open, we pray thee, the eyes of our faith, that we may behold thee in all thy works; through the same thy Son Jesus Christ our Lord. *Amen.*

Tuesday in Easter Week.

GRANT, we beseech thee, Almighty God, that we who celebrate with reverence the Paschal feast, may be found worthy to attain to everlasting joys; through Jesus Christ our Lord. *Amen.*

The First Sunday after Easter.

ALMIGHTY Father, who hast given thine only Son to die for our sins, and to rise again for our justification; Grant us so to put away the leaven of malice and wickedness, that we may always serve thee in pureness of living and truth; through the merits of the same thy Son Jesus Christ our Lord. *Amen.*

The Second Sunday after Easter.

ALMIGHTY God, who hast given thine only Son to be unto us both a sacrifice for sin, and also an ensample of godly life; Give us grace that we may always most thankfully receive that his inestimable benefit, and also daily endeavour ourselves to follow the blessed steps of his most holy life; through the same thy Son Jesus Christ our Lord. *Amen.*

The Third Sunday after Easter.

ALMIGHTY God, who showest to them that are in error the light of thy truth, to the intent that they may return into the way of righteousness; Grant unto all those who are admitted into the fellowship of Christ's Religion, that they may avoid those things that are contrary to their profession, and follow all such things as are agreeable to the same; through our Lord Jesus Christ. *Amen.*

Wednesday in Easter Week

O God, whose blessed Son made himself known to his disciples in the breaking of bread; Open the eyes of our faith, that we may behold him in all his redeeming work; who lives and reigns with you, in the unity of the Holy Spirit, one God, now and for ever. *Amen.*

Monday in Easter Week

Grant, we pray, Almighty God, that we who celebrate with awe the Paschal feast may be found worthy to attain to everlasting joys; through Jesus Christ our Lord, who lives and reigns with you and the Holy Spirit, one God, now and for ever. *Amen.*

Friday in Easter Week

Almighty Father, who gave your only Son to die for our sins and to rise for our justification: Give us grace so to put away the leaven of malice and wickedness, that we may always serve you in pureness of living and truth; through Jesus Christ your Son our Lord, who lives and reigns with you and the Holy Spirit, one God, now and for ever. *Amen.*

Proper 15 *The Sunday closest to August 17*

Almighty God, you have given your only Son to be for us a sacrifice for sin, and also an example of godly life: Give us grace to receive thankfully the fruits of his redeeming work, and to follow daily in the blessed steps of his most holy life; through Jesus Christ your Son our Lord, who lives and reigns with you and the Holy Spirit, one God, now and for ever. *Amen.*

The Fourth Sunday after Easter.

Deus, qui fidelium mentes unius efficis uoluntati, da populis tuis id amare quod praecipis, id desiderare quod promittis, ut inter mundanas uarietates ibi nostra fixa sint corda ubi uera sunt gaudia: per. [Gel., 551.]

O ALMIGHTY God, who alone canst order the unruly wills and affections of sinful men; Grant unto thy people, that they may love the thing which thou commandest, and desire that which thou dost promise; that so, among the sundry and manifold changes of the world, our hearts may surely there be fixed, where true joys are to be found, through Jesus Christ our Lord. *Amen.*

The Fifth Sunday after Easter, commonly called Rogation Sunday.

Deus, a quo bona cuncta procedunt, largire supplicibus, ut cogitemus te inspirante quae recta sunt et te gubernante eadem faciamus: per. [Gel., 556.]

O LORD, from whom all good things do come; grant to us thy humble servants, that by thy holy inspiration we may think those things that are[24] good, and by thy merciful guiding may perform the same, through our Lord Jesus Christ. *Amen.*

Ascensiontide

The Ascension-Day.

Concede quaesumus omnipotens deus, ut qui hodierna die unigenitum tuum redemptorem nostrum ad caelos ascendisse credimus, ipsi quoque mente in caelestibus habitemus. Per dominum. [Greg., 497.]

GRANT, we beseech thee, Almighty God, that like as we do believe thy only begotten Son our Lord Jesus Christ to have ascended into the heavens; so we may also in heart and mind thither ascend, and with him continually dwell, who liveth and reigneth with thee and the Holy Ghost, one God, world without end. *Amen.*

The Sunday after Ascension Day.

O GOD, the kyng of glory, whiche haste exalted thine only sonne Iesus Christe, wyth greate triumphe vnto thy kingdom in heauen: we beseche thee leaue vs not comfortles, but sende to vs thine holy gost to comforte vs, and exalte vs vnto the same place, whyther our sauioure Christe is gone before: who lyueth and reigneth. &c. [1549, The Sondaye after the Ascencion.]

O GOD, the king of glory, who hast exalted thine only Son Jesus Christ with great triumph unto thy kingdom in heaven; we beseech thee, leave us not comfortless; but send to us thine Holy Ghost to comfort us, and exalt us unto the same place whither our Saviour Christ is gone before; who liveth and reigneth with thee and the Holy Ghost, one God, world without end. *Amen.*

[24]"be good" [1662].

The Fourth Sunday after Easter.

O ALMIGHTY God, who alone canst order the unruly wills and affections of sinful men; Grant unto thy people, that they may love the thing which thou commandest, and desire that which thou dost promise; that so, among the sundry and manifold changes of the world, our hearts may surely there be fixed, where true joys are to be found; through Jesus Christ our Lord. *Amen.*

Fifth Sunday in Lent

Almighty God, you alone can bring into order the unruly wills and affections of sinners: Grant your people grace to love what you command and desire what you promise; that, among the swift and varied changes of the world, our hearts may surely there be fixed where true joys are to be found; through Jesus Christ our Lord, who lives and reigns with you and the Holy Spirit, one God, now and for ever. *Amen.*

The Fifth Sunday after Easter, commonly called Rogation Sunday.

O LORD, from whom all good things do come; Grant to us thy humble servants, that by thy holy inspiration we may think those things that are good, and by thy merciful guiding may perform the same; through our Lord Jesus Christ. *Amen.*

Proper 5 *The Sunday closest to June 8*

O God, from whom all good proceeds: Grant that by your inspiration we may think those things that are right, and by your merciful guiding may do them; through Jesus Christ our Lord, who lives and reigns with you and the Holy Spirit, one God, for ever and ever. *Amen.*

The Ascension Day.

GRANT, we beseech thee, Almighty God, that like as we do believe thy only-begotten Son our Lord Jesus Christ to have ascended into the heavens; so we may also in heart and mind thither ascend, and with him continually dwell, who liveth and reigneth with thee and the Holy Ghost, one God, world without end. *Amen.*

Ascension Day

Grant, we pray, Almighty God, that as we believe your only-begotten Son our Lord Jesus Christ to have ascended into heaven, so we may also in heart and mind there ascend, and with him continually dwell; who lives and reigns with you and the Holy Spirit, one God, for ever and ever. *Amen.*

The Sunday after Ascension Day.

O GOD, the King of glory, who hast exalted thine only Son Jesus Christ with great triumph unto thy kingdom in heaven; We beseech thee, leave us not comfortless; but send to us thine Holy Ghost to comfort us, and exalt us unto the same place whither our Saviour Christ is gone before, who liveth and reigneth with thee and the same Holy Ghost, one God, world without end. *Amen.*

Seventh Sunday of Easter:
The Sunday after Ascension Day

O God, the King of glory, you have exalted your only Son Jesus Christ with great triumph to your kingdom in heaven: Do not leave us comfortless, but send us your Holy Spirit to strengthen us, and exalt us to that place where our Savior Christ has gone before; who lives and reigns with you and the Holy Spirit, one God, in glory everlasting. *Amen.*

Whitsuntide

Sources	1662-1871	1892

Whitsunday.

Deus qui hodierna die corda fidelium sancti spiritus inlustratione docuisti, da nobis in eodem spiritu recta sapere, et de eius consolatione gaudere. Per. [Greg., 526.]

O[25] GOD, who as at this time didst teach the hearts of thy faithful people, by sending[26] to them the light of thy Holy Spirit; grant us by the same Spirit to have a right judgment in all things, and evermore to rejoice in his holy comfort; through the merits of Christ Jesus our Saviour, who liveth and reigneth with thee, in the unity of the same Spirit, one God, world without end. *Amen.*

Monday in Whitsun-Week.

O GOD, who as at this time didst teach....

Tuesday in Whitsun-Week.

O GOD, who as at this time didst teach....

Da quaesumus ecclesiae tuae misericors deus, ut sancto spiritu congregata hostili nullatenus incursione turbetur. Per. [Greg., 542.]

Trinity Season

Trinity-Sunday

Omnipotens sempiterne deus qui dedisti famulis tuis in confessione uere fidei eterne trinitatis gloriam agnoscere. et in potencia maiestatis adorare unitatem.

ALMIGHTY and everlasting God, who hast given unto us thy servants grace, by the confession of a true faith, to acknowledge the glory of the eternal Trinity,

[25]"O" omitted [1662 & 1786]. [26]"by the sending" [1662 & 1786].

1928	1979-II
Pentecost, commonly called Whitsunday.	**The Day of Pentecost: Whitsunday**
O GOD, who as at this time didst teach the hearts of thy faithful people, by sending to them the light of thy Holy Spirit; Grant us by the same Spirit to have a right judgment in all things, and evermore to rejoice in his holy comfort; through the merits of Christ Jesus our Saviour, who liveth and reigneth with thee, in the unity of the same Spirit, one God, world without end. *Amen.*	O God, who on this day taught the hearts of your faithful people by sending to them the light of your Holy Spirit: Grant us by the same Spirit to have a right judgment in all things, and evermore to rejoice in his holy comfort; through Jesus Christ your Son our Lord, who lives and reigns with you, in the unity of the Holy Spirit, one God, for ever and ever. *Amen.*
	Of the Holy Spirit
ALMIGHTY and most merciful God, grant, we beseech thee, that by the indwelling of thy Holy Spirit, we may be enlightened and strengthened for thy service; through Jesus Christ our Lord, who liveth and reigneth with thee in the unity of the same Spirit ever, one God, world without end. *Amen.*	Almighty and most merciful God, grant that by the indwelling of your Holy Spirit we may be enlightened and strengthened for your service; through Jesus Christ our Lord, who lives and reigns with you, in the unity of the Holy Spirit, one God, now and for ever. *Amen.*
Monday in Whitsun Week.	
SEND, we beseech thee, Almighty God, thy Holy Spirit into our hearts, that he may direct and rule us according to thy will, comfort us in all our afflictions, defend us from all error, and lead us into all truth; through Jesus Christ our Lord, who with thee and the same Holy Spirit liveth and reigneth, one God, world without end. *Amen.*	
Tuesday in Whitsun Week.	**Proper 16** *The Sunday closest to August 24*
GRANT, we beseech thee, merciful God, that thy Church, being gathered together in unity by thy Holy Spirit, may manifest thy power among all peoples, to the glory of thy Name; through Jesus Christ our Lord, who liveth and reigneth with thee and the same Spirit, one God, world without end. *Amen.*	Grant, O merciful God, that your Church, being gathered together in unity by your Holy Spirit, may show forth your power among all peoples, to the glory of your Name; through Jesus Christ our Lord, who lives and reigns with you and the Holy Spirit, one God, for ever and ever. *Amen.*

Trinity Sunday.	**First Sunday after Pentecost: Trinity Sunday**
ALMIGHTY and everlasting God, who hast given unto us thy servants grace, by the confession of a true faith, to acknowledge the glory of the eternal Trinity,	Almighty and everlasting God, you have given to us your servants grace, by the confession of a true faith, to acknowledge the glory of the eternal Trinity, and in the

quesumus ut eiusdem fidei firmitate ab omnibus semper muniamur aduersis. Qui uiuis. [Sarum, In die sancte trinitatis.]

and in the power of the divine Majesty to worship the Unity, we beseech thee that thou wouldest keep us stedfast in this faith, and evermore defend us from all adversities, who livest and reignest, one God, world without end. *Amen.*

The First Sunday after Trinity.

Deus, in te sperantium fortitudo, adesto propitius inuocationibus nostris, et quia sine te nihil potest mortalis infirmitas, praesta auxilium gratiae tuae, ut in exequendis mandatis tuis et uoluntate tibi et actione placeamus: per dominum. [Gel., 566.]

O GOD, the strength of all those who put their trust in thee; mercifully accept our prayers; and because, through the weakness of our mortal nature, we can do no good thing without thee, grant us the help of thy grace, that in keeping thy commandments we may please thee, both in will and deed, through Jesus Christ our Lord. *Amen.*

The Second Sunday after Trinity.

Sanctae nominis tui, domine, timorem pariter et amorem fac nos habere perpetuum, quia nunquam tuam gubernationem distitues, quos in solidatate tuae dilectionis instituis: per. [Gel., 586.]

O LORD, who never failest to help and govern those[27] whom thou dost bring up in thy stedfast fear and love; keep us, we beseech thee, under the protection of thy good providence, and make us to have a perpetual fear and love of thy holy Name, through Jesus Christ our Lord. *Amen.*

The Third Sunday after Trinity.

Deprecationem nostram quaesumus domine benignus exaudi, et quibus supplicandi praestas affectum, tribue defensionis auxilium. Per. [Greg., 263.]

O LORD, we beseech thee mercifully to hear us; and grant that we, to whom thou hast given an hearty desire to pray, may, by thy mighty aid, be defended and comforted in all dangers and adversities; through Jesus Christ our Lord. *Amen.*

The Fourth Sunday after Trinity.

Protector in te sperantium deus, sine quo nihil est ualidum, nihil sanctum, multiplica super nos misericordiam tuam, ut te rectore te duce, sic transeamus per bona temporalia, ut non amittamus aeterna. Per. [Greg., supp., 1138.]

O GOD, the protector of all that trust in thee, without whom nothing is strong, nothing is holy; increase and multiply upon us thy mercy; that, thou being our ruler and guide, we may so pass through things temporal, that we finally lose not the things eternal: Grant this, O heavenly Father, for Jesus Christ's sake our Lord. *Amen.*

The Fifth Sunday after Trinity.

Da nobis, domine deus noster, ut et mundi cursus pacifico nobis tuo ordine dirigatur, et aeclesia tua tranquilla deuotione laetetur: per. [Ver., 633.]

GRANT, O Lord, we beseech thee, that the course of this world may be so peaceably ordered by thy governance, that thy Church may joyfully serve thee in all godly quietness, through Jesus Christ our Lord. *Amen.*

The Sixth Sunday after Trinity.

Deus qui diligentibus te bona inuisibilia praeparasti, infunde cordibus nostris tui amoris affectum, ut te in omnibus et super omnia diligentes, promissiones tuas quae omne desiderium superant consequamur. Per. [Greg., 1144.

O GOD, who hast prepared for those who[28] love thee such good things as pass man's understanding; pour into our hearts such love toward thee, that we, loving thee above all things, may obtain thy promises, which exceed all that we can desire, through Jesus Christ our Lord. *Amen.*

---

[27]"them" [1662 &1786].

[28]"them that" [1662].

and in the power of the Divine Majesty to worship the Unity; We beseech thee that thou wouldest keep us stedfast in this faith, and evermore defend us from all adversities, who livest and reignest, one God, world without end. *Amen.*

power of your divine Majesty to worship the Unity: Keep us steadfast in this faith and worship, and bring us at last to see you in your one and eternal glory, O Father; who with the Son and Holy Spirit live and reign, one God, for ever and ever. *Amen.*

The First Sunday after Trinity.

O GOD, the strength of all those who put their trust in thee; Mercifully accept our prayers; and because, through the weakness of our mortal nature, we can do no good thing without thee, grant us the help of thy grace, that in keeping thy commandments we may please thee, both in will and deed; through Jesus Christ our Lord. *Amen.*

Sixth Sunday after the Epiphany

O God, the strength of all who put their trust in you: Mercifully accept our prayers; and because in our weakness we can do nothing good without you, give us the help of your grace, that in keeping your commandments we may please you both in will and deed; through Jesus Christ our Lord, who lives and reigns with you and the Holy Spirit, one God, for ever and ever. *Amen.*

The Second Sunday after Trinity.

O LORD, who never failest to help and govern those whom thou dost bring up in thy stedfast fear and love; Keep us, we beseech thee, under the protection of thy good providence, and make us to have a perpetual fear and love of thy holy Name; through Jesus Christ our Lord. *Amen.*

Proper 7 *The Sunday closest to June 22*

O Lord, make us have perpetual love and reverence for your holy Name, for you never fail to help and govern those whom you have set upon the sure foundation of your loving-kindness; through Jesus Christ our Lord, who lives and reigns with you and the Holy Spirit, one God, for ever and ever. *Amen.*

The Third Sunday after Trinity.

O LORD, we beseech thee mercifully to hear us; and grant that we, to whom thou hast given an hearty desire to pray, may, by thy mighty aid, be defended and comforted in all dangers and adversities; through Jesus Christ our Lord. *Amen.*

The Fourth Sunday after Trinity.

O GOD, the protector of all that trust in thee, without whom nothing is strong, nothing is holy; Increase and multiply upon us thy mercy; that, thou being our ruler and guide, we may so pass through things temporal, that we finally lose not the things eternal. Grant this, O heavenly Father, for the sake of Jesus Christ our Lord. *Amen.*

Proper 12 *The Sunday closest to July 27*

O God, the protector of all who trust in you, without whom nothing is strong, nothing is holy: Increase and multiply upon us your mercy; that, with you as our ruler and guide, we may so pass through things temporal, that we lose not the things eternal; through Jesus Christ our Lord, who lives and reigns with you and the Holy Spirit, one God, for ever and ever. *Amen.*

The Fifth Sunday after Trinity.

GRANT, O Lord, we beseech thee, that the course of this world may be so peaceably ordered by thy governance, that thy Church may joyfully serve thee in all godly quietness; through Jesus Christ our Lord. *Amen.*

Proper 3 *The Sunday closest to May 25*

Grant, O Lord, that the course of this world may be peaceably governed by your providence; and that your Church may joyfully serve you in confidence and serenity; through Jesus Christ our Lord, who lives and reigns with you and the Holy Spirit, one God, for ever and ever. *Amen.*

The Sixth Sunday after Trinity.

O GOD, who hast prepared for those who love thee such good things as pass man's understanding; Pour into our hearts such love toward thee, that we, loving thee above all things, may obtain thy promises, which exceed all that we can desire; through Jesus Christ our Lord. *Amen.*

Sixth Sunday of Easter

O God, you have prepared for those who love you such good things as surpass our understanding: Pour into our hearts such love toward you, that we, loving you in all things and above all things, may obtain your promises, which exceed all that we can desire; through Jesus Christ our Lord, who lives and reigns with you and the Holy Spirit, one God, for ever and ever. *Amen.*

The Seventh Sunday after Trinity.

Deus uirtutum, cuius est totum quod est optimum, insere pectoribus nostris amorem tui nominis et praesta, ut et nobis relegionis augmentum quae sunt bona nutrias ac uigilantia studium quaesomus nutrita custodias: per. [Gel, 1182.]

LORD of all power and might, who art the author and giver of all good things; graft in our hearts the love of thy Name, increase in us true religion, nourish us with all goodness, and of thy great mercy keep us in the same, through Jesus Christ our Lord. *Amen.*

The Eighth Sunday after Trinity.

Deus, cuius prouidencia in sui disposicione non fallitur, te supplices exoramus, ut noxia cuncta submoueas et omnia nobis profutura concedas: per. [Gel., 1186.]

O GOD, whose never-failing providence ordereth all things both in heaven and earth; we humbly beseech thee to put away from us all hurtful things, and to give us those things which are[29] profitable for us, through Jesus Christ our Lord. *Amen.*

The Ninth Sunday after Trinity.

Largire nobis, domine, quaesumus, spiritum cogitandi quae bona sunt promptius et agendi, ut qui sine te esse non possumus, secundum te uiuiere ualeamus: per. [Ver., 1015.]

GRANT to us, Lord, we beseech thee, the spirit to think and do always such things as are right;[30] that we who cannot do any thing that is good without thee, may by thee be enabled to live according to thy will; through Jesus Christ our Lord. *Amen.*

The Tenth Sunday after Trinity.

Pateant aures misericordiae, domine, precibus supplicancium, ut et petentibus desiderata concedas, fac tibi eos quae sunt placita postulare: per. [Gel., 1195.]

LET thy merciful ears, O Lord, be open to the prayers of thy humble servants; and, that they may obtain their petitions, make them to ask such things as shall please thee, through Jesus Christ our Lord. *Amen.*

The Eleventh Sunday after Trinity.

Deus, qui omnipotenciam tuam parcendo maximae et miserando manifestas, multiplica super nos graciam tuam, ut a tua promissa currentes caelestium bonorum facis esse consortes: per. [Gel., 1198.]

O GOD, who declarest thy almighty power chiefly[31] in showing mercy and pity; mercifully grant unto us such a measure of thy grace, that we, running the way of thy commandments, may obtain thy gracious promises, and be made partakers of thy heavenly treasure; through Jesus Christ our Lord. *Amen.*

The Twelfth Sunday after Trinity.

Uirtutum caelestium deus, qui plura prestas, quam petimus aut meremur: tribue, quaesumus, ut tua nobis misericordia conferatur, quod nostrorum non habet fiducia meritorum: per. [Ver., 917.]

Omnipotens sempiterne deus qui habu[n]dancia pietatis tua et merita supplicum excedis et uota. effunde super nos misericordiam tuam. ut dimittas que consciencia metuit. et adicias quod oracio non presumit. per. [Sarum, Dominica xii. {post festum sancte trinitatis}, but see Ver., 917.]

ALMIGHTY and everlasting God, who art always more ready to hear than we to pray, and art wont to give more than either we desire or deserve; pour down upon us the abundance of thy mercy; forgiving us those things whereof our conscience is afraid, and giving us those good things which we are not worthy to ask, but through the merits and mediation of Jesus Christ thy Son, our Lord. *Amen.*

29"which be" [1662].

30"be rightful" [1662], "are rightful" [1786].

31"most chiefly" [1662 & 1786].

1928	1979-II
The Seventh Sunday after Trinity.	**Proper 17** *The Sunday closest to August 31*
LORD of all power and might, who art the author and giver of all good things; Graft in our hearts the love of thy Name, increase in us true religion, nourish us with all goodness, and of thy great mercy keep us in the same; through Jesus Christ our Lord. *Amen.*	Lord of all power and might, the author and giver of all good things: Graft in our hearts the love of your Name; increase in us true religion; nourish us with all goodness; and bring forth in us the fruit of good works; through Jesus Christ our Lord, who lives and reigns with you and the Holy Spirit, one God for ever and ever. *Amen.*
The Eighth Sunday after Trinity.	**Proper 4** *The Sunday closest to June 1*
O GOD, whose never-failing providence ordereth all things both in heaven and earth; We humbly beseech thee to put away from us all hurtful things, and to give us those things which are profitable for us; through Jesus Christ our Lord. *Amen.*	O God, your never-failing providence sets in order all things both in heaven and earth: Put away from us, we entreat you, all hurtful things, and give us those things which are profitable for us; through Jesus Christ our Lord, who lives and reigns with you and the Holy Spirit, one God, for ever and ever. *Amen.*
The Ninth Sunday after Trinity.	**Proper 14** *The Sunday closest to August 10*
GRANT to us, Lord, we beseech thee, the spirit to think and do always such things as are right; that we, who cannot do any thing that is good without thee, may by thee be enabled to live according to thy will; through Jesus Christ our Lord. *Amen.*	Grant to us, Lord, we pray, the spirit to think and do always those things that are right, that we, who cannot exist without you, may by you be enabled to live according to your will; through Jesus Christ our Lord, who lives and reigns with you and the Holy Spirit, one God, for ever and ever. *Amen.*
The Tenth Sunday after Trinity.	
LET thy merciful ears, O Lord, be open to the prayers of thy humble servants; and, that they may obtain their petitions, make them to ask such things as shall please thee; through Jesus Christ our Lord. *Amen.*	
The Eleventh Sunday after Trinity.	**Proper 21** *The Sunday closest to September 28*
O GOD, who declarest thy almighty power chiefly in showing mercy and pity; Mercifully grant unto us such a measure of thy grace, that we, running the way of thy commandments, may obtain thy gracious promises, and be made partakers of thy heavenly treasure; through Jesus Christ our Lord. *Amen.*	O God, you declare your almighty power chiefly in showing mercy and pity: Grant us the fullness of your grace, that we, running to obtain your promises, may become partakers of your heavenly treasure; through Jesus Christ our Lord, who lives and reigns with you and the Holy Spirit, one God, for ever and ever. *Amen.*
The Twelfth Sunday after Trinity.	**Proper 22 The Sunday closest to October 5**
ALMIGHTY and everlasting God, who art always more ready to hear than we to pray, and art wont to give more than either we desire or deserve; Pour down upon us the abundance of thy mercy; forgiving us those things whereof our conscience is afraid, and giving us those good things which we are not worthy to ask, but through the merits and mediation of Jesus Christ, thy Son, our Lord. *Amen.*	Almighty and everlasting God, you are always more ready to hear than we to pray, and to give more than we either desire or deserve: Pour upon us the abundance of your mercy, forgiving us those things of which our conscience is afraid, and giving us those good things for which we are not worthy to ask, except through the merits and mediation of Jesus Christ our Savior; who lives and reigns with you and the Holy Spirit, one God, for ever and ever. *Amen.*

The Thirteenth Sunday after Trinity.

Omnipotens et misericors deus, de cuius munere uenit, ut tibi a fidelibus tuis dignae et laudabiliter seruiatur: tribue, ut ad promissiones tuas sine offensione curramus: per. [Ver., 574.]

ALMIGHTY and merciful God, of whose only gift it cometh that thy faithful people do unto thee true and laudable service; grant, we beseech thee, that we may so faithfully serve thee in this life, that we fail not finally to attain thy heavenly promises, through the merits of Jesus Christ our Lord. *Amen.*

The Fourteenth Sunday after Trinity.

Omnipotens sempiterne deus, da nobis fidei spei et caritatis aumentum; et ut mereamur adsequi quod promittis, fac nos amare quod praecipis: per. [Ver., 598.]

ALMIGHTY and everlasting God, give unto us the increase of faith, hope, and charity: and, that we may obtain that which thou dost promise, make us to love that which thou dost command, through Jesus Christ our Lord. *Amen.*

The Fifteenth Sunday after Trinity.

Custodi, domine, quaesumus, aecclesiam tuam propitiacione perpetua, et quia sine te labitur humana mortalitas, tuis semper auxiliis et abstrahatur a noxiis et ad salutaria dirigatur: per. [Gel., 1213.]

KEEP, we beseech thee, O Lord, thy Church with thy perpetual mercy; And, because the frailty of man without thee cannot but fall, keep us ever by thy help from all things hurtful, and lead us to all things profitable to our salvation, through Jesus Christ our Lord. *Amen.*

The Sixteenth Sunday after Trinity.

Ecclesiam tuam, domine, miseracio continuata mundet et muniat, et quia sine te non potest salua consistere, tuo semper munere gubernetur: per. [Gel., 1218.]

O LORD, we beseech thee, let thy continual pity cleanse and defend thy Church; and, because it cannot continue in safety without thy succour, preserve it evermore by thy help and goodness, through Jesus Christ our Lord. *Amen.*

The Seventeenth Sunday after Trinity.

Tua nos domine quaesumus gratia semper et praeueniat et sequatur, ac bonis operibus iugiter prestet esse intentos. Per. [Greg., 966.]

LORD, we pray thee that thy grace may always prevent and follow us; and make us continually to be given to all good works, through Jesus Christ our Lord. *Amen.*

The Eighteenth Sunday after Trinity.

Da, quaesumus, domine, populo tuo diabolica uitare contagia et te solum domine puro corde sectare: per. [Gel., 1226.]

LORD, we beseech thee, grant thy people grace to withstand the temptations of the world, the flesh, and the devil; and with pure hearts and minds to follow thee, the only God; through Jesus Christ our Lord. *Amen.*

The Nineteenth Sunday after Trinity.

Dirigat corda nostra, domine, quaesumus, tuae miserationes operatio, quia tibi sine te placere non possimus: per. [Gel., 1230.]

O GOD, forasmuch as without thee we are not able to please thee; mercifully grant that thy Holy Spirit may in all things direct and rule our hearts, through Jesus Christ our Lord. *Amen.*

The Twentieth Sunday after Trinity.

Omnipotens et misericors deus, uniuersa nobis aduersantia propitiationis exclude, ut mente et corpore pariter expediti quae tua sunt liberis mentibus exequamur: per. [Gel., 1234.]

O ALMIGHTY and most merciful God, of thy bountiful goodness keep us, we beseech thee, from all things that may hurt us; that we, being ready both in body and soul, may cheerfully accomplish those things which

The Thirteenth Sunday after Trinity.

ALMIGHTY and merciful God, of whose only gift it cometh that thy faithful people do unto thee true and laudable service; Grant, we beseech thee, that we may so faithfully serve thee in this life, that we fail not finally to attain thy heavenly promises; through the merits of Jesus Christ our Lord. *Amen.*

Proper 26 *The Sunday closest to November 2*

Almighty and merciful God, it is only by your gift that your faithful people offer you true and laudable service: Grant that we may run without stumbling to obtain your heavenly promises; through Jesus Christ our Lord, who lives and reigns with you and the Holy Spirit, one God, now and for ever. *Amen.*

The Fourteenth Sunday after Trinity.

ALMIGHTY and everlasting God, give unto us the increase of faith, hope, and charity; and, that we may obtain that which thou dost promise, make us to love that which thou dost command; through Jesus Christ our Lord. *Amen.*

Proper 25 *The Sunday closest to October 26*

Almighty and everlasting God, increase in us the gifts of faith, hope, and charity; and, that we may obtain what you promise, make us love what you command; through Jesus Christ our Lord, who lives and reigns with you and the Holy Spirit, one God, for ever and ever. *Amen.*

The Fifteenth Sunday after Trinity.

KEEP, we beseech thee, O Lord, thy Church with thy perpetual mercy; and, because the frailty of man without thee cannot but fall, keep us ever by thy help from all things hurtful, and lead us to all things profitable to our salvation; through Jesus Christ our Lord. *Amen.*

The Sixteenth Sunday after Trinity.

O LORD, we beseech thee, let thy continual pity cleanse and defend thy Church; and, because it cannot continue in safety without thy succour, preserve it evermore by thy help and goodness; through Jesus Christ our Lord. *Amen.*

Proper 13 *The Sunday closest to August 3*

Let your continual mercy, O Lord, cleanse and defend your Church; and, because it cannot continue in safety without your help, protect and govern it always by your goodness; through Jesus Christ our Lord, who lives and reigns with you and the Holy Spirit, one God, for ever and ever. *Amen.*

The Seventeenth Sunday after Trinity.

LORD, we pray thee that thy grace may always prevent and follow us, and make us continually to be given to all good works; through Jesus Christ our Lord. *Amen.*

Proper 23 *The Sunday closest to October 12*

Lord, we pray that your grace may always precede and follow us, that we may continually be given to good works; through Jesus Christ our Lord, who lives and reigns with you and the Holy Spirit, one God, now and for ever. *Amen.*

The Eighteenth Sunday after Trinity.

LORD, we beseech thee, grant thy people grace to withstand the temptations of the world, the flesh, and the devil; and with pure hearts and minds to follow thee, the only God; through Jesus Christ our Lord. *Amen.*

The Nineteenth Sunday after Trinity.

O GOD, forasmuch as without thee we are not able to please thee; Mercifully grant that thy Holy Spirit may in all things direct and rule our hearts; through Jesus Christ our Lord. *Amen.*

Proper 19 *The Sunday closest to September 14*

O God, because without you we are not able to please you, mercifully grant that your Holy Spirit may in all things direct and rule our hearts; through Jesus Christ our Lord, who lives and reigns with you and the Holy Spirit, one God, now and for ever. *Amen.*

The Twentieth Sunday after Trinity.

O ALMIGHTY and most merciful God, of thy bountiful goodness keep us, we beseech thee, from all things that may hurt us; that we, being ready both in body and soul, may cheerfully accomplish those things which

Proper 2 *The Sunday closest to May 18*

Almighty and merciful God, in your goodness keep us, we pray, from all things that may hurt us, that we, being ready both in mind and body, may accomplish with free hearts those things which belong to your pur-

thou commandest;[32] through Jesus Christ our Lord. *Amen.*

The Twenty-first Sunday after Trinity.

Largire, quaesumus, domine, fidelibus tuis indulgenciam placatus et pacem, ut pariter ab omnibus mundentur offensis [et secura] tibi mente deseruiant: per. [Gel., 1238.]

GRANT, we beseech thee, merciful Lord, to thy faithful people pardon and peace; that they may be cleansed from all their sins, and serve thee with a quiet mind, through Jesus Christ our Lord. *Amen.*

The Twenty-second Sunday after Trinity.

Familiam tuam quaesumus domine continua pietate custodi, ut a cunctis aduersitatibus te protegente sit libera, et in bonis actibus tuo nomini sit deuota. Per. [Greg., 1192.]

LORD, we beseech thee to keep thy household the Church in continual godliness; that through thy protection it may be free from all adversities, and devoutly given to serve thee in good works, to the glory of thy Name, through Jesus Christ our Lord. *Amen.*

The Twenty-third Sunday after Trinity.

Deus refugium nostrum et uirtus, adesto piis ecclesiae tuae precibus auctor ipse pietatis, et praesta ut quo fideliter petimus, efficaciter consequamur. Per. [Greg. 1195.]

O GOD, our refuge and strength, who art the author of all godliness; be ready, we beseech thee, to hear the devout prayers of thy Church; and grant that those things which we ask faithfully we may obtain effectually; through Jesus Christ our Lord. *Amen.*

The Twenty-fourth Sunday after Trinity.

Absolue quaesumus domine tuorum delicta populorum et a peccatorum nostrorum nexibus quae pro nostra fragilitate contraximus tua benignitate liberemur. [Greg., 702.]

O LORD, we beseech thee, absolve thy people from their offences; that through thy bountiful goodness we may all be delivered from the bands of those sins, which by our frailty we have committed. Grant this, O heavenly Father, for Jesus Christ's sake, our blessed Lord and Saviour. *Amen.*

THE TWENTY-FIFTH SUNDAY AFTER TRINITY. | THE SUNDAY NEXT BEFORE ADVENT.

Excita domine quaesumus tuorum fidelium uoluntates, ut diuini operis fructum propensius exsequentes, pietatis tuae remedia maiora percipiant. Per. [Greg., 894.]

STIR up, we beseech thee, O Lord, the wills of thy faithful people; that they, plenteously bringing forth the fruit of good works, may by[33] thee be plenteously rewarded, through Jesus Christ our Lord. *Amen.*

Holy Days

Saint Andrew's Day.

ALmightie god which didst geue such grace vnto thy holy Apostle Saincte Andrewe, that he redily obeyed the callyng of thy sone Iesus Christ, and followed hym without delaye: Graunte vnto vs all, that we being

ALMIGHTY God, who didst give such grace unto thy holy Apostle Saint Andrew, that he readily obeyed the calling of thy Son Jesus Christ, and followed him without delay; Grant unto us all, that we, being called by

[32]"that thou wouldest have done" [1662]; "which thou wouldest have done" [1786].

[33]"of" [1662].

thou commandest; through Jesus Christ our Lord. *Amen.*

pose; through Jesus Christ our Lord, who lives and reigns with you and the Holy Spirit, one God, now and for ever. *Amen.*

The Twenty-first Sunday after Trinity.

GRANT, we beseech thee, merciful Lord, to thy faithful people pardon and peace, that they may be cleansed from all their sins, and serve thee with a quiet mind; through Jesus Christ our Lord. *Amen.*

Grant to thy faithful people pardon and peace, that we may be cleansed from all our sins, and serve thee with a quiet mind. *Amen.* [4th petition, Prayers of the People, Burial I.]

The Twenty-second Sunday after Trinity.

LORD, we beseech thee to keep thy household the Church in continual godliness; that through thy protection it may be free from all adversities, and devoutly given to serve thee in good works, to the glory of thy Name; through Jesus Christ our Lord. *Amen.*

The Twenty-third Sunday after Trinity.

O GOD, our refuge and strength, who art the author of all godliness; Be ready, we beseech thee, to hear the devout prayers of thy Church; and grant that those things which we ask faithfully we may obtain effectually; through Jesus Christ our Lord. *Amen.*

The Twenty-fourth Sunday after Trinity.

O LORD, we beseech thee, absolve thy people from their offences; that through thy bountiful goodness we may all be delivered from the bands of those sins, which by our frailty we have committed. Grant this, O heavenly Father, for the sake of Jesus Christ, our blessed Lord and Saviour. *Amen.*

The Sunday next before Advent.

STIR up, we beseech thee, O Lord, the wills of thy faithful people; that they, plenteously bringing forth the fruit of good works, may by thee be plenteously rewarded; through Jesus Christ our Lord. *Amen.*

Saint Andrew the Apostle. [November 30.]

ALMIGHTY God, who didst give such grace unto thy holy Apostle Saint Andrew, that he readily obeyed the calling of thy Son Jesus Christ, and followed him without delay; Grant unto us all, that we, being called by

Saint Andrew *November 30*

Almighty God, who gave such grace to your apostle Andrew that he readily obeyed the call of your Son Jesus Christ, and brought his brother with him: Give us, who are called by your holy Word, grace to follow

called by the holy worde, maye furthwith geue ouer our selfes, obediently to folow thy holy commaudements: through thesame Iesus Chryste our Lorde. [1552, Sainct Andrewes daye.]

thy holy Word, may forthwith give up ourselves obediently to fulfil thy holy commandments, through the same Jesus Christ our Lord. *Amen.*

Saint Thomas the Apostle

ALmightie euerlyuing God, whiche for the more confirmacion of the fayth, didst suffer thy holy Apostle Thomas, to be doubtfull in thy sonnes resurreccion: graunte vs so perfectly, and without al doubt to beleue in thy sone Iesus Christe, that our faith in thy sight neuer be reproued: heare vs, O Lorde, through thesame Iesus Christe: to with thee and the holy gost be all honour. &c. [1549, Saincte Thomas the Apostle.]

ALMIGHTY and everliving God, who, for the greater confirmation[34] of the faith, didst suffer thy holy Apostle Thomas to be doubtful in thy Son's resurrection; grant us so perfectly, and without all doubt, to believe in thy Son Jesus Christ, that our faith in thy sight may never be reproved. Hear us, O Lord, through the same Jesus Christ, to whom, with thee and the Holy Ghost, be all honour and glory, now and for evermore. *Amen.*

The Conversion of Saint Paul.

Deus qui uniuersum mundum beati pauli apostoli tui predicacione docuisti. da nobis quesumus ut qui eius hodie conuersionem colimus. per eius ad te exempla gradiamur. per. [Sarum, In conuersione sancti pauli.]

O GOD, who, through the preaching of the blessed Apostle Saint Paul, hast caused the light of the Gospel to shine throughout the world; grant, we beseech thee, that we, having his wonderful conversion in remembrance, may show forth our thankfulness unto thee for the same, by following the holy doctrine which he taught, through Jesus Christ our Lord. *Amen.*

The Presentation of Christ in the Temple, commonly called The Purification of Saint Mary the Virgin.

Omnipotens sempiterne deus, maiestatem tuam supplices exoramus, ut sicut unigenitus filius tuus hodierna die cum nostrae carnis substantia in templo est praesentatus, ita nos facias purificatis tibi mentibus praesentari. Per dominum nostrum. [Greg., 124.]

ALMIGHTY and everliving God, we humbly beseech thy Majesty, that, as thy only begotten Son was this day presented in the Temple in substance of our flesh; so we may be presented unto thee with pure and clean hearts, by the same thy Son Jesus Christ our Lord. *Amen.*

Saint Matthias's Day.

ALmyghtie God, whiche in the place of the traytor Iudas, didst chose thy faythfull seruaunte Mathie, to bee the noumber of thy twelue Apostles: graunte that thy church being alway preserued from false Apostles, may be ordred and guided by faythfull and true pastors: Through Iesus Christ our Lorde. [1549, Sainct Mathies daie.]

O ALMIGHTY God, who into the place of the traitor Judas didst choose thy faithful servant Matthias to be of the number of the twelve Apostles; grant that thy Church, being alway preserved from false Apostles, may be ordered and guided by faithful and true Pastors, through Jesus Christ our Lord. *Amen.*

The Annunciation of the Blessed Virgin Mary.

Gratiam tuam domine, mentibus nostris infunde, ut qui angelo nuntiante christi filii tui incarnationem cognouimus, per passionem eius et crucem ad resurrectionis gloriam perducamur. Per. [Greg., 143.]

WE beseech thee, O Lord, pour thy grace into our hearts; that, as we have known the Incarnation of thy Son Jesus Christ by the message of an Angel; so by his cross and passion we may be brought unto the glory of his Resurrection, through the same Jesus Christ our Lord. *Amen.*

Saint Mark's Day.

ALmightye GOD, whiche haste instructed thy holye Churche, with the heauenly doctrine of thy Euangelist

O ALMIGHTY God, who hast instructed thy holy Church with the heavenly doctrine of thy Evangelist

[34] "more confirmation" [1662 & 1786].

thy holy Word, may forthwith give up ourselves obediently to fulfil thy holy commandments; through the same Jesus Christ our Lord. *Amen.*

Saint Thomas the Apostle.
[December 21.]

ALMIGHTY and everliving God, who, for the greater confirmation of the faith, didst suffer thy holy Apostle Thomas to be doubtful in thy Son's resurrection; Grant us so perfectly, and without all doubt, to believe in thy Son Jesus Christ, that our faith in thy sight may never be reproved. Hear us, O Lord, through the same Jesus Christ, to whom, with thee and the Holy Ghost, be all honour and glory, now and for evermore. *Amen.*

The Conversion of Saint Paul
[January 25.]

O GOD, who, through the preaching of the blessed Apostle Saint Paul, hast caused the light of the Gospel to shine throughout the world; Grant, we beseech thee, that we, having his wonderful conversion in remembrance, may show forth our thankfulness unto thee for the same, by following the holy doctrine which he taught; through Jesus Christ our Lord. *Amen.*

The Presentation of Christ in the Temple, commonly called The Purification of Saint Mary the Virgin.
[February 2.]

ALMIGHTY and everliving God, we humbly beseech thy Majesty, that, as thy only-begotten Son was this day presented in the temple in substance of our flesh, so we may be presented unto thee with pure and clean hearts, by the same thy Son Jesus Christ our Lord. *Amen.*

Saint Matthias the Apostle.
[February 24.]

O ALMIGHTY God, who into the place of the traitor Judas didst choose thy faithful servant Matthias to be of the number of the twelve Apostles; Grant that thy Church, being alway preserved from false Apostles, may be ordered and guided by faithful and true pastors; through Jesus Christ our Lord. *Amen.*

The Annunciation of the blessed Virgin Mary.
[March 25.]

WE beseech thee, O Lord, pour thy grace into our hearts; that, as we have known the incarnation of thy Son Jesus Christ by the message of an angel, so by his cross and passion we may be brought unto the glory of his resurrection; through the same Jesus Christ our Lord. *Amen.*

Saint Mark the Evangelist.
[April 25.]

O ALMIGHTY God, who hast instructed thy holy Church with the heavenly doctrine of thy Evangelist

him without delay, and to bring those near to us into his gracious presence; who lives and reigns with you and the Holy Spirit, one God, now and for ever. *Amen.*

Saint Thomas *December 21*

Everliving God, who strengthened your apostle Thomas with firm and certain faith in your Son's resurrection: Grant us so perfectly and without doubt to believe in Jesus Christ, our Lord and our God, that our faith may never be found wanting in your sight; through him who lives and reigns with you and the Holy Spirit, one God, now and for ever. *Amen.*

Conversion of Saint Paul *January 25*

O God, by the preaching of your apostle Paul you have caused the light of the Gospel to shine throughout the world: Grant, we pray, that we, having his wonderful conversion in remembrance, may show ourselves thankful to you by following his holy teaching; through Jesus Christ our Lord, who lives and reigns with you, in the unity of the Holy Spirit, one God, now and for ever. *Amen.*

The Presentation *February 2*

Almighty and everliving God, we humbly pray that, as your only-begotten Son was this day presented in the temple, so we may be presented to you with pure and clean hearts by Jesus Christ our Lord; who lives and reigns with you and the Holy Spirit, one God, now and for ever. *Amen.*

Saint Matthias *February 24*

Almighty God, who in the place of Judas chose your faithful servant Matthias to be numbered among the Twelve: Grant that your Church, being delivered from false apostles, may always be guided and governed by faithful and true pastors; through Jesus Christ our Lord, who lives and reigns with you, in the unity of the Holy Spirit, one God, now and for ever. *Amen.*

The Annunciation *March 25*

Pour your grace into our hearts, O Lord, that we who have known the incarnation of your Son Jesus Christ, announced by an angel to the Virgin Mary, may by his cross and passion be brought to the glory of his resurrection; who lives and reigns with you, in the unity of the Holy Spirit, one God, now and for ever. *Amen.*

Sainct Marke: geue vs grace so to bee establyshed by thy holy gospell, that we be not, like children, caried away with euery blast of vayne Doctrine: Through Iesus Christ our Lorde. [1549, Sainct Markes Day.]

Saint Mark; give us grace that, being not like children carried away with every blast of vain doctrine, we may be established in the truth of thy holy Gospel, through Jesus Christ our Lord. *Amen.*

Saint Philip and Saint James's Day.

ALmightie God, whome truely to knowe is euerlasting lyfe: Graunte vs perfectelye to knowe thy sonne Iesus Christe, to be the waye, the trueth, and the life, as thou haste taught saint Philip, and other the Apostles: Through Iesus Christe our Lorde. [1549, Sainct Philip and James.]

O ALMIGHTY God, whom truly to know is everlasting life; grant us perfectly to know thy Son Jesus Christ to be the way, the truth, and the life; that, following the steps of thy holy Apostles, Saint Philip and Saint James, we may stedfastly walk in the way that leadeth to eternal life, through the same thy Son Jesus Christ our Lord. *Amen.*

Saint Barnabas the Apostle.

LOrde almightie, whiche haste indued thy holy Apostle Barnabas, with singular giftes of thy holy gost: let vs not be destitute of thy manifolde giftes, nor yet of grace to vse them alwaye to thy honoure and glory: Through Iesus Christ our Lorde. [1549, Saynct Barnabe Apostle.]

O LORD God Almighty, who didst endue thy holy Apostle Barnabas with singular gifts of the Holy Ghost; leave us not, we beseech thee, destitute of thy manifold gifts, nor yet of grace to use them alway to thy honour and glory; through Jesus Christ our Lord. *Amen.*

Saint John Baptits's Day.

ALmyghtie God, by whose prouidence thy seruaunte Iohn Baptiste was wonderfully borne, and sente to prepare the waye of thy sonne our sauioure, by preachinge of penaunce: make vs so to folowe hys doctrine and holy lyfe, that we may truly repent according to his preachyng, and after his example constantly speake the trueth, boldly rebuke vice, and paciently suffer for the truethes sake: through Iesus Christe our lorde. [1549, Saynct Iohn Baptist.]

ALMIGHTY God, by whose providence thy servant John Baptist was wonderfully born, and sent to prepare the way of thy Son our Saviour by preaching repentance;[35] make us so to follow his doctrine and holy life, that we may truly repent according to his preaching; and after his example constantly speak the truth, boldly rebuke vice, and patiently suffer for the truth's sake; through Jesus Christ our Lord. *Amen.*

Saint Peter's Day.

ALmightie God, whiche by thy sonne Iesus Christ hast geuen to thy Apostle Sayncte Peter many excellente giftes, and commaundest him earnestly to fede thy flocke: make we beseche thee, all byshops and pastors diligently to preache thy holy worde, and the people obedientlye to folowe the same, that they may receyue the croune of euerlasting glorye, through Iesus Christ our Lord. [1549, Sainct Peters Daye.]

O ALMIGHTY God, who by thy Son Jesus Christ didst give to thy Apostle Saint Peter many excellent gifts, and commandedst him earnestly to feed thy flock; make, we beseech thee, all Bishops and Pastors diligently to preach thy holy Word, and the people obediently to follow the same, that they may receive the crown of everlasting glory, through thy Son Jesus Christ our Lord. *Amen.*

Saint James the Apostle.

GRaunt O mercyful God, that as thyne holye Apostle Iames leauing his father and al that he had, without delay, was obediente vnto the calling of thy sonne Iesus Christ, and folowed him: So we forsaking al worldly and carnal affeccions, may be euermore ready to folow thy commaundementes: through Iesus Christ our Lorde. [1549, Sainct Iames the Apostle.]

GRANT, O merciful God, that, as thine holy Apostle Saint James, leaving his father and all that he had, without delay was obedient unto the calling of thy Son Jesus Christ, and followed him; so we, forsaking all worldly and carnal affections, may be evermore ready to follow thy holy commandments, through the same Jesus Christ our Lord. *Amen.*

[35]"by preaching of repentance: [1662 & 1789]; "by the preaching of repentance; [1786].

Saint Mark; Give us grace that, being not like children carried away with every blast of vain doctrine, we may be established in the truth of thy holy Gospel; through Jesus Christ our Lord. *Amen.*

Saint Philip and Saint James, Apostles.
[May 1.]

O ALMIGHTY God, whom truly to know is everlasting life; Grant us perfectly to know thy Son Jesus Christ to be the way, the truth, and the life; that, following the steps of thy holy Apostles, Saint Philip and Saint James, we may stedfastly walk in the way that leadeth to eternal life; through the same thy Son Jesus Christ our Lord. *Amen.*

Saint Barnabas the Apostle.
[June 11.]

O LORD God Almighty, who didst endue thy holy Apostle Barnabas with singular gifts of the Holy Ghost; Leave us not, we beseech thee, destitute of thy manifold gifts, nor yet of grace to use them alway to thy honour and glory; through Jesus Christ our Lord. *Amen.*

Saint John Baptist.
[June 24.]

ALMIGHTY God, by whose providence thy servant John Baptist was wonderfully born, and sent to prepare the way of thy Son our Saviour by preaching repentance; Make us so to follow his doctrine and holy life, that we may truly repent according to his preaching; and after his example constantly speak the truth, boldly rebuke vice, and patiently suffer for the truth's sake; through the same thy Son Jesus Christ our Lord. *Amen.*

The Nativity of Saint John the Baptist *June 24*

Almighty God, by whose providence your servant John the Baptist was wonderfully born, and sent to prepare the way of your Son our Savior by preaching repentance: Make us so to follow his teaching and holy life, that we may truly repent according to his preaching; and, following his example, constantly speak the truth, boldly rebuke vice, and patiently suffer for the truth's sake; through Jesus Christ your Son our Lord, who lives and reigns with you and the Holy Spirit, one God, for ever and ever. *Amen.*

Saint Peter the Apostle.
[June 29.]

O ALMIGHTY God, who by thy Son Jesus Christ didst give to thy Apostle Saint Peter many excellent gifts, and commandedst him earnestly to feed thy flock; Make, we beseech thee, all Bishops and Pastors diligently to preach thy holy Word, and the people obediently to follow the same, that they may receive the crown of everlasting glory; through the same thy Son Jesus Christ our Lord. *Amen.*

Saint James the Apostle.
[July 25.]

GRANT, O merciful God, that, as thine holy Apostle Saint James, leaving his father and all that he had, without delay was obedient unto the calling of thy Son Jesus Christ, and followed him; so we, forsaking all worldly and carnal affections, may be evermore ready to follow thy holy commandments; through the same Jesus Christ our Lord. *Amen.*

THE TRANSFIGURATION OF CHRIST.

O God, who on the mount didst reveal to chosen witnesses thine only-begotten Son wonderfully transfigured, in raiment white and glistening; Mercifully grant that we also, being delivered from the disquietude of this world, may be permitted to behold the King in his beauty, who with thee O Father and thee O Holy Ghost, liveth and reigneth one God, world without end. *Amen.* [Wm. Reed Huntington, "For the Transfiguration," in *Materia Ritualis*. Huntington notes, "Cento of Collect and Secret for the Day. Sarum."]

O GOD, who on the mount didst reveal to chosen witnesses thine only-begotten Son wonderfully transfigured, in raiment white and glistering; Mercifully grant that we, being delivered from the disquietude of this world, may be permitted to behold the King in his beauty, who with thee, O Father, and thee, O Holy Ghost, liveth and reigneth, one God, world without end. *Amen.*

Saint Bartholomew the Apostle.

O Almyghtie and euerlasting God, whiche hast geuen grace to thy apostle Bartholomewe truelye to beleue and to preache thy word: graunt we beseche thee, vnto thy churche, both to loue that he beleued, & to preache that he taught: through Christe our Lorde. [1549, Sainct Bartholomewe.]

O ALMIGHTY and everlasting God, who didst give to thine Apostle Bartholomew grace truly to believe and to preach thy Word; grant, we beseech thee, unto thy Church, to love that Word which he believed, and both to preach and receive the same, through Jesus Christ our Lord. *Amen.*

Saint Matthew the Apostle.

ALmightie God, which by thy blessed sonne diddest call Mathewe from the receipte of custome to be an Apostle and Euangelist: Graunt vs grace to forsake all couetous desyres and inordinate loue of riches, and to folowe thy sayed sonne Iesus Christ: who lyueth and reigneth. &c. [1549, Sainct Mathewe.]

O ALMIGHTY God, who by thy blessed Son didst call Matthew from the receipt of custom to be an Apostle and Evangelist; grant us grace to forsake all covetous desires, and inordinate love of riches, and to follow the same thy Son Jesus Christ, who liveth and reigneth with thee and the Holy Ghost, one God, world without end. *Amen.*

SAINT MICHAEL AND ALL ANGELS.

Deus qui miro ordine angelorum ministeria hominumque dispensas, concede propitius ut quibus tibi ministrantibus in caelo semper adsistitur, ab his in terra nostra uita muniatur. Per. [Greg., 726.]

O EVERLASTING God, who hast ordained and constituted the services of Angels and men in a wonderful order; mercifully grant that, as thy holy Angels always do thee service in heaven; so by thy appointment, they may succour and defend us on earth, through Jesus Christ our Lord. *Amen.*

Saint Luke the Evangelist.

ALmightie God whiche calledst Luke the phisicion, whose prayse is in the gospel, to be a phisicion of the soule; it maye please thee by the holsome medicines of hys doctryne, to heale al the diseases of our soules: through thy sonne Iesus Christe our Lorde. [1549, Sainct Luke Euangelist.]

ALMIGHTY God, who calledst Luke the Physician, whose praise is in the Gospel, to be an Evangelist, and Physician of the soul; may it please thee that, by the wholesome medicines of the doctrine delivered by him, all the diseases of our souls may be healed, through the merits of thy Son Jesus Christ our Lord. *Amen.*

The Transfiguration of Christ.
[August 6.]

O GOD, who on the mount didst reveal to chosen witnesses thine only-begotten Son wonderfully transfigured, in raiment white and glistering; Mercifully grant that we, being delivered from the disquietude of this world, may be permitted to behold the King in his beauty, who with thee, O Father, and thee, O Holy Ghost, liveth and reigneth, one God, world without end. *Amen.*

The Transfiguration *August 6*

O God, who on the holy mount revealed to chosen witnesses your well-beloved Son, wonderfully transfigured, in raiment white and glistening: Mercifully grant that we, being delivered from the disquietude of this world, may by faith behold the King in his beauty; who with you, O Father, and you, O Holy Spirit, lives and reigns, one God, for ever and ever. *Amen.*

Saint Bartholomew the Apostle.
[August 24.]

O ALMIGHTY and everlasting God, who didst give to thine Apostle Bartholomew grace truly to believe and to preach thy Word; Grant, we beseech thee, unto thy Church, to love that Word which he believed, and both to preach and receive the same; through Jesus Christ our Lord. *Amen.*

Saint Bartholomew *August 24*

Almighty and everlasting God, who gave to your apostle Bartholomew grace truly to believe and to preach your Word: Grant that your Church may love what he believed and preach what he taught; through Jesus Christ our Lord, who lives and reigns with you and the Holy Spirit, one God, for ever and ever. *Amen.*

Saint Matthew, Apostle and Evangelist.
[September 21.]

O ALMIGHTY God, who by thy blessed Son didst call Matthew from the receipt of custom to be an Apostle and Evangelist; Grant us grace to forsake all covetous desires, and inordinate love of riches, and to follow the same thy Son Jesus Christ, who liveth and reigneth with thee and the Holy Ghost, one God, world without end. *Amen.*

Saint Michael and all Angels.
[September 29.]

O EVERLASTING God, who hast ordained and constituted the services of Angels and men in a wonderful order; Mercifully grant that, as thy holy Angels always do thee service in heaven, so, by thy appointment, they may succour and defend us on earth; through Jesus Christ our Lord. *Amen.*

Saint Michael and All Angels *September 29*

Everlasting God, you have ordained and constituted in a wonderful order the ministries of angels and mortals: Mercifully grant that, as your holy angels always serve and worship you in heaven, so by your appointment they may help and defend us here on earth; through Jesus Christ our Lord, who lives and reigns with you and the Holy Spirit, one God, for ever and ever. *Amen.*

St. Luke the Evangelist.
[October 18.]

Saint Luke *October 18*

ALmightie God, whiche hast builded the congregacion vpon the foundacion of the Apostles and prophetes, Iesu Christ hymselfe beyng the head corner stone: graunte vs so to bee ioyned together in vnitie of spirite by theyr doctrine, that we may be made an holye temple acceptable to thee: throughe Iesus Christe our Lorde. [1549, Symon and Iude Apostles.]

Saint Simon and Saint Jude, Apostles.

O ALMIGHTY God, who hast built thy Church upon the foundation of the Apostles and Prophets, Jesus Christ himself being the head corner-stone; grant us so to be joined together in unity of spirit by their doctrine, that we may be made an holy temple acceptable unto thee, through the same Jesus Christ our Lord. *Amen.*

ALmightie GOD, whiche hast knitte together thy electe in one Comunion and felowship in the misticall body of thy sonne Christe our Lorde: graunt vs grace so to folow thy holy Saynctes in all vertues, and godly lyuyng, that we maye come to those vnspeakeable ioyes, whiche thou hast prepared for all them that vnfaynedly loue thee: through Iesus Christe. [1549, All Sainctes.]

All Saints' Day

O ALMIGHTY God, who hast knit together thine elect in one communion and fellowship, in the mystical body of thy Son Christ our Lord; grant us grace so to follow thy blessed Saints in all virtuous and godly living, that we may come to those unspeakable joys which thou hast prepared for those who[36] unfeignedly love thee, through the same thy Son Jesus Christ our Lord. *Amen.*

Omnipotens sepmiterne deus, qui in sanctorum cordibus flammam tuae dilectionis accendis, da mentibus eandem fidem caritatisque uirtutem, ut quorum gaudemus triumphis, proficiamur exemplis: per. [Miss. Goth., 455.]

Deus qui nobis per singulos annos huius sancti templi tui consecrationis reparas diem, et sacris semper mysteriis repraesentas incolomes, exaudi preces populi tui, et praesta ut quisquis hoc templum beneficia petiturus ingreditur, cuncta se impetrasse laetetur. Per. [Greg., 1262.]

ALMIGHTY God, whom year by year we praise for the dedication of this church, and who hast preserved us in safety to worship therein; Hear, we beseech thee, the prayers of thy people, and grant that whosoever in this place shall make his supplication before thee, may by the granting of his petitions be filled with joy to the

[36]"them that" [1662].

ALMIGHTY God, who didst inspire thy servant Saint Luke the Physician, to set forth in the Gospel the love and healing power of thy Son; Manifest in thy Church the like power and love, to the healing of our bodies and our souls; through the same thy Son Jesus Christ our Lord. *Amen.*

Saint Simon and Saint Jude, Apostles. [October 28.]

O ALMIGHTY God, who hast built thy church upon the foundation of the Apostles and Prophets, Jesus Christ himself being the head corner-stone; Grant us so to be joined together in unity of spirit by their doctrine, that we may be made an holy temple acceptable unto thee; through the same Jesus Christ our Lord. *Amen.*

All Saints' Day. [November 1.]

O ALMIGHTY God, who hast knit together thine elect in one communion and fellowship, in the mystical body of thy Son Christ our Lord; Grant us grace so to follow thy blessed Saints in all virtuous and godly living, that we may come to those unspeakable joys which thou hast prepared for those who unfeignedly love thee; through Jesus Christ our Lord. *Amen.*

A Saint's Day.

ALMIGHTY and everlasting God, who dost enkindle the flame of thy love in the hearts of the Saints; Grant to us, thy humble servants, the same faith and power of love; that, as we rejoice in their triumphs, we may profit by their examples, through Jesus Christ our Lord. *Amen.*

Or this

O ALMIGHTY God, who hast called us to faith in thee, and hast compassed us about with so great a cloud of witnesses; Grant that we, encouraged by the good examples of thy Saints, and especially of thy servant [Saint ——], may persevere in running the race that is set before us, until at length, through thy mercy, we, with them, attain to thine eternal joy; through him who is the author and finisher of our faith, thy Son Jesus Christ our Lord. *Amen.*

Feast of the Dedication of a Church.

O GOD, whom year by year we praise for the dedication of this church; Hear, we beseech thee, the prayers of thy people, and grant that whosoever shall worship before thee in this place, may obtain thy merciful aid and protection; through Jesus Christ our Lord. *Amen.*

Almighty God, who inspired your servant Luke the physician to set forth in the Gospel the love and healing power of your Son: Graciously continue in your Church this love and power to heal, to the praise and glory of your Name; through Jesus Christ our Lord, who lives and reigns with you, in the unity of the Holy Spirit, one God, now and for ever. Amen.

Proper 8 *The Sunday closest to June 29*

Almighty God, you have built your Church upon the foundation of the apostles and prophets, Jesus Christ himself being the chief cornerstone: Grant us so to be joined together in unity of spirit by their teaching, that we may be made a holy temple acceptable to you; through Jesus Christ our Lord, who lives and reigns with you and the Holy Spirit, one God, for ever and ever. *Amen.*

All Saints' Day *November 1*

Almighty God, you have knit together your elect in one communion and fellowship in the mystical body of your Son Christ our Lord: Give us grace so to follow your blessed saints in all virtuous and godly living, that we may come to those ineffable joys that you have prepared for those who truly love you; through Jesus Christ our Lord, who with you and the Holy Spirit lives and reigns, one God, in glory everlasting. *Amen.*

Of a Martyr

Almighty and everlasting God, who kindled the flame of your love in the heart of your holy martyr *N.*: Grant to us, your humble servants, a like faith and power of love, that we who rejoice in *her* triumph may profit by *her* example; through Jesus Christ our Lord, who lives and reigns with you and the Holy Spirit, one God, for ever and ever. *Amen.*

Of a Saint

Almighty God, you have surrounded us with a great cloud of witnesses: Grant that we, encouraged by the good example of your servant *N.*, may persevere in running the race that is set before us, until at last we may with *him* attain to your eternal joy; through Jesus Christ, the pioneer and perfecter of our faith, who lives and reigns with you and the Holy Spirit, one God, for ever and ever. *Amen.*

glory of thy holy Name, through Jesus Christ our Lord. *Amen.* [Scottish 1912, At the Dedication Festival.]

Almighty God, Lord of Heaven & Earth, in whom we live, & move, & have our Being; who dost good unto all men, making thy Sunne to rise on ye evill & on the good, & sending Raine on ye just, & on ye unjust; Favourably behold us thy people, who call upon thy Name, & send us thy Blessing from Heaven in Giving us fruitful Seasons, & filling our Hearts with food & gladnes, that both our hearts & mouths may be continually filled with thy praises, giving thanks to thee in thy holy church through Jesus Christ our Lord. Amen. [John Cosin.]

O MOST merciful Father, who of thy gracious goodness hast heard the devout prayers of thy Church, and turned our dearth and scarcity into cheapness and plenty;[38] We give thee humble thanks for this thy special bounty; beseeching thee to continue thy loving-kindness unto us, that our land may yield us her fruits of increase, to thy glory and our comfort; through Jesus Christ our Lord. *Amen.* [1662-1928, Thanksgiving For Plenty.]

O MOST merciful Father, who hast blessed the labours of the husbandman in the returns of the fruits of the earth; We give thee humble and hearty thanks for this thy bounty; beseeching thee to continue thy loving-kindness to us; that our land may still yield her increase, to thy glory and our comfort: through Jesu Christ our Lord. *Amen.* [1786-1871, in "A Form of Prayer and Thanksgiving To Almighty God, for the Fruits of the Earth..." which provided special alterations and additions to Morning Prayer.]

[37]Usually attributed to William Heathcote DeLancey.

[38]"cheapness and" deleted from 1789 on.

[39]Attributed to W. E. Scudmore.

The Embber Days At the Four Seasons.

O ALMIGHTY God, who hast committed to the hands of men the ministry of reconciliation; We humbly beseech thee, by the inspiration of thy Holy Spirit, to put it into the hearts of many to offer themselves for this ministry; that thereby mankind may be drawn to thy blessed kingdom; through Jesus Christ our Lord. *Amen.*[37]

The Rogation Days
Being the Three Days before Ascension Day.

ALMIGHTY God, Lord of heaven and earth; We beseech thee to pour forth thy blessing upon this land, and to give us a fruitful season; that we, constantly receiving thy bounty, may evermore give thanks unto thee in thy holy Church; through Jesus Christ our Lord. *Amen.*

Independence Day [July 4.]

O ETERNAL God, through whose mighty power our fathers won their liberties of old; Grant, we beseech thee, that we and all the people of this land may have grace to maintain these liberties in righteousness and peace; through Jesus Christ our Lord. *Amen.*

Independence Day *July 4*

Lord God Almighty, in whose Name the founders of this country won liberty for themselves and for us, and lit the torch of freedom for nations then unborn: Grant that we and all the people of this land may have grace to maintain our liberties in righteousness and peace; through Jesus Christ our Lord, who lives and reigns with you and the Holy Spirit, one God, for ever and ever. *Amen.*

Thanksgiving Day.

O MOST merciful Father, who hast blessed the labours of the husbandman in the returns of the fruits of the earth; We give thee humble and hearty thanks for this thy bounty; beseeching thee to continue thy loving-kindness to us, that our land may still yield her increase, to thy glory and our comfort; through Jesus Christ our Lord. *Amen.*

At a Marriage.

O ETERNAL God, we humbly beseech thee, favourably to behold these thy servants now (*or* about to be) joined in wedlock according to thy holy ordinance; and grant that they, seeking first thy kingdom and thy righteousness, may obtain the manifold blessings of thy grace; through Jesus Christ our Lord. *Amen.*

At the Burial of the Dead.

O ETERNAL Lord God, who holdest all souls in life; Vouchsafe, we beseech thee, to thy whole Church in paradise and on earth, thy light and thy peace; and grant that we, following the good examples of those who have served thee here and are now at rest, may at the last enter with them into thine unending joy; through Jesus Christ our Lord. *Amen.*[39]

8. For the Departed

Eternal Lord God, you hold all souls in life: Give to your whole Church in paradise and on earth your light and your peace; and grant that we, following the good examples of those who have served you here and are now at rest, may at the last enter with them into your unending joy; through Jesus Christ our Lord, who lives and reigns with you, in the unity of the Holy Spirit, one God, now and for ever. *Amen.*

Deus, cuius misericordiae non est numerus, suscipe pro anima famuli tui *illi* episcopi preaces nostras et lucis ei laeticiaeque in regione sanctorum tuorum societate concide: per. [Gel., 1634. In the Sarum use, this collect was employed at the requiem of a priest, with a new collect appointed for a bishop.]

O GOD, whose mercies cannot be numbered; Accept our prayers on behalf of the soul of thy servant departed, and grant *him* an entrance into the land of life and joy, in the fellowship of thy saints; through Jesus Christ our Lord. *Amen.*

O God, whose mercies cannot be numbered: Accept our prayers on behalf of you servant *N.*, and grant *him* an entrance into the land of light and joy, in the fellowship of your saints; through Jesus Christ our Lord, who lives and reigns with you and the Holy Spirit, one God, now and for ever. *Amen.* [Burial II.]

Family Prayer

Morning Prayer

Bishop Gibson **1789-1892**

FORMS OF PRAYER TO BE USED IN FAMILIES[1]

MORNING PRAYER
TO BE USED IN ALL FAMILIES.[2]

¶ *The Master or Mistress having called together as many of the Family as can conveniently be present, let one of them, or any other whom they shall think most proper, say as follows, all kneeling.*

MORNING PRAYER.

¶ *The Master or Mistress having called together as many of the Family as can conveniently be present, let one of them, or any other whom they shall think proper, say as follows, all kneeling.*

[1]These prayers are not to be found in either the English or the Proposed Book.

[2]from *Family Devotion: or a Plain Exhortation to Morning and Evening Prayer in Families*, by Edmund Gibson, published in 1705 while he was Rector of Lambeth. When Gibson became Bishop of London he gained oversight of the Church in all of the colonies, where his book was immensely popular and provided all the liturgical experience some Anglicans were able to have on a regular basis. Of Gibson's sources, chief was the collection of household prayers Archbishop John Tillotson had compiled for William III.

1928	1979

Forms of Prayer to be used in Families

MORNING PRAYER.

¶ *The Master or Mistress having called together as many of the Family as can conveniently be present, let one of them, or any other who may be appointed, say as followeth, all kneeling, and repeating with him the Lord's Prayer.*

Daily Devotions for Individuals and Families

These devotions follow the basic structure of the Daily Office of the Church.

When more than one person is present, the Reading and the Collect should be read by one person, and the other parts said in unison, or in some other convenient manner. (For suggestions about reading the Psalms, see page 582.)

For convenience, appropriate Psalms, Readings, and Collects are provided in each service. When desired, however, the Collect of the Day, or any of the collects appointed in the Daily Offices, may be used instead.

The Psalms and Readings may be replaced by those appointed in

a) the Lectionary for Sundays, Holy Days, the Common of Saints, and Various Occasions, page 888

b) the Daily Office Lectionary, page 934

c) some other manual of devotion which provides daily selections for the Church Year.

OUR Father, who,...for ever and ever. Amen.

Acknowledgment of God's mercy and preservation, especially the night past.

ALMIGHTY and everlasting God, in whom we live and move, and have our being, and whose mercy is over all thy works: We thy needy creatures, in a thankful sense of thy good providence over us, render Thee our humblest praises for thy preservation of us from the beginning of our lives to this day. Blessed be thy holy name for the continual protection of thy hand, by which we have been defended amidst the changes and chances of this mortal life, and kept and delivered from innumerable dangers, and particularly from the terrors and evil accidents of the past night.

Acknowledgement of God's mercy and preservation, especially through the night past.

ALMIGHTY and everlasting God, in whom we live and move and have our being; We, thy needy creatures, render thee our humble praises, for thy preservation of us from the beginning of our lives to this day, and especially for having delivered us from the dangers of the past night.

[* *When disturbances of any kind befall a family, instead of this say,* that notwithstanding our fears and dangers, we are brought in safety to the beginning of this day.]

To thy watchful Providence we wholly owe it, [* that no disturbance hath come nigh us or our dwelling, but that we have enjoyed quiet and refreshing sleep, and are brought in safety to the beginning of this day.] For these and all thy other mercies, our souls do bless and magnify thy glorious name; humbly beseeching Thee to accept this our morning sacrifice of praise and thanksgiving, for his sake, who lay down in the grave, and rose again for us, thy Son our Saviour Jesus Christ. *Amen.*

* *When disturbances of any kind befall a family, instead of this say,* that notwithstanding our dangers, we are brought in safety to the beginning of this day.

To thy watchful providence we owe it, * (that no disturbance hath come nigh us or our dwelling; but that we are brought in safety to the beginning of this day.) For these thy mercies, we bless and magnify thy glorious name; humbly beseeching Thee to accept this our morning sacrifice of praise and thanksgiving, for his sake, who lay down in the grave, and rose again for us, thy Son our Saviour Jesus Christ. *Amen.*

Dedication of soul and body to God's service, with a resolution to be growing daily in goodness.

AND, since it is of thy mercy, O gracious Father, that another day is added to our lives; We here dedicate both our souls and bodies to thee and thy service, to promote thy glory and our own salvation, in a sober, righteous, and godly life. We renounce the devil and all his works, the vanities of this wicked world, and all the sinful lusts of the flesh; desiring nothing so much as to serve Thee faithfully all the days of our lives.[3] And we sincerely resolve so to improve the time which thou shalt be pleased to grant us in this world that we may every day become better Christians, and persevere in holiness and righteousness unto the end.

In which resolutions do thou, O merciful God, confirm and strengthen us; and especially this day keep it steadfastly in the purpose of our hearts to perform them that, as we grow in age, we may grow in grace and in the knowledge of our Lord and Saviour Jesus Christ. *Amen.*

Dedication of soul and body to God's service, with a resolution to be growing daily in goodness.

AND since it is of thy mercy, O gracious Father, that another day is added to our lives; We here dedicate both our souls and our bodies to thee and thy service, in a sober, righteous, and godly life: in which resolution, do thou, O merciful God, confirm and strengthen us; that, as we grow in age, we may grow in grace, and in the knowledge of our Lord and Saviour Jesus Christ. *Amen.*

Family Prayer

Morning Prayer

Prayer for grace to enable us to perform that resolution.

BUT, Lord, thou knowest the weakness and corruption of our nature, and the manifold temptations that we daily meet

Prayer for grace to enable us to perform that resolution.

BUT, O God, who knowest the weakness and corruption of our nature, and the manifold temptations which we

[3]Cf. the rites for Baptism and Confirmation in the 1662 book.

OUR Father, who,...for ever and ever. Amen.

¶ *Here may follow the Collect for the day.*

Acknowledgment of God's Mercy and Preservation, especially through the Night past.

ALMIGHTY and everlasting God, in whom we live and move and have our being; We, thy needy creatures, render thee our humble praises, for thy preservation of us from the beginning of our lives to this day, and especially for having delivered us from the dangers of the past night.

For these thy mercies, we bless and magnify thy glorious Name; humbly beseeching thee to accept this our morning sacrifice of praise and thanksgiving; for his sake who lay down in the grave, and rose again for us, thy Son our Saviour Jesus Christ. *Amen.*

Dedication of Soul and Body to God's Service, with a Resolution to be growing daily in Goodness.

AND since it is of thy mercy, O gracious Father, that another day is added to our lives; We here dedicate both our souls and our bodies to thee and thy service, in a sober, righteous, and godly life:

in which resolution, do thou, O merciful God, confirm and strengthen us; that, as we grow in age, we may grow in grace, and in the knowledge of our Lord and Saviour Jesus Christ. *Amen.*

For Grace to enable us to perform that Resolution.

BUT, O God, who knowest the weakness and corruption of our natures, and the manifold temptations which we daily meet with; We humbly beseech thee to have compassion on our infirmities,

with; We therefore humbly beseech Thee to have compassion upon our infirmities, and to give us the constant assistance of thy Holy Spirit; that we may be effectually restrained from sin, and excited to our duty. And when thou seest us giving way to any temptation, suffer us not to be tempted above that we are able, but stretch out thy helping hand to save and deliver us.

daily meet with; We humbly beseech thee to have compassion on our infirmities, and to give us the constant assistance of thy Holy Spirit; that we may be effectually restrained from sin, and excited to our duty.

Imprint upon our hearts such a dread of thy judgments, and such a grateful sense of thy goodness to us, as may make us both afraid and ashamed to offend thee. And, above all, keep up in our minds a lively remembrance of that great day, in which we must give a strict account of our thoughts, words, and actions; and according to the works done in the body, be eternally rewarded or punished, by him whom thou hast appointed Judge of quick and dead, thy Son Jesus Christ our Lord. *Amen.*

Imprint upon our hearts such a dread of thy judgments, and such a grateful sense of thy goodness to us, as may make us both afraid and ashamed to offend thee. And, above all, keep in our minds a lively remembrance of that great day, in which we must give a strict account of our thoughts, words, and actions; and according to the works done in the body, be eternally rewarded or punished, by him whom thou hast appointed the Judge of quick and dead, thy Son Jesus Christ our Lord. *Amen.*

For grace to guide and keep us the following day.

IN particular, that we may then be able to give account of this day, grant us grace to have Thee and thy law before our eyes, that we may walk in it according to thy will with watchfulness and circumspection. Keep us sober and temperate in our meats and drinks, and diligent in the several callings and professions which thy providence hath appointed us: Grant us patience under any affliction thou shalt see fit to lay on us, and minds always contented with our present condition. Give us grace to be just and upright in all our dealings, quiet and peaceable among our neighbours, full of compassion towards the needy and afflicted, and ever ready to do good to all men, according to the abilities and opportunities which thou shalt give us. That so walking faithfully before thee all our days, and being found watching whenever our appointed time shall come, we may, from a life of righteousness, be translated to a life of glory, through the merits and mediation of Jesus Christ our only Saviour and Redeemer. *Amen.*

For grace to guide and keep us the following day, and for God's blessing on the business of the same.

IN particular, we implore thy grace and protection for the ensuing day. Keep us temperate in our meats and drinks, and diligent in our several callings. Grant us patience under any afflictions thou shalt see fit to lay on us, and minds always contented with our present condition. Give us grace to be just and upright in all our dealings; quiet and peaceable; full of compassion; and ready to do good to all men, according to our abilities and opportunities.

For God's blessing upon the business of the day.

[* AND now we are entering upon the business of the several stations wherein thy providence hath placed us, we humbly beg thy blessing this day upon our honest designs and undertakings. Direct us in all our ways, and prosper the works of our hands:] And as we desire to walk in a constant sense of thy all-seeing providence, so let the same good providence watch over us, and preserve our going out and coming in. Defend us from all dangers and adversities, and be graciously pleased to take us, and all things belonging to us into thy fatherly care and protection. These things, O Lord, and whatever else thou shalt see necessary and convenient, either for our souls, or bodies, or estates, we humbly beg of thee, for the sake of thy Son Jesus Christ, in whose name

* *On Sunday morning, instead of this, say,* And now we are going to the place of thy publick worship, we beseech thee let thy holy Spirit accompany us, and make us devout, serious and attentive, raise our minds from the thoughts of this world, to the consideration of the next, that we fervently join in the prayers and praises of thy church, and listen to our duty with honest hearts, in order to practise it. And give us grace to dedicate this day, as thou

Direct us in all our ways, * [and prosper the works of our hands in the business of our several stations.] Defend us from all dangers and adversities; and be graciously pleased to take us and all things belonging to us, under thy fatherly care and protection. These things, and whatever else thou shalt see necessary and convenient to us we humbly beg, through the merits and mediation of thy Son Jesus Christ our Lord and Saviour. *Amen.*

* *On Sunday morning, instead of this, say,* and let thy Holy Spirit accompany us to the place of thy public worship, making us serious and attentive, and raising our minds from the thoughts of this world to the consideration of the next; that we may fervently join in the prayers and praises of thy Church, and listen to our duty with honest hearts, in order to practice it.

and to give us the constant assistance of thy Holy Spirit; that we may be effectually restrained from sin, and incited to our duty.

Imprint upon our hearts such a dread of thy judgments, and such a grateful sense of thy goodness to us, as may make us both afraid and ashamed to offend thee. And, above all, keep in our minds a lively remembrance of that great day, in which we must give a strict account of our thoughts, words, and actions to him whom thou hast appointed the Judge of quick and dead, thy Son Jesus Christ our Lord. *Amen.*

For Grace to guide and keep us the following Day, and for God's Blessing on the business of the Same.

IN particular, we implore thy grace and protection for the ensuing day. Keep us temperate in all things, and diligent in our several callings. Grant us patience under our afflictions. Give us grace to be just and upright in all our dealings; quiet and peaceable; full of compassion; and ready to do good to all men, according to our abilities and opportunities.

Direct us in all our ways. Defend us from all dangers and adversities; and be graciously pleased to take us, and all who are dear to us, under thy fatherly care and protection. These things, and whatever else thou shalt see to be necessary and convenient to us, we humbly beg, through the merits and mediation of thy Son Jesus Christ, our Lord and Saviour. *Amen.*

and words we conclude our imperfect prayers.

hast appointed us, to thy service, and the care of our souls. Direct us in all our ways, and guide our feet into thy paths.

Our Father, which art....forever and ever. Amen.

THE grace of our Lord Jesus Christ, and the love of God, and the fellowship of the Holy Ghost, be with us all evermore. *Amen.*

Evening Prayer

EVENING PRAYER TO BE USED IN ALL FAMILIES.

¶ *The Family being together, a little before bed-time, let the Master or Mistress, or any other whom they shall think most proper, say as follows, all kneeling.*

MOST gracious and merciful God, who art of purer eyes than to behold iniquity, and hast promised mercy and forgiveness to all them who confess and forsake their sins; we come before thee in an humble sense of our own unworthiness, acknowledging our manifold transgressions of thy righteous laws, in thought, word and deed. We have every day been doing those things which thou hast forbidden, and leaving undone the things which thou hast commanded; so that when we look back upon our past lives, and remember that thou art privy to our most secret sins, we are afraid of thy judgements, and are ashamed to lift up our eyes unto thee.

Confession of sins, with a prayer for contrition and pardon.

* But, O gracious Father, who desirest not the death of a Sinner, look upon us, we beseech thee, in thy Son Jesus Christ, for the merits of his sufferings be thou merciful to our sins. Make us deeply sensible of the great evil of them, and work in us an hearty contrition, and let the remembrance of them be more grievous and afflicting to us, than of any other evil whatsoever; that we worthily lamenting our transgressions, and being brought to a hatred of our sins, and a hearty repentance, may obtain forgiveness at thy hands, who art ever ready to receive humble and penitent sinners; for the sake of thy Son Jesus Christ our only Saviour and Redeemer. *Amen.*

** Here let him who reads, make a short pause, that every one may secretly confess the sins and failings of that day.*

EVENING PRAYER.

¶ *The Family being together, a little before bed-time, let the Master or Mistress, or any other whom they shall think proper, say as follows, all kneeling.*

OUR Father, who...for ever and ever. Amen.

MOST merciful God, who art of purer eyes than to behold iniquity, and hast promised forgiveness to all those who confess and forsake their sins; We come before thee in an humble sense of our own unworthiness, acknowledging our manifold transgressions of thy righteous laws.

Confession of sins, with a prayer for contrition and pardon.

* But, O gracious Father, who desirest not the death of a sinner, look upon us, we beseech thee, in mercy, and forgive us all our transgressions. Make us deeply sensible of the great evil of them; and work in us an hearty contrition; that we may obtain forgiveness at thy hands, who art ever ready to receive humble and penitent sinners; for the sake of thy Son Jesus Christ, our only Saviour and Redeemer. *Amen.*

** Here let him who reads make a short pause, that every one may secretly confess the sins and failings of that day.*

THE grace of our Lord Jesus Christ, and the love of God, and the fellowship of the Holy Ghost, be with us all evermore. *Amen.*

EVENING PRAYER.

¶ *The Family being together, a little before bed-time, let the Master or Mistress, or any other who may be appointed, say as followeth, all kneeling, and repeating with him the Lord's Prayer.*

OUR Father, who...for ever and ever. Amen.

¶ *Here may follow the Collect for the day.*

Confession of Sins, with a Prayer for Contrition and Pardon

MOST merciful God, who art of purer eyes than to behold iniquity, and hast promised forgiveness to all those who confess and forsake their sins; We come before thee in an humble sense of our own unworthiness, acknowledging our manifold transgression of thy righteous laws,

* But, O gracious Father, who desirest not the death of a sinner, look upon us, we beseech thee, in mercy, and forgive us all our transgressions. Make us deeply sensible of the great evil of them; and work in us an hearty contrition; that we may obtain forgiveness at thy hands, who art ever ready to receive humble and penitent sinners; for the sake of thy Son Jesus Christ, our only Saviour and Redeemer. *Amen.*

* *Here let him who reads make a short pause, that every one may secretly confess the sins and failings of that day.*

AND lest, through our own frailty, or the temptations that encompass us, we be drawn again to our former sins; vouchsafe us, we beseech thee, the direction and assistance of thy holy Spirit; that as thou hast put into our hearts these desires and resolutions of amendment, so by the help of thy grace we may bring the same to good effect in a godly, righteous and sober life.

Prayer for grace to reform and grow better.

AND lest, through our own frailty, or the temptations which encompass us, we be drawn again into sin, vouchsafe us, we beseech thee, the direction and assistance of thy Holy Spirit.

Prayer for grace to reform and grow better.

Reform whatever thou findest amiss in the temper and disposition of our souls; that no unclean thoughts, unlawful designs, or inordinate desires, may rest there. Purge our hearts from envy, hatred, and malice: that we may never suffer the sun to go down upon our wrath; but may always go to our rest in peace, charity, and good-will, with a conscience void of offence towards thee, and towards men: That so our hearts being a fit habitation for thy Holy Spirit, he may continually dwell therein; and we whether we wake or sleep, may be under his blessed protection, and have our whole spirit, and soul, and body preserved pure and blameless, unto the coming of our Lord and Saviour Jesus Christ. *Amen.*

Reform whatever is amiss in the temper and disposition of our souls; that no unclean thoughts, unlawful designs, or inordinate desires, may rest there. Purge our hearts from envy, hatred, and malice: that we may never suffer the sun to go down upon our wrath; but may always go to our rest in peace, charity, and good-will, with a conscience void of offence towards thee, and towards men: That so we may be preserved pure and blameless, unto the coming of our Lord and Saviour Jesus Christ. *Amen.*

WITH these prayers in behalf of ourselves, accept, O Lord, as the testimony of our love and charity, our hearty intercessions for all mankind.

The Intercession, general and particular.

Let the light of thy Gospel shine upon all nations; and may as many as have already heard and received it live as becomes it. Be more especially gracious to the Church and nation whereunto we belong. Bless the King and all who by thy providence have authority under him; so rule their hearts and strengthen their hands, that they may neither want will or power to punish wickedness and vice, and to maintain thy true religion among us. Send down thy blessings, temporal and spiritual, upon all our relations, friends, and neighbours. Reward all that have done us good, and pardon all those who have done or wish us evil, and give them repentance and better minds. Be merciful to all who are in any trouble or affliction of mind, body, or estate; and do thou the God of pity and compassion administer to every one help and comfort, according to their several necessities; for his sake who went about doing good to the souls and bodies of men, thy Son our Saviour Jesus Christ. *Amen.*

AND accept, O Lord, our intercessions for all mankind.

The Intercession

Let the light of thy Gospel shine upon all nations; and may as many as have received it, live as becomes it. Be gracious unto thy Church; and grant that every member of the same, in his vocation and ministry, may serve thee faithfully. Bless all in authority over us; and so rule their hearts and strengthen their hands, that they may punish wickedness and vice, and maintain thy true religion and virtue. Send down thy blessings, temporal and spiritual, upon all our relations, friends, and neighbours. Reward all who have done us good, and pardon all those who have done or wish us evil, and give them repentance and better minds. Be merciful to all who are in any trouble; and do thou, the God of pity, administer to them according to their several necessities; for his sake who went about doing good, thy Son our Saviour Jesus Christ. *Amen.*

Family Prayer

Evening Prayer

TO our prayers and intercessions for future blessings, O Lord, we humbly beg leave to add our unfeigned thanks for all thy mercies which from time to time thou hast vouchsafed us; for our being, our reason, and all other endowments and faculties of soul and body; for our health, friends, food, and raiment, and all the other comforts and conveniences of life. Above all, we adore thy tender mercy and compassion to us and all mankind in sending thy only Son into the world, to redeem us from sin and eternal death, and in giving us the knowledge and sense of our duty towards thee. We bless thee for thy patience with us, notwithstanding our many and

The Thanksgiving, general and particular.

TO our prayers, O Lord, we join our unfeigned thanks for all thy mercies, for our being, our reason, and all other endowments and faculties of soul and body; for our health, friends, food, and raiment, and all the other comforts and conveniences of life. Above all, we adore thy mercy in sending thy only Son into the world, to redeem us from sin and eternal death, and in giving us the knowledge and sense of our duty towards thee. We bless thee for thy patience with us, notwithstanding our many and great provocations; for all the directions, assistances,

The Thanksgiving.

Prayer for Grace to reform and grow Better.

AND lest, through our own frailty, or the temptations which encompass us, we be drawn again into sin, vouchsafe us, we be- beseech thee, the direction and assistance of thy Holy Spirit.

Reform whatever is amiss in the temper and disposition of our souls; that no unclean thoughts, unlawful designs, or inordinate desires, may rest there. Purge our hearts from envy, hatred, and malice; that we may never suffer the sun to go down upon our wrath; but may always go to our rest in peace, charity, and good-will, with a conscience void of offence towards thee, and towards men; that so we may be preserved pure and blameless, unto the coming of our Lord and Saviour Jesus Christ. *Amen.*

The Intercession

AND accept, O Lord, our intercessions for all mankind.

Let the light of thy Gospel shine upon all nations; and may as many as have received it, live as becomes it. Be gracious unto thy Church; and grant that every member of the same, in his vocation and ministry, may serve thee faithfully. Bless all in authority over us; and so rule their hearts and strengthen their hands, that they may punish wickedness and vice, and maintain thy true religion and virtue. Send down thy blessings, temporal and spiritual, upon all our relations, friends, and neighbours. Reward all who have done us good, and pardon all those who have done or wish us evil, and give them repentance and better minds. Be merciful to all who are in any trouble; and do thou, the God of pity, administer to them according to their several necessities; for his sake who went about doing good, thy Son our Saviour Jesus Christ. *Amen.*

The Thanksgiving

TO our prayers, O Lord, we join our unfeigned thanks for all thy mercies; for

our being, our reason, and all other endowments and faculties of soul and body; for our health, friends, food, and raiment, and all the other comforts and conveniences of life. Above all, we adore thy mercy in sending thy only Son into the world, to redeem us from sin and eternal death, and in giving us the knowledge and sense of our duty towards thee. We bless thee for thy patience with us, notwithstanding our many and great provocations; for all the directions, assistances, and comforts of thy Holy Spirit; for

great provocations; for all the directions, assistances, and comforts of thy Holy Spirit; for thy continual care and watchful providence over us through the whole course of our lives; and particularly for the mercies and benefits of the past day: beseeching thee to continue these thy blessing to us; and to give us grace to show our sense of them, and all thy other mercies in a sincere obedience to his laws, through whose merits and intercession we receive them all, thy Son our Saviour Jesus Christ. *Amen.*

and comforts of thy Holy Spirit; for thy continual care and watchful providence over us through the whole course of our lives; and particularly for the mercies and benefits of the past day: beseeching thee to continue these thy blessings to us; and to give us grace to show our thankfulness in a sincere obedience to his laws, through whose merits and intercession we receive them all, thy Son our Saviour Jesus Christ. *Amen.*

Prayer for God's protection the following night.

IN a particular manner, we beseech thee to continue thy gracious protection to us this night. Into thy hand we com-commend our souls and bodies, our substance, dwelling, and all things that belong to us. Do thou, our gracious God who neither slumberest nor sleepest, be pleased to take both us and them this night into thy special care and protection.

Defend us from all dangers and mischiefs, and from the dread and fear of them; that we may enjoy such quiet and refreshing sleep as may fit us for the duties of the following day. And Lord, make us ever mindful of that time when we shall lie down in the dust; and grant us grace always to live in such a state, that we may never be afraid to die, but that whether we live, we may live unto thee; or whether we die, we may die unto thee, so that living and dying, we may be thine, through the merits and satisfaction of thy Son Christ Jesus, in whose name and words we conclude our imperfect prayer.

Our Father, which...for ever and ever. Amen.

Prayer for God's protection through the night following.

IN particular, we beseech thee to continue thy gracious protection to us this night.

Defend us from all dangers and mischiefs, and from the fear of them; that we may enjoy such refreshing sleep as may fit us for the duties of the following day. Make us ever mindful of the time when we shall lie down in the dust; and grant us grace always to live in such a state, that we may never be afraid to die: so that, living and dying, we may be thine, through the merits and satisfaction of thy Son Christ Jesus, in whose Name we offer up these our imperfect prayers. *Amen.*

THE grace of our Lord Jesus Christ, and the love of God, and the fellowship of the Holy Ghost, be with us all evermore. *Amen.*

¶ *On Sundays and other days, when it may be convenient, it will be proper to begin with a Chapter, or part of a Chapter, from the New Testament.*

A Shorter Form

thy continual care and watchful providence over us through the whole course of our lives; and particularly for the mercies and benefits of the past day; beseeching thee to continue these thy blessings to us, and to give us grace to show our thankfulness in a sincere obedience to his laws, through whose merits and intercession we received them all, thy Son our Saviour Jesus Christ. *Amen.*

Prayer for God's Protection through the Night following.

IN particular, we beseech thee to continue thy gracious protection to us this night.

Defend us from all dangers and mischiefs, and from the fear of them; that we may enjoy such refreshing sleep as may fit us for the duties of the coming day. And grant us grace always to live in such a state that we may never be afraid to die; so that, living and dying, we may be thine, through the merits and satisfaction of thy Son Christ Jesus, in whose Name we offer up these our imperfect prayers. *Amen.*

THE grace of our Lord Jesus Christ, and the love of God, and the fellowship of the Holy Ghost, be with us all evermore. *Amen.*

¶ *On Sundays, and on other days when it may be convenient, it will be proper to begin with a Chapter, or part of a Chapter, from the New Testament.*

A SHORTER FORM.

MORNING.

In the Morning

From Psalm 51

Open my lips, O Lord, *
　and my mouth shall proclaim your praise.
Create in me a clean heart, O God, *

Family
Prayer

A Shorter Form

1928

¶ *After the reading of a brief portion of Holy Scripture, let the Head of the Household, or some other member of the family, say as followeth, all kneeling, and repeating with him the Lord's Prayer.*

OUR Father, who....for ever and ever. Amen.

O LORD, our heavenly Father, Almighty and everlasting God, who hast safely brought us to the beginning of this day; Defend us in the same with thy mighty power; and grant that this day we fall into no sin, neither run into any kind of danger; but that all our doings, being ordered by thy governance, may be righteous in thy sight; through Jesus Christ our Lord. *Amen.*

¶ *Here may be added any special Prayers.*

THE grace of our Lord Jesus Christ, and the love of God, and the fellowship of the Holy Ghost, be with us all evermore. *Amen.*

1979

and renew a right spirit within me.
Cast me not away from your presence *
and take not your holy Spirit from me.
Give me the joy of your saving help again *
and sustain me with your bountiful Spirit.
Glory to the Father, and to the Son, and to the Holy Spirit: *
as it was in the beginning, is now, and will be for ever. Amen.

A Reading

Blessed be the God and Father of our Lord Jesus Christ! By his great mercy we have been born anew to a living hope through the resurrection of Jesus Christ from the dead. *1 Peter 1:3*

A period of silence may follow.
A hymn or canticle may be used; the Apostles' Creed may be said.
Prayers may be offered for ourselves and others.

The Lord's Prayer.

The Collect

Lord God, almighty and everlasting Father, you have brought us in safety to this new day: Preserve us with your mighty power, that we may not fall into sin, nor be overcome by adversity; and in all we do, direct us to the fulfilling of your purpose; through Jesus Christ our Lord. *Amen.*

At Noon

From Psalm 113

Give praise, you servants of the LORD; *
praise the Name of the LORD.
Let the Name of the LORD be blessed, *
from thhis forth for evermore.
From the rising of the sun to its going down *
let the Name of the LORD be praised.
The LORD is high above all nations, *
and his glory above the heavens.

A Reading

O God, you will keep in perfect peace those whose minds are fixed on you; for in returning and rest we shall be saved; in quietness and trust shall be our strength. *Isaiah 26:3; 30:15*

Prayers may be offered for ourselves and others.

The Lord's Prayer

The Collect

Blessed Savior, at this hour you hung upon the cross, stretching out your loving arms: Grant that all peoples of the earth may look to you and be saved; for your mercies' sake. *Amen.*

or this

Family Prayer

A Shorter Form

134, 135

Lord Jesus Christ, you said to your apostles, "Peace I give to you; my own peace I leave with you:" Regard not our sins, but the faith of your Church, and give to us the peace and unity of that heavenly City, where with the Father and the Holy Spirit you live and reign, now and for ever. *Amen.*

In the Early Evening

This devotion may be used before or after the evening meal.

The Order of Worship for the Evening, page 109, may be used instead.

O gracious Light,
pure brightness of the everliving Father in heaven,
O Jesus Christ, holy and blessed!

Now as we come to the setting of the sun,
and our eyes behold the vesper light,
we sing your praises O God: Father, Son, and Holy Spirit.

You are worthy at all times to be praised by happy voices,
O Son of God, O Giver of life,
and to be glorified through all the worlds.

A Reading

It is not ourselves that we proclaim; we proclaim Christ Jesus as Lord, and ourselves as your servants, for Jesus' sake. For the same God who said, "Out of darkness let light shine," has caused his light to shine within us, to give the light of revelation—the revelation of the glory of God in the face of Jesus Christ. *2 Corinthians 4:5-6*

Prayers may be offered for ourselves and others.

The Lord's Prayer

The Collect

Lord Jesus, stay with us, for evening is at hand and the day is past; be our companion in the way, kindle our hearts, and awaken hope, that we may know you as you are revealed in Scripture and the breaking of bread. Grant this for the sake of your love. *Amen.*

EVENING.

¶ *After the reading of a brief portion of Holy Scripture, let the Head of the Household, or some other member of the family, say as followeth, all kneeling, and repeating with him the Lord's Prayer.*

At the Close of Day

Psalm 134

Behold now, bless the LORD, all you servants of the LORD, *
 you that stand by night in the house of the LORD.
Lift up your hands in the holy place and bless the LORD; *
 the LORD who made heaven and earth bless you out of Zion.

A Reading

Lord, you are in the midst of us and we are called by your Name: Do not forsake us, O Lord our God. *Jeremiah 14:9,22.*

The following may be said

Lord, you now have set your servant free *
 to go in peace as you have promised;

Additional Prayers

For these eyes of mine have seen the Savior, *
whom you have prepared for all the world to see:
A Light to enlighten the nations, *
and the glory of your people Israel.

Prayers for ourselves and other may follow. It is appropriate that prayers of thanksgiving for the blessings of the day, and penitence for our sins, be included.

OUR Father, who....for ever and ever. Amen.

The Lord's Prayer

LIGHTEN our darkness, we beseech thee, O Lord; and by thy great mercy defend us from all perils and dangers of this night; for the love of thy only Son, our Saviour, Jesus Christ. *Amen.*

The Collect
Visit this place, O Lord, and drive far from it all snares of the enemy; let your holy angels dwell with us to preserve us in peace; and let your blessing be upon us always; through Jesus Christ our Lord. *Amen.*

¶ *Here may be added any special Prayers.*

THE Lord bless us and keep us. The Lord make his face to shine upon us, and be gracious unto us. The Lord lift up his countenance upon us, and give us peace, this night and evermore. *Amen.*

The almighty and merciful Lord, Father, Son, and Holy Spirit, bless us and keep us. *Amen.*

ADDITIONAL PRAYERS.

For the Spirit of Prayer.

O ALMIGHTY God, who pourest out on all who desire it, the spirit of grace and of supplication; Deliver us, when we draw nigh to thee, from coldness of heart and wanderings of mind, that with stedfast thoughts and kindled affections, we may worship thee in spirit and in truth; through Jesus Christ our Lord. *Amen.* [William Bright]

O Almighty God, *who pourest* out on all who desire it the spirit of grace and of supplication: Deliver us, when we draw near to *thee,* from coldness of heart and wanderings of mind, that with steadfast thoughts and kindled affections we may worship *thee* in spirit and in truth; through Jesus Christ our Lord. *Amen.* [Prayers and Thanksgivings, 64. *Before Worship.*]

In the Morning.

O GOD, the King eternal, who dividest the day from the darkness, and turnest the shadow of death into the morning; Drive far off from us all wrong desires, incline our hearts to keep thy law, and guide our feet into the way of peace; that having done thy will with cheerfulness while it was day, we may, when the night cometh, rejoice to give thee thanks; through Jesus Christ our Lord. *Amen.* [William Reed Huntington.]

O God, the King eternal, whose light divides the day from the night and turns the shadow of death into the morning: Drive far from us all wrong desires, incline our hearts to keep your law, and guide our feet into the way of peace; that, having done your will with cheerfulness during the day, we may, when night comes, rejoice to give you thanks; through Jesus Christ our Lord. *Amen.* [Morning Prayer II, *A Collect for the Renewal of Life.* See also Morning Prayer I.]

ALMIGHTY God, who alone gavest us the breath of life, and alone canst keep alive in us the holy desires thou dost impart; We beseech thee, for thy compassion's sake, to sanctify all our thoughts and endeavours; that we may neither begin an action without a pure intention nor continue it without thy blessing. And grant that, having the eyes of the mind opened to behold

Family
Prayer

Additional
Prayers

1928	1979
things invisible and unseen, we may in heart be inspired by thy wisdom, and in work be upheld by thy strength, and in the end be accepted of thee as thy faithful servants; through Jesus Christ our Saviour. *Amen.* [Rowland Williams]	
At Night.	
O LORD, support us all the day long, until the shadows lengthen and the evening comes, and the busy world is hushed, and the fever of life is over, and our work is done. Then in thy mercy grant us a safe lodging, and a holy rest, and peace at the last. *Amen.* [George W. Douglas, based on phrases in two of Newman's sermons.]	O Lord, support us all the day long, until the shadows lengthen, and the evening comes, and the busy world is hushed, and the fever of life is over, and our work is done. Then in *thy* mercy, grant us a safe lodging, and a holy rest, and peace at the last. *Amen.* [Prayers and Thanksgivings, 63. *In the Evening.*]
O GOD, who art the life of mortal men, the light of the faithful, the strength of those who labour, and the repose of the dead; We thank thee for the timely blessings of the day, and humbly supplicate thy merciful protection all this night. Bring us, we beseech thee, in safety to the morning hours; through him who died for us and rose again, thy Son, our Saviour Jesus Christ. *Amen.* [William Huntington Reed.]	O God, the life of all who live, the light of the faithful, the strength of those who labor, and the repose of the dead: We thank you for the blessings of the day that is past, and humbly ask for your protection through the coming night. Bring us in safety to the morning hours; through him who died and rose again for us, your Son our Savior Jesus Christ. *Amen.* [Evening Prayer II, A *Collect for Protection.* See also Evening Prayer I.]
Sunday Morning.	
O GOD, who makest us glad with the weekly remembrance of the glorious resurrection of thy Son our Lord; Vouchsafe us this day such blessing through our worship of thee, that the days to come may be spent in thy service; through the same Jesus Christ our Lord. *Amen.* [William Bright.]	O God, you make us glad with the weekly remembrance of the glorious resurrection of your Son our Lord: Give us this day such blessing through our worship of you, that the week to come may be spent in your favor; through Jesus Christ our Lord. *Amen.* [Morning Prayer II, A *Collect for Sundays.* See also Morning Prayer I.]
For Quiet Confidence.	
O GOD of peace, who hast taught us that in returning and rest we shall be saved, in quietness and in confidence shall be our strength; By the might of thy Spirit lift us, we pray thee, to thy presence, where we may be still and know that thou art God; through Jesus Christ our Lord. *Amen.* [John W. Suter, Jr.]	O God of peace, *who hast* taught us that in returning and rest we shall be saved, in quietness and in confidence shall be our strength: By the might of *thy* Spirit lift us, we pray *thee,* to *thy* presence, where we may be still and know that *thou art* God; through Jesus Christ our Lord. *Amen.* [Prayers and Thanksgivings, 59., *For Quiet Confidence.*]
For Guidance.	
O GOD, by whom the meek are guided in judgment, and light riseth up in darkness for the godly; Grant us, in all our doubts and uncertainties, the grace to ask what thou wouldest have us to do, that the Spirit of Wisdom may save us from all false choices, and that in thy light we may see light, and in thy straight path may not stumble; through Jesus Christ our Lord. *Amen.* [William Bright.]	O God, by whom the meek are guided in judgment, and light *riseth* up in darkness for the godly: Grant us, in all our doubts and uncertainties, the grace to ask what *thou wouldest* have us to do, that the Spirit of wisdom may save us from all false choices, and that in *thy* light we may see light, and in *thy* straight path may not stumble; through Jesus Christ our Lord. *Amen.* [Prayers and Thanksgivings, 58. *For Guidance.*]
For Trustfulness.	
O MOST loving Father, who willest us to give thanks for all things, to dread nothing but the loss of thee, and to cast all our care on thee, who carest for us; Preserve us from faithless fears and worldly anxieties, and grant that no clouds of this mortal life may hide from us the light of that love which is immortal, and which thou hast manifested unto us in thy Son, Jesus Christ our Lord. *Amen.* [William Bright.]	Most loving Father, whose will it is for us to give thanks for all things, to fear nothing but the loss of you, and to cast all our care on you who care for us: Preserve us from faithless fears and worldly anxieties, that no clouds of this mortal life may hide from us the light of that love which is immortal, and which you have manifested to us in your Son Jesus Christ our Lord; who lives and reigns with you, in the unity of the Holy Spirit, one God, now and for ever. *Amen.* [Collect for the Eighth Sunday after the Epiphany; see also Collects: Traditional.]
O HEAVENLY Father, thou understandest all thy children; through thy gift of faith we bring our perplexities to the light of thy wisdom, and receive the blessed encouragement of thy sympathy, and a clearer knowledge of thy will. Glory be to thee for all thy gracious gifts. *Amen.* [John W. Suter, Jr.]	

Family Prayer

Additional Prayers

140, 141

For Joy in God's Creation.

O HEAVENLY Father, who hast filled the world with beauty; Open, we beseech thee, our eyes to behold thy gracious hand in all thy works; that rejoicing in thy whole creation, we may learn to serve thee with gladness; for the sake of him by whom all things were made, thy Son, Jesus Christ our Lord. *Amen.* [John W. Suter, Jr.]

O heavenly Father, *who hast* filled the world with beauty: Open our eyes to behold *thy* gracious hand in all *thy* works; that, rejoicing in *thy* whole creation, we may learn to serve *thee* with gladness; for the sake of him through whom all things were made, *thy* Son Jesus Christ our Lord. *Amen.* [Prayers and Thanksgivings, *1. For Joy in God's Creation.*]

Open, O Lord, the eyes of all people to behold thy gracious hand in all thy works, that, rejoicing in thy whole creation, they may honor thee with their substance, and be faithful stewards of thy bounty. [Prayers of the People, Rite I.]

For the Children.

ALMIGHTY God, heavenly Father, who hast blessed us with the joy and care of children; Give us light and strength so to train them, that they may love whatsoever things are true and pure and lovely and of good report, following the example of their Saviour Jesus Christ. *Amen.* [John W. Suter, Jr.]

Almighty God, heavenly Father, you have blessed us with the joy and care of children: Give us calm strength and patient wisdom as we bring them up, that we may teach them to love whatever is just and true and good, following the example of our Savior Jesus Christ. *Amen.* [Prayers and Thanksgivings, *46. For the Care of Children.*]

For the Absent.

O GOD, whose fatherly care reacheth to the uttermost parts of the earth; We humbly beseech thee graciously to behold and bless those whom we love, now absent from us. Defend them from all dangers of soul and body; and grant that both they and we, drawing nearer to thee, may be bound together by thy love in the communion of thy Holy Spirit, and in the fellowship of thy saints; through Jesus Christ our Lord. *Amen.* [Bp. Jonathan Wainwright's *An Order of Family Prayer* (1845).]

O God, whose fatherly care *reacheth* to the uttermost parts of the earth: We humbly beseech *thee* graciously to behold and bless those whom we love, now absent from us. Defend them from all dangers of soul and body; and grant that both they and we, drawing nearer to *thee*, may be bound together by *thy* love in the communion of *thy* Holy Spirit, and in the fellowship of *thy* saints; through Jesus Christ our Lord. *Amen.* [Prayers and Thanksgivings, *52. For the Absent.*]

For Those We Love.

ALMIGHTY God, we entrust all who are dear to us to thy never-failing care and love, for this life and the life to come; knowing that thou art doing for them better things than we can desire or pray for; through Jesus Christ our Lord. *Amen.* [*Family Prayers and Bible Readings* (1876).]

Almighty God, we entrust all who are dear to us to *thy* never-failing care and love, for this life and the life to come, knowing that *thou art* doing for them better things than we can desire or pray for; through Jesus Christ our Lord. *Amen.* [Prayers and Thanksgivings, *54. For those we Love.*]

For the Recovery of a Sick Person.

O MERCIFUL God, giver of life and health; Bless, we pray thee, thy servant, [*N.*], and those who administer to *him* of thy healing gifts; that *he* may be restored to health of body and of mind; through Jesus Christ our Lord. *Amen.* [Scottish, 1912; by Bp. John Dowden.]

For One about to undergo an Operation.

ALMIGHTY God our heavenly Father, we beseech thee graciously to comfort thy servant in *his* suffering, and to bless the means made use of for *his* cure. fill *his* heart with confidence, that though *he* be sometime afraid, *he* yet may put *his* trust in thee; through Jesus Christ our Lord. *Amen.*

Almighty God our heavenly Father, graciously comfort your servant *N.* in *his* suffering, and bless the means made use of for *his* cure. fill *his* heart with confidence that, though at times *he* may be afraid, *he* yet may put *his* trust in you; through Jesus Christ our Lord. *Amen.* [Ministration to the Sick. Prayers for the Sick. *Before an Operation.*]

For a Birthday.

WATCH over thy child, O Lord, as *his* days increase; bless and guide *him* wherever *he* may be, keeping *him* unspotted from the world. Strengthen *him* when *he* stands; comfort *him* when discouraged or sorrowful; raise *him* up if *he* fall; and in *his* heart may thy peace which passeth understanding abide all the days of *his* life; through Jesus Christ our Lord. *Amen.* [Condensed from the Groton School's Graduates Prayer.]

Watch over thy child, O Lord, as *his* days increase; bless and guide *him* wherever *he* may be. Strengthen *him* when *he* stands; comfort *him* when discouraged or sorrowful; raise *him* up if *he* fall; and in *his* heart may thy peace which passeth understanding abide all the days of *his* life; through Jesus Christ our Lord. *Amen.* [Prayers and Thanksgivings, *51. For a Birthday.*]

For a Blessing on the Families of the Land.

ALMIGHTY God, the Father of our Lord Jesus Christ, of whom the whole family in heaven and earth is named; We commend to thy continual care the families of thy people, and the homes in which they dwell, Put far from them, we pray thee, the desire of vain glory, the pride of life, and every root of bitterness. Endue them with faith, temperance, patience, and godliness. Knit together in constant affection those who in holy wedlock have been made one flesh; turn the hearts of the fathers to the children, and the hearts of the children to their fathers; and so kindle charity among us all, that we may be evermore kindly affectioned with brotherly love; through Jesus Christ our Lord. *Amen.* [From "An Office for Harvest-Home" in the *Book of Offices* proposed in 1889.]

For all Poor, Homeless, and Neglected Folk.

O GOD, almighty and merciful, who healest those that are broken in heart, and turnest the sadness of the sorrowful to joy; Let thy fatherly goodness be upon all that thou hast made. Remember in pity such as are this day destitute, homeless, or forgotten of their fellow-men. Bless the congregation of thy poor.

Forgive us wherein we have failed to care for the sick, the helpless, and the needy, and stir us up to love and to good works. Give unto all men the desire of industry and the opportunity of honest labour, that they may dwell peaceably upon the earth.

Lift up those who are cast down; befriend innocent sufferers, sanctify to them the endurance of their wrongs, and mightily deliver them. Cheer with hope all discouraged and unhappy people; and by thy grace preserve from falling those whose penury tempteth them to sin. Hear us, O Lord, for the love of him who for our sakes became poor, thy Son our Saviour Jesus Christ. *Amen.* [From the "An Office for Harvest-Home" in the *Book of Offices* proposed in 1889.]

[4]A prayer with no verbal or structural parallels to this one was included in the abortive 1889 *Book of Offices* under the title "For Insane and Imbecile Persons." See the excerpts from that book, including this prayer, in the documents sections of this volume.

For an Anniversary of One Departed

ALMIGHTY God, we remember this day before thee thy faithful servant [*N.*], and we pray thee that, having opened to *him* the gates of larger life, thou wilt receive *him* more and more into thy joyful service; that *he* may win, with thee and thy servants everywhere, the eternal victory; through Jesus Christ our Lord. *Amen.* [Bp. Charles Slattery.]

Almighty God, we remember before you today your faithful servant *N.*; and we pray that, having opened to *him* the gates of larger life, you will receive *him* more and more into your joyful service, that, with all who have faithfully served you in the past, *he* may share in the eternal victory of Jesus Christ our Lord; who lives and reigns with you, in the unity of the Holy Spirit, one God, for ever and ever. *Amen.* [Collects: Contemporary, 8. *For the Departed.* see also Collects: Traditional.]

For Those in Mental Darkness.

O HEAVENLY Father, we beseech thee to have mercy upon all thy children who are living in mental darkness. Restore them to strength of mind and cheerfulness of spirit, and give them health and peace; through Jesus Christ our Lord. *Amen.*[4]

For a Blessing on the Families of the Land.

ALMIGHTY God, our heavenly Father, who settest the solitary in families; We commend to thy continual care the homes in which thy people dwell. Put far from them, we beseech thee, every root of bitterness, the desire of vain-glory, and the pride of life. fill them with faith, virtue, knowledge, temperance, patience, godliness. Knit together in constant affection those who, in holy wedlock, have been made one flesh; turn the heart of the fathers to the children, and the heart of the children to the fathers; and so enkindle fervent charity among us all, that we be evermore kindly affectioned with brotherly love; through Jesus Christ our Lord. *Amen.*

Almighty God, our heavenly Father, who settest the solitary in families: We commend to thy continual care the homes in which thy people dwell. Put far from them, we beseech thee, every root of bitterness, the desire of vainglory, and the pride of life. fill them with faith, virtue, knowledge, temperance, patience, godliness. Knit together in constant affection those who, in holy wedlock, have been made one flesh. Turn the hearts of the parents to the children, and the hearts of the children to the parents; and so enkindle fervent charity among us all, that we may evermore be kindly affectioned one to another; through Jesus Christ our Lord. *Amen.* [Prayers and Thanksgivings, 45. *For Families.*]

For all Poor, Homeless, and Neglected Folk.

O GOD, Almighty and merciful, who healest those that are broken in heart, and turnest the sadness of the sorrowful to joy; Let thy fatherly goodness be upon all that thou hast made. Remember in pity such as are this day destitute, homeless, or forgotten of their fellow-men. Bless the congregation of thy poor.

Uplift those who are cast down. Mightily befriend innocent sufferers, and sanctify to them the endurance of their wrongs. Cheer with hope all discouraged and unhappy people, and by thy heavenly grace preserve from falling those whose penury tempteth them to sin; though they be troubled on every side, suffer them not to be distressed; though they be perplexed, save them from despair. Grant this, O Lord, for the love of him, who for our sakes became poor, thy Son, our Saviour Jesus Christ. *Amen.*

For the Rich.

O ALMIGHTY God, we beseech thee to send thy grace upon those whom thou hast entrusted with great possessions, that they may praise thee in their lives, honour thee with their wealth, and lead others by their example to seek for that inheritance which thy beloved Son will give to all those who have followed him. Have mercy upon such as neglect to minister to the wants of thy poor; and grant that, remembering the account of their stewardship which they must one day give, they may be faithful almoners of thy bounty, and so at last attain to thy heavenly kingdom; through Jesus Christ our Lord. *Amen.* [From the *Book of Offices* proposed in 1889.]

[5]The 1979 book prints this prayer first.

For Faithfulness in the Use of this World's Goods.

ALMIGHTY God, whose loving hand hath given us all that we possess; Grant us grace that we may honour thee with our substance, and remembering the account which we must one day give, may be faithful stewards of thy bounty; through Jesus Christ our Lord. *Amen.*

A General Intercession.

O GOD, at whose word man goeth forth to his work and to his labour until the evening; Be merciful to all whose duties are difficult or burdensome, and comfort them concerning their toil. Shield from bodily accident and harm the workmen at their work. Protect the efforts of sober and honest industry, and suffer not the hire of the labourers to be kept back by fraud. Incline the heart of employers and of those whom they employ to mutual forbearance, fairness, and good-will. Give the spirit of governance and of a sound mind to all in places of authority. Bless all those who labour in works of mercy or in schools of good learning. Care for all aged persons, and all little children, the sick and the afflicted, and those who travel by land or by sea. Remember all who by reason of weakness are overtasked, or because of poverty are forgotten. Let the sorrowful sighing of the prisoners come before thee; and according to the greatness of thy power, preserve thou those that are appointed to die. Give ear unto our prayer, O merciful and gracious Father, for the love of thy dear Son, our Saviour Jesus Christ. *Amen.* [William Reed Huntington.]

Almighty God, whose loving hand *hath* given us all that we possess: Grant us grace that we may honor *thee* with our substance, and, remembering the account which we must one day give, may be faithful stewards of *thy* bounty, through Jesus Christ our Lord. *Amen.* [Prayers and Thanksgivings, *38. For the Right Use of God's Gifts.*]

O merciful Creator, your hand is open wide to satisfy the needs of every living creature: Make us always thankful for your loving providence; and grant that we, remembering the account that we must one day give, may be faithful stewards of your good gifts; through Jesus Christ our Lord, who with you and the Holy Spirit lives and reigns, one God, for ever and ever. *Amen.* [Collects: Contemporary, *19. For Rogation Days III. For stewardship of creation.* See also Collects: Traditional.]

Grace before Meat.

BLESS, O Father, thy gifts to our use and us to thy service; for Christ's sake. *Amen.*

GIVE us grateful hearts, our Father, for all thy mercies, and make us mindful of the needs of others; through Jesus Christ our Lord. *Amen.*

Grace at Meals

Bless, O Lord, *thy* gifts to our use and us to *thy* service; for Christ's sake. *Amen.*

Give us grateful hearts, our Father, for all *thy* mercies, and make us mindful of the needs of others; through Jesus Christ our Lord. *Amen.*[5]

or this

Blessed are you, O Lord God, King of the Universe, for you give us food to sustain our lives and make our hearts glad; through Jesus Christ our Lord. *Amen.*

or this

For these and all his mercies, God's holy Name be blessed and praised; through Jesus Christ our Lord. *Amen.*

Prayers at Sea

1662 (1775)	1786 (Proposed)	1789-1871	1892

1662 (1775) and 1786 (Proposed):

FORMS OF PRAYER
TO BE USED AT SEA

¶ *The Morning and Evening Service to be used daily at Sea, shall be the same which is appointed in the Book of Common Prayer.*

1662 (1775)	1786 (Proposed)
¶ *These two following Prayers are to be also used in his Majesty's Navy every day.*	¶ *These two following Prayers may be also used in Ships of War.*

O ETERNAL Lord God, who alone spreadest out the heavens, and rulest the raging of the sea; who hast compassed the waters with bounds until day and night come to an end; Be pleased to receive into thy Almighty and most gracious protection the persons of us thy servants, and the Fleet in which we serve. Preserve us from the dangers of the sea, and from

1662 (1775)	1786 (Proposed)
the violence of the enemy; that we may be a safeguard unto our most gracious Sovereign Lord, King GEORGE, and his Dominions, and a security for such as pass on the seas upon their lawful occasions; that the inhabitants of our Island	the violence of the enemy; that we may be a safeguard to the United States of America, and a security for such as pass on the Seas upon their lawful occasions; that the Inhabitants of our Country

may in peace and quietness serve thee our God; and that we may return in safety to enjoy the blessings of the land, with the fruits of our labours, and with a

1789-1871 and 1892:

FORMS OF PRAYER
To be used at Sea.

¶ *The Morning and Evening Services to be used daily at Sea, shall be the same which is appointed in the Book of Common Prayer.*

¶ *These two following Prayers may be also used in Ships of War.*

O ETERNAL Lord God, who alone spreadest out the heavens, and rulest the raging of the Sea; who hast compassed the waters with bounds until day and night come to an end; be pleased to receive into thy Almighty and most gracious protections the persons of us thy servants, and the Fleet [*or*[1] Ship] in which we serve. Preserve us from the dangers of the Sea, and from

the violence of the enemy; that we may be a safeguard unto the United States of America, and a security for such as pass on the Seas upon their lawful occasions; that the inhabitants of our land

may in peace and quietness serve thee our God; and that we may return in safety to enjoy the blessings of the land, with the fruits of our labour; and, with a

[1]Italics added in 1845.

Prayers at Sea

146, 147

1928 1979

thankful remembrance of thy mercies to praise and glorify thy holy Name; through Jesus Christ our Lord. *Amen.*

The Collect

PREVENT us, O Lord, in all our doings, with thy most gracious favour, and further us with thy continual help; that in all our works, begun, continued, and ended in thee, we may glorify thy holy Name, and finally by thy mercy obtain everlasting life; through Jesus Christ our Lord. *Amen.*

¶ *Prayers to be used in Storms at Sea.*

O MOST powerful and glorious Lord God, at whose command the winds blow, and lift up the waves of the sea, and who stillest the rage thereof; We thy creatures, but miserable sinners, do in this our great distress cry unto thee for help: Save, Lord, or else we perish. We confess, when we have been safe, and seen all things quiet about us, we have forgot[2] thee our God, and refused to hearken to the still voice of thy word, and to obey thy commandments: But now we see, how terrible thou art in all thy works of wonder; the great God to be feared above all: And therefore we adore thy Divine Majesty, acknowledging thy power, and imploring thy goodness. Help, Lord, and save us for thy mercy's sake in Jesus Christ thy Son, our Lord. *Amen.*

Or this,

O MOST glorious and gracious Lord God, who dwellest in heaven, but beholdest all things below; Look down, we beseech thee, and hear us, calling out of the depth of misery, and out of the jaws of this death, which is ready now to swallow us up: Save, Lord, or else we perish. The living, the living, shall praise thee: O send thy word of command to rebuke the raging winds, and the roaring sea; that we, being delivered from this distress, may live to serve thee, and to glorify thy Name all the days of our life. Hear, Lord, and save us; for the infinite merits of our blessed Saviour, thy Son, our Lord Jesus Christ. *Amen.*

thankful remembrance of thy mercies, to praise and glorify thy holy Name, through Jesus Christ our Lord. *Amen.*

The Collect

DIRECT us, O Lord, in all our doings, with thy most gracious favour, and further us with thy continual help; that in all our works, begun, continued, and ended in thee, we may glorify thy holy Name, and finally by thy mercy obtain everlasting life; through Jesus Christ our Lord. *Amen.*

Prayers to be used in Storms at Sea. (1789-1871)

Prayers to be used in all Ships in Storms at Sea. (1892)

O MOST powerful and glorious Lord God, at whose command the winds blow, and lift up the waves of the sea, and who stillest the rage thereof; we thy creatures, but miserable sinners, do in this our great distress cry unto thee for help: Save, Lord, or else we perish. We confess, when we have been safe, and seen all things quiet about us, we have forgotten thee our God, and refused to hearken to the still voice of thy word, and to obey thy commandments: But now we see how terrible thou art in all thy works of wonder: the great God to be feared above all: And therefore we adore thy Divine Majesty, acknowledging thy power, and imploring thy goodness. Help, Lord, and save us for thy mercy's sake in Jesus Christ, thy Son our Lord. *Amen.*

¶ *Or this:*

O MOST glorious and gracious Lord God, who dwellest in heaven, but beholdest all things below; Look down, we beseech thee, and hear us, calling out of the depth of misery, and out of the jaws of this death, which is ready now to swallow us up: Save, Lord, or else we perish. The living, the living, shall praise thee: O send thy word of command to rebuke the raging winds, and the roaring sea; that we, being delivered from this distress, may live to serve thee, and to glorify thy Name all the days of our life. Hear, Lord, and save us; for the infinite merits of our blessed Saviour, thy Son, our Lord Jesus Christ. *Amen.*

Short Prayers in respect of a Storm.

THOU, O Lord, who stillest the raging of the sea, hear, hear us, and save us, that we perish not.

O blessed Saviour, who didst save thy disciples ready to perish in a storm, hear us, and save us, we beseech thee.

Lord, have mercy upon us.

Christ, have mercy upon us.

Lord, have mercy upon us.

Prayers at Sea

148, 149

[2]"forgotten" [1786].

O Lord, hear us.
O Christ, hear us.
God the Father, God the Son, God the Holy Ghost, have mercy upon us, save us now and evermore. Amen.

¶ *When there shall be imminent danger, as many as can be spared from necessary service in the Ship shall be called together, and make an humble Confession of their sin to God: In which, every one ought seriously to reflect upon those particular sins of which his conscience shall accuse him; saying as followeth.*

The Confession

ALMIGHTY God, Father of our Lord Jesus Christ, maker of all things, judge of all men....

¶ *Then shall the Priest, if there be any in the Ship, say,*

ALMIGHTY God, our heavenly Father, who of his great mercy hath promised....

¶ *Then shall they together say the Lord's Prayer.*

Our Father, who... but deliver us from evil. Amen.

The Prayer to be said before a Fight at Sea against any Enemy.

O Most powerful and glorious Lord God, the Lord of hosts, that[3] rulest and commandest all things; Thou sittest in the Throne judging right; and therefore we make our Address to thy divine Majesty in this our necessity; that thou wouldest take the cause into thine own hand, and judge between us and our Enemies. Stir up thy strength, O Lord, and come and help us; for thou givest not alway the battle to the strong, but canst save by many or by few. O let not our sins now cry against us for vengeance; but hear us thy poor servants begging mercy, and imploring thy help, and that thou

The Prayer to be said before a Fight at Sea against any Enemy.

O Most powerful and glorious Lord God, the Lord of hosts, that rulest and commandest all things; thou sittest in the throne judging right; And therefore we make our address to thy Divine Majesty in this our necessity, that thou wouldest take the cause into thine own hand, and judge between us and our Enemies. Stir up thy strength, O Lord, and come and help us; for thou givest not away[4] the battle to the strong, but canst save by many or by few. O let not our sins now cry against us for vengeance; but hear us thy poor servants begging mercy, and imploring thy help, and that thou

[3] "who" [1786].

[4] *sic.*

1662 (1775) / 1786 (Proposed)	1789-1871 / 1892
wouldest be a defence unto us against the face of the enemy: Make it appear that thou art our Saviour and mighty Deliverer, through Jesus Christ our Lord. *Amen.*	wouldest be a defence unto us against the face of the enemy: Make it appear that thou art our Saviour and mighty Deliverer, through Jesus Christ our Lord. *Amen.*
Short Prayer for single Persons that cannot meet to join in Prayer with others, by reason of the fight or storm.	*Short Prayers for single Persons, who cannot meet to join in Prayer with others, by reason of the fight, or Storm.*
General Prayers.	*General Prayers.*
LORD, be merciful to us sinners, and save us for thy mercies sake. Thou art the great God, who hast made and rulest all things: O deliver us for the Name's sake.	LORD, be merciful to us sinners, and save us for thy mercies[5] sake. Thou art the great God, who hast made and rulest all things: O deliver us for the Name's sake.
Thou art the great God to be feared above all: O save us, that we may praise thee.	Thou art the great God to be feared above all: O save us, that we may praise thee.
Special Prayers with respect to the Enemy.	*Special Prayers with respect to the Enemy.*
THOU, O Lord, art just and powerful: O defend our cause against the face of the enemy.	THOU, O Lord, art just and powerful: O defend our cause against the face of the enemy.
O God, thou art a strong tower of defence to all that flee[6] unto thee: O save us from the violence of the enemy.	O God, thou art a strong tower of defence to all who fly unto thee: O save us from the violence of the enemy.
O Lord of hosts, fight for us, that we may glorify thee.	O Lord of Hosts, fight for us, that we may glorify thee.
O suffer us not to sink under the weight of our sins, or the violence of the enemy.	O suffer us not to sink under the weight of our sins, or the violence of the enemy.
O Lord, arise, help us, and deliver us for thy Name's sake.	O Lord, arise, help us, and deliver us for thy Name's sake.
Short Prayers in respect of a Storm	*Short Prayers in respect of a Storm.*
THOU, O Lord, that[7] stillest the raging of the sea, hear, hear us, and save us, that we perish not.	THOU, O Lord, who stillest the raging of the sea, hear, hear us, and save us, that we perish not.
O blessed Saviour, that[8] didst save thy disciples ready to perish in a storm, hear us, and save us, we beseech thee.	O blessed Saviour, who didst save thy disciples ready to perish in a storm; hear us, and save us, we beseech thee.
Lord, have mercy upon us. Christ, have mercy upon us. Lord, have mercy upon us. O Lord, hear us. O Christ, hear us.	Lord, have mercy upon us. Christ, have mercy upon us. Lord, have mercy upon us. O Lord, hear us. O Christ, hear us.
God the Father, God the Son, God the Holy Ghost have mercy upon us, save us now and evermore. Amen.	God the Father, God the Son, God the Holy Ghost, have mercy upon us, save us now and evermore. Amen.
1662: OUR Father, which... and ever. Amen. 1786: OUR Father, who... ever and ever. *Amen.*	Our Father, who... but deliver us from evil. Amen.

[5]mercy's [1845-1892].

[6]"all who fly" [1786].

[7]"who" [1786].

[8]"who" [1786].

1662 (1775)	1786 (Proposed)	1789-1871	1892
¶ *When there shall be imminent danger, as many as can be spared from necessary service in the Ship shall be called together, and make an humble Confession of their sins to God: in which every one ought seriously to reflect upon those particular sins of which his conscience shall accuse him; saying as followeth,*		¶ *When there shall be imminent danger, as many as can be spared from necessary service in the ship shall be called together, and make an humble Confession of their sin*[9] *to God: in which every one ought seriously to reflect upon those particular sins of which his Conscience shall accuse him; saying as followeth:*	
The Confession.		*The Confession.*	
ALMIGHTY God, Father of our Lord Jesus Christ,....		ALMIGHTY God, Father of our Lord Jesus Christ,....	
¶ *Then shall the Priest, if there be any in the Ship, pronounce this Absolution.*	¶ *Then shall the Minister, if there be any in the Ship, say,*	¶ *Then shall the Priest,*[10] *if there be any in the ship, say,*	
ALMIGHTY God, our heavenly Father....		ALMIGHTY God, our heavenly Father....	
Thanksgiving after a Storm.		*Thanksgiving after a Storm.*	
Jubilate Deo. Psal. lxvi.	*From* Psalm 66.	*Jubilate Deo.* From Psalm lxvi.[11]	
[here follow all 18 vv., with *Gloria Patri.*]	[here follow vv. 1-4, 6-10, 12, 14-18, but without *Gloria Patri.*]	[here follow vv. 1-4, 6-10, 12, 14-18, with *Gloria Patri.*]	
Confitemini Domino. Psal. cvii.	*From* Psalm 107.	*Confitemini Domino.* From Psalm cvii.[12]	
[here follow all 43 vv., with *Gloria Patri.*]	[here follow vv. 21-32, with *Gloria Patri.*]	[here follow vv. 25-32, with *Gloria Patri.*]	
			O COME, let us give thanks unto the Lord, for he is gracious: and his mercy endureth for ever. Great is the Lord, and greatly to be praised; let the redeemed of the Lord say so: whom he hath delivered from the merciless rage of the sea. The Lord is gracious, and full of compassion: slow to anger, and of great mercy. He hath not dealt with

[9]"sins" until 1843.

[10]"Minister" from 1789 until 1822, when it was corrected among a list of typographical errors.

[11]"Psalm lxvi. *Jubilate Deo*" [1789-1793]. "Psalm 66. *Jubilate Deo*" [1822-1838]. "*Jubilate Deo.* Psalm lxvi." [1845]. The reading given above dates from 1871.

[12]"Psalm cvii. *Confitemini Domino.*" [1790-1793]. etc., as in note 8.

us according to our sins: neither rewarded us according to our iniquities.

But as the heaven is high above the earth: so great hath been his mercy towards us.

We found trouble and heaviness: we were even at death's door.

The waters of the sea had well-nigh covered us: the proud waters had well-nigh gone over our soul.

The sea roared: and the stormy wind lifted up the waves thereof.

We were carried up as it were to heaven, and then down again into the deep: our soul melted within us, because of trouble.

Then cried we unto thee, O Lord: and thou didst deliver us out of our distress.

Blessed be thy Name, who didst not despise the prayer of thy servants: but didst hear our cry, and hast saved us.

Thou didst send forth thy commandment: and the windy storm ceased, and was turned into a calm.

O let us therefore praise the Lord for his goodness: and declare the wonders that he hath done, and still doeth for the children of men!

Praised be the Lord daily: even the Lord that helpeth us, and poureth his benefits upon us.

He is our God, even the God of whom cometh salvation: God is the Lord, by whom we have escaped death.

Thou, Lord, hast made us glad through the operation of thy hands: and we will triumph in thy praise.

Blessed be the Lord God: even the Lord God, who only doeth wondrous things;

And blessed be the

Name of his Majesty for ever: and let every one of us say, Amen, Amen.

Glory be to the Father, and to the Son: and to the Holy Ghost;

As it was in the beginning, is now, and ever shall be: world without end. Amen.

Collects of Thanksgiving.

O MOST blessed and glorious Lord God, who art of infinite goodness and mercy; We thy poor creatures, whom thou hast made and preserved, holding our souls in life, and now rescuing us out of the jaws of death, humbly present ourselves again before thy Divine Majesty, to offer a sacrifice of praise and thanksgiving, for that thou heardest us when we called in our trouble, and didst not cast out our prayer, which we made before thee in our great distress: Even when we gave all for lost, our ship, our goods, our lives, then didst thou mercifully look upon us, and wonderfully command a deliverance; for which we, now being in safety, do give all praise and glory to thy holy Name; through Jesus Christ our Lord. *Amen.*

Or this:

O MOST mighty and gracious good God, thy mercy is over all thy works, but in special manner hath been extended toward us, whom thou hast so powerfully and wonderfully defended. Thou hast shewed us terrible things, and wonders in the deep, that we might see how powerful and gracious a God thou art; how able and ready to help them that[13] trust in thee. Thou hast shewed us how both winds and seas obey thy command; that we may learn, even from them, hereafter to obey thy voice, and to do thy will. We therefore bless and glorify thy Name, for this thy mercy in saving us, when we were ready to perish. And, we beseech thee, make us as truly sensible now of thy mercy, as we were then of the danger: And give us hearts always ready to express our thankfulness, not only by words, but also by our lives, in being more obedient to thy holy commandments. Continue, we beseech thee, this thy goodness to us; that we, whom thou hast saved, may serve thee in holiness and righteousness all the days of our life; through Jesus Christ our Lord and Saviour. *Amen.*

A Hymn of Praise and Thanksgiving after a dangerous Tempest.

O COME, let us give thanks unto the Lord...[14]

2 Cor. xiii. 14.

Collects of Thanksgiving.

O MOST blessed and glorious Lord God, who art of infinite goodness and mercy; we, thy poor creatures, whom thou hast made and preserved, holding our souls in life, and now rescuing us out of the jaws of death, humbly present ourselves again before thy Divine Majesty, to offer a sacrifice of praise and thanksgiving, for that thou heardest us when we called in our trouble, and didst not cast out our prayer, which we made before thee in our great distress; even when we gave all for lost, our Ship, our Goods, our Lives, then didst thou mercifully look upon us, and wonderfully command a deliverance; for which we, now being in safety, do give all praise and glory to thy holy Name, through Jesus Christ our Lord. *Amen.*

¶ *Or this:*

O MOST mighty and gracious good God, thy mercy is over all thy works, but in special manner hath been extended towards us, whom thou hast so powerfully and wonderfully defended. Thou hast shewed us terrible things, and wonders in the deep, that we might see how powerful and gracious a God thou art; how able and ready to help those who trust in thee. Thou hast showed us how both Winds and Seas obey thy command; that we may learn, even from them, hereafter to obey thy voice, and to do thy will. We therefore bless and glorify thy Name, for this thy mercy in saving us, when we were ready to perish. And, we beseech thee, make us as truly sensible now of thy mercy, as we were then of the danger; and give us hearts always ready to express our thankfulness, not only by words, but also by our lives, in being more obedient to thy holy commandments. Continue, we beseech thee, this thy goodness to us; that we, whom thou hast saved, may serve thee in holiness and righteousness all the days of our life, through Jesus Christ our Lord and Saviour. *Amen.*

A Hymn of Praise and Thanksgiving after a dangerous Tempest.

O COME, let us give thanks unto the Lord...[14]

[13]"those who" [1786].

[14]For this text, see above, 1892.

The grace of our Lord Jesus Christ, the love of God, and the fellowship of the Holy Ghost, be with us all evermore. *Amen.*

After Victory or Deliverance from An Enemy

1662 (1775)	1786 (Proposed)
¶ A *Psalm or Hymn of Praise and Thanksgiving after Victory*	¶ A *Psalm or Hymn of Praise and Thanksgiving after Victory.*

IF the Lord had not been on our side, now may we say : if the Lord himself had not been on our side, when men rose up against us,

They had swallowed us up quick : when they were so wrathfully displeased at us.

Yea, the waters had drowned us, and the stream had gone over our soul : the deep waters of the proud had gone over our soul.

But praised be the Lord : who hath not given us over as a prey unto them.

The Lord hath wrought : a mighty salvation for us.

We gat not this by our own sword, neither was it our own arm that saved us : but thy right hand, and thine arm, and the light of thy countenance, because thou hadst a favour unto us.

The Lord hath appeared for us : the Lord hath covered our heads, and made us to stand in the day of battle.

The Lord hath appeared for us : the Lord hath overthrown our enemies, and dashed in pieces those that rose up against us.

Therefore not unto us, O Lord, not unto us : but unto thy Name be given the glory.

The Lord hath done great things for us : the Lord hath done great things for us, for which we rejoice.

Our help standeth in the Name of the Lord : who hath made heaven and earth.

Blessed be the name of the Lord : from this time forth for evermore.

Glory be to the Father, and to the Son : and to the Holy Ghost;

As it was in the beginning, is now, and ever shall be : world without end. Amen.[16]

¶ *After this Hymn may be sung the* Te Deum.

¶ *Then this Collect.*

O ALMIGHTY God, the Sovereign Commander of all the world, in whose hand is power and might which none is able to withstand; We bless and magnify thy great and glorious Name for this happy Victory, the whole glory whereof do we ascribe to thee, who art the only giver of Victory. And, we beseech thee, give us grace to improve this great mercy to thy glory, the advancement of thy Gospel, the honour of our Sovereign,[17] and, as much as in us lieth, to the good of

Thanksgiving after a Victory

1789-1871	1892
A *Psalm or Hymn of Praise and Thanksgiving after Victory.*	A *Psalm or Hymn of Praise and Thanksgiving.*

IF the Lord had not been on our side, now may we say :[15] if the Lord himself had not been on our side, when men rose up against us;

They had swallowed us up quick : when they were so wrathfully displeased at us.

Yea, the waters had drowned us, and the stream had gone over our soul : the deep waters of the proud had gone over our soul.

But praised be the Lord : who hath not given us over as a prey unto them.

The Lord hath wrought : a mighty salvation for us.

We got not this by our own sword, neither was it our own arm that saved us : but thy right hand, and thine arm, and the light of thy countenance, because thou hadst a favour unto us.

The Lord hath appeared for us : the Lord hath covered our heads, and made us to stand in the day of battle.

The Lord hath appeared for us : the Lord hath overthrown our enemies, and dashed in pieces those that rose up against us.

Therefore not unto us, O Lord, not unto us : but unto thy Name be given the glory.

The Lord hath done great things for us : the Lord hath done great things for us, for which we rejoice.

Our help standeth in the Name of the Lord : who hath made heaven and earth.

Blessed be the Name of the Lord : from this time forth for evermore.

Glory be to the Father, and to the Son : and to the Holy Ghost;

As it was in the beginning, is now, and ever shall be : world without end. Amen.

¶ *After this Hymn may be said the* Te Deum.

¶ *Then this Collect.*

O ALMIGHTY God, the Sovereign Commander of all the world, in whose hand is power and might, which none is able to withstand; we bless and magnify thy great and glorious Name for this happy victory, the whole glory whereof do we ascribe to thee, who art the only giver of victory. And, we beseech thee, give us grace to improve this great mercy to thy Glory, the advancement of thy Gospel, the honour of our Country, and, as much as in us lieth, to the good of all

Prayers at Sea

[15]The "musical colon" was restored to the American text in 1892; it is present in English editions in use before the American Revolution.

[16]add "Glory be to the Father, &c.
"As it was in the beginning, &c." [1786].

[17]"honour of our country" [1786].

1662 (1775) / 1786 (Proposed)		1789-1871 / 1892	
all mankind. And, we beseech thee, give us such a sense of this great mercy, as may engage us to a true thankfulness, such as may appear in our lives by an humble, holy, and obedient walking before thee all our days, through Jesus Christ our Lord; to whom with thee and the Holy Spirit, as for all thy mercies, so in particular for this Victory and Deliverance, be all glory and honour, world without end. *Amen.*		mankind. And, we beseech thee, give us such a sense of this great mercy, as may engage us to a true thankfulness, such as may appear in our lives by an humble, holy, and obedient walking before thee all our days, through Jesus Christ our Lord; to whom, with thee and the Holy Spirit, as for all thy mercies, so in particular for this victory and deliverance, be all glory and honour, world without end. *Amen.*	
2 Cor. xiii. 14.		2 Cor. xiii. 14.	
THE grace of our Lord Jesus Christ, and the love of God, and the fellowship of the Holy Ghost, be with us all evermore. *Amen.*		THE grace of our Lord Jesus Christ, and the love of God, and the fellowship of the Holy Ghost, be with us all evermore. *Amen.*	
At the Burial of their Dead at Sea.		¶ *At the Burial of their Dead*[18] *at Sea,*	[*At the Burial of the Dead at Sea.*][19]
			[¶ *The same office may be used; but in the Sentence of Committal, the Minister shall say,*
¶ *The Office in the Common Prayer-book may be used; only instead of these words* [We therefore commit *his* body to the ground, earth to earth, &c.] *say,* We therefore commit *his* body to the deep, to be turned into corruption, looking for the resurrection of the body, (when the sea shall give up her dead,) and the life of the world to come, through our Lord Jesus Christ; who at his coming shall change our vile body, that it may be like his glorious body, according to the mighty working whereby he is able to subdue all things to himself.	¶ *At the Burial of their Dead at Sea, the Office in the Common Prayer Book may be used; only instead of these Words,* "We therefore commit his Body to the Ground, Earth to Earth, &c." *say,* We therefore commit his Body to the Deep, to be turned into Corruption.	*The Office in the Common Prayer Book may be used; only instead of these words,* We therefor commit his Body to the Ground, Earth to Earth, &c., *say,* We therefore commit *his* Body to the Deep, to be turned into corruption, looking for the resurrection of the Body, when the Sea shall give up her Dead, and the life of the world to come, through our Lord Jesus Christ; who at his coming shall change our vile Body, that it may be like his glorious Body, according to the mighty working whereby he is able to subdue all things unto himself.[20]	We therefore commit *his* body to the deep, looking for the general Resurrection in the last day, and the life of the world to come, through our Lord Jesus Christ; at whose second coming in glorious majesty to judge the world, the sea shall give up her dead; and the corruptible bodies of those who sleep in him shall be changed, and made like unto his glorious body; according to the mighty working whereby he is able to subdue all things unto himself.]

[18]"the Dead" from 1793 until 1845.

[19]This paragraph and the two which follow are included in the 1892 Burial rite rather than in the prayers at sea.

[20]"to himself" [1789-1832], following the English, except "unto" in 1818.

Articles of Religion

1662(1775) **1786 (Proposed)**

ARTICLES
AGREED UPON
BY THE ARCHBISHOPS AND BISHOPS OF BOTH PROVINCES, AND THE WHOLE CLERGY,

In the Convocation holden at London *in the Year* 1562, *for the avoiding of Diversities of Opinions, and for the establishing of Consent touching true Religion: Reprinted by His Majesty's Commandment, with His Royal Declaration prefixed thereto.*

HIS MAJESTY'S DECLARATION

BEING by God's Ordinance, according to Our just Title, *Defender of the Faith, and Supreme Governor of the Church, within these Our Dominions,* We hold it most agreeable to this Our Kingly Office, and Our own religious Zeal, to conserve and maintain the Church committed to Our Charge, in Unity of true Religion, and in the Bond of Peace; and not to suffer unnecessary Disputations, Altercations, or Questions to be raised, which may nourish Faction both in the Church and Commonwealth. We have therefore, upon mature Deliberation, and with the Advice of so many of Our Bishops as might conveniently be called together,

ARTICLES OF RELIGION

[1]In the English book from 1662 on, the Articles stand at the end of the book, followed by a single page of "Table of Affinity and Kindred" outlining degrees of relationship within which marriage could not be contracted in England. In the United States, in the proposed book of 1786 the Articles stood before the Psalter. From 1789 until 1801 the prayer book contained no Articles. From their adoption until 1892, the Articles were placed immediately before the ordination rites. In the 1892 and 1928 books they stand at the very end of the volume. In 1979 they were included in a selection of "Historical Documents" along with the Chalcedonian Definition, the Athanasian Creed, The Preface to the 1549 Prayer Book, and the Chicago-Lambeth Quadrilateral.

1801-1979

ARTICLES OF RELIGION[1]

As established by the Bishops, the Clergy, and Laity of the Protestant Episcopal Church in the United States of America, in Convention, on the twelfth day of September, in the Year of our Lord 1801.

thought fit to make this Declaration following:

That the Articles of the Church of *England* (which have been allowed and authorized heretofore, and which Our Clergy generally have subscribed unto) do contain the true Doctrine of the Church of *England* agreeable to God's Word: which We do therefore ratify and confirm, requiring all Our loving Subjects to continue in the uniform Profession thereof and prohibiting the least difference from the said Articles; which to that End We command to be new printed, and this Our Declaration to be published therewith.

That We are Supreme Governor of the Church of *England:* And that if any Difference arise about the external Policy concerning the *Injunctions, Canons,* and other *Constitutions* whatsoever thereto belonging, the Clergy in their Convocation is to order and settle them, having first obtained leave under Our Broad Seal so to do: and We approving their said Ordinances and Constitutions: providing that none be made contrary to the Laws and Customs of the Land.

That out of Our Princely Care that the Churchmen may do the Work which is proper unto them, the Bishops and Clergy, from time to time in Convocation, upon their humble Desire, shall have Licence under Our Broad Seal to deliberate of, and to do all such Things, as, being made plain by them, and assented unto by Us, shall concern the settled Continuance of the Doctrine and Discipline of the Church of *England,* now established; from which We will not endure any varying or departing in the least Degree.

That for the present, though some differences have been ill raised, yet We take comfort in this, that all Clergymen within Our Realm have always most willingly subscribed to the Articles established; which is an argument to Us, that they all agree in the true, usual, literal meaning of the said Articles; and that even in those curious points, in which the present differences lie, men of all sorts take the Articles of the Church of *England* to be for them; which is an argument again, that none of them intend any desertion of the Articles established.

That therefore in these both curious and unhappy differences which have for so many hundred years, in different times and places, exercised the Church of Christ, We will, that all further curious search be laid aside, and these disputes shut up in God's promises, as they be generally set forth to us in the holy Scriptures, and the general meaning of the Articles of the Church of *England* according to them. And that no man hereafter shall either print, or preach, to draw the Article aside any way, but shall submit to it in the plain and full meaning thereof: and shall not put his own sense or comment to be the meaning of the Article, but shall take it in the literal and grammatical sense.

Articles of Religion

That if any public Reader in either of Our Universities, or any Head or Master of a College, or any other person respectively in either of them, shall affix any new sense to any Article, or shall publickly read, determine, or hold any publick Disputation, or suffer any such to be held either way, in either the Universities or Colleges respectively; or if any Divine in the Universities shall preach or print any thing either way, other than is already established in Convocation with
166, 167 our Royal Assent: he, or they the Offenders, shall be

1662(1775)	1786 (Proposed)
liable to Our displeasure, and the Church's censure in Our Commission Ecclesiastical, as well as any other: And We will see there shall be due Execution upon them.	
I. *Of Faith in the Holy Trinity.* THERE is but one living and true God, everlasting, without body, parts, or passions; of infinite power, wisdom, and goodness; the Maker, the Preserver of all things both visible and invisible. And in unity of this Godhead there be three Persons, of one substance, power, and eternity; the Father, the Son, and the Holy Ghost.	I. *Of Faith in the Holy Trinity.* THERE is but one living, true, and Eternal God, the Father Almighty; without body, parts or passions; of infinite Power, Wisdom, and Goodness, the Maker and preserver of all things both visible and invisible:
II. *Of the Word or Son of God, which was made very Man.* THE Son, which is the Word of the Father, begotten from everlasting of the Father, the very and eternal God, and of one substance with the Father, took Man's nature in the womb of the blessed Virgin, of her substance: so that two whole and perfect Natures, that is to say, the Godhead and Manhood, were joined together in one Person, never to be divided, whereof is one Christ, very God, and very Man; who truly suffered, was crucified, dead, and buried, to reconcile his Father to us, and to be a sacrifice, not only for original guilt, but also for all actual sins of men.[3]	And one Lord Jesus Christ, Son of God, begotten of the Father before all worlds, very and true God; who came down from heaven, took man's nature in the womb of the Blessed Virgin of her substance, and was God and man in one person, whereof is one Christ; who truly suffered, was crucified, dead and buried, to reconcile his Father to us, and to be a sacrifice for the sins of all men;
III. *Of the going down of Christ into Hell.* AS Christ died for us, and was buried; so also is it to be believed, that he went down into Hell.	
IV. *Of the Resurrection of Christ.* CHRIST did truly rise again from death, and took again his body, with flesh, bones, and all things appertaining to the perfection of Man's nature; wherewith he ascended into Heaven, and there sitteth, until he return to judge all men at the last day.	He rose again from death, ascended into heaven, and there sitteth until he shall return to judge the world at the last day;
V. *Of the Holy Ghost.* THE Holy Ghost, proceeding from the Father and the Son, is of one substance, majesty, and glory, with the Father and the Son, very and eternal God.	And one Holy Spirit, the Lord and Giver of Life, of the same divine nature with the Father and the Son.
VI. *Of the Sufficiency of the Holy Scriptures for Salvation.* HOLY Scripture containeth all things necessary to salvation: so that whatsoever is not read therein, nor may be proved thereby, is not to be required of any man, that it should be believed as an article of the Faith, or be thought requisite or necessary to salvation. In the name of the Holy Scripture we do understand those canonical Books of the Old and New Testament, of whose authority was never any doubt in the Church.	II. *Of the Sufficiency of the Holy Scriptures for Salvation.* HOLY Scripture containeth all things necessary to salvation: so that whatsoever is not read therein, nor may be proved thereby, is not to be required of any man, that it should be believed as an article of the Faith, or be thought requisite or necessary to salvation. In the name of the Holy Scripture we do understand those canonical Books of the Old and New Testament, [of whose authority was never any doubt in the Church.][4]

[2] 1928-1979 drop the "ART." throughout.

[3] A number of eighteenth century editions of the prayer book missed "all" in this clause, an error that was adopted in the American version of the Articles.

[4] The words placed in brackets in this edition were struck out by the Convention of 1785. Apparently acting on its own authority, the editorial committee responsible for the Proposed Book reinserted them.

ART. I. *Of Faith in the Holy Trinity.*[2]

THERE is but one living and true God, everlasting, without body, parts, or passions; of infinite power, wisdom, and goodness; the Maker, the Preserver of all things both visible and invisible. And in unity of this Godhead there be three Persons, of one substance, power, and eternity; the Father, the Son, and the Holy Ghost.

ART. II. *Of the Word or Son of God, which was made very Man.*

THE Son, which is the Word of the Father, begotten from everlasting of the Father, the very and eternal God, and of one substance with the Father, took Man's nature in the womb of the blessed Virgin, of her substance: so that two whole and perfect Natures, that is to say, the Godhead and Manhood, were joined together in one Person, never to be divided, whereof is one Christ, very God, and very Man; who truly suffered, was crucified, dead, and buried, to reconcile his Father to us, and to be a sacrifice, not only for original guilt, but also for actual sins of men.

ART. III. *Of the going down of Christ into Hell.*

AS Christ died for us, and was buried; so also is it to be believed, that he went down into Hell.

ART. IV. *Of the Resurrection of Christ.*

CHRIST did truly rise again from death, and took again his body, with flesh, bones, and all things appertaining to the perfection of Man's nature; wherewith he ascended into Heaven, and there sitteth, until he return to judge all men at the last day.

ART. V. *Of the Holy Ghost.*

THE Holy Ghost, proceeding from the Father and the Son, is of one substance, majesty, and glory, with the Father and the Son, very and eternal God.

ART. VI. *Of the Sufficiency of the Holy Scriptures for Salvation.*

HOLY Scripture containeth all things necessary to salvation: so that whatsoever is not read therein, nor may be proved thereby, is not to be required of any man, that it should be believed as an article of the Faith, or be thought requisite or necessary to salvation. In the name of the Holy Scripture we do understand those canonical Books of the Old and New Testament, of whose authority was never any doubt in the Church.

1662(1775)	1786 (Proposed)
OF THE NAMES AND NUMBER OF THE CANONICAL BOOKS.	OF THE NAMES AND NUMBER OF THE CANONICAL BOOKS.
Genesis, Exodus, Leviticus, Numbers, Deuteronium, Joshue, Judges, Ruth, The 1 Book of Samuel, The 2 Book of Samuel, The 1 Book of Kings, The 2 Book of Kings *The 1 Book of Chronicles, The 2 Book of Chronicles, The 1 Book of Esdras, The 2 Book of Esdras, The Book of Hester, The Book of Job, The Psalms, The Proverbs, Ecclesiastes or Preacher, Cantica, or Songs of Solomon, 4 Prophets the greater, 12 Prophets the less.*	*Genesis, Exodus, Leviticus, Numbers, Deuteronomy, Joshua, Judges, Ruth, The First Book of Samuel, The Second Book of Samuel, The First Book of Kings, The Second Book of Kings* *The First Book of Chronicles, The Second Book of Chronicles, The First Book of Esdras, The Second Book of Esdras, The Book of Hester, The Book of Job, The Psalms, The Proverbs, Ecclesiastes or Preacher, Cantica, or Songs of Solomon, Four Prophets the greater, Twelve Prophets the less.*
And the other Books (as *Hierome* saith) the Church doth read for example of life and instruction of manners; but yet doth it not apply them to establish any doctrine; such are these following:	And the other Books (as *Hierome* saith) the Church doth read for example of life and instruction of manners; but yet doth it not apply them to establish any doctrine; such are these following:
The 3 Book of Esdras, The 4 Book of Esdras The Book of Tobias, The Book of Judith, The rest of the Book of Hester, The Book of Wisdom, Jesus the Son of Sirach, *Baruch the Prophet The Song of the three Children The Story of Susanna, Of Bel and the Dragon, The Prayer of Manasses, The 1 Book of Maccabees, The 2 Book of Maccabees.*	*The third Book of Esdras, The Fourth Book of Esdras, The Book of Tobias, The Book of Judith, The rest of the Book of Hester, The Book of Wisdom, Jesus the Son of Sirach,* *Baruch the Prophet, The Song of the Three Children, The Story of Susanna, Of Bel and the Dragon, The Prayer of Manasses, The First Book of Maccabees, The Second Book of Maccabees.*
All the Books of the New Testament, as they are commonly received, we do receive, and account them Canonical.	All the Books of the New Testament, as they are commonly received, we do receive, and account Canonical.
VII. *Of the Old Testament.*	III. *Of the Old and New Testament.*
THE Old Testament is not contrary to the New: for both in the Old and New Testament everlasting life is offered to Mankind by Christ, who is the only Mediator between God and Man, being both God and Man. Wherefore they are not to be heard, which feign that the old Fathers did look only for transitory promises. Although the Law given from God by Moses, as touching Ceremonies and Rites, do not bind Christian men, nor the Civil precepts thereof ought of necessity to be received in any commonwealth; yet notwithstanding, no Christian man whatsoever is free from the obedience of the Commandments which are called Moral.	THERE is a perfect harmony and agreement between the Old Testament and the New, for in both everlasting life is offered to Mankind by Christ, who is the only Mediator between God and man: and although the law given by Moses, as to ceremonies and the civil precepts of it, doth not bind Christians; yet all such are obliged to observe the moral commandments which he delivered.
VIII. *Of the three Creeds.*	IV. *Of the Creed.*[7]
THE three Creeds, *Nicene* Creed, *Athanasius's* Creed, and that which is commonly called the *Apostles* Creed, ought thoroughly to be received and believed: for they may be proved by most certain warrants of Holy Scripture.	THE Creed, commonly called the *Apostles' Creed* ought to be received and believed: because it may be proved by the Holy Scripture.

[5]The 1662 spellings of Deuteronomy, Joshua, and Esther were retained until 1845.

[6]italicized until 1928, but the spelling has not been modernized.

[7]The General Convention had adopted "Of Creeds," but the editorial committee put this reading in its place.

[8]Italics for personal and place names are general removed in 1928 and 1979.

Of the Names and Number of the Canonical Books.

Genesis,
Exodus,
Leviticus,
Numbers,
Deuteronomy,[5]
Joshua,
Judges,
Ruth,
The First Book of Samuel,
The Second Book of Samuel,
The First Book of Kings,
The Second Book of Kings
The First Book of Chronicles,
The Second Book of Chronicles,
The First Book of Esdras,
The Second Book of Esdras,
The Book of Ester,
The Book of Job,
The Psalms,
The Proverbs,
Ecclesiastes or Preacher,
Cantica, or Songs of Solomon,
Four Prophets the greater,
Twelve Prophets the less.

And the other Books (as Hierome[6] saith) the Church doth read for example of life and instruction of manners; but yet doth it not apply them to establish any doctrine; such are these following:

The Third Book of Esdras,
The Fourth Book of Esdras,
The Book of Tobias,
The Book of Judith,
The Rest of the Book of Esther,
The Book of Wisdom,
Jesus the Son of Sirach,
Baruch the Prophet,
The Song of the Three Children,
The Story of Susanna,
Of Bel and the Dragon,
The Prayer of Manasses,
The First Book of Maccabees,
The Second Book of Maccabees.

All the Books of the New Testament, as they are commonly received, we do receive, and account Canonical.

ART. VII. *Of the Old Testament.*

THE Old Testament is not contrary to the New: for both in the Old and New Testament everlasting life is offered to Mankind by Christ, who is the only Mediator between God and Man, being both God and Man. Wherefore they are not to be heard, which feign that the old Fathers did look only for transitory promises. Although the Law given from God by Moses, as touching Ceremonies and Rites, do not bind Christian men, nor the Civil precepts thereof ought of necessity to be received in any commonwealth; yet notwithstanding, no Christian man whatsoever is free from the obedience of the Commandments which are called Moral.

ART. VIII. *Of the Creeds.*

THE *Nicene*[8] Creed, and that which is commonly called the *Apostles* Creed, ought thoroughly to be received and believed: for they may be proved by most certain warrants of Holy Scripture.

1662 (1775)

IX. *Of Original or Birth-Sin.*

ORIGINAL sin standeth not in the following of *Adam*, (as the *Pelagians* do vainly talk;) but it is the fault and corruption of the Nature of every man, that naturally is engendered of the offspring of *Adam*; whereby man is very far gone from original righteousness, and is of his own nature inclined to evil, so that the flesh lusteth always contrary to the Spirit; and therefore in every person born into this world, it deserveth God's wrath and damnation. And this infection of nature doth remain, yea in them that are regenerated; whereby the lust of the flesh, called in Greek, *phronema sarkos*,[9] (which some do expound the wisdom, some sensuality, some the affection, some the desire, of the flesh,) is not subject to the Law of God. And although there is no condemnation for them that believe and are baptized; yet the Apostle doth confess, that concupiscence and lust hath of itself the nature of sin.

X. *Of Free-Will.*

THE condition of Man after the fall of *Adam* is such, that he cannot turn and prepare himself, by his own natural strength and good works, to faith, and calling upon God. Wherefore we have no power to do good works pleasant and acceptable to God, without the grace of God by Christ preventing us, that we may have a good will, and working with us, when we have that good will.

XI. *Of the Justification of Man.*

WE are accounted righteous before God, only for the merit of our Lord and Saviour Jesus Christ by Faith, and not for our own works or deservings. Wherefore, that we are justified by Faith only, is a most wholesome doctrine,[14] and very full of comfort, as more largely is expressed in the Homily of Justification.

XII. *Of Good Works.*

ALBEIT that Good Works, which are the fruits of Faith, and follow after Justification, cannot put away our sins, and endure the severity of God's judgment; yet are they pleasing and acceptable to God in Christ, and do spring out necessarily of a true and lively Faith; insomuch that by them a lively Faith may be as evidently known as a tree discerned by the fruit.

XIII. *Of Works before Justification.*

WORKS done before the grace of Christ, and the Inspiration of his Spirit, are not pleasant to God, forasmuch as they spring not of faith in Jesus Christ; neither

1786 (Proposed)

V. *Of Original Sin.*

BY the fall of Adam the Nature of Man is become greatly corrupted,[10] having departed from its primitive innocence, and that original righteousness in which it was at first created by God. For we are now so inclined naturally[11] to do evil that the flesh is continually striving to act contrary to the Spirit of God, which corrupt inclination still remains even in the regenerate. But although there is no man living who sinneth not, yet we must use our sincere endeavours to keep the whole law of God, so far as we possibly can.

VI. *Of Free-Will.*

THE condition of Man after the fall of *Adam* is such, that he cannot turn and prepare himself, by his own natural strength and good works, to faith, and calling upon God. Wherefore we have no power to do good works pleasant and acceptable to God, without the grace of God by Christ giving[13] a good will, and working with us, when we have that good will.

VII. *Of the Justification of Man.*

WE are accounted righteous before God, only for the merit of our Lord and Saviour Jesus Christ by Faith, and not for our own works or deservings. Wherefore, that we are justified by Faith only, is a most wholesome doctrine and very full of comfort.

VIII. *Of Good Works.*

ALTHOUGH[15] Good Works, which are the fruits of Faith, and follow after Justification, cannot put away our sins, and endure the severity of God's judgment; yet are they pleasing and acceptable to God in Christ, and do spring out necessarily of a true and lively Faith; insomuch that by them a lively Faith may be as evidently known as a tree discerned by the fruit.

---

[9] given in Greek characters here and in the American version.

[10] The Convention had adopted "is become so corrupt, as to be greatly depraved." This reading is the work of the editorial committee.

[11] The Convention had adopted "so naturally inclined."

[12] given in Greek characters here and in the English original.

[13] The Convention had adopted "giving us."

[14] 1775 actually has "docrine."

[15] The Convention had adopted "Albeit that."

ART. IX. *Of Original or Birth-Sin.*

ORIGINAL sin standeth not in the following of *Adam,* (as the *Pelagians* do vainly talk;) but it is the fault and corruption of the Nature of every man, that naturally is engendered of the offspring of *Adam;* whereby man is very far gone from original righteousness, and is of his own nature inclined to evil, so that the flesh lusteth always contrary to the Spirit; and therefore in every person born into this world, it deserveth God's wrath and damnation. And this infection of nature doth remain, yea in them that are regenerated; whereby the lust of the flesh, called in Greek, *phronema sarkos,*[12] (which some do expound the wisdom, some sensuality, some the affection, some the desire, of the flesh,) is not subject to the Law of God. And although there is no condemnation for them that believe and are baptized; yet the Apostle doth confess, that concupiscence and lust hath of itself the nature of sin.

ART. X. *Of Free-Will.*

THE condition of Man after the fall of *Adam* is such, that he cannot turn and prepare himself, by his own natural strength and good works, to faith, and calling upon God. Wherefore we have no power to do good works pleasant and acceptable to God, without the grace of God by Christ preventing us, that we may have a good will, and working with us, when we have that good will.

ART. XI. *Of the Justification of Man.*

WE are accounted righteous before God, only for the merit of our Lord and Saviour Jesus Christ by Faith, and not for our own works or deservings. Wherefore, that we are justified by Faith only, is a most wholesome Doctrine, and very full of comfort, as more largely is expressed in the Homily of Justification.

ART. XII. *Of Good Works.*

ALBEIT that Good Works, which are the fruits of Faith, and follow after Justification, cannot put away our sins, and endure the severity of God's judgment; yet are they pleasing and acceptable to God in Christ, and do spring out necessarily of a true and lively Faith; insomuch that by them a lively Faith may be as evidently known as a tree discerned by the fruit.

ART. XIII. *Of Works before Justification.*

WORKS done before the grace of Christ, and the Inspiration of his Spirit, are not pleasant to God, forasmuch as they spring not of faith in Jesus Christ; neither

1662(1775)

do they make men meet to receive grace, or (as the School-authors say) deserve grace of congruity; yea rather, for that they are not done as God hath willed and commanded them to be done, we doubt not but they have the nature of sin.

XIV. *Of Works of Supererogation.*

VOLUNTARY Works besides, over and above, God's Commandments, which they call Works of Supererogation, cannot be taught without arrogancy and impiety; for then men do declare, that they do not only render unto God as much as they are bound to do, but that they do more for his sake, than of bounden duty is required; whereas Christ saith plainly, When ye have done all that are commanded to you, say, We are unprofitable servants.

XV. *Of Christ alone without Sin.*

CHRIST in the truth of our nature was made like unto us in all things, sin only except, from which he was clearly void, both in his flesh and in his spirit. He came to be the Lamb without spot, who, by sacrifice of himself once made, should take away the sins of the world; and sin (as Saint *John* saith) was not in him. But all we the rest, although baptized, and born again in Christ, yet offend in many things; and if we say we have no sin, we deceive ourselves, and the truth is not in us.

1786 (Proposed)

IX. *Of Christ alone without Sin.*

CHRIST, by taking human nature on him, was made like unto us in all things, sin only excepted. He was a lamb without spot, and by the sacrifice of himself once offered, made atonement and propitiation for the sins of the world; and sin was not in him. But all man kind[16] besides, although baptized and born again in Christ, do offend in many things. For if we say we have no sin we deceive ourselves, and the truth is not in us.

1662(1775)

XVI. *Of Sin after Baptism.*

NOT every deadly sin willingly committed after Baptism is sin against the Holy Ghost, and unpardonable. Wherefore the grant of repentance is not to be denied to such as fall into sin after Baptism. After we have received the Holy Ghost, we may depart from grace given, and fall into sin, and by the grace of God we may arise again, and amend our lives. And therefore they are to be condemned, which say, they can no more sin as long as they live here, or deny the place of forgiveness to such as truly repent.

1786 (Proposed)

X. *Of Sin after Baptism.*

THEY who fall into sin after Baptism may be renewed by repentance; for although after we have received God's grace, we may depart from it by falling into sin, yet, through the assistance of his Holy Spirit, we may by repentance and the amendment of our lives, be restored again to his favour. God will not deny forgiveness[17] of sins to those who truly repent, and do that which is lawful and right; but all such through his mercy in Christ Jesus, shall save their souls alive.

1662(1775)

XVII. *Of Predestination and Election.*

PREDESTINATION to Life is the everlasting purpose of God, whereby (before the foundations of the world were laid) he hath constantly decreed by his counsel secret to us, to deliver from curse and damnation those whom he hath chosen in Christ out of mankind, and to bring them by Christ to everlasting salvation, as vessels made to honour. Wherefore, they which he endued with so excellent a benefit of God, be called according to God's purpose by his Spirit working in due season: they through Grace obey the calling: they be justified freely: they be made sons of God by adoption: they be made like the image of his only-begotten Son Jesus Christ: they walk religiously in good works, and at length, by God's mercy, they attain to everlasting felicity.

As the godly consideration of Predestination, and our Election in Christ, is full of sweet, pleasant, and

1786 (Proposed)

XI. *Of Predestination*

PREDESTINATION to life, with respect to every Man's Salvation, is the everlasting purpose of God, secret to us:

and the right knowledge of what is revealed concerning it, is full of comfort to such truly religious

[16] *sic.*

[17] The Convention had adopted "repentance."

do they make men meet to receive grace, or (as the School-authors say) deserve grace of congruity; yea rather, for that they are not done as God hath willed and commanded them to be done, we doubt not but they have the nature of sin.

ART. XIV. *Of Works of Supererogation.*

VOLUNTARY Works besides, over and above, God's Commandments, which they call Works of Supererogation, cannot be taught without arrogancy and impiety; for by them men do declare, that they do not only render unto God as much as they are bound to do, but that they do more for his sake, than of bounden duty is required: whereas Christ saith plainly, When ye have done all that are commanded to you, say, We are unprofitable servants.

Art. XV. *Of Christ alone without Sin.*

CHRIST in the truth of our nature was made like unto us in all things, sin only except, from which he was clearly void, both in his flesh and in his spirit. He came to be the Lamb without spot, who, by sacrifice of himself once made, should take away the sins of the world; and sin (as Saint *John* saith) was not in him. But all we the rest, although baptized, and born again in Christ, yet offend in many things; and if we say we have no sin, we deceive ourselves, and the truth is not in us.

ART. XVI. *Of Sin after Baptism.*

NOT every deadly sin willingly committed after Baptism is sin against the Holy Ghost, and unpardonable. Wherefore the grant of repentance is not to be denied to such as fall into sin after Baptism. After we have received the Holy Ghost, we may depart from grace given, and fall into sin, and by the grace of God we may arise again, and amend our lives. And therefore they are to be condemned, which say, they can no more sin as long as they live here, or deny the place of forgiveness to such as truly repent.

ART. XVII. *Of Predestination and Election.*

PREDESTINATION to Life is the everlasting purpose of God, whereby (before the foundations of the world were laid) he hath constantly decreed by his counsel secret to us, to deliver from curse and damnation those whom he hath chosen in Christ out of mankind, and to bring them by Christ to everlasting salvation, as vessels made to honour. Wherefore, they which be endued with so excellent a benefit of God, be called according to God's purpose by his Spirit working in due season: they through Grace obey the calling: they be justified freely: they be made sons of God by adoption: they be made like the image of his only begotten-Son Jesus Christ: they walk religiously in good works, and at length, by God's mercy, they attain to everlasting felicity.

As the godly consideration of Predestination, and our Election in Christ, is full of sweet, pleasant, and unspeakable comfort to godly persons, and such as feel in themselves the working of the Spirit of Christ, mortifying the works of the flesh, and their earthly members, and drawing up their mind to high and heavenly things, as well because it doth greatly establish and confirm their faith of eternal Salvation to be enjoyed through Christ, as because it doth fervently kindle their love towards God: So, for curious and carnal persons, lacking the Spirit of Christ, to have continually before their eyes the sentence of God's Predestination, is a most dangerous downfall, whereby the Devil doth thrust them either into desperation, or into wretchlessness of most unclean living, no less perilous than desperation.

Furthermore, we must receive God's promises in such wise, as they be generally set forth to us in Holy Scripture: and, in our doings, that Will of God is to be followed, which we have expressly declared unto us in the Word of God.

XVIII. *Of obtaining eternal Salvation only by the Name of Christ.*

THEY also are to be had accursed that presume to say, That every man shall be saved by the Law or Sect which he professeth, so that he be diligent to frame his life according to that Law, and the light of Nature. For Holy Scripture doth set out unto us only the Name of Jesus Christ, whereby men must be saved.

XIX. *Of the Church.*

THE visible Church of Christ is a congregation of faithful men, in the which the pure Word of God is preached, and the Sacraments be duly ministered according to Christ's ordinance, in all those things that of necessity are requisite to the same.

As the Church of *Hierusalem, Alexandria,* and *Antioch,* have erred; so also the Church of *Rome* hath erred, not only in their living and manner of Ceremonies, but also in matters of Faith.

XX. *Of the Authority of the Church.*

THE Church hath power to decree Rites or Ceremonies, and authority in Controversies of Faith: and yet it is not lawful for the Church to ordain any thing that is contrary to God's Word written, neither may it so expound one place of Scripture, that it be repugnant to another. Wherefore, although the Church be a witness and a keeper of Holy Writ, yet, as it ought not to decree any thing against the same, so beside the same ought it not to enforce anything to believed for necessity of Salvation.

Christians, as feel in themselves the spirit of Christ, mortifying the works of their flesh, and their earthly affections, and raising their minds to heavenly things.

But we must receive God's promises as they are[18] generally declared in Holy Scripture, and do his will, as therein is expressly directed: for without holiness of life no man shall be saved.

XII. *Of obtaining eternal Salvation only by the Name of Christ.*

THEY are to be accounted presumptuous, who say, That every man shall be saved by the Law or Sect which he professeth, so that he be diligent to frame his life according to that Law, and the light of Nature. For Holy Scripture doth set out unto us only the Name of Jesus Christ, whereby men must be saved.

XIII. *Of the Church and its Authority.*

THE visible Church of Christ is a congregation of faithful men, wherein the true Word[19] of God is preached and the Sacraments administered[20] according to Christ's ordinance in all things requisite and necessary,[21]

and every Church hath power to ordain, change, and abolish rites and ceremonies for the more decent and good government thereof: so that all things be done to edifying. But it is not lawful for the Church to ordain anything contrary to God's Word, nor so to expound the Scripture, as to make one part seem repugnant to another; nor to decree or enforce anything to be believed as necessary to Salvation that is not contained in the Scriptures.[23]

---

[18]The Convention had adopted "they be."

[19]The Convention had adopted "pure Word."

[20]The Convention had adopted "are duly administered."

[21]The Convention had adopted "necessary and requisite."

[22]Spelling modernized in 1845.

[23]The Convention had adopted "that is contrary to God's Holy Word."

unspeakable comfort to godly persons, and such as feel in themselves the working of the Spirit of Christ, mortifying the works of the flesh, and their earthly members, and drawing up their mind to high and heavenly things, as well because it doth greatly establish and confirm their faith of eternal Salvation to be enjoyed through Christ, as because it doth fervently kindle their love towards God: So, for curious and carnal persons, lacking the Spirit of Christ, to have continually before their eyes the sentence of God's Predestination, is a most dangerous downfall, whereby the Devil doth thrust them either into desperation, or into wretchlessness of most unclean living, no less perilous than desperation.

Furthermore, we must receive God's promises in such wise, as they be generally set forth to us in Holy Scripture: and, in our doings, that Will of God is to be followed, which we have expressly declared unto us in the Word of God.

ART. XVIII. *Of obtaining eternal Salvation only by the Name of Christ.*

THEY also are to be had accursed that presume to say, That every man shall be saved by the Law or Sect which he professeth, so that he be diligent to frame his life according to that Law, and the light of Nature. For Holy Scripture doth set out unto us only the Name of Jesus Christ, whereby men must be saved.

ART. XIX. *Of the Church.*

THE visible Church of Christ is a congregation of faithful men, in the which the pure Word of God is preached, and the Sacraments be duly ministered according to Christ's ordinance, in all those things that of necessity are requisite to the same.

As the Church of *Jerusalem, Alexandria,* and *Antioch,*[22] have erred; so also the Church of *Rome* hath erred, not only in their living and manner of Ceremonies, but also in matters of Faith.

ART. XX. *Of the Authority of the Church.*

THE Church hath power to decree Rites or Ceremonies, and authority in Controversies of Faith: and yet it is not lawful for the Church to ordain any thing that is contrary to God's Word written, neither may it so expound one place of Scripture, that it be repugnant to another. Wherefore, although the Church be a witness and a keeper of Holy Writ, yet, as it ought not to decree any thing against the same, so beside the same ought it not to enforce anything to believed for necessity of Salvation.

XXI. *Of the Authority of General Councils.*

GENERAL Councils may not be gathered together without the commandment and will of Princes. And when they be gathered together, (forasmuch as they be an assembly of men, whereof all be not governed with the Spirit and Word of God,) they may err, and sometimes have erred, even in things pertaining unto God. Wherefore things ordained by them as necessary to salvation have neither strength nor authority, unless it may be declared that they be taken out of holy Scripture.

General Councils and Churches are liable to err, and have erred, even in matters of faith and doctrine, as well as in their ceremonies.

XXII. *Of Purgatory.*

THE Romish Doctrine concerning Purgatory, Pardons, Worshipping and Adoration, as well of Images as of Reliques, and also Invocation of Saints, is a fond thing, vainly invented, and grounded upon no warranty of Scripture, but rather repugnant to the Word of God.

XXIII. *Of Ministering in the Congregation.*

IT is not lawful for any man to take upon him the office of public preaching, or ministering the Sacraments in the Congregation, before he be lawfully called, and sent to execute the same. And those we ought to judge lawfully called and sent, which be chosen and called to this work by men who have public authority given unto them in the Congregation, to call and send Ministers into the Lord's vineyard.

XIV. *Of Ministering in the Congregation.*

IT is not lawful for any man to take upon him the office of public preaching, or ministering the Sacraments in the Congregation, before he be lawfully called, and sent to execute the same. And those we ought to judge lawfully called and sent, who are chosen and called to this work by men who have public authority given unto them in the Congregation, to call and send Ministers into the Lord's vineyard.

XXIV. *Of Speaking in the Congregation in such a Tongue as the people understandeth.*

IT is a thing plainly repugnant to the Word of God, and the custom of the Primitive Church, to have public Prayer in the Church, or to minister the Sacraments, in a tongue not understanded of the people.

XXV. *Of the Sacraments.*

SACRAMENTS ordained of Christ be not only badges or tokens of Christian men's profession, but rather they be certain sure witnesses, and effectual signs of grace, and God's good will towards us, by the which he doth work invisibly in us, and doth not only quicken, but also strengthen and confirm our Faith in him.

There are two Sacraments ordained of Christ our Lord in the Gospel, that is to say, Baptism, and the Supper of the Lord.

The Sacraments were not ordained of Christ to be gazed upon, or to be carried about, but that we should duly use them. And in such only as worthily receive the same, they have a wholesome effect or operation: but they that receive them unworthily, purchase to themselves damnation, as Saint *Paul* saith.

XV. *Of the Sacraments.*

SACRAMENTS ordained by Christ are not merely badges or tokens of Christian men's profession, but rather certain sure witnesses, and effectual signs of grace, and God's good will towards us, by which he doth work invisibly in us, and doth not only quicken, but also strengthen and confirm our Faith in him.

There are two Sacraments ordained of Christ our Lord in the Gospel, that is to say, Baptism, and the Supper of the Lord.

---

[24]This passage appeared as a footnote at the bottom of the page on which the title to the Article appeared, until 1928, when it was printed in brackets in place of the text of Article XXI. (Hence arose the fact that Americans had only thirty-eight articles, whilst retaining the titles of all thirty-nine.) The note explaining the absence of Article XXI. is to modern eyes disingenuous: the fact was that citizens of a republic with no state interest in religion who were also members of a nearly-orphaned church in an already pluralistic religious culture simply had no idea how an authentic General Council might be called for the Christian Church, and in this perplexity they were arguably ahead of their time.

[25]Spelling modernized in 1838.

ART. XXI *Of the Authority of General Councils.**

*The Twenty-first of the former Articles is omitted; because it is partly of a local and civil nature, and is provided for, as to the remaining parts of it, in other Articles.[24]

ART. XXII. *Of Purgatory.*

THE Romish Doctrine concerning Purgatory, Pardons, Worshipping and Adoration, as well of Images as of Relics,[25] and also Invocation of Saints, is a fond thing, vainly invented, and grounded upon no warranty of Scripture, but rather repugnant to the Word of God.

ART. XXIII. *Of Ministering in the Congregation.*

IT is not lawful for any man to take upon him the office of public preaching, or ministering the Sacraments in the Congregation, before he be lawfully called, and sent to execute the same. And those we ought to judge lawfully called and sent, which be chosen and called to this work by men who have public authority given unto them in the Congregation, to call and send Ministers into the Lord's vineyard.

ART. XXIV. *Of Speaking in the Congregation in such a Tongue as the people understandeth.*

IT is a thing plainly repugnant to the Word of God, and the custom of the Primitive Church, to have public Prayer in the Church, or to minister the Sacraments, in a tongue not understanded of the people.

ART. XXV. *Of the Sacraments.*

SACRAMENTS ordained of Christ be not only badges or tokens of Christian men's profession, but rather they be certain sure witnesses, and effectual signs of grace, and God's good will towards us, by the which he doth work invisibly in us, and doth not only quicken, but also strengthen and confirm our Faith in him.

There are two Sacraments ordained of Christ our Lord in the Gospel, that is to say, Baptism, and the Supper of the Lord.

The Sacraments were not ordained of Christ to be gazed upon, or to be carried about, but that we should duly use them. And in such only as worthily receive the same, they have a wholesome effect or operation: but they that receive them unworthily, purchase to themselves damnation, as Saint *Paul* saith.

XXVI. *Of the Unworthiness of the Ministers, which hinders not the effect of the Sacraments.*

ALTHOUGH in the visible Church the evil be ever mingled with the good, and sometimes the evil have chief authority in the Ministration of the Word and Sacraments, yet forasmuch as they do not the same in their own name, but in Christ's, and do minister by his commission and authority, we may use their Ministry, both in hearing the Word of God, and in the receiving of the Sacraments. Neither is the effect of Christ's ordinance taken away by their wickedness, nor the grace of God's gifts diminished from such as by faith, and rightly, do receive the Sacraments ministered unto them; which be effectual, because of Christ's institution and promise, although they be ministered by evil men.

Nevertheless, it appertaineth to the discipline of the Church, that inquiry be made of evil Ministers, and that they be accused by those that have knowledge of their offences; and finally, being found guilty, by just judgment be deposed.

XXVII. *Of Baptism.*

BAPTISM is not only a sign of profession, and mark of difference, whereby Christian men are discerned from others that be not christened, but it is also a sign of Regeneration or New-Birth, whereby, as by an instrument, they that receive Baptism rightly are grafted into the Church; the promises of the forgiveness of sin, and of our adoption to be the sons of God by the Holy Ghost, are visibly signed and sealed; Faith is confirmed, and Grace increased by virtue of prayer unto God.

The Baptism of young Children is in any wise to be retained in the Church, as most agreeable to the institution of Christ.

XVI. *Of Baptism.*

BAPTISM is not merely a sign of profession, and mark of difference, whereby Christian men are discerned from others that are not christened, but it is also a sign of Regeneration or New-Birth, whereby, as by an instrument, they who receive Baptism rightly are grafted into the Church; the promises of the forgiveness of sin, and of our adoption to be the sons of God by the Holy Ghost, are visibly signed and sealed; Faith is confirmed, and Grace increased by virtue of prayer unto God.[26]

XXVIII. *Of the Lord's Supper.*

THE Supper of the Lord is not only a sign of the love that Christians ought to have among themselves one to another; but rather it is a Sacrament of our Redemption by Christ's death: insomuch that to such as rightly, worthily, and with faith, receive the same, the Bread which we break is a partaking of the Body of Christ; and likewise the Cup of Blessing is a partaking of the Blood of Christ.

Transubstantiation (or the change of the substance of bread and Wine) in the Supper of the Lord, cannot be proved by Holy Writ; but is repugnant to the plain words of Scripture, overthroweth the nature of a Sacrament, and hath given occasion to many superstitions.

The Body of Christ is given, taken, and eaten, in the Supper, only after an heavenly and spiritual manner. And the mean whereby the Body of Christ is received and eaten in the Supper, is Faith.

The Sacrament of the Lord's Supper was not by Christ's ordinance reserved, carried about, lifted up, or worshipped.

XVII. *Of the Lord's Supper.*

THE Supper of the Lord is not merely a Sign of the love that Christians ought to have among themselves one to another; but rather is a Sacrament of our Redemption by Christ's death: insomuch that to such as rightly, worthily, and with faith, receive the same, the Bread which we break is a partaking of the Body of Christ; and likewise the Cup of Blessing is a partaking of the Blood of Christ.

Transubstantiation (or the change of the substance of bread and Wine) in the Supper of the Lord, cannot be proved by Holy Writ; but is repugnant to the plain words of Scripture, overthroweth the nature of a Sacrament, and hath given occasion to many superstitions.

The Body of Christ is given, taken, and eaten, in the Supper of the Lord, only after an heavenly and spiritual manner. And the mean whereby the Body of Christ is received and eaten in the Supper, is Faith.

[26]The slight verbal changes in this paragraph were made by the editorial committee.

ART. XXVI. *Of the Unworthiness of the Ministers, which hinders not the effect of the Sacraments.*

ALTHOUGH in the visible Church the evil be ever mingled with the good, and sometimes the evil have chief authority in the Ministration of the Word and Sacraments, yet forasmuch as they do not the same in their own name, but in Christ's, and do minister by his commission and authority, we may use their Ministry, both in hearing the Word of God and in receiving the Sacraments. Neither is the effect of Christ's ordinance taken away by their wickedness, nor the grace of God's gifts diminished from such as by faith, and rightly, do receive the Sacraments ministered unto them; which be effectual, because of Christ's institution and promise, although they be ministered by evil men.

ART. XXVII. *Of Baptism.*

BAPTISM is not only a sign of profession, and mark of difference, whereby Christian men are discerned from others that be not christened, but it is also a sign of Regeneration or New-Birth, whereby, as by an instrument, they that receive Baptism rightly are grafted into the Church; the promises of the forgiveness of sin, and of our adoption to be the sons of God by the Holy Ghost, are visibly signed and sealed; Faith is confirmed, and Grace increased by virtue of prayer unto God.

The Baptism of young Children is in any wise to be retained in the Church, as most agreeable with the institution of Christ.

ART. XXVIII. *Of the Lord's Supper.*

THE Supper of the Lord is not only a sign of the love that Christians ought to have among themselves one to another; but rather it is a Sacrament of our Redemption by Christ's death: insomuch that to such as rightly, worthily, and with faith, receive the same, the Bread which we break is a partaking of the Body of Christ; and likewise the Cup of Blessing is a partaking of the Blood of Christ.

Transubstantiation (or the change of the substance of bread and Wine) in the Supper of the Lord, cannot be proved by Holy Writ; but is repugnant to the plain words of Scripture, overthroweth the nature of a Sacrament, and hath given occasion to many superstitions.

The Body of Christ is given, taken, and eaten, in the Supper, only after an heavenly and spiritual manner. And the mean whereby the Body of Christ is received and eaten in the Supper, is Faith.

The Sacrament of the Lord's Supper was not by Christ's ordinance reserved, carried about, lifted up, or worshipped.

XXIX. *Of the Wicked, which eat not the Body of Christ in the use of the Lord's Supper.*

THE Wicked, and such as be void of a lively faith, although they do carnally and visibly press with their teeth (as Saint *Augustine* saith) the Sacrament of the Body and Blood of Christ; yet in no wise are they partakers of Christ; but rather, to their condemnation, do eat and drink the sign or Sacrament of so great a thing.

XXX. *Of both Kinds.*

THE Cup of the Lord is not to be denied to the Lay-people: for both the parts of the Lord's Sacrament, by Christ's ordinance and commandment, ought to be ministered to all Christian men alike.

XXXI. *Of the one Oblation of Christ finished upon the Cross.*

THE offering of Christ once made is that perfect redemption, propitiation, and satisfaction, for all the sins of the whole world, both original and actual; and there is none other satisfaction for sin, but that alone. Wherefore the sacrifice of Masses, in which it was commonly said, that the Priest did offer Christ for the quick and the dead, to have remission of pain or guilt, were blasphemous fables, and dangerous deceits.

XVIII. *Of the one Oblation of Christ upon the Cross.*

THE offering of Christ once made is that perfect redemption, propitiation, and satisfaction, for all the sins of the whole world, both original and actual; and there is none other satisfaction for sin, but that alone.

XXXII. *Of the Marriage of Priests.*

BISHOPS, Priests, and Deacons, are not commanded by God's Law, either to vow the estate of single life, or to abstain from marriage: therefore it is lawful for them, as for all other Christian men, to marry at their own discretion, as they shall judge the same to serve better to godliness.

XXXIII. *Of excommunicate Persons, how they are to be avoided.*

THAT person which by open denunciation of the church is rightly cut off from the unity of the Church, and excommunicated, ought to be taken of the whole multitude of the faithful, as an Heathen and Publican, until he be openly reconciled by penance, and received into the Church by a Judge that hath authority thereunto.

XXXIV. *Of the Traditions of the Church.*

IT is not necessary that Traditions and Ceremonies be in all places one, or utterly like; for at all times they have been divers, and may be changed according to the diversity of countries, times, and men's manners, so that nothing be ordained against God's Word. Whosoever, through his private judgment, willingly and purposely, doth openly break the Traditions and Ceremonies of the Church, which be not repugnant to the Word of God, and be ordained and approved by common authority, ought to be rebuked openly, (that other[28] may fear to do the like,) as he that offendeth against the common order of the Church, and hurteth

[27]Changed to the plural in 1845.

[28]*sic.*

ART. XXIX. *Of the Wicked, which eat not the Body of Christ in the use of the Lord's Supper.*

THE Wicked, and such as be void of a lively faith, although they do carnally and visibly press with their teeth (as Saint *Augustine* saith) the Sacrament of the Body and Blood of Christ: yet in no wise are they partakers of Christ; but rather, to their condemnation, do eat and drink the sign or Sacrament of so great a thing.

ART. XXX. *Of both Kinds.*

THE Cup of the Lord is not to be denied to the Lay-people: for both the parts of the Lord's Sacrament, by Christ's ordinance and commandment, ought to be ministered to all Christian men alike.

ART. XXXI. *Of the one Oblation of Christ finished upon the Cross.*

THE Offering of Christ once made is that perfect redemption, propitiation, and satisfaction, for all the sins of the whole world, both original and actual; and there is none other satisfaction for sin, but that alone. Wherefore the sacrifices[27] of Masses, in which it was commonly said, that the Priest did offer Christ for the quick and the dead, to have remission of pain or guilt, were blasphemous fables, and dangerous deceits.

ART. XXXII. *Of the Marriage of Priests.*

BISHOPS, Priests, and Deacons, are not commanded by God's Law, either to vow the estate of single life, or to abstain from marriage: therefore it is lawful for them, as for all other Christian men, to marry at their own discretion, as they shall judge the same to serve better to godliness.

ART. XXXIII. *Of excommunicate Persons, how they are to be avoided.*

THAT person which by open denunciation of the Church is rightly cut off from the unity of the Church, and excommunicated, ought to be taken of the whole multitude of the faithful, as an Heathen and Publican, until he be openly reconciled by penance, and received into the Church by a Judge that hath authority thereunto.

ART. XXXIV. *Of the Traditions of the Church.*

IT is not necessary that Traditions and Ceremonies be in all places one, or utterly like; for at all times they have been divers, and may be changed according to the diversity of countries, times, and men's manners, so that nothing be ordained against God's Word. Whosoever, through his private judgment, willingly and purposely, doth openly break the Traditions and Ceremonies of the Church, which be not repugnant to the Word of God, and be ordained and approved by common authority, ought to be rebuked openly, (that others may fear to do the like,) as he that offendeth against the common order of the Church, and hurteth the authority of the Magistrate, and woundeth the consciences of the weak brethren.

Every particular or national Church hath authority to ordain, change, and abolish, Ceremonies or Rites of the Church ordained only by man's authority, so that all things be done to edifying.

XXXV. *Of the Homilies.*

THE Second Book of Homilies, the several titles whereof we have joined under this Article, doth contain a godly and wholesome Doctrine, and necessary for these times, as doth the former Book of Homilies, which were set forth in the time of *Edward the Sixth;* and therefore we judge them to be read in Church by the Ministers, diligently and distinctly, that they may be understanded of the people.

OF THE NAMES OF THE HOMILIES.

1 *Of the right Use of the Church.*
2 *Against Peril of Idolatry.*
3 *Of repairing and keeping clean of Churches.*
4 *Of good Works: first of Fasting.*
5 *Against Gluttony and Drunkenness.*
6 *Against Excess of Apparel.*
7 *Of Prayer.*
8 *Of the Place and Time of Prayer.*
9 *That Common Prayers and Sacraments ought to be ministered in a known tongue.*
10 *Of the reverend Estimation of God's Word.*
11 *Of Alms-doing.*
12 *Of the Nativity of Christ.*
13 *Of the Passion of Christ.*
14 *Of the Resurrection of Christ.*
15 *Of the worthy receiving of the Sacrament of the Body and Blood of Christ.*
16 *Of the Gifts of the Holy Ghost.*
17 *For the Rogation-days.*
18 *Of the State of Matrimony.*
19 *Of Repentance.*
20 *Against Idleness.*
21 *Against Rebellion.*

XXXVI. *Of Consecration of Bishops and Ministers.*

THE Book of Consecration of Archbishops and Bishops, and Ordering of Priests and Deacons, lately set forth in the time of *Edward* the Sixth, and confirmed at the same time by authority of Parliament, doth contain all things necessary to such Consecration

XIX. *Of Consecration and Ordination.*[30]

THE Book of Consecration of Bishops and Ordering of Priests and Deacons, excepting such parts as require any Oaths inconsistent with the American revolution, is to be adopted, as containing all things necessary to such Consecration and Ordering.

[29]This note, with the brackets, was adopted with the Articles in 1801.

[30]The Convention had adopted the title, "Of Consecration and Ordination of Bishops and Ministers."

the authority of the Magistrate, and woundeth the consciences of the weak brethren.

Every particular or national Church hath authority to ordain, change, and abolish, Ceremonies or Rites of the Church ordained only by man's authority, so that all things be done to edifying.

ART. XXXV. *Of the Homilies.*

THE Second Book of Homilies, the several titles whereof we have joined under this Article, doth contain a godly and wholesome Doctrine, and necessary for these times, as doth the former Book of Homilies, which were set forth in the time of *Edward the Sixth;* and therefore we judge them to be read in Church by the Ministers, diligently and distinctly, that they may be understanded of the people.

Of the Names of the Homilies

1 *Of the right Use of the Church.*
2 *Against Peril of Idolatry.*
3 *Of repairing and keeping clean of Churches.*
4 *Of good Works: first of Fasting.*
5 *Against Gluttony and Drunkenness.*
6 *Against Excess of Apparel.*
7 *Of Prayer.*
8 *Of the Place and Time of Prayer.*
9 *That Common Prayers and Sacraments ought to be ministered in a known tongue.*
10 *Of the reverend Estimation of God's Word.*
11 *Of Alms-doing.*
12 *Of the Nativity of Christ.*
13 *Of the Passion of Christ.*
14 *Of the Resurrection of Christ.*
15 *Of the worthy receiving of the Sacrament of the Body and Blood of Christ.*
16 *Of the Gifts of the Holy Ghost.*
17 *For the Rogation-days.*
18 *Of the State of Matrimony.*
19 *Of Repentance.*
20 *Against Idleness.*
21 *Against Rebellion.*

[This Article is received in this Church, so far as it declares the Books of Homilies to be an explication of Christian doctrine, and instructive in piety and morals. But all references to the constitution and laws of England are considered as inapplicable to the circumstances of this Church; which also suspends the order for the reading of said Homilies in churches, until a revision of them may be conveniently made, for the clearing of them, as well from obsolete words and phrases, as from the local references.][29]

ART. XXXVI. *Of Consecration of Bishops and Ministers.*

THE Book of Consecration of Bishops, and Ordering of Priests and Deacons, as set forth by the General Convention of this Church in 1792, doth contain all things necessary to such Consecration and Ordering; neither hath it any thing that, of itself, is superstitious and

and Ordering: neither hath it any thing, that of itself is superstitious and ungodly. And therefore whosoever are consecrated or ordered according to the Rites of that Book, since the second year of the forenamed King *Edward* unto this time, or hereafter shall be consecrated or ordered according to the same Rites; we decree all such to be rightly, orderly, and lawfully consecrated and ordered.

XXXVII. *Of the civil Magistrates.*

THE King's Majesty hath the chief power in this Realm of *England,* and other his Dominions, unto whom the chief Government of all Estates of this Realm, whether they be Ecclesiastical or Civil, in all causes doth appertain, and is not, nor ought to be, subject to any foreign Jurisdiction.

Where we attribute to the King's Majesty the chief government, by which Titles we understand the minds of some slanderous folks to be offended; we give not to our Princes the ministering either of God's Word, or of the Sacraments, the which thing the Injunctions also lately set forth by *Elizabeth* our Queen do most plainly testify; but that only prerogative, which we see to have been given always to all godly Princes in holy Scriptures by God himself; that is, that they should rule all states and degrees committed to their charge by God, whether they be Ecclesiastical or Temporal, and restrain with the civil sword the stubborn and evil-doers.

The bishop of *Rome* hath no jurisdiction in this Realm of *England.*

The Laws of the Realm may punish Christian men with death, for heinous and grievous offences.

It is lawful for Christian men, at the commandment of the Magistrate, to wear weapons, and serve in the wars.

XXXVIII. *Of Christian Men's Goods, which are not common.*

THE Riches and Goods of Christians are not common, as touching the right, title, and possession of the same; as certain Anabaptists do falsely boast. Notwithstanding, every man ought, of such things as he possesseth, liberally to give alms to the poor, according to his ability.

XXXIX. *Of a Christian Man's Oath.*

AS we confess that vain and rash Swearing is forbidden Christian men by our Lord Jesus Christ, and *James* his Apostle, so we judge, that Christian Religion doth not prohibit, but that a man may swear when the Magistrate requireth, in a cause of faith and charity, so it be done according to the Prophet's teaching, in justice, judgment, and truth.

XX. *Of a Christian Man's Oath.*

THE Christian Religion doth not prohibit any man from taking an oath, when required by the Magistrate in testimony of truth; but all vain and rash swearing is forbidden by the Holy Scriptures.

THE RATIFICATION.

THIS Book of Articles before rehearsed, is again approved, and allowed to be holden and executed within the Realm, by the assent and consent of our Sovereign Lady ELIZA-

[31]Italics removed in 1928.

ungodly. And, therefore, whosoever are consecrated or ordered according to said Form, we decree all such to be rightly, orderly, and lawfully consecrated and ordered.

ART. XXXVII. *Of the Power of the Civil Magistrates.*

THE Power of the Civil Magistrate extendeth to all men, as well Clergy as Laity, in all things temporal; but hath no authority in things purely spiritual. And we hold it to be the duty of all men who are professors of the Gospel, to pay respectful obedience to the Civil Authority, regularly and legitimately constituted.

ART. XXXVIII. *Of Christian Men's Goods, which are not common.*

THE Riches and Goods of Christians are not common, as touching the right, title, and possession of the same; as certain Anabaptists do falsely boast. Notwithstanding, every man ought, of such things as he possesseth, liberally to give alms to the poor, according to his ability.

ART. XXXIX. *Of a Christian Man's Oath.*

AS we confess that vain and rash Swearing is forbidden Christian men by our Lord Jesus Christ, and *James*[31] his Apostle, so we judge, that Christian Religion doth not prohibit, but that a man may swear when the Magistrate requireth, in a cause of faith and charity, so it be done according to the Prophet's teaching, in justice, judgment, and truth.

BETH, by the grace of God, of England, France, and Ireland, queen, Defender of the Faith, &c. Which Articles were deliberately read and confirmed again by the subscription of the hands of the Archbishop and Bishops of the Upper-house, and by the subscription of the whole Clergy of the Nether-house in their Convocation, in the Year of our Lord, 1571.

A TABLE OF THE ARTICLES.

The Psalter

1789-1871	1892

THE PSALTER,

OR

PSALMS OF DAVID.

THE FIRST DAY.

Morning Prayer.

Psalm i. *Beatus vir, qui non abiit.*

BLESSED is the man that hath not walked in the counsel of the ungodly, nor stood in the way of sinners, and hath not sat in the seat of the scornful.

2 But his delight is in the law of the LORD ; and in his law will he exercise himself day and night.

3 And he shall be like a tree planted by the water-side, that will bring forth his fruit in due season.

4 His leaf also shall not wither ; and look, whatsoever he doeth, it shall prosper.

5 As for the ungodly, it is not so with them ; but they are like the chaff, which the wind scattereth away from the face of the earth.

6 Therefore the ungodly shall not be able to stand in the judgment, neither the sinners in the congregation of the righteous.

7 But the LORD knoweth the way of the righteous ; and the way of the ungodly shall perish.

The Psalter,

OR

PSALMS OF DAVID

THE FIRST DAY.

Morning Prayer.

PSALM 1. *Beatus vir qui non abiit.*

BLESSED is the man that hath not walked in the counsel of the ungodly, nor stood in the way of sinners : and hath not sat in the seat of the scornful.

2 But his delight is in the law of the LORD : and in his law will he exercise himself day and night.

3 And he shall be like a tree planted by the water-side : that will bring forth his fruit in due season.

4 His leaf also shall not wither : and look, whatsoever he doeth, it shall prosper.

5 As for the ungodly, it is not so with them : but they are like the chaff, which the wind scattereth away from the face of the earth.

6 Therefore the ungodly shall not be able to stand in the judgment : neither the sinners in the congregation of the righteous.

7 But the LORD knoweth the way of the righteous : and the way of the ungodly shall perish.

The Psalter

190, 191

1928

The Psalter or Psalms of David

BOOK I.

The First Day.

Morning Prayer.

Psalm 1. *Beatus vir qui non abiit.*

BLESSED is the man that hath not walked in the
counsel of the ungodly, nor stood in the way of
sinners, * and hath not sat in the seat of the scornful.
2 But his delight is in the law of the LORD; * and in
his law will he exercise himself day and night.
3 And he shall be like a tree planted by the water-
side, * that will bring forth his fruit in due season.
4 His leaf also shall not wither; * and look, whatsoever he doeth, it shall prosper.
5 As for the ungodly, it is not so with them; * but
they are like the chaff, which the wind scattereth away
from the face of the earth.
6 Therefore the ungodly shall not be able to stand
in the judgment, * neither the sinners in the congregation of the righteous.
7 But the LORD knoweth the way of the righteous; * and the way of the ungodly shall perish.

1979

The Psalter

Book One

First Day: Morning Prayer

1 *Beatus vir qui non abiit*

1 Happy are they who have not walked in the counsel of
the wicked, *
nor lingered in the way of sinners,
nor sat in the seats of the scornful!

2 Their delight is in the law of the LORD, *
and they meditate on his law day and night.

3 They are like trees planted by streams of water,
bearing fruit in due season, with leaves that do not wither; *
everything they do shall prosper.

4 It is not so with the wicked; *
they are like chaff which the wind blows away.

5 Therefore the wicked shall not stand upright when
judgment comes, *
nor the sinner in the council of the righteous.

6 For the LORD knows the way of the righteous, *
but the way of the wicked is doomed.

1789-1871

Psalm ii. *Quare fremuerunt gentes?*

WHY do thé heathen so furiously rage together? and why do the people imagine a vain thing?

2 The kings of the earth stand up, and the rulers take counsel together against the LORD, and against his Anointed :

3 Let us break their bonds asunder, and cast away their cords from us.

4 He that dwelleth in heaven shall laugh them to scorn : the Lord shall have them in derision.

5 Then shall he speak unto them in his wrath, and vex them in his sore displeasure.

6 Yet have I set my King upon my holy hill of Sion.

7 I will preach the law, whereof the LORD hath said unto me, Thou art my Son, this day have I begotten thee.

8 Desire of me, and I shall give thee the heathen for thine inheritance, and the utmost parts of the earth for thy possession.

9 Thou shalt bruise them with a rod of iron, and break them in pieces like a potter's vessel.

10 Be wise now therefore, O ye kings ; be learned, ye that are judges of the earth.

11 Serve the LORD in fear, and rejoice unto him with reverence.

12 Kiss the Son, lest he be angry, and so ye perish from the right way, if his wrath be kindled, yea but a little. Blessed[1] are all they that put their trust in him.

1892

PSALM 2. *Quare fremuerunt gentes?*

WHY do the heathen so furiously rage together : and why do the people imagine a vain thing?

2 The kings of the earth stand up, and the rulers take counsel together : against the LORD, and against his Anointed :

3 Let us break their bonds asunder : and cast away their cords from us.

4 He that dwelleth in heaven shall laugh them to scorn : the Lord shall have them in derision.

5 Then shall he speak unto them in his wrath : and vex them in his sore displeasure :

6 Yet have I set my King : upon my holy hill of Sion.

7 I will preach the law, whereof the LORD hath said unto me : Thou art my Son, this day have I begotten thee.

8 Desire of me, and I shall give thee the heathen for thine inheritance : and the utmost parts of the earth for thy possession.

9 Thou shalt bruise them with a rod of iron : and break them in pieces like a potter's vessel.

10 Be wise now therefore, O ye kings : be learned, ye that are judges of the earth.

11 Serve the LORD in fear : and rejoice unto him with reverence.

12 Kiss the Son, lest he be angry, and so ye perish from the right way : if his wrath be kindled, yea but a little. Blessed are all they that put their trust in him.

1789-1871

Psalm iii. *Domine, quid multiplicati?*

LORD, how are they increased that trouble me! many are they that rise against me.

2 Many one there be that say of my soul, There is no help for him in his God.

3 But thou, O LORD, art my defender ; thou art my worship, and the lifter up of my head.

4 I did call upon the LORD with my voice, and he heard me out of his holy hill.

5 I laid me down and slept, and rose up again ; for the LORD sustained me.

1892

PSALM 3. *Domine, quid multiplicati?*

LORD, how are they increased that trouble me : many are they that rise against me.

2 Many one there be that say of my soul : There is no help for him in his God.

3 But thou, O LORD, art my defender : thou art my worship, and the lifter up of my head.

4 I did call upon the LORD with my voice : and he heard me out of his holy hill.

5 I laid me down and slept, and rose up again : for the LORD sustained me.

[1]"little. blessed" prior to 1845.

1928

Psalm 2. *Quare fremuerunt gentes?*

WHY do the heathen so furiously rage together? * and why do the people imagine a vain thing?

2 The kings of the earth stand up, and the rulers take counsel together * against the LORD, and against his Anointed:

3 Let us break their bonds asunder, * and cast away their cords from us.

4 He that dwelleth in heaven shall laugh them to scorn: * the Lord shall have them in derision.

5 Then shall he speak unto them in his wrath, * and vex them in his sore displeasure:

6 Yet have I set my King * upon my holy hill of Sion.

7 I will rehearse the decree; * the LORD hath said unto me, Thou art my Son, this day have I begotten thee.

8 Desire of me, and I shall give thee the nations for thine inheritance, * and the utmost parts of the earth for thy possession.

9 Thou shalt bruise them with a rod of iron, * and break them in pieces like a potter's vessel.

10 Be wise now therefore, O ye kings; * be instructed, ye that are judges of the earth.

11 Serve the LORD in fear, * and rejoice unto him with reverence.

12 Kiss the Son, lest he be angry, and so ye perish from the right way, if his wrath be kindled, yea but a little. * Blessed are all they that put their trust in him.

1979

2 *Quare fremuerunt gentes?*

1 Why are the nations in an uproar? *
Why do the peoples mutter empty threats?

2 Why do the kings of the earth rise up in revolt,
and the princes plot together, *
against the LORD and against his Anointed?

3 "Let us break their yoke," they say; *
"let us cast off their bonds from us."

4 He whose throne is in heaven is laughing; *
the LORD has them in derision.

5 Then he speaks to them in his wrath, *
and his rage fills them with terror.

6 "I myself have set my king *
upon my holy hill of Zion."

7 Let me announce the decree of the LORD: *
he said to me, "You are my Son;
this day have I begotten you.

8 Ask of me, and I will give you the nations for your inheritance *
and the ends of the earth for your possession.

9 You shall crush them with an iron rod *
and shatter them like a piece of pottery."

10 And now, you kings, be wise; *
be warned, you rulers of the earth.

11 Submit to the LORD with fear, *
and with trembling bow before him;

12 Lest he be angry and you perish; *
for his wrath is quickly kindled.

13 Happy are they all *
who take refuge in him!

1928

Psalm 3. *Domine, quid multiplicati?*

LORD, how are they increased that trouble me! * many are they that rise against me.

2 Many one there be that say of my soul, * There is no help for him in his God.

3 But thou, O LORD, art my defender; * thou art my worship, and the lifter up of my head.

4 I did call upon the LORD with my voice, * and he heard me out of his holy hill.

5 I laid me down and slept, and rose up again; * for the LORD sustained me.

1979

3 *Domine, quid multiplicati*

1 LORD, how many adversaries I have! *
how many there are who rise up against me!

2 How many there are who say of me, *
"There is no help for him in his God."

3 But you, O LORD, are a shield about me; *
you are my glory, the one who lifts up my head.

4 I call aloud upon the LORD, *
and he answers me from his holy hill;

5 I lie down and go to sleep; *
I wake again, because the LORD sustains me.

1789-1871

6 I will not be afraid for ten thousands of the people, that have set themselves against me round about.

7 Up, LORD, and help me, O my God! For thou smitest all mine enemies upon the cheek-bone ; thou hast broken the teeth of the ungodly.

8 Salvation belongeth unto the LORD ; and thy blessing is upon thy people.

Psalm iv. *Cum invocarem.*

HEAR me, when I call, O God of my righteousness : thou hast set me at liberty, when I was in trouble ; have mercy upon me, and hearken unto my prayer.

2 O ye sons of men, how long will ye blaspheme mine honour, and have such pleasure in vanity, and seek after falsehood?[2]

3 Know this also, that the LORD hath chosen to himself the man that is godly ; when I call upon the LORD he will hear me.

4 Stand in awe, and sin not ; commune with your own heart, and in your chamber, and be still.

5 Offer the sacrifice of righteousness, and put your trust in the LORD.

6 There be many that say, Who will show us any good?

7 LORD, lift thou up the light of thy countenance upon us.

8 Thou hast put gladness in my heart, since the time that their corn, and wine and oil increased.

9 I will lay me down in peace, and take my rest ; for it is thou, LORD, only, that makest me dwell in safety.

Psalm v. *Verba mea auribus.*

PONDER my words, O LORD, consider my meditation.

2 O hearken thou unto the voice of my calling, my King and my God : for unto thee will I make my prayer.

3 My voice shalt thou hear betimes, O LORD ; early in the morning will I direct my prayer unto thee, and will look up.

4 For thou art the God that hast no pleasure in wickedness ; neither shall any evil dwell with thee.

5 Such as be foolish shall not stand in thy sight ; for thou hatest all them that work vanity.

[2]"leasing" in the English book (1775).

1892

6 I will not be afraid for ten thousands of the people : that have set themselves against me round about.

7 Up, LORD, and help me, O my God : for thou smitest all mine enemies upon the cheek-bone ; thou hast broken the teeth of the ungodly.

8 Salvation belongeth unto the LORD : and thy blessing is upon thy people.

PSALM 4. *Cum invocarem.*

HEAR me when I call, O God of my righteousness : thou hast set me at liberty when I was in trouble ; have mercy upon me, and hearken unto my prayer.

2 O ye sons of men, how long will ye blaspheme mine honour : and have such pleasure in vanity, and seek after falsehood?

3 Know this also, that the LORD hath chosen to himself the man that is godly : when I call upon the LORD he will hear me.

4 Stand in awe, and sin not : commune with your own heart, and in your chamber, and be still.

5 Offer the sacrifice of righteousness : and put your trust in the LORD.

6 There be many that say : Who will show us any good?

7 LORD, lift thou up : the light of thy countenance upon us.

8 Thou hast put gladness in my heart : since the time that their corn and wine and oil increased.

9 I will lay me down in peace, and take my rest : for it is thou, LORD, only, that makest me dwell in safety.

PSALM 5. *Verba mea auribus.*

PONDER my words, O LORD : consider my meditation.

2 O hearken thou unto the voice of my calling, my King and my God : for unto thee will I make my prayer.

3 My voice shalt thou hear betimes, O LORD : early in the morning will I direct my prayer unto thee, and will look up.

4 For thou art the God that hast no pleasure in wickedness : neither shall any evil dwell with thee.

5 Such as be foolish shall not stand in thy sight : for thou hatest all them that work vanity.

6 I will not be afraid for ten thousands of the people, * that have set themselves against me round about.

7 Up, LORD, and help me, O my God, * for thou smitest all mine enemies upon the cheek-bone; thou hast broken the teeth of the ungodly.

8 Salvation belongeth unto the LORD; * and thy blessing is upon thy people.

6 I do not fear the multitudes of people *
who set themselves against me all around.

7 Rise up, O LORD; set me free, O my God; *
surely, you will strike all my enemies across the face,
you will break the teeth of the wicked.

8 Deliverance belongs to the LORD. *
Your blessing be upon your people!

Psalm 4. *Cum invocarem.*

HEAR me when I call, O God of my righteousness: * thou hast set me at liberty when I was in trouble; have mercy upon me, and hearken unto my prayer.

2 O ye sons of men, how long will ye blaspheme mine honour, * and have such pleasure in vanity, and seek after falsehood?

3 Know this also, that the LORD hath chosen to himself the man that is godly; * when I call upon the LORD he will hear me.

4 Stand in awe, and sin not; * commune with your own heart, and in your chamber, and be still.

5 Offer the sacrifice of righteousness, * and put your trust in the LORD.

6 There be many that say, * Who will show us any good?

7 LORD, lift thou up * the light of thy countenance upon us.

8 Thou hast put gladness in my heart; * yea, more than when their corn and wine and oil increase.

9 I will lay me down in peace, and take my rest; * for it is thou, LORD, only, that makest me dwell in safety.

4 *Cum invocarem*

1 Answer me when I call, O God, defender of my cause; *
you set me free when I am hard-pressed;
have mercy on me and hear my prayer.

2 "You mortals, how long will you dishonor my glory; *
how long will you worship dumb idols
and run after false gods?"

3 Know that the LORD does wonders for the faithful; *
when I call upon the LORD, he will hear me.

4 Tremble, then, and do not sin; *
speak to your heart in silence upon your bed.

5 Offer the appointed sacrifices *
and put your trust in the LORD.

6 Many are saying,
"Oh that we might see better times!" *
Lift up the light of your countenance upon us, O LORD.

7 You have put gladness in my heart, *
more than when grain and wine and oil increase.

8 I lie down in peace; at once I fall asleep; *
for only you, LORD, make me dwell in safety.

Psalm 5. *Verba mea auribus.*

PONDER my words, O LORD, * consider my meditation.

2 O hearken thou unto the voice of my calling, my King and my God; * for unto thee will I make my prayer.

3 My voice shalt thou hear betimes, O LORD; * early in the morning will I direct my prayer unto thee, and will look up.

4 For thou art the God that hast no pleasure in wickedness; * neither shall any evil dwell with thee.

5 Such as be foolish shall not stand in thy sight; * for thou hatest all them that work iniquity.

5 *Verba mea auribus*

1 Give ear to my words, O LORD; *
consider my meditation.

2 Hearken to my cry for help, my King and my God, *
for I make my prayer to you.

3 In the morning, LORD, you hear my voice; *
early in the morning I make my appeal and watch for you.

4 For you are not a God who takes pleasure in wickedness, *
and evil cannot dwell with you.

5 Braggarts cannot stand in your sight; *
you hate all those who work wickedness.

1789-1871

6 Thou shalt destroy them that speak lies :[3] the LORD will abhor both the blood-thirsty and deceitful man.

7 But as for me, I will come into thine house, even upon the multitude of thy mercy ; and in thy fear will I worship toward thy holy temple.

8 Lead me, O LORD, in thy righteousness, because of mine enemies ; make thy way plain before my face.

9 For there is no faithfulness in his mouth ; their inward parts are very wickedness.

10 Their throat is an open sepulchre ; they flatter with their tongue.

11 Destroy thou them, O God ; let them perish through their own imaginations ; cast them out in the multitude of their ungodliness ; for they have rebelled against thee.

12 And let all them that put their trust in thee rejoice : they shall ever be giving of thanks, because thou defendest them ; they that love thy Name shall be joyful in thee ;

13 For thou, LORD, wilt give thy blessing unto the righteous, and with thy favourable kindness wilt thou defend him, as with a shield.

1892

6 Thou shalt destroy them that speak lies : the LORD will abhor both the blood-thirsty and deceitful man.

7 But as for me, I will come into thine house, even upon the multitude of thy mercy : and in thy fear will I worship toward thy holy temple.

8 Lead me, O LORD, in thy righteousness, because of mine enemies : make thy way plain before my face.

9 For there is no faithfulness in his mouth : their inward parts are very wickedness.

10 Their throat is an open sepulchre : they flatter with their tongue.

11 Destroy thou them, O God ; let them perish through their own imaginations : cast them out in the multitude of their ungodliness ; for they have rebelled against thee.

12 And let all them that put their trust in thee rejoice : they shall ever be giving of thanks, because thou defendest them ; they that love thy Name shall be joyful in thee ;

13 For thou, LORD, wilt give thy blessing unto the righteous : and with thy favourable kindness wilt thou defend him as with a shield.

1789-1871

Evening Prayer.

Psalm vi. *Domine, ne in furore.*

O LORD, rebuke me not in thine indignation, neither chasten me in thy displeasure.

2 Have mercy upon me, O LORD, for I am weak ; O LORD, heal me, for my bones are vexed.

3 My soul also is sore troubled : but, LORD, how long wilt thou punish me?

4 Turn thee, O LORD, and deliver my soul ; O save me, for thy mercy's[4] sake.

5 For in death no man remembereth thee ; and who will give thee thanks in the pit?

6 I am weary of my groaning : every night wash I my bed, and water my couch with my tears.

7 My beauty is gone for very trouble, and worn away because of all mine enemies.

8 Away from me, all ye that work vanity ; for the LORD hath heard the voice of my weeping.

1892

Evening Prayer.

PSALM 6. *Domine, ne in furore.*

O LORD, rebuke me not in thine indignation : neither chasten me in thy displeasure.

2 Have mercy upon me, O LORD, for I am weak : O LORD, heal me, for my bones are vexed.

3 My soul also is sore troubled : but, LORD, how long wilt thou punish me?

4 Turn thee, O LORD, and deliver my soul : O save me, for thy mercy's sake.

5 For in death no man remembereth thee : and who will give thee thanks in the pit?

6 I am weary of my groaning ; every night wash I my bed : and water my couch with my tears.

7 My beauty is gone for very trouble : and worn away because of all mine enemies.

8 Away from me, all ye that work vanity : for the LORD hath heard the voice of my weeping.

[3] "leasing" in the English book.

[4] "mercies" prior to 1822 ; "mercies'" prior to 1845.

1928

6 Thou shalt destroy them that speak lies: * the LORD will abhor both the blood-thirsty and deceitful man.

7 But as for me, in the multitude of thy mercy I will come into thine house; * and in thy fear will I worship toward thy holy temple.

8 Lead me, O LORD, in thy righteousness, because of mine enemies; * make thy way plain before my face.

9 For there is no faithfulness in their mouth; * their inward parts are very wickedness.

10 Their throat is an open sepulchre; * they flatter with their tongue.

11 Destroy thou them, O God; let them perish through their own imaginations; * cast them out in the multitude of their ungodliness; for they have rebelled against thee.

12 And let all them that put their trust in thee rejoice: * they shall ever be giving of thanks, because thou defendest them; they that love thy Name shall be joyful in thee;

13 For thou, LORD, wilt give thy blessing unto the righteous, * and with thy favourable kindness wilt thou defend him as with a shield.

Evening Prayer.

Psalm 6. *Domine, ne in furore.*

O LORD, rebuke me not in thine indignation, * neither chasten me in thy displeasure.

2 Have mercy upon me, O LORD, for I am weak; * O LORD, heal me, for my bones are vexed.

3 My soul also is sore troubled: * but, LORD, how long wilt thou punish me?

4 Turn thee, O LORD, and deliver my soul; * O save me, for thy mercy's sake.

5 For in death no man remembereth thee; * and who will give thee thanks in the pit?

6 I am weary of my groaning; * every night wash I my bed, and water my couch with my tears.

7 My beauty is gone for very trouble, * and worn away because of all mine enemies.

8 Away from me, all ye that work iniquity; * for the LORD hath heard the voice of my weeping.

1979

6 You destroy those who speak lies; *
the bloodthirsty and deceitful, O LORD, you abhor.

7 But as for me, through the greatness of your mercy I will
go into your house; *
I will bow down toward your holy temple in awe of you.

8 Lead me, O LORD, in your righteousness,
because of those who lie in wait for me; *
make your way straight before me.

9 For there is no truth in their mouth; *
there is destruction in their heart;

10 Their throat is an open grave; *
they flatter with their tongue.

11 Declare them guilty, O God; *
let them fall, because of their schemes.

12 Because of their many transgressions cast them out, *
for they have rebelled against you.

13 But all who take refuge in you will be glad; *
they will sing out their joy for ever.

14 You will shelter them, *
so that those who love your Name may exult in you.

15 For you, O LORD, will bless the righteous; *
you will defend them with your favor as with a shield.

First Day: Evening Prayer

6 *Domine, ne in furore*

1 LORD, do not rebuke me in your anger; *
do not punish me in your wrath.

2 Have pity on me, LORD, for I am weak; *
heal me, LORD, for my bones are racked.

3 My spirit shakes with terror; *
how long, O LORD, how long?

4 Turn, O LORD, and deliver me; *
save me for your mercy's sake.

5 For in death no one remembers you; *
and who will give you thanks in the grave?

6 I grow weary because of my groaning; *
every night I drench my bed
and flood my couch with tears.

7 My eyes are wasted with grief *
and worn away because of all my enemies.

8 Depart from me, all evildoers, *
for the LORD has heard the sound of my weeping.

1789-1871

9 The LORD hath heard my petition ; the LORD will receive my prayer.

10 All mine enemies shall be confounded, and sore vexed ; they shall be turned back, and put to shame suddenly.

Psalm vii. *Domine, Deus meus.*

O LORD my God, in thee have I put my trust : save me from all them that persecute me, and deliver me ;

2 Lest he devour my soul like a lion, and tear it in pieces, while there is none to help.

3 O LORD my God, if I have done any such thing ; or if there be any wickedness in my hands ;

4 If I have rewarded evil unto him that dealt friendly with me ; yea, I have delivered him that without any cause is mine enemy ;

5 Then let mine enemy persecute my soul, and take me ; yea, let him tread my life down upon the earth, and lay mine honour in the dust.

6 Stand up, O LORD, in thy wrath, and lift up thyself, because of the indignation of mine enemies ; arise up for me in the judgment that thou hast commanded.

7 And so shall the congregation of the people come about thee : for their sakes therefore lift up thyself again.

8 The LORD shall judge the people : give sentence with me, O LORD, according to my righteousness, and according to the innocency that is in me.

9 O let the wickedness of the ungodly come to an end ; but guide thou the just.

10 For the righteous God trieth the very hearts and reins.

11 My help cometh of God, who preserveth them that are true of heart.

12 God is a righteous Judge, strong and patient ; and God is provoked every day.

13 If a man will not turn, he will whet his sword ; he hath bent his bow, and made it ready.

14 He hath prepared for him the instruments of death ; he ordaineth his arrows against the persecutors.

15 Behold, he travaileth with mischief ; he hath conceived sorrow, and brought forth ungodliness.

16 He hath graven and digged up a pit, and is fallen himself into the destruction that he made for other.

1892

9 The LORD hath heard my petition : the LORD will receive my prayer.

10 All mine enemies shall be confounded, and sore vexed : they shall be turned back, and put to shame suddenly.

PSALM 7. *Domine, Deus meus.*

O LORD my God, in thee have I put my trust : save me from all them that persecute me, and deliver me ;

2 Lest he devour my soul like a lion, and tear it in pieces : while there is none to help.

3 O LORD my God, if I have done any such thing : or if there be any wickedness in my hands ;

4 If I have rewarded evil unto him that dealt friendly with me : yea, I have delivered him that without any cause is mine enemy ;

5 Then let mine enemy persecute my soul, and take me : yea, let him tread my life down upon the earth, and lay mine honour in the dust.

6 Stand up, O LORD, in thy wrath, and lift up thyself, because of the indignation of mine enemies : arise up for me in the judgment that thou hast commanded.

7 And so shall the congregation of the people come about thee : for their sakes therefore lift up thyself again.

8 The LORD shall judge the people ; give sentence with me, O LORD : according to my righteousness, and according to the innocency that is in me.

9 O let the wickedness of the ungodly come to an end : but guide thou the just.

10 For the righteous God : trieth the very hearts and reins.

11 My help cometh of God : who preserveth them that are true of heart.

12 God is a righteous Judge, strong and patient : and God is provoked every day.

13 If a man will not turn, he will whet his sword : he hath bent his bow, and made it ready.

14 He hath prepared him the instruments of death : he ordaineth his arrows against the persecutors.

15 Behold, he travaileth with mischief : he hath conceived sorrow, and brought forth ungodliness.

16 He hath graven and digged up a pit : and is fallen himself into the destruction that he made for other.

1928

9 The LORD hath heard my petition; * the LORD will receive my prayer.

10 All mine enemies shall be confounded, and sore vexed; * they shall be turned back, and put to shame suddenly.

Psalm 7. *Domine, Deus meus.*

O LORD my God, in thee have I put my trust: * save me from all them that persecute me, and deliver me;

2 Lest he devour my soul like a lion, and tear it in pieces, * while there is none to help.

3 O LORD my God, if I have done any such thing; * or if there be any wickedness in my hands;

4 If I have rewarded evil unto him that dealt friendly with me; * (yea, I have delivered him that without any cause is mine enemy;)

5 Then let mine enemy persecute my soul, and take me; * yea, let him tread my life down upon the earth, and lay mine honour in the dust.

6 Stand up, O LORD, in thy wrath, and lift up thyself, because of the indignation of mine enemies; * arise up for me in the judgment that thou hast commanded.

7 And so shall the congregation of the peoples come about thee: * for their sakes therefore lift up thyself again.

8 The LORD shall judge the peoples: give sentence with me, O LORD, * according to my righteousness, and according to the innocency that is in me.

9 O let the wickedness of the ungodly come to an end; * but guide thou the just.

10 For the righteous God * trieth the very hearts and reins.

11 My help cometh of God, * who preserveth them that are true of heart.

12 God is a righteous Judge, strong and patient; * and God is provoked every day.

13 If a man will not turn, he will whet his sword; * he hath bent his bow, and made it ready.

14 He hath prepared him the instruments of death; * he ordaineth his arrows against the persecutors.

15 Behold, the ungodly travaileth with iniquity; * he hath conceived mischief, and brought forth falsehood.

16 He hath graven and digged up a pit, * and is fallen himself into the destruction that he made for other.

1979

9 The LORD has heard my supplication; *
the LORD accepts my prayer.

10 All my enemies shall be confounded and quake with fear; *
they shall turn back and suddenly be put to shame.

7 *Domine, Deus Meus*

1 O LORD my God, I take refuge in you; *
save and deliver me from all who pursue me;

2 Lest like a lion they tear me in pieces *
and snatch me away with none to deliver me.

3 O LORD my God, if I have done these things: *
if there is any wickedness in my hands,

4 If I have repaid my friend with evil, *
or plundered him who without cause is my enemy;

5 Then let my enemy pursue and overtake me, *
trample my life into the ground,
and lay my honor in the dust.

6 Stand up, O LORD, in your wrath; *
rise up against the fury of my enemies.

7 Awake, O my God, decree justice; *
let the assembly of the peoples gather round you.

8 Be seated on your lofty throne, O Most High; *
O LORD, judge the nations.

9 Give judgment for me according to my
righteousness, O LORD, *
and according to my innocence, O Most High.

10 Let the malice of the wicked come to an end,
but establish the righteous; *
for you test the mind and heart, O righteous God.

11 God is my shield and defense; *
he is the savior of the true in heart.

12 God is a righteous judge; *
God sits in judgment every day.

13 If they will not repent, God will whet his sword; *
he will bend his bow and make it ready.

14 He has prepared his weapons of death; *
he makes his arrows shafts of fire.

15 Look at those who are in labor with wickedness, *
who conceive evil, and give birth to a lie.

16 They dig a pit and make it deep *
and fall into the hole that they have made.

17 For his travail shall come upon his own head, and his wickedness shall fall on his own pate.
18 I will give thanks unto the LORD, according to his righteousness; and I will praise the Name of the LORD Most High.

Psalm viii. *Domine, Dominus noster.*

O LORD, our Governor, how excellent is thy Name in all the world; thou that hast set thy glory above the heavens!
2 Out of the mouth of very babes and sucklings hast thou ordained strength, because of thine enemies, that thou mightest still the enemy and the avenger.
3 For I will consider thy heavens, even the works of thy fingers; the moon and the stars which thou hast ordained.
4 What is man, that thou art mindful of him? and the son of man, that thou visitest him?
5 Thou madest him lower than the angels, to crown him with glory and worship.
6 Thou makest him to have dominion of the works of thy hands; and thou hast put all things in subjection under his feet;
7 All sheep and oxen; yea, and the beasts of the field;
8 The fowls of the air, and the fishes of the sea; and whatsoever walketh through the paths of the seas.
9 O LORD our Governor, how excellent is thy Name in all the world!

THE SECOND DAY.

Morning Prayer.

Psalm ix. *Confitebor tibi.*

I WILL give thanks unto thee, O LORD, with my whole heart; I will speak of all thy marvellous works.
2 I will be glad and rejoice in thee; yea, my songs will I make of thy Name, O thou Most Highest.
3 While mine enemies are driven back, they shall fall and perish at thy presence.
4 For thou hast maintained my right and my cause; thou art set in the throne that judgest right.
5 Thou hast rebuked the heathen, and destroyed the ungodly; thou hast put out their name for ever and ever.

17 For his travail shall come upon his own head: and his wickedness shall fall on his own pate.
18 I will give thanks unto the LORD, according to his righteousness: and I will praise the Name of the LORD Most High.

PSALM 8. *Domine, Dominus noster.*

O LORD our Governor, how excellent is thy Name in all the world: thou that hast set thy glory above the heavens!
2 Out of the mouth of very babes and sucklings hast thou ordained strength, because of thine enemies: that thou mightest still the enemy and the avenger.
3 For I will consider thy heavens, even the works of thy fingers: the moon and the stars which thou hast ordained.
4 What is man, that thou art mindful of him: and the son of man, that thou visitest him?
5 Thou madest him lower than the angels: to crown him with glory and worship.
6 Thou makest him to have dominion of the works of thy hands: and thou hast put all things in subjection under his feet:
7 All sheep and oxen: yea, and the beasts of the field;
8 The fowls of the air, and the fishes of the sea: and whatsoever walketh through the paths of the seas.
9 O LORD our Governor: how excellent is thy Name in all the world!

THE SECOND DAY.

Morning Prayer.

PSALM 9. *Confitebor tibi.*

I WILL give thanks unto thee, O LORD, with my whole heart: I will speak of all thy marvellous works.
2 I will be glad and rejoice in thee: yea, my songs will I make of thy Name, O thou Most Highest.
3 While mine enemies are driven back: they shall fall and perish at thy presence.
4 For thou hast maintained my right and my cause: thou art set in the throne that judgest right.
5 Thou hast rebuked the heathen, and destroyed the ungodly: thou hast put out their name for ever and ever.

17 For his travail shall come upon his own head, * and his wickedness shall fall on his own pate.

18 I will give thanks unto the LORD, according to his righteousness; * and I will praise the Name of the LORD Most High.

Psalm 8. *Domine, Dominus noster.*

O LORD our Governor, how excellent is thy Name in all the world; * thou that hast set thy glory above the heavens!

2 Out of the mouth of very babes and sucklings hast thou ordained strength, because of thine enemies, * that thou mightest still the enemy and the avenger.

3 When I consider thy heavens, even the work of thy fingers; * the moon and the stars which thou hast ordained;

4 What is man, that thou art mindful of him? * and the son of man, that thou visitest him?

5 Thou madest him lower than the angels, * to crown him with glory and worship.

6 Thou makest him to have dominion of the works of thy hands; * and thou hast put all things in subjection under his feet:

7 All sheep and oxen; * yea, and the beasts of the field;

8 The fowls of the air, and the fishes of the sea; * and whatsoever walketh through the paths of the seas.

9 O LORD our Governor, * how excellent is thy Name in all the world!

The Second Day.

Morning Prayer.

Psalm 9. *Confitebor tibi.*

I WILL give thanks unto thee, O LORD, with my whole heart; * I will speak of all thy marvellous works.

2 I will be glad and rejoice in thee; * yea, my songs will I make of thy Name, O thou Most Highest.

3 While mine enemies are driven back, * they shall fall and perish at thy presence.

4 For thou hast maintained my right and my cause; * thou art set in the throne that judgest right.

5 Thou hast rebuked the heathen, and destroyed the ungodly; * thou hast put out their name for ever and ever.

17 Their malice turns back upon their own head; *
their violence falls on their own scalp.

18 I will bear witness that the LORD is righteous; *
I will praise the Name of the LORD Most High.

8 *Domine, Dominus noster*

1 O LORD our Governor, *
how exalted is your Name in all the world!

2 Out of the mouths of infants and children *
your majesty is praised above the heavens.

3 You have set up a stronghold against your adversaries, *
to quell the enemy and the avenger.

4 When I consider your heavens, the work of your fingers, *
the moon and the stars you have set in their courses,

5 What is man that you should be mindful of him? *
the son of man that you should seek him out?

6 You have made him but little lower than the angels; *
you adorn him with glory and honor;

7 You give him mastery over the works of your hands; *
you put all things under his feet:

8 All sheep and oxen, *
even the wild beasts of the field,

9 The birds of the air, the fish of the sea, *
and whatsoever walks in the paths of the sea.

10 O LORD our Governor, *
how exalted is your Name in all the world!

Second Day: Morning Prayer

9 *Confitebor tibi*

1 I will give thanks to you, O LORD, with my whole heart; *
I will tell of all your marvelous works.

2 I will be glad and rejoice in you; *
I will sing to your Name, O Most High.

3 When my enemies are driven back, *
they will stumble and perish at your presence.

4 For you have maintained my right and my cause; *
you sit upon your throne judging right.

5 You have rebuked the ungodly and destroyed the wicked; *
you have blotted out their name for ever and ever.

1789-1871

6 O thou enemy, destructions are come to a perpetual end ; even as the cities which thou hast destroyed, their memorial is perished with them.

7 But the LORD shall endure for ever ; he hath also prepared his seat for judgment.

8 For he shall judge the world in righteousness, and minister true judgment unto the people.

9 The LORD also will be a defence for the oppressed, even a refuge in due time of trouble.

10 And they that know thy Name will put their trust in thee ; for thou, LORD, hast never failed them that seek thee.

11 O praise the LORD which dwelleth in Sion ; show the people of his doings.

12 For when he maketh inquisition for blood, he remembereth them, and forgetteth not the complaint of the poor.

13 Have mercy upon me, O LORD ; consider the trouble which I suffer of them that hate me, thou that liftest me up from the gates of death ;

14 That I may show all thy praises within the ports of the daughter of Sion : I will rejoice in thy salvation.

15 The heathen are sunk down in the pit that they made ; in the same net which they hid privily is their foot taken.

16 The LORD is known to execute judgment ; the ungodly is trapped in the work of his own hands.

17 The wicked shall be turned into hell, and all the people that forget God.

18 For the poor shall not alway be forgotten ; the patient abiding of the meek shall not perish for ever.

19 Up, LORD, and let not man have the upper hand ; let the heathen be judged in thy sight.

20 Put them in fear, O LORD, that the heathen may know themselves to be but men.

Psalm x. *Ut quid, Domine?*

WHY standest thou so far off, O LORD, and hidest thy face in the needful time of trouble?

2 The ungodly, for his own lust, doth persecute the poor : let them be taken in the crafty wiliness that they have imagined.

3 For the ungodly hath made boast of his own heart's desire, and speaketh good of the covetous, whom GOD abhorreth.

4 The ungodly is so proud, that he careth not for God, neither is God in all his thoughts.

1892

6 O thou enemy, destructions are come to a perpetual end : even as the cities which thou hast destroyed, their memorial is perished with them.

7 But the LORD shall endure for ever : he hath also prepared his seat for judgment.

8 For he shall judge the world in righteousness : and minister true judgment unto the people.

9 The LORD also will be a defence for the oppressed : even a refuge in due time of trouble.

10 And they that know thy Name will put their trust in thee : for thou, LORD, hast never failed them that seek thee.

11 O praise the LORD which dwelleth in Sion : show the people of his doings.

12 For when he maketh inquisition for blood, he remembereth them : and forgetteth not the complaint of the poor.

13 Have mercy upon me, O LORD ; consider the trouble which I suffer of them that hate me : thou that liftest me up from the gates of death ;

14 That I may show all thy praises within the ports of the daughter of Sion : I will rejoice in thy salvation.

15 The heathen are sunk down in the pit that they made : in the same net which they hid privily is their foot taken.

16 The LORD is known to execute judgment : the ungodly is trapped in the work of his own hands.

17 The wicked shall be turned into hell : and all the people that forget God.

18 For the poor shall not alway be forgotten : the patient abiding of the meek shall not perish for ever.

19 Up, LORD, and let not man have the upper hand : let the heathen be judged in thy sight.

20 Put them in fear, O LORD : that the heathen may know themselves to be but men.

PSALM 10. *Ut quid, Domine?*

WHY standest thou so far off, O LORD : and hidest thy face in the needful time of trouble?

2 The ungodly, for his own lust, doth persecute the poor : let them be taken in the crafty wiliness that they have imagined.

3 For the ungodly hath made boast of his own heart's desire : and speaketh good of the covetous, whom God abhorreth.

4 The ungodly is so proud, that he careth not for God : neither is God in all his thoughts.

6 O thou enemy, thy destructions are come to a perpetual end; * even as the cities which thou hast destroyed, whose memorial is perished with them.

7 But the LORD shall endure for ever; * he hath also prepared his seat for judgment.

8 For he shall judge the world in righteousness, * and minister true judgment unto the people.

9 The LORD also will be a defence for the oppressed, * even a refuge in due time of trouble.

10 And they that know thy Name will put their trust in thee; * for thou, LORD, hast never failed them that seek thee.

11 O praise the LORD which dwelleth in Sion; * show the people of his doings.

12 For when he maketh inquisition for blood, he remembereth them, * and forgetteth not the complaint of the poor.

13 Have mercy upon me, O LORD; consider the trouble which I suffer of them that hate me, * thou that liftest me up from the gates of death;

14 That I may show all thy praises within the gates of the daughter of Sion: * I will rejoice in thy salvation.

15 The heathen are sunk down in the pit that they made; * in the same net which they hid privily is their foot taken.

16 The LORD is known to execute judgment; * the ungodly is trapped in the work of his own hands.

17 The wicked shall be turned to destruction, * and all the people that forget God.

18 For the poor shall not alway be forgotten; * the patient abiding of the meek shall not perish for ever.

19 Up, LORD, and let not man have the upper hand; * let the heathen be judged in thy sight.

20 Put them in fear, O LORD, * that the heathen may know themselves to be but men.

6 As for the enemy, they are finished, in perpetual ruin, *
their cities ploughed under, the memory of them perished;

7 But the LORD is enthroned for ever; *
he has set up his throne for judgment.

8 It is he who rules the world with righteousness; *
he judges the peoples with equity.

9 The LORD will be a refuge for the oppressed, *
a refuge in time of trouble.

10 Those who know your Name will put their trust in you, *
for you never forsake those who seek you, O LORD.

11 Sing praise to the LORD who dwells in Zion; *
proclaim to the peoples the things he has done.

12 The Avenger of blood will remember them; *
he will not forget the cry of the afflicted.

13 Have pity on me, O LORD; *
see the misery I suffer from those who hate me,
O you who lift me up from the gate of death;

14 So that I may tell of all your praises
and rejoice in your salvation *
in the gates of the city of Zion.

15 The ungodly have fallen into the pit they dug, *
and in the snare they set is their own foot caught.

16 The LORD is known by his acts of justice; *
the wicked are trapped in the works of their own hands.

17 The wicked shall be given over to the grave, *
and also all the peoples that forget God.

18 For the needy shall not always be forgotten, *
and the hope of the poor shall not perish for ever.

19 Rise up, O LORD, let not the ungodly have the upper hand; *
let them be judged before you.

20 Put fear upon them, O LORD; *
let the ungodly know they are but mortal.

Psalm 10. *Ut quid, Domine?*

WHY standest thou so far off, O LORD, * and hidest thy face in the needful time of trouble?

2 The ungodly, for his own lust, doth persecute the poor: * let them be taken in the crafty wiliness that they have imagined.

3 For the ungodly hath made boast of his own heart's desire, * and speaketh good of the covetous, whom the LORD abhorreth.

4 The ungodly is so proud, that he careth not for God, * neither is God in all his thoughts.

10 *Ut quid, Domine?*

1 Why do you stand so far off, O LORD, *
and hide yourself in time of trouble?

2 The wicked arrogantly persecute the poor, *
but they are trapped in the schemes they have devised.

3 The wicked boast of their heart's desire; *
the covetous curse and revile the LORD.

4 The wicked are so proud that they care not for God; *
their only thought is, "God does not matter."

5 His ways are alway[5] grievous ; thy judgments are far above out of his sight, and therefore defieth he all his enemies.

6 For he hath said in his heart, Tush! I shall never be cast down, there shall no harm happen unto me.

7 His mouth is full of cursing, deceit, and fraud ; under his tongue is ungodliness and vanity.

8 He sitteth lurking in the thievish corners of the streets, and privily in his lurking dens doth he murder the innocent ; his eyes are set against the poor.

9 For he lieth waiting secretly ; even as a lion lurketh he in his den, that he may ravish the poor.

10 He doth ravish the poor, when he getteth him into his net.

11 He falleth down, and humbleth himself, that the congregation of the poor may fall into the hands of his captains.

12 He hath said in his heart, Tush! God hath forgotten ; he hideth away his face, and he will never see it.

13 Arise, O LORD God, and lift up thine hand ; forget not the poor.

14 Wherefore should the wicked blaspheme God, while he doth say in his heart, Tush! thou God carest not for it?

15 Surely thou hast seen it ; for thou beholdest ungodliness and wrong,

16 That thou mayest take the matter into thy hand : the poor committeth himself unto thee ; for thou art the helper of the friendless.

17 Break thou the power of the ungodly and malicious ; take away his ungodliness, thou shalt find none.

18 The LORD is King for ever and ever, and the heathen are perished out of the land.

19 LORD, thou hast heard the desire of the poor ; thou preparest their heart, and thine ear hearkeneth thereto ;

20 To help the fatherless and poor unto their right, that the man of the earth be no more exalted against them.

5 His ways are alway grievous : thy judgments are far above out of his sight, and therefore defieth he all his enemies.

6 For he hath said in his heart, Tush, I shall never be cast down : there shall no harm happen unto me.

7 His mouth is full of cursing, deceit, and fraud : under his tongue is ungodliness and vanity.

8 He sitteth lurking in the thievish corners of the streets : and privily in his lurking dens doth he murder the innocent ; his eyes are set against the poor.

9 For he lieth waiting secretly ; even as a lion lurketh he in his den : that he may ravish the poor.

10 He doth ravish the poor : when he getteth him into his net.

11 He falleth down, and humbleth himself : that the congregation of the poor may fall into the hands of his captains.

12 He hath said in his heart, Tush, God hath forgotten : he hideth away his face, and he will never see it.

13 Arise, O LORD God, and lift up thine hand : forget not the poor.

14 Wherefore should the wicked blaspheme God : while he doth say in his heart, Tush, thou God carest not for it?

15 Surely thou hast seen it : for thou beholdest ungodliness and wrong,

16 That thou mayest take the matter into thy hand : the poor committeth himself unto thee ; for thou art the helper of the friendless.

17 Break thou the power of the ungodly and malicious : take away his ungodliness, and thou shalt find none.

18 The LORD is King for ever and ever : and the heathen are perished out of the land.

19 LORD, thou hast heard the desire of the poor : thou preparest their heart, and thine ear hearkeneth thereto ;

20 To help the fatherless and poor unto their right : that the man of the earth be no more exalted against them.

Psalm xi. *In Domino confido.*

IN the LORD put I my trust ; how say ye then to my soul, that she should flee as a bird unto the hill?

2 For lo, the ungodly bend their bow, and make ready their arrows within the quiver, that they may privily shoot at them which are true of heart.

3 For the foundations will be cast down ; and what hath the righteous done?

PSALM 11. *In Domino confido.*

IN the LORD put I my trust : how say ye then to my soul, that she should flee as a bird unto the hill?

2 For lo, the ungodly bend their bow, and make ready their arrows within the quiver : that they may privily shoot at them which are true of heart.

3 For the foundations will be cast down : and what hath the righteous done?

[5] "always" in the English book.

1928

5 His ways are alway grievous; * thy judgments are far above out of his sight, and therefore defieth he all his enemies.

6 For he hath said in his heart, Tush, I shall never be cast down, * there shall no harm happen unto me.

7 His mouth is full of cursing, deceit, and fraud; * under his tongue is ungodliness and vanity.

8 He sitteth lurking in the thievish corners of the streets, * and privily in his lurking dens doth he murder the innocent; his eyes are set against the poor.

9 For he lieth waiting secretly; even as a lion lurketh he in his den, * that he may ravish the poor.

10 He doth ravish the poor, * when he getteth him into his net.

11 He falleth down, and humbleth himself, * that the congregation of the poor may fall into the hands of his captains.

12 He hath said in his heart, Tush, God hath forgotten; * he hideth away his face, and he will never see it.

13 Arise, O LORD God, and lift up thine hand; * forget not the poor.

14 Wherefore should the wicked blaspheme God, * while he doth say in his heart, Tush, thou God carest not for it?

15 Surely thou hast seen it; * for thou beholdest ungodliness and wrong, that thou mayest take the matter into thy hand.

16 The poor committeth himself unto thee; * for thou art the helper of the friendless.

17 Break thou the power of the ungodly and malicious; * search out his ungodliness, until thou find none.

18 The LORD is King for ever and ever, * and the heathen are perished out of the land.

19 LORD, thou hast heard the desire of the poor; * thou preparest their heart, and thine ear hearkeneth;

20 To help the fatherless and poor unto their right, * that the man of the earth be no more exalted against them.

1979

5 Their ways are devious at all times;
your judgments are far above out of their sight; *
they defy all their enemies.

6 They say in their heart, "I shall not be shaken; *
no harm shall happen to me ever."

7 Their mouth is full of cursing, deceit, and oppression; *
under their tongue are mischief and wrong.

8 They lurk in ambush in public squares
and in secret places they murder the innocent; *
they spy out the helpless.

9 They lie in wait, like a lion in a covert;
they lie in wait to seize upon the lowly; *
they seize the lowly and drag them away in their net.

10 The innocent are broken and humbled before them; *
the helpless fall before their power.

11 They say in their heart, "God has forgotten; *
he hides his face; he will never notice."

12 Rise up, O LORD;
lift up your hand, O God; *
do not forget the afflicted.

13 Why should the wicked revile God? *
why should they say in their heart, "You do not care"?

14 Surely, you behold trouble and misery; *
you see it and take it into your own hand.

15 The helpless commit themselves to you, *
for you are the helper of orphans.

16 Break the power of the wicked and evil; *
search out their wickedness until you find none.

17 The LORD is King for ever and ever; *
the ungodly shall perish from his land.

18 The LORD will hear the desire of the humble; *
you will strengthen their heart and your ears shall hear;

19 To give justice to the orphan and oppressed, *
so that mere mortals may strike terror no more.

Psalm 11. *In Domino confido.*

IN the LORD put I my trust; * how say ye then to my soul, that she should flee as a bird unto the hill?

2 For lo, the ungodly bend their bow, and make ready their arrows within the quiver, * that they may privily shoot at them which are true of heart.

3 If the foundations be destroyed, * what can the righteous do?

11 *In Domino confido*

1 In the LORD have I taken refuge; *
how then can you say to me,
"Fly away like a bird to the hilltop;

2 For see how the wicked bend the bow
and fit their arrows to the string, *
to shoot from ambush at the true of heart.

3 When the foundations are being destroyed, *
what can the righteous do?"

4 The LORD is in his holy temple ; the LORD'S seat is in heaven.
5 His eyes consider the poor, and his eyelids try the children of men.
6 The LORD alloweth the righteous: but the ungodly, and him that delighteth in wickedness, doth his soul abhor.
7 Upon the ungodly he shall rain snares, fire and brimstone, storm and tempest: this shall be their portion to drink.
8 For the righteous LORD loveth righteousness ; his countenance will behold the thing that is just.

4 The LORD is in his holy temple : the LORD'S seat is in heaven.
5 His eyes consider the poor : and his eyelids try the children of men.
6 The LORD alloweth the righteous: but the ungodly, and him that delighteth in wickedness, doth his soul abhor.
7 Upon the ungodly he shall rain snares, fire and brimstone, storm and tempest: this shall be their portion to drink.
8 For the righteous LORD loveth righteousness : his countenance will behold the thing that is just.

Evening Prayer.

Psalm xii. *Salvum me fac.*

HELP me, LORD, for there is not one godly man left ; for the faithful are minished from among the children of men.
2 They talk of vanity every one with his neighbour ; they do but flatter with their lips, and dissemble in their double heart.
3 The LORD shall root out all deceitful lips, and the tongue that speaketh proud things :
4 Which have said, With our tongue will we prevail ; we are they that ought to speak : who is lord over us?
5 Now, for the comfortless troubles' sake of the needy, and because of the deep sighing of the poor,
6 I will up, saith the LORD ; and will help every one from him that swelleth against him, and will set him at rest.
7 The words of the LORD are pure words ; even as the silver which from the earth is tried, and purified seven times in the fire.
8 Thou shalt keep them, O LORD ; thou shalt preserve him from this generation for ever.
9 The ungodly walk on every side : when they are exalted, the children of men are put to rebuke.

Evening Prayer.

PSALM 12. *Salvum me fac.*

HELP me, LORD, for there is not one godly man left : for the faithful are minished from among the children of men.
2 They talk of vanity every one with his neighbour : they do but flatter with their lips, and dissemble in their double heart.
3 The LORD shall root out all deceitful lips : and the tongue that speaketh proud things ;
4 Which have said, With our tongue will we prevail : we are they that ought to speak, who is lord over us?
5 Now, for the comfortless troubles' sake of the needy : and because of the deep sighing of the poor,
6 I will up, saith the LORD : and will help every one from him that swelleth against him, and will set him at rest.
7 The words of the LORD are pure words : even as the silver which from the earth is tried, and purified seven times in the fire.
8 Thou shalt keep them, O LORD: thou shalt preserve him from this generation for ever.
9 The ungodly walk on every side : when they are exalted, the children of men are put to rebuke.

Psalm xiii. *Usque quo, Domine?*

HOW long wilt thou forget me, O LORD ; for ever? how long wilt thou hide thy face from me?
2 How long shall I seek counsel in my soul, and be so vexed in my heart? how long shall mine enemies triumph over me?

PSALM 13. *Usquequo, Domine?*

HOW long wilt thou forget me, O LORD ; for ever : how long wilt thou hide thy face from me?
2 How long shall I seek counsel in my soul, and be so vexed in my heart : how long shall mine enemies triumph over me?

4 The LORD is in his holy temple; * the LORD'S seat is in heaven.

5 His eyes consider the poor, * and his eyelids try the children of men.

6 The LORD approveth the righteous: * but the ungodly, and him that delighteth in wickedness, doth his soul abhor.

7 Upon the ungodly he shall rain snares, fire and brimstone, storm and tempest: * this shall be their portion to drink.

8 For the righteous LORD loveth righteousness; * his countenance will behold the thing that is just.

4 The LORD is in his holy temple; *
the LORD'S throne is in heaven.

5 His eyes behold the inhabited world; *
his piercing eye weighs our worth.

6 The LORD weighs the righteous as well as the wicked, *
but those who delight in violence he abhors.

7 Upon the wicked he shall rain coals of fire and
burning sulphur; *
a scorching wind shall be their lot.

8 For the LORD is righteous;
he delights in righteous deeds; *
and the just shall see his face.

Evening Prayer.

Psalm 12. *Salvum me fac.*

HELP me, LORD, for there is not one godly man left; * for the faithful are minished from among the children of men.

2 They talk of vanity every one with his neighbour; * they do but flatter with their lips, and dissemble in their double heart.

3 The LORD shall root out all deceitful lips, * and the tongue that speaketh proud things;

4 Which have said, With our tongue will we prevail; * we are they that ought to speak; who is lord over us?

5 Now, for the comfortless troubles' sake of the needy, * and because of the deep sighing of the poor,

6 I will up, saith the LORD; * and will help every one from him that swelleth against him, and will set him at rest.

7 The words of the LORD are pure words; * even as the silver which from the earth is tried, and purified seven times in the fire.

8 Thou shalt keep them, O LORD; * thou shalt preserve them from this generation for ever.

9 The ungodly walk on every side: * when they are exalted, the children of men are put to rebuke.

Second Day: Evening Prayer

12 *Salvum me fac*

1 Help me, LORD, for there is no godly one left; *
the faithful have vanished from among us.

2 Everyone speaks falsely with his neighbor; *
with a smooth tongue they speak from a double heart.

3 Oh, that the LORD would cut off all smooth tongues, *
and close the lips that utter proud boasts!

4 Those who say, "With our tongue will we prevail; *
our lips are our own; who is lord over us?"

5 "Because the needy are oppressed,
and the poor cry out in misery, *
I will rise up," says the LORD,
"and give them the help they long for."

6 The words of the LORD are pure words, *
like silver refined from ore
and purified seven times in the fire.

7 O LORD, watch over us *
and save us from this generation for ever.

8 The wicked prowl on every side, *
and that which is worthless is highly prized by everyone.

Psalm 13. *Usquequo, Domine?*

HOW long wilt thou forget me, O LORD; for ever? * how long wilt thou hide thy face from me?

2 How long shall I seek counsel in my soul, and be so vexed in my heart? * how long shall mine enemy triumph over me?

13 *Usquequo, Domine?*

1 How long, O LORD?
will you forget me for ever? *
how long will you hide your face from me?

2 How long shall I have perplexity in my mind,
and grief in my heart, day after day? *
how long shall my enemy triumph over me?

3 Consider, and hear me, O LORD my God ; lighten mine eyes, that I sleep not in death ;
4 Lest mine enemy say, I have prevailed against him : for if I be cast down, they that trouble me will rejoice at it.
5 But my trust is in thy mercy, and my heart is joyful in thy salvation.
6 I will sing of the LORD, because he hath dealt so lovingly with me ; yea, I will praise the Name of the Lord most Highest.

Psalm xiv. *Dixit insipiens.*

THE fool hath said in his heart, There is no God.
2 They are corrupt, and become abominable in their doings ; there is none that doeth good, no not one.
3 The LORD looked down from heaven upon the children of men, to see if there were any that would understand, and seek after God :
4 But they are all gone out of the way, they are altogether become abominable ; there is none that doeth good, no not one.
5 Their throat is an open sepulchre ; with their tongues have they deceived : the poison of asps is under their lips.
6 Their mouth is full of cursing and bitterness ; their feet are swift to shed blood.
7 Destruction and unhappiness is in their ways, and the way of peace have they not known ; there is no fear of God before their eyes.
8 Have they no knowledge, that they are all such workers of mischief, eating up my people as it were bread, and call not upon the LORD?
9 There were they brought in great fear, even where no fear was ; for God is in the generation of the righteous.
10 As for you, ye have made a mock at the counsel of the poor ; because he putteth his trust in the LORD.
11 Who shall give salvation unto Israel out of Sion? When the LORD turneth the captivity of his people, then shall Jacob rejoice, and Israel shall be glad.

THE THIRD DAY.

Morning Prayer.

Psalm xv. *Domine, quis habitabit?*

LORD, who shall dwell in thy tabernacle? or who shall rest upon thy holy hill?
2 Even he that leadeth an uncorrupt life, and doeth the thing which is right, and speaketh the truth from his heart.

3 Consider, and hear me, O LORD my God : lighten mine eyes, that I sleep not in death ;
4 Lest mine enemy say, I have prevailed against him : for if I be cast down, they that trouble me will rejoice at it.
5 But my trust is in thy mercy : and my heart is joyful in thy salvation.
6 I will sing of the LORD, because he hath dealt so lovingly with me : yea, I will praise the Name of the Lord most highest.

PSALM 14. *Dixit insipiens.*

THE fool hath said in his heart : There is no God.
2 They are corrupt, and become abominable in their doings : there is none that doeth good, no not one.
3 The LORD looked down from heaven upon the children of men : to see if there were any that would understand, and seek after God.
4 But they are all gone out of the way, they are altogether become abominable : there is none that doeth good, no not one.
5 Their throat is an open sepulchre ; with their tongues have they deceived : the poison of asps is under their lips.
6 Their mouth is full of cursing and bitterness : their feet are swift to shed blood.
7 Destruction and unhappiness is in their ways, and the way of peace have they not known : there is no fear of God before their eyes.
8 Have they no knowledge, that they are all such workers of mischief : eating up my people as it were bread, and call not upon the LORD?
9 There were they brought in great fear, even where no fear was : for God is in the generation of the righteous.
10 As for you, ye have made a mock at the counsel of the poor : because he putteth his trust in the LORD.
11 Who shall give salvation unto Israel out of Sion? When the LORD turneth the captivity of his people : then shall Jacob rejoice, and Israel shall be glad.

THE THIRD DAY.

Morning Prayer.

PSALM 15. *Domine, quis habitabit?*

LORD, who shall dwell in thy tabernacle : or who shall rest upon thy holy hill?
2 Even he that leadeth an uncorrupt life : and doeth the thing which is right, and speaketh the truth from his heart.

3 Consider, and hear me, O LORD my God; * lighten mine eyes, that I sleep not in death;
4 Lest mine enemy say, I have prevailed against him: * for if I be cast down, they that trouble me will rejoice at it.
5 But my trust is in thy mercy, * and my heart is joyful in thy salvation.
6 I will sing of the LORD, because he hath dealt so lovingly with me; * yea, I will praise the Name of the Lord Most Highest.

3 Look upon me and answer me, O LORD my God; *
give light to my eyes, lest I sleep in death;

4 Lest my enemy say, "I have prevailed over him," *
and my foes rejoice that I have fallen.

5 But I put my trust in your mercy; *
my heart is joyful because of your saving help.

6 I will sing to the LORD, for he has dealt with me richly; *
I will praise the Name of the Lord Most High.

Psalm 14. *Dixit insipiens.*

THE fool hath said in his heart, * There is no God.
2 They are corrupt, and become abominable in their doings; * there is none that doeth good, no not one.
3 The LORD looked down from heaven upon the children of men, * to see if there were any that would understand, and seek after God.
4 But they are all gone out of the way, they are altogether become abominable; * there is none that doeth good, no not one.
5 Have they no knowledge, that they are all such workers of mischief, * eating up my people as it were bread, and call not upon the LORD?
6 There were they brought in great fear, even where no fear was; * for God is in the generation of the righteous.
7 As for you, ye have made a mock at the counsel of the poor; * because he putteth his trust in the LORD.
8 Who shall give salvation unto Israel out of Sion? * When the LORD turneth the captivity of his people, then shall Jacob rejoice, and Israel shall be glad.

14 *Dixit insipiens*

1 The fool has said in his heart, "There is no God." *
All are corrupt and commit abominable acts;
there is none who does any good.

2 The LORD looks down from heaven upon us all, *
to see if there is any who is wise,
if there is one who seeks after God.

3 Every one has proved faithless;
all alike have turned bad; *
there is none who does good; no, not one.

4 Have they no knowledge, all those evildoers *
who eat up my people like bread
and do not call upon the LORD?

5 See how they tremble with fear, *
because God is in the company of the righteous.

6 Their aim is to confound the plans of the afflicted, *
but the LORD is their refuge.

7 Oh, that Israel's deliverance would come out of Zion! *
when the LORD restores the fortunes of his people,
Jacob will rejoice and Israel be glad.

The Third Day.

Morning Prayer.

Psalm 15. *Domine, quis habitabit?*

LORD, who shall dwell in thy tabernacle? * or who shall rest upon thy holy hill?
2 Even he that leadeth an uncorrupt life, * and doeth the thing which is right, and speaketh the truth from his heart.

Third Day: Morning Prayer

15 *Domine, quis habitabit?*

1 LORD, who may dwell in your tabernacle? *
who may abide upon your holy hill?

2 Whoever leads a blameless life and does what is right, *
who speaks the truth from his heart.

3 He that hath used no deceit in his tongue, nor done evil to his neighbour, and hath not slandered his neighbour.

4 He that setteth not by himself, but is lowly in his own eyes, and maketh much of them that fear the LORD.

5 He that sweareth unto his neighbour, and disappointeth him not, though it were to his own hindrance.

6 He that hath not given his money upon usury, nor taken reward against the innocent.

7 Whoso doeth these things shall never fall.

3 He that hath used no deceit in his tongue, nor done evil to his neighbour : and hath not slandered his neighbour.

4 He that setteth not by himself, but is lowly in his own eyes : and maketh much of them that fear the LORD.

5 He that sweareth unto his neighbour, and disappointeth him not : though it were to his own hindrance.

6 He that hath not given his money upon usury : nor taken reward against the innocent.

7 Whoso doeth these things : shall never fall.

Psalm xvi. *Conserva me, Domine.*

PRESERVE me, O God ; for in thee have I put my trust.

2 O my soul, thou hast said unto the LORD, Thou art my God ; my goods are nothing unto thee.

3 All my delight is upon the saints that are in the earth, and upon such as excel in virtue.

4 But they that run after another god shall have great trouble.

5 Their drink-offerings of blood will I not offer, neither make mention of their names within my lips.

6 The LORD himself is the portion of mine inheritance, and of my cup ; thou shalt maintain my lot.

7 The lot is fallen unto me in a fair ground ; yea, I have a goodly heritage.

8 I will thank the LORD for giving me warning ; my reins also chasten me in the night-season.

9 I have set GOD alway before me ; for he is on my right hand, therefore I shall not fall.

10 Wherefore my heart was glad, and my glory rejoiced : my flesh also shall rest in hope.

11 For why? thou shalt not leave my soul in hell ; neither shall thou suffer thy Holy One to see corruption.

12 Thou shalt show me the path of life : in thy presence is the fulness of joy, and at thy right hand there is pleasure for evermore.

PSALM 16. *Conserva me, Domine.*

PRESERVE me, O God : for in thee have I put my trust.

2 O my soul, thou hast said unto the LORD : Thou art my God ; my goods are nothing unto thee.

3 All my delight is upon the saints that are in the earth : and upon such as excel in virtue.

4 But they that run after another god : shall have great trouble.

5 Their drink-offerings of blood will I not offer . neither make mention of their names within my lips.

6 The LORD himself is the portion of mine inheritance, and of my cup : thou shalt maintain my lot.

7 The lot is fallen unto me in a fair ground : yea, I have a goodly heritage.

8 I will thank the LORD for giving me warning : my reins also chasten me in the night season.

9 I have set GOD alway before me : for he is on my right hand, therefore I shall not fall.

10 Wherefore my heart was glad and my glory rejoiced : my flesh also shall rest in hope.

11 For why? thou shalt not leave my soul in hell : neither shall thou suffer thy Holy One to see corruption.

12 Thou shalt show me the path of life ; in thy presence is the fulness of joy : and at thy right hand there is pleasure for evermore.

3 He that hath used no deceit in his tongue, nor done evil to his neighbour, * and hath not slandered his neighbour.

4 He that setteth not by himself, but is lowly in his own eyes, * and maketh much of them that fear the LORD.

5 He that sweareth unto his neighbour, and disappointeth him not, * though it were to his own hindrance.

6 He that hath not given his money upon usury, * nor taken reward against the innocent.

7 Whoso doeth these things * shall never fall.

3 There is no guile upon his tongue;
he does no evil to his friend; *
he does not heap contempt upon his neighbor.

4 In his sight the wicked is rejected, *
but he honors those who fear the LORD.

5 He has sworn to do no wrong *
and does not take back his word.

6 He does not give his money in hope of gain, *
nor does he take a bribe against the innocent.

7 Whoever does these things *
shall never be overthrown.

Psalm 16. *Conserva me, Domine.*

PRESERVE me, O God; * for in thee have I put my trust.

2 O my soul, thou hast said unto the LORD, * Thou art my God; I have no good like unto thee.

3 All my delight is upon the saints that are in the earth, * and upon such as excel in virtue.

4 But they that run after another god * shall have great trouble.

5 Their drink-offerings of blood will I not offer, * neither make mention of their names within my lips.

6 The LORD himself is the portion of mine inheritance, and of my cup; * thou shalt maintain my lot.

7 The lot is fallen unto me in a fair ground; * yea, I have a goodly heritage.

8 I will thank the LORD for giving me warning; * my reins also chasten me in the night season.

9 I have set the LORD alway before me; * for he is on my right hand, therefore I shall not fall.

10 Wherefore my heart is glad and my glory rejoiceth: * my flesh also shall rest in hope.

11 For why? thou shalt not leave my soul in hell; * neither shalt thou suffer thy Holy One to see corruption.

12 Thou shalt show me the path of life: in thy presence is the fulness of joy, * and at thy right hand there is pleasure for evermore.

16 *Conserva me, Domine*

1 Protect me, O God, for I take refuge in you; *
I have said to the LORD, "You are my Lord,
my good above all other."

2 All my delight is upon the godly that are in the land, *
upon those who are noble among the people.

3 But those who run after other gods *
shall have their troubles multiplied.

4 Their libations of blood I will not offer, *
nor take the names of their gods upon my lips.

5 O LORD, you are my portion and my cup; *
it is you who uphold my lot.

6 My boundaries enclose a pleasant land; *
indeed, I have a goodly heritage.

7 I will bless the LORD who gives me counsel; *
my heart teaches me, night after night.

8 I have set the LORD always before me; *
because he is at my right hand I shall not fall.

9 My heart, therefore, is glad, and my spirit rejoices; *
my body also shall rest in hope.

10 For you will not abandon me to the grave, *
nor let your holy one see the Pit.

11 You will show me the path of life; *
in your presence there is fullness of joy,
and in your right hand are pleasures for evermore.

Psalm xvii. *Exaudi, Domine.*

HEAR the right, O LORD, consider my complaint, and hearken unto my prayer, that goeth not out of feigned lips.

2 Let my sentence come forth from thy presence ; and let thine eyes look upon the thing that is equal.

3 Thou has proved and visited mine heart in the night-season ; thou hast tried me, and shalt find no wickedness in me ; for I am utterly purposed that my mouth shall not offend.

4 Because of men's works that are done against the words of thy lips, I have kept me from the ways of the destroyer.

5 O hold thou up my goings in thy paths, that my footsteps slip not.

6 I have called upon thee, O God, for thou shalt hear me : incline thine ear to me, and hearken unto my words.

7 Show thy marvellous loving-kindness, thou that art the Saviour of them which put their trust in thee, from such as resist thy right hand.

8 Keep me as the apple of an eye ; hide me under the shadow of thy wings.

9 From the ungodly, that trouble me ; mine enemies compass me round about, to take away my soul.

10 They are inclosed in their own fat, and their mouth speaketh proud things.

11 They lie waiting in our way on every side, turning their eyes down to the ground ;

12 Like as a lion that is greedy of his prey, and as it were a lion's whelp lurking in secret places.

13 Up, LORD, disappoint him, and cast him down ; deliver my soul from the ungodly, which is a sword of thine ;

14 From the men of thy hand, O LORD, from the men, I say, and from the evil world ; which have their portion in this life, whose bellies thou fillest with thy hid treasure.

15 They have children at their desire, and leave the rest of their substance for their babes.

16 But as for me, I will behold thy presence in righteousness ; and when I awake up after thy likeness, I shall be satisfied with it.

PSALM 17. *Exaudi, Domine.*

HEAR the right, O LORD, consider my complaint : and hearken unto my prayer, that goeth not out of feigned lips.

2 Let my sentence come forth from thy presence : and let thine eyes look upon the thing that is equal.

3 Thou hast proved and visited mine heart in the night season ; thou hast tried me, and shalt find no wickedness in me : for I am utterly purposed that my mouth shall not offend.

4 Because of men's works that are done against the words of thy lips : I have kept me from the ways of the destroyer.

5 O hold thou up my goings in thy paths : that my footsteps slip not.

6 I have called upon thee, O God, for thou shalt hear me : incline thine ear to me, and hearken unto my words.

7 Show thy marvellous loving-kindness, thou that art the Saviour of them which put their trust in thee : from such as resist thy right hand.

8 Keep me as the apple of an eye : hide me under the shadow of thy wings,

9 From the ungodly, that trouble me : mine enemies compass me round about, to take away my soul.

10 They are inclosed in their own fat : and their mouth speaketh proud things.

11 They lie waiting in our way on every side : turning their eyes down to the ground ;

12 Like as a lion that is greedy of his prey : and as it were a lion's whelp lurking in secret places.

13 Up, LORD, disappoint him, and cast him down : deliver my soul from the ungodly, which is a sword of thine ;

14 From the men of thy hand, O LORD, from the men, I say, and from the evil world : which have their portion in this life, whose bellies thou fillest with thy hid treasure.

15 They have children at their desire : and leave the rest of their substance for their babes.

16 But as for me, I will behold thy presence in righteousness : and when I awake up after thy likeness, I shall be satisfied with it.

Psalm 17. *Exaudi, Domine.*

HEAR the right, O LORD, consider my complaint, * and hearken unto my prayer, that goeth not out of feigned lips.

2 Let my sentence come forth from thy presence; * and let thine eyes look upon the thing that is equal.

3 Thou has proved and visited mine heart in the night season; thou hast tried me, and shalt find no wickedness in me; * for I am utterly purposed that my mouth shall not offend.

4 As for the works of men, * by the word of thy lips I have kept me from the ways of the destroyer.

5 O hold thou up my goings in thy paths, * that my footsteps slip not.

6 I have called upon thee, O God, for thou shalt hear me: * incline thine ear to me, and hearken unto my words.

7 Show thy marvellous loving-kindness, thou that art the Saviour of them which put their trust in thee, * from such as resist thy right hand.

8 Keep me as the apple of an eye; * hide me under the shadow of thy wings,

9 From the ungodly, that trouble me; * mine enemies compass me round about, to take away my soul.

10 They are inclosed in their own fat, * and their mouth speaketh proud things.

11 They lie waiting in our way on every side, * watching to cast us down to the ground;

12 Like as a lion that is greedy of his prey, * and as it were a lion's whelp lurking in secret places.

13 Up, LORD, disappoint him, and cast him down; * deliver my soul from the ungodly, by thine own sword;

14 Yea, by thy hand, O LORD; from the men of the evil world; * which have their portion in this life, whose bellies thou fillest with thy hid treasure.

15 They have children at their desire, * and leave the rest of their substance for their babes.

16 But as for me, I shall behold thy presence in righteousness; * and when I awake up after thy likeness, I shall be satisfied.

17 *Exaudi, Domine*

1 Hear my plea of innocence, O LORD;
give heed to my cry; *
listen to my prayer, which does not come from lying lips.

2 Let my vindication come forth from your presence; *
let your eyes be fixed on justice.

3 Weigh my heart, summon me by night, *
melt me down; you will find no impurity in me.

4 I give no offense with my mouth as others do; *
I have heeded the words of your lips.

5 My footsteps hold fast to the ways of your law; *
in your paths my feet shall not stumble.

6 I call upon you, O God, for you will answer me; *
incline your ear to me and hear my words.

7 Show me your marvelous loving-kindness, *
O Savior of those who take refuge at your right hand
from those who rise up against them.

8 Keep me as the apple of your eye; *
hide me under the shadow of your wings,

9 From the wicked who assault me, *
from my deadly enemies who surround me.

10 They have closed their heart to pity, *
and their mouth speaks proud things.

11 They press me hard,
now they surround me, *
watching how they may cast me to the ground,

12 Like a lion, greedy for its prey, *
and like a young lion lurking in secret places.

13 Arise, O LORD; confront them and bring them down; *
deliver me from the wicked by your sword.

14 Deliver me, O LORD, by your hand *
from those whose portion in life is this world;

15 Whose bellies you fill with your treasure, *
who are well supplied with children
and leave their wealth to their little ones.

16 But at my vindication I shall see your face; *
when I awake, I shall be satisfied, beholding
your likeness.

1789-1871

Evening Prayer.

Psalm xviii. *Diligam te, Domine.*

I WILL love thee, O LORD, my strength. The LORD is my stony rock, and my defence, My Saviour ; my God, and my might, in whom I will trust ; my buckler, the horn also of my salvation, and my refuge.

2 I will call upon the LORD, which is worthy to be praised ; so shall I be safe from mine enemies.

3 The sorrows of death compassed me, and the overflowings of ungodliness made me afraid.

4 The pains of hell came about me ; the snares of death overtook me.

5 In my trouble I will call upon the LORD, and complain unto my God :

6 So shall he hear my voice out of his holy temple, and my complaint shall come before him ; it shall enter even into his ears.

7 The earth trembled and quaked, the very foundations also of the hills shook, and were removed, because he was wroth.

8 There went a smoke out in his presence, and a consuming fire out of his mouth, so that coals were kindled at it.

9 He bowed the heavens also, and came down, and it was dark under his feet.

10 He rode upon the Cherubim,[6] and did fly ; he came flying upon the wings of the wind.

11 He made darkness his secret place, his pavilion round about him with dark water, and thick clouds to cover him.

12 At the brightness of his presence his clouds removed ; hailstones and coals of fire.

13 The LORD also thundered out of heaven, and the Highest gave his thunder ; hailstones and coals of fire.

14 He sent out his arrows, and scattered them ; he cast forth lightnings, and destroyed them.

15 The springs of waters were seen, and the foundations of the round world were discovered at thy chiding, O LORD, at the blasting of the breath of thy displeasure.

16 He shall send down from on high to fetch me, and shall take me out of many waters.

17 He shall deliver me from my strongest enemy, and from them which hate me ; for they were too mighty for me.

[6]"Cherubins" in the English book ; "Cherubims" prior to 1793 standard.

1892

Evening Prayer.

PSALM 18. *Diligam te, Domine.*

I WILL love thee, O LORD, my strength. The LORD is my stony rock, and my defence : My Saviour, my God, and my might, in whom I will trust, my buckler, the horn also of my salvation, and my refuge.

2 I will call upon the LORD, which is worthy to be praised : so shall I be safe from mine enemies.

3 The sorrows of death compassed me : and the overflowings of ungodliness made me afraid.

4 The pains of hell came about me : the snares of death overtook me.

5 In my trouble I will call upon the LORD : and complain unto my God :

6 So he heard my voice out of his holy temple : and my complaint shall come before him ; it entered even into his ears.

7 The earth trembled and quaked : the very foundations also of the hills shook, and were removed, because he was wroth.

8 There went a smoke out in his presence : and a consuming fire out of his mouth, so that coals were kindled at it.

9 He bowed the heavens also, and came down : and it was dark under his feet.

10 He rode upon the Cherubim, and did fly : he came flying upon the wings of the wind.

11 He made darkness his secret place : his pavilion round about him with dark water, and thick clouds to cover him.

12 At the brightness of his presence his clouds removed : hailstones and coals of fire.

13 The LORD also thundered out of heaven, and the Highest gave his thunder : hailstones and coals of fire.

14 He sent out his arrows, and scattered them : he cast forth lightnings, and destroyed them.

15 The springs of waters were seen, and the foundations of the round world were discovered at thy chiding, O LORD : at the blasting of the breath of thy displeasure.

16 He shall send down from on high to fetch me : and shall take me out of many waters.

17 He shall deliver me from my strongest enemy, and from them which hate me : for they are too mighty for me.

Evening Prayer.

Psalm 18. *Diligam te, Domine.*

I WILL love thee, O LORD, my strength. * The LORD is my stony rock, and my defence;

2 My Saviour, my God, and my might, in whom I will trust; * my buckler, the horn also of my salvation, and my refuge.

3 I will call upon the LORD, which is worthy to be praised; * so shall I be safe from mine enemies.

4 The sorrows of death compassed me, * and the overflowings of ungodliness made me afraid.

5 The pains of hell came about me; * the snares of death overtook me.

6 In my trouble I called upon the LORD, * and complained unto my God:

7 So he heard my voice out of his holy temple, * and my complaint came before him; it entered even into his ears.

8 The earth trembled and quaked, * the very foundations also of the hills shook, and were removed, because he was wroth.

9 There went a smoke out in his presence, * and a consuming fire out of his mouth, so that coals were kindled at it.

10 He bowed the heavens also, and came down, * and it was dark under his feet.

11 He rode upon the Cherubim, and did fly; * he came flying upon the wings of the wind.

12 He made darkness his secret place, * his pavilion round about him with dark water, and thick clouds to cover him.

13 At the brightness of his presence his clouds removed; * hailstones and coals of fire.

14 The LORD also thundered out of heaven, and the Highest gave his thunder; * hailstones and coals of fire.

15 He sent out his arrows, and scattered them; * he cast forth lightnings, and destroyed them.

16 The springs of waters were seen, and the foundations of the round world were discovered, * at thy chiding, O LORD, at the blasting of the breath of thy displeasure.

17 He sent down from on high to fetch me, * and took me out of many waters.

Third Day: Evening Prayer

18

Part I *Diligam te, Domine.*

1 I love you, O LORD my strength, *
O LORD my stronghold, my crag, and my haven.

2 My God, my rock in whom I put my trust, *
my shield, the horn of my salvation, and my refuge;
you are worthy of praise.

3 I will call upon the LORD, *
and so shall I be saved from my enemies.

4 The breakers of death rolled over me, *
and the torrents of oblivion made me afraid.

5 The cords of hell entangled me, *
and the snares of death were set for me.

6 I called upon the LORD in my distress *
and cried out to my God for help.

7 He heard my voice from his heavenly dwelling; *
my cry of anguish came to his ears.

8 The earth reeled and rocked; *
the roots of the mountains shook;
they reeled because of his anger.

9 Smoke rose from his nostrils
and a consuming fire out of his mouth; *
hot burning coals blazed forth from him.

10 He parted the heavens and came down *
with a storm cloud under his feet.

11 He mounted on cherubim and flew; *
he swooped on the wings of the wind.

12 He wrapped darkness about him; *
he made dark waters and thick clouds his pavilion.

13 From the brightness of his presence, through the clouds, *
burst hailstones and coals of fire.

14 The LORD thundered out of heaven; *
the Most High uttered his voice.

15 He loosed his arrows and scattered them; *
he hurled thunderbolts and routed them.

16 The beds of the seas were uncovered,
and the foundations of the world laid bare, *
at your battle cry, O LORD,
at the blast of the breath of your nostrils.

17 He reached down from on high and grasped me; *
he drew me out of great waters.

1789-1871

18 They prevented me in the day of my trouble ; but the LORD was my upholder.

19 He brought me forth also into a place of liberty ; he brought me forth, even because he had a favour unto me.

20 The LORD shall reward me after my righteous dealing, according to the cleanness of my hands shall he recompense me.

21 Because I have kept the ways of the LORD, and have not forsaken my God, as the wicked doth.

22 For I have an eye unto all his laws, and will not cast out his commandments from me.

23 I was also uncorrupt before him, and eschewed mine own wickedness.

24 Therefore shall the LORD reward me after my righteous dealing, and according unto the cleanness of my hands in his eyesight.

25 With the holy thou shalt be holy, and with a perfect man thou shalt be perfect.

26 With the clean thou shalt be clean, and with the froward thou shalt learn frowardness.

27 For thou shalt save the people that are in adversity, and shalt bring down the high looks of the proud.

28 Thou also shalt light my candle ; the LORD my God shall make my darkness to be light.

29 For in thee I shall discomfit an host of men, and with the help of my God I shall leap over the wall.

30 The way of God is an undefiled way ; the word of the LORD also is tried in the fire : he is the defender of all them that put their trust in him.

31 For who is God, but the LORD? or who hath any strength, except our God?

32 It is God that girdeth me with strength of war, and maketh my way perfect.

33 He maketh my feet like harts' feet, and setteth me up on high.

34 He teacheth mine hands to fight, and mine arms shall bend even a bow of steel.

35 Thou hast given me the defence of thy salvation ; thy right hand also shall hold me up, and thy loving correction shall make me great.

36 Thou shalt make room enough under me for to go, that my footsteps shall not slide.

1892

18 They prevented me in the day of my trouble : but the LORD was my upholder.

19 He brought me forth also into a place of liberty : he brought me forth, even because he had a favour unto me.

20 The LORD shall reward me after my righteous dealing : according to the cleanness of my hands shall he recompense me.

21 Because I have kept the ways of the LORD : and have not forsaken my God, as the wicked doth.

22 For I have an eye unto all his laws : and will not cast out his commandments from me.

23 I was also uncorrupt before him : and eschewed mine own wickedness.

24 Therefore shall the LORD reward me after my righteous dealing : and according unto the cleanness of my hands in his eyesight.

25 With the holy thou shalt be holy : and with a perfect man thou shalt be perfect.

26 With the clean thou shalt be clean : and with the froward thou shalt learn frowardness.

27 For thou shalt save the people that are in adversity : and shalt bring down the high looks of the proud.

28 Thou also shalt light my candle : the LORD my God shall make my darkness to be light.

29 For in thee I shall discomfit an host of men : and with the help of my God I shall leap over the wall.

30 The way of God is an undefiled way : the word of the LORD also is tried in the fire ; he is the defender of all them that put their trust in him.

31 For who is God, but the LORD : or who hath any strength, except our God?

32 It is God that girdeth me with strength of war : and maketh my way perfect.

33 He maketh my feet like harts' feet : and setteth me up on high.

34 He teacheth mine hands to fight : and mine arms shall break even a bow of steel.

35 Thou hast given me the defence of thy salvation : thy right hand also shall hold me up, and thy loving correction shall make me great.

36 Thou shalt make room enough under me for to go : that my footsteps shall not slide.

18 He delivered me from my strongest enemy, and from them which hate me; * for they were too mighty for me.

19 They came upon me in the day of my trouble; * but the LORD was my upholder.

20 He brought me forth also into a place of liberty; * he brought me forth, even because he had a favour unto me.

21 The LORD rewarded me after my righteous dealing, * according to the cleanness of my hands did he recompense me.

22 Because I have kept the ways of the LORD, * and have not forsaken my God, as the wicked doth.

23 For I have an eye unto all his laws, * and will not cast out his commandments from me.

24 I was also uncorrupt before him, * and eschewed mine own wickedness.

25 Therefore the LORD rewarded me after my righteous dealing, * and according unto the cleanness of my hands in his eyesight.

26 With the holy thou shalt be holy, * and with a perfect man thou shalt be perfect.

27 With the clean thou shalt be clean, * and with the froward thou shalt be froward.

28 For thou shalt save the people that are in adversity, * and shalt bring down the high looks of the proud.

29 Thou also shalt light my candle; * the LORD my God shall make my darkness to be light.

30 For in thee I shall discomfit an host of men, * and with the help of my God I shall leap over the wall.

31 The way of God is an undefiled way: * the word of the LORD also is tried in the fire; he is the defender of all them that put their trust in him.

32 For who is God, but the LORD? * or who hath any strength, except our God?

33 It is God that girdeth me with strength of war, * and maketh my way perfect.

34 He maketh my feet like harts' feet, * and setteth me up on high.

35 He teacheth mine hands to fight, * and mine arms shall bend even a bow of steel.

36 Thou hast given me the defence of thy salvation; * thy right hand also shall hold me up, and thy loving correction shall make me great.

18 He delivered me from my strong enemies
and from those who hated me; *
for they were too mighty for me.

19 They confronted me in the day of my disaster; *
but the LORD was my support.

20 He brought me out into an open place; *
he rescued me because he delighted in me.

Psalm 18: Part II *Et retribuet mihi*

21 The LORD rewarded me because of my righteous dealing; *
because my hands were clean he rewarded me;

22 For I have kept the ways of the LORD *
and have not offended against my God;

23 For all his judgments are before my eyes, *
and his decrees I have not put away from me;

24 For I have been blameless with him *
and have kept myself from iniquity;

25 Therefore the LORD rewarded me according to my righteous dealing, *
because of the cleanness of my hands in his sight.

26 With the faithful you show yourself faithful, O God; *
with the forthright you show yourself forthright.

27 With the pure you show yourself pure, *
but with the crooked you are wily.

28 You will save a lowly people, *
but you will humble the haughty eyes.

29 You, O LORD, are my lamp; *
my God, you make my darkness bright.

30 With you I will break down an enclosure; *
with the help of my God I will scale any wall.

31 As for God, his ways are perfect;
the words of the LORD are tried in the fire; *
he is a shield to all who trust in him.

32 For who is God, but the LORD? *
who is the Rock, except our God?

33 It is God who girds me about with strength *
and makes my way secure.

34 He makes me sure-footed like a deer *
and lets me stand firm on the heights.

35 He trains my hands for battle *
and my arms for bending even a bow of bronze.

36 You have given me your shield of victory; *
your right hand also sustains me;
your loving care makes me great.

1789-1871

37 I will follow upon mine enemies, and overtake them ; neither will I turn again till I have destroyed them.

38 I will smite them, that they shall not be able to stand, but fall under my feet.

39 Thou hast girded me with strength unto the battle ; thou shalt throw down mine enemies under me.

40 Thou hast made mine enemies also to turn their backs upon me, and I shall destroy them that hate me.

41 They shall cry, but there shall be none to help them ; yea, even unto the LORD shall they cry, but he shall not hear them.

42 I will beat them as small as the dust before the wind : I will cast them out as the clay in the streets.

43 Thou shalt deliver me from the strivings of the people, and thou shalt make me the head of the heathen.

44 A people whom I have not known shall serve me.

45 As soon as they hear of me, they shall obey me ; but the strange children shall dissemble with me.

46 The strange children shall fail, and be afraid out of their prisons.

47 The LORD liveth ; and blessed be my strong helper, and praised be the God of my salvation :

48 Even the God that seeth that I be avenged, and subdueth the people unto me.

49 It is he that delivereth me from my cruel enemies, and setteth me up above mine adversaries : thou shalt rid me from the wicked man.

50 For this cause will I give thanks unto thee, O LORD, among the Gentiles, and sing praises unto thy Name.

51 Great prosperity giveth he unto his King, and showeth loving-kindness unto David, his Anointed, and unto his seed for evermore.

THE FOURTH DAY.

Morning Prayer.

Psalm xix. *Cæli enarrant.*

THE heavens declare the glory of God ; and the firmament showeth his handy-work.

2 One day telleth another ; and one night certifieth another.

3 There is neither speech nor language ; but their voices are heard among them.

1892

37 I will follow upon mine enemies, and overtake them : neither will I turn again till I have destroyed them.

38 I will smite them, that they shall not be able to stand : but fall under my feet.

39 Thou hast girded me with strength unto the battle : thou shalt throw down mine enemies under me.

40 Thou hast made mine enemies also to turn their backs upon me : and I shall destroy them that hate me.

41 They shall cry, but there shall be none to help them : yea, even unto the LORD shall they cry, but he shall not hear them.

42 I will beat them as small as the dust before the wind : I will cast them out as the clay in the streets.

43 Thou shalt deliver me from the strivings of the people : and thou shalt make me the head of the heathen.

44 A people whom I have not known : shall serve me.

45 As soon as they hear of me, they shall obey me : but the strange children shall dissemble with me.

46 The strange children shall fail : and be afraid out of their prisons.

47 The LORD liveth ; and blessed be my strong helper : and praised be the God of my salvation :

48 Even the God that seeth that I be avenged : and subdueth the people unto me.

49 It is he that delivereth me from my cruel enemies, and setteth me up above mine adversaries : thou shalt rid me from the wicked man.

50 For this cause will I give thanks unto thee, O LORD, among the Gentiles : and sing praises unto thy Name.

51 Great prosperity giveth he unto his King : and showeth loving-kindness unto David his anointed, and unto his seed for evermore.

THE FOURTH DAY.

Morning Prayer.

PSALM 19. *Cæli enarrant.*

THE heavens declare the glory of God : and the firmament showeth his handy-work.

2 One day telleth another : and one night certifieth another.

3 There is neither speech nor language : but their voices are heard among them.

37 Thou shalt make room enough under me for to go, * that my footsteps shall not slide.

38 I will follow upon mine enemies, and overtake them; * neither will I turn again till I have destroyed them.

39 I will smite them, that they shall not be able to stand, * but fall under my feet.

40 Thou hast girded me with strength unto the battle; * thou shalt throw down mine enemies under me.

41 Thou hast made mine enemies also to turn their backs upon me, * and I shall destroy them that hate me.

42 They shall cry, but there shall be none to help them; * yea, even unto the LORD shall they cry, but he shall not hear them.

43 I will beat them as small as the dust before the wind: * I will cast them out as the clay in the streets.

44 Thou shalt deliver me from the strivings of the people, * and thou shalt make me the head of the nations; a people whom I have not known shall serve me.

45 As soon as they hear of me, they shall obey me; * the strangers shall feign obedience unto me.

46 The strangers shall fail, * and come trembling out of their strongholds.

47 The LORD liveth; and blessed be my strong helper, * and praised be the God of my salvation;

48 Even the God that seeth that I be avenged, * and subdueth the people unto me.

49 It is he that delivereth me from my cruel enemies, and setteth me up above mine adversaries: * thou shalt rid me from the wicked man.

50 For this cause will I give thanks unto thee, O LORD, among the Gentiles, * and sing praises unto thy Name.

51 Great prosperity giveth he unto his King, * and showeth loving-kindness unto David his anointed, and unto his seed for evermore.

The Fourth Day.

Morning Prayer.

Psalm 19. *Cæli enarrant.*

THE heavens declare the glory of God; * and the firmament showeth his handy-work.

2 One day telleth another; * and one night certifieth another.

3 There is neither speech nor language; * but their voices are heard among them.

37 You lengthen my stride beneath me, *
and my ankles do not give way.

38 I pursue my enemies and overtake them; *
I will not turn back till I have destroyed them.

39 I strike them down, and they cannot rise; *
they fall defeated at my feet.

40 You have girded me with strength for the battle; *
you have cast down my adversaries beneath me;
you have put my enemies to flight.

41 I destroy those who hate me;
they cry out, but there is none to help them; *
they cry to the LORD, but he does not answer.

42 I beat them small like dust before the wind; *
I trample them like mud in the streets.

43 You deliver me from the strife of the peoples; *
you put me at the head of the nations.

44 A people I have not known shall serve me;
no sooner shall they hear than they shall obey me; *
strangers will cringe before me.

45 The foreign peoples will lose heart; *
they shall come trembling out of their strongholds.

46 The LORD lives! Blessed is my Rock! *
Exalted is the God of my salvation!

47 He is the God who gave me victory *
and cast down the peoples beneath me.

48 You rescued me from the fury of my enemies;
you exalted me above those who rose against me; *
you saved me from my deadly foe.

49 Therefore will I extol you among the nations, O LORD, *
and sing praises to your Name.

50 He multiplies the victories of his king; *
he shows loving-kindness to his anointed,
to David and his descendants for ever.

Fourth Day: Morning Prayer

19 *Cæli enarrant*

1 The heavens declare the glory of God, *
and the firmament shows his handiwork.

2 One day tells it tale to another, *
and one night imparts knowledge to another.

3 Although they have no words or language, *
and their voices are not heard,

1789-1871

4 Their sound is gone out into all lands ; and their words into the ends of the world.

5 In them hath he set a tabernacle for the sun ; which cometh forth as a bridegroom out of his chamber, and rejoiceth as a giant to run his course.

6 It goeth forth from the uttermost part of the heaven, and runneth about unto the end of it again ; and there is nothing hid from the heat thereof.

7 The law of the LORD is an undefiled law, converting the soul ; the testimony of the LORD is sure, and giveth wisdom unto the simple.

8 The statutes of the LORD are right, and rejoice the heart ; the commandment of the LORD is pure, and giveth light unto the eyes.

9 The fear of the LORD is clean, and endureth for ever ; the judgments of the LORD are true, and righteous altogether.

10 More to be desired are they than gold, yea, than much fine gold ; sweeter also than honey, and the honey-comb.

11 Moreover, by them is thy servant taught ; and in keeping of them there is great reward.

12 Who can tell how oft he offendeth? O cleanse thou me from my secret faults.

13 Keep thy servant also from presumptuous sins, lest they get the dominion over me ; so shall I be undefiled, and innocent from the great offence.

14 Let the words of mouth, and the meditation of my heart, be alway acceptable in thy sight,

15 O LORD, my strength and my redeemer.

1892

4 Their sound is gone out into all lands : and their words into the ends of the world.

5 In them hath he set a tabernacle for the sun : which cometh forth as a bridegroom out of his chamber, and rejoiceth as a giant to run his course.

6 It goeth forth from the uttermost part of the heaven, and runneth about unto the end of it again : and there is nothing hid from the heat thereof.

7 The law of the LORD is an undefiled law, converting the soul : the testimony of the LORD is sure, and giveth wisdom unto the simple.

8 The statutes of the LORD are right, and rejoice the heart : the commandment of the LORD is pure, and giveth light unto the eyes.

9 The fear of the LORD is clean, and endureth for ever : the judgments of the LORD are true, and righteous altogether.

10 More to be desired are they than gold, yea, than much fine gold : sweeter also than honey, and the honey-comb.

11 Moreover, by them is thy servant taught : and in keeping of them there is great reward.

12 Who can tell how oft he offendeth : O cleanse thou me from my secret faults.

13 Keep thy servant also from presumptuous sins, lest they get the dominion over me : so shall I be undefiled, and innocent from the great offence.

14 Let the words of mouth, and the meditation of my heart, be alway acceptable in thy sight,

15 O LORD, my strength and my redeemer.

The Psalter

Psalm xx. *Exaudiat te Dominus.*

THE LORD hear thee in the day of trouble ; the Name of the God of Jacob defend thee :

2 Send thee help from the sanctuary, and strengthen thee out of Sion :

3 Remember all thy offerings, and accept thy burnt-sacrifice :

PSALM 20. *Exaudiat te Dominus.*

THE LORD hear thee in the day of trouble : the Name of the God of Jacob defend thee :

2 Send thee help from the sanctuary : and strengthen thee out of Sion :

3 Remember all thy offerings : and accept thy burnt-sacrifice :

1928

4 Their sound is gone out into all lands; * and their words into the ends of the world.

5 In them hath he set a tabernacle for the sun; * which cometh forth as a bridegroom out of his chamber, and rejoiceth as a giant to run his course.

6 It goeth forth from the uttermost part of the heaven, and runneth about unto the end of it again; * and there is nothing hid from the heat thereof.

7 The law of the LORD is an undefiled law, converting the soul; * the testimony of the LORD is sure, and giveth wisdom unto the simple.

8 The statutes of the LORD are right, and rejoice the heart; * the commandment of the LORD is pure, and giveth light unto the eyes.

9 The fear of the LORD is clean, and endureth for ever; * the judgments of the LORD are true, and righteous altogether.

10 More to be desired are they than gold, yea, than much fine gold; * sweeter also than honey, and the honey-comb.

11 Moreover, by them is thy servant taught; * and in keeping of them there is great reward.

12 Who can tell how oft he offendeth? * O cleanse thou me from my secret faults.

13 Keep thy servant also from presumptuous sins, lest they get the dominion over me; * so shall I be undefiled, and innocent from the great offence.

14 Let the words of mouth, and the meditation of my heart, be alway acceptable in thy sight, * O LORD, my strength and my redeemer.

Psalm 20. *Exaudiat te Dominus.*

THE LORD hear thee in the day of trouble; * the Name of the God of Jacob defend thee:

2 Send thee help from the sanctuary, * and strengthen thee out of Sion:

3 Remember thy offerings, * and accept thy burnt-sacrifice:

1979

4 Their sound has gone out into all lands, *
and their message to the ends of the world.

5 In the deep has he set a pavilion for the sun; *
it comes forth like a bridegroom out of his chamber;
it rejoices like a champion to run its course.

6 It goes forth from the uttermost edge of the heavens
and runs about to the end of it again; *
nothing is hidden from its burning heat.

7 The law of the LORD is perfect
and revives the soul; *
the testimony of the LORD is sure
and gives wisdom to the innocent.

8 The statutes of the LORD are just
and rejoice the heart; *
the commandment of the LORD is clear
and gives light to the eyes.

9 The fear of the LORD is clean
and endures for ever; *
the judgments of the LORD are true
and righteous altogether.

10 More to be desired are they than gold,
more than much fine gold, *
sweeter far than honey,
than honey in the comb.

11 By them also is your servant enlightened, *
and in keeping them there is great reward.

12 Who can tell how often he offends? *
cleanse me from my secret faults.

13 Above all, keep your servant from presumptuous sins;
let them not get dominion over me; *
then shall I be whole and sound,
and innocent of a great offense.

14 Let the words of my mouth and the meditation of my heart be acceptable in your sight, *
O LORD, my strength and my redeemer.

20 *Exaudiat te Dominus*

1 May the LORD answer you in the day of trouble, *
the Name of the God of Jacob defend you;

2 Send you help from his holy place *
and strengthen you out of Zion;

3 Remember all your offerings *
and accept your burnt sacrifice;

4 Grant thee thy heart's desire, and fulfil all thy mind.

5 We will rejoice in thy salvation, and triumph in the Name of the Lord our God : the LORD perform all thy petitions.

6 Now know I that the LORD helpeth his Anointed, and will hear him from his holy heaven, even with the wholesome strength of his right hand.

7 Some put their trust in chariots, and some in horses ; but we will remember the Name of the LORD our God.

8 They are brought down and fallen ; but we are risen and stand upright.

9 Save, LORD ; and hear us, O King of heaven, when we call upon thee.

Psalm xxi. *Domine, in virtute tua.*

THE King shall rejoice in thy strength, O LORD ; exceeding glad shall he be of thy salvation.

2 Thou hast given him his heart's desire, and hast not denied him the request of his lips.

3 For thou shalt prevent him with the blessing of goodness, and shalt set a crown of pure gold upon his head.

4 He asked life of thee ; and thou gavest him a long life, even for ever and ever.

5 His honour is great in thy salvation ; glory and great worship shalt thou lay upon him.

6 For thou shalt give him everlasting felicity, and make him glad with the joy of thy countenance.

7 And why? because the King putteth his trust in the LORD ; and in the mercy of the Most Highest he shall not miscarry.

8 All thine enemies shall feel thine hand ; thy right hand shall find out them that hate thee.

9 Thou shalt make them like a fiery oven in time of thy wrath : the LORD shall destroy them in his displeasure, and the fire shall consume them.

10 Their fruit shalt thou root out of the earth, and their seed from among the children of men.

11 For they intended mischief against thee, and imagined such a device as they are not able to perform.

12 Therefore shalt thou put them to flight, and the strings of thy bow shalt thou make ready against the face of them.

4 Grant thee thy heart's desire : and fulfil all thy mind.

5 We will rejoice in thy salvation, and triumph in the Name of the Lord our God : the LORD perform all thy petitions.

6 Now know I that the LORD helpeth his anointed, and will hear him from his holy heaven : even with the wholesome strength of his right hand.

7 Some put their trust in chariots, and some in horses : but we will remember the Name of the LORD our God.

8 They are brought down and fallen : but we are risen and stand upright.

9 Save, LORD ; and hear us, O King of heaven : when we call upon thee.

PSALM 21. *Domine, in virtute tua.*

THE King shall rejoice in thy strength, O LORD : exceeding glad shall he be of thy salvation.

2 Thou hast given him his heart's desire : and hast not denied him the request of his lips.

3 For thou shalt prevent him with the blessings of goodness : and shalt set a crown of pure gold upon his head.

4 He asked life of thee ; and thou gavest him a long life : even for ever and ever.

5 His honour is great in thy salvation : glory and great worship shalt thou lay upon him.

6 For thou shalt give him everlasting felicity : and make him glad with the joy of thy countenance.

7 And why? because the King putteth his trust in the LORD : and in the mercy of the Most Highest he shall not miscarry.

8 All thine enemies shall feel thine hand : thy right hand shall find out them that hate thee.

9 Thou shalt make them like a fiery oven in time of thy wrath : the LORD shall destroy them in his displeasure, and the fire shall consume them.

10 Their fruit shalt thou root out of the earth : and their seed from among the children of men.

11 For they intended mischief against thee : and imagined such a device as they are not able to perform.

12 Therefore shalt thou put them to flight : and the strings of thy bow shalt thou make ready against the face of them.

4 Grant thee thy heart's desire, * and fulfil all thy mind.

5 We will rejoice in thy salvation, and triumph in the Name of the Lord our God: * the LORD perform all thy petitions.

6 Now know I that the LORD helpeth his anointed, and will hear him from his holy heaven, * even with the wholesome strength of his right hand.

7 Some put their trust in chariots, and some in horses: * but we will remember the Name of the LORD our God.

8 They are brought down and fallen; * but we are risen and stand upright.

9 Save, LORD; and hear us, O King of heaven, * when we call upon thee.

4 Grant you your heart's desire *
and prosper all your plans.

5 We will shout for joy at your victory
and triumph in the Name of our God; *
may the LORD grant all your requests.

6 Now I know that the LORD gives victory to his anointed; *
he will answer him out of his holy heaven,
with the victorious strength of his right hand.

7 Some put their trust in chariots and some in horses, *
but we will call upon the Name of the LORD our God.

8 They collapse and fall down, *
but we will arise and stand upright.

9 O LORD, give victory to the king *
and answer us when we call.

Psalm 21. *Domine, in virtute tua.*

THE King shall rejoice in thy strength, O LORD; * exceeding glad shall he be of thy salvation.

2 Thou hast given him his heart's desire, * and hast not denied him the request of his lips.

3 For thou shalt meet him with the blessing of goodness, * and shalt set a crown of pure gold upon his head.

4 He asked life of thee; and thou gavest him a long life, * even for ever and ever.

5 His honour is great in thy salvation; * glory and great worship shalt thou lay upon him.

6 For thou shalt give him everlasting felicity, * and make him glad with the joy of thy countenance.

7 And why? because the King putteth his trust in the LORD; * and in the mercy of the Most Highest he shall not miscarry.

8 All thine enemies shall feel thine hand; * thy right hand shall find out them that hate thee.

9 Thou shalt make them like a fiery oven in time of thy wrath: * the LORD shall destroy them in his displeasure, and the fire shall consume them.

10 Their fruit shalt thou root out of the earth, * and their seed from among the children of men.

11 For they intended mischief against thee, * and imagined such a device as they are not able to perform.

12 Therefore shalt thou put them to flight, * and the strings of thy bow shalt thou make ready against the face of them.

21 *Domine, in virtute tua*

1 The king rejoices in your strength, O LORD; *
how greatly he exults in your victory!

2 You have given him his heart's desire; *
you have not denied him the request of his lips.

3 For you meet him with blessings of prosperity, *
and set a crown of fine gold upon his head.

4 He asked you for life, and you gave it to him: *
length of days, for ever and ever.

5 His honor is great, because of your victory; *
splendor and majesty have you bestowed upon him.

6 For you will give him everlasting felicity *
and will make him glad with the joy of your presence.

7 For the king puts his trust in the LORD; *
because of the loving-kindness of the Most High, he
will not fall.

8 Your hand will lay hold upon all your enemies; *
your right hand will seize all those who hate you.

9 You will make them like a fiery furnace *
at the time of your appearing, O LORD;

10 You will swallow them up in your wrath, *
and fire shall consume them.

11 You will destroy their offspring from the land *
and their descendants from among the peoples of the earth.

12 Though they intend evil against you
and devise wicked schemes, *
yet they shall not prevail.

13 Be thou exalted, LORD, in thine own strength ; so will we sing, and praise thy power.

Evening Prayer.

Psalm xxii. *Deus, Deus meus!*

MY God! my God! look upon me ; why hast thou forsaken me? and art so far from my health, and from the words of my complaint?

2 O my God, I cry in the day-time, but thou hearest not ; and in the night-season also I take no rest.

3 And thou continuest holy, O thou Worship of Israel.

4 Our fathers hoped in thee ; they trusted in thee, and thou didst deliver them.

5 They called upon thee, and were holpen ; they put their trust in thee, and were not confounded.

6 But as for me, I am a worm, and no man ; a very scorn of men, and the outcast of the people.

7 All they that see me laugh me to scorn ; they shoot out their lips, and shake their heads, saying,

8 He trusted in the GOD, that he would deliver him ; let him deliver him, if he will have him.

9 But thou art he that took me out of my mother's womb ; thou wast my hope, when I hanged yet upon my mother's breasts.

10 I have been left unto thee ever since I was born ; thou art my God even from my mother's womb.

11 O go not from me ; for trouble is hard at hand, and there is none to help me.

12 Many oxen are come about me ; fat bulls of Basan close me in on every side.

13 They gape upon me with their mouths, as it were a ramping and a roaring lion.

14 I am poured out like water, and all my bones are out of joint ; my heart also in the midst of my body is even like melting wax.

15 My strength is dried up like a potsherd, and my tongue cleaveth to my gums, and thou shalt bring me into the dust of death.

13 Be thou exalted, LORD, in thine own strength : so will we sing, and praise thy power.

Evening Prayer.

PSALM 22. *Deus, Deus meus.*

MY God, my God, look upon me ; why hast thou forsaken me : and art so far from my health, and from the words of my complaint?

2 O my God, I cry in the day-time, but thou hearest not : and in the night season also I take no rest.

3 And thou continuest holy : O thou Worship of Israel.

4 Our fathers hoped in thee : they trusted in thee, and thou didst deliver them.

5 They called upon thee, and were holpen : they put their trust in thee, and were not confounded.

6 But as for me, I am a worm, and no man : a very scorn of men, and the outcast of the people.

7 All they that see me laugh me to scorn : they shoot out their lips, and shake their heads, saying,

8 He trusted in the LORD, that he would deliver him : let him deliver him, if he will have him.

9 But thou art he that took me out of my mother's womb : thou wast my hope, when I hanged yet upon my mother's breasts.

10 I have been left unto thee ever since I was born : thou art my God even from my mother's womb.

11 O go not from me ; for trouble is hard at hand : and there is none to help me.

12 Many oxen are come about me : fat bulls of Basan close me in on every side.

13 They gape upon me with their mouths : as it were a ramping and a roaring lion.

14 I am poured out like water, and all my bones are out of joint : my heart also in the midst of my body is even like melting wax.

15 My strength is dried up like a potsherd, and my tongue cleaveth to my gums : and thou shalt bring me into the dust of death.

13 Be thou exalted, LORD, in thine own strength; *
so will we sing, and praise thy power.

Evening Prayer.

Psalm 22. *Deus, Deus meus.*

MY God, my God, look upon me; why hast thou
forsaken me? * and art so far from my health, and from
the words of my complaint?
2 O my God, I cry in the day-time, but thou hearest
not; * and in the night season also I take no rest.
3 And thou continuest holy, * O thou Worship of
Israel.
4 Our fathers hoped in thee; * they trusted in thee,
and thou didst deliver them.
5 They called upon thee, and were holpen; * they
put their trust in thee, and were not confounded.
6 But as for me, I am a worm, and no man; * a very
scorn of men, and the outcast of the people.
7 All they that see me laugh me to scorn; * they
shoot out their lips, and shake their heads, saying,
8 He trusted in the LORD, that he would deliver
him; * let him deliver him, if he will have him.
9 But thou art he that took me out of my mother's
womb; * thou wast my hope, when I hanged yet upon
my mother's breasts.
10 I have been left unto thee ever since I was
born; * thou art my God even from my mother's womb.
11 O go not from me; for trouble is hard at hand, *
and there is none to help me.
12 Many oxen are come about me; * fat bulls of
Bashan close me in on every side.
13 They gape upon me with their mouths, * as it
were a ramping and a roaring lion.
14 I am poured out like water, and all my bones are
out of joint; * my heart also in the midst of my body is
even like melting wax.
15 My strength is dried up like a potsherd, and my
tongue cleaveth to my gums, * and thou bringest me
into the dust of death.

13 For you will put them to flight *
and aim your arrows at them.

14 Be exalted, O LORD, in your might; *
we will sing and praise your power.

Fourth Day: Evening Prayer

22 *Deus, Deus meus*

1 My God, my God, why have you forsaken me? *
and are so far from my cry
and from the words of my distress?

2 O my God, I cry in the daytime, but you do not answer; *
by night as well, but I find no rest.

3 Yet you are the Holy One, *
enthroned upon the praises of Israel.

4 Our forefathers put their trust in you; *
they trusted, and you delivered them.

5 They cried out to you and were delivered; *
they trusted in you and were not put to shame.

6 But as for me, I am a worm and no man, *
scorned by all and despised by the people.

7 All who see me laugh me to scorn; *
they curl their lips and wag their heads, saying,

8 "He trusted in the LORD; let him deliver him; *
let him rescue him, if he delights in him."

9 Yet you are he who took me out of the womb, *
and kept me safe upon my mother's breast.

10 I have been entrusted to you ever since I was born; *
you were my God when I was still in my
mother's womb.

11 Be not far from me, for trouble is near, *
and there is none to help.

12 Many young bulls encircle me; *
strong bulls of Bashan surround me.

13 They open wide their jaws at me, *
like a ravening and a roaring lion.

14 I am poured out like water;
all my bones are out of joint; *
my heart within my breast is melting wax.

15 My mouth is dried out like a pot-sherd;
my tongue sticks to the roof of my mouth; *
and you have laid me in the dust of the grave.

16 For many dogs are come about me, and council[7] of the wicked layeth siege against me.

17 They pierced my hands and my feet : I may tell all my bones : they stand staring and looking upon me.

18 They part my garments among them, and cast lots upon my vesture.

19 But be not thou far from me, O LORD ; thou art my succour, haste thee to help me.

20 Deliver my soul from the sword, my darling from the power of the dog.

21 Save me from the lion's mouth ; thou hast heard me also from among the horns of the unicorns.

22 I will declare thy Name unto my brethren ; in the midst of the congregation will I praise thee.

23 O praise the LORD, ye that fear him : magnify him, all ye of the seed of Jacob ; and fear him, all ye seed of Israel.

24 For he hath not despised nor abhorred the low estate of the poor ; he hath not hid his face from him ; but when he called unto him he heard him.

25 My praise is of thee in the great congregation ; my vows will I perform in the sight of them that fear him.

26 The poor shall eat, and be satisfied ; they that seek after the LORD, shall praise him : your heart shall live for ever.

27 All the ends of the world shall remember themselves, and be turned unto the LORD ; and all the kindreds of the nations shall worship before him.

28 For the kingdom is the LORD'S, and he is the Governor among the people.

29 All such as be fat upon the earth have eaten, and worshipped.

30 All they that go down into the dust shall kneel before him ; and no man hath quickened his own soul.

31 My seed shall serve him : they shall be counted unto the Lord for a generation.

32 They shall come, and shall declare his righteousness unto a people that shall be born, whom the Lord hath made.

16 For many dogs are come about me : and the council of the wicked layeth siege against me.

17 They pierced my hands and my feet ; I may tell all my bones : they stand staring and looking upon me.

18 They part my garments among them : and cast lots upon my vesture.

19 But be not thou far from me, O LORD : thou art my succour, haste thee to help me.

20 Deliver my soul from the sword : my darling from the power of the dog.

21 Save me from the lion's mouth : thou hast heard me also from among the horns of the unicorns.

22 I will declare thy Name unto my brethren : in the midst of the congregation will I praise thee.

23 O praise the LORD, ye that fear him : magnify him, all ye of the seed of Jacob ; and fear him, all ye seed of Israel.

24 For he hath not despised nor abhorred the low estate of the poor : he hath not hid his face from him ; but when he called unto him he heard him.

25 My praise is of thee in the great congregation : my vows will I perform in the sight of them that fear him.

26 The poor shall eat, and be satisfied : they that seek after the LORD shall praise him ; your heart shall live for ever.

27 All the ends of the world shall remember themselves, and be turned unto the LORD : and all the kindreds of the nations shall worship before him.

28 For the kingdom is the LORD'S : and he is the Governor among the nations.

29 All such as be fat upon the earth : have eaten, and worshipped.

30 All they that go down into the dust shall kneel before him : and no man hath quickened his own soul.

31 My seed shall serve him : they shall be counted unto the Lord for a generation.

32 They shall come, and the heavens shall declare his righteousness : unto a people that shall be born, whom the Lord hath made.

[7]"counsel" prior to 1845.

1928

16 For many dogs are come about me, * and council of the wicked layeth siege against me.

17 They pierced my hands and my feet: I may tell all my bones: * they stand staring and looking upon me.

18 They part my garments among them, * and cast lots upon my vesture.

19 But be not thou far from me, O LORD; * thou art my succour, haste thee to help me.

20 Deliver my soul from the sword, * my darling from the power of the dog.

21 Save me from the lion's mouth; * thou hast heard me also from among the horns of the unicorns.

22 I will declare thy Name unto my brethren; * in the midst of the congregation will I praise thee.

23 O praise the LORD, ye that fear him: * magnify him, all ye of the seed of Jacob; and fear him, all ye seed of Israel.

24 For he hath not despised nor abhorred the low estate of the poor; * he hath not hid his face from him; but when he called unto him he heard him.

25 My praise is of thee in the great congregation; * my vows will I perform in the sight of them that fear him.

26 The poor shall eat, and be satisfied; they that seek after the LORD shall praise him: * your heart shall live for ever.

27 All the ends of the world shall remember themselves, and be turned unto the LORD; * and all the kindreds of the nations shall worship before him.

28 For the kingdom is the LORD'S, * and he is the Governor among the nations.

29 All such as be fat upon the earth * have eaten, and worshipped.

30 All they that go down into the dust shall kneel before him; * and no man hath quickened his own soul.

31 My seed shall serve him: * they shall be counted unto the Lord for a generation.

32 They shall come, and shall declare his righteousness * unto a people that shall be born, whom the Lord hath made.

1979

16 Packs of dogs close me in,
and gangs of evildoers circle around me; *
they pierce my hands and my feet;
I can count all my bones.

17 They stare and gloat over me; *
they divide my garments among them;
they cast lots for my clothing.

18 Be not far away, O LORD; *
you are my strength; hasten to help me.

19 Save me from the sword, *
my life from the power of the dog.

20 Save me from the lion's mouth, *
my wretched body from the horns of wild bulls.

21 I will declare your Name to my brethren; *
in the midst of the congregation I will praise you.

22 Praise the LORD, you that fear him; *
stand in awe of him, O offspring of Israel;
all you of Jacob's line, give glory.

23 For he does not despise nor abhor the poor in their poverty;
neither does he hide his face from them; *
but when they cry to him he hears them.

24 My praise is of him in the great assembly; *
I will perform my vows in the presence of those who worship him.

25 The poor shall eat and be satisfied,
and those who seek the LORD shall praise him: *
"May your heart live for ever!"

26 All the ends of the earth shall remember and turn to the LORD, *
and all the families of the nations shall bow before him.

27 For kingship belongs to the LORD; *
he rules over the nations.

28 To him alone all who sleep in the earth bow down in worship; *
all who go down to the dust fall before him.

29 My soul shall live for him;
my descendants shall serve him; *
they shall be known as the LORD'S for ever.

30 They shall come and make known to a people yet unborn *
the saving deeds that he has done.

Psalm xxiii. *Dominus regit me.*

THE LORD is my shepherd ; therefore can I lack nothing.

2 He shall feed me in a green pasture, and lead me forth beside the waters of comfort.

3 He shall convert my soul, and bring me forth in the paths of righteousness for his Name's sake.

4 Yea, though I walk through the valley of the shadow of death, I will fear no evil ; for thou art with me ; thy rod and thy staff comfort me.

5 Thou shalt prepare a table before me against them that trouble me ; thou hast anointed my head with oil, and my cup shall be full.

6 Surely thy loving-kindness and mercy shall follow me all the days of my life ; and I will dwell in the house of the LORD for ever.

PSALM 23. *Dominus regit me.*

THE LORD is my shepherd : therefore can I lack nothing.

2 He shall feed me in a green pasture : and lead me forth beside the waters of comfort.

3 He shall convert my soul : and bring me forth in the paths of righteousness for his Name's sake.

4 Yea, though I walk through the valley of the shadow of death, I will fear no evil : for thou art with me ; thy rod and thy staff comfort me.

5 Thou shalt prepare a table before me against them that trouble me : thou hast anointed my head with oil, and my cup shall be full.

6 But thy loving-kindness and mercy shall follow me all the days of my life : and I will dwell in the house of the LORD for ever.

THE FIFTH DAY.

Morning Prayer.

Psalm xxiv. Domini est terra.

THE earth is the LORD'S, and all that therein is ; the compass of the world, and they that dwell therein.

2 For he hath founded it upon the seas, and prepared it upon the floods.

3 Who shall ascend into the hill of the LORD? or who shall rise up in his holy place?

4 Even he that hath clean hands, and a pure heart ; and that hath not lift up his mind unto vanity, nor sworn to deceive his neighbour.

5 He shall receive the blessing from the LORD, and righteousness from the God of his salvation.

6 This is the generation of them that seek him ; even of them that seek thy face, O Jacob.

7 Lift up your heads, O ye gates ; and be ye lift up, ye everlasting doors ; and the King of glory shall come in.

8 Who is the King of glory? It is the LORD strong and mighty, even the LORD mighty in battle.

9 Lift up your heads, O ye gates ; and be ye lift up, ye everlasting doors ; and the King of glory shall come in.

THE FIFTH DAY.

Morning Prayer.

PSALM 24. *Domini est terra.*

THE earth is the LORD'S, and all that therein is : the compass of the world, and they that dwell therein.

2 For he hath founded it upon the seas : and prepared it upon the floods.

3 Who shall ascend into the hill of the LORD : or who shall rise up in his holy place?

4 Even he that hath clean hands, and a pure heart : and that hath not lift up his mind unto vanity, nor sworn to deceive his neighbour.

5 He shall receive the blessing from the LORD : and righteousness from the God of his salvation.

6 This is the generation of them that seek him : even of them that seek thy face, O Jacob.

7 Lift up your heads, O ye gates ; and be ye lift up, ye everlasting doors : and the King of glory shall come in.

8 Who is the King of glory : It is the LORD strong and mighty, even the LORD mighty in battle.

9 Lift up your heads, O ye gates ; and be ye lift up, ye everlasting doors : and the King of glory shall come in.

Psalm 23. *Dominus regit me.*

THE LORD is my shepherd; * therefore can I lack
nothing.
2 He shall feed me in a green pasture, * and lead
me forth beside the waters of comfort.
3 He shall convert my soul, * and bring me forth in
the paths of righteousness for his Name's sake.
4 Yea, though I walk through the valley of the
shadow of death, I will fear no evil; * for thou art with
me; thy rod and thy staff comfort me.
5 Thou shalt prepare a table before me in the presence of them that trouble me; * thou hast anointed my
head with oil, and my cup shall be full.
6 Surely thy loving-kindness and mercy shall follow
me all the days of my life; * and I will dwell in the
house of the LORD for ever.

The Fifth Day.

Morning Prayer.

Psalm 24. *Domini est terra.*

THE earth is the LORD'S, and all that therein is; * the
compass of the world, and they that dwell therein.
2 For he hath founded it upon the seas, * and stablished it upon the floods.
3 Who shall ascend into the hill of the LORD? * or
who shall rise up in his holy place?
4 Even he that hath clean hands, and a pure
heart; * and that hath not lift up his mind unto vanity,
nor sworn to deceive his neighbour.
5 He shall receive the blessing from the LORD, *
and righteousness from the God of his salvation.
6 This is the generation of them that seek him; *
even of them that seek thy face, O God of Jacob.
7 Lift up your heads, O ye gates; and be ye lift up,
ye everlasting doors; * and the King of glory shall come
in.
8 Who is the King of glory? * It is the LORD strong
and mighty, even the LORD mighty in battle.
9 Lift up your heads, O ye gates; and be ye lift up,
ye everlasting doors; * and the King of glory shall come
in.

23 *Dominus regit me*

1 The LORD is my shepherd; *
I shall not be in want.

2 He makes me lie down in green pastures *
and leads me beside still waters.

3 He revives my soul *
and guides me along right pathways for his Name's sake.

4 Though I walk through the valley of the shadow of death,
I shall fear no evil; *
for you are with me;
your rod and your staff, they comfort me.

5 You spread a table before me in the presence of those
who trouble me; *
you have anointed my head with oil,
and my cup is running over.

6 Surely your goodness and mercy shall follow me all the days
of my life, *
and I will dwell in the house of the LORD for ever.

Fifth Day: Morning Prayer

24 *Domini est terra*

1 The earth is the LORD'S and all that is in it, *
the world and all who dwell therein.

2 For it is he who founded it upon the seas *
and made it firm upon the rivers of the deep.

3 "Who can ascend the hill of the LORD? *
and who can stand in his holy place?"

4 "Those who have clean hands and a pure heart, *
who have not pledged themselves to falsehood,
nor sworn by what is a fraud.

5 They shall receive a blessing from the LORD *
and a just reward from the God of their salvation."

6 Such is the generation of those who seek him, *
of those who seek your face, O God of Jacob.

7 Lift up your heads, O gates;
lift them high, O everlasting doors; *
and the King of glory shall come in.

8 "Who is this King of glory?" *
"The LORD, strong and mighty,
The LORD, mighty in battle."

9 Lift up your heads, O gates;
lift them high, O everlasting doors; *
and the King of glory shall come in.

10 Who is this King of glory? Even the LORD of hosts, he is the King of glory.

Psalm xxv. *Ad te, Domine, levavi.*

UNTO thee, O LORD, will I lift up my soul ; my God, I have put my trust in thee : O let me not be confounded, neither let mine enemies triumph over me.

2 For all they that hope in thee shall not be ashamed ; but such as transgress without a cause shall be put to confusion.

3 Show me thy ways, O LORD, and teach me thy paths.

4 Lead me forth in thy truth, and learn me : for thou art the God of my salvation ; in thee hath been my hope all the day long.

5 Call to remembrance, O LORD, thy tender mercies, and thy loving-kindnesses, which have been ever of old.

6 O remember not the sins and offences of my youth ; but according to thy mercy think thou upon me, O LORD, for thy goodness.

7 Gracious and righteous is the LORD ; therefore will he teach sinners in the way.

8 Them that are meek shall he guide in judgment ; and such as are gentle, them shall he learn his way.

9 All the paths of the LORD are mercy and truth, unto such as keep his covenant, and his testimonies.

10 For thy Name's sake, O LORD, be merciful unto my sin ; for it is great.

11 What man is he that feareth the LORD? him shall he teach in the way that he shall choose.

12 His soul shall dwell at ease, and his seed shall inherit the land.

13 The secret of the LORD is among them that fear him ; and he will show them his covenant.

14 Mine eyes are ever looking unto the LORD ; for he shall pluck my feet out of the net.

15 Turn thee unto me, and have mercy upon me ; for I am desolate, and in misery.

16 The sorrows of my heart are enlarged : O bring thou me out of my troubles.

17 Look upon my adversity and misery, and forgive me all my sin.

10 Who is this King of glory : Even the LORD of hosts, he is the King of glory.

PSALM 25. *Ad te, Domine, levavi.*

UNTO thee, O LORD, will I lift up my soul ; my God, I have put my trust in thee : O let me not be confounded, neither let mine enemies triumph over me.

2 For all they that hope in thee shall not be ashamed : but such as transgress without a cause shall be put to confusion.

3 Show me thy ways, O LORD : and teach me thy paths.

4 Lead me forth in thy truth, and learn me : for thou art the God of my salvation ; in thee hath been my hope all the day long.

5 Call to remembrance, O LORD, thy tender mercies : and thy loving-kindnesses, which have been ever of old.

6 O remember not the sins and offences of my youth : but according to thy mercy think thou upon me, O LORD, for thy goodness.

7 Gracious and righteous is the LORD : therefore will he teach sinners in the way.

8 Them that are meek shall he guide in judgment : and such as are gentle, them shall he learn his way.

9 All the paths of the LORD are mercy and truth : unto such as keep his covenant and his testimonies.

10 For thy Name's sake, O LORD : be merciful unto my sin ; for it is great.

11 What man is he that feareth the LORD : him shall he teach in the way that he shall choose.

12 His soul shall dwell at ease : and his seed shall inherit the land.

13 The secret of the LORD is among them that fear him : and he will show them his covenant.

14 Mine eyes are ever looking unto the LORD : for he shall pluck my feet out of the net.

15 Turn thee unto me, and have mercy upon me : for I am desolate, and in misery.

16 The sorrows of my heart are enlarged : O bring thou me out of my troubles.

17 Look upon my adversity and misery : and forgive me all my sin.

10 Who is this King of glory? * Even the LORD of
hosts, he is the King of glory.

Psalm 25. *Ad te, Domine, levavi.*

UNTO thee, O LORD, will I lift up my soul; my God, I
have put my trust in thee: * O let me not be
confounded, neither let mine enemies triumph over
me.
2 For all they that hope in thee shall not be
ashamed; * but such as transgress without a cause shall
be put to confusion.
3 Show me thy ways, O LORD, * and teach me thy
paths.
4 Lead me forth in thy truth, and learn me: * for
thou art the God of my salvation; in thee hath been my
hope all the day long.
5 Call to remembrance, O LORD, thy tender
mercies, * and thy loving-kindnesses, which have been
ever of old.
6 O remember not the sins and offences of my
youth; * but according to thy mercy think thou upon
me, O LORD, for thy goodness.
7 Gracious and righteous is the LORD; * therefore
will he teach sinners in the way.
8 Them that are meek shall he guide in judgment; * and such as are gentle, them shall he learn his
way.
9 All the paths of the LORD are mercy and truth, *
unto such as keep his covenant and his testimonies.
10 For thy Name's sake, O LORD, * be merciful
unto my sin; for it is great.
11 What man is he that feareth the LORD? * him
shall he teach in the way that he shall choose.
12 His soul shall dwell at ease, * and his seed shall
inherit the land.
13 The secret of the LORD is among them that fear
him; * and he will show them his covenant.
14 Mine eyes are ever looking unto the LORD; * for
he shall pluck my feet out of the net.
15 Turn thee unto me, and have mercy upon me; *
for I am desolate, and in misery.
16 The sorrows of my heart are enlarged: * O bring
thou me out of my troubles.
17 Look upon my adversity and misery, * and
forgive me all my sin.

10 "Who is he, this King of glory?" *
"The LORD of hosts,
he is the King of glory."

25 *Ad te, Domine, levavi*

1 To you, O LORD, I lift up my soul;
my God, I put my trust in you; *
let me not be humiliated,
nor let my enemies triumph over me.

2 Let none who look to you be put to shame; *
let the treacherous be disappointed in their schemes.

3 Show me your ways, O LORD, *
and teach me your paths.

4 Lead me in your truth and teach me, *
for you are the God of my salvation;
in you have I trusted all the day long.

5 Remember, O LORD, your compassion and love, *
for they are from everlasting.

6 Remember not the sins of my youth and my transgressions; *
remember me according to your love
and for the sake of your goodness, O LORD.

7 Gracious and upright is the LORD; *
therefore he teaches sinners in his way.

8 He guides the humble in doing right *
and teaches his way to the lowly.

9 All the paths of the LORD are love and faithfulness *
to those who keep his covenant and his testimonies.

10 For your Name's sake, O LORD, *
forgive my sin, for it is great.

11 Who are they who fear the LORD? *
he will teach them the way that they should choose.

12 They shall dwell in prosperity, *
and their offspring shall inherit the land.

13 The LORD is a friend to those who fear him *
and will show them his covenant.

14 My eyes are ever looking to the LORD,
for he shall pluck my feet out of the net.

15 Turn to me and have pity on me, *
for I am left alone and in misery.

16 The sorrows of my heart have increased; *
bring me out of my troubles.

17 Look upon my adversity and misery *
and forgive me all my sin.

1789-1871

18 Consider mine enemies, how many they are ;
and they bear a tyrannous hate against me.
19 O keep my soul, and deliver me : let me not be
confounded, for I have put my trust in thee.
20 Let perfectness and righteous dealing wait upon
me ; for my hope hath been in thee.
21 Deliver Israel, O God, out of all his troubles.

Psalm xxvi. *Judica me, Domine.*

BE thou my Judge, O LORD, for I have walked innocently : my trust hath been also in the LORD, therefore shall I not fall.
2 Examine me, O LORD, and prove me ; try out my
reins and my heart.
3 For thy loving-kindness is ever before mine eyes ;
and I will walk in thy truth.
4 I have not dwelt with vain persons ; neither will I
have fellowship with the deceitful.
5 I have hated the congregation of the wicked ; and
will not sit among the ungodly.
6 I will wash my hands in innocency, O LORD ; and
so will I go to thine altar ;
7 That I may show the voice of thanksgiving, and
tell of all thy wondrous works.
8 LORD, I have loved the habitation of thy house,
and the place where thine honour dwelleth.
9 O shut not up my soul with the sinners, nor my
life with the blood-thirsty ;
10 In whose hands is wickedness, and their right
hand is full of gifts.
11 But as for me, I will walk innocently : O deliver
me, and be merciful unto me.
12 My foot standeth right : I will praise the LORD in
the congregations.

Evening Prayer.

Psalm xxvii. *Dominus illuminatio.*

THE LORD is my light and my salvation ; whom then shall I fear? the LORD is the strength of my life ; of whom then shall I be afraid?

1892

18 Consider mine enemies, how many they are :
and they bear a tyrannous hate against me.
19 O keep my soul, and deliver me : let me not be
confounded, for I have put my trust in thee.
20 Let perfectness and righteous dealing wait upon
me : for my hope hath been in thee.
21 Deliver Israel, O God : out of all his troubles.

PSALM 26. *Judica me, Domine.*

BE thou my Judge, O LORD, for I have walked innocently : my trust hath been also in the LORD, therefore shall I not fall.
2 Examine me, O LORD, and prove me : try out my
reins and my heart.
3 For thy loving-kindness is ever before mine eyes :
and I will walk in thy truth.
4 I have not dwelt with vain persons : neither will I
have fellowship with the deceitful.
5 I have hated the congregation of the wicked : and
will not sit among the ungodly.
6 I will wash my hands in innocency, O LORD : and
so will I go to thine altar ;
7 That I may show the voice of thanksgiving : and
tell of all thy wondrous works.
8 LORD, I have loved the habitation of thy house :
and the place where thine honour dwelleth.
9 O shut not up my soul with the sinners : nor my
life with the blood-thirsty ;
10 In whose hands is wickedness : and their right
hand is full of gifts.
11 But as for me, I will walk innocently : O deliver
me, and be merciful unto me.
12 My foot standeth right : I will praise the LORD in
the congregations.

Evening Prayer.

PSALM 27. *Dominus illuminatio.*

THE LORD is my light and my salvation ; whom then shall I fear : the LORD is the strength of my life ; of whom then shall I be afraid?

18 Consider mine enemies, how many they are; *
and they bear a tyrannous hate against me.
19 O keep my soul, and deliver me: * let me not be
confounded, for I have put my trust in thee.
20 Let perfectness and righteous dealing wait upon
me; * for my hope hath been in thee.
21 Deliver Israel, O God, * out of all his troubles.

18 Look upon my enemies, for they are many, *
and they bear a violent hatred against me.

19 Protect my life and deliver me; *
let me not be put to shame, for I have trusted in you.

20 Let integrity and uprightness preserve me, *
for my hope has been in you.

21 Deliver Israel, O God, *
out of all his troubles.

Psalm 26. *Judica me, Domine.*

BE thou my Judge, O LORD, for I have walked innocently: * my trust hath been also in the LORD, therefore shall I not fall.
2 Examine me, O LORD, and prove me; * try out
my reins and my heart.
3 For thy loving-kindness is ever before mine
eyes; * and I will walk in thy truth.
4 I have not dwelt with vain persons; * neither will
I have fellowship with the deceitful.
5 I have hated the congregation of the wicked; *
and will not sit among the ungodly.
6 I will wash my hands in innocency, O LORD; *
and so will I go to thine altar;
7 That I may show the voice of thanksgiving, * and
tell of all thy wondrous works.
8 LORD, I have loved the habitation of thy house, *
and the place where thine honour dwelleth.
9 O shut not up my soul with the sinners, * nor my
life with the blood-thirsty;
10 In whose hands is wickedness, * and their right
hand is full of gifts.
11 But as for me, I will walk innocently: * O deliver
me, and be merciful unto me.
12 My foot standeth right: * I will praise the LORD
in the congregations.

26 *Judica me, Domine*

1 Give judgment for me, O LORD,
for I have lived with integrity; *
I have trusted in the LORD and have not faltered.

2 Test me, O LORD, and try me; *
examine my heart and my mind.

3 For your love is before my eyes; *
I have walked faithfully with you.

4 I have not sat with the worthless, *
nor do I consort with the deceitful.

5 I have hated the company of evildoers; *
I will not sit down with the wicked.

6 I will wash my hands in innocence, O LORD, *
that I may go in procession round your altar,

7 Singing aloud a song of thanksgiving *
and recounting all your wonderful deeds.

8 LORD, I love the house in which you dwell *
and the place where your glory abides.

9 Do not sweep me away with sinners, *
nor my life with those who thirst for blood,

10 Whose hands are full of evil plots, *
and their right hand full of bribes.

11 As for me, I will live with integrity; *
redeem me, O LORD, and have pity on me.

12 My foot stands on level ground; *
in the full assembly I will bless the LORD.

Evening Prayer.

Psalm 27. *Dominus illuminatio.*

THE LORD is my light and my salvation; whom then
shall I fear? * the LORD is the strength of my life; of
whom then shall I be afraid?

Fifth Day: Evening Prayer

27 *Dominus illuminatio*

1 The LORD is my light and my salvation;
whom then shall I fear? *
the LORD is the strength of my life;
of whom then shall I be afraid?

1789-1871

2 When the wicked, even mine enemies and my foes, came upon me to eat up my flesh, they stumbled and fell.

3 Though an host of men were laid against me, yet shall not my heart be afraid ; and though there rose up war against me, yet will I put my trust in him.

4 One thing have I desired of the LORD, which I will require, even that I may dwell in the house of the LORD all the days of my life, to behold the fair beauty of the LORD, and to visit his temple.

5 For in the time of trouble he shall hide me in his tabernacle ; yea, in the secret place of his dwelling shall he hide me, and set me up upon a rock of stone.

6 And now shall he lift up mine head above mine enemies round about me.

7 Therefore will I offer in his dwelling an oblation, with great gladness : I will sing and speak praises unto the LORD.

8 Hearken unto my voice, O LORD, when I cry unto thee ; have mercy upon me, and hear me.

9 My heart hath talked of thee, Seek ye my face : Thy face, LORD, will I seek.

10 O hide not thou thy face from me, nor cast thy servant away in displeasure.

11 Thou hast been my succour ; leave me not, neither forsake me, O God of my salvation.

12 When my father and my mother forsake me, the LORD taketh me up.

13 Teach me thy way, O LORD, and lead me in the right way, because of mine enemies.

14 Deliver me not over into the will of mine adversaries : for there are false witnesses risen up against me, and such as speak wrong.

15 I should utterly have fainted, but that I believe verily to see the goodness of the LORD in the land of the living.

16 O tarry thou the LORD'S leisure ; be strong, and he shall comfort thine heart ; and put thou thy trust in the LORD.

1892

2 When the wicked, even mine enemies and my foes, came upon me to eat up my flesh : they stumbled and fell.

3 Though an host of men were laid against me, yet shall not my heart be afraid : and though there rose up war against me, yet will I put my trust in him.

4 One thing have I desired of the LORD, which I will require : even that I may dwell in the house of the LORD all the days of my life, to behold the fair beauty of the LORD, and to visit his temple.

5 For in the time of trouble he shall hide me in his tabernacle : yea, in the secret place of his dwelling shall he hide me, and set me up upon a rock of stone.

6 And now shall he lift up mine head : above mine enemies round about me.

7 Therefore will I offer in his dwelling an oblation, with great gladness : I will sing and speak praises unto the LORD.

8 Hearken unto my voice, O LORD, when I cry unto thee : have mercy upon me, and hear me.

9 My heart hath talked of thee, Seek ye my face : Thy face, LORD, will I seek.

10 O hide not thou thy face from me : nor cast thy servant away in displeasure.

11 Thou hast been my succour : leave me not, neither forsake me, O God of my salvation.

12 When my father and my mother forsake me : the LORD taketh me up.

13 Teach me thy way, O LORD : and lead me in the right way, because of mine enemies.

14 Deliver me not over into the will of mine adversaries : for there are false witnesses risen up against me, and such as speak wrong.

15 I should utterly have fainted : but that I believe verily to see the goodness of the LORD in the land of the living.

16 O tarry thou the LORD'S leisure : be strong, and he shall comfort thine heart ; and put thou thy trust in the LORD.

1928

2 When the wicked, even mine enemies and my foes, came upon me to eat up my flesh, * they stumbled and fell.

3 Though an host of men were laid against me, yet shall not my heart be afraid; * and though there rose up war against me, yet will I put my trust in him.

4 One thing have I desired of the LORD, which I will require; * even that I may dwell in the house of the LORD all the days of my life, to behold the fair beauty of the LORD, and to visit his temple.

5 For in the time of trouble he shall hide me in his tabernacle; * yea, in the secret place of his dwelling shall he hide me, and set me up upon a rock of stone.

6 And now shall he lift up mine head * above mine enemies round about me.

7 Therefore will I offer in his dwelling an oblation, with great gladness: * I will sing and speak praises unto the LORD.

8 Hearken unto my voice, O LORD, when I cry unto thee; * have mercy upon me, and hear me.

9 My heart hath talked of thee, Seek ye my face: * Thy face, LORD, will I seek.

10 O hide not thou thy face from me, * nor cast thy servant away in displeasure.

11 Thou hast been my succour; * leave me not, neither forsake me, O God of my salvation.

12 When my father and my mother forsake me, * the LORD taketh me up.

13 Teach me thy way, O LORD, * and lead me in the right way, because of mine enemies.

14 Deliver me not over into the will of mine adversaries: * for there are false witnesses risen up against me, and such as speak wrong.

15 I should utterly have fainted, * but that I believe verily to see the goodness of the LORD in the land of the living.

16 O tarry thou the LORD'S leisure; * be strong, and he shall comfort thine heart; and put thou thy trust in the LORD.

1979

2 When evildoers came upon me to eat up my flesh, *
it was they, my foes and my adversaries, who stumbled and fell.

3 Though an army should encamp against me, *
yet my heart shall not be afraid;

4 And though war should rise up against me, *
yet will I put my trust in him.

5 One thing have I asked of the LORD;
one thing I seek; *
that I may dwell in the house of the LORD all the days of my life;

6 To behold the fair beauty of the LORD *
and to seek him in his temple.

7 For in the day of trouble he shall keep me safe in his shelter; *
he shall hide me in the secrecy of his dwelling
and set me high upon a rock.

8 Even now he lifts up my head *
above my enemies round about me.

9 Therefore I will offer in his dwelling an oblation
with sounds of great gladness; *
I will sing and make music to the LORD.

10 Hearken to my voice, O LORD, when I call; *
have mercy on me and answer me.

11 You speak in my heart and say, "Seek my face." *
Your face, LORD, will I seek.

12 Hide not your face from me, *
nor turn away your servant in displeasure.

13 You have been my helper;
cast me not away; *
do not forsake me, O God of my salvation.

14 Though my father and my mother forsake me, *
the LORD will sustain me.

15 Show me your way, O LORD; *
lead me on a level path, because of my enemies.

16 Deliver me not into the hand of my adversaries, *
for false witnesses have risen up against me,
and also those who speak malice.

17 What if I had not believed
that I should see the goodness of the LORD *
in the land of the living!

18 O tarry and await the LORD'S pleasure;
be strong, and he shall comfort your heart; *
wait patiently for the LORD.

Psalm xxviii. *Ad te, Domine.*

UNTO thee will I cry, O LORD, my strength : think no scorn of me ; lest, if thou make as though thou hearest not, I become like them that go down into the pit.

2 Hear the voice of my humble petitions, when I cry unto thee ; when I hold up my hands towards the mercy-seat of thy holy temple.

3 O pluck me not away, neither destroy me with the ungodly and wicked doers, which speak friendly to their neighbours, but imagine mischief in their hearts.

4 Reward them according to their deeds, and according to the wickedness of their own inventions.

5 Recompense them after the work of their hands ; pay them that they have deserved.

6 For they regard not in their mind the works of the LORD, nor the operation of his hands ; therefore shall he break them down, and not build them up.

7 Praised be the LORD ; for he hath heard the voice of my humble petitions.

8 The LORD is my strength, and my shield ; my heart hath trusted in him, and I am helped ; therefore my heart danceth for joy, and in my song will I praise him.

9 The LORD is my strength, and he is the wholesome defence of his Anointed.

10 O save thy people, and give thy blessing unto thine inheritance : feed them, and set them up for ever.

PSALM 28. *Ad te, Domine.*

UNTO thee will I cry, O LORD, my strength : think no scorn of me ; lest, if thou make as though thou hearest not, I become like them that go down into the pit.

2 Hear the voice of my humble petitions, when I cry unto thee : when I hold up my hands towards the mercy-seat of thy holy temple.

3 O pluck me not away, neither destroy me with the ungodly and wicked doers : which speak friendly to their neighbours, but imagine mischief in their hearts.

4 Reward them according to their deeds : and according to the wickedness of their own inventions.

5 Recompense them after the work of their hands : pay them that they have deserved.

6 For they regard not in their mind the works of the LORD, nor the operation of his hands : therefore shall he break them down, and not build them up.

7 Praised be the LORD : for he hath heard the voice of my humble petitions.

8 The LORD is my strength, and my shield ; my heart hath trusted in him, and I am helped : therefore my heart danceth for joy, and in my song will I praise him.

9 The LORD is my strength : and he is the wholesome defence of his anointed.

10 O save thy people, and give thy blessing unto thine inheritance : feed them, and set them up for ever.

Psalm xxix. *Afferte Domino.*

BRING unto the LORD, O ye mighty, bring young rams unto the LORD ; ascribe unto the LORD worship and strength.

2 Give the LORD the honour due unto his Name ; worship the LORD with holy worship.

3 It is the LORD that commandeth the waters ; it is the glorious God that maketh the thunder.

4 It is the LORD that ruleth the sea ; the voice of the LORD is mighty in operation ; the voice of the LORD is a glorious voice.

5 The voice of the LORD breaketh the cedar trees ; yea, the LORD breaketh the cedars of Libanus.

PSALM 29. *Afferte Domino.*

BRING unto the LORD, O ye mighty, bring young rams unto the LORD : ascribe unto the LORD worship and strength.

2 Give the LORD the honour due unto his Name : worship the LORD with holy worship.

3 It is the LORD that commandeth the waters : it is the glorious God that maketh the thunder.

4 It is the LORD that ruleth the sea ; the voice of the LORD is mighty in operation : the voice of the LORD is a glorious voice.

5 The voice of the LORD breaketh the cedar-trees : yea, the LORD breaketh the cedars of Libanus.

Psalm 28. *Ad te, Domine.*

UNTO thee will I cry, O LORD, my strength: * think no scorn of me; lest, if thou make as though thou hearest not, I become like them that go down into the pit.

2 Hear the voice of my humble petitions, when I cry unto thee; * when I hold up my hands towards the mercy-seat of thy holy temple.

3 O pluck me not away, neither destroy me with the ungodly and wicked doers, * which speak friendly to their neighbours, but imagine mischief in their hearts.

4 Reward them according to their deeds, * and according to the wickedness of their own inventions.

5 Recompense them after the work of their hands; * pay them that they have deserved.

6 For they regard not in their mind the works of the LORD, nor the operation of his hands; * therefore shall he break them down, and not build them up.

7 Praised be the LORD; * for he hath heard the voice of my humble petitions.

8 The LORD is my strength, and my shield; my heart hath trusted in him, and I am helped; * therefore my heart danceth for joy, and in my song will I praise him.

9 The LORD is my strength, * and he is the wholesome defence of his anointed.

10 O save thy people, and give thy blessing unto thine inheritance: * feed them, and set them up for ever.

28 *Ad te, Domine*

1 O LORD, I call to you;
my Rock, do not be deaf to my cry; *
lest, if you do not hear me,
I become like those who go down to the Pit.

2 Hear the voice of my prayer when I cry out to you, *
when I lift up my hands to your holy of holies.

3 Do not snatch me away with the wicked or with the evildoers, *
who speak peaceably with their neighbors,
while strife is in their hearts.

4 Repay them according to their deeds, *
and according to the wickedness of their actions.

5 According to the work of their hands repay them, *
and give them their just deserts.

6 They have no understanding of the LORD'S doings,
nor of the works of his hands; *
therefore he will break them down and not build them up.

7 Blessed is the LORD! *
for he has heard the voice of my prayer.

8 The LORD is my strength and my shield; *
my heart trusts in him, and I have been helped;

9 Therefore my heart dances for joy, *
and in my song will I praise him.

10 The LORD is the strength of his people, *
a safe refuge for his anointed.

11 Save your people and bless your inheritance; *
shepherd them and carry them for ever.

Psalm 29. *Afferte Domino.*

ASCRIBE unto the LORD, O ye mighty, * ascribe unto the LORD worship and strength.

2 Ascribe unto the LORD the honour due unto his Name; * worship the LORD with holy worship.

3 The voice of the LORD is upon the waters; * it is the glorious God that maketh the thunder.

4 It is the LORD that ruleth the sea; the voice of the LORD is mighty in operation; * the voice of the LORD is a glorious voice.

5 The voice of the LORD breaketh the cedar-trees; * yea, the LORD breaketh the cedars of Lebanon.

29 *Afferte Domino*

1 Ascribe to the LORD, you gods, *
ascribe to the LORD glory and strength.

2 Ascribe to the LORD the glory due his Name; *
worship the LORD in the beauty of holiness.

3 The voice of the LORD is upon the waters;
the God of glory thunders; *
the LORD is upon the mighty waters.

4 The voice of the LORD is a powerful voice; *
the voice of the LORD is a voice of splendor.

5 The voice of the LORD breaks the cedar trees; *
the LORD breaks the cedars of Lebanon;

6 He maketh them also to skip like a calf; Libanus also, and Sirion, like a young unicorn.
7 The voice of the LORD divideth the flames of fire; the voice of the LORD shaketh the wilderness; yea, the LORD shaketh the wilderness of Cades.
8 The voice of the LORD maketh the hinds to bring forth young, and discovereth the thick bushes: in his temple doth every man speak of his honour.
9 The LORD sitteth above the water-flood, and the LORD remaineth a King for ever.
10 The LORD shall give strength unto his people; the LORD shall give his people the blessing of peace.

6 He maketh them also to skip like a calf: Libanus also, and Sirion, like a young unicorn.
7 The voice of the LORD divideth the flames of fire; the voice of the LORD shaketh the wilderness: yea, the LORD shaketh the wilderness of Cades.
8 The voice of the LORD maketh the hinds to bring forth young, and discovereth the thick bushes: in his temple doth every man speak of his honour.
9 The LORD sitteth above the water-flood: and the LORD remaineth a King for ever.
10 The LORD shall give strength unto his people: the LORD shall give his people the blessing of peace.

THE SIXTH DAY.

Morning Prayer.

Psalm xxx. *Exaltabo te, Domine.*

I WILL magnify thee, O LORD; for thou hast set me up, and not made my foes to triumph over me.
2 O LORD, my God, I cried unto thee; and thou hast healed me.
3 Thou, LORD, hast brought my soul out of hell: thou hast kept my life from them that go down to the pit.
4 Sing praises unto the LORD, O ye saints of his; and give thanks unto him, for a remembrance of his holiness.
5 For his wrath endureth but the twinkling of an eye, and in his pleasure is life; heaviness may endure for a night, but joy cometh in the morning.
6 And in my prosperity I said, I shall never be removed: thou, LORD, of thy goodness, hast made my hill so strong.
7 Thou didst turn thy face from me, and I was troubled.
8 Then cried I unto thee, O LORD; and gat me to my LORD right humbly.
9 What profit is there in my blood, when I go down into the pit?
10 Shall the dust give thanks unto thee? or shall it declare thy truth?
11 Hear, O LORD, and have mercy upon me; LORD, be thou my helper.
12 Thou hast turned my heaviness into joy; thou hast put off my sackcloth, and girded me with gladness:

THE SIXTH DAY.

Morning Prayer.

PSALM 30. *Exaltabo te, Domine.*

I WILL magnify thee, O LORD; for thou hast set me up: and not made my foes to triumph over me.
2 O LORD my God, I cried unto thee: and thou hast healed me.
3 Thou, LORD, hast brought my soul out of hell: thou hast kept my life from them that go down into the pit.
4 Sing praises unto the LORD, O ye saints of his: and give thanks unto him, for a remembrance of his holiness.
5 For his wrath endureth but the twinkling of an eye, and in his pleasure is life: heaviness may endure for a night, but joy cometh in the morning.
6 And in my prosperity I said, I shall never be removed: thou, LORD, of thy goodness, hast made my hill so strong.
7 Thou didst turn thy face from me: and I was troubled.
8 Then cried I unto thee, O LORD: and gat me to my LORD right humbly.
9 What profit is there in my blood: when I go down to the pit?
10 Shall the dust give thanks unto thee: or shall it declare thy truth?
11 Hear, O LORD, and have mercy upon me: LORD, be thou my helper.
12 Thou hast turned my heaviness into joy: thou hast put off my sackcloth, and girded me with gladness:

1928

6 He maketh them also to skip like a calf; * Lebanon also, and Sirion, like a young unicorn.

7 The voice of the LORD divideth the flames of fire; the voice of the LORD shaketh the wilderness; * yea, the LORD shaketh the wilderness of Kadesh.

8 The voice of the LORD maketh the hinds to bring forth young, and strippeth bare the forests: * in his temple doth every thing speak of his honour.

9 The LORD sitteth above the water-flood, * and the LORD remaineth a King for ever.

10 The LORD shall give strength unto his people; * the LORD shall give his people the blessing of peace.

The Sixth Day.

Morning Prayer.

Psalm 30. *Exaltabo te, Domine.*

I WILL magnify thee, O LORD; for thou hast set me up, * and not made my foes to triumph over me.

2 O LORD my God, I cried unto thee; * and thou hast healed me.

3 Thou, LORD, hast brought my soul out of hell: * thou hast kept my life, that I should not go down into the pit.

4 Sing praises unto the LORD, O ye saints of his; * and give thanks unto him, for a remembrance of his holiness.

5 For his wrath endureth but the twinkling of an eye, and in his pleasure is life; * heaviness may endure for a night, but joy cometh in the morning.

6 And in my prosperity I said, I shall never be removed: * thou, LORD, of thy goodness, hast made my hill so strong.

7 Thou didst turn thy face from me, * and I was troubled.

8 Then cried I unto thee, O LORD; * and gat me to my LORD right humbly.

9 What profit is there in my blood, * when I go down into the pit?

10 Shall the dust give thanks unto thee? * or shall it declare thy truth?

11 Hear, O LORD, and have mercy upon me; * LORD, be thou my helper.

12 Thou hast turned my heaviness into joy; * thou hast put off my sackcloth, and girded me with gladness:

1979

6 He makes Lebanon skip like a calf, *
and Mount Hermon like a young wild ox.

7 The voice of the LORD splits the flames of fire;
the voice of the LORD shakes the wilderness; *
the LORD shakes the wilderness of Kadesh.

8 The voice of the LORD makes the oak trees writhe *
and strips the forests bare.

9 And in the temple of the LORD *
all are crying, "Glory!"

10 The LORD sits enthroned above the flood; *
the LORD sits enthroned as King for evermore.

11 The LORD shall give strength to his people; *
the LORD shall give his people the blessing of peace.

Sixth Day: Morning Prayer

30 *Exaltabo te, Domine*

1 I will exalt you, O LORD,
because you have lifted me up *
and have not let my enemies triumph over me.

2 O LORD my God, I cried out to you, *
and you restored me to health.

3 You brought me up, O LORD, from the dead; *
you restored my life as I was going down to the grave.

4 Sing to the LORD, you servants of his; *
give thanks for the remembrance of his holiness.

5 For his wrath endures but the twinkling of an eye, *
his favor for a lifetime.

6 Weeping may spend the night, *
but joy comes in the morning.

7 While I felt secure, I said,
"I shall never be disturbed. *
You, LORD, with your favor, made me as strong as the mountains."

8 Then you hid your face, *
and I was filled with fear.

9 I cried to you, O LORD; *
I pleaded with the LORD, saying,

10 "What profit is there in my blood, if I go down to the Pit? *
will the dust praise you or declare your faithfulness?

11 Hear, O LORD, and have mercy upon me; *
O LORD, be my helper."

12 You have turned my wailing into dancing; *
you have put off my sack-cloth and clothed me with joy.

1789-1871

13 Therefore shall every good man sing of thy praise without ceasing. O my God, I will give thanks unto thee for ever.

Psalm xxxi. *In te, Domine, speravi.*

IN thee, O LORD, have I put my trust ; let me never be put to confusion ; deliver me in thy righteousness.

2 Bow down thine ear to me ; make haste to deliver me.

3 And be thou my strong rock, and house of defence, that thou mayest save me.

4 For thou art my strong rock, and my castle : be thou also my guide, and lead me for thy Name's sake.

5 Draw me out of the net that they have laid privily for me ; for thou art my strength.

6 Into thy hands I commend my spirit ; for thou hast redeemed me, O LORD, thou God of truth.

7 I have hated them that hold of superstitious vanities, and my trust hath been in the LORD.

8 I will be glad, and rejoice in thy mercy ; for thou hast considered my trouble, and hast known my soul in adversities.

9 Thou hast not shut me up into the hand of the enemy ; but hast set my feet in a large room.

10 Have mercy upon me, O LORD, for I am in trouble, and mine eye is consumed for very heaviness ; yea, my soul and my body.

11 For my life is waxen old with heaviness, and my years with mourning.

12 My strength faileth me, because of mine iniquity, and my bones are consumed.

13 I became a reproof among all mine enemies, but especially among my neighbours ; and they of mine acquaintance were afraid of me ; and they that did see me without, conveyed themselves from me.

14 I am clean forgotten as a dead man out of mind ; I am become like a broken vessel.

1892

13 Therefore shall every good man sing of thy praise without ceasing : O my God, I will give thanks unto thee for ever.

PSALM 31. *In te, Domine, speravi.*

IN thee, O LORD, have I put my trust : let me never be put to confusion ; deliver me in thy righteousness.

2 Bow down thine ear to me : make haste to deliver me.

3 And be thou my strong rock, and house of defence : that thou mayest save me.

4 For thou art my strong rock, and my castle : be thou also my guide, and lead me for thy Name's sake.

5 Draw me out of the net that they have laid privily for me : for thou art my strength.

6 Into thy hands I commend my spirit : for thou hast redeemed me, O LORD, thou God of truth.

7 I have hated them that hold of superstitious vanities : and my trust hath been in the LORD.

8 I will be glad and rejoice in thy mercy : for thou hast considered my trouble, and hast known my soul in adversities.

9 Thou hast not shut me up into the hand of the enemy : but hast set my feet in a large room.

10 Have mercy upon me, O LORD, for I am in trouble : and mine eye is consumed for very heaviness ; yea, my soul and my body.

11 For my life is waxen old with heaviness : and my years with mourning.

12 My strength faileth me, because of mine iniquity : and my bones are consumed.

13 I became a reproof among all mine enemies, but especially among my neighbours : and they of mine acquaintance were afraid of me ; and they that did see me without, conveyed themselves from me.

14 I am clean forgotten as a dead man out of mind : I am become like a broken vessel.

13 Therefore shall every good man sing of thy praise without ceasing. * O my God, I will give thanks unto thee for ever.

Psalm 31. *In te, Domine, speravi.*

IN thee, O LORD, have I put my trust; let me never be put to confusion; * deliver me in thy righteousness.

2 Bow down thine ear to me; * make haste to deliver me.

3 And be thou my strong rock, and house of defence, * that thou mayest save me.

4 For thou art my strong rock, and my castle: * be thou also my guide, and lead me for thy Name's sake.

5 Draw me out of the net that they have laid privily for me; * for thou art my strength.

6 Into thy hands I commend my spirit; * for thou hast redeemed me, O LORD, thou God of truth.

7 I have hated them that hold of lying vanities, * and my trust hath been in the LORD.

8 I will be glad and rejoice in thy mercy; * for thou hast considered my trouble, and hast known my soul in adversities.

9 Thou hast not shut me up into the hand of the enemy; * but hast set my feet in a large room.

10 Have mercy upon me, O LORD, for I am in trouble, * and mine eye is consumed for very heaviness; yea, my soul and my body.

11 For my life is waxen old with heaviness, * and my years with mourning.

12 My strength faileth me, because of mine iniquity, * and my bones are consumed.

13 I became a reproach among all mine enemies, but especially among my neighbours; * and they of mine acquaintance were afraid of me; and they that did see me without, conveyed themselves from me.

14 I am clean forgotten as a dead man out of mind; * I am become like a broken vessel.

13 Therefore my heart sings to you without ceasing; *
O LORD my God, I will give you thanks for ever.

31 *In te, Domine, speravi*

1 In you, O LORD, have I taken refuge;
let me never be put to shame; *
deliver me in your righteousness.

2 Incline your ear to me; *
make haste to deliver me.

3 Be my strong rock, a castle to keep me safe,
for you are my crag and my stronghold; *
for the sake of your Name, lead me and guide me.

4 Take me out of the net that they have secretly set for me, *
for you are my tower of strength.

5 Into your hands I commend my spirit, *
for you have redeemed me,
O LORD, O God of truth.

6 I hate those who cling to worthless idols, *
and I put my trust in the LORD.

7 I will rejoice and be glad because of your mercy; *
for you have seen my affliction;
you know my distress.

8 You have not shut me up in the power of the enemy; *
you have set my feet in an open place.

9 Have mercy on me, O LORD, for I am in trouble; *
my eye is consumed with sorrow,
and also my throat and my belly.

10 For my life is wasted with grief,
and my years with sighing; *
my strength fails me because of affliction,
and my bones are consumed.

11 I have become a reproach to all my enemies and even to my neighbors,
a dismay to those of my acquaintance; *
when they see me in the street they avoid me.

12 I am forgotten like a dead man, out of mind; *
I am as useless as a broken pot.

13 For I have heard the whispering of the crowd;
fear is all around; *
they put their heads together against me;
they plot to take my life.

14 But as for me, I have trusted in you, O LORD. *
I have said, "You are my God.

1789-1871

15 For I have heard the blasphemy of the multitude, and fear is on every side; while they conspire together against me, and take their counsel to take away my life.

16 But my hope hath been in thee, O LORD; I have said, Thou art my God.

17 My time is in thy hand; deliver me from the hand of mine enemies, and from them that persecute me.

18 Show thy servant the light of thy countenance, and save me for thy mercy's sake.

19 Let me not be confounded, O LORD, for I have called upon thee; let the ungodly be put to confusion, and be put to silence in the grave.

20 Let the lying lips be put to silence, which cruelly, disdainfully, and despitefully speak against the righteous.

21 O how plentiful is thy goodness, which thou hast laid up for them that fear thee, and that thou hast prepared for them that put their trust in thee, even before the sons of men!

22 Thou shalt hide them in the covert of thine own presence from the provoking of all men: thou shalt keep them secretly in thy tabernacle from the strife of tongues.

23 Thanks be to the LORD; for he hath showed me marvellous great kindness in a strong city.

24 And when I made haste, I said, I am cast out of the sight of thine eyes.

25 Nevertheless, thou heardest the voice of my prayer, when I cried unto thee.

26 O love the LORD, all ye his saints; for the LORD preserveth them that are faithful, and plenteously rewardeth the proud doer.

27 Be strong, and he shall establish your heart, all ye that put your trust in the LORD.

Evening Prayer.

Psalm xxxii. *Beati, quorum.*

BLESSED is he whose unrighteousness is forgiven, and whose sin is covered.

2 Blessed is the man unto whom the LORD imputeth no sin, and in whose spirit there is no guile.

3 For whilst I held my tongue, my bones consumed away through my daily complaining.

4 For thy hand is heavy upon me day and night, and my moisture is like the drought in summer.

5 I will acknowledge my sin unto thee; and mine unrighteousness have I not hid.

1892

15 For I have heard the blasphemy of the multitude: and fear is on every side; while they conspire together against me, and take their counsel to take away my life.

16 But my hope hath been in thee, O LORD: I have said, Thou art my God.

17 My time is in thy hand; deliver me from the hand of mine enemies: and from them that persecute me.

18 Show thy servant the light of thy countenance: and save me for thy mercy's sake.

19 Let me not be confounded, O LORD, for I have called upon thee: let the ungodly be put to confusion, and be put to silence in the grave.

20 Let the lying lips be put to silence: which cruelly, disdainfully, and despitefully speak against the righteous.

21 O how plentiful is thy goodness, which thou hast laid up for them that fear thee: and that thou hast prepared for them that put their trust in thee, even before the sons of men!

22 Thou shalt hide them privily by thine own presence from the provoking of all men: thou shalt keep them secretly in thy tabernacle from the strife of tongues.

23 Thanks be to the LORD: for he hath showed me marvellous great kindness in a strong city.

24 And when I made haste, I said: I am cast out of the sight of thine eyes.

25 Nevertheless, thou heardest the voice of my prayer: when I cried unto thee.

26 O love the LORD, all ye his saints: for the LORD preserveth them that are faithful, and plenteously rewardeth the proud doer.

27 Be strong, and he shall establish your heart: all ye that put your trust in the LORD.

Evening Prayer.

PSALM 32. *Beati quorum.*

BLESSED is he whose unrighteousness is forgiven: and whose sin is covered.

2 Blessed is the man unto whom the LORD imputeth no sin: and in whose spirit there is no guile.

3 For whilst I held my tongue: my bones consumed away through my daily complaining.

4 For thy hand is heavy upon me day and night: and my moisture is like the drought in summer.

5 I will acknowledge my sin unto thee: and mine unrighteousness have I not hid.

15 For I have heard the blasphemy of the multitude, and fear is on every side; * while they conspire together against me, and take their counsel to take away my life.

16 But my hope hath been in thee, O LORD; * I have said, Thou art my God.

17 My times are in thy hand; deliver me from the hand of mine enemies, * and from them that persecute me.

18 Show thy servant the light of thy countenance, * and save me for thy mercy's sake.

19 Let me not be confounded, O LORD, for I have called upon thee; * let the ungodly be put to confusion, and be put to silence in the grave.

20 Let the lying lips be put to silence, * which cruelly, disdainfully, and despitefully speak against the righteous.

21 O how plentiful is thy goodness, which thou hast laid up for them that fear thee, * and that thou hast prepared for them that put their trust in thee, even before the sons of men!

22 Thou shalt hide them in the covert of thine own presence from the plottings of men: * thou shalt keep them secretly in thy tabernacle from the strife of tongues.

23 Thanks be to the LORD; * for he hath showed me marvellous great kindness in a strong city.

24 But in my haste I said, * I am cast out of the sight of thine eyes.

25 Nevertheless, thou heardest the voice of my prayer, * when I cried unto thee.

26 O love the LORD, all ye his saints; * for the LORD preserveth them that are faithful, and plenteously rewardeth the proud doer.

27 Be strong, and he shall establish your heart, * all ye that put your trust in the LORD.

Evening Prayer.

Psalm 32. *Beati quorum.*

BLESSED is he whose unrighteousness is forgiven, * and whose sin is covered.

2 Blessed is the man unto whom the LORD imputeth no sin, * and in whose spirit there is no guile.

3 For whilst I held my tongue, * my bones consumed away through my daily complaining.

4 For thy hand was heavy upon me day and night, * and my moisture was like the drought in summer.

5 I acknowledged my sin unto thee; * and mine unrighteousness have I not hid.

15 My times are in your hand; *
rescue me from the hand of my enemies,
and from those who persecute me.

16 Make your face to shine upon your servant, *
and in your loving-kindness save me."

17 LORD, let me not be ashamed for having called upon you; *
rather, let the wicked be put to shame;
let them be silent in the grave.

18 Let the lying lips be silenced which speak against the righteous, *
haughtily, disdainfully, and with contempt.

19 How great is your goodness, O LORD!
which you have laid up for those who fear you; *
which you have done in the sight of all
for those who put their trust in you.

20 You hide them in the covert of your presence from those who slander them; *
you keep them in your shelter from the strife of tongues.

21 Blessed be the LORD! *
for he has shown me the wonders of his love in a besieged city.

22 Yet I said in my alarm,
"I have been cut off from the sight of your eyes." *
Nevertheless, you heard the sound of my entreaty
when I cried out to you.

23 Love the LORD, all you who worship him; *
the LORD protects the faithful,
but repays to the full those who act haughtily.

24 Be strong and let your heart take courage, *
all you who wait for the LORD.

Sixth Day: Evening Prayer

32 *Beati quorum*

1 Happy are they whose transgressions are forgiven, *
and whose sin is put away!

2 Happy are they to whom the LORD imputes no guilt, *
and in whose spirit there is no guile!

3 While I held my tongue, my bones withered away, *
because of my groaning all day long.

4 For your hand was heavy upon me day and night; *
my moisture was dried up as in the heat of summer.

5 Then I acknowledged my sin to you, *
and did not conceal my guilt.

6 I said, I will confess my sins unto the LORD ; and so thou forgavest the wickedness of my sin.

7 For this shall every one that is godly make his prayer unto thee, in a time when thou mayest be found ; surely the great water-floods they shall not come nigh him.

8 Thou art a place to hide me in ; thou shalt preserve me from trouble ; thou shalt compass me about with songs of deliverance.

9 I will inform thee, and teach thee in the way wherein thou shalt go ; and I will guide thee with mine eye.

10 Be ye not like to horse and mule, which have no understanding ; whose mouths must be held with bit and bridle, lest they fall upon thee.

11 Great plagues remain for the ungodly ; but whoso putteth his trust in the LORD, mercy embraceth him on every side.

12 Be glad, O ye righteous, and rejoice in the LORD ; and be joyful, all ye that are true of heart.

6 I said, I will confess my sins unto the LORD : and so thou forgavest the wickedness of my sin.

7 For this shall every one that is godly make his prayer unto thee, in a time when thou mayest be found : but in the great water-floods they shall not come nigh him.

8 Thou art a place to hide me in ; thou shalt preserve me from trouble : thou shalt compass me about with songs of deliverance.

9 I will inform thee, and teach thee in the way wherein thou shalt go : and I will guide thee with mine eye.

10 Be ye not like to horse and mule, which have no understanding : whose mouths must be held with bit and bridle, lest they fall upon thee.

11 Great plagues remain for the ungodly : but whoso putteth his trust in the LORD, mercy embraceth him on every side.

12 Be glad, O ye righteous, and rejoice in the LORD : and be joyful, all ye that are true of heart.

Psalm xxxiii. *Exultate, justi.*

REJOICE in the LORD, O ye righteous ; for it becometh well the just to be thankful.

2 Praise the LORD with harp ; sing praises unto him with the lute, and instrument of ten strings.

3 Sing unto the LORD a new song ; sing praises lustily unto him with a good courage.

4 For the word of the LORD is true ; and all his works are faithful.

5 He loveth righteousness and judgment ; the earth is full of the goodness of the LORD.

6 By the word of the LORD were the heavens made ; and all the hosts of them by the breath of his mouth.

7 He gathereth the waters of the sea together, as it were upon an heap ; and layeth up the deep, as in a treasure-house.

8 Let all the earth fear the LORD : stand in awe of him, all ye that dwell in the world.

9 For he spake, and it was done ; he commanded, and it stood fast.

10 The LORD bringeth the counsel of the heathen to nought, and maketh the devices of the people to be of none effect, and casteth out the counsels of princes.

11 The counsel of the LORD shall endure for ever, and the thoughts of his heart from generation to generation.

PSALM 33. *Exultate, justi.*

REJOICE in the LORD, O ye righteous : for it becometh well the just to be thankful.

2 Praise the LORD with harp : sing praises unto him with the lute, and instrument of ten strings.

3 Sing unto the LORD a new song : sing praises lustily unto him with a good courage.

4 For the word of the LORD is true : and all his works are faithful.

5 He loveth righteousness and judgment : the earth is full of the goodness of the LORD.

6 By the word of the LORD were the heavens made : and all the hosts of them by the breath of his mouth.

7 He gathereth the waters of the sea together, as it were upon an heap : and layeth up the deep, as in a treasure-house.

8 Let all the earth fear the LORD : stand in awe of him, all ye that dwell in the world.

9 For he spake, and it was done : he commanded, and it stood fast.

10 The LORD bringeth the counsel of the heathen to nought : and maketh the devices of the people to be of none effect, and casteth out the counsels of princes.

11 The counsel of the LORD shall endure for ever : and the thoughts of his heart from generation to generation.

6 I said, I will confess my sins unto the LORD; * and so thou forgavest the wickedness of my sin.

7 For this shall every one that is godly make his prayer unto thee, in a time when thou mayest be found; * surely the great water-floods shall not come nigh him.

8 Thou art a place to hide me in; thou shalt preserve me from trouble; * thou shalt compass me about with songs of deliverance.

9 I will inform thee, and teach thee in the way wherein thou shalt go; * and I will guide thee with mine eye.

10 Be ye not like to horse and mule, which have no understanding; * whose mouths must be held with bit and bridle, else they will not obey thee.

11 Great plagues remain for the ungodly; * but whoso putteth his trust in the LORD, mercy embraceth him on every side.

12 Be glad, O ye righteous, and rejoice in the LORD; * and be joyful, all ye that are true of heart.

6 I said, "I will confess my transgressions to the LORD." *
Then you forgave me the guilt of my sin.

7 Therefore all the faithful will make their prayer to you in time of trouble; *
when the great waters overflow, they shall not reach them.

8 You are my hiding-place;
you preserve me from trouble; *
you surround me with shouts of deliverance.

9 "I will instruct you and teach you in the way that you should go; *
I will guide you with my eye.

10 Do not be like horse or mule, which have no understanding; *
who must be fitted with bit and bridle,
or else they will not stay near you."

11 Great are the tribulations of the wicked; *
but mercy embraces those who trust in the LORD.

12 Be glad, you righteous, and rejoice in the LORD; *
shout for joy, all who are true of heart.

Psalm 33. *Exultate, justi.*

REJOICE in the LORD, O ye righteous; * for it becometh well the just to be thankful.

2 Praise the LORD with harp; * sing praises unto him with the lute, and instrument of ten strings.

3 Sing unto the LORD a new song; * sing praises lustily unto him with a good courage.

4 For the word of the LORD is true; * and all his works are faithful.

5 He loveth righteousness and judgment; * the earth is full of the goodness of the LORD.

6 By the word of the LORD were the heavens made; * and all the host of them by the breath of his mouth.

7 He gathereth the waters of the sea together, as it were upon an heap; * and layeth up the deep, as in a treasure-house.

8 Let all the earth fear the LORD: * stand in awe of him, all ye that dwell in the world.

9 For he spake, and it was done; * he commanded, and it stood fast.

10 The LORD bringeth the counsel of the heathen to nought, * and maketh the devices of the people to be of none effect, and casteth out the counsels of princes.

11 The counsel of the LORD shall endure for ever, * and the thoughts of his heart from generation to generation.

33 *Exultate, justi*

1 Rejoice in the LORD, you righteous; *
it is good for the just to sing praises.

2 Praise the LORD with the harp; *
play to him upon the psaltery and lyre.

3 Sing for him a new song; *
sound a fanfare with all your skill upon the trumpet.

4 For the word of the LORD is right, *
and all his works are sure.

5 He loves righteousness and justice; *
the loving-kindness of the LORD fills the whole earth.

6 By the word of the LORD were the heavens made, *
by the breath of his mouth all the heavenly hosts.

7 He gathers up the waters of the ocean as in a water-skin *
and stores up the depths of the sea.

8 Let all the earth fear the LORD; *
let all who dwell in the world stand in awe of him.

9 For he spoke, and it came to pass; *
he commanded, and it stood fast.

10 The LORD brings the will of the nations to naught; *
he thwarts the designs of the peoples.

11 But the LORD'S will stands fast for ever, *
and the designs of his heart from age to age.

1789-1871

12 Blessed are the people whose God is the Lord JEHOVAH ; and blessed are the folk that he hath chosen to him, to be his inheritance.
13 The LORD looked down from heaven, and beheld all the children of men ; from the habitation of his dwelling, he considereth all them that dwell on the earth.
14 He fashioneth all the hearts of them, and understandeth all their works.
15 There is no king that can be saved by the multitude of an host ; neither is any mighty man delivered by much strength.
16 A horse is counted but a vain thing to save a man ; neither shall he deliver any man by his great strength.
17 Behold, the eye of the LORD is upon them that fear him, and upon them that put their trust in his mercy ;
18 To deliver their soul from death, and to feed them in the time of dearth.
19 Our soul hath patiently tarried for the LORD ; for he is our help and our shield.
20 For our heart shall rejoice in him ; because we have hoped in his holy Name.
21 Let thy merciful kindness, O LORD, be upon us, like as we do put our trust in thee.

1892

12 Blessed are the people whose God is the Lord JEHOVAH : and blessed are the folk that he hath chosen to him, to be his inheritance.
13 The LORD looked down from heaven, and beheld all the children of men : from the habitation of his dwelling, he considereth all them that dwell on the earth.
14 He fashioneth all the hearts of them : and understandeth all their works.
15 There is no king that can be saved by the multitude of an host : neither is any mighty man delivered by much strength.
16 A horse is counted but a vain thing to save a man : neither shall he deliver any man by his great strength.
17 Behold, the eye of the LORD is upon them that fear him : and upon them that put their trust in his mercy ;
18 To deliver their soul from death : and to feed them in the time of dearth.
19 Our soul hath patiently tarried for the LORD : for he is our help and our shield.
20 For our heart shall rejoice in him : because we have hoped in his holy Name.
21 Let thy merciful kindness, O LORD, be upon us : like as we do put our trust in thee.

Psalm xxxiv. *Benedicam Domino.*[8]

I WILL alway give thanks unto the LORD ; his praise shall ever be in my mouth.
2 My soul shall make her boast in the LORD ; the humble shall hear thereof, and be glad.
3 O praise the LORD with me, and let us magnify his Name together.
4 I sought the LORD, and he heard me ; yea, he delivered me out of all my fear.
5 They had an eye unto him, and were lightened ; and their faces were not ashamed.
6 Lo, the poor crieth, and the LORD heareth him ; yea, and saveth him out of all his troubles.
7 The angel of the LORD tarrieth round about them that fear him, and delivereth them.
8 O taste, and see, how gracious the LORD is : blessed is the man that trusteth in him.
9 O fear the LORD, ye that are his saints ; for they that fear him lack nothing.

PSALM 34. *Benedicam Dominum.*

I WILL alway give thanks unto the LORD : his praise shall ever be in my mouth.
2 My soul shall make her boast in the LORD : the humble shall hear thereof, and be glad.
3 O praise the LORD with me : and let us magnify his Name together.
4 I sought the LORD, and he heard me : yea, he delivered me out of all my fear.
5 They had an eye unto him, and were lightened : and their faces were not ashamed.
6 Lo, the poor crieth, and the LORD heareth him : yea, and saveth him out of all his troubles.
7 The angel of the LORD tarrieth round about them that fear him : and delivereth them.
8 O taste, and see, how gracious the LORD is : blessed is the man that trusteth in him.
9 O fear the LORD, ye that are his saints : for they that fear him lack nothing.

[8]note change in 1892.

12 Blessed are the people whose God is the Lord JEHOVAH; * and blessed are the folk that he hath chosen to him, to be his inheritance.

13 The LORD looketh down from heaven, and beholdeth all the children of men; * from the habitation of his dwelling, he considereth all them that dwell on the earth.

14 He fashioneth all the hearts of them, * and understandeth all their works.

15 There is no king that can be saved by the multitude of an host; * neither is any mighty man delivered by much strength.

16 A horse is counted but a vain thing to save a man; * neither shall he deliver any man by his great strength.

17 Behold, the eye of the LORD is upon them that fear him, * and upon them that put their trust in his mercy;

18 To deliver their soul from death, * and to feed them in the time of dearth.

19 Our soul hath patiently tarried for the LORD; * for he is our help and our shield.

20 For our heart shall rejoice in him; * because we have hoped in his holy Name.

21 Let thy merciful kindness, O LORD, be upon us, * like as we do put our trust in thee.

Psalm 34. *Benedicam Dominum.*

I WILL alway give thanks unto the LORD; * his praise shall ever be in my mouth.

2 My soul shall make her boast in the LORD; * the humble shall hear thereof, and be glad.

3 O praise the LORD with me, * and let us magnify his Name together.

4 I sought the LORD, and he heard me; * yea, he delivered me out of all my fear.

5 They had an eye unto him, and were lightened; * and their faces were not ashamed.

6 Lo, the poor crieth, and the LORD heareth him; * yea, and saveth him out of all his troubles.

7 The angel of the LORD tarrieth round about them that fear him, * and delivereth them.

8 O taste, and see, how gracious the LORD is: * blessed is the man that trusteth in him.

9 O fear the LORD, ye that are his saints; * for they that fear him lack nothing.

12 Happy is the nation whose God is the LORD! *
happy the people he has chosen to be his own!

13 The LORD looks down from heaven, *
and beholds all the people in the world.

14 From where he sits enthroned he turns his gaze *
on all who dwell on the earth.

15 He fashions all the hearts of them *
and understands all their works.

16 There is no king that can be saved by a mighty army; *
a strong man is not delivered by his great strength.

17 The horse is a vain hope for deliverance; *
for all its strength it cannot save.

18 Behold, the eye of the LORD is upon those who fear him, *
on those who wait upon his love,

19 To pluck their lives from death, *
and to feed them in time of famine.

20 Our soul waits for the LORD; *
he is our help and our shield.

21 Indeed, our heart rejoices in him, *
for in his holy Name we put our trust.

22 Let you loving-kindness, O LORD, be upon us, *
as we have put our trust in you.

34 *Benedicam Dominum*

1 I will bless the LORD at all times; *
his praise shall ever be in my mouth.

2 I will glory in the LORD; *
let the humble hear and rejoice.

3 Proclaim with me the greatness of the LORD; *
let us exalt his Name together.

4 I sought the LORD, and he answered me *
and delivered me out of all my terror.

5 Look upon him and be radiant, *
and let not your faces be ashamed.

6 I called in my affliction and the LORD heard me *
and saved me from all my troubles.

7 The angel of the LORD encompasses those who fear him, *
and he will deliver them.

8 Taste and see that the LORD is good; *
happy are they who trust in him!

9 Fear the LORD, you that are his saints, *
for those who fear him lack nothing.

1789-1871	1892
10 The lions do lack, and suffer hunger ; but they who seek the LORD shall want no manner of thing that is good.	10 The lions do lack, and suffer hunger : but they who seek the LORD shall want no manner of thing that is good.
11 Come, ye children, and hearken unto me ; I will teach you the fear of the LORD.	11 Come, ye children, and hearken unto me : I will teach you the fear of the LORD.
12 What man is he that lusteth to live, and would fain see good days?	12 What man is he that lusteth to live : and would fain see good days?
13 Keep thy tongue from evil, and thy lips, that they speak no guile.	13 Keep thy tongue from evil : and thy lips, that they speak no guile.
14 Eschew evil, and do good ; seek peace, and ensue it.	14 Eschew evil, and do good : seek peace, and ensue it.
15 The eyes of the LORD are over the righteous, and his ears are open unto their prayers.	15 The eyes of the LORD are over the righteous : and his ears are open unto their prayers.
16 The countenance of the LORD is against them that do evil, to root out the remembrance of them from the earth.	16 The countenance of the LORD is against them that do evil : to root out the remembrance of them from the earth.
17 The righteous cry, and the LORD heareth them, and delivereth them out of all their troubles.	17 The righteous cry, and the LORD heareth them : and delivereth them out of all their troubles.
18 The LORD is nigh unto them that are of a contrite heart, and will save such as be of an humble spirit.	18 The LORD is nigh unto them that are of a contrite heart : and will save such as be of an humble spirit.
19 Great are the troubles of the righteous ; but the LORD delivereth him out of all.	19 Great are the troubles of the righteous : but the LORD delivereth him out of all.
20 He keepeth all his bones, so that not one of them is broken.	20 He keepeth all his bones : so that not one of them is broken.
21 But misfortune shall slay the ungodly ; and they that hate the righteous shall be desolate.	21 But misfortune shall slay the ungodly : and they that hate the righteous shall be desolate.
22 The LORD delivereth the souls of his servants ; and all they that put their trust in him shall not be destitute.	22 The LORD delivereth the souls of his servants : and all they that put their trust in him shall not be destitute.
THE SEVENTH DAY.	THE SEVENTH DAY.
Morning Prayer.	**Morning Prayer.**
Psalm xxxv. *Judica me, Domine.*[9]	PSALM 35. *Judica, Domine.*
PLEAD thou my cause, O LORD, with them that strive with me, and fight thou against them that fight against me.	PLEAD thou my cause, O LORD, with them that strive with me : and fight thou against them that fight against me.
2 Lay hand upon the shield and buckler, and stand up to help me.	2 Lay hand upon the shield and buckler : and stand up to help me.
3 Bring forth the spear, and stop the way against them that persecute me : say unto my soul, I am thy salvation.	3 Bring forth the spear, and stop the way against them that persecute me : say unto my soul, I am thy salvation.
4 Let them be confounded, and put to shame, that seek after my soul ; let them be turned back, and brought to confusion, that imagine mischief for me.	4 Let them be confounded, and put to shame, that seek after my soul : let them be turned back, and brought to confusion, that imagine mischief for me.
5 Let them be as the dust before the wind, and the angel of the LORD scattering them.	5 Let them be as the dust before the wind : and the angel of the LORD scattering them.

[9]*Judica, Domine* prior to 1822.

1928

10 The lions do lack, and suffer hunger; * but they
who seek the LORD shall want no manner of thing that
is good.
11 Come, ye children, and hearken unto me; * I
will teach you the fear of the LORD.
12 What man is he that lusteth to live, * and would
fain see good days?
13 Keep thy tongue from evil, * and thy lips, that
they speak no guile.
14 Eschew evil, and do good; * seek peace, and
ensue it.
15 The eyes of the LORD are over the righteous, *
and his ears are open unto their prayers.
16 The countenance of the LORD is against them
that do evil, * to root out the remembrance of them
from the earth.
17 The righteous cry, and the LORD heareth
them, * and delivereth them out of all their troubles.
18 The LORD is nigh unto them that are of a
contrite heart, * and will save such as be of an humble
spirit.
19 Great are the troubles of the righteous; * but
the LORD delivereth him out of all.
20 He keepeth all his bones, * so that not one of
them is broken.
21 But misfortune shall slay the ungodly; * and
they that hate the righteous shall be desolate.
22 The LORD delivereth the souls of his servants; *
and all they that put their trust in him shall not be
destitute.

The Seventh Day.

Morning Prayer.

Psalm 35. *Judica, Domine.*

PLEAD thou my cause, O LORD, with them that strive
with me, * and fight thou against them that fight
against me.
2 Lay hand upon the shield and buckler, * and
stand up to help me.
3 Bring forth the spear, and stop the way against
them that pursue me: * say unto my soul, I am thy
salvation.
4 Let them be confounded, and put to shame, that
seek after my soul; * let them be turned back, and
brought to confusion, that imagine mischief for me.
5 Let them be as the dust before the wind, * and
the angel of the LORD scattering them.

1979

10 The young lions lack and suffer hunger, *
but those who seek the LORD lack nothing that is good.

11 Come, children, and listen to me; *
I will teach you the fear of the LORD.

12 Who among you loves life *
and desires long life to enjoy prosperity?

13 Keep your tongue from evil-speaking *
and your lips from lying words.

14 Turn from evil and do good; *
seek peace and pursue it.

15 The eyes of the LORD are upon the righteous, *
and his ears are open to their cry.

16 The face of the LORD is against those who do evil, *
to root out the remembrance of them from the earth.

17 The righteous cry, and the LORD hears them *
and delivers them from all their troubles.

18 The LORD is near to the brokenhearted *
and will save those whose spirits are crushed.

19 Many are the troubles of the righteous, *
but the LORD will deliver him out of them all.

20 He will keep safe all his bones; *
not one of them shall be broken.

21 Evil shall slay the wicked, *
and those who hate the righteous will be punished.

22 The LORD ransoms the life of his servants, *
and none will be punished who trust in him.

Seventh Day: Morning Prayer

35 *Judica, Domine*

1 Fight those who fight me, O LORD; *
attack those who are attacking me.

2 Take up shield and armor *
and rise up to help me.

3 Draw the sword and bar the way against those
who pursue me; *
say to my soul, "I am your salvation."

4 Let those who seek after my life be shamed and humbled; *
let those who plot my ruin fall back and be dismayed.

5 Let them be like chaff before the wind, *
and let the angel of the LORD drive them away.

1789-1871

6 Let their way be dark and slippery, and let the angel of the LORD persecute them.

7 For they have privily laid their net to destroy me without a cause ; yea, even without a cause have they made a pit for my soul.

8 Let a sudden destruction come upon him unawares, and his net that he hath laid privily catch himself ; that he may fall into his own mischief.

9 And, my soul, be joyful in the LORD ; it shall rejoice in his salvation.

10 All my bones shall say, LORD, who is like unto thee, who deliverest the poor from him that is too strong for him ; yea, the poor, and him that is in misery, from him that spoileth him?

11 False witnesses did rise up : they laid to my charge things that I knew not.

12 They rewarded me evil for good, to the great discomfort of my soul.

13 Nevertheless, when they were sick, I put on sackcloth, and humbled my soul with fasting ; and my prayer shall turn into mine own bosom.

14 I behaved myself as though it had been my friend or my brother ; I went heavily, as one that mourneth for his mother.

15 But in mine adversity they rejoiced, and gathered themselves together ; yea, the very abjects came together against me unawares, making mouths at me, and ceased not.

16 With the flatterers were busy mockers, who gnashed upon me with their teeth.

17 Lord, how long wilt thou look upon this? O deliver my soul from the calamities which they bring on me, and my darling from the lions.

18 So will I give thee thanks in the great congregation ; I will praise thee among much people.

19 O let not them that are mine enemies triumph over me ungodly ; neither let them wink with their eyes, that hate me without a cause.

20 And why? their communing is not for peace ; but they imagine deceitful words against them that are quiet in the land.

21 They gaped upon me with their mouths, and said, Fie on thee! fie on thee! we saw it with our eyes.

22 This thou hast seen, O LORD ; hold not thy tongue then ; go not far from me, O Lord.

23 Awake, and stand up to judge my quarrel ; avenge thou my caûse, my God and my Lord.

1892

6 Let their way be dark and slippery : and let the angel of the LORD pursue them.

7 For they have privily laid their net to destroy me without a cause : yea, even without a cause have they made a pit for my soul.

8 Let a sudden destruction come upon him unawares, and his net that he hath laid privily catch himself : that he may fall into his own mischief.

9 And, my soul, be joyful in the LORD : it shall rejoice in his salvation.

10 All my bones shall say, LORD, who is like unto thee, who deliverest the poor from him that is too strong for him : yea, the poor, and him that is in misery, from him that spoileth him?

11 False witnesses did rise up : they laid to my charge things that I knew not.

12 They rewarded me evil for good : to the great discomfort of my soul.

13 Nevertheless, when they were sick, I put on sackcloth, and humbled my soul with fasting : and my prayer shall turn into mine own bosom.

14 I behaved myself as though it had been my friend or my brother : I went heavily, as one that mourneth for his mother.

15 But in mine adversity they rejoiced, and gathered themselves together : yea, the very abjects came together against me unawares, making mouths at me, and ceased not.

16 With the flatterers were busy mockers : who gnashed upon me with their teeth.

17 Lord, how long wilt thou look upon this : O deliver my soul from the calamities which they bring on me, and my darling from the lions.

18 So will I give thee thanks in the great congregation : I will praise thee among much people.

19 O let not them that are mine enemies triumph over me ungodly : neither let them wink with their eyes, that hate me without a cause.

20 And why? their communing is not for peace : but they imagine deceitful words against them that are quiet in the land.

21 They gaped upon me with their mouths, and said : Fie on thee! fie on thee! we saw it with our eyes.

22 This thou hast seen, O LORD : hold not thy tongue then, go not far from me, O Lord.

23 Awake, and stand up to judge my quarrel : avenge thou my cause, my God and my Lord.

1928

6 Let their way be dark and slippery, * and let the angel of the LORD pursue them.

7 For they have privily laid their net to destroy me without a cause; * yea, even without a cause have they made a pit for my soul.

8 Let a sudden destruction come upon him unawares, and his net that he hath laid privily catch himself; * that he may fall into his own mischief.

9 And my soul shall be joyful in the LORD; * it shall rejoice in his salvation.

10 All my bones shall say, LORD, who is like unto thee, who deliverest the poor from him that is too strong for him; * yea, the poor, and him that is in misery, from him that spoileth him?

11 False witnesses did rise up: * they laid to my charge things that I knew not.

12 They rewarded me evil for good, * to the great discomfort of my soul.

13 Nevertheless, when they were sick, I put on sackcloth, and humbled my soul with fasting; * and my prayer shall turn into mine own bosom.

14 I behaved myself as though it had been my friend or my brother; * I went heavily, as one that mourneth for his mother.

15 But in mine adversity they rejoiced, and gathered themselves together; * yea, the very abjects came together against me unawares, making mouths at me, and ceased not.

16 With the flatterers were busy mockers, * who gnashed upon me with their teeth.

17 Lord, how long wilt thou look upon this? * O deliver my soul from the calamities which they bring on me, and my darling from the lions.

18 So will I give thee thanks in the great congregation; * I will praise thee among much people.

19 O let not them that are mine enemies triumph over me ungodly; * neither let them wink with their eyes, that hate me without a cause.

20 And why? their communing is not for peace; * but they imagine deceitful words against them that are quiet in the land.

21 They gaped upon me with their mouths, and said, * Fie on thee! fie on thee! we saw it with our eyes.

22 This thou hast seen, O LORD; * hold not thy tongue then; go not far from me, O Lord.

23 Awake, and stand up to judge my quarrel; * avenge thou my cause, my God and my Lord.

1979

6 Let their way be dark and slippery, *
and let the angel of the LORD pursue them.

7 For they have secretly spread a net for me without a cause; *
without a cause they have dug a pit to take me alive.

8 Let ruin come upon them unawares; *
let them be caught in the net they hid;
let them fall into the pit they dug.

9 Then I will be joyful in the LORD; *
I will glory in his victory.

10 My very bones will say, "LORD, who is like you? *
You deliver the poor from those who are too strong for them,
the poor and needy from those who rob them."

11 Malicious witnesses rise up against me; *
they charge me with matters I know nothing about.

12 They pay me evil in exchange for good; *
my soul is full of despair.

13 But when they were sick I dressed in sack-cloth *
and humbled myself by fasting;

14 I prayed with my whole heart,
as one would for a friend or a brother; *
I behaved like one who mourns for his mother,
bowed down and grieving.

15 But when I stumbled, they were glad and gathered together;
they gathered against me; *
strangers whom I did not know tore me to pieces and would not stop.

16 They put me to the test and mocked me; *
they gnashed at me with their teeth.

17 O LORD, how long will you look on? *
rescue me from the roaring beasts,
and my life from the young lions.

18 I will give you thanks in the great congregation; *
I will praise you in the mighty throng.

19 Do not let my treacherous foes rejoice over me, *
nor let those who hate me without a cause wink at each other.

20 For they do not plan for peace, *
but invent deceitful schemes against the quiet in the land.

21 They opened their mouths at me and said, *
"Aha! we saw it with our own eyes."

22 You saw it, O LORD; do not be silent; *
O LORD, be not far from me.

23 Awake, arise, to my cause! *
to my defense, my God and my Lord!

1789-1871

24 Judge me, O LORD my God, according to thy righteousness ; and let them not triumph over me.

25 Let them not say in their hearts, There! there! so would we have it ; neither let them say, We have devoured him.

26 Let them be put to confusion and shame together, that rejoice at my trouble ; let them be clothed with rebuke and dishonour, that boast themselves against me.

27 Let them be glad and rejoice, that favour my righteous dealing ; yea, let them say alway, Blessed be the LORD, who hath pleasure in the prosperity of his servant.

28 And as for my tongue, it shall be talking of thy righteousness, and of thy praise, all the day long.

Psalm xxxvi. *Dixit injustus.*

MY heart showeth me the wickedness of the ungodly, that there is no fear of God before his eyes.

2 For he flattereth himself in his own sight, until his abominable sin be found out.

3 The words of his mouth are unrighteous and full of deceit : he hath left off to behave himself wisely, and to do good.

4 He imagineth mischief upon his bed, and hath set himself in no good way ; neither doth he abhor any thing that is evil.

5 Thy mercy, O LORD, reacheth unto the heavens, and thy faithfulness unto the clouds.

6 Thy righteousness standeth like the strong mountains : thy judgments are like the great deep.

7 Thou, LORD, shalt save both man and beast : how excellent is thy mercy, O God! and the children of men shall put their trust under the shadow of thy wings.

8 They shall be satisfied with the plenteousness of thy house ; and thou shalt give them drink of thy pleasures, as out of the river.

9 For with thee is the well of life ; and in thy light shall we see light.

10 O continue forth thy loving-kindness unto them that know thee, and thy righteousness unto them that are true of heart.

11 O let not the foot of pride come against me ; and let not the hand of the ungodly cast me down.

12 There are they fallen, all that work wickedness ; they are cast down, and shall not be able to stand.

1892

24 Judge me, O LORD my God, according to thy righteousness : and let them not triumph over me.

25 Let them not say in their hearts, There! there! so would we have it : neither let them say, We have devoured him.

26 Let them be put to confusion and shame together, that rejoice at my trouble : let them be clothed with rebuke and dishonour, that boast themselves against me.

27 Let them be glad and rejoice, that favour my righteous dealing : yea, let them say alway, Blessed be the LORD, who hath pleasure in the prosperity of his servant.

28 And as for my tongue, it shall be talking of thy righteousness : and of thy praise, all the day long.

PSALM 36. *Dixit injustus.*

MY heart showeth me the wickedness of the ungodly : that there is no fear of God before his eyes.

2 For he flattereth himself in his own sight : until his abominable sin be found out.

3 The words of his mouth are unrighteous and full of deceit : he hath left off to behave himself wisely, and to do good.

4 He imagineth mischief upon his bed, and hath set himself in no good way : neither doth he abhor any thing that is evil.

5 Thy mercy, O LORD, reacheth unto the heavens : and thy faithfulness unto the clouds.

6 Thy righteousness standeth like the strong mountains : thy judgments are like the great deep.

7 Thou, LORD, shalt save both man and beast ; how excellent is thy mercy, O God : and the children of men shall put their trust under the shadow of thy wings.

8 They shall be satisfied with the plenteousness of thy house : and thou shalt give them drink of thy pleasures, as out of the river.

9 For with thee is the well of life : and in thy light shall we see light.

10 O continue forth thy loving-kindness unto them that know thee : and thy righteousness unto them that are true of heart.

11 O let not the foot of pride come against me : and let not the hand of the ungodly cast me down.

12 There are they fallen, all that work wickedness : they are cast down, and shall not be able to stand.

24 Judge me, O LORD my God, according to thy righteousness; * and let them not triumph over me.

25 Let them not say in their hearts, There! there! so would we have it; * neither let them say, We have devoured him.

26 Let them be put to confusion and shame together, that rejoice at my trouble; * let them be clothed with rebuke and dishonour, that boast themselves against me.

27 Let them be glad and rejoice, that favour my righteous dealing; * yea, let them say alway, Blessed be the LORD, who hath pleasure in the prosperity of his servant.

28 And as for my tongue, it shall be talking of thy righteousness, * and of thy praise, all the day long.

24 Give me justice, O LORD my God,
according to you righteousness; *
do not let them triumph over me.

25 Do not let them say in their hearts,
"Aha! just what we want!" *
Do not let them say, "We have swallowed him up."

26 Let all who rejoice at my ruin be ashamed and disgraced; *
let those who boast against me be clothed with
dismay and shame.

27 Let those who favor my cause sing out with joy and be glad; *
let them say always, "Great is the LORD,
who desires the prosperity of his servant."

28 And my tongue shall be talking of your righteousness *
and of your praise all the day long.

Psalm 36. *Dixit injustus.*

MY heart showeth me the wickedness of the ungodly, * that there is no fear of God before his eyes.

2 For he flattereth himself in his own sight, * until his abominable sin be found out.

3 The words of his mouth are unrighteous and full of deceit: * he hath left off to behave himself wisely, and to do good.

4 He imagineth mischief upon his bed, and hath set himself in no good way; * neither doth he abhor any thing that is evil.

5 Thy mercy, O LORD, reacheth unto the heavens, * and thy faithfulness unto the clouds.

6 Thy righteousness standeth like the strong mountains: * thy judgments are like the great deep.

7 Thou, LORD, shalt save both man and beast: how excellent is thy mercy, O God! * and the children of men shall put their trust under the shadow of thy wings.

8 They shall be satisfied with the plenteousness of thy house; * and thou shalt give them drink of thy pleasures, as out of the river.

9 For with thee is the well of life; * and in thy light shall we see light.

10 O continue forth thy loving-kindness unto them that know thee, * and thy righteousness unto them that are true of heart.

11 O let not the foot of pride come against me; * and let not the hand of the ungodly cast me down.

12 There are they fallen, all that work wickedness; * they are cast down, and shall not be able to stand.

36 *Dixit injustus*

1 There is a voice of rebellion deep in the heart of the wicked; *
there is no fear of God before his eyes.

2 He flatters himself in his own eyes *
that his hateful sin will not be found out.

3 The words of his mouth are wicked and deceitful; *
he has left off acting wisely and doing good.

4 He thinks up wickedness upon his bed
and has set himself in no good way; *
he does not abhor that which is evil.

5 Your love, O LORD, reaches to the heavens, *
and your faithfulness to the clouds.

6 Your righteousness is like the strong mountains,
your justice like the great deep; *
you save both man and beast, O LORD.

7 How priceless is your love, O God! *
your people take refuge under the
shadow of your wings.

8 They feast upon the abundance of your house; *
you give them drink from the river of your delights.

9 For with you is the well of life, *
and in your light we see light.

10 Continue your loving-kindness to those who know you, *
and your favor to those who are true of heart.

11 Let not the foot of the proud come near me, *
nor the hand of the wicked push me aside.

12 See how they are fallen, those who work wickedness! *
they are cast down and shall not be able to rise.

Evening Prayer.

Psalm xxxvii. *Noli æmulari.*

FRET not thyself because of the ungodly ; neither be thou envious against the evil doers.

2 For they shall soon be cut down like the grass, and withered even as the green herb.

3 Put thou thy trust in the LORD, and be doing good ; dwell in the land, and verily thou shalt be fed.

4 Delight thou in the LORD, and he shall give thee thy heart's desire.

5 Commit thy way unto the LORD, and put thy trust in him, and he shall bring it to pass.

6 He shall make thy righteousness as clear as the light, and thy just dealing as the noon-day.

7 Hold thee still in the LORD, and abide patiently upon him : but grieve not thyself at him whose way doth prosper, against the man that doeth after evil counsels.

8 Leave off from wrath, and let go displeasure : fret not thyself, else shalt thou be moved to do evil.

9 Wicked doers shall be rooted out ; and they that patiently abide the LORD, those shall inherit the land.

10 Yet a little while, and the ungodly shall be clean gone : thou shalt look after his place, and he shall be away.

11 But the meek-spirited shall possess the earth, and shall be refreshed in the multitude of peace.

12 The ungodly seeketh counsel against the just, and gnasheth upon him with his teeth.

13 The Lord shall laugh him to scorn ; for he hath seen that his day is coming.

14 The ungodly have drawn out the sword, and have bent their bow, to cast down the poor and needy, and to slay such as are of a right conversation.

15 Their sword shall go through their own heart, and their bow shall be broken.

16 A small thing that the righteous hath, is better than great riches of the ungodly.

17 For the arms of the ungodly shall be broken, and the LORD upholdeth the righteous.

18 The LORD knoweth the days of the godly ; and their inheritance shall endure for ever.

Evening Prayer.

PSALM 37. *Noli æmulari.*

FRET not thyself because of the ungodly : neither be thou envious against the evil doers.

2 For they shall soon be cut down like the grass : and be withered even as the green herb.

3 Put thou thy trust in the LORD, and be doing good : dwell in the land, and verily thou shalt be fed.

4 Delight thou in the LORD : and he shall give thee thy heart's desire.

5 Commit thy way unto the LORD, and put thy trust in him : and he shall bring it to pass.

6 He shall make thy righteousness as clear as the light : and thy just dealing as the noon-day.

7 Hold thee still in the LORD, and abide patiently upon him : but grieve not thyself at him whose way doth prosper, against the man that doeth after evil counsels.

8 Leave off from wrath, and let go displeasure : fret not thyself, else shalt thou be moved to do evil.

9 Wicked doers shall be rooted out : and they that patiently abide the LORD, those shall inherit the land.

10 Yet a little while, and the ungodly shall be clean gone : thou shalt look after his place, and he shall be away.

11 But the meek-spirited shall possess the earth : and shall be refreshed in the multitude of peace.

12 The ungodly seeketh counsel against the just : and gnasheth upon him with his teeth.

13 The Lord shall laugh him to scorn : for he hath seen that his day is coming.

14 The ungodly have drawn out the sword, and have bent their bow : to cast down the poor and needy, and to slay such as are of a right conversation.

15 Their sword shall go through their own heart : and their bow shall be broken.

16 A small thing that the righteous hath : is better than great riches of the ungodly.

17 For the arms of the ungodly shall be broken : and the LORD upholdeth the righteous.

18 The LORD knoweth the days of the godly : and their inheritance shall endure for ever.

Evening Prayer.

Psalm 37. *Noli æmulari.*

FRET not thyself because of the ungodly; * neither be thou envious against the evil doers.

2 For they shall soon be cut down like the grass, * and withered even as the green herb.

3 Put thou thy trust in the LORD, and be doing good; * dwell in the land, and verily thou shalt be fed.

4 Delight thou in the LORD, * and he shall give thee thy heart's desire.

5 Commit thy way unto the LORD, and put thy trust in him, * and he shall bring it to pass.

6 He shall make thy righteousness as clear as the light, * and thy just dealing as the noon-day.

7 Hold thee still in the LORD, and abide patiently upon him: * but grieve not thyself at him whose way doth prosper, against the man that doeth after evil counsels.

8 Leave off from wrath, and let go displeasure: * fret not thyself, else shalt thou be moved to do evil.

9 Wicked doers shall be rooted out; * and they that patiently abide the LORD, those shall inherit the land.

10 Yet a little while, and the ungodly shall be clean gone: * thou shalt look after his place, and he shall be away.

11 But the meek-spirited shall possess the earth, * and shall be refreshed in the multitude of peace.

12 The ungodly seeketh counsel against the just, * and gnasheth upon him with his teeth.

13 The Lord shall laugh him to scorn; * for he hath seen that his day is coming.

14 The ungodly have drawn out the sword, and have bent their bow, * to cast down the poor and needy, and to slay such as be upright in their ways.

15 Their sword shall go through their own heart, * and their bow shall be broken.

16 A small thing that the righteous hath, * is better than great riches of the ungodly.

17 For the arms of the ungodly shall be broken, * and the LORD upholdeth the righteous.

18 The LORD knoweth the days of the godly; * and their inheritance shall endure for ever.

Seventh Day: Evening Prayer

37

Part I *Noli æmulari*

1 Do not fret yourself because of evildoers; *
do not be jealous of those who do wrong.

2 For they shall soon wither like the grass, *
and like the green grass fade away.

3 Put your trust in the LORD and do good; *
dwell in the land and feed on its riches.

4 Take delight in the LORD, *
and he shall give you your heart's desire.

5 Commit your way to the LORD and put your trust in him, *
and he will bring it to pass.

6 He will make your righteousness as clear as the light *
and your just dealing as the noonday.

7 Be still before the LORD *
and wait patiently for him.

8 Do not fret yourself over the one who prospers, *
the one who succeeds in evil schemes.

9 Refrain from anger, leave rage alone; *
do not fret yourself; it leads only to evil.

10 For evildoers shall be cut off, *
but those who wait upon the LORD shall possess the land.

11 In a little while the wicked shall be no more; *
you shall search out their place, but they will not be there.

12 But the lowly shall possess the land; *
they will delight in abundance of peace.

13 The wicked plot against the righteous *
and gnash at them with their teeth.

14 The LORD laughs at the wicked, *
because he sees that their day will come.

15 The wicked draw their sword and bend their bow
to strike down the poor and needy, *
to slaughter those who are upright in their ways.

16 Their sword shall go through their own heart, *
and their bow shall be broken.

17 The little that the righteous has *
is better than great riches of the wicked.

18 For the power of the wicked shall be broken, *
but the LORD upholds the righteous.

1789-1871	1892
19 They shall not be confounded in the perilous time ; and in the days of dearth they shall have enough.	19 They shall not be confounded in the perilous time : and in the days of dearth they shall have enough.
20 As for the ungodly, they shall perish, and the enemies of the LORD shall consume as the fat of lambs : yea, even as the smoke shall they consume away.	20 As for the ungodly, they shall perish, and the enemies of the LORD shall consume as the fat of lambs : yea, even as the smoke shall they consume away.
21 The ungodly borroweth, and payeth not again ; but the righteous is merciful and liberal.	21 The ungodly borroweth, and payeth not again : but the righteous is merciful and liberal.
22 Such as are blessed of God, shall possess the land ; and they that are cursed of him, shall be rooted out.	22 Such as are blessed of God, shall possess the land : and they that are cursed of him, shall be rooted out.
23 The LORD ordereth a good man's going, and maketh his way acceptable to himself.	23 The LORD ordereth a good man's goings : and maketh his way acceptable to himself.
24 Though he fall, he shall not be cast away ; for the LORD upholdeth him with his hand.	24 Though he fall, he shall not be cast away : for the LORD upholdeth him with his hand.
25 I have been young, and now am old ; and yet saw I never the righteous forsaken, nor his seed begging their bread.	25 I have been young, and now am old : and yet saw I never the righteous forsaken, nor his seed begging their bread.
26 The righteous is ever merciful, and lendeth ; and his seed is blessed.	26 The righteous is ever merciful, and lendeth : and his seed is blessed.
27 Flee from evil, and do the thing that is good ; and dwell for evermore.	27 Flee from evil, and do the thing that is good : and dwell for evermore.
28 For the LORD loveth the thing that is right ; he forsaketh not his that be godly, but they are preserved for ever.	28 For the LORD loveth the thing that is right : he forsaketh not his that be godly, but they are preserved for ever.
29 The unrighteous shall be punished ; as for the seed of the ungodly, it shall be rooted out.	29 The unrighteous shall be punished : as for the seed of the ungodly, it shall be rooted out.
30 The righteous shall inherit the land, and dwell therein for ever.	30 The righteous shall inherit the land : and dwell therein for ever.
31 The mouth of the righteous is exercised in wisdom, and his tongue will be talking of judgment.	31 The mouth of the righteous is exercised in wisdom : and his tongue will be talking of judgment.
32 The law of his God is in his heart, and his goings shall not slide.	32 The law of his God is in his heart : and his going shall not slide.
33 The ungodly seeth the righteous, and seeketh occasion to slay him.	33 The ungodly seethed the righteous : and seeketh occasion to slay him.
34 The LORD will not leave him in his hand, nor condemn him when he is judged.	34 The LORD will not leave him in his hand : nor condemn him when he is judged.
35 Hope thou in the LORD, and keep his way, and he shall promote thee, that thou shalt possess the land : when the ungodly shall perish, thou shalt see it.	35 Hope thou in the LORD, and keep his way, and he shall promote thee, that thou shalt possess the land : when the ungodly shall perish, thou shalt see it.
36 I myself have seen the ungodly in great power, and flourishing like a green bay-tree.	36 I myself have seen the ungodly in great power : and flourishing like a green bay-tree.
37 I went by, and lo, he was gone : I sought him, but his place could no where be found.	37 I went by, and lo, he was gone : I sought him, but his place could no where be found.

19 They shall not be confounded in the perilous time; * and in the days of dearth they shall have enough.

20 As for the ungodly, they shall perish, and the enemies of the LORD shall consume as the fat of lambs: * yea, even as the smoke shall they consume away.

21 The ungodly borroweth, and payeth not again; * but the righteous is merciful and liberal.

22 Such as are blessed of God, shall possess the land; * and they that are cursed of him, shall be rooted out.

23 The LORD ordereth a good man's going, * and maketh his way acceptable to himself.

24 Though he fall, he shall not be cast away; * for the LORD upholdeth him with his hand.

25 I have been young, and now am old; * and yet saw I never the righteous forsaken, nor his seed begging their bread.

26 The righteous is ever merciful, and lendeth; * and his seed is blessed.

27 Flee from evil, and do the thing that is good; * and dwell for evermore.

28 For the LORD loveth the thing that is right; * he forsaketh not his that be godly, but they are preserved for ever.

29 The unrighteous shall be punished; * as for the seed of the ungodly, it shall be rooted out.

30 The righteous shall inherit the land, * and dwell therein for ever.

31 The mouth of the righteous is exercised in wisdom, * and his tongue will be talking of judgment.

32 The law of his God is in his heart, * and his going shall not slide.

33 The ungodly watcheth the righteous, * and seeketh occasion to slay him.

34 The LORD will not leave him in his hand, * nor condemn him when he is judged.

35 Hope thou in the LORD, and keep his way, and he shall promote thee, that thou shalt possess the land: * when the ungodly shall perish, thou shalt see it.

36 I myself have seen the ungodly in great power, * and flourishing like a green bay-tree.

37 I went by, and lo, he was gone: * I sought him, but his place could no where be found.

Psalm 37: Part II *Novit Dominus*

19 The LORD cares for the lives of the godly, *
and their inheritance shall last for ever.

20 They shall not be ashamed in bad times, *
and in days of famine they shall have enough.

21 As for the wicked, they shall perish, *
and the enemies of the LORD, like the glory of the meadows, shall vanish;
they shall vanish like smoke.

22 The wicked borrow and do not repay, *
but the righteous are generous in giving.

23 Those who are blessed by God shall possess the land, *
but those who are cursed by him shall be destroyed.

24 Our steps are directed by the LORD; *
he strengthens those in whose way he delights.

25 If they stumble, they shall not fall headlong, *
for the LORD holds them by the hand.

26 I have been young and now I am old, *
but never have I seen the righteous forsaken,
or their children begging bread.

27 The righteous are always generous in their lending, *
and their children shall be a blessing.

28 Turn from evil, and do good, *
and dwell in the land for ever.

29 For the LORD loves justice; *
he does not forsake his faithful ones.

30 They shall be kept safe for ever, *
but the offspring of the wicked shall be destroyed.

31 The righteous shall possess the land *
and dwell in it for ever.

32 The mouth of the righteous utters wisdom, *
and their tongue speaks what is right.

33 The law of their God is in their heart, *
and their footsteps shall not falter.

34 The wicked spy on the righteous *
and seek occasion to kill them.

35 The LORD will not abandon them to their hand, *
nor let them be found guilty when brought to trial.

36 Wait upon the LORD and keep his way; *
he will raise you up to possess the land,
and when the wicked are cut off, you will see it.

37 I have seen the wicked in their arrogance, *
flourishing like a tree in full leaf.

1789-1871

38 Keep innocency, and take heed unto the thing that is right; for that shall bring a man peace at the last.

39 As for the transgressors, they shall perish together; and the end of the ungodly is, they shall be rooted out at the last.

40 But the salvation of the righteous cometh of the LORD; who is also their strength in the time of trouble.

41 And the LORD shall stand by them, and save them: he shall deliver them from the ungodly, and shall save them, because they put their trust in him.

THE EIGHTH DAY.

Morning Prayer.

Psalm xxxviii *Domine, ne in furore.*

PUT me not to rebuke, O LORD, in thine anger; neither chasten me in thy heavy displeasure:

2 For thine arrows stick fast in me, and thy hand presseth me sore.

3 There is no health in my flesh, because of thy displeasure; neither is there any rest in my bones, by reason of my sin.

4 For my wickednesses are gone over my head, and are like a sore burden, too heavy for me to bear.

5 My wounds stink, and are corrupt, through my foolishness.

6 I am brought into so great trouble and misery, that I go mourning all the day long.

7 For my loins are filled with a sore disease, and there is no whole part in my body.

8 I am feeble and sore smitten; I have roared for the very disquietness of my heart.

9 Lord, thou knowest all my desire; and my groaning is not hid from thee.

10 My heart panteth, my strength hath failed me, and the sight of mine eyes is gone from me.

11 My lovers and my neighbours did stand looking upon my trouble, and my kinsmen stood afar off.

12 They also that sought after my life laid snares for me; and they that went about to do me evil talked of wickedness, and imagined deceit all the day long.

13 As for me, I was like a deaf man, and heard not; and as one that is dumb, who doth not open his mouth.

1892

38 Keep innocency, and take heed unto the thing that is right: for that shall bring a man peace at the last.

39 As for the transgressors, they shall perish together: and the end of the ungodly is, they shall be rooted out at the last.

40 But the salvation of the righteous cometh of the LORD: who is also their strength in the time of trouble.

41 And the LORD shall stand by them, and save them: he shall deliver them from the ungodly, and shall save them, because they put their trust in him.

THE EIGHTH DAY.

Morning Prayer.

PSALM 38. *Domine, ne in furore.*

PUT me not to rebuke, O LORD, in thine anger: neither chasten me in thy heavy displeasure:

2 For thine arrows stick fast in me: and thy hand presseth me sore.

3 There is no health in my flesh, because of thy displeasure: neither is there any rest in my bones, by reason of my sin.

4 For my wickednesses are gone over my head: and are like a sore burden, too heavy for me to bear.

5 My wounds stink, and are corrupt: through my foolishness.

6 I am brought into so great trouble and misery: that I go mourning all the day long.

7 For my loins are filled with a sore disease: and there is no whole part in my body.

8 I am feeble and sore smitten: I have roared for the very disquietness of my heart.

9 Lord, thou knowest all my desire: and my groaning is not hid from thee.

10 My heart panteth, my strength hath failed me: and the light of mine eyes is gone from me.

11 My lovers and my neighbours did stand looking upon my trouble: and my kinsmen stood afar off.

12 They also that sought after my life laid snares for me: and they that went about to do me evil talked of wickedness, and imagined deceit all the day long.

13 As for me, I was like a deaf man, and heard not: and as one that is dumb, who doth not open his mouth.

38 Keep innocency, and take heed unto the thing that is right; * for that shall bring a man peace at the last.

39 As for the transgressors, they shall perish together; * and the end of the ungodly is, they shall be rooted out at the last.

40 But the salvation of the righteous cometh of the LORD; * who is also their strength in the time of trouble.

41 And the LORD shall stand by them, and save them: * he shall deliver them from the ungodly, and shall save them, because they put their trust in him.

The Eighth Day.

Morning Prayer.

Psalm 38. *Domine, ne in furore.*

PUT me not to rebuke, O LORD, in thine anger; * neither chasten me in thy heavy displeasure:

2 For thine arrows stick fast in me, * and thy hand presseth me sore.

3 There is no health in my flesh, because of thy displeasure; * neither is there any rest in my bones, by reason of my sin.

4 For my wickednesses are gone over my head, * and are like a sore burden, too heavy for me to bear.

5 My wounds stink, and are corrupt, * through my foolishness.

6 I am brought into so great trouble and misery, * that I go mourning all the day long.

7 For my loins are filled with a sore disease, * and there is no whole part in my body.

8 I am feeble and sore smitten; * I have roared for the very disquietness of my heart.

9 Lord, thou knowest all my desire; * and my groaning is not hid from thee.

10 My heart panteth, my strength hath failed me, * and the light of mine eyes is gone from me.

11 My lovers and my neighbours did stand looking upon my trouble, * and my kinsmen stood afar off.

12 They also that sought after my life laid snares for me; * and they that went about to do me evil talked of wickedness, and imagined deceit all the day long.

13 As for me, I was like a deaf man, and heard not; * and as one that is dumb, who doth not open his mouth.

38 I went by, and behold, they were not there; *
I searched for them, but they could not be found.

39 Mark those who are honest;
observe the upright; *
for there is a future for the peaceable.

40 Transgressors shall be destroyed, one and all; *
the future of the wicked is cut off.

41 But the deliverance of the righteous comes from the LORD; *
he is their stronghold in time of trouble.

42 The LORD will help them and rescue them; *
he will rescue them from the wicked and deliver them,
because they seek refuge in him.

Eighth Day: Morning Prayer

38 *Domine, ne in furore*

1 O LORD, do not rebuke me in your anger; *
do not punish me in your wrath.

2 For your arrows have already pierced me, *
and your hand presses hard upon me.

3 There is no health in my flesh,
because of your indignation; *
there is no soundness in my body, because of my sin.

4 For my iniquities overwhelm me; *
like a heavy burden they are too much for me to bear.

5 My wounds stink and fester *
by reason of my foolishness.

6 I am utterly bowed down and prostrate; *
I go about in mourning all the day long.

7 My loins are filled with searing pain; *
there is no health in my body.

8 I am utterly numb and crushed; *
I wail, because of the groaning of my heart.

9 O LORD, you know all my desires, *
and my sighing is not hidden from you.

10 My heart is pounding, my strength has failed me, *
and the brightness of my eyes is gone from me.

11 My friends and companions draw back from my affliction; *
my neighbors stand afar off.

12 Those who seek after my life lay snares for me; *
those who strive to hurt me speak of my ruin
and plot treachery all the day long.

13 But I am like the deaf who do not hear, *
like those who are mute and do not open their mouth.

1789-1871

14 I became even as a man that heareth not, and in whose mouth are no reproofs.

15 For in thee, O LORD, have I put my trust; thou shalt answer for me, O Lord my God.

16 I have required that they, even mine enemies, should not triumph over me; for when my foot slipt, they rejoiced greatly against me.

17 And I truly am set in the plague, and my heaviness is ever in my sight.

18 For I will confess my wickedness, and be sorry for my sin.

19 But mine enemies live, and are mighty; and they that hate me wrongfully are many in number.

20 They also that reward evil for good are against me; because I follow the thing that good is.

21 Forsake me not, O LORD my God; be not thou far from me.

22 Haste thee to help me, O Lord God of my salvation.

1892

14 I became even as a man that heareth not: and in whose mouth are no reproofs.

15 For in thee, O LORD, have I put my trust: thou shalt answer for me, O Lord my God.

16 I have required that they, even mine enemies, should not triumph over me: for when my foot slipt, they rejoiced greatly against me.

17 And I truly am set in the plague: and my heaviness is ever in my sight.

18 For I will confess my wickedness: and be sorry for my sin.

19 But mine enemies live, and are mighty: and they that hate me wrongfully are many in number.

20 They also that reward evil for good are against me: because I follow the thing that good is.

21 Forsake me not, O LORD my God: be not thou far from me.

22 Haste thee to help me: O Lord God of my salvation.

1789-1871

Psalm xxxix, *Dixi, custodiam.*

I SAID, I will take heed to my ways, that I offend not in my tongue.

2 I will keep my mouth as it were with a bridle, while the ungodly is in my sight.

3 I held my tongue, and spake nothing: I kept silence, yea, even from good words; but it was pain and grief to me.

4 My heart was hot within me: and while I was thus musing the fire kindled, and at the last I spake with my tongue;

5 LORD, let me know mine end, and the number of my days; that I may be certified how long I have to live.

6 Behold, thou hast made my days as it were a span long, and mine age is even as nothing in respect of thee; and verily every man living is altogether vanity.

7 For man walketh in a vain shadow, and disquieteth himself in vain; he heapeth up riches, and cannot tell who shall gather them.

8 And now, Lord, what is my hope? Truly my hope is even in thee.

9 Deliver me from all mine offences; and make me not a rebuke unto the foolish.

1892

PSALM 39. *Dixi, Custodiam.*

I SAID, I will take heed to my ways: that I offend not in my tongue.

2 I will keep my mouth as it were with a bridle: while the ungodly is in my sight.

3 I held my tongue, and spake nothing: I kept silence, yea, even from good words; but it was pain and grief to me.

4 My heart was hot within me; and while I was thus musing the fire kindled: and at the last I spake with my tongue:

5 LORD, let me know mine end, and the number of my days: that I may be certified how long I have to live.

6 Behold, thou hast made my days as it were a span long, and mine age is even as nothing in respect of thee; and verily every man living is altogether vanity.

7 For man walketh in a vain shadow, and disquieteth himself in vain: he heapeth up riches, and cannot tell who shall gather them.

8 And now, Lord, what is my hope: truly my hope is even in thee.

9 Deliver me from all mine offences: and make me not a rebuke unto the foolish.

14 I became even as a man that heareth not, * and in whose mouth are no reproofs.

15 For in thee, O LORD, have I put my trust; * thou shalt answer for me, O Lord my God.

16 I have required that they, even mine enemies, should not triumph over me; * for when my foot slipt, they rejoiced greatly against me.

17 And I truly am set in the plague, * and my heaviness is ever in my sight.

18 For I will confess my wickedness, * and be sorry for my sin.

19 But mine enemies live, and are mighty; * and they that hate me wrongfully are many in number.

20 They also that reward evil for good are against me; * because I follow the thing that good is.

21 Forsake me not, O LORD my God; * be not thou far from me.

22 Haste thee to help me, * O Lord God of my salvation.

14 I have become like one who does not hear *
and from whose mouth comes no defense.

15 For in you, O LORD, have I fixed my hope; *
you will answer me, O Lord my God.

16 For I said, "Do not let them rejoice at my expense, *
those who gloat over me when my foot slips."

17 Truly, I am on the verge of falling, *
and my pain is always with me.

18 I will confess my iniquity *
and be sorry for my sin.

19 Those who are my enemies without cause are mighty, *
and many in number are those who wrongfully hate me.

20 Those who repay evil for good slander me, *
because I follow the course that is right.

21 O LORD, do not forsake me; *
be not far from me, O my God.

22 Make haste to help me, *
O Lord of my salvation.

Psalm 39. *Dixi, Custodiam.*

I SAID, I will take heed to my ways, * that I offend not in my tongue.

2 I will keep my mouth as it were with a bridle, * while the ungodly is in my sight.

3 I held my tongue, and spake nothing: * I kept silence, yea, even from good words; but it was pain and grief to me.

4 My heart was hot within me: and while I was thus musing the fire kindled, * and at the last I spake with my tongue:

5 LORD, let me know mine end, and the number of my days; * that I may be certified how long I have to live.

6 Behold, thou hast made my days as it were a span long, and mine age is even as nothing in respect of thee; * and verily every man living is altogether vanity.

7 For man walketh in a vain shadow, and disquieteth himself in vain; * he heapeth up riches, and cannot tell who shall gather them.

8 And now, Lord, what is my hope? * truly my hope is even in thee.

9 Deliver me from all mine offences; * and make me not a rebuke unto the foolish.

39 *Dixi, Custodiam*

1 I said, "I will keep watch upon my ways, *
so that I do not offend with my tongue.

2 I will put a muzzle on my mouth *
while the wicked are in my presence."

3 So I held my tongue and said nothing; *
I refrained from rash words;
but my pain became unbearable.

4 My heart was hot within me;
while I pondered, the fire burst into flame; *
I spoke out with my tongue:

5 LORD, let me know my end and the number of my days, *
so that I may know how short my life is.

6 You have given me a mere handful of days,
and my lifetime is as nothing in your sight; *
truly, even those who stand erect are but a puff of wind.

7 We walk about like a shadow,
and in vain we are in turmoil; *
we heap up riches and cannot tell who will gather them.

8 And now, what is my hope? *
O Lord, my hope is in you.

9 Deliver me from all my transgressions *
and do not make me the taunt of the fool.

10 I became dumb, and opened not my mouth ; for it was thy doing.
11 Take thy plague away from me: I am even consumed by the means of thy heavy hand.
12 When thou with rebukes dost chasten man for sin, thou makest his beauty to consume away, like as it were a moth fretting a garment : every man therefore is but vanity.
13 Hear my prayer, O LORD, and with thine ears consider my calling ; hold not thy peace at my tears ;
14 For I am a stranger with thee : and a sojourner, as all my fathers were.
15 O spare me a little, that I may recover my strength, before I go hence, and be no more seen.

Psalm xl. *Expectans expectavi.*

I WAITED patiently for the LORD, and he inclined unto me, and heard my calling.
2 He brought me also out of the horrible pit, out of the mire and clay, and set my feet upon the rock, and ordered my goings.
3 And he hath put a new song in my mouth, even a thanksgiving unto our God.
4 Many shall see it, and fear, and shall put their trust in the LORD.
5 Blessed is the man that hath set his hope in the LORD, and turned not unto the proud, and to such as go about with lies.
6 O LORD my God, great are the wondrous works which thou hast done, like as be also thy thoughts, which are to us-ward ; and yet there is no man that ordereth them unto thee.
7 If I should declare them, and speak of them, they should be more than I am able to express.
8 Sacrifice and meat-offering thou wouldest not, but mine ears hast thou opened.
9 Burnt-offering and sacrifice for sin hast thou not required : then said I, Lo, I come ;
10 In the volume of the book it is written of me, that I should fulfil thy will, O my God : I am content to do it ; yea, thy law is within my heart.
11 I have declared thy righteousness in the great congregation : lo, I will not refrain my lips, O LORD, and that thou knowest.

10 I became dumb, and opened not my mouth : for it was thy doing.
11 Take thy plague away from me: I am even consumed by the means of thy heavy hand.
12 When thou with rebukes dost chasten man for sin, thou makest his beauty to consume away, like as it were a moth fretting a garment : every man therefore is but vanity.
13 Hear my prayer, O LORD, and with thine ears consider my calling : hold not thy peace at my tears ;
14 For I am a stranger with thee, and a sojourner : as all my fathers were.
15 O spare me a little, that I may recover my strength : before I go hence, and be no more seen.

PSALM 40. *Expectans expectavi.*

I WAITED patiently for the LORD : and he inclined unto me, and heard my calling.
2 He brought me also out of the horrible pit, out of the mire and clay : and set my feet upon the rock, and ordered my goings.
3 And he hath put a new song in my mouth : even a thanksgiving unto our God.
4 Many shall see it, and fear : and shall put their trust in the LORD.
5 Blessed is the man that hath set his hope in the LORD : and turned not unto the proud, and to such as go about with lies.
6 O LORD my God, great are the wondrous works which thou hast done, like as be also thy thoughts, which are to us-ward : and yet there is no man that ordereth them unto thee.
7 If I should declare them, and speak of them : they should be more than I am able to express.
8 Sacrifice and meat-offering thou wouldest not : but mine ears hast thou opened.
9 Burnt-offering and sacrifice for sin hast thou not required : then said I, Lo, I come ;
10 In the volume of the book it is written of me, that I should fulfil thy will, O my God : I am content to do it ; yea, thy law is within my heart.
11 I have declared thy righteousness in the great congregation : lo, I will not refrain my lips, O LORD, and that thou knowest.

10 I became dumb, and opened not my mouth; * for it was thy doing.

11 Take thy plague away from me: * I am even consumed by the means of thy heavy hand.

12 When thou with rebukes dost chasten man for sin, thou makest his beauty to consume away, like as it were a moth fretting a garment: * every man therefore is but vanity.

13 Hear my prayer, O LORD, and with thine ears consider my calling; * hold not thy peace at my tears;

14 For I am a stranger with thee, and a sojourner, * as all my fathers were.

15 O spare me a little, that I may recover my strength, * before I go hence, and be no more seen.

Psalm 40. *Expectans expectavi.*

I WAITED patiently for the LORD, * and he inclined unto me, and heard my calling.

2 He brought me also out of the horrible pit, out of the mire and clay, * and set my feet upon the rock, and ordered my goings.

3 And he hath put a new song in my mouth, * even a thanksgiving unto our God.

4 Many shall see it, and fear, * and shall put their trust in the LORD.

5 Blessed is the man that hath set his hope in the LORD, * and turned not unto the proud, and to such as go about with lies.

6 O LORD my God, great are the wondrous works which thou hast done, like as be also thy thoughts, which are to us-ward; * and yet there is no man that ordereth them unto thee.

7 If I should declare them, and speak of them, * they should be more than I am able to express.

8 Sacrifice and offering thou wouldest not, * but mine ears hast thou opened.

9 Burnt-offering and sacrifice for sin hast thou not required: * then said I, Lo, I come;

10 In the volume of the book it is written of me, that I should fulfil thy will, O my God: * I am content to do it; yea, thy law is within my heart.

11 I have declared thy righteousness in the great congregation: * lo, I will not refrain my lips, O LORD, and that thou knowest.

10 I fell silent and did not open my mouth, *
for surely it was you that did it.

11 Take your affliction from me; *
I am worn down by the blows of your hand.

12 With rebukes for sin you punish us;
like a moth you eat away all that is dear to us; *
truly, everyone is but a puff of wind.

13 Hear my prayer, O LORD,
and give ear to my cry; *
hold not your peace at my tears.

14 For I am but a sojourner with you, *
a wayfarer, as all my forebears were.

15 Turn your gaze from me, that I may be glad again, *
before I go my way and am no more.

40 *Expectans, expectavi*

1 I waited patiently upon the LORD; *
he stooped to me and heard my cry.

2 He lifted me out of the desolate pit, out of the mire and clay; *
he set my feet upon a high cliff and made my footing sure.

3 He put a new song in my mouth,
a song of praise to our God; *
many shall see, and stand in awe,
and put their trust in the LORD.

4 Happy are they who trust in the LORD! *
they do not resort to evil spirits or turn to false gods.

5 Great things are they that you have done, O LORD my God!
how great your wonders and your plans for us! *
there is none who can be compared with you.

6 Oh, that I could make them known and tell them! *
but they are more than I can count.

7 In sacrifice and offering you take no pleasure *
(you have given me ears to hear you);

8 Burnt-offering and sin-offering you have not required, *
and so I said, "Behold, I come.

9 In the roll of the book it is written concerning me: *
'I love to do your will, O my God;
your law is deep in my heart.'"

10 I proclaimed righteousness in the great congregation; *
behold, I did not restrain my lips;
and that, O LORD, you know.

11 Your righteousness have I not hidden in my heart;
I have spoken of your faithfulness and your deliverance; *
I have not concealed your love and faithfulness from the great congregation.

12 I have not hid thy righteousness within my heart; my talk hath been of thy truth, and of thy salvation.

13 I have not kept back thy loving mercy and truth from the great congregation.

14 Withdraw not thou thy mercy from me, O LORD; let thy loving-kindness and thy truth alway preserve me.

15 For innumerable troubles are come about me; my sins have taken such hold upon me, that I am not able to look up; yea, they are more in number than the hairs of my head, and my heart hath failed me.

16 O LORD, let it be thy pleasure to deliver me; make haste, O LORD, to help me.

17 Let them be ashamed, and confounded together, that seek after my soul to destroy it; let them be driven backward, and put to rebuke, that wish me evil.

18 Let them be desolate, and rewarded with shame, that say unto me, Fie upon thee! fie upon thee!

19 Let all those that seek thee, be joyful and glad in thee; and let such as love thy salvation, say alway, The LORD be praised!

20 As for me, I am poor and needy; but the Lord careth for me.

21 Thou art my helper and redeemer; make no long tarrying, O my God.

12 I have not hid thy righteousness within my heart: my talk hath been of thy truth, and of thy salvation.

13 I have not kept back thy loving mercy and truth: from the great congregation.

14 Withdraw not thou thy mercy from me, O LORD: let thy loving-kindness and thy truth alway preserve me.

15 For innumerable troubles are come about me; my sins have taken such hold upon me, that I am not able to look up: yea, they are more in number than the hairs of my head, and my heart hath failed me.

16 O LORD, let it be thy pleasure to deliver me: make haste, O LORD, to help me.

17 Let them be ashamed, and confounded together, that seek after my soul to destroy it: let them be driven backward, and put to rebuke, that wish me evil.

18 Let them be desolate, and rewarded with shame: that say unto me, Fie upon thee! fie upon thee!

19 Let all those that seek thee, be joyful and glad in thee: and let such as love thy salvation, say alway, The LORD be praised.

20 As for me, I am poor and needy: but the Lord careth for me.

21 Thou art my helper and redeemer: make no long tarrying, O my God.

Evening Prayer.

Psalm xli. *Beatus qui intelligit.*

BLESSED is he that considereth the poor and needy; the LORD shall deliver him in the time of trouble.

2 The LORD preserve him, and keep him alive, that he may be blessed upon earth; and deliver not thou him into the will of his enemies.

3 The LORD comfort him when he lieth sick upon his bed; make thou all his bed in his sickness.

4 I said, LORD, be merciful unto me; heal my soul, for I have sinned against thee.

5 Mine enemies speak evil of me, When shall he die, and his name perish?

6 And if he come to see me, he speaketh vanity, and his heart conceiveth falsehood within himself; and when he cometh forth, he telleth it.

7 All mine enemies whisper together against me; even against me do they imagine this evil.

8 Let the sentence of guiltiness proceed against him; and now that he lieth, let him rise up no more.

Evening Prayer.

PSALM 41. *Beatus qui intelligit.*

BLESSED is he that considereth the poor and needy: the LORD shall deliver him in the time of trouble.

2 The LORD preserve him, and keep him alive, that he may be blessed upon earth: and deliver not thou him into the will of his enemies.

3 The LORD comfort him when he lieth sick upon his bed: make thou all his bed in his sickness.

4 I said, LORD, be merciful unto me: heal my soul, for I have sinned against thee.

5 Mine enemies speak evil of me: When shall he die, and his name perish?

6 And if he come to see me, he speaketh vanity: and his heart conceiveth falsehood within himself; and when he cometh forth, he telleth it.

7 All mine enemies whisper together against me: even against me do they imagine this evil.

8 Let the sentence of guiltiness proceed against him: and now that he lieth, let him rise up no more.

12 I have not hid thy righteousness within my
heart; * my talk hath been of thy truth, and of thy
salvation.
13 I have not kept back thy loving mercy and
truth * from the great congregation.
14 Withdraw not thou thy mercy from me, O
LORD; * let thy loving-kindness and thy truth alway
preserve me.
15 For innumerable troubles are come about me;
my sins have taken such hold upon me, that I am not
able to look up; * yea, they are more in number than
the hairs of my head, and my heart hath failed me.
16 O LORD, let it be thy pleasure to deliver me; *
make haste, O LORD, to help me.

17 Let them be ashamed, and confounded
together, that seek after my soul to destroy it; * let
them be driven backward, and put to rebuke, that wish
me evil.
18 Let them be desolate, and rewarded with
shame, * that say unto me, Fie upon thee! fie upon
thee!
19 Let all those that seek thee, be joyful and glad in
thee; * and let such as love thy salvation, say alway,
The LORD be praised.
20 As for me, I am poor and needy; * but the Lord
careth for me.
21 Thou art my helper and redeemer; * make no
long tarrying, O my God.

Evening Prayer.

Psalm 41. *Beatus qui intelligit.*

BLESSED is he that considereth the poor and needy; *
the LORD shall deliver him in the time of trouble.
2 The LORD preserve him, and keep him alive, that
he may be blessed upon earth; * and deliver not thou
him into the will of his enemies.
3 The LORD comfort him when he lieth sick upon
his bed; * make thou all his bed in his sickness.
4 I said, LORD, be merciful unto me; * heal my soul,
for I have sinned against thee.
5 Mine enemies speak evil of me, * When shall he
die, and his name perish?
6 And if he come to see me, he speaketh vanity, *
and his heart conceiveth falsehood within himself; and
when he cometh forth, he telleth it.
7 All mine enemies whisper together against me; *
even against me do they imagine this evil.
8 An evil disease, say they, cleaveth fast unto
him; * and now that he lieth, he shall rise up no more.

12 You are the LORD;
do not withhold your compassion from me; *
let your love and your faithfulness keep me safe for ever,

13 For innumerable troubles have crowded upon me;
my sins have overtaken me, and I cannot see; *
they are more in number than the hairs of my head,
and my heart fails me.

14 Be pleased, O LORD, to deliver me; *
O LORD, make haste to help me.

15 Let them be ashamed and altogether dismayed
who seek after my life to destroy it; *
let them draw back and be disgraced
who take pleasure in my misfortune.

16 Let those who say "Aha!" and gloat over me be confounded, *
because they are ashamed.

17 Let all who seek you rejoice in you and be glad; *
let those who love your salvation continually say,
"Great is the LORD!"

18 Though I am poor and afflicted, *
the Lord will have regard for me.

19 You are my helper and my deliverer; *
do not tarry, O my God.

Eighth Day: Evening Prayer

41 *Beatus qui intelligit*

1 Happy are they who consider the poor and needy! *
the LORD will deliver them in the time of trouble.

2 The LORD preserves them and keeps them alive,
so that they may be happy in the land; *
he does not hand them over to the will of their enemies.

3 The LORD sustains them on their sickbed *
and ministers to them in their illness.

4 I said, "LORD, be merciful to me; *
heal me, for I have sinned against you."

5 My enemies are saying wicked things about me: *
"When will he die, and his name perish?"

6 Even if they come to see me, they speak empty words; *
their heart collects false rumors;
they go outside and spread them.

7 All my enemies whisper together about me *
and devise evil against me.

8 "A deadly thing," they say, "has fastened on him; *
he has taken to his bed and will never get up again."

9 Yea, even mine own familiar friend whom I trusted, who did also eat of my bread, hath laid great wait for me.
10 But be thou merciful unto me, O LORD ; raise thou me up again, and I shall reward them.
11 By this I know thou favourest me, that mine enemy doth not triumph against me.
12 And when I am in health, thou upholdest me, and shalt set me before thy face for ever.
13 Blessed be the LORD God of Israel, world without end. Amen.

9 Yea, even mine own familiar friend whom I trusted : who did also eat of my bread, hath laid great wait for me.
10 But be thou merciful unto me, O LORD : raise thou me up again, and I shall reward them.
11 By this I know thou favourest me : that mine enemy doth not triumph against me.
12 And when I am in my health, thou upholdest me : and shalt set me before thy face for ever.
13 Blessed be the LORD God of Israel : world without end. Amen.

Psalm xlii. *Quemadmodum.*

LIKE as the hart desireth the water-brooks, so longeth my soul after thee, O God.
2 My soul is athirst for God, yea, even for the living God : when shall I come to appear before the presence of God?
3 My tears have been my meat day and night, while they daily say unto me, Where is now thy God?
4 Now when I think thereupon, I pour out my heart by myself; for I went with the multitude, and brought them forth into the house of God ;
5 In the voice of praise and thanksgiving, among such as keep holy-day.
6 Why art thou so full of heaviness, O my soul? and why art thou so disquieted within me?
7 O put thy trust in God ; for I will yet give him thanks for the help of his countenance.
8 My God, my soul is vexed within me ; therefore will I remember thee from the land of Jordan, from the little hill of Hermon.
9 One deep calleth another, because of the noise of the water-pipes ; all thy waves and storms are gone over me.
10 The LORD hath granted his loving-kindness in the day-time ; and in the night-season did I sing of him, and made my prayer unto the God of my life.
11 I will say unto the God of my strength, Why hast thou forgotten me? why go I thus heavily, while the enemy oppresseth me?

PSALM 42. *Quemadmodum.*

LIKE as the hart desireth the water-brooks : so longeth my soul after thee, O God.
2 My soul is athirst for God, yea, even for the living God : when shall I come to appear before the presence of God?
3 My tears have been my meat day and night : while they daily say unto me, Where is now thy God?
4 Now when I think thereupon, I pour out my heart by myself: for I went with the multitude, and brought them forth into the house of God ;
5 In the voice of praise and thanksgiving : among such as keep holy-day.
6 Why art thou so full of heaviness, O my soul : and why art thou so disquieted within me?
7 Put thy trust in God : for I will yet give him thanks for the help of his countenance.
8 My God, my soul is vexed within me : therefore will I remember thee concerning the land of Jordan, and the little hill of Hermon.
9 One deep calleth another, because of the noise of thy water-pipes : all thy waves and storms are gone over me.
10 The LORD hath granted his loving-kindness in the day-time : and in the night season did I sing of him, and make my prayer unto the God of my life.
11 I will say unto the God of my strength, Why hast thou forgotten me : why go I thus heavily, while the enemy oppresseth me?

9 Yea, even mine own familiar friend whom I
trusted, * who did also eat of my bread, hath laid great
wait for me.
10 But be thou merciful unto me, O LORD; * raise
thou me up again, and I shall reward them.
11 By this I know thou favourest me, * that mine
enemy doth not triumph against me.
12 And in my innocency thou upholdest me, * and
shalt set me before thy face for ever.

13 Blessed be the LORD God of Israel, * world
without end. Amen.

BOOK II.

Psalm 42. *Quemadmodum.*

LIKE as the hart desireth the water-brooks, * so
longeth my soul after thee, O God.
2 My soul is athirst for God, yea, even for the living
God: * when shall I come to appear before the presence of God?
3 My tears have been my meat day and night, *
while they daily say unto me, Where is now thy God?
4 Now when I think thereupon, I pour out my
heart by myself; * for I went with the multitude, and
brought them forth into the house of God;
5 In the voice of praise and thanksgiving, * among
such as keep holy-day.
6 Why art thou so full of heaviness, O my soul? *
and why art thou so disquieted within me?
7 O put thy trust in God; * for I will yet thank him,
which is the help of my countenance, and my God.

8 My soul is vexed within me; * therefore will I
remember thee from the land of Jordan, from Hermon
and the little hill.
9 One deep calleth another, because of the noise of
thy water-floods; * all thy waves and storms are gone
over me.
10 The LORD will grant his loving-kindness in the
day-time; * and in the night season will I sing of him,
and make my prayer unto the God of my life.
11 I will say unto the God of my strength, Why hast
thou forgotten me? * why go I thus heavily, while the
enemy oppresseth me?

9 Even my best friend, whom I trusted,
who broke bread with me, *
has lifted up his heel and turned against me.

10 But you, O LORD, be merciful to me and raise me up, *
and I shall repay them.

11 By this I know you are pleased with me, *
that my enemy does not triumph over me.

12 In my integrity you hold me fast, *
and shall set me before your face for ever.

13 Blessed be the LORD God of Israel, *
from age to age. Amen. Amen.

Book Two

42 *Quemadmodum*

1 As the deer longs for the water-brooks, *
so longs my soul for you, O God.

2 My soul is athirst for God, athirst for the living God; *
when shall I come to appear before the presence of God?

3 My tears have been my food day and night, *
while all day long they say to me,
"Where now is your God?"

4 I pour out my soul when I think on these things: *
how I went with the multitude and led them into the
house of God,

5 With the voice of praise and thanksgiving, *
among those who keep holy-day.

6 Why are you so full of heaviness, O my soul? *
and why are you so disquieted within me?

7 Put your trust in God; *
for I will yet give thanks to him,
who is the help of my countenance, and my God.

8 My soul is heavy within me; *
therefore I will remember you from the land of Jordan,
and from the peak of Mizar among the heights of Hermon.

9 One deep calls to another in the noise of your cataracts; *
all your rapids and floods have gone over me.

10 The LORD grants his loving-kindness in the daytime; *
in the night season his song is with me,
a prayer to the God of my life.

11 I will say to the God of my strength,
"Why have you forgotten me? *
and why do I go so heavily while the enemy
oppresses me?"

1789-1871	1892
12 My bones are smitten asunder as with a sword, while mine enemies that trouble me cast me in the teeth ;	12 My bones are smitten asunder as with a sword : while mine enemies that trouble me cast me in the teeth ;
13 Namely, while they say daily unto me, Where is now thy God?	13 Namely, while they say daily unto me : Where is now thy God?
14 Why art thou so vexed, O my soul? and why art thou so disquieted within me?	14 Why art thou so vexed, O my soul : and why art thou so disquieted within me?
15 O put thy trust in God ; for I will yet thank him, which is the help of my countenance, and my God.	15 O put thy trust in God : for I will yet thank him, which is the help of my countenance, and my God.
Psalm xliii. *Judica me, Deus.*	PSALM 43. *Judica me, Deus.*
GIVE sentence with me, O God, and defend my cause against the ungodly people ; O deliver me from the deceitful and wicked man.	GIVE sentence with me, O God, and defend my cause against the ungodly people : O deliver me from the deceitful and wicked man.
2 For thou art the God of my strength, why hast thou put me from thee? and why go I so heavily, while the enemy oppresseth me?	2 For thou art the God of my strength ; why hast thou put me from thee : and why go I so heavily, while the enemy oppresseth me?
3 O send out thy light and thy truth, that they may lead me, and bring me unto thy holy hill, and to thy dwelling ;	3 O send out thy light and thy truth, that they may lead me : and bring me unto thy holy hill, and to thy dwelling.
4 And that I may go unto the altar of God, even unto the God of my joy and gladness ; and upon the harp will I give thanks unto thee, O God, my God.	4 And that I may go unto the altar of God, even unto the God of my joy and gladness : and upon the harp will I give thanks unto thee, O God, my God.
5 Why art thou so heavy, O my soul? and why art thou so disquieted within me?	5 Why art thou so heavy, O my soul? : and why art thou so disquieted within me?
6 O put thy trust in God ; for I will yet give him thanks, which is the help of my countenance, and my God.	6 O put thy trust in God : for I will yet give him thanks, which is the help of my countenance, and my God.
THE NINTH DAY.	THE NINTH DAY.
Morning Prayer.	**Morning Prayer.**
Psalm xliv. *Deus, auribus.*	PSALM 44. *Deus, auribus.*
WE have heard with our ears, O God, our fathers have told us what thou hast done in their time of old ;	WE have heard with our ears, O God, our fathers have told us : what thou hast done in their time of old :
2 How thou hast driven out the heathen with thy hand, and planted them in ; how thou hast destroyed the nations, and cast them out.	2 How thou hast driven out the heathen with thy hand, and planted them in ; how thou hast destroyed the nations, and cast them out.
3 For they gat not the land in possession through their own sword, neither was it their own arm that helped them :	3 For they gat not the land in possession through their own sword : neither was it their own arm that helped them ;

12 My bones are smitten asunder as with a sword, * while mine enemies that trouble me cast me in the teeth;

13 Namely, while they say daily unto me, * Where is now thy God?

14 Why art thou so vexed, O my soul? * and why art thou so disquieted within me?

15 O put thy trust in God; * for I will yet thank him, which is the help of my countenance, and my God.

Psalm 43. *Judica me, Deus.*

GIVE sentence with me, O God, and defend my cause against the ungodly people; * O deliver me from the deceitful and wicked man.

2 For thou art the God of my strength; why hast thou put me from thee? * and why go I so heavily, while the enemy oppresseth me?

3 O send out thy light and thy truth, that they may lead me, * and bring me unto thy holy hill, and to thy dwelling;

4 And that I may go unto the altar of God, even unto the God of my joy and gladness; * and upon the harp will I give thanks unto thee, O God, my God.

5 Why art thou so heavy, O my soul? * and why art thou so disquieted within me?

6 O put thy trust in God; * for I will yet give him thanks, which is the help of my countenance, and my God.

The Ninth Day.

Morning Prayer.

Psalm 44. *Deus, auribus.*

WE have heard with our ears, O God, our fathers have told us * what thou hast done in their time of old:

2 How thou hast driven out the heathen with thy hand, and planted our fathers in; * how thou hast destroyed the nations, and made thy people to flourish.

3 For they gat not the land in possession through their own sword, * neither was it their own arm that helped them;

12 While my bones are being broken, *
my enemies mock me to my face;

13 All day long they mock me *
and say to me, "Where is now your God?"

14 Why are you so full of heaviness, O my soul? *
and why are you so disquieted within me?

15 Put your trust in God; *
for I will yet give thanks to him,
who is the help of my countenance, and my God.

43 *Judica me, Deus*

1 Give judgment for me, O God,
and defend my cause against an ungodly people; *
deliver me from the deceitful and the wicked.

2 For you are the God of my strength;
why have you put me from you? *
and why do I go so heavily while the enemy oppresses me?

3 Send out your light and your truth, that they may lead me, *
and bring me to your holy hill
and to your dwelling;

4 That I may go to the altar of God,
to the God of my joy and gladness; *
and on the harp I will give thanks to you, O God my God.

5 Why are you so full of heaviness, O my soul? *
and why are you so disquieted within me?

6 Put your trust in God; *
for I will yet give thanks to him,
who is the help of my countenance, and my God.

Ninth Day: Morning Prayer

44 *Deus, auribus*

1 We have heard with our ears, O God,
our forefathers have told us, *
the deeds you did in their days,
in the days of old.

2 How with your hand you drove the peoples out
and planted our forefathers in the land; *
how you destroyed nations and made your people flourish.

3 For they did not take the land by their sword,
nor did their arm win the victory for them; *
but your right hand, your arm, and the light of your countenance,
because you favored them.

1789-1871

4 But thy right hand, and thine arm, and the light of thy countenance ; because thou hadst a favour unto them.

5 Thou art my King, O God ; send help unto Jacob.

6 Through thee will we overthrow our enemies, and in thy Name will we tread them under that rise up against us.

7 For I will not trust in my bow, it is not my sword that shall help me ;

8 But it is thou that savest us from our enemies, and puttest them to confusion that hate us.

9 We make our boast of God all day long, and will praise thy Name for ever.

10 But now thou art far off, and puttest us to confusion ; and goest not forth with our armies.

11 Thou makest us to turn our backs upon our enemies, so that they which hate us spoil our goods.

12 Thou lettest us be eaten up like sheep, and hast scattered us among the heathen.

13 Thou sellest thy people for nought, and takest no money for them.

14 Thou makest us to be rebuked of our neighbours, to be laughed to scorn, and had in derision of them that are round about us.

15 Thou makest us to be a by-word among the heathen, and that the people shake their heads at us.

16 My confusion is daily before me, and the shame of my face hath covered me ;

17 For the voice of the slanderer and blasphemer, for the enemy and avenger.

18 And though all this be come upon us, yet do we not forget thee, nor behave ourselves frowardly in thy covenant.

19 Our heart is not turned back, neither our steps gone out of thy way ;

20 No, not when thou hast smitten us into the place of dragons, and covered us with the shadow of death.

21 If we have forgotten the Name of our God, and holden up our hands to any strange god, shall not God search it out? for he knoweth the very secrets of the heart.

22 For thy sake also are we killed all the day long, and are counted as sheep appointed to be slain.

23 Up, Lord, why sleepest thou? awake, and be not absent from us for ever.

24 Wherefore hidest thou thy face, and forgettest our misery and trouble?

1892

4 But thy right hand, and thine arm, and the light of thy countenance : because thou hadst a favour unto them.

5 Thou art my King, O God : send help unto Jacob.

6 Through thee will we overthrow our enemies : and in thy Name will we tread them under that rise up against us.

7 For I will not trust in my bow : it is not my sword that shall help me ;

8 But it is thou that savest us from our enemies : and puttest them to confusion that hate us.

9 We make our boast of God all day long : and will praise thy Name for ever.

10 But now thou art far off, and puttest us to confusion : and goest not forth with our armies.

11 Thou makest us to turn our backs upon our enemies : so that they which hate us spoil our goods.

12 Thou lettest us be eaten up like sheep : and hast scattered us among the heathen.

13 Thou sellest thy people for nought : and takest no money for them.

14 Thou makest us to be rebuked of our neighbours : to be laughed to scorn, and had in derision of them that are round about us.

15 Thou makest us to be a by-word among the heathen : and that the people shake their heads at us.

16 My confusion is daily before me : and the shame of my face hath covered me ;

17 For the voice of the slanderer and blasphemer : for the enemy and avenger.

18 And though all this be come upon us, yet do we not forget thee : nor behave ourselves frowardly in thy covenant.

19 Our heart is not turned back : neither our steps gone out of thy way ;

20 No, not when thou hast smitten us into the place of dragons : and covered us with the shadow of death.

21 If we have forgotten the Name of our God, and holden up our hands to any strange god : shall not God search it out? for he knoweth the very secrets of the heart.

22 For thy sake also are we killed all the day long : and are counted as sheep appointed to be slain.

23 Up, Lord, why sleepest thou : awake, and be not absent from us for ever.

24 Wherefore hidest thou thy face : and forgettest our misery and trouble?

1928

4 But thy right hand, and thine arm, and the light
of thy countenance; * because thou hadst a favour
unto them.
5 Thou art my King, O God; * send help unto
Jacob.
6 Through thee will we overthrow our enemies, *
and in thy Name will we tread them under that rise up
against us.
7 For I will not trust in my bow, * it is not my sword
that shall help me;
8 But it is thou that savest us from our enemies, *
and puttest them to confusion that hate us.
9 We make our boast of God all day long, * and will
praise thy Name for ever.
10 But now thou art far off, and puttest us to
confusion, * and goest not forth with our armies.
11 Thou makest us to turn our backs upon our
enemies, * so that they which hate us spoil our goods.
12 Thou lettest us be eaten up like sheep, * and
hast scattered us among the heathen.
13 Thou sellest thy people for nought, * and takest
no money for them.
14 Thou makest us to be rebuked of our neighbours, * to be laughed to scorn, and had in derision of
them that are round about us.
15 Thou makest us to be a by-word among the
nations, * and that the peoples shake their heads at us.
16 My confusion is daily before me, * and the
shame of my face hath covered me;
17 For the voice of the slanderer and blasphemer, *
for the enemy and avenger.
18 And though all this be come upon us, yet do we
not forget thee, * nor behave ourselves frowardly in thy
covenant.
19 Our heart is not turned back, * neither our
steps gone out of thy way;
20 No, not when thou hast smitten us into the
place of dragons, * and covered us with the shadow of
death.
21 If we have forgotten the Name of our God, and
holden up our hands to any strange god, * shall not
God search it out? for he knoweth the very secrets of
the heart.
22 For thy sake also are we killed all the day long, *
and are counted as sheep appointed to be slain.
23 Up, Lord, why sleepest thou? * awake, and be
not absent from us for ever.
24 Wherefore hidest thou thy face, * and forgettest
our misery and trouble?

1979

4 You are my King and my God; *
you command victories for Jacob.

5 Through you we pushed back our adversaries; *
through your Name we trampled on those who
rose up against us.

6 For I do not rely on my bow, *
and my sword does not give me the victory.

7 Surely, you gave us victory over our adversaries *
and put those who hate us to shame.

8 Every day we gloried in God, *
and we will praise your Name for ever.

9 Nevertheless, you have rejected and humbled us *
and do not go forth with our armies.

10 You have made us fall back before our adversary, *
and our enemies have plundered us.

11 You have made us like sheep to be eaten *
and have scattered us among the nations.

12 You are selling your people for a trifle *
and are making no profit on the sale of them.

13 You have made us the scorn of our neighbors, *
a mockery and derision to those around us.

14 You have made us a byword among the nations, *
a laughing-stock among the peoples.

15 My humiliation is daily before me, *
and shame has covered my face;

16 Because of the taunts of the mockers and the blasphemers, *
because of the enemy and avenger.

17 All this has come upon us; *
yet we have not forgotten you,
nor have we betrayed your covenant.

18 Our heart never turned back, *
nor did our footsteps stray from your path;

19 Though you thrust us down into a place of misery, *
and covered us over with deep darkness.

20 If we have forgotten the Name of our God, *
or stretched out our hand to some strange god,

21 Will not God find it out? *
for he knows the secrets of the heart.

22 Indeed, for your sake we are killed all the day long; *
we are accounted as sheep for the slaughter.

23 Awake, O Lord! why are you sleeping? *
Arise! do not reject us for ever.

24 Why have you hidden your face *
and forgotten our affliction and oppression?

1789-1871	1892
25 For our soul is brought low, even unto the dust ; our belly cleaveth unto the ground.	25 For our soul is brought low, even unto the dust : our belly cleaveth unto the ground.
26 Arise, and help us, and deliver us, for thy mercy's sake.	26 Arise, and help us : and deliver us, for thy mercy's sake.
Psalm xlv. *Eructavit cor meum.*	PSALM 45. *Eructavit cor meum.*
MY heart is inditing of a good matter ; I speak of the things which I have made unto the King.	MY heart is inditing of a good matter : I speak of the things which I have made unto the King.
2 My tongue is the pen of a ready writer.	2 My tongue is the pen : of a ready writer.
3 Thou art fairer than the children of men ; full of grace are thy lips, because God hath blessed thee for ever.	3 Thou art fairer than the children of men : full of grace are thy lips, because God hath blessed thee for ever.
4 Gird thee with thy sword upon thy thigh, O thou Most Mighty, according to thy worship and renown.	4 Gird thee with thy sword upon thy thigh, O thou Most Mighty : according to thy worship and renown.
5 Good luck have thou with thine honour : ride on, because of the word of truth, of meekness, and righteousness ; and thy right hand shall teach thee terrible things.	5 Good luck have thou with thine honour : ride on, because of the word of truth, of meekness, and righteousness ; and thy right hand shall teach thee terrible things.
6 Thy arrows are very sharp, and the people shall be subdued unto thee, even in the midst among the King's enemies.	6 Thy arrows are very sharp, and the people shall be subdued unto thee : even in the midst among the King's enemies.
7 Thy seat, O God, endureth for ever ; the sceptre of thy kingdom is a right sceptre.	7 Thy seat, O God, endureth for ever : the sceptre of thy kingdom is a right sceptre.
8 Thou hast loved righteousness, and hated iniquity ; wherefore God, even thy God, hath anointed thee with the oil of gladness above thy fellows.	8 Thou hast loved righteousness, and hated iniquity : wherefore God, even thy God, hath anointed thee with the oil of gladness above thy fellows.
9 All thy garments smell of myrrh, aloes, and cassia ; out of the ivory palaces, whereby they have made thee glad.	9 All thy garments smell of myrrh, aloes, and cassia : out of the ivory palaces, whereby they have made thee glad.
10 Kings' daughters were among thy honourable women ; upon thy right hand did stand the queen in a vesture of gold, wrought about with divers colours.	10 Kings' daughters were among thy honourable women : upon thy right hand did stand the queen in a vesture of gold, wrought about with divers colours.
11 Hearken, O daughter, and consider ; incline thine ear ; forget also thine own people, and thy father's house.	11 Hearken, O daughter, and consider, incline thine ear : forget also thine own people, and thy father's house.
12 So shall the King have pleasure in thy beauty ; for he is thy Lord God, and worship thou him.	12 So shall the King have pleasure in thy beauty : for he is thy Lord God, and worship thou him.
13 And the daughter of Tyre shall be there with a gift ; like as the rich also among the people shall make their supplication before thee.	13 And the daughter of Tyre shall be there with a gift : like as the rich also among the people shall make their supplication before thee.
14 The King's daughter is all glorious within ; her clothing is of wrought gold.	14 The King's daughter is all glorious within : her clothing is of wrought gold.
15 She shall be brought unto the King in raiment of needlework : the virgins that be her fellows shall bear her company, and shall be brought unto thee.	15 She shall be brought unto the King in raiment of needlework : the virgins that be her fellows shall bear her company, and shall be brought unto thee.
16 With joy and gladness shall they be brought, and shall enter into the King's palace.	16 With joy and gladness shall they be brought : and shall enter into the King's palace.

25 For our soul is brought low, even unto the dust; * our belly cleaveth unto the ground.

26 Arise, and help us, * and deliver us, for thy mercy's sake.

Psalm 45. *Eructavit cor meum.*

MY heart overfloweth with a good matter; I speak the things which I have made concerning the King. * My tongue is the pen of a ready writer.

2 Thou art fairer than the children of men; * full of grace are thy lips, because God hath blessed thee for ever.

3 Gird thee with thy sword upon thy thigh, O thou Most Mighty, * according to thy worship and renown.

4 Good luck have thou with thine honour: * ride on, because of the word of truth, of meekness, and righteousness; and thy right hand shall teach thee terrible things.

5 Thy arrows are very sharp in the heart of the King's enemies, * and the people shall be subdued unto thee.

6 Thy seat, O God, endureth for ever; * the sceptre of thy kingdom is a right sceptre.

7 Thou hast loved righteousness, and hated iniquity; * wherefore God, even thy God, hath anointed thee with the oil of gladness above thy fellows.

8 All thy garments smell of myrrh, aloes, and cassia; * out of the ivory palaces, whereby they have made thee glad.

9 Kings' daughters are among thy honourable women; * upon thy right hand doth stand the queen in a vesture of gold, wrought about with divers colours.

10 Hearken, O daughter, and consider; incline thine ear; * forget also thine own people, and thy father's house.

11 So shall the King have pleasure in thy beauty; * for he is thy Lord, and worship thou him.

12 And the daughter of Tyre shall be there with a gift; * like as the rich also among the people shall make their supplication before thee.

13 The King's daughter is all glorious within; * her clothing is of wrought gold.

14 She shall be brought unto the King in raiment of needlework: * the virgins that be her fellows shall bear her company, and shall be brought unto thee.

15 With joy and gladness shall they be brought, * and shall enter into the King's palace.

16 Instead of thy fathers, thou shalt have children, * whom thou mayest make princes in all lands.

25 We sink down into the dust; *
our body cleaves to the ground.

26 Rise up, and help us, *
and save us, for the sake of your steadfast love.

45 *Eructavit cor meum*

1 My heart is stirring with a noble song;
let me recite what I have fashioned for the king; *
my tongue shall be the pen of a skilled writer.

2 You are the fairest of men; *
grace flows from your lips,
because God has blessed you for ever.

3 Strap your sword upon your thigh, O mighty warrior, *
in your pride and in your majesty.

4 Ride out and conquer in the cause of truth *
and for the sake of justice.

5 Your right hand will show you marvelous things; *
your arrows are very sharp, O mighty warrior.

6 The peoples are falling at your feet, *
and the king's enemies are losing heart.

7 Your throne, O God, endures for ever and ever, *
a scepter of righteousness is the scepter of your kingdom;
you love righteousness and hate iniquity.

8 Therefore God, your God, has anointed you *
with the oil of gladness above your fellows.

9 All your garments are fragrant with myrrh, aloes, and cassia, *
and the music of strings from ivory palaces makes you glad.

10 Kings' daughters stand among the ladies of the court; *
on your right hand is the queen,
adorned with the gold of Ophir.

11 "Hear, O daughter; consider and listen closely; *
forget your people and your father's house.

12 The king will have pleasure in your beauty; *
he is your master; therefore do him honor.

13 The people of Tyre are here with a gift; *
the rich among the people seek your favor."

14 All glorious is the princess as she enters; *
her gown is cloth-of-gold.

15 In embroidered apparel she is brought to the king; *
after her the bridesmaids follow in procession.

16 With joy and gladness they are brought, *
and enter into the palace of the king.

17 Instead of thy fathers, thou shalt have children, whom thou mayest make princes in all lands.

18 I will remember thy Name from one generation to another ; therefore shall the people give thanks unto thee, world without end.

17 Instead of thy fathers, thou shalt have children : whom thou mayest make princes in all lands.

18 I will remember thy Name from one generation to another : therefore shall the people give thanks unto thee, world without end.

Psalm xlvi. *Deus noster refugium.*

GOD is our hope and strength, a very present help in trouble.

2 Therefore will we not fear, though the earth be moved, and though the hills be carried into the midst of the sea.

3 Though the waters thereof rage and swell, and though the mountains shake at the tempest of the same.

4 The rivers of the flood thereof shall make glad the city of God ; the holy place of the tabernacle of the Most Highest.

5 God is in the midst of her, therefore shall she not be removed ; God shall help her, and that right early.

6 The heathen make much ado, and the kingdoms are moved ; but God hath showed his voice, and the earth shall melt away.

7 The LORD of hosts is with us ; the God of Jacob is our refuge.

8 O come hither, and behold the works of the LORD, what destruction he hath brought upon the earth.

9 He maketh wars to cease in all the world ; he breaketh the bow, and knappeth the spear in sunder, and burneth the chariots in the fire.

10 Be still then, and know that I am God : I will be exalted among the heathen, and I will be exalted in the earth.

11 The LORD of hosts is with us ; the God of Jacob is our refuge.

PSALM 46. *Deus noster refugium.*

GOD is our hope and strength : a very present help in trouble.

2 Therefore will we not fear, though the earth be moved : and though the hills be carried into the midst of the sea ;

3 Though the waters thereof rage and swell : and though the mountains shake at the tempest of the same.

4 The rivers of the flood thereof shall make glad the city of God : the holy place of the tabernacle of the Most Highest.

5 God is in the midst of her, therefore shall she not be removed : God shall help her, and that right early.

6 The heathen make much ado, and the kingdoms are moved : but God hath showed his voice, and the earth shall melt away.

7 The LORD of hosts is with us : the God of Jacob is our refuge.

8 O come hither, and behold the works of the LORD : what destruction he hath brought upon the earth.

9 He maketh wars to cease in all the world : he breaketh the bow, and knappeth the spear in sunder, and burneth the chariots in the fire.

10 Be still then, and know that I am God : I will be exalted among the heathen, and I will be exalted in the earth.

11 The LORD of hosts is with us : the God of Jacob is our refuge.

Evening Prayer.

Psalm xlvii. *Omnes gentes, plaudite.*

O CLAP your hands together, all ye peoples : O sing unto God with the voice of melody.

Evening Prayer.

PSALM 47. *Omnes gentes, plaudite.*

O CLAP your hands together, all ye people : O sing unto God with the voice of melody.

1928

17 I will make thy Name to be remembered from one generation to another; * therefore shall the people give thanks unto thee, world without end.

Psalm 46. *Deus noster refugium.*

GOD is our hope and strength, * a very present help in trouble.

2 Therefore will we not fear, though the earth be moved, * and though the hills be carried into the midst of the sea;

3 Though the waters thereof rage and swell, * and though the mountains shake at the tempest of the same.

4 There is a river, the streams whereof make glad the city of God; * the holy place of the tabernacle of the Most Highest.

5 God is in the midst of her, therefore shall she not be removed; * God shall help her, and that right early.

6 The nations make much ado, and the kingdoms are moved; * but God hath showed his voice, and the earth shall melt away.

7 The LORD of hosts is with us; * the God of Jacob is our refuge.

8 O come hither, and behold the works of the LORD, * what destruction he hath brought upon the earth.

9 He maketh wars to cease in all the world; * he breaketh the bow, and knappeth the spear in sunder, and burneth the chariots in the fire.

10 Be still then, and know that I am God: * I will be exalted among the nations, and I will be exalted in the earth.

11 The LORD of hosts is with us; * the God of Jacob is our refuge.

Evening Prayer.

Psalm 47. *Omnes gentes, plaudite.*

O CLAP your hands together, all ye peoples: * O sing unto God with the voice of melody.

1979

17 "In place of fathers, O king, you shall have sons; *
you shall make them princes over all the earth.

18 I will make your name to be remembered
from one generation to another; *
therefore nations will praise you forever and ever."

46 *Deus noster refugium*

1 God is our refuge and strength, *
a very present help in trouble.

2 Therefore we will not fear, though the earth be moved, *
and though the mountains be toppled into the depths of the sea;

3 Though its waters rage and foam, *
and though the mountains tremble at its tumult.

4 The LORD of hosts is with us; *
the God of Jacob is our stronghold.

5 There is a river whose streams make glad the city of God, *
the holy habitation of the Most High.

6 God is in the midst of her;
she shall not be overthrown; *
God shall help her at the break of day.

7 The nations make much ado, and the kingdoms are shaken; *
God has spoken, and the earth shall melt away.

8 The LORD of hosts is with us; *
the God of Jacob is our stronghold.

9 Come now and look upon the works of the LORD, *
what awesome things he has done on earth.

10 It is he who makes war to cease in all the world; *
he breaks the bow, and shatters the spear,
and burns the shields with fire.

11 "Be still, then, and know that I am God; *
I will be exalted among the nations;
I will be exalted in the earth."

12 The LORD of hosts is with us *
the God of Jacob is our stronghold.

Ninth Day: Evening Prayer

47 *Omnes gentes, plaudite*

1 Clap your hands, all you peoples; *
shout to God with a cry of joy.

2 For the LORD is high, and to be feared ; he is the great King upon all the earth.
3 He shall subdue the people under us, and the nations under our feet.
4 He shall choose out an heritage for us, even the worship of Jacob, whom he loved.
5 God is gone up with a merry noise, and the LORD with the sound of the trump.
6 O sing praises, sing praises unto our God ; sing praises, sing praises unto our King.
7 For God is the King of all the earth : sing ye praises with understanding.
8 God reigneth over the heathen ; God sitteth upon his holy seat.
9 The princes of the people are joined unto the people of the God of Abraham ; for God, which is very high exalted, doth defend the earth, as it were with a shield.

Psalm xlviii. *Magnus Dominus.*

GREAT is the LORD, and highly to be praised in the city of our God, even upon his holy hill.
2 The hill of Sion is a fair place, and the joy of the whole earth ; upon the north side lieth the city of the great King : God is well known in her palaces as a sure refuge.
3 For lo, the kings of the earth were gathered, and gone by together.
4 They marvelled to see such things ; they were astonished, and suddenly cast down.
5 Fear came there upon them ; and sorrow, as upon a woman in her travail.
6 Thou shalt break the ships of the sea through the east-wind.
7 Like as we have heard, so have we seen in the city of the LORD of hosts, in the city of our God ; God upholdeth the same for ever.
8 We wait for thy loving-kindness, O God, in the midst of thy temple.
9 O God, according to thy Name, so is thy praise unto the world's end ; thy right hand is full of righteousness.

2 For the LORD is high, and to be feared : he is the great King upon all the earth.
3 He shall subdue the people under us : and the nations under our feet.
4 He shall choose out an heritage for us : even the worship of Jacob, whom he loved.
5 God is gone up with a merry noise : and the LORD with the sound of the trump.
6 O sing praises, sing praises unto our God : O sing praises, sing praises unto our King.
7 For God is the King of all the earth : sing ye praises with understanding.
8 God reigneth over the heathen : God sitteth upon his holy seat.
9 The princes of the people are joined unto the people of the God of Abraham : for God, which is very high exalted, doth defend the earth, as it were with a shield.

PSALM 48. *Magnus Dominus.*

GREAT is the LORD, and highly to be praised : in the city of our God, even upon his holy hill.
2 The hill of Sion is a fair place, and the joy of the whole earth : upon the north side lieth the city of the great King ; God is well known in her palaces as a sure refuge.
3 For lo, the kings of the earth : are gathered, and gone by together.
4 They marvelled to see such things : they were astonished, and suddenly cast down.
5 Fear came there upon them, and sorrow : as upon a woman in her travail.
6 Thou shalt break the ships of the sea : through the east-wind.
7 Like as we have heard, so have we seen in the city of the LORD of hosts, in the city of our God : God upholdeth the same for ever.
8 We wait for thy loving-kindness, O God : in the midst of thy temple.
9 O God, according to thy Name, so is thy praise unto the world's end : thy right hand is full of righteousness.

2 For the LORD is high, and to be feared; * he is the
great King upon all the earth.
3 He shall subdue the peoples under us, * and the
nations under our feet.
4 He shall choose out an heritage for us, * even the
excellency of Jacob, whom he loved.
5 God is gone up with a merry noise, * and the
LORD with the sound of the trump.
6 O sing praises, sing praises unto our God; * sing
praises, sing praises unto our King.
7 For God is the King of all the earth: * sing ye
praises with understanding.
8 God reigneth over the nations; * God sitteth
upon his holy seat.
9 The princes of the peoples are joined unto the
people of the God of Abraham; * for God, which is
very high exalted, doth defend the earth, as it were
with a shield.

2 For the LORD Most High is to be feared; *
he is the great King over all the earth.

3 He subdues the peoples under us, *
and the nations under our feet.

4 He chooses our inheritance for us, *
the pride of Jacob whom he loves.

5 God has gone up with a shout, *
the LORD with the sound of the ram's-horn.

6 Sing praises to God, sing praises; *
sing praises to our King, sing praises.

7 For God is King of all the earth; *
sing praises with all your skill.

8 God reigns over the nations; *
God sits upon his holy throne.

9 The nobles of the peoples have gathered together *
with the people of the God of Abraham.

10 The rulers of the earth belong to God, *
and he is highly exalted.

Psalm 48. *Magnus Dominus.*

GREAT is the LORD, and highly to be praised * in the
city of our God, even upon his holy hill.
2 The hill of Sion is a fair place, and the joy of the
whole earth; * upon the north side lieth the city of the
great King: God is well known in her palaces as a sure
refuge.
3 For lo, the kings of the earth * were gathered,
and gone by together.
4 They marvelled to see such things; * they were
astonished, and suddenly cast down.
5 Fear came there upon them; and sorrow, * as
upon a woman in her travail.
6 Thou dost break the ships of the sea * through
the east-wind.
7 Like as we have heard, so have we seen in the
city of the LORD of hosts, in the city of our God; * God
upholdeth the same for ever.
8 We wait for thy loving-kindness, O God, * in the
midst of thy temple.
9 O God, according to thy Name, so is thy praise
unto the world's end; * thy right hand is full of righteousness.

48 *Magnus Dominus*

1 Great is the LORD, and highly to be praised; *
in the city of our God is his holy hill.

2 Beautiful and lofty, the joy of all the earth, is the hill of Zion, *
the very center of the world and the city of the great King.

3 God is in her citadels; *
he is known to be her sure refuge.

4 Behold, the kings of the earth assembled *
and marched forward together.

5 They looked and were astounded; *
they retreated and fled in terror.

6 Trembling seized them there; *
they writhed like a woman in childbirth,
like ships of the sea when the east wind shatters them.

7 As we have heard, so have we seen,
in the city of the LORD of hosts, in the city of our God; *
God has established her for ever.

8 We have waited in silence on your loving-kindness, O God, *
in the midst of your temple.

9 Your praise, like your Name, O God, reaches to the world's end; *
your right hand is full of justice.

1789-1871

10 Let the Mount Sion rejoice, and the daughter of Judah be glad, because of thy judgments.

11 Walk about Sion, and go round about her ; and tell the towers thereof.

12 Mark well her bulwarks, set up her houses, that ye may tell them that come after.

13 For this God is our God for ever and ever : he shall be our guide unto death.

Psalm xlix. *Audite hæc, omnes.*

O HEAR ye this, all ye people ; ponder it with your ears, all ye that dwell in the world ;

2 High and low, rich and poor, one with another.

3 My mouth shall speak of wisdom, and my heart shall muse of understanding.

4 I will incline mine ear to the parable, and show my dark speech upon the harp.

5 Wherefore should I fear in the days of wickedness, and when the wickedness of my heels compasseth me round about?

6 There be some that put their trust in their goods, and boast themselves in the multitude of their riches.

7 But no man may deliver his brother, nor make agreement unto God for him ;

8 For it cost more to redeem their souls, so that he must let that alone for ever ;

9 Yea, though he live long, and see not the grave.

10 For he seeth that wise men also die and perish together, as well as the ignorant and foolish, and leave their riches for other.

11 And yet they think that their houses shall continue for ever, and that their dwelling-places shall endure from one generation to another ; and call the lands after their own names.

12 Nevertheless, man will not abide in honour, seeing he may be compared unto the beasts that perish ; this is the way of them.

13 This is their foolishness, and their posterity praise their saying.

1892

10 Let the mount Sion rejoice, and the daughter of Judah be glad : because of thy judgments.

11 Walk about Sion, and go round about her : and tell the towers thereof.

12 Mark well her bulwarks, set up her houses : that ye may tell them that come after.

13 For this God is our God for ever and ever : he shall be our guide unto death.

PSALM 49. *Audite hæc, omnes.*

O HEAR ye this, all ye people : ponder it with your ears, all ye that dwell in the world ;

2 High and low, rich and poor : one with another.

3 My mouth shall speak of wisdom : and my heart shall muse of understanding.

4 I will incline mine ear to the parable : and show my dark speech upon the harp.

5 Wherefore should I fear in the days of wickedness : and when the wickedness of my heels compasseth me round about?

6 There be some that put their trust in their goods : and boast themselves in the multitude of their riches.

7 But no man may deliver his brother : nor make agreement unto God for him ;

8 For it cost more to redeem their souls : so that he must let that alone for ever ;

9 Yea, though he live long : and see not the grave.

10 For he seeth that wise men also die and perish together : as well as the ignorant and foolish, and leave their riches for other.

11 And yet they think that their houses shall continue for ever : and that their dwelling-places shall endure from one generation to another ; and call the lands after their own names.

12 Nevertheless, man will not abide in honour : seeing he may be compared unto the beasts that perish ; this is the way of them.

13 This is their foolishness : and their posterity praise their saying.

10 Let the mount Sion rejoice, and the daughters of Judah be glad, * because of thy judgments.

11 Walk about Sion, and go round about her; * and tell the towers thereof.

12 Mark well her bulwarks, consider her palaces, * that ye may tell them that come after.

13 For this God is our God for ever and ever: * he shall be our guide unto death.

Psalm 49. *Audite hæc, omnes.*

O HEAR ye this, all ye people; * ponder it with your ears, all ye that dwell in the world;

2 High and low, rich and poor, * one with another.

3 My mouth shall speak of wisdom, * and my heart shall muse of understanding.

4 I will incline mine ear to the parable, * and show my dark speech upon the harp.

5 Wherefore should I fear in the days of evil, * when wickedness at my heels compasseth me round about?

6 There be some that put their trust in their goods, * and boast themselves in the multitude of their riches.

7 But no man may deliver his brother, * nor give a ransom unto God for him,

8 (For it cost more to redeem their souls, * so that he must let that alone for ever;)

9 That he shall live alway, * and not see the grave.

10 For he seeth that wise men also die and perish together, * as well as the ignorant and foolish, and leave their riches for other.

11 And yet they think that their houses shall continue for ever, and that their dwelling-places shall endure from one generation to another; * and call the lands after their own names.

12 Nevertheless, man being in honour abideth not, * seeing he may be compared unto the beasts that perish;

13 This their way is very foolishness; * yet their posterity praise their saying.

10 Let Mount Zion be glad
and the cities of Judah rejoice, *
because of your judgments.

11 Make the circuit of Zion;
walk round about her; *
count the number of her towers.

12 Consider well her bulwarks;
examine her strongholds; *
that you may tell those who come after.

13 This God is our God for ever and ever; *
he shall be our guide for evermore.

49 *Audite hæc, omnes*

1 Hear this, all you peoples;
hearken, all you who dwell in the world, *
you of high degree and low, rich and poor together.

2 My mouth shall speak of wisdom, *
and my heart shall meditate on understanding.

3 I will incline my ear to a proverb *
and set forth my riddle upon the harp.

4 Why should I be afraid in evil days, *
when the wickedness of those at my heels surrounds me,

5 The wickedness of those who put their trust in their goods, *
and boast of their great riches?

6 We can never ransom ourselves, *
or deliver to God the price of our life;

7 For the ransom of our life is so great, *
that we should never have enough to pay it,

8 In order to live for ever and ever, *
and never see the grave.

9 For we see that the wise die also;
like the dull and stupid they perish *
and leave their wealth to those who come after them.

10 Their graves shall be their homes for ever,
their dwelling places from generation to generation, *
though they call the lands after their own names.

11 Even though honored, they cannot live for ever; *
they are like the beasts that perish.

12 Such is the way of those who foolishly trust in themselves, *
and the end of those who delight in their own words.

13 Like a flock of sheep they are destined to die;
Death is their shepherd; *
they go down straightway to the grave.

14 They lie in hell like sheep ; death gnaweth upon them, and the righteous shall have dominion[10] over them in the morning : their beauty shall consume in the sepulchre out of their dwelling.

15 But God hath delivered my soul from the place of hell ; for he shall receive me.

16 Be not thou afraid, though one be made rich, or if the glory of his house be increased ;

17 For he shall carry nothing away with him when he dieth, neither shall his pomp follow him.

18 For while he lived, he counted himself an happy man ; and so long as thou doest well unto thyself, men will speak good of thee.

19 He shall follow the generation of his fathers, and shall never see light.

20 Man being in honour hath no understanding, but is compared unto the beasts that perish.

THE TENTH DAY.

Morning Prayer.

Psalm l. *Deus deorum.*

THE LORD, even the most mighty God, hath spoken, and called the world, from the rising up of the sun unto the going down thereof.

2 Out of Sion hath God appeared in perfect beauty.

3 Our God shall come, and shall not keep silence ; there shall go before him a consuming fire, and a mighty tempest shall be stirred up round about him.

4 He shall call the heaven from above, and the earth, that he may judge his people.

5 Gather my saints together unto me ; those that have made a covenant with me with sacrifice.

6 And the heavens shall declare his righteousness ; for God is Judge himself.

7 Hear, O my people, and I will speak ; I myself will testify against thee, O Israel ; for I am God, even thy God.

8 I will not reprove thee because of thy sacrifices, or for thy burnt-offerings ; because they were not alway before me.

9 I will take no bullock out of thine house, nor he-goats out of thy folds.

10 For all the beasts of the forest are mine, and so are the cattle upon a thousand hills.

14 They lie in the hell like sheep ; death gnaweth upon them, and the righteous shall have domination over them in the morning : their beauty shall consume in the sepulchre out of their dwelling.

15 But God hath delivered my soul from the place of hell : for he shall receive me.

16 Be not thou afraid, though one be made rich : or if the glory of his house be increased ;

17 For he shall carry nothing away with him when he dieth : neither shall his pomp follow him.

18 For while he lived, he counted himself an happy man : and so long as thou doest well unto thyself, men will speak good of thee.

19 He shall follow the generation of his fathers : and shall never see light.

20 Man being in honour hath no understanding : but is compared unto the beasts that perish.

THE TENTH DAY.

Morning Prayer.

PSALM 50. *Deus deorum.*

THE LORD, even the Most Mighty God, hath spoken : and called the world, from the rising up of the sun unto the going down thereof.

2 Out of Sion hath God appeared : in perfect beauty.

3 Our God shall come, and shall not keep silence : there shall go before him a consuming fire, and a mighty tempest shall be stirred up round about him.

4 He shall call the heaven from above : and the earth, that he may judge his people

5 Gather my saints together unto me : those that have made a covenant with me with sacrifice.

6 And the heavens shall declare his righteousness : for God is Judge himself.

7 Hear, O my people, and I will speak : I myself will testify against thee, O Israel ; for I am God, even thy God.

8 I will not reprove thee because of thy sacrifices, or for thy burnt-offerings : they were not alway before me.

9 I will take no bullock out of thine house : nor he-goats out of thy folds.

10 For all the beasts of the forest are mine : and so are the cattle upon a thousand hills.

[10] "domination" in the English book.

14 They lie in the grave like sheep; death is their
shepherd; and the righteous shall have dominion over
them in the morning: * their beauty shall consume in
the sepulchre, and have no abiding.
15 But God hath delivered my soul from the power
of the grave; * for he shall receive me.
16 Be not thou afraid, though one be made rich, *
or if the glory of his house be increased;
17 For he shall carry nothing away with him when
he dieth, * neither shall his pomp follow him.
18 For while he lived, he counted himself an happy
man; * and so long as thou doest well unto thyself, men
will speak good of thee.
19 He shall follow the generation of his fathers, *
and shall never see light.
20 Man that is in honour but hath no understanding * is compared unto the beasts that perish.

The Tenth Day.

Morning Prayer.

Psalm 50. *Deus deorum.*

THE LORD, even the Most Mighty God, hath
spoken, * and called the world, from the rising up of
the sun unto the going down thereof.
2 Out of Sion hath God appeared * in perfect
beauty.
3 Our God shall come, and shall not keep silence; *
there shall go before him a consuming fire, and a
mighty tempest shall be stirred up round about him.
4 He shall call the heaven from above, * and the
earth, that he may judge his people
5 Gather my saints together unto me; * those that
have made a covenant with me with sacrifice.
6 And the heavens shall declare his righteousness; * for God is Judge himself.
7 Hear, O my people, and I will speak; * I myself
will testify against thee, O Israel; for I am God, even
thy God.
8 I will not reprove thee because of thy sacrifices; *
as for thy burnt-offerings, they are alway before me.
9 I will take no bullock out of thine house, * nor
he-goats out of thy folds.
10 For all the beasts of the forest are mine, * and so
are the cattle upon a thousand hills.

14 Their form shall waste away, *
and the land of the dead shall be their home.

15 But God will ransom my life; *
he will snatch me from the grasp of death.

16 Do not be envious when some become rich, *
or when the grandeur of their house increases;

17 For they will carry nothing away at their death, *
nor will their grandeur follow them.

18 Though they thought highly of themselves while they lived, *
and were praised for their success,

19 They shall join the company of their forebears, *
who will never see the light again.

20 Those who are honored, but have no understanding, *
are like the beasts that perish.

Tenth Day: Morning Prayer

50 *Deus deorum*

1 The LORD, the God of gods, has spoken; *
he has called the earth from the rising of the sun to
its setting.

2 Out of Zion, perfect in its beauty, *
God reveals himself in glory.

3 Our God will come and will not keep silence; *
before him there is a consuming flame,
and round about him a raging storm.

4 He calls the heavens and the earth from above *
to witness the judgment of his people.

5 "Gather before me my loyal followers, *
those who have made a covenant with me
and sealed it with sacrifice."

6 Let the heavens declare the rightness of his cause; *
for God himself is judge.

7 Hear, O my people, and I will speak:
"O Israel, I will bear witness against you; *
for I am God, your God.

8 I do not accuse you because of your sacrifices; *
your offerings are always before me.

9 I will take no bull-calf from your stalls, *
nor he-goats out of your pens;

10 For all the beasts of the forest are mine, *
the herds in their thousands upon the hills.

1789-1871

11 I know all the fowls upon the mountains, and the wild beasts of the field are in my sight.

12 If I be hungry, I will not tell thee ; for the whole world is mine, and all that is therein.

13 Thinkest thou that I will eat bulls' flesh, and drink the blood of goats?

14 Offer unto God thanksgiving, and pay thy vows unto the Most Highest.

15 And call upon me in the time of trouble ; so will I hear thee, and thou shalt praise me.

16 But unto the ungodly said God, Why dost thou preach my laws, and takest my covenant in thy mouth ;

17 Whereas thou hatest to be reformed, and hast cast my words behind thee?

18 When thou sawest a thief, thou consentedst unto him ; and hast been partaker with the adulterers.

19 Thou hast let thy mouth speak wickedness, and with thy tongue thou hast set forth deceit.

20 Thou sattest and spakest against thy brother ; yea, and hast slandered thine own mother's son.

21 These things hast thou done, and I held my tongue, and thou thoughtest wickedly, that I am even such a one as thyself ; but I will reprove thee, and set before thee the things that thou hast done.

22 O consider this, ye that forget God, lest I pluck you away, and there be none to deliver you.

23 Whoso offereth me thanks and praise, he honoureth me ; and to him that ordereth his conversation right, will I show the salvation of God.

1892

11 I know all the fowls upon the mountains : and the wild beasts of the field are in my sight.

12 If I be hungry, I will not tell thee : for the whole world is mine, and all that is therein.

13 Thinkest thou that I will eat bulls' flesh : and drink the blood of goats?

14 Offer unto God thanksgiving : and pay thy vows unto the Most Highest.

15 And call upon me in the time of trouble : so will I hear thee, and thou shalt praise me.

16 But unto the ungodly said God : Why dost thou preach my laws, and takest my covenant in thy mouth ;

17 Whereas thou hatest to be reformed : and hast cast my words behind thee?

18 When thou sawest a thief, thou consentedst unto him : and hast been partaker with the adulterers.

19 Thou hast let thy mouth speak wickedness : and with thy tongue thou hast set forth deceit.

20 Thou sattest and spakest against thy brother : yea, and hast slandered thine own mother's son.

21 These things hast thou done, and I held my tongue, and thou thoughtest wickedly, that I am even such a one as thyself : but I will reprove thee, and set before thee the things that thou hast done.

22 O consider this, ye that forget God : lest I pluck you away, and there be none to deliver you.

23 Whoso offereth me thanks and praise, he honoureth me : and to him that ordereth his conversation right, will I show the salvation of God.

Psalm li. *Miserere mei, Deus.*

HAVE mercy upon me, O God, after thy great goodness ; according to the multitude of thy mercies do away mine offences.

2 Wash me throughly from my wickedness, and cleanse me from my sin.

3 For I acknowledge my faults, and my sin is ever before me.

4 Against thee only have I sinned, and done this evil in thy sight, that thou mightest be justified in thy saying, and clear when thou art judged.

PSALM 51. *Miserere mei, Deus.*

HAVE mercy upon me, O God, after thy great goodness : according to the multitude of thy mercies do away mine offences.

2 Wash me throughly from my wickedness : and cleanse me from my sin.

3 For I acknowledge my faults : and my sin is ever before me.

4 Against thee only have I sinned, and done this evil in thy sight : that thou mightest be justified in thy saying, and clear when thou art judged.

11 I know all the fowls upon the mountains, * and the wild beasts of the field are in my sight.

12 If I be hungry, I will not tell thee; * for the whole world is mine, and all that is therein.

13 Thinkest thou that I will eat bulls' flesh, * and drink the blood of goats?

14 Offer unto God thanksgiving, * and pay thy vows unto the Most Highest.

15 And call upon me in the time of trouble; * so will I hear thee, and thou shalt praise me.

16 But unto the ungodly saith God, * Why dost thou preach my laws, and takest my covenant in thy mouth;

17 Whereas thou hatest to be reformed, * and hast cast my words behind thee?

18 When thou sawest a thief, thou consentedst unto him; * and hast been partaker with the adulterers.

19 Thou hast let thy mouth speak wickedness, * and with thy tongue thou hast set forth deceit.

20 Thou sattest and spakest against thy brother; * yea, and hast slandered thine own mother's son.

21 These things hast thou done, and I held my tongue, and thou thoughtest wickedly, that I am even such a one as thyself; * but I will reprove thee, and set before thee the things that thou hast done.

22 O consider this, ye that forget God, * lest I pluck you away, and there be none to deliver you.

23 Whoso offereth me thanks and praise, he honoureth me; * and to him that ordereth his way aright, will I show the salvation of God.

11 I know every bird in the sky, *
and the creatures of the fields are in my sight.

12 If I were hungry, I would not tell you, *
for the whole world is mine and all that is in it.

13 Do you think I eat the flesh of bulls, *
or drink the blood of goats?

14 Offer to God a sacrifice of thanksgiving *
and make good your vows to the Most High.

15 Call upon me in the day of trouble; *
I will deliver you, and you shall honor me.

16 But to the wicked God says: *
"Why do you recite my statutes,
and take my covenant upon your lips;

17 Since you refuse discipline, *
and toss my words behind your back?

18 When you see a thief, you make him your friend, *
and you cast in your lot with adulterers.

19 You have loosed your lips for evil, *
and harnessed your tongue to a lie.

20 You are always speaking evil of your brother *
and slandering your own mother's son.

21 These things you have done, and I kept still, *
and you thought that I am like you."

22 "I have made my accusation; *
I have put my case in order before your eyes.

23 Consider this well, you who forget God, *
lest I rend you and there be none to deliver you.

24 Whoever offers me the sacrifice of thanksgiving
honors me; *
but to those who keep in my way will I show
the salvation of God."

Psalm 51. *Miserere mei, Deus.*

HAVE mercy upon me, O God, after thy great goodness; * according to the multitude of thy mercies do away mine offences.

2 Wash me throughly from my wickedness, * and cleanse me from my sin.

3 For I acknowledge my faults, * and my sin is ever before me.

4 Against thee only have I sinned, and done this evil in thy sight; * that thou mightest be justified in thy saying, and clear when thou shalt judge.

51 *Miserere mei, Deus*

1 Have mercy on me, O God, according to your
loving-kindness; *
in your great compassion blot out my offenses.

2 Wash me through and through from my wickedness *
and cleanse me from my sin.

3 For I know my transgressions, *
and my sin is ever before me.

4 Against you only have I sinned *
and done what is evil in your sight.

5 Behold, I was shapen in wickedness, and in sin hath my mother conceived me.

6 But lo, thou requirest truth in the inward parts, and shalt make me to understand wisdom secretly.

7 Thou shalt purge me with hyssop, and I shall be clean ; thou shalt wash me, and I shall be whiter than snow.

8 Thou shalt make me hear of joy and gladness, that the bones which thou hast broken may rejoice.

9 Turn thy face from my sins, and put out all my misdeeds.

10 Make me a clean heart, O God, and renew a right spirit within me.

11 Cast me not away from thy presence, and take not thy holy Spirit from me.

12 O give me the comfort of thy help again, and stablish me with thy free Spirit.

13 Then shall I teach thy ways unto the wicked, and sinners shall be converted unto thee.

14 Deliver me from blood-guiltiness, O God, thou that art the God of my health ; and my tongue shall sing of thy righteousness.

15 Thou shalt open my lips, O Lord, and my mouth shall show thy praise.

16 For thou desirest no sacrifice, else would I give it thee ; but thou delightest not in burnt-offerings.

17 The sacrifice of God is a troubled spirit : a broken and contrite heart, O God, shalt thou not despise.

18 O be favourable and gracious unto Sion ; build thou the walls of Jerusalem.

19 Then shalt thou be pleased with the sacrifice of righteousness, with the burnt-offerings and oblations ; then shall they offer young bullocks upon thine altar.

5 Behold, I was shapen in wickedness : and in sin hath my mother conceived me.

6 But lo, thou requirest truth in the inward parts : and shalt make me to understand wisdom secretly.

7 Thou shalt purge me with hyssop, and I shall be clean : thou shalt wash me, and I shall be whiter than snow.

8 Thou shalt make me hear of joy and gladness : that the bones which thou hast broken may rejoice.

9 Turn thy face from my sins : and put out all my misdeeds.

10 Make me a clean heart, O God : and renew a right spirit within me.

11 Cast me not away from thy presence : and take not thy holy Spirit from me.

12 O give me the comfort of thy help again : and stablish me with thy free Spirit.

13 Then shall I teach thy ways unto the wicked : and sinners shall be converted unto thee.

14 Deliver me from blood-guiltiness, O God, thou that art the God of my health : and my tongue shall sing of thy righteousness.

15 Thou shalt open my lips, O Lord : and my mouth shall show thy praise.

16 For thou desirest no sacrifice, else would I give it thee : but thou delightest not in burnt-offerings.

17 The sacrifice of God is a troubled spirit : a broken and contrite heart, O God, shalt thou not despise.

18 O be favourable and gracious unto Sion : build thou the walls of Jerusalem.

19 Then shalt thou be pleased with the sacrifice of righteousness, with the burnt-offerings and oblations : then shall they offer young bullocks upon thine altar.

Psalm lii. *Quid gloriaris?*

WHY boastest thou thyself, thou tyrant, that thou canst do mischief ;

2 Whereas the goodness of God endureth yet daily?

PSALM 52. *Quid gloriaris?*

WHY boastest thou thyself, thou tyrant : that thou canst do mischief ;

2 Whereas the goodness of God : endureth yet daily?

5 Behold, I was shapen in wickedness, * and in sin
hath my mother conceived me.
6 But lo, thou requirest truth in the inward parts, *
and shalt make me to understand wisdom secretly.
7 Thou shalt purge me with hyssop, and I shall be
clean; * thou shalt wash me, and I shall be whiter than
snow.
8 Thou shalt make me hear of joy and gladness, *
that the bones which thou hast broken may rejoice.
9 Turn thy face from my sins, * and put out all my
misdeeds.
10 Make me a clean heart, O God, * and renew a
right spirit within me.
11 Cast me not away from thy presence, * and take
not thy holy Spirit from me.
12 O give me the comfort of thy help again, * and
stablish me with thy free Spirit.
13 Then shall I teach thy ways unto the wicked, *
and sinners shall be converted unto thee.
14 Deliver me from blood-guiltiness, O God, thou
that art the God of my health; * and my tongue shall
sing of thy righteousness.
15 Thou shalt open my lips, O Lord, * and my
mouth shall show thy praise.
16 For thou desirest no sacrifice, else would I give it
thee; * but thou delightest not in burnt-offerings.
17 The sacrifice of God is a troubled spirit: * a
broken and contrite heart, O God, shalt thou not
despise.
18 O be favourable and gracious unto Sion; * build
thou the walls of Jerusalem.
19 Then shalt thou be pleased with the sacrifice of
righteousness, with the burnt-offerings and oblations; *
then shall they offer young bullocks upon thine altar.

5 And so you are justified when you speak *
and upright in your judgment.

6 Indeed, I have been wicked from my birth, *
a sinner from my mother's womb.

7 For behold, you look for truth deep within me, *
and will make me understand wisdom secretly.

8 Purge me from my sin, and I shall be pure; *
wash me, and I shall be clean indeed.

9 Make me hear of joy and gladness, *
that the body you have broken may rejoice.

10 Hide your face from my sins *
and blot out all my iniquities.

11 Create in me a clean heart, O God, *
and renew a right spirit within me.

12 Cast me not away from your presence *
and take not your holy Spirit from me.

13 Give me the joy of your saving help again *
and sustain me with your bountiful Spirit.

14 I shall teach your ways to the wicked, *
and sinners shall return to you.

15 Deliver me from death, O God, *
and my tongue shall sing of your righteousness,
O God of my salvation.

16 Open my lips, O Lord, *
and my mouth shall proclaim your praise.

17 Had you desired it, I would have offered sacrifice, *
but you take no delight in burnt-offerings.

18 The sacrifice of God is a troubled spirit; *
a broken and contrite heart, O God, you will not despise.

19 Be favorable and gracious to Zion, *
and rebuild the walls of Jerusalem.

20 Then you will be pleased with the appointed sacrifices,
with burnt-offerings and oblations; *
then shall they offer young bullocks upon your altar.

Psalm 52. *Quid gloriaris?*

WHY boastest thou thyself, thou tyrant, * that thou
canst do mischief;
2 Whereas the goodness of God * endureth yet
daily?

52 *Quid gloriaris?*

1 You tyrant, why do you boast of wickedness *
against the godly all day long?

2 You plot ruin;
your tongue is like a sharpened razor, *
O worker of deception.

3 Thy tongue imagineth wickedness, and with lies thou cuttest like a sharp razor.

4 Thou hast loved unrighteousness more than goodness, and to talk of lies more than righteousness.

5 Thou hast loved to speak all words that may do hurt, O thou false tongue!

6 Therefore shall God destroy thee for ever; he shall take thee, and pluck thee out of thy dwelling, and root thee out of the land of the living.

7 The righteous also shall see this, and fear, and shall laugh him to scorn;

8 Lo, this is the man that took not God for his strength; but trusted unto the multitude of his riches, and strengthened himself in his wickedness.

9 As for me, I am like a green olive-tree in the house of God; my trust is in the tender mercy of God for ever and ever.

10 I will always give thanks unto thee for that thou hast done; and I will hope in thy Name, for thy saints like it well.

Evening Prayer.

Psalm liii. *Dixit insipiens.*

THE foolish body hath said in his heart, There is no God.

2 Corrupt are they, and become abominable in their wickedness; there is none that doeth good.

3 God looked down from heaven upon the children of men, to see if there were any that would understand, and seek after God.

4 But they are all gone out of the way, they are altogether become abominable; there is also none that doeth good, no not one.

5 Are not they without understanding that work wickedness, eating up my people as if they would eat bread? they have not called upon God.

6 They were afraid where no fear was; for God hath broken the bones of him that besieged thee; thou hast put them to confusion, because God hath despised them.

7 O that the salvation were given unto Israel out of Sion! Oh, that the Lord would deliver his people out of captivity!

8 Then should Jacob rejoice, and Israel should be right glad.

Psalm liv. *Deus, in Nomine.*

SAVE me, O God, for thy Name's sake, and avenge me in thy strength.

3 Thy tongue imagineth wickedness: and with lies thou cuttest like a sharp razor.

4 Thou hast loved unrighteousness more than goodness: and talk of lies more than righteousness.

5 Thou hast loved to speak all words that may do hurt: O thou false tongue.

6 Therefore shall God destroy thee for ever: he shall take thee, and pluck thee out of thy dwelling, and root thee out of the land of the living.

7 The righteous also shall see this, and fear: and shall laugh him to scorn:

8 Lo, this is the man that took not God for his strength: but trusted unto the multitude of his riches, and strengthened himself in his wickedness.

9 As for me, I am like a green olive-tree in the house of God: my trust is in the tender mercy of God for ever and ever.

10 I will alway give thanks unto thee for that thou hast done: and I will hope in thy Name, for thy saints like it well.

Evening Prayer.

PSALM 53. *Dixit insipiens.*

THE foolish body hath said in his heart: There is no God.

2 Corrupt are they, and become abominable in their wickedness: there is none that doeth good.

3 God looked down from heaven upon the children of men: to see if there were any that would understand, and seek after God.

4 But they are all gone out of the way, they are altogether become abominable: there is also none that doeth good, no not one.

5 Are not they without understanding that work wickedness: eating up my people as if they would eat bread? they have not called upon God.

6 They were afraid where no fear was: for God hath broken the bones of him that besieged thee; thou hast put them to confusion, because God hath despised them.

7 O that the salvation were given unto Israel out of Sion: O that the Lord would deliver his people out of captivity!

8 Then should Jacob rejoice: and Israel should be right glad.

PSALM 54. *Deus, in Nomine.*

SAVE me, O God, for thy Name's sake: and avenge me in thy strength.

3 Thy tongue imagineth wickedness, * and with lies thou cuttest like a sharp razor.

4 Thou hast loved unrighteousness more than goodness, * and falsehood more than righteousness.

5 Thou hast loved to speak all words that may do hurt, * O thou false tongue.

6 Therefore shall God destroy thee for ever; * he shall take thee, and pluck thee out of thy dwelling, and root thee out of the land of the living.

7 The righteous also shall see this, and fear, * and shall laugh him to scorn:

8 Lo, this is the man that took not God for his strength; * but trusted unto the multitude of his riches, and strengthened himself in his wickedness.

9 As for me, I am like a green olive-tree in the house of God; * my trust is in the tender mercy of God for ever and ever.

10 I will alway give thanks unto thee for that thou hast done; * and I will hope in thy Name, for thy saints like it well.

3 You love evil more than good *
and lying more than speaking the truth.

4 You love all words that hurt, *
O you deceitful tongue.

5 Oh, that God would demolish you utterly, *
topple you, and snatch you from your dwelling,
and root you out of the land of the living!

6 The righteous shall see and tremble, *
and they shall laugh at him, saying,

7 "This is the one who did not take God for a refuge, *
but trusted in great wealth
and relied upon wickedness."

8 But I am like a green olive tree in the house of God; *
I trust in the mercy of God for ever and ever.

9 I will give you thanks for what you have done *
and declare the goodness of your Name in the presence of the godly.

Evening Prayer.

Psalm 53. *Dixit insipiens.*

THE foolish body hath said in his heart, * There is no God.

2 Corrupt are they, and become abominable in their wickedness; * there is none that doeth good.

3 God looked down from heaven upon the children of men, * to see if there were any that would understand, and seek after God.

4 But they are all gone out of the way, they are altogether become abominable; * there is also none that doeth good, no not one.

5 Are not they without understanding that work wickedness, * eating up my people as if they would eat bread? they have not called upon God.

6 They were afraid where no fear was; * for God hath broken the bones of him that besieged thee; thou hast put them to confusion, because God hath despised them.

7 O that the salvation were given unto Israel out of Sion! * O that the Lord would deliver his people out of captivity!

8 Then should Jacob rejoice, * and Israel should be right glad.

Tenth Day: Evening Prayer

53 *Dixit insipiens*

1 The fool has said in his heart, "There is no God." *
All are corrupt and commit abominable acts;
there is none who does any good.

2 God looks down from heaven upon us all, *
to see if there is any who is wise,
if there is one who seeks after God.

3 Every one has proved faithless;
all alike have turned bad; *
there is none who does good; no, not one.

4 Have they no knowledge, those evildoers *
who eat up my people like bread
and do not call upon God?

5 See how greatly they tremble,
such trembling as never was; *
for God has scattered the bones of the enemy;
they are put to shame, because God has rejected them.

6 Oh, that Israel's deliverance would come out of Zion! *
when God restores the fortunes of his people
Jacob will rejoice and Israel be glad.

Psalm 54. *Deus, in Nomine.*

SAVE me, O God, for thy Name's sake, * and avenge me in thy strength.

54 *Deus, in nomine*

1 Save me, O God, by your Name; *
in your might, defend my cause.

1789-1871

2 Hear my prayer, O God, and hearken unto the words of my mouth.
3 For strangers are risen up against me; and tyrants, which have not God before their eyes, seek after my soul.
4 Behold, God is my helper; the Lord is with them that uphold my soul.
5 He shall reward evil unto mine enemies: destroy thou them in thy truth.
6 An offering of a free heart will I give thee, and praise thy Name, O LORD; because it is so comfortable.
7 For he hath delivered me out of all my trouble; and mine eye hath seen his desire upon mine enemies.

Psalm lv. *Exaudi, Deus.*

HEAR my prayer, O God, and hide not thyself from my petition.
2 Take heed unto me, and hear me, how I mourn in my prayer, and am vexed.
3 The enemy crieth so, and the ungodly cometh on so fast; for they are minded to do me some mischief, so maliciously are they set against me.
4 My heart is disquieted within me, and the fear of death is fallen upon me.
5 Fearfulness and trembling are come upon me, and an horrible dread hath overwhelmed me.
6 And I said, Oh, that I had wings like a dove! for then would I flee away, and be at rest.
7 Lo, then would I get me away far off, and remain in the wilderness.
8 I would make haste to escape, because of the stormy wind and tempest.
9 Destroy their tongues, O Lord, and divide them; for I have spied unrighteousness and strife in the city.
10 Day and night they go about within the walls thereof: mischief also and sorrow are in the midst of it.
11 Wickedness is therein; deceit and guile go not out of their streets.
12 For it is not an open enemy that hath done me this dishonour; for then I could have borne it;

1892

2 Hear my prayer, O God: and hearken unto the words of my mouth.
3 For strangers are risen up against me: and tyrants, which have not God before their eyes, seek after my soul.
4 Behold, God is my helper: the Lord is with them that uphold my soul.
5 He shall reward evil unto mine enemies: destroy thou them in thy truth.
6 An offering of a free heart will I give thee, and praise thy Name, O LORD: because it is so comfortable.
7 For he hath delivered me out of all my trouble: and mine eye hath seen his desire upon mine enemies.

PSALM 55. *Exaudi, Deus.*

HEAR my prayer, O God: and hide not thyself from my petition.
2 Take heed unto me, and hear me: how I mourn in my prayer, and am vexed;
3 The enemy crieth so, and the ungodly cometh on so fast: for they are minded to do me some mischief, so maliciously are they set against me.
4 My heart is disquieted within me: and the fear of death is fallen upon me.
5 Fearfulness and trembling are come upon me: and an horrible dread hath overwhelmed me.
6 And I said, O that I had wings like a dove: for then would I flee away, and be at rest.
7 Lo, then would I get me away far off: and remain in the wilderness.
8 I would make haste to escape: because of the stormy wind and tempest.
9 Destroy their tongues, O Lord, and divide them: for I have spied unrighteousness and strife in the city.
10 Day and night they go about within the walls thereof: mischief also and sorrow are in the midst of it.
11 Wickedness is therein: deceit and guile go not out of her streets.
12 For it is not an open enemy that hath done me this dishonour: for then I could have borne it;

2 Hear my prayer, O God, * and hearken unto the words of my mouth.

3 For strangers are risen up against me; * and tyrants, which have not God before their eyes, seek after my soul.

4 Behold, God is my helper; * the Lord is with them that uphold my soul.

5 He shall reward evil unto mine enemies: * destroy thou them in thy truth.

6 An offering of a free heart will I give thee, and praise thy Name, O LORD; * because it is so comfortable.

7 For he hath delivered me out of all my trouble; * and mine eye hath seen his desire upon mine enemies.

Psalm 55. *Exaudi, Deus.*

HEAR my prayer, O God, * and hide not thyself from my petition.

2 Take heed unto me, and hear me, * how I mourn in my prayer, and am vexed;

3 The enemy crieth so, and the ungodly cometh on so fast; * for they are minded to do me some mischief, so maliciously are they set against me.

4 My heart is disquieted within me, * and the fear of death is fallen upon me.

5 Fearfulness and trembling are come upon me, * and an horrible dread hath overwhelmed me.

6 And I said, O that I had wings like a dove! * for then would I flee away, and be at rest.

7 Lo, then would I get me away far off, * and remain in the wilderness.

8 I would make haste to escape, * because of the stormy wind and tempest.

9 Destroy their tongues, O Lord, and divide them; * for I have spied unrighteousness and strife in the city.

10 Day and night they go about within the walls thereof: * mischief also and sorrow are in the midst of it.

11 Wickedness is therein; * deceit and guile go not out of her streets.

12 For it is not an open enemy that hath done me this dishonour; * for then I could have borne it;

2 Hear my prayer, O God; *
give ear to the words of my mouth.

3 For the arrogant have risen up against me,
and the ruthless have sought my life, *
those who have no regard for God.

4 Behold, God is my helper; *
it is the Lord who sustains my life.

5 Render evil to those who spy on me; *
in your faithfulness, destroy them.

6 I will offer you a freewill sacrifice *
and praise your Name, O LORD, for it is good.

7 For you have rescued me from every trouble, *
and my eye has seen the ruin of my foes.

55 *Exaudi, Deus*

1 Hear my prayer, O God; *
do not hide yourself from my petition.

2 Listen to me and answer me; *
I have no peace, because of my cares.

3 I am shaken by the noise of the enemy *
and by the pressure of the wicked;

4 For they have cast an evil spell upon me *
and are set against me in fury.

5 My heart quakes within me, *
and the terrors of death have fallen upon me.

6 Fear and trembling have come over me, *
and horror overwhelms me.

7 And I said, "Oh, that I had wings like a dove! *
I would fly away and be at rest.

8 I would flee to a far-off place *
and make my lodging in the wilderness.

9 I would hasten to escape *
from the stormy wind and tempest."

10 Swallow them up, O Lord;
confound their speech; *
for I have seen violence and strife in the city.

11 Day and night the watchmen make their rounds upon her walls, *
but trouble and misery are in the midst of her.

12 There is corruption at her heart; *
her streets are never free of oppression and deceit.

1789-1871

13 Neither was it mine adversary that did magnify himself against me; for then peradventure I would have hid myself from him:

14 But it was even thou, my companion, my guide, and mine own familiar friend.

15 We took sweet counsel together, and walked in the house of God as friends.

16 Let death come hastily upon them, and let them go down quick into hell; for wickedness is in their dwellings, and among them.

17 As for me, I will call upon God, and the LORD shall save me.

18 In the evening, and morning, and at noon-day will I pray, and that instantly; and he shall hear my voice.

19 It is he that hath delivered my soul in peace from the battle that was against me; for there were many with me.

20 Yea, even God, that endureth for ever, shall hear me, and bring them down; for they will not turn, nor fear God.

21 He laid his hands upon such as be at peace with him, and he brake his covenant.

22 The words of his mouth were softer than butter, having war in his heart; his words were smoother than oil, and yet be they very swords.

23 O cast thy burden upon the LORD, and he shall nourish thee, and shall not suffer the righteous to fall for ever.

24 And as for them, thou, O God, shalt bring them into the pit of destruction.

25 The blood-thirsty and deceitful men shall not live out half their days: nevertheless, my trust shall be in thee, O Lord.

THE ELEVENTH DAY.

Morning Prayer.

Psalm lvi. *Miserere mei, Deus.*

BE merciful unto me, O God, for man goeth about to devour me; he is daily fighting, and troubling me.

2 Mine enemies are daily in hand to swallow me up; for they be many that fight against me, O thou Most Highest.

1892

13 Neither was it mine adversary that did magnify himself against me: for then peradventure I would have hid myself from him;

14 But it was even thou, my companion: my guide, and mine own familiar friend.

15 We took sweet counsel together: and walked in the house of God as friends.

16 Let death come hastily upon them, and let them go down quick into hell: for wickedness is in their dwellings, and among them.

17 As for me, I will call upon God: and the LORD shall save me.

18 In the evening, and morning, and at noon-day will I pray, and that instantly: and he shall hear my voice.

19 It is he that hath delivered my soul in peace from the battle that was against me: for there were many with me.

20 Yea, even God, that endureth for ever, shall hear me, and bring them down: for they will not turn, nor fear God.

21 He laid his hands upon such as be at peace with him: and he brake his covenant.

22 The words of his mouth were softer than butter, having war in his heart: his words were smoother than oil, and yet be they very swords.

23 O cast thy burden upon the LORD, and he shall nourish thee: and shall not suffer the righteous to fall for ever.

24 And as for them: thou, O God, shalt bring them into the pit of destruction.

25 The blood-thirsty and deceitful men shall not live out half their days: nevertheless, my trust shall be in thee, O Lord.

THE ELEVENTH DAY.

Morning Prayer.

PSALM 56. *Miserere mei, Deus.*

BE merciful unto me, O God, for man goeth about to devour me: he is daily fighting, and troubling me.

2 Mine enemies are daily in hand to swallow me up: for they be many that fight against me, O thou most Highest.

13 Neither was it mine adversary that did magnify himself against me; * for then peradventure I would have hid myself from him;

14 But it was even thou, my companion, * my guide, and mine own familiar friend.

15 We took sweet counsel together, * and walked in the house of God as friends.

16 Let death come hastily upon them, and let them go down alive into the pit; * for wickedness is in their dwellings, and among them.

17 As for me, I will call upon God, * and the LORD shall save me.

18 In the evening, and morning, and at noon-day will I pray, and that instantly; * and he shall hear my voice.

19 It is he that hath delivered my soul in peace from the battle that was against me; * for there were many that strove with me.

20 Yea, even God, that endureth for ever, shall hear me, and bring them down; * for they will not turn, nor fear God.

21 He laid his hands upon such as be at peace with him, * and he brake his covenant.

22 The words of his mouth were softer than butter, having war in his heart; * his words were smoother than oil, and yet be they very swords.

23 O cast thy burden upon the LORD, and he shall nourish thee, * and shall not suffer the righteous to fall for ever.

24 And as for them, * thou, O God, shalt bring them into the pit of destruction.

25 The blood-thirsty and deceitful men shall not live out half their days: * nevertheless, my trust shall be in thee, O Lord.

The Eleventh Day.

Morning Prayer.

Psalm 56. *Miserere mei, Deus.*

BE merciful unto me, O God, for man goeth about to devour me; * he is daily fighting, and troubling me.

2 Mine enemies are daily at hand to swallow me up; * for they be many that fight against me, O thou Most Highest.

13 For had it been an adversary who taunted me,
then I could have borne it; *
or had it been an enemy who vaunted himself against me,
then I could have hidden from him.

14 But it was you, a man after my own heart, *
my companion, my own familiar friend.

15 We took sweet counsel together, *
and walked with the throng in the house of God.

16 Let death come upon them suddenly;
let them go down alive into the grave; *
for wickedness is in their dwellings, in their very midst.

17 But I will call upon God, *
and the LORD will deliver me.

18 In the evening, in the morning, and at noonday,
I will complain and lament, *
and he will hear my voice.

19 He will bring me safely back from the battle
waged against me; *
for there are many who fight me.

20 God, who is enthroned of old, will hear me and
bring them down; *
they never change; they do not fear God.

21 My companion stretched forth his hand against his comrade; *
he has broken his covenant.

22 His speech is softer than butter, *
but war is in his heart.

23 His words are smoother than oil, *
but they are drawn swords.

24 Cast your burden upon the LORD,
and he will sustain you; *
he will never let the righteous stumble.

25 For you will bring the bloodthirsty and deceitful *
down to the pit of destruction, O God.

26 They shall not live out half their days, *
but I will put my trust in you.

Eleventh Day: Morning Prayer

56 *Miserere mei, Deus*

1 Have mercy on me, O God,
for my enemies are hounding me; *
all day long they assault and oppress me.

2 They hound me all the day long; *
truly there are many who fight against me, O Most High.

3 Nevertheless, though I am sometime afraid, yet put I my trust in thee.
4 I will praise God, because of his word : I have put my trust in God, and will not fear what flesh can do unto me.
5 They daily mistake my words ; all that they imagine is to do me evil.
6 They hold all together, and keep themselves close, and mark my steps, when they lay wait for my soul.
7 Shall they escape for their wickedness? thou, O God, in thy displeasure shalt cast them down.
8 Thou tellest my wanderings :[11] put my tears into thy bottle : are not these things noted in thy book?
9 Whensoever I call upon thee, then shall mine enemies be put to flight : this I know ; for God is on my side.
10 In God's word will I rejoice ; in the LORD'S word will I comfort me.
11 Yea, in God have I put my trust ; I will not be afraid what man can do unto me.
12 Unto thee, O God, will I pay my vows ; unto thee will I give thanks.
13 For thou hast delivered my soul from death, and my feet from falling, that I may walk before God in the light of the living.

3 Nevertheless, though I am sometime afraid : yet put I my trust in thee.
4 I will praise God, because of his word : I have put my trust in God, and will not fear what flesh can do unto me.
5 They daily mistake my words : all that they imagine is to do me evil.
6 They hold all together, and keep themselves close : and mark my steps when they lay wait for my soul.
7 Shall they escape for their wickedness : thou, O God, in thy displeasure shalt cast them down.
8 Thou tellest my wanderings ; put my tears into thy bottle : are not these things noted in thy book?
9 Whensoever I call upon thee, then shall mine enemies be put to flight : this I know ; for God is on my side.
10 In God's word will I rejoice : in the LORD'S word will I comfort me.
11 Yea, in God have I put my trust : I will not be afraid what man can do unto me.
12 Unto thee, O God, will I pay my vows : unto thee will I give thanks.
13 For thou hast delivered my soul from death, and my feet from falling : that I may walk before God in the light of the living.

Psalm lvii. *Miserere mei, Deus.*

BE merciful unto me, O God, be merciful unto me ; for my soul trusteth in thee ; and under the shadow of thy wings shall be my refuge, until this tyranny be overpast.
2 I will call unto the most high God, even unto the God that shall perform the cause which I have in hand.
3 He shall send from heaven, and save me from the reproof of him that would eat me up.
4 God shall send forth his mercy and truth : my soul is among lions.
5 And I lie even among the children of men, that are set on fire, whose teeth are spears and arrows, and their tongue a sharp sword.

PSALM 57. *Miserere mei, Deus.*

BE merciful unto me, O God, be merciful unto me ; for my soul trusteth in thee : and under the shadow of thy wings shall be my refuge, until this tyranny be overpast.
2 I will call unto the Most High God : even unto the God that shall perform the cause which I have in hand.
3 He shall send from heaven : and save me from the reproof of him that would eat me up.
4 God shall send forth his mercy and truth : my soul is among lions ;
5 And I lie even among the children of men, that are set on fire : whose teeth are spears and arrows, and their tongue a sharp sword.

[11] "fittings" in the English book.

3 Nevertheless, though I am sometime afraid, * yet
put I my trust in thee.
4 I will praise God, because of his word: * I have
put my trust in God, and will not fear what flesh can do
unto me.
5 They daily mistake my words; * all that they
imagine is to do me evil.
6 They hold all together, and keep themselves
close, * and mark my steps when they lay wait for my
soul.
7 Shall they escape for their wickedness? * thou, O
God, in thy displeasure shalt cast them down.
8 Thou tellest my wanderings; put my tears into thy
bottle: * are not these things noted in thy book?
9 Whensoever I call upon thee, then shall mine
enemies be put to flight: * this I know; for God is on my
side.
10 In God's word will I rejoice; * in the LORD'S
word will I comfort me.
11 Yea, in God have I put my trust; * I will not be
afraid what man can do unto me.
12 Unto thee, O God, will I pay my vows; * unto
thee will I give thanks.
13 For thou hast delivered my soul from death, and
my feet from falling, * that I may walk before God in
the light of the living.

3 Whenever I am afraid, *
I will put my trust in you.

4 In God, whose word I praise,
In God I trust and will not be afraid, *
for what can flesh do to me?

5 All day long they damage my cause; *
their only thought is to do me evil.

6 They band together; they lie in wait; *
they spy upon my footsteps;
because they seek my life.

7 Shall they escape despite their wickedness? *
O God, in your anger, cast down the peoples.

8 You have noted my lamentation;
put my tears into your bottle; *
are they not recorded in your book?

9 Whenever I call upon you, my enemies will be put to flight; *
this I know, for God is on my side.

10 In God the LORD, whose word I praise,
in God I trust and will not be afraid, *
for what can mortals do to me?

11 I am bound by the vow I made to you, O God; *
I will present to you thank-offerings;

12 For you have rescued my soul from death and my feet from stumbling, *
that I may walk before God in the light of the living.

Psalm 57. *Miserere mei, Deus.*

BE merciful unto me, O God, be merciful unto me; for
my soul trusteth in thee; * and under the shadow of
thy wings shall be my refuge, until this tyranny be
overpast.
2 I will call unto the Most High God, * even unto
the God that shall perform the cause which I have in
hand.
3 He shall send from heaven, * and save me from
the reproof of him that would eat me up.
4 God shall send forth his mercy and truth: * my
soul is among lions;
5 And I lie even among the children of men, that
are set on fire, * whose teeth are spears and arrows,
and their tongue a sharp sword.

57 *Miserere mei, Deus*

1 Be merciful to me, O God, be merciful,
for I have taken refuge in you; *
in the shadow of your wings will I take refuge
until this time of trouble has gone by.

2 I will call upon the Most High God, *
the God who maintains my cause.

3 He will send from heaven and save me;
he will confound those who trample upon me; *
God will send forth his love and his faithfulness.

4 I lie in the midst of lions that devour the people; *
their teeth are spears and arrows,
their tongue a sharp sword.

5 They have laid a net for my feet,
and I am bowed low; *
they have dug a pit before me,
but have fallen into it themselves.

1789-1871	1892
6 Set up thyself, O God, above the heavens ; and thy glory above all the earth.	6 Set up thyself, O God, above the heavens : and thy glory above all the earth.
7 They have laid a net for my feet, and pressed down my soul ; they have digged a pit before me, and are fallen into the midst of it themselves.	7 They have laid a net for my feet, and pressed down my soul : they have digged a pit before me, and are fallen into the midst of it themselves.
8 My heart is fixed, O God, my heart is fixed ; I will sing and give praise.	8 My heart is fixed, O God, my heart is fixed : I will sing and give praise.
9 Awake up, my glory ; awake, lute and harp : I myself will awake right early.	9 Awake up, my glory ; awake, lute and harp : I myself will awake right early.
10 I will give thanks unto thee, O Lord, among the people ; and I will sing unto thee among the nations.	10 I will give thanks unto thee, O Lord, among the people : and I will sing unto thee among the nations.
11 For the greatness of thy mercy reacheth unto the heavens, and thy truth unto the clouds.	11 For the greatness of thy mercy reacheth unto the heavens : and thy truth unto the clouds.
12 Set up thyself, O God, above the heavens ; and thy glory above all the earth.	12 Set up thyself, O God, above the heavens : and thy glory above all the earth.

1789-1871	1892
Psalm lviii. *Si vere utique.*	PSALM 58. *Si vere utique.*
ARE your minds set upon righteousness, O ye congregation? and do ye judge the thing that is right, O ye sons of men?	ARE your minds set upon righteousness, O ye congregation : and do ye judge the thing that is right, O ye sons of men?
2 Yea, ye imagine mischief in your heart upon the earth, and your hands deal with wickedness.	2 Yea, ye imagine mischief in your heart upon the earth : and your hands deal with wickedness.
3 The ungodly are froward, even from their mother's womb ; as soon as they are born, they go astray, and speak lies.	3 The ungodly are froward, even from their mother's womb : as soon as they are born, they go astray, and speak lies.
4 They are as venomous as the poison of a serpent, even like the deaf adder, that stoppeth her ears ;	4 They are as venomous as the poison of a serpent : even like the deaf adder, that stoppeth her ears ;
5 Which refuseth to hear the voice of the charmer, charm he never so wisely.	5 Which refuseth to hear the voice of the charmer : charm he never so wisely.
6 Break their teeth, O God, in their mouths ; smite the jaw-bones of the lions, O LORD : let them fall away like water that runneth apace ; and when they shoot their arrows let them be rooted out.	6 Break their teeth, O God, in their mouths ; smite the jaw-bones of the lions, O LORD : let them fall away like water that runneth apace ; and when they shoot their arrows let them be rooted out.
7 Let them consume away like a snail, and be like the untimely fruit of a woman ; and let them not see the sun.	7 Let them consume away like a snail, and be like the untimely fruit of a woman : and let them not see the sun.
8 Or ever your pots be made hot with thorns, so let indignation vex him, even as a thing that is raw.	8 Or ever your pots be made hot with thorns : so let indignation vex him, even as a thing that is raw.
9 The righteous shall rejoice when he seeth the vengeance ; he shall wash his footsteps in the blood of the ungodly.	9 The righteous shall rejoice when he seeth the vengeance : he shall wash his footsteps in the blood of the ungodly.
10 So that a man shall say, Verily there is a reward for the righteous ; doubtless there is a God that judgeth the earth.	10 So that a man shall say, Verily there is a reward for the righteous : doubtless there is a God that judgeth the earth.

6 Set up thyself, O God, above the heavens; * and thy glory above all the earth.

7 They have laid a net for my feet, and pressed down my soul; * they have digged a pit before me, and are fallen into the midst of it themselves.

8 My heart is fixed, O God, my heart is fixed; * I will sing and give praise.

9 Awake up, my glory; awake, lute and harp: * I myself will awake right early.

10 I will give thanks unto thee, O Lord, among the peoples; * and I will sing unto thee among the nations.

11 For the greatness of thy mercy reacheth unto the heavens, * and thy truth unto the clouds.

12 Set up thyself, O God, above the heavens; * and thy glory above all the earth.

Psalm 58. *Si vere utique.*

ARE your minds set upon righteousness, O ye congregation? * and do ye judge the thing that is right, O ye sons of men?

2 Yea, ye imagine mischief in your heart upon the earth, * and your hands deal with wickedness.

3 The ungodly are froward, even from their mother's womb; * as soon as they are born, they go astray, and speak lies.

4 They are as venomous as the poison of a serpent, * even like the deaf adder, that stoppeth her ears;

5 Which refuseth to hear the voice of the charmer, * charm he never so wisely.

6 Break their teeth, O God, in their mouths; * smite the jaw-bones of the lions, O LORD.

7 Let them fall away like water that runneth apace; * when they shoot their arrows, let them be rooted out.

8 Let them consume away like a snail, and be like the untimely fruit of a woman; * and let them not see the sun.

9 Or ever your pots be made hot with thorns, * he shall take them away with a whirlwind, the green and the burning alike.

10 The righteous shall rejoice when he seeth the vengeance; * he shall wash his footsteps in the blood of the ungodly.

11 So that a man shall say, Verily there is a reward for the righteous; * doubtless there is a God that judgeth the earth.

6 Exalt yourself above the heavens, O God, *
and your glory over all the earth.

7 My heart is firmly fixed, O God, my heart is fixed; *
I will sing and make melody.

8 Wake up, my spirit;
awake, lute and harp; *
I myself will waken the dawn.

9 I will confess you among the peoples, O LORD; *
I will sing praise to you among the nations.

10 For your loving-kindness is greater than the heavens, *
and your faithfulness reaches to the clouds.

11 Exalt yourself above the heavens, O God, *
and your glory over all the earth.

58 *Si vere utique*

1 Do you indeed decree righteousness, you rulers? *
do you judge the peoples with equity?

2 No; you devise evil in your hearts, *
and your hands deal out violence in the land.

3 The wicked are perverse from the womb; *
liars go astray from their birth.

4 They are as venomous as a serpent, *
they are like the deaf adder which stops its ears,

5 Which does not heed the voice of the charmer, *
no matter how skillful his charming.

6 O God, break their teeth in their mouths; *
pull the fangs of the young lions, O LORD.

7 Let them vanish like water that runs off; *
let them wither like trodden grass.

8 Let them be like the snail that melts away, *
like a stillborn child that never sees the sun.

9 Before they bear fruit, let them be cut down like a brier; *
like thorns and thistles let them be swept away.

10 The righteous will be glad when they see the vengeance; *
they will bathe their feet in the blood of the wicked.

11 And they will say,
"Surely, there is a reward for the righteous; *
surely, there is a God who rules in the earth."

Evening Prayer.

Psalm lix. *Eripe me de inimicis.*

DELIVER me from mine enemies, O God ; defend me from them that rise up against me.

2 O deliver me from the wicked doers, and save me from the blood-thirsty men.

3 For lo, they lie waiting for my soul ; the mighty men are gathered against me, without any offence or fault of me, O LORD.

4 They run and prepare themselves without my fault ; arise thou therefore to help me, and behold.

5 Stand up, O LORD God of hosts, thou God of Israel, to visit all the heathen, and be not merciful unto them that offend of malicious wickedness.

6 They go to and fro in the evening, they grin like a dog, and run about through the city.

7 Behold, they speak with their mouth, and swords are in their lips ; for who doth hear?

8 But thou, O LORD, shalt have them in derision, and thou shalt laugh all the heathen to scorn.

9 My strength will I ascribe unto thee ; for thou art the God of my refuge.

10 God showeth me his goodness plenteously ; and God shall let me see my desire upon mine enemies.

11 Slay them not, lest my people forget it ; but scatter them abroad among the people, and put them down, O Lord our defence.

12 For the sin of their mouth, and for the words of their lips, they shall be taken in their pride : and why? their preaching is of cursing and lies.

13 Consume them in thy wrath, consume them, that they may perish ; and know that it is God that ruleth in Jacob, and unto the ends of the world.

14 And in the evening they will return, grin like a dog, and will go about the city.

15 They will run here and there for meat, and grudge if they be not satisfied.

16 As for me, I will sing of thy power, and will praise thy mercy betimes in the morning ; for thou hast been my defence and refuge in the day of my trouble.

17 Unto thee, O my strength, will I sing ; for thou, O God, art my refuge, and my merciful God.

Evening Prayer.

PSALM 59. *Eripe me de inimicis.*

DELIVER me from mine enemies, O God : defend me from them that rise up against me.

2 O deliver me from the wicked doers : and save me from the blood-thirsty men.

3 For lo, they lie waiting for my soul : the mighty men are gathered against me, without any offence or fault of me, O LORD.

4 They run and prepare themselves without my fault : arise thou therefore to help me, and behold.

5 Stand up, O LORD God of hosts, thou God of Israel, to visit all the heathen : and be not merciful unto them that offend of malicious wickedness.

6 They go to and fro in the evening : they grin like a dog, and run about through the city.

7 Behold, they speak with their mouth, and swords are in their lips : for who doth hear?

8 But thou, O LORD, shalt have them in derision : and thou shalt laugh all the heathen to scorn.

9 My strength will I ascribe unto thee : for thou art the God of my refuge.

10 God showeth me his goodness plenteously : and God shall let me see my desire upon mine enemies.

11 Slay them not, lest my people forget it : but scatter them abroad among the people, and put them down, O Lord our defence.

12 For the sin of their mouth, and for the words of their lips, they shall be taken in their pride : and why? their preaching is of cursing and lies.

13 Consume them in thy wrath, consume them, that they may perish : and know that it is God that ruleth in Jacob, and unto the ends of the world.

14 And in the evening they will return : grin like a dog, and will go about the city.

15 They will run here and there for meat : and grudge if they be not satisfied.

16 As for me, I will sing of thy power, and will praise thy mercy betimes in the morning : for thou hast been my defence and refuge in the day of my trouble.

17 Unto thee, O my strength, will I sing : for thou, O God, art my refuge, and my merciful God.

Evening Prayer.

Psalm 59. *Eripe me de inimicis.*

DELIVER me from mine enemies, O God; * defend me from them that rise up against me.

2 O deliver me from the wicked doers, * and save me from the blood-thirsty men.

3 For lo, they lie waiting for my soul; * the mighty men are gathered against me, without any offence or fault of me, O LORD.

4 They run and prepare themselves without my fault; * arise thou therefore to help me, and behold.

5 Stand up, O LORD God of hosts, thou God of Israel, to visit all the heathen, * and be not merciful unto them that offend of malicious wickedness.

6 They go to and fro in the evening, * they grin like a dog, and run about through the city.

7 Behold, they speak with their mouth, and swords are in their lips; * for who doth hear?

8 But thou, O LORD, shalt have them in derision, * and thou shalt laugh all the heathen to scorn.

9 My strength will I ascribe unto thee; * for thou art the God of my refuge.

10 God showeth me his goodness plenteously; * and God shall let me see my desire upon mine enemies.

11 Slay them not, lest my people forget it; * but scatter them abroad among the people, and put them down, O Lord our defence.

12 For the sin of their mouth, and for the words of their lips, they shall be taken in their pride: * and why? their talk is of cursing and lies.

13 Consume them in thy wrath, consume them, that they may perish; * and know that it is God that ruleth in Jacob, and unto the ends of the world.

14 And in the evening they will return, * grin like a dog, and will go about the city.

15 They will run here and there for meat, * and grudge if they be not satisfied.

16 As for me, I will sing of thy power, and will praise thy mercy betimes in the morning; * for thou hast been my defence and refuge in the day of my trouble.

17 Unto thee, O my strength, will I sing; * for thou, O God, art my refuge, and my merciful God.

Eleventh Day: Evening Prayer

59 *Eripe me de inimicis*

1 Rescue me from my enemies, O God; *
protect me from those who rise up against me.

2 Rescue me from evildoers *
and save me from those who thirst for my blood.

3 See how they lie in wait for my life,
how the mighty gather together against me; *
not for any offense or fault of mine, O LORD.

4 Not because of any guilt of mine *
they run and prepare themselves for battle.

5 Rouse yourself, come to my side, and see; *
for you, LORD God of hosts, are Israel's God.

6 Awake, and punish all the ungodly; *
show no mercy to those who are faithless and evil.

7 They go to and fro in the evening; *
they snarl like dogs and run about the city.

8 Behold, they boast with their mouths,
and taunts are on their lips; *
"For who," they say, "will hear us?"

9 But you, O LORD, you laugh at them; *
you laugh all the ungodly to scorn.

10 My eyes are fixed on you, O my Strength; *
for you, O God, are my stronghold.

11 My merciful God comes to meet me; *
God will let me look in triumph on my enemies.

12 Slay them, O God, lest my people forget; *
send them reeling by your might
and put them down, O Lord our shield.

13 For the sins of their mouths, for the words of their lips,
for the cursing and lies that they utter, *
let them be caught in their pride.

14 Make an end of them in your wrath; *
make an end of them, and they shall be no more.

15 Let everyone know that God rules in Jacob, *
and to the ends of the earth.

16 They go to and fro in the evening; *
they snarl like dogs and run about the city.

17 They forage for food, *
and if they are not filled, they howl.

18 For my part, I will sing of your strength; *
I will celebrate your love in the morning;

Psalm lx. *Deus, repulisti nos.*

O GOD, thou hast cast us out, and scattered us abroad ; thou hast also been displeased : O turn thee unto us again.

2 Thou hast moved the land, and divided it : heal the sores thereof, for it shaketh.

3 Thou hast showed thy people heavy things ; thou hast given us a drink of deadly wine.

4 Thou hast given a token for such as fear thee, that they may triumph because of the truth.

5 Therefore were thy beloved delivered : help me with thy right hand, and hear me.

6 God hath spoken in his holiness, I will rejoice, and divide Sichem, and mete out the valley of Succoth.

7 Gilead is mine, and Manasses is mine ; Ephraim also is the strength of my head ; Judah is my law-giver :

8 Moab is my wash-pot ; over Edom will I cast out my shoe ; Philistia, be thou glad of me.

9 Who will lead me into the strong city? who will bring me into Edom?

10 Hast not thou cast us out, O God? wilt not thou, O God, go out with our hosts?

11 O be thou our help in trouble ; for vain is the help of man.

12 Through God will we do great acts ; for it is he that shall tread down our enemies.

PSALM 60. *Deus, repulisti nos.*

O GOD, thou hast cast us out, and scattered us abroad : thou hast also been displeased ; O turn thee unto us again.

2 Thou hast moved the land, and divided it : heal the sores thereof, for it shaketh.

3 Thou hast showed thy people heavy things : thou hast given us a drink of deadly wine.

4 Thou hast given a token for such as fear thee : that they may triumph because of the truth.

5 Therefore were thy beloved delivered : help me with thy right hand, and hear me.

6 God hath spoken in his holiness, I will rejoice, and divide Sichem : and mete out the valley of Succoth.

7 Gilead is mine, and Manasses is mine : Ephraim also is the strength of my head ; Judah is my law-giver ;

8 Moab is my wash-pot ; over Edom will I cast out my shoe : Philistia, be thou glad of me.

9 Who will lead me into the strong city : who will bring me into Edom?

10 Hast not thou cast us out, O God : wilt not thou, O God, go out with our hosts?

11 O be thou our help in trouble : for vain is the help of man.

12 Through God will we do great acts : for it is he that shall tread down our enemies.

Psalm lxi. *Exaudi, Deus.*

HEAR my crying, O God, give ear unto my prayer.

2 From the ends of the earth will I call upon thee, when my heart is in heaviness.

3 O set me up upon the rock that is higher than I ; for thou hast been my hope, and a strong tower for me against the enemy.

PSALM 61. *Exaudi, Deus.*

HEAR my crying, O God : give ear unto my prayer.

2 From the ends of the earth will I call upon thee : when my heart is in heaviness.

3 O set me up upon the rock that is higher than I : for thou hast been my hope, and a strong tower for me against the enemy.

19 For you have become my stronghold, *
a refuge in the day of my trouble.

20 To you, O my Strength, will I sing; *
for you, O God, are my stronghold and my merciful God.

Psalm 60. *Deus, repulisti nos.*

O GOD, thou hast cast us out, and scattered us abroad; * thou hast also been displeased: O turn thee unto us again.

2 Thou hast moved the land, and divided it: * heal the sores thereof, for it shaketh.

3 Thou hast showed thy people heavy things; * thou hast given us a drink of deadly wine.

4 Thou hast given a token for such as fear thee, * that they may triumph because of the truth.

5 Therefore were thy beloved delivered: * help me with thy right hand, and hear me.

6 God hath spoken in his holiness, I will rejoice, and divide Shechem, * and mete out the valley of Succoth.

7 Gilead is mine, and Manasseh is mine; * Ephraim also is the strength of my head; Judah is my law-giver;

8 Moab is my wash-pot; over Edom will I cast out my shoe; * Philistia, be thou glad of me.

9 Who will lead me into the strong city? * who will bring me into Edom?

10 Hast not thou cast us out, O God? * wilt not thou, O God, go out with our hosts?

11 O be thou our help in trouble; * for vain is the help of man.

12 Through God will we do great acts; * for it is he that shall tread down our enemies.

60 *Deus, repulisti nos*

1 O God, you have cast us off and broken us; *
you have been angry;
oh, take us back to you again.

2 You have shaken the earth and split it open; *
repair the cracks in it, for it totters.

3 You have made your people know hardship; *
you have given us wine that makes us stagger.

4 You have set up a banner for those who fear you, *
to be a refuge from the power of the bow.

5 Save us by your right hand and answer us, *
that those who are dear to you may be delivered.

6 God spoke from his holy place and said: *
"I will exult and parcel out Shechem;
I will divide the valley of Succoth.

7 Gilead is mine and Manasseh is mine; *
Ephraim is my helmet and Judah my scepter.

8 Moab is my wash-basin,
on Edom I throw down my sandal to claim it, *
and over Philistia will I shout in triumph."

9 Who will lead me into the strong city? *
who will bring me into Edom?

10 Have you not cast us off, O God? *
you no longer go out, O God, with our armies.

11 Grant us your help against the enemy, *
for vain is the help of man.

12 With God we will do valiant deeds, *
and he shall tread our enemies under foot.

Psalm 61. *Exaudi, Deus.*

HEAR my crying, O God, * give ear unto my prayer.

2 From the ends of the earth will I call upon thee, * when my heart is in heaviness.

3 O set me up upon the rock that is higher than I; * for thou hast been my hope, and a strong tower for me against the enemy.

61 *Exaudi, Deus*

1 Hear my cry, O God, *
and listen to my prayer.

2 I call upon you from the ends of the earth
with heaviness in my heart; *
set me upon the rock that is higher than I.

3 For you have been my refuge, *
a strong tower against the enemy.

4 I will dwell in thy tabernacle for ever, and my trust shall be under the covering of thy wings.

5 For thou, O Lord, hast heard my desires, and hast given an heritage unto those that fear thy Name.

6 Thou shalt grant the King a long life, that his years may endure throughout all generations.

7 He shall dwell before God for ever : O prepare thy loving mercy and faithfulness, that they may preserve him.

8 So will I alway sing praise unto thy Name, that I may daily perform my vows.

4 I will dwell in thy tabernacle for ever : and my trust shall be under the covering of thy wings.

5 For thou, O Lord, hast heard my desires : and hast given an heritage unto those that fear thy Name.

6 Thou shalt grant the King a long life : that his years may endure throughout all generations.

7 He shall dwell before God for ever : O prepare thy loving mercy and faithfulness, that they may preserve him.

8 So will I alway sing praise unto thy Name : that I may daily perform my vows.

THE TWELFTH DAY.

Morning Prayer.

Psalm lxii. *Nonne Deo?*

MY soul truly waiteth still upon God ; for of him cometh my salvation.

2 He verily is my strength and my salvation ; he is my defence, so that I shall not greatly fall.

3 How long will ye imagine mischief against every man? Ye shall be slain all the sort of you ; yea, as a tottering wall shall ye be, and like a broken hedge.

4 Their device is only how to put him out whom God will exalt ; their delight is in lies ; they give good words with their mouth, but curse with their heart.

5 Nevertheless, my soul, wait thou still upon God ; for my hope is in him.

6 He truly is my strength and my salvation ; he is my defence, so that I shall not fall.

7 In God is my health and my glory ; the rock of my might, and in God is my trust.

8 O put your trust in him alway, ye people ; pour out your hearts before him, for God is our hope.

9 As for the children of men, they are but vanity ; the children of men are deceitful upon the weights ; they are altogether lighter than vanity itself.

10 O trust not in wrong and robbery ; give not yourselves unto vanity : if riches increase, set not your heart upon them.

11 God spake once, and twice I have also heard the same, that power belongeth unto God ;

12 And that thou, Lord, art merciful ; for thou rewardest every man according to his work.

THE TWELFTH DAY.

Morning Prayer.

PSALM 62. *Nonne Deo?*

MY soul truly waiteth still upon God : for of him cometh my salvation.

2 He verily is my strength and my salvation : he is my defence, so that I shall not greatly fall.

3 How long will ye imagine mischief against every man : ye shall be slain all the sort of you ; yea, as a tottering wall shall ye be, and like a broken hedge.

4 Their device is only how to put him out whom God will exalt : their delight is in lies ; they give good words with their mouth, but curse with their heart.

5 Nevertheless, my soul, wait thou still upon God : for my hope is in him.

6 He truly is my strength and my salvation : he is my defence, so that I shall not fall.

7 In God is my health and my glory : the rock of my might ; and in God is my trust.

8 O put your trust in him alway, ye people : pour out your hearts before him, for God is our hope.

9 As for the children of men, they are but vanity : the children of men are deceitful upon the weights ; they are altogether lighter than vanity itself.

10 O trust not in wrong and robbery ; give not yourselves unto vanity : if riches increase, set not your heart upon them.

11 God spake once, and twice I have also heard the same : that power belongeth unto God ;

12 And that thou, Lord, art merciful : for thou rewardest every man according to his work.

4 I will dwell in thy tabernacle for ever, * and my trust shall be under the covering of thy wings.
5 For thou, O Lord, hast heard my desires, * and hast given an heritage unto those that fear thy Name.
6 Thou shalt grant the King a long life, * that his years may endure throughout all generations.
7 He shall dwell before God for ever: * O prepare thy loving mercy and faithfulness, that they may preserve him.
8 So will I alway sing praise unto thy Name, * that I may daily perform my vows.

The Twelfth Day.

Morning Prayer.

Psalm 62. *Nonne Deo?*

MY soul truly waiteth still upon God; * for of him cometh my salvation.
2 He verily is my strength and my salvation; * he is my defence, so that I shall not greatly fall.
3 How long will ye imagine mischief against every man? * Ye shall be slain all the sort of you; yea, as a tottering wall shall ye be, and like a broken hedge.
4 Their device is only how to put him out whom God will exalt; * their delight is in lies; they give good words with their mouth, but curse with their heart.
5 Nevertheless, my soul, wait thou still upon God; * for my hope is in him.
6 He truly is my strength and my salvation; * he is my defence, so that I shall not fall.
7 In God is my health and my glory; * the rock of my might; and in God is my trust.
8 O put your trust in him alway, ye people; * pour out your hearts before him, for God is our hope.
9 As for the children of men, they are but vanity; the children of men are deceitful; * upon the weights they are altogether lighter than vanity itself.
10 O trust not in wrong and robbery; give not yourselves unto vanity: * if riches increase, set not your heart upon them.
11 God spake once, and twice I have also heard the same, * that power belongeth unto God;
12 And that thou, Lord, art merciful; * for thou rewardest every man according to his work.

4 I will dwell in your house for ever; *
I will take refuge under the cover of your wings.

5 For you, O God, have heard my vows; *
you have granted me the heritage of those who fear your Name.

6 Add length of days to the king's life; *
let his years extend over many generations.

7 Let him sit enthroned before God for ever; *
bid love and faithfulness watch over him.

8 So will I always sing the praise of your Name, *
and day by day I will fulfill my vows.

Twelfth Day: Morning Prayer

62 *Nonne Deo?*

1 For God alone my soul in silence waits; *
from him comes my salvation.

2 He alone is my rock and my salvation, *
my stronghold, so that I shall not be greatly shaken.

3 How long will you assail me to crush me,
all of you together, *
as if you were a leaning fence, a toppling wall?

4 They seek only to bring me down from my place of honor; *
lies are their chief delight.

5 They bless with their lips, *
but in their hearts they curse.

6 For God alone my soul in silence waits; *
truly, my hope is in him.

7 He alone is my rock and my salvation, *
my stronghold, so that I shall not be shaken.

8 In God is my safety and my honor; *
God is my strong rock and my refuge.

9 Put your trust in him always, O people, *
pour out your hearts before him, for God is our refuge.

10 Those of high degree are but a fleeting breath, *
even those of low estate cannot be trusted.

11 On the scales they are lighter than a breath, *
all of them together.

12 Put no trust in extortion;
in robbery take no empty pride; *
though wealth increase, set not your heart upon it.

13 God has spoken once, twice have I heard it, *
that power belongs to God.

Psalm lxiii. *Deus, Deus meus.*

O GOD, thou art my God ; early will I seek thee.

2 My soul thirsteth for thee ; my flesh also longeth after thee, in a barren and dry land where no water is.

3 Thus have I looked for thee in holiness, that I might behold thy power and glory.

4 For thy loving-kindness is better than the life itself : my lips shall praise thee.

5 As long as I live will I magnify thee in[12] this manner, and lift up my hands in thy Name.

6 My soul shall be satisfied, even as it were with marrow and fatness, when my mouth praiseth thee with joyful lips.

7 Have I not remembered thee in my bed, and thought upon thee when I was waking?

8 Because thou hast been my helper ; therefore under the shadow of thy wings will I rejoice.

9 My soul hangeth upon thee ; thy right hand hath upholden me.

10 These also that seek the hurt of my soul, they shall go under the earth.

11 Let them fall upon the edge of the sword, that they may be a portion for foxes.

12 But the King shall rejoice in God ; all they also that swear by him shall be commended ; for the mouth of them that speak lies shall be stopped.

PSALM 63. *Deus, Deus meus.*

O GOD, thou art my God : early will I seek thee.

2 My soul thirsteth for thee, my flesh also longeth after thee : in a barren and dry land where no water is.

3 Thus have I looked for thee in holiness : that I might behold thy power and glory.

4 For thy loving-kindness is better than the life itself : my lips shall praise thee.

5 As long as I live will I magnify thee in this manner : and lift up my hands in thy Name.

6 My soul shall be satisfied, even as it were with marrow and fatness : when my mouth praiseth thee with joyful lips.

7 Have I not remembered thee in my bed : and thought upon thee when I was waking?

8 Because thou hast been my helper : therefore under the shadow of thy wings will I rejoice.

9 My soul hangeth upon thee : thy right hand hath upholden me.

10 These also that seek the hurt of my soul : they shall go under the earth.

11 Let them fall upon the edge of the sword : that they may be a portion for foxes.

12 But the King shall rejoice in God ; all they also that swear by him shall be commended : for the mouth of them that speak lies shall be stopped.

Psalm lxiv. *Exaudi, Deus.*

HEAR my voice, O God, in my prayer ; preserve my life from fear of the enemy.

2 Hide me from the gathering together of the froward, and from the insurrection of wicked doers.

3 Who have whet their tongue like a sword, and shoot out their arrows, even bitter words ;

4 That they may privily shoot at him that is perfect : suddenly do they hit him, and fear not.

5 They encourage themselves in mischief, and commune among themselves, how they may lay snares ; and say, that no man shall see them.

PSALM 64. *Exaudi, Deus.*

HEAR my voice, O God, in my prayer : preserve my life from fear of the enemy.

2 Hide me from the gathering together of the froward : and from the insurrection of wicked doers.

3 Who have whet their tongue like a sword : and shoot out their arrows, even bitter words ;

4 That they may privily shoot at him that is perfect : suddenly do they hit him, and fear not.

5 They encourage themselves in mischief : and commune among themselves, how they may lay snares ; and say, that no man shall see them.

---

[12]"on" in the English book.

14 Steadfast love is yours, O Lord, *
for you repay everyone according to his deeds.

Psalm 63. *Deus, Deus meus.*

O GOD, thou art my God; * early will I seek thee.
2 My soul thirsteth for thee, my flesh also longeth
after thee, * in a barren and dry land where no water
is.
3 Thus have I looked for thee in the sanctuary, *
that I might behold thy power and glory.
4 For thy loving-kindness is better than the life
itself: * my lips shall praise thee.
5 As long as I live will I magnify thee in this
manner, * and lift up my hands in thy Name.
6 My soul shall be satisfied, even as it were with
marrow and fatness, * when my mouth praiseth thee
with joyful lips.
7 Have I not remembered thee in my bed, * and
thought upon thee when I was waking?
8 Because thou hast been my helper; * therefore
under the shadow of thy wings will I rejoice.
9 My soul hangeth upon thee; * thy right hand
hath upholden me.
10 These also that seek the hurt of my soul, * they
shall go under the earth.
11 Let them fall upon the edge of the sword, * that
they may be a portion for foxes.
12 But the King shall rejoice in God; all they also
that swear by him shall be commended; * for the
mouth of them that speak lies shall be stopped.

63 *Deus, Deus meus*

1 O God, you are my God; eagerly I seek you; *
my soul thirsts for you, my flesh faints for you,
as in a barren and dry land where there is no water.

2 Therefore I have gazed upon you in your holy place, *
that I might behold your power and your glory.

3 For your loving-kindness is better than life itself; *
my lips shall give you praise.

4 So will I bless you as long as I live *
and lift up my hands in your Name.

5 My soul is content, as with marrow and fatness, *
and my mouth praises you with joyful lips,

6 When I remember you upon my bed, *
and meditate on you in the night watches.

7 For you have been my helper, *
and under the shadow of your wings I will rejoice.

8 My soul clings to you; *
and your right hand holds me fast.

9 May those who seek my life to destroy it *
go down into the depths of the earth;

10 Let them fall upon the edge of the sword, *
and let them be food for jackals.

11 But the king will rejoice in God;
all those who swear by him will be glad; *
for the mouth of those who speak lies shall be stopped.

Psalm 64. *Exaudi, Deus.*

HEAR my voice, O God, in my prayer; * preserve my
life from fear of the enemy.
2 Hide me from the gathering together of the
froward, * and from the insurrection of wicked doers.
3 Who have whet their tongue like a sword, * and
shoot out their arrows, even bitter words;
4 That they may privily shoot at him that is
perfect: * suddenly do they hit him, and fear not.
5 They encourage themselves in mischief, * and
commune among themselves, how they may lay snares;
and say, that no man shall see them.

64 *Exaudi, Deus*

1 Hear my voice, O God, when I complain; *
protect my life from fear of the enemy.

2 Hide me from the conspiracy of the wicked, *
from the mob of evildoers.

3 They sharpen their tongue like a sword, *
and aim their bitter words like arrows,

4 That they may shoot down the blameless from ambush; *
they shoot without warning and are not afraid.

5 They hold fast to their evil course; *
they plan how they may hide their snares.

6 They imagine wickedness, and practise it; that they keep secret among themselves, every man in the deep of his heart.

7 But God shall suddenly shoot at them with a swift arrow, that they shall be wounded.

8 Yea, their own tongues shall make them fall; insomuch that whoso seeth them shall laugh them to scorn.

9 And all men that see it shall say, This hath God done; for they shall perceive that it is his work.

10 The righteous shall rejoice in the LORD, and put his trust in him; and all they that are true of heart shall be glad.

6 They imagine wickedness, and practise it: that they keep secret among themselves, every man in the deep of his heart.

7 But God shall suddenly shoot at them with a swift arrow: that they shall be wounded.

8 Yea, their own tongues shall make them fall: insomuch that whoso seeth them shall laugh them to scorn.

9 And all men that see it shall say, This hath God done: for they shall perceive that it is his work.

10 The righteous shall rejoice in the LORD, and put his trust in him: and all they that are true of heart shall be glad.

Evening Prayer.

Psalm lxv. *Te decet hymnus.*

THOU, O God, art praised in Sion; and unto thee shall the vow be performed in Jerusalem.

2 Thou that hearest the prayer, unto thee shall all flesh come.

3 My misdeeds prevail against me: O be thou merciful unto our sins.

4 Blessed is the man whom thou choosest, and receivest unto thee: he shall dwell in thy court, and shall be satisfied with the pleasures of thy house, even of thy holy temple.

5 Thou shalt show us wonderful things in thy righteousness, O God of our salvation; thou that art the hope of all the ends of the earth, and of them that remain in the broad sea.

6 Who in his strength setteth fast the mountains, and is girded about with power.

7 Who stilleth the raging of the sea, and the noise of his waves, and the madness of the people.

8 They also that dwell in the uttermost parts of the earth shall be afraid at thy tokens, thou that makest the out-goings of the morning and evening to praise thee.

9 Thou visitest the earth, and blessest it; thou makest it very plenteous.

10 The river of God is full of water: thou preparest their corn, for so thou providest for the earth.

11 Thou waterest her furrows; thou sendest rain into the little valleys thereof; thou makest it soft with the drops of rain, and blessest the increase of it.

Evening Prayer.

PSALM 65. *Te decet hymnus.*

THOU, O God, art praised in Sion: and unto thee shall the vow be performed in Jerusalem.

2 Thou that hearest the prayer: unto thee shall all flesh come.

3 My misdeeds prevail against me: O be thou merciful unto our sins.

4 Blessed is the man whom thou choosest, and receivest unto thee: he shall dwell in thy court, and shall be satisfied with the pleasures of thy house, even of thy holy temple.

5 Thou shalt show us wonderful things in thy righteousness, O God of our salvation: thou that art the hope of all the ends of the earth, and of them that remain in the broad sea.

6 Who in his strength setteth fast the mountains: and is girded about with power.

7 Who stilleth the raging of the sea: and the noise of his waves, and the madness of the people.

8 They also that dwell in the uttermost parts of the earth shall be afraid at thy tokens: thou that makest the out-goings of the morning and evening to praise thee.

9 Thou visitest the earth, and blessest it: thou makest it very plenteous.

10 The river of God is full of water: thou preparest their corn, for so thou providest for the earth.

11 Thou waterest her furrows; thou sendest rain into the little valleys thereof: thou makest it soft with the drops of rain, and blessest the increase of it.

6 They imagine wickedness, and practise it; * that they keep secret among themselves, every man in the deep of his heart.
7 But God shall suddenly shoot at them with a swift arrow, * that they shall be wounded.
8 Yea, their own tongues shall make them fall; * insomuch that whoso seeth them shall laugh them to scorn.
9 And all men that see it shall say, This hath God done; * for they shall perceive that it is his work.
10 The righteous shall rejoice in the LORD, and put his trust in him; * and all they that are true of heart shall be glad.

Evening Prayer.

Psalm 65. *Te decet hymnus.*

THOU, O God, art praised in Sion; * and unto thee shall the vow be performed in Jerusalem.
2 Thou that hearest the prayer, * unto thee shall all flesh come.
3 My misdeeds prevail against me: * O be thou merciful unto our sins.
4 Blessed is the man whom thou choosest, and receivest unto thee: * he shall dwell in thy court, and shall be satisfied with the pleasures of thy house, even of thy holy temple.
5 Thou shalt show us wonderful things in thy righteousness, O God of our salvation; * thou that art the hope of all the ends of the earth, and of them that remain in the broad sea.
6 Who in his strength setteth fast the mountains, * and is girded about with power.
7 Who stilleth the raging of the sea, * and the noise of his waves, and the madness of the peoples.
8 They also that dwell in the uttermost parts of the earth shall be afraid at thy tokens, * thou that makest the out-goings of the morning and evening to praise thee.
9 Thou visitest the earth, and blessest it; * thou makest it very plenteous.
10 The river of God is full of water: * thou preparest their corn, for so thou providest for the earth.
11 Thou waterest her furrows; thou sendest rain into the little valleys thereof; * thou makest it soft with the drops of rain, and blessest the increase of it.

6 They say, "Who will see us?
who will find out our crimes? *
we have thought out a perfect plot."

7 The human mind and heart are a mystery; *
but God will loose an arrow at them,
and suddenly they will be wounded.

8 He will make them trip over their tongues, *
and all who see them will shake their heads.

9 Everyone will stand in awe and declare God's deeds; *
they will recognize his works.

10 The righteous will rejoice in the LORD and put their trust in him, *
and all who are true of heart will glory.

Twelfth Day: Evening Prayer

65 *Te decet hymnus*

1 You are to be praised, O God, in Zion; *
to you shall vows be performed in Jerusalem.

2 To you that hear prayer shall all flesh come, *
because of their transgressions.

3 Our sins are stronger than we are, *
but you will blot them out.

4 Happy are they whom you choose
and draw to your courts to dwell there! *
they will be satisfied by the beauty of your house,
by the holiness of your temple.

5 Awesome things will you show us in your righteousness,
O God of our salvation, *
O Hope of all the ends of the earth
and of the seas that are far away.

6 You make fast the mountains by your power; *
they are girded about with might.

7 You still the roaring of the seas, *
the roaring of their waves,
and the clamor of the peoples.

8 Those who dwell at the ends of the earth will tremble at your marvelous signs; *
you make the dawn and the dusk to sing for joy.

9 You visit the earth and water it abundantly;
you make it very plenteous; *
the river of God is full of water.

10 You prepare the grain, *
for so you provide for the earth.

11 You drench the furrows and smooth out the ridges; *
with heavy rain you soften the ground and bless its increase.

1789-1871

12 Thou crownest the year with thy goodness ; and thy clouds drop fatness.

13 They shall drop upon the dwellings of the wilderness ; and the little hills shall rejoice on every side.

14 The folds shall be full of sheep ; the valleys also shall stand so thick with corn, that they shall laugh and sing.

Psalm lxvi. *Jubilate Deo.*

O BE joyful in God, all ye lands ; sing praises unto the honour of his Name ; make his praise to be glorious.

2 Say unto God, O how wonderful art thou in thy works ; through the greatness of thy power shall thine enemies be found liars unto thee.

3 For all the world shall worship thee, sing of thee, and praise thy Name.

4 O come hither, and behold the works of God ; how wonderful he is in his doing toward the children of men.

5 He turned the sea into dry land, so that they went through the water on foot ; there did we rejoice thereof.

6 He ruleth with his power for ever ; his eyes behold the people : and such as will not believe shall not be able to exalt themselves.

7 O praise our God, ye people, and make the voice of his praise to be heard ;

8 Who holdeth our soul in life ; and suffereth not our feet to slip.

9 For thou, O God, hast proved us ; thou also hast tried us, like as silver is tried.

10 Thou broughtest us into the snare ; and laidest trouble upon our loins.

11 Thou sufferedst men to ride over our heads ; we went through fire and water, and thou broughtest us out into a wealthy place.

12 I will go into thine house with burnt-offerings : and will pay thee my vows, which I promised with my lips, and spake with my mouth, when I was in trouble.

13 I will offer unto thee fat burnt-sacrifices, with the incense of rams ; I will offer bullocks and goats.

1892

12 Thou crownest the year with thy goodness : and thy clouds drop fatness.

13 They shall drop upon the dwellings of the wilderness : and the little hills shall rejoice on every side.

14 The folds shall be full of sheep : the valleys also shall stand so thick with corn, that they shall laugh and sing.

PSALM 66. *Jubilate Deo.*

O BE joyful in God, all ye lands : sing praises unto the honour of his Name ; make his praise to be glorious.

2 Say unto God, O how wonderful art thou in thy works : through the greatness of thy power shall thine enemies be found liars unto thee.

3 For all the world shall worship thee : sing of thee, and praise thy Name.

4 O come hither, and behold the works of God : how wonderful he is in his doing toward the children of men.

5 He turned the sea into dry land : so that they went through the water on foot ; there did we rejoice thereof.

6 He ruleth with his power for ever ; his eyes behold the people : and such as will not believe shall not be able to exalt themselves.

7 O praise our God, ye people : and make the voice of his praise to be heard ;

8 Who holdeth our soul in life : and suffereth not our feet to slip.

9 For thou, O God, hast proved us : thou also hast tried us, like as silver is tried.

10 Thou broughtest us into the snare : and laidest trouble upon our loins.

11 Thou sufferedst men to ride over our heads : we went through fire and water, and thou broughtest us out into a wealthy place.

12 I will go into thine house with burnt-offerings : and will pay thee my vows which I promised with my lips, and spake with my mouth, when I was in trouble.

13 I will offer unto thee fat burnt-sacrifices, with the incense of rams : I will offer bullocks and goats.

12 Thou crownest the year with thy goodness; * and thy clouds drop fatness.

13 They shall drop upon the dwellings of the wilderness; * and the little hills shall rejoice on every side.

14 The folds shall be full of sheep; * the valleys also shall stand so thick with corn, that they shall laugh and sing.

Psalm 66. *Jubilate Deo.*

O BE joyful in God, all ye lands; * sing praises unto the honour of his Name; make his praise to be glorious.

2 Say unto God, O how wonderful art thou in thy works! * through the greatness of thy power shall thine enemies bow down unto thee.

3 For all the world shall worship thee, * sing of thee, and praise thy Name.

4 O come hither, and behold the works of God; * how wonderful he is in his doing toward the children of men.

5 He turned the sea into dry land, * so that they went through the water on foot; there did we rejoice thereof.

6 He ruleth with his power for ever; his eyes behold the nations: * and such as will not believe shall not be able to exalt themselves.

7 O praise our God, ye peoples, * and make the voice of his praise to be heard;

8 Who holdeth our soul in life; * and suffereth not our feet to slip.

9 For thou, O God, hast proved us; * thou also hast tried us, like as silver is tried.

10 Thou broughtest us into the snare; * and laidest trouble upon our loins.

11 Thou sufferedst men to ride over our heads; * we went through fire and water, and thou broughtest us out into a wealthy place.

12 I will go into thine house with burnt-offerings, and will pay thee my vows, * which I promised with my lips, and spake with my mouth, when I was in trouble.

13 I will offer unto thee fat burnt-sacrifices, with the incense of rams; * I will offer bullocks and goats.

12 You crown the year with your goodness, *
and your paths overflow with plenty.

13 May the fields of the wilderness be rich for grazing, *
and the hills be clothed with joy.

14 May the meadows cover themselves with flocks,
and the valleys cloak themselves with grain; *
let them shout for joy and sing.

66 *Jubilate Deo*

1 Be joyful in God, all you lands; *
sing the glory of his Name;
sing the glory of his praise.

2 Say to God, "How awesome are your deeds! *
because of your great strength your enemies
cringe before you.

3 All the earth bows down before you, *
sings to you, sings out your Name."

4 Come now and see the works of God, *
how wonderful he is in his doing toward all people.

5 He turned the sea into dry land,
so that they went through the water on foot, *
and there we rejoiced in him.

6 In his might he rules for ever;
his eyes keep watch over the nations; *
let no rebel rise up against him.

7 Bless our God, you peoples; *
make the voice of his praise to be heard;

8 Who holds our souls in life, *
and will not allow our feet to slip.

9 For you, O God, have proved us; *
you have tried us just as silver is tried.

10 You brought us into the snare; *
you laid heavy burdens upon our backs.

11 You let enemies ride over our heads;
we went through fire and water; *
but you brought us out into a place of refreshment.

12 I will enter your house with burnt-offerings
and will pay you my vows, *
which I promised with my lips
and spoke with my mouth when I was in trouble.

13 I will offer you sacrifices of fat beasts
with the smoke of rams; *
I will give you oxen and goats.

1789-1871

14 O come hither, and hearken, all ye that fear God ; and I will tell you what he hath done for my soul.
15 I called unto him with my mouth, and gave him praises with my tongue.
16 If I incline unto wickedness with mine heart, the Lord will not hear me.
17 But God hath heard me ; and considered the voice of my prayer.
18 Praised be God, who hath not cast out my prayer, nor turned his mercy from me.

Psalm lxvii. *Deus misereatur.*

GOD be merciful unto us, and bless us, and show us the light of his countenance, and be merciful unto us ;
2 That thy way may be known upon earth, thy saving health among all nations.
3 Let the people praise thee, O God ; yea, let all the people praise thee.
4 O let the nations rejoice and be glad ; for thou shalt judge the folk righteously, and govern the nations upon earth.
5 Let the people praise thee, O God ; yea,[13] let all the people praise thee.
6 Then shall the earth bring forth her increase ; and God, even our own God, shall give us his blessing.
7 God shall bless us ; and all the ends of the world shall fear him.

THE THIRTEENTH DAY.

Morning Prayer.

Psalm lxviii. *Exurgat Deus.*

LET God arise, and let his enemies be scattered ; let them also that hate him flee before him.
2 Like as the smoke vanisheth, so shalt thou drive them away ; and like as wax melteth at the fire, so let the ungodly perish at the presence of God.
3 But let the righteous be glad, and rejoice before God ; let them also be merry and joyful.
4 O sing unto God, and sing praises unto his Name ; magnify him that rideth upon the heavens, as it were upon an horse ; praise him in his Name JAH, and rejoice before him.

1892

14 O come hither, and hearken, all ye that fear God : and I will tell you what he hath done for my soul.
15 I called unto him with my mouth : and gave him praises with my tongue.
16 If I incline unto wickedness with mine heart : the Lord will not hear me.
17 But God hath heard me : and considered the voice of my prayer.
18 Praised be God, who hath not cast out my prayer : nor turned his mercy from me.

PSALM 67. *Deus misereatur.*

GOD be merciful unto us, and bless us : and show us the light of his countenance, and be merciful unto us ;
2 That thy way may be known upon earth : thy saving health among all nations.
3 Let the people praise thee, O God : yea, let all the people praise thee.
4 O let the nations rejoice and be glad : for thou shalt judge the folk righteously, and govern the nations upon earth.
5 Let the people praise thee, O God : yea, let all the people praise thee.
6 Then shall the earth bring forth her increase : and God, even our own God, shall give us his blessing.
7 God shall bless us : and all the ends of the world shall fear him.

THE THIRTEENTH DAY.

Morning Prayer.

PSALM 68. *Exsurgat Deus.*

LET God arise, and let his enemies be scattered : let them also that hate him flee before him.
2 Like as the smoke vanisheth, so shalt thou drive them away : and like as wax melteth at the fire, so let the ungodly perish at the presence of God.
3 But let the righteous be glad, and rejoice before God : let them also be merry and joyful.
4 O sing unto God, and sing praises unto his Name : magnify him that rideth upon the heavens, as it were upon a horse ; praise him in his Name JAH, and rejoice before him.

[13] "yea" added in 1822.

14 O come hither, and hearken, all ye that fear God; * and I will tell you what he hath done for my soul.

15 I called unto him with my mouth, * and gave him praises with my tongue.

16 If I incline unto wickedness with mine heart, * the Lord will not hear me.

17 But God hath heard me; * and considered the voice of my prayer.

18 Praised be God, who hath not cast out my prayer, * nor turned his mercy from me.

Psalm 67. *Deus misereatur.*

GOD be merciful unto us, and bless us, * and show us the light of his countenance, and be merciful unto us;

2 That thy way may be known upon earth, * thy saving health among all nations.

3 Let the peoples praise thee, O God; * yea, let all the peoples praise thee.

4 O let the nations rejoice and be glad; * for thou shalt judge the folk righteously, and govern the nations upon earth.

5 Let the peoples praise thee, O God; * yea, let all the peoples praise thee.

6 Then shall the earth bring forth her increase; * and God, even our own God, shall give us his blessing.

7 God shall bless us; * and all the ends of the world shall fear him.

The Thirteenth Day.

Morning Prayer.

Psalm 68. *Exurgat Deus.*

LET God arise, and let his enemies be scattered; * let them also that hate him flee before him.

2 Like as the smoke vanisheth, so shalt thou drive them away; * and like as wax melteth at the fire, so let the ungodly perish at the presence of God.

3 But let the righteous be glad, and rejoice before God; * let them also be merry and joyful.

4 O sing unto God, and sing praises unto his Name; magnify him that rideth upon the heavens; * praise him in his Name JAH, and rejoice before him.

14 Come and listen, all you who fear God, *
and I will tell you what he has done for me.

15 I called out to him with my mouth, *
and his praise was on my tongue.

16 If I had found evil in my heart, *
the Lord would not have heard me;

17 But in truth God has heard me; *
he has attended to the voice of my prayer.

18 Blessed be God, who has not rejected my prayer, *
nor withheld his love from me.

67 *Deus misereatur*

1 May God be merciful to us and bless us, *
show us the light of his countenance and come to us.

2 Let your ways be known upon earth, *
your saving health among all nations.

3 Let the peoples praise you, O God; *
let all the peoples praise you.

4 Let the nations be glad and sing for joy, *
for you judge the peoples with equity
and guide all the nations upon earth.

5 Let the peoples praise you, O God; *
let all the peoples praise you.

6 The earth has brought forth her increase; *
may God, our own God, give us his blessing.

7 May God give us his blessing, *
and may all the ends of the earth stand in awe of him.

Thirteenth Day: Morning Prayer

68 *Exsurgat Deus*

1 Let God arise, and let his enemies be scattered; *
let those who hate him flee before him.

2 Let them vanish like smoke when the wind drives it away; *
as the wax melts at the fire, so let the wicked perish at the presence of God.

3 But the let righteous be glad and rejoice before God; *
let them also be merry and joyful.

4 Sing to God, sing praises to his Name;
exalt him who rides upon the heavens; *
YAHWEH is his Name, rejoice before him!

1789-1871

5 He is a Father of the fatherless, and defendeth the cause of the widows ; even God in his holy habitation.

6 He is the God that maketh men to be of one mind in an house, and bringeth the prisoners out of captivity ; but letteth the runagates continue in scarceness.

7 O God, when thou wentest forth before the people ; when thou wentest through the wilderness,

8 The earth shook, and the heavens dropped at the presence of God ; even as Sinai also was moved at the presence of God, who is the God of Israel.

9 Thou, O God, sentest a gracious rain upon thine inheritance, and refreshedst it when it was weary.

10 Thy congregation shall dwell therein ; for thou, O God, hast of thy goodness prepared for the poor.

11 The Lord gave the word ; great was the company of the preachers.

12 Kings with their armies did flee, and were discomfited, and they of the household divided the spoil.

13 Though ye have lain[14] among the pots, yet shall ye be as the wings of a dove that is covered with silver wings, and her feathers like gold.

14 When the Almighty scattered kings for their sake, then were they as white as snow in Salmon.

15 As the hill of Basan, so is God's hill ; even an high hill, as the hill of Basan.

16 Why hop ye so, ye high hills? this is God's hill, in the which it pleaseth him to dwell ; yea, the LORD will abide in it for ever.

17 The chariots of God are twenty thousand, even thousands of angels ; and the LORD is among them as in the holy place of Sinai.

18 Thou art gone up on high, thou hast led captivity captive, and received gifts for men ; yea, even for thine enemies, that the LORD God might dwell among them.

19 Praised be the Lord daily, even the God who helpeth us, and poureth his benefits upon us.

20 He is our God, even the God of whom cometh salvation : GOD is the Lord, by whom we escape death.

21 God shall wound the head of his enemies, and the hairy scalp of such a one as goeth on still in his wickedness.

22 The Lord hath said, I will bring my people again, as I did from Basan ; mine own will I bring again, as I did sometime from the deep of the sea.

1892

5 He is a Father of the fatherless, and defendeth the cause of the widows : even God in his holy habitation.

6 He is the God that maketh men to be of one mind in an house, and bringeth the prisoners out of captivity : but letteth the runagates continue in scarceness.

7 O God, when thou wentest forth before the people : when thou wentest through the wilderness.

8 The earth shook, and the heavens dropped at the presence of God : even as Sinai also was moved at the presence of God, who is the God of Israel.

9 Thou, O God, sentest a gracious rain upon thine inheritance : and refreshedst it when it was weary.

10 Thy congregation shall dwell therein : for thou, O God, hast of thy goodness prepared for the poor.

11 The Lord gave the word : great was the company of the preachers.

12 Kings with their armies did flee, and were discomfited : and they of the household divided the spoil.

13 Though ye have lain among the pots, yet shall ye be as the wings of a dove : that is covered with silver wings, and her feathers like gold.

14 When the Almighty scattered kings for their sake : then were they as white as snow in Salmon.

15 As the hill of Basan, so is God's hill : even an high hill, as the hill of Basan.

16 Why hop ye so, ye high hills? this is God's hill, in the which it pleaseth him to dwell : yea, the LORD will abide in it for ever.

17 The chariots of God are twenty thousand, even thousands of angels : and the LORD is among them as in the holy place of Sinai.

18 Thou art gone up on high, thou hast led captivity captive, and received gifts for men : yea, even for thine enemies, that the LORD God might dwell among them.

19 Praised be the LORD daily : even the God who helpeth us, and poureth his benefits upon us.

20 He is our God, even the God of whom cometh salvation : GOD is the Lord, by whom we escape death.

21 God shall wound the head of his enemies : and the hairy scalp of such a one as goeth on still in his wickedness.

22 The Lord hath said, I will bring my people again, as I did from Basan : mine own will I bring again, as I did sometime from the deep of the sea.

[14]"lien" in the English book.

1928

5 He is a Father of the fatherless, and defendeth the cause of the widows; * even God in his holy habitation.

6 He is the God that maketh men to be of one mind in an house, and bringeth the prisoners out of captivity; * but letteth the runagates continue in scarceness.

7 O God, when thou wentest forth before the people; * when thou wentest through the wilderness.

8 The earth shook, and the heavens dropped at the presence of God; * even as Sinai also was moved at the presence of God, who is the God of Israel.

9 Thou, O God, sentest a gracious rain upon thine inheritance, * and refreshedst it when it was weary.

10 Thy congregation shall dwell therein; * for thou, O God, hast of thy goodness prepared for the poor.

11 The Lord gave the word; * great was the company of women that bare the tidings.

12 Kings with their armies did flee, and were discomfited, * and they of the household divided the spoil.

13 Though ye have lain among the sheep-folds, yet shall ye be as the wings of a dove * that is covered with silver wings, and her feathers like gold.

14 When the Almighty scattered kings for their sake, * then were they as white as snow in Salmon.

15 As the hill of Bashan, so is God's hill; * even an high hill, as the hill of Bashan.

16 Why mock ye so, ye high hills? this is God's hill, in the which it pleaseth him to dwell; * yea, the LORD will abide in it for ever.

17 The chariots of God are twenty thousand, even thousands of angels; * and the LORD is among them as in the holy place of Sinai.

18 Thou art gone up on high, thou hast led captivity captive, and received gifts from men; * yea, even from thine enemies, that the LORD God might dwell among them.

19 Praised be the LORD daily, * even the God who helpeth us, and poureth his benefits upon us.

20 He is our God, even the God of whom cometh salvation: * GOD is the Lord, by whom we escape death.

21 God shall wound the head of his enemies, * and the hairy scalp of such a one as goeth on still in his wickedness.

22 The Lord hath said, I will bring my people again, as I did from Bashan; * mine own will I bring again, as I did sometime from the deep of the sea.

1979

5 Father of orphans, defender of widows, *
God in his holy habitation!

6 God gives the solitary a home and brings forth prisoners into freedom; *
but the rebels shall live in dry places.

7 O God, when you went forth before your people, *
when you marched through the wilderness,

8 The earth shook, and the skies poured down rain,
at the presence of God, the God of Sinai, *
at the presence of God, the God of Israel.

9 You sent a gracious rain, O God, upon your inheritance; *
you refreshed the land when it was weary.

10 Your people found their home in it; *
in your goodness, O God, you have made provision for the poor.

11 The Lord gave the word; *
great was the company of women who bore the tidings:

12 "Kings with their armies are fleeing away; *
the women at home are dividing their spoils."

13 Though you lingered among the sheepfolds, *
you shall be like a dove whose wings are covered with silver,
whose feathers are like green gold.

14 When the Almighty scattered kings, *
it was like snow falling in Zalmon.

15 O mighty mountain, O hill of Bashan! *
O rugged mountain, O hill of Bashan!

16 Why do you look with envy, O rugged mountain,
at the hill which God chose for his resting place? *
truly, the LORD will dwell there for ever.

17 The chariots of God are twenty thousand,
even thousands of thousands; *
the Lord comes in holiness from Sinai.

18 You have gone up on high and led captivity captive;
you have received gifts even from your enemies, *
that the LORD God might dwell among them.

19 Blessed be the Lord day by day, *
the God of our salvation, who bears our burdens.

20 He is our God, the God of our salvation; *
God is the LORD, by whom we escape death.

21 God shall crush the heads of his enemies, *
and the hairy scalp of those who go on still in their wickedness.

22 The LORD has said, "I will bring them back from Bashan; *
I will bring them back from the depths of the sea;

23 That thy foot may be dipped in the blood of thine enemies, and that the tongue of thy dogs may be red through the same.

24 It is well seen, O God, how thou goest; how thou, my God and King, goest in the sanctuary.

25 The singers go before, the minstrels follow after, in the midst are the damsels playing with the timbrels.

26 Give thanks, O Israel, unto God the Lord in the congregations, from the ground of the heart.

27 There is little Benjamin their ruler, and the princes of Judah their council;[15] the princes of Zabulon,[16] and the princes of Nephthali.

28 Thy God hath sent forth strength for thee; stablish the thing, O God, that thou hast wrought in us,

29 For thy temple's sake at Jerusalem; so shall kings bring presents unto thee.

30 When the company of the spear-men, and multitude of the mighty are scattered abroad among the beasts of the people, so that they humbly bring pieces of silver; and when he hath scattered the people that delight in war.

31 Then shall the princes come out of Egypt; the Morians' land shall soon stretch out her hands unto God.

32 Sing unto God, O ye kingdoms of the earth; O sing praises unto the Lord;

33 Who sitteth in the heavens over all, from the beginning: lo, he doth send out his voice; yea, and that a mighty voice.

34 Ascribe ye the power to God over Israel; his worship and strength is in the clouds.

35 O God, wonderful art thou in thy holy places: even the God of Israel, he will give strength and power unto his people. Blessed be God.

Evening Prayer.

Psalm lxix. *Salvum me fac.*

SAVE me, O God; for the waters are come in, even unto my soul.

2 I stick fast in the deep mire, where no ground is; I am come into deep waters, so that the floods run over me.

[15]"counsel" in the English book.

[16]"Zebulon," 1793.

23 That thy foot may be dipped in the blood of thine enemies: and that the tongue of thy dogs may be red through the same.

24 It is well seen, O God, how thou goest: how thou, my God and King, goest in the sanctuary.

25 The singers go before, the minstrels follow after: in the midst are the damsels playing with the timbrels.

26 Give thanks, O Israel, unto God the Lord in the congregations: from the ground of the heart.

27 There is little Benjamin their ruler, and the princes of Judah their council: the princes of Zabulon, and the princes of Nephthali.

28 Thy God hath sent forth strength for thee: stablish the thing, O God, that thou hast wrought in us,

29 For thy temple's sake at Jerusalem: so shall kings bring presents unto thee.

30 When the company of the spearmen and multitude of the mighty are scattered abroad among the beasts of the people, so that they humbly bring pieces of silver: and when he hath scattered the people that delight in war;

31 Then shall the princes come out of Egypt: the Morians' land shall soon stretch out her hands unto God.

32 Sing unto God, O ye kingdoms of the earth: O sing praises unto the Lord;

33 Who sitteth in the heavens over all, from the beginning: lo, he doth send out his voice; yea, and that a mighty voice.

34 Ascribe ye the power to God over Israel: his worship and strength is in the clouds.

35 O God, wonderful art thou in thy holy places: even the God of Israel, he will give strength and power unto his people. Blessed be God.

Evening Prayer.

PSALM 69. *Salvum me fac.*

SAVE me, O God: for the waters are come in, even unto my soul.

2 I stick fast in the deep mire, where no ground is: I am come into deep waters, so that the floods run over me.

23 That thy foot may be dipped in the blood of
thine enemies, * and that the tongue of thy dogs may
be red through the same.
24 It is well seen, O God, how thou goest; * how
thou, my God and King, goest in the sanctuary.
25 The singers go before, the minstrels follow
after, * in the midst of the damsels playing with the
timbrels.
26 Give thanks unto God the Lord in the congregation, * ye that are of the fountain of Israel.
27 There is little Benjamin their ruler, and the
princes of Judah their council; * the princes of Zebulon, and the princes of Naphthali.
28 Thy God hath sent forth strength for thee; *
stablish the thing, O God, that thou hast wrought in
us,
29 For thy temple's sake at Jerusalem; * so shall
kings bring presents unto thee.
30 Rebuke thou the dragon and the bull, with the
leaders of the heathen, so that they humbly bring
pieces of silver; * scatter thou the peoples that delight
in war;
31 Then shall the princes come out of Egypt; * the
Morians' land shall soon stretch out her hands unto
God.
32 Sing unto God, O ye kingdoms of the earth; * O
sing praises unto the Lord;
33 Who sitteth in the heavens over all, from the
beginning: * lo, he doth send out his voice; yea, and
that a mighty voice.
34 Ascribe ye the power to God over Israel; * his
worship and strength is in the clouds.
35 O God, wonderful art thou in thy holy places: *
even the God of Israel, he will give strength and power
unto his people. Blessed be God.

Evening Prayer.

Psalm 69. *Salvum me fac.*

SAVE me, O God; * for the waters are come in, even
unto my soul.
2 I stick fast in the deep mire, where no ground
is; * I am come into deep waters, so that the floods run
over me.

23 That your foot may be dipped in blood, *
the tongues of your dogs in the blood of your enemies."

24 They see your procession, O God, *
your procession into the sanctuary, my God and my King.

25 The singers go before, musicians follow after, *
in the midst of maidens playing upon the hand-drums.

26 Bless God in the congregation; *
bless the LORD, you that are of the fountain of Israel.

27 There is Benjamin, least of the tribes, at the head;
the princes of Judah in a company; *
and the princes of Zebulon and Naphtali.

28 Send forth your strength, O God; *
establish, O God, what you have wrought for us.

29 Kings shall bring gifts to you, *
for your temple's sake at Jerusalem.

30 Rebuke the wild beast of the reeds, *
and the peoples, a herd of wild bulls with its calves.

31 Trample down those who lust after silver; *
scatter the peoples that delight in war.

32 Let tribute be brought out of Egypt; *
let Ethiopia stretch out her hands to God.

33 Sing to God, O kingdoms of the earth; *
sing praises to the Lord.

34 He rides in the heavens, the ancient heavens; *
he sends forth his voice, his mighty voice.

35 Ascribe power to God; *
his majesty is over Israel;
his strength is in the skies.

36 How wonderful is God in his holy places! *
the God of Israel giving strength and power to his people!
Blessed be God!

Thirteenth Day: Evening Prayer

69 *Salvum me fac*

1 Save me, O God, *
for the waters have risen up to my neck.

2 I am sinking in deep mire, *
and there is no firm ground for my feet.

1789-1871

3 I am weary of crying ; my throat is dry ; my sight faileth me for waiting so long upon my God.

4 They that hate me without a cause are more than the hairs of my head ; they that are mine enemies, and would destroy me guiltless, are mighty.

5 I paid them the things that I never took : God, thou knowest my simpleness, and my faults are not hid from thee.

6 Let not them that trust in thee, O Lord GOD of hosts, be ashamed for my cause ; let not those that seek thee be confounded through me, O Lord God of Israel.

7 And why? for thy sake have I suffered reproof ; shame hath covered my face.

8 I am become a stranger unto my brethren, even an alien unto my mother's children.

9 For the zeal of thine house hath even eaten me ; and the rebukes of them that rebuked thee are fallen upon me.

10 I wept, and chastened myself with fasting, and that was turned to my reproof.

11 I put on sackcloth also, and they jested upon me.

12 They that sit in the gate speak against me, and the drunkards make songs upon me.

13 But, LORD, I make my prayer unto thee in an acceptable time.

14 Hear me, O God, in the multitude of thy mercy, even in the truth of thy salvation.

15 Take me out of the mire, that I sink not ; O let me be delivered from them that hate me, and out of the deep waters.

16 Let not the water-flood drown me, neither let the deep swallow me up ; and let not the pit shut her mouth upon me.

17 Hear me, O LORD, for thy loving-kindness is comfortable ; turn thee unto me according to the multitude of thy mercies.

18 And hide not thy face from thy servant ; for I am in trouble : O haste thee, and hear me.

19 Draw nigh unto my soul, and save it ; O deliver me, because of mine enemies.

20 Thou hast known my reproof, my shame, and my dishonour : mine adversaries are all in thy sight.

1892

3 I am weary of crying ; my throat is dry : my sight faileth me for waiting so long upon my God.

4 They that hate me without a cause are more than the hairs of my head : they that are mine enemies, and would destroy me guiltless, are mighty.

5 I paid them the things that I never took : God, thou knowest my simpleness, and my faults are not hid from thee.

6 Let not them that trust in thee, O Lord GOD of hosts, be ashamed for my cause : let not those that seek thee be confounded through me, O Lord God of Israel.

7 And why? for thy sake have I suffered reproof : shame hath covered my face.

8 I am become a stranger unto my brethren : even an alien unto my mother's children.

9 For the zeal of thine house hath even eaten me : and the rebukes of them that rebuked thee are fallen upon me.

10 I wept, and chastened myself with fasting : and that was turned to my reproof.

11 I put on sackcloth also : and they jested upon me.

12 They that sit in the gate speak against me : and the drunkards make songs upon me.

13 But, LORD, I make my prayer unto thee : in an acceptable time.

14 Hear me, O God, in the multitude of thy mercy : even in the truth of thy salvation.

15 Take me out of the mire, that I sink not : O let me be delivered from them that hate me, and out of the deep waters.

16 Let not the water-flood drown me, neither let the deep swallow me up : and let not the pit shut her mouth upon me.

17 Hear me, O LORD, for thy loving-kindness is comfortable : turn thee unto me according to the multitude of thy mercies.

18 And hide not thy face from thy servant, for I am in trouble : O haste thee, and hear me.

19 Draw nigh unto my soul, and save it : O deliver me, because of mine enemies.

20 Thou hast known my reproof, my shame, and my dishonour : mine adversaries are all in thy sight.

1928

3 I am weary of crying; my throat is dry; * my sight faileth me for waiting so long upon my God.

4 They that hate me without a cause are more than the hairs of my head; * they that are mine enemies, and would destroy me guiltless, are mighty.

5 I paid them the things that I never took: * God, thou knowest my simpleness, and my faults are not hid from thee.

6 Let not them that trust in thee, O Lord GOD of hosts, be ashamed for my cause; * let not those that seek thee be confounded through me, O Lord God of Israel.

7 And why? for thy sake have I suffered reproof; * shame hath covered my face.

8 I am become a stranger unto my brethren, * even an alien unto my mother's children.

9 For the zeal of thine house hath even eaten me; * and the rebukes of them that rebuked thee are fallen upon me.

10 I wept, and chastened myself with fasting, * and that was turned to my reproof.

11 I put on sackcloth also, * and they jested upon me.

12 They that sit in the gate speak against me, * and the drunkards make songs upon me.

13 But, LORD, I make my prayer unto thee * in an acceptable time.

14 Hear me, O God, in the multitude of thy mercy, * even in the truth of thy salvation.

15 Take me out of the mire, that I sink not; * O let me be delivered from them that hate me, and out of the deep waters.

16 Let not the water-flood drown me, neither let the deep swallow me up; * and let not the pit shut her mouth upon me.

17 Hear me, O LORD, for thy loving-kindness is comfortable; * turn thee unto me according to the multitude of thy mercies.

18 And hide not thy face from thy servant; for I am in trouble: * O haste thee, and hear me.

19 Draw nigh unto my soul, and save it; * O deliver me, because of mine enemies.

20 Thou hast known my reproach, my shame, and my dishonour: * mine adversaries are all in thy sight.

1979

3 I have come into deep waters, *
and the torrent washes over me.

4 I have grown weary with my crying;
my throat is inflamed; *
my eyes have failed from looking for my God.

5 Those who hate me without a cause are more than the hairs of my head;
my lying foes who would destroy me are mighty. *
Must I then give back what I never stole?

6 O God, you know my foolishness, *
and my faults are not hidden from you.

7 Let not those who hope in you be put to shame through me, Lord GOD of hosts; *
let not those who seek you be disgraced because of me, O God of Israel.

8 Surely, for your sake have I suffered reproach, *
and shame has covered my face.

9 I have become a stranger to my own kindred, *
and alien to my mother's children.

10 Zeal for your house has eaten me up; *
the scorn of those who scorn you has fallen upon me.

11 I humbled myself with fasting, *
but that was turned to my reproach.

12 I put on sack-cloth also, *
and became a byword among them.

13 Those who sit at the gate murmur against me, *
and the drunkards make songs about me.

14 But as for me, this is my prayer to you, *
at the time you have set, O LORD.

15 "In your great mercy, O God, *
answer me with your unfailing help.

16 Save me from the mire; do not let me sink; *
let me be rescued from those who hate me
and out of the deep waters.

17 Let not the torrent of waters wash over me,
neither let the deep swallow me up *
do not let the Pit shut its mouth upon me.

18 Answer me, O LORD, for your love is kind; *
in your great compassion, turn to me."

19 "Hide not your face from your servant; *
be swift and answer me, for I am in distress.

20 Draw near to me and redeem me; *
because of my enemies deliver me.

21 Thy rebuke hath broken my heart ; I am full of heaviness : I looked for some to have pity on me, but there was no man, neither found I any to comfort me.

22 They gave me gall to eat ; and when I was thirsty they gave me vinegar to drink.

23 Let their table be made a snare to take themselves withal ; and let the things that should have been for their wealth be unto them an occasion of falling.

24 Let their eyes be blinded, that they see not ; and ever bow thou down their backs.

25 Pour out thine indignation upon them, and let thy wrathful displeasure take hold of them.

26 Let their habitation be void, and no man to dwell in their tents.

27 For they persecute him whom thou hast smitten ; and they talk how they may vex them whom thou hast wounded.

28 Let them fall from one wickedness to another, and not come into thy righteousness.

29 Let them be wiped out of the book of the living, and not be written among the righteous.

30 As for me, when I am poor and in heaviness, thy help, O God, shall lift me up.

31 I will praise the Name of God with a song, and magnify it with thanksgiving.

32 This also shall please the LORD better than a bullock that hath horns and hoofs.

33 The humble shall consider this, and be glad : seek ye after God, and your soul shall live.

34 For the LORD heareth the poor, and despiseth not his prisoners.

35 Let heaven and earth praise him : the sea, and all that moveth therein.

36 For God will save Sion, and build the cities of Judah, that men may dwell there, and have it in possession.

37 The posterity also of his servants shall inherit it ; and they that love his Name shall dwell therein.

21 Thy rebuke hath broken my heart ; I am full of heaviness : I looked for some to have pity on me, but there was no man, neither found I any to comfort me.

22 They gave me gall to eat : and when I was thirsty they gave me vinegar to drink.

23 Let their table be made a snare to take themselves withal : and let the things that should have been for their wealth be unto them an occasion of falling.

24 Let their eyes be blinded, that they see not : and ever bow thou down their backs.

25 Pour out thine indignation upon them : and let thy wrathful displeasure take hold of them.

26 Let their habitation be void : and no man to dwell in their tents.

27 For they persecute him whom thou hast smitten : and they talk how they may vex them whom thou hast wounded.

28 Let them fall from one wickedness to another : and not come into thy righteousness.

29 Let them be wiped out of the book of the living : and not be written among the righteous.

30 As for me, when I am poor and in heaviness : thy help, O God, shall lift me up.

31 I will praise the Name of God with a song : and magnify it with thanksgiving.

32 This also shall please the LORD : better than a bullock that hath horns and hoofs.

33 The humble shall consider this, and be glad : seek ye after God, and your soul shall live.

34 For the LORD heareth the poor : and despiseth not his prisoners.

35 Let heaven and earth praise him : the sea, and all that moveth therein.

36 For God will save Sion, and build the cities of Judah : that men may dwell there, and have it in possession.

37 The posterity also of his servants shall inherit it : and they that love his Name shall dwell therein.

Psalm lxx. *Deus, in adjutorium.*

316, 317 HASTE thee, O God, to deliver me ; make haste to
help me, O LORD.

PSALM 70. *Deus, in adjutorium.*

HASTE thee, O God, to deliver me : make haste to help me, O LORD.

21 Reproach hath broken my heart; I am full of heaviness: * I looked for some to have pity on me, but there was no man, neither found I any to comfort me.

22 They gave me gall to eat; * and when I was thirsty they gave me vinegar to drink.

23 Let their table be made a snare to take themselves withal; * and let the things that should have been for their wealth be unto them an occasion of falling.

24 Let their eyes be blinded, that they see not; * and ever bow thou down their backs.

25 Pour out thine indignation upon them, * and let thy wrathful displeasure take hold of them.

26 Let their habitation be void, * and no man to dwell in their tents.

27 For they persecute him whom thou hast smitten; * and they talk how they may vex them whom thou hast wounded.

28 Let them fall from one wickedness to another, * and not come into thy righteousness.

29 Let them be wiped out of the book of the living, * and not be written among the righteous.

30 As for me, when I am poor and in heaviness, * thy help, O God, shall lift me up.

31 I will praise the Name of God with a song, * and magnify it with thanksgiving.

32 This also shall please the LORD * better than a bullock that hath horns and hoofs.

33 The humble shall consider this, and be glad: * seek ye after God, and your soul shall live.

34 For the LORD heareth the poor, * and despiseth not his prisoners.

35 Let heaven and earth praise him: * the sea, and all that moveth therein.

36 For God will save Sion, and build the cities of Judah, * that men may dwell there, and have it in possession.

37 The posterity also of his servants shall inherit it; * and they that love his Name shall dwell therein.

21 You know my reproach, my shame, and my dishonor; *
my adversaries are all in your sight."

22 Reproach has broken my heart, and it cannot be healed; *
I looked for sympathy, but there was none,
for comforters, but I could find no one.

23 They gave me gall to eat, *
and when I was thirsty, they gave me vinegar to drink.

24 Let the table before them be a trap *
and their sacred feasts a snare.

25 Let their eyes be darkened, that they may not see, *
and give them continual trembling in their loins.

26 Pour out your indignation upon them, *
and let the fierceness of your anger overtake them.

27 Let their camp be desolate, *
and let there be none to dwell in their tents.

28 For they persecute him whom you have stricken *
and add to the pain of those whom you have pierced.

29 Lay to their charge guilt upon guilt, *
and let them not receive your vindication.

30 Let them be wiped out of the book of the living *
and not be written among the righteous.

31 As for me, I am afflicted and in pain; *
your help, O God, will lift me up on high.

32 I will praise the Name of God in song; *
I will proclaim his greatness with thanksgiving.

33 This will please the LORD more than an offering of oxen, *
more than bullocks with horns and hoofs.

34 The afflicted shall see and be glad; *
you who seek God, your heart shall live.

35 For the LORD listens to the needy, *
and his prisoners he does not despise.

36 Let the heavens and the earth praise him, *
the seas and all that moves in them;

37 For God will save Zion and rebuild the cities of Judah; *
they shall live there and have it in possession.

38 The children of his servants will inherit it, *
and those who love his Name will dwell therein.

Psalm 70. *Deus, in adjutorium.*

HASTE thee, O God, to deliver me; * make haste to help me, O LORD.

70 *Deus, in adjutorium*

1 Be pleased, O God, to deliver me; *
O LORD, make haste to help me.

2 Let them be ashamed and confounded that seek after my soul ; let them be turned backward and put to confusion that wish me evil.

3 Let them for their reward be soon brought to shame, that cry over me, There! there!

4 But let all those that seek thee be joyful and glad in thee : and let all such as delight in thy salvation say alway, The Lord be praised!

5 As for me, I am poor and in misery : haste thee unto me, O God.

6 Thou art my helper, and my redeemer : O LORD, make no long tarrying.

2 Let them be ashamed and confounded that seek after my soul : let them be turned backward and put to confusion that wish me evil.

3 Let them for their reward be soon brought to shame : that cry over me, There! there!

4 But let all those that seek thee be joyful and glad in thee : and let all such as delight in thy salvation say alway, The Lord be praised.

5 As for me, I am poor and in misery : haste thee unto me, O God.

6 Thou art my helper, and my redeemer : O LORD, make no long tarrying.

THE FOURTEENTH DAY.

Morning Prayer.

Psalm lxxi. *In te, Domine, speravi.*

IN thee, O LORD, have I put my trust ; let me never be put to confusion, but rid me, and deliver me, in thy righteousness ; incline thine ear unto me, and save me.

2 Be thou my stronghold, whereunto I may alway resort : thou hast promised to help me, for thou art my house of defence, and my castle.

3 Deliver me, O my God, out of the hand of the ungodly, out of the hand of the unrighteous and cruel man.

4 For thou, O Lord GOD, art the thing that I long for : thou art my hope, even from my youth.

5 Through thee have I been holden up ever since I was born : thou art he that took me out of my mother's womb : my praise shall be always of thee.

6 I am become as it were a monster unto many, but my sure trust is in thee.

7 O let my mouth be filled with thy praise, that I may sing of thy glory and honour all the day long.

8 Cast me not away in the time of age ; forsake me not when my strength faileth me.

9 For mine enemies speak against me ; and they that lay wait for my soul take their counsel together, saying, God hath forsaken him ; persecute him, and take him, for there is none to deliver him.

10 Go not far from me, O God ; my God, haste thee to help me.

11 Let them be confounded and perish that are against my soul ; let them be covered with shame and dishonour that seek to do me evil.

12 As for me, I will patiently abide alway, and will praise thee more and more.

THE FOURTEENTH DAY.

Morning Prayer.

PSALM 71. *In te, Domine, speravi.*

IN thee, O LORD, have I put my trust ; let me never be put to confusion : but rid me, and deliver me in thy righteousness ; incline thine ear unto me, and save me.

2 Be thou my stronghold, whereunto I may alway resort : thou hast promised to help me, for thou art my house of defence, and my castle.

3 Deliver me, O my God, out of the hand of the ungodly : out of the hand of the unrighteous and cruel man.

4 For thou, O Lord GOD, art the thing that I long for : thou art my hope, even from my youth.

5 Through thee have I been holden up ever since I was born : thou art he that took me out of my mother's womb : my praise shall be alway of thee.

6 I am become as it were a monster unto many : but my sure trust is in thee.

7 O let my mouth be filled with thy praise : that I may sing of thy glory and honour all the day long.

8 Cast me not away in the time of age : forsake me not when my strength faileth me.

9 For mine enemies speak against me ; and they that lay wait for my soul take their counsel together, saying : God hath forsaken him ; persecute him, and take him, for there is none to deliver him.

10 Go not far from me, O God : my God, haste thee to help me.

11 Let them be confounded and perish that are against my soul : let them be covered with shame and dishonour that seek to do me evil.

12 As for me, I will patiently abide alway : and will praise thee more and more.

2 Let them be ashamed and confounded that seek
after my soul; * let them be turned backward and put
to confusion that wish me evil.
3 Let them for their reward be soon brought to
shame, * that cry over me, There! there!
4 But let all those that seek thee be joyful and glad
in thee: * and let all such as delight in thy salvation say
alway, The Lord be praised.
5 As for me, I am poor and in misery: * haste thee
unto me, O God.
6 Thou art my helper, and my redeemer: * O
LORD, make no long tarrying.

The Fourteenth Day.

Morning Prayer.

Psalm 71. *In te, Domine, speravi.*

IN thee, O LORD, have I put my trust; let me never be
put to confusion, * but rid me and deliver me in thy
righteousness; incline thine ear unto me, and save me.
2 Be thou my stronghold, whereunto I may alway
resort: * thou hast promised to help me, for thou art
my house of defence, and my castle.
3 Deliver me, O my God, out of the hand of the
ungodly, * out of the hand of the unrighteous and
cruel man.
4 For thou, O Lord GOD, art the thing that I long
for: * thou art my hope, even from my youth.
5 Through thee have I been holden up ever since I
was born: * thou art he that took me out of my
mother's womb: my praise shall be alway of thee.
6 I am become as it were a monster unto many, *
but my sure trust is in thee.
7 O let my mouth be filled with thy praise, * that I
may sing of thy glory and honour all the day long.
8 Cast me not away in the time of age; * forsake me
not when my strength faileth me.
9 For mine enemies speak against me; * and they
that lay wait for my soul take their counsel together,
saying,
10 God hath forsaken him; * persecute him, and
take him, for there is none to deliver him.
11 Go not far from me, O God; * my God, haste
thee to help me.
12 Let them be confounded and perish that are
against my soul; * let them be covered with shame and
dishonour that seek to do me evil.

2 Let those who seek my life be ashamed
and altogether dismayed; *
let those who take pleasure in my misfortune
draw back and be disgraced.

3 Let those who say to me "Aha!" and gloat over me turn back, *
because they are ashamed.

4 Let all who seek you rejoice and be glad in you; *
let those who love your salvation say for ever,
"Great is the LORD!"

5 But as for me, I am poor and needy; *
come to me speedily, O God.

6 You are my helper and my deliverer; *
O LORD, do not tarry.

Fourteenth Day: Morning Prayer

71 *In te, Domine, speravi*

1 In you, O LORD, have I taken refuge; *
let me never be ashamed.

2 In your righteousness, deliver me and set me free; *
incline your ear to me and save me.

3 Be my strong rock, a castle to keep me safe; *
you are my crag and my stronghold.

4 Deliver me, my God, from the hand of the wicked, *
from the clutches of the evildoer and the oppressor.

5 For you are my hope, O Lord GOD, *
my confidence since I was young.

6 I have been sustained by you ever since I was born;
from my mother's womb you have been my strength; *
my praise shall be always of you.

7 I have become a portent to many; *
but you are my refuge and my strength. *

8 Let my mouth be full of your praise *
and your glory all the day long.

9 Do not cast me off in my old age; *
forsake me not when my strength fails.

10 For my enemies are talking against me, *
and those who lie in wait for my life take counsel together.

11 They say, "God has forsaken him;
go after him and seize him; *
because there is none who will save."

12 O God, be not far from me; *
come quickly to help me, O my God.

13 My mouth shall daily speak of thy righteousness and salvation ; for I know no end thereof.

14 I will go forth in the strength of the Lord GOD, and will make mention of thy righteousness only.

15 Thou, O God, hast taught me from my youth up until now ; therefore will I tell of thy wondrous works.

16 Forsake me not, O God, in mine old age, when I am gray-headed, until I have showed thy strength unto this generation, and thy power to all them that are yet for to come.

17 Thy righteousness, O God, is very high, and great things are they that thou hast done : O God, who is like unto thee!

18 O what great troubles and adversities hast thou showed me! and yet didst thou turn and refresh me ; yea, and broughtest me from the deep of the earth again.

19 Thou hast brought me to great honour, and comforted me on every side :

20 Therefore will I praise thee, and thy faithfulness, O God, playing upon an instrument of music : unto thee will I sing upon the harp, O thou Holy One of Israel.

21 My lips will be glad when I sing unto thee ; and so will my soul whom thou hast delivered.

22 My tongue also shall talk of thy righteousness all the day long ; for they are confounded and brought unto shame that seek to do me evil.

Psalm lxxii. *Deus, judicium.*

GIVE the King thy judgments, O God, and thy righteousness unto the King's son.

2 Then shall he judge thy people according unto right, and defend the poor.

3 The mountains also shall bring peace, and the little hills righteousness unto the people.

4 He shall keep the simple folk by their right, defend the children of the poor, and punish the wrong doer.

13 My mouth shall daily speak of thy righteousness and salvation : for I know no end thereof.

14 I will go forth in the strength of the Lord GOD : and will make mention of thy righteousness only.

15 Thou, O God, hast taught me from my youth up until now : therefore will I tell of thy wondrous works.

16 Forsake me not, O God, in mine old age, when I am gray-headed : until I have showed thy strength unto this generation, and thy power to all them that are yet for to come.

17 Thy righteousness, O God, is very high : and great things are they that thou hast done, O God ; who is like unto thee!

18 O what great troubles and adversities hast thou showed me! and yet didst thou turn and refresh me : yea, and broughtest me from the deep of the earth again.

19 Thou hast brought me to great honour : and comforted me on every side :

20 Therefore will I praise thee, and thy faithfulness, O God, playing upon an instrument of music : unto thee will I sing upon the harp, O thou Holy One of Israel.

21 My lips will be fain when I sing unto thee : and so will my soul whom thou hast delivered.

22 My tongue also shall talk of thy righteousness all the day long : for they are confounded and brought unto shame that seek to do me evil.

PSALM 72. *Deus, judicium.*

GIVE the King thy judgments, O God : and thy righteousness unto the King's son.

2 Then shall he judge thy people according unto right : and defend the poor.

3 The mountains also shall bring peace : and the little hills righteousness unto the people.

4 He shall keep the simple folk by their right : defend the children of the poor, and punish the wrong doer.

1928

13 As for me, I will patiently abide alway, * and will
praise thee more and more.
14 My mouth shall daily speak of thy righteousness
and salvation; * for I know no end thereof.
15 I will go forth in the strength of the Lord GOD, *
and will make mention of thy righteousness only.
16 Thou, O God, hast taught me from my youth up
until now; * therefore will I tell of thy wondrous works.
17 Forsake me not, O God, in mine old age, when I
am gray-headed, * until I have showed thy strength
unto this generation, and thy power to all them that
are yet for to come.
18 Thy righteousness, O God, is very high, * and
great things are they that thou hast done: O God, who
is like unto thee!
19 O what great troubles and adversities hast thou
showed me! and yet didst thou turn and refresh me; *
yea, and broughtest me from the deep of the earth
again.
20 Thou hast brought me to great honour, * and
comforted me on every side:
21 Therefore will I praise thee, and thy faithfulness,
O God, playing upon an instrument of music: * unto
thee will I sing upon the harp, O thou Holy One of
Israel.
22 My lips will be glad when I sing unto thee; * and
so will my soul whom thou hast delivered.
23 My tongue also shall talk of thy righteousness all
the day long; * for they are confounded and brought
unto shame that seek to do me evil.

1979

13 Let those who set themselves against me be put to shame and be disgraced; *
let those who seek to do me evil be covered with scorn and reproach.

14 But I shall always wait in patience, *
and shall praise you more and more.

15 My mouth shall recount your mighty acts
and saving deeds all day long; *
though I cannot know the number of them.

16 I will begin with the mighty works of the Lord GOD; *
I will recall your righteousness, yours alone.

17 O God, you have taught me since I was young, *
and to this day I tell of your wonderful works.

18 And now that I am old and gray-headed, O God, do not forsake me, *
till I make known your strength to this generation
and your power to all who are to come.

19 Your righteousness, O God, reaches to the heavens; *
you have done great things;
who is like you, O God?

20 You have showed me great troubles and adversities, *
but you will restore my life
and bring me up again from the deep places of the earth.

21 You strengthen me more and more; *
you enfold and comfort me,

22 Therefore I will praise you upon the lyre for your faithfulness, O my God; *
I will sing to you with the harp, O Holy One of Israel.

23 My lips will sing with joy when I play to you, *
and so will my soul, which you have redeemed.

24 My tongue will proclaim your righteousness all day long, *
for they are ashamed and disgraced who sought to do me harm.

Psalm 72. *Deus, judicium.*

GIVE the King thy judgments, O God, * and thy righteousness unto the King's son.
2 Then shall he judge thy people according unto
right, * and defend the poor.
3 The mountains also shall bring peace, * and the
little hills righteousness unto the people.
4 He shall keep the simple folk by their right, *
defend the children of the poor, and punish the wrong
doer.

72 *Deus, judicium*

1 Give the King your justice, O God, *
and your righteousness to the King's Son;

2 That he may rule your people righteously *
and the poor with justice;

3 That the mountains may bring prosperity to the people, *
and the little hills bring righteousness.

4 He shall defend the needy among the people; *
he shall rescue the poor and crush the oppressor.

1789-1871

5 They shall fear thee, as long as the sun and moon endureth, from one generation to another.

6 He shall come down like the rain into a fleece of wool, even as the drops that water the earth.

7 In his time shall the righteous flourish ; yea, and abundance of peace, so long as the moon endureth.

8 His dominion shall be also from the one sea to the other, and from the flood unto the world's end.

9 They that dwell in the wilderness shall kneel before him ; his enemies shall lick the dust.

10 The kings of Tharsis and of the isles shall give presents ; the kings of Arabia and Saba shall bring gifts.

11 All kings shall fall down before him ; all nations shall do him service.

12 For he shall deliver the poor when he crieth ; the needy also, and him that hath no helper.

13 He shall be favourable to the simple and needy, and shall preserve the souls of the poor.

14 He shall deliver their souls from falsehood and wrong ; and dear shall their blood be in his sight.

15 He shall live, and unto him shall be given of the gold of Arabia ; prayer shall be made ever unto him, and daily shall he be praised.

16 There shall be an heap of corn in the earth, high upon the hills ; his fruit shall shake like Libanus, and shall be green in the city like grass upon the earth.

17 His Name shall endure for ever ; his Name shall remain under the sun amongst[17] the posterities, which shall be blessed through him ; and all the heathen shall praise him.

18 Blessed be the LORD God, even the God of Israel, which only doeth wondrous things ;

19 And blessed be the Name of his Majesty for ever : and all the earth shall be filled with his Majesty. Amen, Amen.

1892

5 They shall fear thee, as long as the sun and moon endureth : from one generation to another.

6 He shall come down like the rain into a fleece of wool : even as the drops that water the earth.

7 In his time shall the righteous flourish : yea, and abundance of peace, so long as the moon endureth.

8 His dominion shall be also from the one sea to the other : and from the flood unto the world's end.

9 They that dwell in the wilderness shall kneel before him : his enemies shall lick the dust.

10 The kings of Tharsis and of the isles shall give presents : the kings of Arabia and Saba shall bring gifts.

11 All kings shall fall down before him : all nations shall do him service.

12 For he shall deliver the poor when he crieth : the needy also, and him that hath no helper.

13 He shall be favourable to the simple and needy : and shall preserve the souls of the poor.

14 He shall deliver their souls from falsehood and wrong : and dear shall their blood be in his sight.

15 He shall live, and unto him shall be given of the gold of Arabia : prayer shall be made ever unto him, and daily shall he be praised.

16 There shall be an heap of corn in the earth, high upon the hills : his fruit shall shake like Libanus : and shall be green in the city like grass upon the earth.

17 His Name shall endure for ever ; his Name shall remain under the sun among the posterities : which shall be blessed through him ; and all the heathen shall praise him.

18 Blessed be the LORD God, even the God of Israel : which only doeth wondrous things ;

19 And blessed be the Name of his majesty for ever : and all the earth shall be filled with his majesty. Amen. Amen.

[17] "among" prior to 1793.

1928

5 They shall fear thee, as long as the sun and moon endureth, * from one generation to another.

6 He shall come down like the rain upon the mown grass, * even as the drops that water the earth.

7 In his time shall the righteous flourish; * yea, and abundance of peace, so long as the moon endureth.

8 His dominion shall be also from the one sea to the other, * and from the River unto the world's end.

9 They that dwell in the wilderness shall kneel before him; * his enemies shall lick the dust.

10 The kings of Tarshish and of the isles shall give presents; * the kings of Arabia and Saba shall bring gifts.

11 All kings shall fall down before him; * all nations shall do him service.

12 For he shall deliver the poor when he crieth; * the needy also, and him that hath no helper.

13 He shall be favourable to the simple and needy, * and shall preserve the souls of the poor.

14 He shall deliver their souls from falsehood and wrong; * and dear shall their blood be in his sight.

15 He shall live, and unto him shall be given of the gold of Arabia; * prayer shall be made ever unto him, and daily shall he be praised.

16 There shall be an heap of corn in the earth, high upon the hills; the fruit thereof shall shake like Lebanon: * and they of the city shall flourish like grass upon the earth.

17 His Name shall endure for ever; his Name shall remain under the sun among the posterities, which shall be blessed in him; * and all the nations shall praise him.

18 Blessed be the LORD God, even the God of Israel, * which only doeth wondrous things;

19 And blessed be the Name of his majesty for ever: * and all the earth shall be filled with his majesty. Amen, Amen.

1979

5 He shall live as long as the sun and moon endure, *
from one generation to another.

6 He shall come down like rain upon the mown field, *
like showers that water the earth.

7 In his time shall the righteous flourish; *
there shall be abundance of peace till the moon shall be no more.

8 He shall rule from sea to sea, *
and from the River to the ends of the earth.

9 His foes shall bow down before him, *
and his enemies lick the dust.

10 The kings of Tarshish and of the isles shall pay tribute, *
and the kings of Arabia and Saba offer gifts.

11 All kings shall bow down before him, *
and all the nations do him service.

12 For he shall deliver the poor who cries out in distress, *
and the oppressed who has no helper.

13 He shall have pity on the lowly and poor; *
he shall preserve the lives of the needy.

14 He shall redeem their lives from oppression and violence, *
and dear shall their blood be in his sight.

15 Long may he live!
and may there be given to him gold from Arabia; *
may prayer be made for him always,
and may they bless him all the day long.

16 May there be abundance of grain on the earth,
growing thick even on the hilltops; *
may its fruit flourish like Lebanon,
and its grain like grass upon the earth.

17 May his Name remain for ever
and be established as long as the sun endures; *
may all the nations bless themselves in him and call him blessed.

18 Blessed be the Lord GOD, the God of Israel, *
who alone does wondrous deeds!

19 And blessed be his glorious Name for ever! *
and may all the earth be filled with his glory.
Amen. Amen.

Evening Prayer.

Psalm lxxiii. *Quam bonus Israel!*

TRULY God is loving unto Israel : even unto such as are of a clean heart.

2 Nevertheless, my feet were almost gone, my treadings had well-nigh slipt.

3 And why? I was grieved at the wicked : I do also see the ungodly in such prosperity.

4 For they are in no peril of death ; but are lusty and strong.

5 They come in no misfortune like other folk ; neither are they plagued like other men.

6 And this is the cause that they are so holden with pride, and overwhelmed with cruelty.

7 Their eyes swell with fatness, and they do even what they lust.

8 They corrupt other, and speak of wicked blasphemy ; their talking is against the Most High.

9 For they stretch forth their mouth unto the heaven, and their tongue goeth through the world.

10 Therefore fall the people unto them, and thereout suck they no small advantage.

11 Tush, say they, how should God perceive it? is there knowledge in the Most High?

12 Lo, these are the ungodly, these prosper in the world, and these have riches in possession : and I said, Then have I cleansed my heart in vain, and washed my hands in innocency.

13 All the day long have I been punished, and chastened every morning.

14 Yea, and I had almost said even as they ; but lo, then I should have condemned the generation of thy children.

15 Then thought I to understand this ; but it was too hard for me,

16 Until I went into the sanctuary of God : then understood I the end of these men ;

17 Namely, how thou dost set them in slippery places, and castest them down, and destroyest them.

18 O how suddenly do they consume, perish, and come to a fearful end!

19 Yea, even like as a dream when one awaketh ; so shalt thou make their image to vanish out of the city.

Evening Prayer.

PSALM 73. *Quam bonus Israel!*

TRULY God is loving unto Israel : even unto such as are of a clean heart.

2 Nevertheless, my feet were almost gone : my treadings had well-nigh slipt.

3 And why? I was grieved at the wicked : I do also see the ungodly in such prosperity.

4 For they are in no peril of death : but are lusty and strong.

5 They come in no misfortune like other folk : neither are they plagued like other men.

6 And this is the cause that they are so holden with pride : and overwhelmed with cruelty.

7 Their eyes swell with fatness : and they do even what they lust.

8 They corrupt other, and speak of wicked blasphemy : their talking is against the most High.

9 For they stretch forth their mouth unto the heaven : and their tongue goeth through the world.

10 Therefore fall the people unto them : and thereout suck they no small advantage.

11 Tush, say they, how should God perceive it : is there knowledge in the Most High?

12 Lo, these are the ungodly, these prosper in the world, and these have riches in possession : and I said, Then have I cleansed my heart in vain, and washed my hands in innocency.

13 All the day long have I been punished : and chastened every morning.

14 Yea, and I had almost said even as they : but lo, then I should have condemned the generation of thy children.

15 Then thought I to understand this : but it was too hard for me,

16 Until I went into the sanctuary of God : then understood I the end of these men ;

17 Namely, how thou dost set them in slippery places : and castest them down, and destroyest them.

18 O how suddenly do they consume : perish, and come to a fearful end!

19 Yea, even like as a dream when one awaketh : so shalt thou make their image to vanish out of the city.

BOOK III.

Evening Prayer.

Psalm 73. *Quam bonus Israel!*

TRULY God is loving unto Israel: * even unto such as are of a clean heart.

2 Nevertheless, my feet were almost gone, * my treadings had well-nigh slipt.

3 And why? I was grieved at the wicked: * I do also see the ungodly in such prosperity.

4 For they are in no peril of death; * but are lusty and strong.

5 They come in no misfortune like other folk; * neither are they plagued like other men.

6 And this is the cause that they are so holden with pride, * and cruelty covereth them as a garment.

7 Their eyes swell with fatness, * and they do even what they lust.

8 They corrupt other, and speak of wicked blasphemy; * their talking is against the Most High.

9 For they stretch forth their mouth unto the heaven, * and their tongue goeth through the world.

10 Therefore fall the people unto them, * and thereout suck they no small advantage.

11 Tush, say they, how should God perceive it? * is there knowledge in the Most High?

12 Lo, these are the ungodly, * these prosper in the world, and these have riches in possession:

13 And I said, Then have I cleansed my heart in vain, * and washed my hands in innocency.

14 All the day long have I been punished, * and chastened every morning.

15 Yea and I had almost said even as they; * but lo, then I should have condemned the generation of thy children.

16 Then thought I to understand this; * but it was too hard for me,

17 Until I went into the sanctuary of God: * then understood I the end of these men;

18 Namely, how thou dost set them in slippery places, * and castest them down, and destroyest them.

19 O how suddenly do they consume, * perish, and come to a fearful end!

Book Three

Fourteenth Day: Evening Prayer

73 *Quam bonus Israel!*

1 Truly, God is good to Israel, *
to those who are pure in heart.

2 But as for me, my feet had nearly slipped; *
I had almost tripped and fallen;

3 Because I envied the proud: *
and saw the prosperity of the wicked:

4 For they suffer no pain, *
and their bodies are sleek and sound;

5 In the misfortunes of others they have no share; *
they are not afflicted as others are;

6 Therefore they wear their pride like a necklace *
and wrap their violence about them like a cloak.

7 Their iniquity comes from gross minds, *
and their hearts overflow with wicked thoughts.

8 They scoff and speak maliciously; *
out of their haughtiness they plan oppression.

9 They set their mouths against the heavens, *
and their evil speech runs through the world.

10 And so the people turn to them *
and find in them no fault.

11 They say, "How should God know? *
is there knowledge in the Most High?"

12 So then, these are the wicked; *
always at ease, they increase their wealth.

13 In vain have I kept my heart clean, *
and washed my hands in innocence.

14 I have been afflicted all day long, *
and punished every morning.

15 Had I gone on speaking this way, *
I should have betrayed the generation of your children.

16 When I tried to understand these things, *
it was too hard for me;

17 Until I entered the sanctuary of God *
and discerned the end of the wicked.

18 Surely, you set them in slippery places; *
you cast them down in ruin.

19 Oh, how suddenly do they come to destruction, *
come to an end, and perish from terror!

20 Thus my heart was grieved, and it went even through my reins.
21 So foolish was I, and ignorant, even as it were a beast before thee.
22 Nevertheless, I am alway by thee ; for thou hast holden me by my right hand.
23 Thou shalt guide me with thy counsel, and after that receive me with glory.
24 Whom have I in heaven but thee? and there is none upon earth that I desire in comparison of thee.
25 My flesh and my heart faileth ; but God is the strength of my heart, and my portion for ever.
26 For lo, they that forsake thee shall perish ; thou hast destroyed all them that commit fornication against thee.
27 But it is good for me to hold me fast by God, to put my trust in the Lord GOD, and to speak of all thy works in the gates of the daughter of Sion.

20 Thus my heart was grieved : and it went even through my reins.
21 So foolish was I, and ignorant : even as it were a beast before thee.
22 Nevertheless, I am alway by thee : for thou hast holden me by my right hand.
23 Thou shalt guide me with thy counsel : and after that receive me with glory.
24 Whom have I in heaven but thee : and there is none upon earth that I desire in comparison of thee.
25 My flesh and my heart faileth : but God is the strength of my heart, and my portion for ever.
26 For lo, they that forsake thee shall perish : thou hast destroyed all them that commit fornication against thee.
27 But it is good for me to hold me fast by God, to put my trust in the Lord GOD : and to speak of all thy works in the gates of the daughter of Sion.

Psalm lxxiv. *Ut quid, Deus?*

O GOD, wherefore art thou absent from us so long? why is thy wrath so hot against the sheep of thy pasture?
2 O think upon thy congregation, whom thou hast purchased, and redeemed of old.
3 Think upon the tribe of thine inheritance, and Mount Sion, wherein thou hast dwelt.
4 Lift up thy feet, that thou mayest utterly destroy every enemy, which hath done evil in thy sanctuary.
5 Thine adversaries roar in the midst of thy congregations, and set up their banners for tokens.
6 He that hewed timber afore out of the thick trees, was known to bring it to an excellent work.
7 But now they break down all the carved work thereof with axes and hammers.
8 They have set fire upon thy holy places, and have defiled the dwelling-place of thy Name, even unto the ground.

PSALM 74. *Ut quid, Deus?*

O GOD, wherefore art thou absent from us so long : why is thy wrath so hot against the sheep of thy pasture?
2 O think upon thy congregation : whom thou hast purchased, and redeemed of old.
3 Think upon the tribe of thine inheritance : and Mount Sion, wherein thou hast dwelt.
4 Lift up thy feet, that thou mayest utterly destroy every enemy : which hath done evil in thy sanctuary.
5 Thine adversaries roar in the midst of thy congregations : and set up their banners for tokens.
6 He that hewed timber afore out of the thick trees : was known to bring it to an excellent work.
7 But now they break down all the carved work thereof : with axes and hammers.
8 They have set fire upon thy holy places : and have defiled the dwelling-place of thy Name, even unto the ground.

20 Yea, even like as a dream when one awaketh; *
so shalt thou make their image to vanish out of the
city.
21 Thus my heart was grieved, * and it went even
through my reins.
22 So foolish was I, and ignorant, * even as it were
a beast before thee.
23 Nevertheless, I am alway by thee; * for thou
hast holden me by my right hand.
24 Thou shalt guide me with thy counsel, * and
after that receive me with glory.
25 Whom have I in heaven but thee? * and there is
none upon earth that I desire in comparison of thee.
26 My flesh and my heart faileth; * but God is the
strength of my heart, and my portion for ever.
27 For lo, they that forsake thee shall perish; * thou
hast destroyed all them that are unfaithful unto thee.
28 But it is good for me to hold me fast by God, to
put my trust in the Lord GOD, * and to speak of all thy
works in the gates of the daughter of Sion.

20 Like a dream when one awakens, O Lord, *
when you arise you will make their image vanish.

21 When my mind became embittered, *
I was sorely wounded in my heart.

22 I was stupid and had no understanding; *
I was like a brute beast in your presence.

23 Yet I am always with you; *
you hold me by my right hand.

24 You will guide me by your counsel, *
and afterwards receive me with glory.

25 Whom have I in heaven but you? *
and having you I desire nothing upon earth.

26 Though my flesh and my heart should waste away, *
God is the strength of my heart and my portion for ever.

27 Truly, those who forsake you will perish; *
you destroy all who are unfaithful.

28 But it is good for me to be near God; *
I have made the Lord GOD my refuge.

29 I will speak of all your works *
in the gates of the city of Zion.

Psalm 74. *Ut quid, Deus?*

O GOD, wherefore art thou absent from us so long? *
why is thy wrath so hot against the sheep of thy
pasture?
2 O think upon thy congregation, * whom thou
hast purchased, and redeemed of old.
3 Think upon the tribe of thine inheritance, * and
Mount Sion, wherein thou hast dwelt.
4 Lift up thy feet, that thou mayest utterly destroy
every enemy, * which hath done evil in thy sanctuary.
5 Thine adversaries roar in the midst of thy congregations, * and set up their banners for tokens.
6 He that hewed timber afore out of the thick
trees, * was known to bring it to an excellent work.
7 But now they break down all the carved work
thereof * with axes and hammers.
8 They have set fire upon thy holy places, * and
have defiled the dwelling-place of thy Name, even unto
the ground.

74 *Ut quid, Deus?*

1 O God, why have you utterly cast us off? *
why is your wrath so hot against the sheep of your pasture?

2 Remember your congregation that you purchased long ago, *
the tribe you redeemed to be your inheritance,
and Mount Zion where you dwell.

3 Turn your steps toward the endless ruins; *
the enemy has laid waste everything in your sanctuary.

4 Your adversaries roared in your holy place; *
they set up their banners as tokens of victory.

5 They were like men coming up with axes to a grove of trees; *
they broke down all your carved work with hatchets
and hammers.

6 They set fire to your holy place; *
they defiled the dwelling-place of your Name
and razed it to the ground.

7 They said to themselves, "Let us destroy them altogether." *
They burned down all the meeting-places of God
in the land.

8 There are no signs for us to see;
there is no prophet left; *
there is not one among us who knows how long.

1789-1871

9 Yea, they said in their hearts, Let us make havoc of them altogether: thus have they burnt up all the houses of God in the land.

10 We see not our tokens; there is not one prophet more; no, not one is there among us, that understandeth any more.

11 O God, how long shall the adversary do this dishonour? how long shall the enemy blaspheme thy Name? for ever?

12 Why withdrawest thou thy hand? why pluckest thou not thy right hand out of thy bosom to consume the enemy?

13 For God is my King of old; the help that is done upon earth, he doeth it himself.

14 Thou didst divide the sea through thy power; thou brakest the heads of the dragons in the waters.

15 Thou smotest the heads of Leviathan in pieces, and gavest him to be meat for the people in the wilderness.

16 Thou broughtest out fountains and waters out of the hard rocks; thou driedst up mighty waters.

17 The day is thine, and the night is thine; thou hast prepared the light and the sun.

18 Thou hast set all the borders of the earth; thou hast made summer and winter.

19 Remember this, O LORD, how the enemy hath rebuked; and how the foolish people hath blasphemed thy Name.

20 O deliver not the soul of thy turtle-dove unto the multitude of the enemies; and forget not the congregation of the poor for ever.

21 Look upon the covenant; for all the earth is full of darkness and cruel habitations.

22 O let not the simple go away ashamed; but let the poor and needy give praise unto thy Name.

23 Arise, O God, maintain thine own cause; remember how the foolish man blasphemeth thee daily.

24 Forget not the voice of thine enemies: the presumption of them that hate thee increaseth ever more and more.

THE FIFTEENTH DAY.

Morning Prayer.

Psalm lxxv. *Confitebimur tibi.*

UNTO thee, O God, do we give thanks; yea, unto thee do we give thanks.

2 Thy Name also is so nigh; and that do thy wondrous works declare.

3 When I receive the congregation, I shall judge according unto right.

1892

9 Yea, they said in their hearts, Let us make havoc of them altogether: thus have they burnt up all the houses of God in the land.

10 We see not our tokens; there is not one prophet more: no, not one is there among us, that understandeth any more.

11 O God, how long shall the adversary do this dishonour: how long shall the enemy blaspheme thy Name? for ever?

12 Why withdrawest thou thy hand: why pluckest thou not thy right hand out of thy bosom to consume the enemy?

13 For God is my King of old: the help that is done upon earth, he doeth it himself.

14 Thou didst divide the sea through thy power: thou brakest the heads of the dragons in the waters.

15 Thou smotest the heads of leviathan in pieces: and gavest him to be meat for the people in the wilderness.

16 Thou broughtest out fountains and waters out of the hard rocks: thou driedst up mighty waters.

17 The day is thine, and the night is thine: thou hast prepared the light and the sun.

18 Thou hast set all the borders of the earth: thou hast made summer and winter.

19 Remember this, O LORD, how the enemy hath rebuked: and how the foolish people hath blasphemed thy Name.

20 O deliver not the soul of thy turtle-dove unto the multitude of the enemies: and forget not the congregation of the poor for ever.

21 Look upon the covenant: for all the earth is full of darkness and cruel habitations.

22 O let not the simple go away ashamed: but let the poor and needy give praise unto thy Name.

23 Arise, O God, maintain thine own cause: remember how the foolish man blasphemeth thee daily.

24 Forget not the voice of thine enemies: the presumption of them that hate thee increaseth ever more and more.

THE FIFTEENTH DAY.

Morning Prayer.

PSALM 75. *Confitebimur tibi.*

UNTO thee, O God, do we give thanks: yea, unto thee do we give thanks.

2 Thy Name also is so nigh: and that do thy wondrous works declare.

3 When I receive the congregation: I shall judge according unto right.

9 Yea, they said in their hearts, Let us make havoc of them altogether: * thus have they burnt up all the houses of God in the land.

10 We see not our tokens; there is not one prophet more; * no, not one is there among us, that understandeth any more.

11 O God, how long shall the adversary do this dishonour? * shall the enemy blaspheme thy Name for ever?

12 Why withdrawest thou thy hand? * why pluckest thou not thy right hand out of thy bosom to consume the enemy?

13 For God is my King of old; * the help that is done upon earth, he doeth it himself.

14 Thou didst divide the sea through thy power; * thou brakest the heads of the dragons in the waters.

15 Thou smotest the heads of leviathan in pieces, * and gavest him to be meat for the people of the wilderness.

16 Thou broughtest out fountains and waters out of the hard rocks; * thou driedst up mighty waters.

17 The day is thine, and the night is thine; * thou hast prepared the light and the sun.

18 Thou hast set all the borders of the earth; * thou hast made summer and winter.

19 Remember this, O LORD, how the enemy hath rebuked; * and how the foolish people hath blasphemed thy Name.

20 O deliver not the soul of thy turtle-dove unto the multitude of the enemies; * and forget not the congregation of the poor for ever.

21 Look upon the covenant; * for all the earth is full of darkness and cruel habitations.

22 O let not the simple go away ashamed; * but let the poor and needy give praise unto thy Name.

23 Arise, O God, maintain thine own cause; * remember how the foolish man blasphemeth thee daily.

24 Forget not the voice of thine enemies: * the presumption of them that hate thee increaseth ever more and more.

The Fifteenth Day.

Morning Prayer.

Psalm 75. *Confitebimur tibi.*

UNTO thee, O God, do we give thanks; * yea, unto thee do we give thanks.

2 Thy Name also is so nigh; * and that do thy wondrous works declare.

3 In the appointed time, saith God, * I shall judge according unto right.

9 How long, O God, will the adversary scoff? *
will the enemy blaspheme your Name for ever?

10 Why do you draw back your hand? *
why is your right hand hidden in your bosom?

11 Yet God is my King from ancient times, *
victorious in the midst of the earth.

12 You divided the sea by your might *
and shattered the heads of the dragons upon the waters;

13 You crushed the heads of Leviathan *
and gave him to the people of the desert for food.

14 You split open spring and torrent; *
you dried up ever-flowing rivers.

15 Yours is the day, yours also the night; *
you established the moon and the sun.

16 You fixed all the boundaries of the earth; *
you made both summer and winter.

17 Remember, O LORD, how the enemy scoffed. *
how a foolish people despised your Name.

18 Do not hand over the life of your dove to wild beasts; *
never forget the lives of your poor.

19 Look upon your covenant; *
the dark places of the earth are haunts of violence.

20 Let not the oppressed turn away ashamed; *
let the poor and needy praise your Name.

21 Arise, O God, maintain your cause; *
remember how fools revile you all day long.

22 Forget not the clamor of your adversaries, *
the unending tumult of those who rise up against you.

Fifteenth Day: Morning Prayer

75 *Confitebimur tibi*

1 We give you thanks, O God, we give you thanks, *
calling upon your Name and declaring all your wonderful deeds.

2 "I will appoint a time," says God; *
"I will judge with equity.

3 Though the earth and all its inhabitants are quaking, *
I will make its pillars fast.

4 The earth is weak, and all the inhabiters thereof: I bear up the pillars of it.
5 I said unto the fools, Deal not so madly; and to the ungodly, Set not up your horn.
6 Set not up your horn on high, and speak not with a stiff neck.
7 For promotion cometh neither from the east, nor from the west, nor yet from the south.
8 And why? God is the Judge; he putteth down one, and setteth up another.
9 For in the hand of the LORD there is a cup, and the wine is red; it is full mixt, and he poureth out of the same.
10 As for the dregs thereof, all the ungodly of the earth shall drink them, and suck them out.
11 But I will talk of the God of Jacob, and praise him for ever.
12 All the horns of the ungodly also will I break, and the horns of the righteous shall be exalted.

4 The earth is weak, and all the inhabiters thereof: I bear up the pillars of it.
5 I said unto the fools, Deal not so madly: and to the ungodly, Set not up your horn.
6 Set not up your horn on high: and speak not with a stiff neck.
7 For promotion cometh neither from the east, nor from the west: nor yet from the south.
8 And why? God is the Judge: he putteth down one, and setteth up another.
9 For in the hand of the LORD there is a cup, and the wine is red: it is full mixt, and he poureth out of the same.
10 As for the dregs thereof: all the ungodly of the earth shall drink them, and suck them out.
11 But I will talk of the God of Jacob: and praise him for ever.
12 All the horns of the ungodly also will I break: and the horns of the righteous shall be exalted.

Psalm lxxvi. *Notus in Judæa.*

IN Jewry is God known; his Name is great in Israel.
2 At Salem is his tabernacle, and his dwelling in Sion.
3 There brake he the arrows of the bow, the shield, the sword, and the battle.
4 Thou art of more honour and might than the hills of the robbers.
5 The proud are robbed, they have slept their sleep; and all the men whose hands were mighty have found nothing.
6 At thy rebuke, O God of Jacob, both the chariot and horse are fallen.
7 Thou, even thou art to be feared; and who may stand in thy sight when thou art angry?
8 Thou didst cause thy judgment to be heard from heaven; the earth trembled, and was still,
9 When God arose to judgment, and to help all the meek upon earth.
10 The fierceness of man shall turn to thy praise; and the fierceness of them shalt thou refrain.
11 Promise unto the LORD your God, and keep it, all ye that are round about him; bring presents unto him that ought to be feared.
12 He shall refrain the spirit of princes, and is wonderful among the kings of the earth.

PSALM 76. *Notus in Judæa.*

IN Jewry is God known: his Name is great in Israel.
2 At Salem is his tabernacle: and his dwelling in Sion.
3 There brake he the arrows of the bow: the shield, the sword, and the battle.
4 Thou art of more honour and might: then the hills of the robbers.
5 The proud are robbed, they have slept their sleep: and all the men whose hands were mighty have found nothing.
6 At thy rebuke, O God of Jacob: both the chariot and horse are fallen.
7 Thou, even thou art to be feared: and who may stand in thy sight when thou art angry?
8 Thou didst cause thy judgment to be heard from heaven: the earth trembled, and was still,
9 When God arose to judgment: and to help all the meek upon earth.
10 The fierceness of man shall turn to thy praise: and the fierceness of them shalt thou refrain.
11 Promise unto the LORD your God, and keep it, all ye that are round about him: bring presents unto him that ought to be feared.
12 He shall refrain the spirit of princes: and is wonderful among the kings of the earth.

4 The earth is weak, and all the inhabiters
thereof: * I bear up the pillars of it.
5 I said unto the fools, Deal not so madly; * and to
the ungodly, Set not up your horn.
6 Set not up your horn on high, * and speak not
with a stiff neck.
7 For promotion cometh neither from the east, nor
from the west, * nor yet from the south.
8 And why? God is the Judge; * he putteth down
one, and setteth up another.
9 For in the hand of the LORD there is a cup, and
the wine is red; * it is full mixt, and he poureth out of
the same.
10 As for the dregs thereof, * all the ungodly of the
earth shall drink them, and suck them out.
11 But I will talk of the God of Jacob, * and praise
him for ever.
12 All the horns of the ungodly also will I break, *
and the horns of the righteous shall be exalted.

Psalm 76. *Notus in Judæa.*

IN Judah is God known; * his Name is great in Israel.
2 At Salem is his tabernacle, * and his dwelling in
Sion.
3 There brake he the arrows of the bow, * the
shield, the sword, and the battle.
4 Thou art glorious in might, * when thou comest
from the hills of the robbers.
5 The proud are robbed, they have slept their
sleep; * and all the men whose hands were mighty
have found nothing.
6 At thy rebuke, O God of Jacob, * both the chariot and horse are fallen.
7 Thou, even thou art to be feared; * and who may
stand in thy sight when thou art angry?
8 Thou didst cause thy judgment to be heard from
heaven; * the earth trembled, and was still,
9 When God arose to judgment, * and to help all
the meek upon earth.
10 The fierceness of man shall turn to thy praise; *
and the fierceness of them shalt thou refrain.
11 Promise unto the LORD your God, and keep it,
all ye that are round about him; * bring presents unto
him that ought to be feared.
12 He shall refrain the spirit of princes, * and is
wonderful among the kings of the earth.

4 I will say to the boasters, 'Boast no more,' *
and to the wicked, 'Do not toss your horns;

5 Do not toss your horns so high, *
nor speak with a proud neck.'"

6 For judgment is neither from the east nor from the west, *
nor yet from the wilderness or the mountains.

7 It is God who judges; *
he puts down one and lifts up another.

8 For in the LORD'S hand there is a cup,
full of spiced and foaming wine, which he pours out, *
and all the wicked of the earth shall drink and
drain the dregs.

9 But I will rejoice for ever; *
I will sing praises to the God of Jacob.

10 He shall break off all the horns of the wicked; *
but the horns of the righteous shall be exalted.

76 *Notus in Judæa*

1 In Judah is God known; *
his Name is great in Israel.

2 At Salem is his tabernacle, *
and his dwelling is in Zion.

3 There he broke the flashing arrows, *
the shield, the sword, and the weapons of battle.

4 How glorious you are! *
more splendid than the everlasting mountains!

5 The strong of heart have been despoiled;
they sink into sleep; *
none of the warriors can lift a hand.

6 At your rebuke, O God of Jacob, *
both horse and rider lie stunned.

7 What terror you inspire! *
who can stand before you when you are angry?

8 From heaven you pronounced judgment; *
the earth was afraid and was still;

9 When God rose up to judgment *
and to save all the oppressed of the earth.

10 Truly, wrathful Edom will give you thanks, *
and the remnant of Hamath will keep your feasts.

11 Make a vow to the LORD your God and keep it; *
let all around him bring gifts to him who is worthy
to be feared.

12 He breaks the spirit of princes, *
and strikes terror in the kings of the earth.

Psalm lxxvii. *Voce mea ad Dominum.*

I WILL cry unto God with my voice ; even unto God will I cry with my voice, and he shall hearken unto me.

2 In the time of my trouble I sought the Lord : my sore ran, and ceased not in the night-season ; my soul refused comfort.

3 When I am in heaviness, I will think upon God ; when my heart is vexed, I will complain.

4 Thou holdest mine eyes waking : I am so feeble that I cannot speak.

5 I have considered the days of old, and the years that are past.

6 I call to remembrance my song, and in the night I commune with mine own heart, and search out my spirit.[18]

7 Will the Lord absent himself for ever? and will he be no more intreated?

8 Is his mercy clean gone for ever? and is his promise come utterly to an end for evermore?

9 Hath God forgotten to be gracious? and will he shut up his loving-kindness in displeasure?

10 And I said, It is mine own infirmity ; but I will remember the years of the right hand of the Most Highest.

11 I will remember the works of the LORD, and call to mind thy wonders of old time.

12 I will think also of all thy works, and my talking shall be of thy doings.

13 Thy way, O God, is holy : who is so great a God as our God?

14 Thou art the God that doest[19] wonders, and hast declared thy power among the people.

15 Thou hast mightily delivered thy people, even the sons of Jacob and Joseph.

16 The waters saw thee, O God, the waters saw thee, and were afraid ; the depths also were troubled.

17 The clouds poured out water, the air thundered, and thine arrows went abroad.

18 The voice of thy thunder was heard round about : the lightnings shone upon the ground ; the earth was moved, and shook withal.

19 Thy way is in the sea, and thy paths in the great waters, and thy footsteps are not known.

PSALM 77. *Voce mea ad Dominum.*

I WILL cry unto God with my voice : even unto God will I cry with my voice, and he shall hearken unto me.

2 In the time of my trouble I sought the Lord : my sore ran, and ceased not in the night season ; my soul refused comfort.

3 When I am in heaviness, I will think upon God : when my heart is vexed, I will complain.

4 Thou holdest mine eyes waking : I am so feeble that I cannot speak.

5 I have considered the days of old : and the years that are past.

6 I call to remembrance my song : and in the night I commune with mine own heart, and search out my spirit.

7 Will the Lord absent himself for ever : and will he be no more intreated?

8 Is his mercy clean gone for ever : and is his promise come utterly to an end for evermore?

9 Hath God forgotten to be gracious : and will he shut up his loving-kindness in displeasure?

10 And I said, It is mine own infirmity : but I will remember the years of the right hand of the Most Highest.

11 I will remember the works of the LORD : and call to mind thy wonders of old time.

12 I will think also of thy works : and my talking shall be of thy doings.

13 Thy way, O God, is holy : who is so great a God as our God?

14 Thou art the God that doest wonders : and hast declared thy power among the people.

15 Thou hast mightily delivered thy people : even the sons of Jacob and Joseph.

16 The waters saw thee, O God, the waters saw thee, and were afraid : the depths also were troubled.

17 The clouds poured out water, the air thundered : and thine arrows went abroad.

18 The voice of thy thunder was heard round about : the lightnings shone upon the ground ; the earth was moved, and shook withal.

19 Thy way is in the sea, and thy paths in the great waters : and thy footsteps are not known.

[18]"spirits" prior to 1845.

[19]"doeth" prior to 1845.

Psalm 77. *Voce mea ad Dominum.*

I WILL cry unto God with my voice; * even unto God
will I cry with my voice, and he shall hearken unto me.
2 In the time of my trouble I sought the Lord: * I
stretched forth my hands unto him, and ceased not in
the night season; my soul refused comfort.
3 When I am in heaviness, I will think upon God; *
when my heart is vexed, I will complain.
4 Thou holdest mine eyes waking: * I am so feeble
that I cannot speak.
5 I have considered the days of old, * and the years
that are past.
6 I call to remembrance my song, * and in the night
I commune with mine own heart, and search out my
spirit.
7 Will the Lord absent himself for ever? * and will
he be no more intreated?
8 Is his mercy clean gone for ever? * and is his
promise come utterly to an end for evermore?
9 Hath God forgotten to be gracious? * and will he
shut up his loving-kindness in displeasure?
10 And I said, It is mine own infirmity; * but I will
remember the years of the right hand of the Most
Highest.
11 I will remember the works of the LORD, * and
call to mind thy wonders of old time.
12 I will think also of thy works, * and my talking
shall be of thy doings.
13 Thy way, O God, is holy: * who is so great a God
as our God?
14 Thou art the God that doest wonders, * and
hast declared thy power among the peoples.
15 Thou hast mightily delivered thy people, * even
the sons of Jacob and Joseph.
16 The waters saw thee, O God, the waters saw
thee, and were afraid; * the depths also were troubled.
17 The clouds poured out water, the air thundered, * and thine arrows went abroad.
18 The voice of thy thunder was heard round
about: * the lightnings shone upon the ground; the
earth was moved, and shook withal.
19 Thy way is in the sea, and thy paths in the great
waters, * and thy footsteps are not known.

77 *Voce mea ad Dominum*

1 I will cry aloud to God; *
I will cry aloud, and he will hear me.

2 In the day of my trouble I sought the Lord; *
my hands were stretched out by night and did not tire;
I refused to be comforted.

3 I think of God, I am restless, *
I ponder, and my spirit faints.

4 You will not let my eyelids close; *
I am troubled and I cannot speak.

5 I consider the days of old; *
I remember the years long past;

6 I commune with my heart in the night; *
I ponder and search my mind.

7 Will the Lord cast me off for ever? *
will he no more show his favor?

8 Has his loving-kindness come to an end for ever? *
has his promise failed for evermore?

9 Has God forgotten to be gracious? *
has he, in his anger, withheld his compassion?

10 And I said, "My grief is this: *
the right hand of the Most High has lost its power."

11 I will remember the works of the LORD, *
and call to mind your wonders of old time.

12 I will meditate on all your acts *
and ponder your mighty deeds.

13 Your way, O God, is holy; *
who is so great a god as our God?

14 You are the God who works wonders *
and have declared your power among the peoples.

15 By your strength you have redeemed your people, *
the children of Jacob and Joseph.

16 The waters saw you, O God;
the waters saw you and trembled; *
the very depths were shaken.

17 The clouds poured out water;
the skies thundered; *
your arrows flashed to and fro;

18 The sound of your thunder was in the whirlwind;
your lightnings lit up the world; *
the earth trembled and shook.

19 Your way was in the sea,
and your paths in the great waters, *
yet your footsteps were not seen.

20 Thou leddest thy people like sheep, by the hand of Moses and Aaron.

Evening Prayer.

Psalm lxxviii. *Attendite popule.*

HEAR my law, O my people ; incline your ears unto the words of my mouth.

2 I will open my mouth in a parable ; I will declare hard sentences of old ;

3 Which we have heard and known, and such as our fathers have told us ;

4 That we should not hide them from the children of the generations to come ; but to show the honour of the LORD, his mighty and wonderful works that he hath done.

5 He made a covenant with Jacob, and gave Israel a law, which he commanded our forefathers to teach their children ;

6 That their posterity might know it, and the children which were yet unborn ;

7 To the intent that when they came up, they might show their children the same ;

8 That they might put their trust in God ; and not to forget the works of God, but to keep his commandments ;

9 And not to be as their forefathers, a faithless and stubborn generation ; a generation that set not their heart aright, and whose spirit cleaveth not steadfastly unto God ;

10 Like as the children of Ephraim ; who being harnessed, and carrying bows, turned themselves back in the day of battle.

11 They kept not the covenant of God, and would not walk in his law ;

12 But forgat what he had done, and the wonderful works that he had showed for them.

13 Marvellous things did he in the sight of our forefathers, in the land of Egypt, even in the field of Zoan.

14 He divided the sea, and let them go through ; he made the waters to stand on an heap.

15 In the day-time also he led them with a cloud, and all the night through with a light of fire.

20 Thou leddest thy people like sheep : by the hand of Moses and Aaron.

Evening Prayer.

PSALM 78. *Attendite, popule.*

HEAR my law, O my people : incline your ears unto the words of my mouth.

2 I will open my mouth in a parable : I will declare hard sentences of old ;

3 Which we have heard and known : and such as our fathers have told us ;

4 That we should not hide them from the children of the generations to come : but to show the honour of the LORD, his mighty and wonderful works that he hath done.

5 He made a covenant with Jacob, and gave Israel a law : which he commanded our forefathers to teach their children ;

6 That their posterity might know it : and the children which were yet unborn ;

7 To the intent that when they came up : they might show their children the same ;

8 That they might put their trust in God : and not to forget the works of God, but to keep his commandments ;

9 And not to be as their forefathers, a faithless and stubborn generation : a generation that set not their heart aright, and whose spirit cleaveth not stedfastly unto God ;

10 Like as the children of Ephraim : who being harnessed, and carrying bows, turned themselves back in the day of battle.

11 They kept not the covenant of God : and would not walk in his law ;

12 But forgat what he had done : and the wonderful works that he had showed for them.

13 Marvellous things did he in the sight of our forefathers, in the land of Egypt : even in the field of Zoan.

14 He divided the sea, and let them go through : he made the waters to stand up on an heap.

15 In the day-time also he led them with a cloud : and all the night through with a light of fire.

20 Thou leddest thy people like sheep, * by the hand of Moses and Aaron.

Evening Prayer.

Psalm 78. *Attendite, popule.*

HEAR my law, O my people; * incline your ears unto the words of my mouth.

2 I will open my mouth in a parable; * I will declare hard sentences of old;

3 Which we have heard and known, * and such as our fathers have told us;

4 That we should not hide them from the children of the generations to come; * but to show the honour of the LORD, his mighty and wonderful works that he hath done.

5 He made a covenant with Jacob, and gave Israel a law, * which he commanded our forefathers to teach their children;

6 That their posterity might know it, * and the children which were yet unborn;

7 To the intent that when they came up, * they might show their children the same;

8 That they might put their trust in God; * and not to forget the works of God, but to keep his commandments;

9 And not to be as their forefathers, a faithless and stubborn generation; * a generation that set not their heart aright, and whose spirit clave not stedfastly unto God;

10 Like as the children of Ephraim; * who being harnessed, and carrying bows, turned themselves back in the day of battle.

11 They kept not the covenant of God, * and would not walk in his law;

12 But forgat what he had done, * and the wonderful works that he had showed for them.

13 Marvellous things did he in the sight of our forefathers, in the land of Egypt, * even in the field of Zoan.

14 He divided the sea, and let them go through; * he made the waters to stand up on an heap.

15 In the day-time also he led them with a cloud, * and all the night through with a light of fire.

20 You led your people like a flock *
by the hand of Moses and Aaron.

Fifteenth Day: Evening Prayer

78

Part I *Attendite, popule*

1 Hear my teaching, O my people; *
incline your ears to the words of my mouth.

2 I will open my mouth in a parable; *
I will declare the mysteries of ancient times.

3 That which we have heard and known,
and what our forefathers have told us, *
we will not hide from their children.

4 We will recount to generations to come
the praiseworthy deeds and the power of the LORD, *
and the wonderful works he has done.

5 He gave his decrees to Jacob
and established a law for Israel, *
which he commanded them to teach their children;

6 That the generations to come might know,
and the children yet unborn; *
that they in their turn might tell it to their children;

7 So that they might put their trust in God, *
and not forget the deeds of God,
but keep his commandments;

8 And not be like their forefathers,
a stubborn and rebellious generation, *
a generation whose heart was not steadfast,
and whose spirit was not faithful to God.

9 The people of Ephraim, armed with the bow, *
turned back in the day of battle;

10 They did not keep the covenant of God, *
and refused to walk in his law;

11 They forgot what he had done, *
and the wonders he had shown them.

12 He worked marvels in the sight of their forefathers, *
in the land of Egypt, in the field of Zoan.

13 He split open the sea and let them pass through; *
he made the waters stand up like walls.

14 He led them with a cloud by day, *
and all the night through with a glow of fire.

15 He split the hard rocks in the wilderness *
and gave them drink as from the great deep.

16 He clave the hard rocks in the wilderness, and gave them drink thereof, as it had been out of the great depth.

17 He brought waters out of the stony rock, so that it gushed out like the rivers.

18 Yet for all this they sinned more against him, and provoked the Most Highest in the wilderness.

19 They tempted God in their hearts, and required meat for their lust.

20 They spake against God also, saying, Shall God prepare a table in the wilderness?

21 He smote the stony rock indeed, that the water gushed out, and the streams flowed withal ; but can he give bread also, or provide flesh for his people?

22 When the LORD heard this, he was wroth ; so the fire was kindled in Jacob, and there came up heavy displeasure against Israel ;

23 Because they believed not in God, and put not their trust in his help.

24 So he commanded the clouds above, and opened the doors of heaven.

25 He rained down manna also upon them for to eat, and gave them food from heaven.

26 So man did eat angels' food ; for he sent them meat enough.

27 He caused the east-wind to blow under heaven ; and through his power he brought in the southwest-wind.

28 He rained flesh upon them as thick as dust, and feathered fowls like as the sand of the sea.

29 He let it fall among their tents, even round about their habitation.

30 So they did eat, and were well filled ; for he gave them their own desire : they were not disappointed of their lust.

31 But while the meat was yet in their mouths, the heavy wrath of God came upon them, and slew the wealthiest of them ; yea, and smote down the chosen men that were in Israel.

32 But for all this they sinned yet more, and believed not his wondrous works.

33 Therefore their days did he consume in vanity, and their years in trouble.

34 When he slew them, they sought him, and turned them early, and inquired after God.

16 He clave the hard rocks in the wilderness : and gave them drink thereof, as it had been out of the great depth.

17 He brought waters out of the stony rock : so that it gushed out like the rivers.

18 Yet for all this they sinned more against him : and provoked the Most Highest in the wilderness.

19 They tempted God in their hearts : and required meat for their lust.

20 They spake against God also, saying : Shall God prepare a table in the wilderness?

21 He smote the stony rock indeed, that the water gushed out, and the streams flowed withal : but can he give bread also, or provide flesh for his people?

22 When the LORD heard this, he was wroth : so the fire was kindled in Jacob, and there came up heavy displeasure against Israel ;

23 Because they believed not in God : and put not their trust in his help.

24 So he commanded the clouds above : and opened the doors of heaven.

25 He rained down manna also upon them for to eat : and gave them food from heaven.

26 So man did eat angels' food : for he sent them meat enough.

27 He caused the east-wind to blow under heaven : and through his power he brought in the southwest-wind.

28 He rained flesh upon them as thick as dust : and feathered fowls like as the sand of the sea.

29 He let it fall among their tents : even round about their habitation.

30 So they did eat, and were well filled ; for he gave them their own desire : they were not disappointed of their lust.

31 But while the meat was yet in their mouths, the heavy wrath of God came upon them, and slew the wealthiest of them : yea, and smote down the chosen men that were in Israel.

32 But for all this they sinned yet more : and believed not his wondrous works.

33 Therefore their days did he consume in vanity : and their years in trouble.

34 When he slew them, they sought him : and turned them early, and inquired after God.

1928

16 He clave the hard rocks in the wilderness, * and
gave them drink thereof, as it had been out of the great
depth.
17 He brought waters out of the stony rock, * so
that it gushed out like the rivers.
18 Yet for all this they sinned more against him, *
and provoked the Most Highest in the wilderness.
19 They tempted God in their hearts, * and
required meat for their lust.
20 They spake against God also, saying, * Shall
God prepare a table in the wilderness?
21 He smote the stony rock indeed, that the water
gushed out, and the streams flowed withal; * but can
he give bread also, or provide flesh for his people?
22 When the LORD heard this, he was wroth; * so
the fire was kindled in Jacob, and there came up heavy
displeasure against Israel;
23 Because they believed not in God, * and put not
their trust in his help.
24 So he commanded the clouds above, * and
opened the doors of heaven.
25 He rained down manna also upon them for to
eat, * and gave them food from heaven.
26 So man did eat angels' food; * for he sent them
meat enough.
27 He caused the east-wind to blow under
heaven; * and through his power he brought in the
southwest-wind.
28 He rained flesh upon them as thick as dust, *
and feathered fowls like as the sand of the sea.
29 He let it fall among their tents, * even round
about their habitation.
30 So they did eat, and were well filled; for he gave
them their own desire: * they were not disappointed of
their lust.
31 But while the meat was yet in their mouths the
heavy wrath of God came upon them, and slew the
wealthiest of them; * yea, and smote down the chosen
men that were in Israel.
32 But for all this they sinned yet more, * and
believed not his wondrous works.
33 Therefore their days did he consume in
vanity, * and their years in trouble.
34 When he slew them, they sought him, * and
turned them early, and inquired after God.

1979

16 He brought streams out of the cliff, *
and the waters gushed out like rivers.

17 But they went on sinning against him, *
rebelling in the desert against the Most High.

18 They tested God in their hearts, *
demanding food for their craving.

19 They railed against God and said, *
"Can God set a table in the wilderness?

20 True, he struck the rock, the waters gushed out, and the gullies overflowed; *
but is he able to give bread
or to provide meat for his people?"

21 When the LORD heard this, he was full of wrath; *
a fire was kindled against Jacob,
and his anger mounted against Israel;

22 For they had no faith in God, *
nor did they put their trust in his saving power.

23 So he commanded the clouds above *
and opened the doors of heaven.

24 He rained down manna upon them to eat *
and gave them grain from heaven.

25 So mortals ate the bread of angels; *
be provided for them food enough.

26 He caused the east wind to blow in the heavens *
and led out the south wind by his might.

27 He rains down flesh upon them like dust *
and wingèd birds like the sand of the sea.

28 He let it fall in the midst of their camp *
and round about their dwellings.

29 So they ate and were well filled, *
for he gave them what they craved.

30 But they did not stop their craving, *
though the food was still in their mouths.

31 So God's anger mounted against them; *
he slew their strongest men
and laid low the youth of Israel.

32 In spite of all this, they went on sinning *
and had no faith in his wonderful works.

33 So he brought their days to an end like a breath *
and their years in sudden terror.

34 Whenever he slew them, they would seek him, *
and repent, and diligently search for God.

35 And they remembered that God was their strength, and that the High God was their redeemer.
36 Nevertheless, they did but flatter him with their mouth, and dissembled with him in their tongue.
37 For their heart was not whole with him, neither continued they stedfast in his covenant.
38 But he was so merciful, that he forgave their misdeeds, and destroyed them not.
39 Yea, many a time turned he his wrath away, and would not suffer his whole displeasure to arise.
40 For he considered that they were but flesh, and that they were even a wind that passeth away, and cometh not again.
41 Many a time did they provoke him in the wilderness, and grieved him in the desert.
42 They turned back, and tempted God, and moved the Holy One in Israel.
43 They thought not of his hand, and of the day when he delivered them from the hand of the enemy ;
44 How he had wrought his miracles in Egypt, and his wonders in the field of Zoan.
45 He turned their waters into blood, so that they might not drink of the rivers.
46 He sent lice among them, and devoured them up ; and frogs to destroy them.
47 He gave their fruit unto the caterpillar, and their labour unto the grasshopper.
48 He destroyed their vines with hailstones, and their mulberry-trees with the frost.
49 He smote their cattle also with hailstones, and their flocks with hot thunderbolts.
50 He cast upon them the furiousness of his wrath, anger, displeasure, and trouble : and sent evil angels among them.
51 He made a way to his indignation, and spared not their soul from death ; but gave their life over to the pestilence ;
52 And smote all the firstborn in Egypt, the most principal and mightiest in the dwellings of Ham.
53 But as for his own people, he led them forth like sheep, and carried them in the wilderness like a flock.

35 And they remembered that God was their strength : and that the High God was their redeemer.
36 Nevertheless, they did but flatter him with their mouth : and dissembled with him in their tongue.
37 For their heart was not whole with him : neither continued they stedfast in his covenant.
38 But he was so merciful, that he forgave their misdeeds : and destroyed them not.
39 Yea, many a time turned he his wrath away : and would not suffer his whole displeasure to arise.
40 For he considered that they were but flesh : and that they were even a wind that passeth away, and cometh not again.
41 Many a time did they provoke him in the wilderness : and grieved him in the desert.
42 They turned back, and tempted God : and moved the Holy One in Israel.
43 They thought not of his hand : and of the day when he delivered them from the hand of the enemy ;
44 How he had wrought his miracles in Egypt : and his wonders in the field of Zoan.
45 He turned their waters into blood : so that they might not drink of the rivers.
46 He sent lice among them, and devoured them up : and frogs to destroy them.
47 He gave their fruit unto the caterpillar : and their labour unto the grasshopper.
48 He destroyed their vines with hailstones : and their mulberry-trees with the frost.
49 He smote their cattle also with hailstones : and their flocks with hot thunderbolts.
50 He cast upon them the furiousness of his wrath, anger, displeasure, and trouble : and sent evil angels among them.
51 He made a way to his indignation, and spared not their soul from death : but gave their life over to the pestilence ;
52 And smote all the firstborn in Egypt : the most principal and mightiest in the dwellings of Ham.
53 But as for his own people, he led them forth like sheep : and carried them in the wilderness like a flock.

1928

35 And they remembered that God was their
strength, * and that the High God was their redeemer.
36 Nevertheless, they did but flatter him with their
mouth, * and dissembled with him in their tongue.
37 For their heart was not whole with him, *
neither continued they stedfast in his covenant.
38 But he was so merciful, that he forgave their
misdeeds, * and destroyed them not.
39 Yea, many a time turned he his wrath away, *
and would not suffer his whole displeasure to arise.
40 For he considered that they were but flesh, *
and that they were even a wind that passeth away, and
cometh not again.

41 Many a time did they provoke him in the
wilderness, * and grieved him in the desert.
42 They turned back, and tempted God, * and
provoked the Holy One of Israel.
43 They thought not of his hand, * and of the day
when he delivered them from the hand of the enemy;
44 How he had wrought his miracles in Egypt, *
and his wonders in the field of Zoan.
45 He turned their waters into blood, * so that they
might not drink of the rivers.
46 He sent flies among them, and devoured them
up; * and frogs to destroy them.
47 He gave their fruit unto the caterpillar, * and
their labour unto the grasshopper.
48 He destroyed their vines with hailstones, * and
their mulberry-trees with the frost.
49 He smote their cattle also with hailstones, * and
their flocks with hot thunderbolts.
50 He cast upon them the furiousness of his wrath,
anger, displeasure, and trouble: * and sent evil angels
among them.
51 He made a way to his indignation, and spared
not their soul from death; * but gave their life over to
the pestilence;
52 And smote all the firstborn in Egypt, * the most
principal and mightiest in the dwellings of Ham.
53 But as for his own people, he led them forth like
sheep, * and carried them in the wilderness like a
flock.

1979

35 They would remember that God was their rock, *
and the Host High God their redeemer.

36 But they flattered him with their mouths *
and lied to him with their tongues.

37 Their heart was not steadfast toward him, *
and they were not faithful to his covenant.

38 But he was so merciful that he forgave their sins
and did not destroy them; *
many times he held back his anger
and did not permit his wrath to be roused.

39 For he remembered that they were but flesh, *
a breath that goes forth and does not return.

Psalm 78: Part II *Quoties exacerbaverunt*

40 How often the people disobeyed him in the wilderness *
and offended him in the desert!

41 Again and again they tempted God *
and provoked the Holy One of Israel.

42 They did not remember his power *
in the day when he ransomed them from the enemy;

43 How he wrought his signs in Egypt *
and his omens in the field of Zoan.

44 He turned their rivers into blood, *
so that they could not drink of their streams.

45 He sent swarms of flies among them, which ate them up, *
and frogs, which destroyed them.

46 He gave their crops to the caterpillar, *
the fruit of their toil to the locust.

47 He killed their vines with hail *
and their sycamores with frost.

48 He delivered their cattle to hailstones *
and their livestock to hot thunderbolts.

49 He poured out upon them his blazing anger: *
fury, indignation, and distress,
a troop of destroying angels.

50 He gave full rein to his anger;
he did not spare their souls from death; *
but delivered their lives to the plague.

51 He struck down all the firstborn of Egypt, *
the flower of manhood in the dwellings of Ham.

52 He led out his people like sheep *
and guided them in the wilderness like a flock.

53 He led them to safety, and they were not afraid; *
but the sea overwhelmed their enemies.

1789-1871

54 He brought them out safely, that they should not fear, and overwhelmed their enemies with the sea.

55 And brought them within the borders of his sanctuary, even to his mountain, which he purchased with his right hand.

56 He cast out the heathen also before them, caused their land to be divided among them for an heritage, and made the tribes of Israel to dwell in their tents.

57 So they tempted and displeased the most high God, and kept not his testimonies ;

58 But turned their backs, and fell away like their forefathers ; starting aside like a broken bow.

59 For they grieved him with their hill-altars, and provoked him to displeasure with their images.

60 When God heard this, he was wroth, and took sore displeasure at Israel ;

61 So that he forsook the tabernacle in Silo, even the tent that he had pitched among men.

62 He delivered their power into captivity, and their beauty into the enemy's hand.

63 He gave his people over also unto the sword, and was wroth with his inheritance.

64 The fire consumed their young men, and their maidens were not given to marriage.

65 Their priests were slain with the sword, and there were no widows to make lamentation.

66 So the Lord awaked as one out of sleep, and like a giant refreshed with wine.

67 He smote his enemies in the hinder parts, and put them to a perpetual shame.

68 He refused the tabernacle of Joseph, and chose not the tribe of Ephraim ;

69 But chose the tribe of Judah, even the hill of Sion which he loved.

70 And there he built his temple on high, and laid the foundation of it like the ground which he hath made continually.

71 He chose David also his servant, and took him away from the sheep-folds :

72 As he was following the ewes great with young ones he took him, that he might feed Jacob his people, and Israel his inheritance.

73 So he fed them with a faithful and true heart, and ruled them prudently with all his power.

1892

54 He brought them out safely, that they should not fear : and overwhelmed their enemies with the sea.

55 And brought them within the borders of his sanctuary : even to his mountain, which he purchased with his right hand.

56 He cast out the heathen also before them : caused their land to be divided among them for an heritage, and made the tribes of Israel to dwell in their tents.

57 So they tempted and displeased the Most High God : and kept not his testimonies.

58 But turned their backs, and fell away like their forefathers : starting aside like a broken bow.

59 For they grieved him with their hill-altars : and provoked him to displeasure with their images.

60 When God heard this, he was wroth : and took sore displeasure at Israel ;

61 So that he forsook the tabernacle in Silo : even the tent that he had pitched among men.

62 He delivered their power into captivity : and their beauty into the enemy's hand.

63 He gave his people over also unto the sword : and was wroth with his inheritance.

64 The fire consumed their young men : and their maidens were not given to marriage.

65 Their priests were slain with the sword : and there were no widows to make lamentation.

66 So the Lord awaked as one out of sleep : and like a giant refreshed with wine.

67 He smote his enemies in the hinder parts : and put them to a perpetual shame.

68 He refused the tabernacle of Joseph : and chose not the tribe of Ephraim ;

69 But chose the tribe of Judah : even the hill of Sion which he loved.

70 And there he built his temple on high : and laid the foundation of it like the ground which he hath made continually.

71 He chose David also his servant : and took him away from the sheep-folds.

72 As he was following the ewes great with their young ones he took him : that he might feed Jacob his people, and Israel his inheritance.

73 So he fed them with a faithful and true heart : and ruled them prudently with all his power.

1928

54 He brought them out safely, that they should
not fear, * and overwhelmed their enemies with the
sea.
55 And brought them within the borders of his
sanctuary, * even to this mountain, which he
purchased with his right hand.
56 He cast out the heathen also before them, *
caused their land to be divided among them for an
heritage, and made the tribes of Israel to dwell in their
tents.
57 Yet they tempted and displeased the Most High
God, * and kept not his testimonies.
58 They turned their backs, and fell away like their
forefathers; * starting aside like a broken bow.
59 For they grieved him with their hill-altars, * and
provoked him to displeasure with their images.
60 When God heard this, he was wroth, * and took
sore displeasure at Israel;
61 So that he forsook the tabernacle in Shiloh, *
even the tent that he had pitched among men.
62 He delivered their power into captivity, * and
their beauty into the enemy's hand.
63 He gave his people over also unto the sword, *
and was wroth with his inheritance.
64 The fire consumed their young men, * and their
maidens were not given in marriage.
65 Their priests were slain with the sword, * and
there were no widows to make lamentation.
66 So the Lord awaked as one out of sleep, * and
like a giant refreshed with wine.
67 He drave his enemies backward, * and put them
to a perpetual shame.
68 He refused the tabernacle of Joseph, * and
chose not the tribe of Ephraim;
69 But chose the tribe of Judah, * even the hill of
Sion which he loved.
70 And there he built his temple on high, * and
laid the foundation of it like the ground which he hath
made continually.
71 He chose David also his servant, * and took him
away from the sheep-fold.
72 As he was following the ewes with their young
he took him, * that he might feed Jacob his people, and
Israel his inheritance.
73 So he fed them with a faithful and true heart, *
and ruled them prudently with all his power.

1979

54 He brought them to his holy land, *
the mountain his right hand had won.

55 He drove out the Canaanites before them
and apportioned an inheritance to them by lot; *
he made the tribes of Israel to dwell in their tents.

56 But they tested the Most High God, and defied him; *
and did not keep his commandments.

57 They turned away and were disloyal like their fathers; *
they were undependable like a warped bow.

58 They grieved him with their hill-altars *
and provoked his displeasure with their idols.

59 When God heard this, he was angry *
and utterly rejected Israel.

60 He forsook the shrine at Shiloh, *
the tabernacle where he had lived among his people.

61 He delivered the ark into captivity, *
his glory into the adversary's hand.

62 He gave his people to the sword *
and was angered against his inheritance.

63 The fire consumed their young men; *
there were no wedding songs for their maidens.

64 Their priest fell by the sword, *
and their widows made no lamentation.

65 Then the LORD woke as though from sleep, *
like a warrior refreshed with wine.

66 He struck his enemies on the backside *
and put them to perpetual shame.

67 He rejected the tent of Joseph *
and did not choose the tribe of Ephraim;

68 He chose instead the tribe of Judah *
and Mount Zion, which he loved.

69 He built his sanctuary like the heights of heaven, *
like the earth which he founded for ever.

70 He chose David his servant, *
and took him away from the sheepfolds.

71 He brought him from following the ewes, *
to be a shepherd over Jacob his people
and over Israel his inheritance.

72 So he shepherded them with a faithful and true heart *
and guided them with the skillfulness of his hands.

1789-1871

THE SIXTEENTH DAY.

Morning Prayer.

Psalm lxxix. *Deus, venerunt.*

O GOD, the heathen are come into thine inheritance; thy holy temple have they defiled, and made Jerusalem an heap of stones.

2 The dead bodies of thy servants have they given to be meat unto the fowls of the air, and the flesh of thy saints unto the beasts of the land.

3 Their blood have they shed like water on every side of Jerusalem, and there was no man to bury them.

4 We are become an open shame to our enemies, a very scorn and derision unto them that are round about us.

5 LORD, how long wilt thou be angry? shall thy jealousy burn like fire for ever?

6 Pour out thine indignation upon the heathen that have not known thee; and upon the kingdoms that have not called upon thy Name.

7 For they have devoured Jacob, and laid waste his dwelling-place.

8 O remember not our old sins, but have mercy upon us, and that soon; for we are come to great misery.

9 Help us, O God of our salvation, for the glory of thy Name: O deliver us, and be merciful unto our sins, for thy Name's sake.

10 Wherefore do the heathen say, Where is now their God?

11 O let the vengeance of thy servants' blood that is shed, be openly showed upon the heathen, in our sight.

12 O let the sorrowful sighing of the prisoners come before thee; according to the greatness of thy power, preserve thou those that are appointed to die.

13 And for the blasphemy wherewith our neighbours have blasphemed thee, reward thou them, O Lord, sevenfold into their bosom.

14 So we, that are thy people, and sheep of thy pasture, shall give thee thanks for ever, and will alway be showing forth thy praise from generation to generation.

1892

THE SIXTEENTH DAY.

Morning Prayer.

PSALM 79. *Deus, venerunt.*

O GOD, the heathen are come into thine inheritance: thy holy temple have they defiled, and made Jerusalem an heap of stones.

2 The dead bodies of thy servants have they given to be meat unto the fowls of the air: and the flesh of thy saints unto the beasts of the land.

3 Their blood have they shed like water on every side of Jerusalem: and there was no man to bury them.

4 We are become an open shame to our enemies: a very scorn and derision unto them that are round about us.

5 LORD, how long wilt thou be angry: shall thy jealousy burn like fire for ever?

6 Pour out thine indignation upon the heathen that have not known thee: and upon the kingdoms that have not called upon thy Name.

7 For they have devoured Jacob: and laid waste his dwelling-place.

8 O remember not our old sins, but have mercy upon us, and that soon: for we are come to great misery.

9 Help us, O God of our salvation, for the glory of thy Name: O deliver us, and be merciful unto our sins, for thy Name's sake.

10 Wherefore do the heathen say: Where is now their God?

11 O let the vengeance of thy servants' blood that is shed: be openly showed upon the heathen, in our sight.

12 O let the sorrowful sighing of the prisoners come before thee: according to the greatness of thy power, preserve thou those that are appointed to die.

13 And for the blasphemy wherewith our neighbours have blasphemed thee: reward thou them, O Lord, seven-fold into their bosom.

14 So we, that are thy people, and sheep of thy pasture, shall give thee thanks for ever: and will alway be showing forth thy praise from generation to generation.

The Sixteenth Day.

Morning Prayer.

Psalm 79. *Deus, venerunt.*

O GOD, the heathen are come into thine inheritance; * thy holy temple have they defiled, and made Jerusalem an heap of stones.

2 The dead bodies of thy servants have they given to be meat unto the fowls of the air, * and the flesh of thy saints unto the beasts of the land.

3 Their blood have they shed like water on every side of Jerusalem, * and there was no man to bury them.

4 We are become an open shame to our enemies, * and very scorn and derision unto them that are round about us.

5 LORD, how long wilt thou be angry? * shall thy jealousy burn like fire for ever?

6 Pour out thine indignation upon the heathen that have not known thee; * and upon the kingdoms that have not called upon thy Name.

7 For they have devoured Jacob, * and laid waste his dwelling-place.

8 O remember not our old sins, but have mercy upon us, and that soon; * for we are come to great misery.

9 Help us, O God of our salvation, for the glory of thy Name: * O deliver us, and be merciful unto our sins, for thy Name's sake.

10 Wherefore do the heathen say, * Where is now their God?

11 O let the vengeance of thy servants' blood that is shed, * be openly showed upon the heathen, in our sight.

12 O let the sorrowful sighing of the prisoners come before thee; * according to the greatness of thy power, preserve thou those that are appointed to die.

13 And for the blasphemy wherewith our neighbours have blasphemed thee, * reward thou them, O Lord, sevenfold into their bosom.

14 So we, that are thy people, and sheep of thy pasture, shall give thee thanks for ever, * and will alway be showing forth thy praise from generation to generation.

Sixteenth Day: Morning Prayer

79 *Deus, venerunt*

1 O God, the heathen have come into your inheritance;
they have profaned your holy temple; *
they have made Jerusalem a heap of rubble.

2 They have given the bodies of your servants as food for the birds of the air, *
and the flesh of your faithful ones to the beasts of the field.

3 They have shed their blood like water on every side of Jerusalem, *
and there was no one to bury them.

4 We have become a reproach to our neighbors, *
an object of scorn and derision to those around us.

5 How long will you be angry, O LORD? *
will your fury blaze like fire for ever?

6 Pour out your wrath upon the heathen who have not known you *
and upon the kingdoms that have not called upon your Name.

7 For they have devoured Jacob *
and made his dwelling a ruin.

8 Remember not our past sins;
let your compassion be swift to meet us; *
for we have been brought very low.

9 Help us, O God our Savior, for the glory of your Name; *
deliver us and forgive us our sins, for your Name's sake.

10 Why should the heathen say, "Where is their God?" *
Let it be known among the heathen and in our sight
that you avenge the shedding of your servants' blood.

11 Let the sorrowful sighing of the prisoners come before you, *
and by your great might spare those who are condemned to die.

12 May the revilings with which they reviled you, O Lord, *
return seven-fold into their bosoms.

13 For we are your people and the sheep of your pasture; *
we will give you thanks for ever
and show forth your praise from age to age.

1789-1871

Psalm lxxx. *Qui regis Israel.*

HEAR, O thou Shepherd of Israel, thou that leadest Joseph like a sheep ; show thyself also, thou that sittest upon the Cherubim.[20]

2 Before Ephraim, Benjamin, and Manasses, stir up thy strength, and come and help us.

3 Turn us again, O God ; show the light of thy countenance, and we shall be whole.

4 O LORD God of hosts, how long wilt thou be angry with thy people that prayeth?

5 Thou feedest them with the bread of tears, and givest them plenteousness of tears to drink.

6 Thou hast made us a very strife unto our neighbours, and our enemies laugh us to scorn.

7 Turn us again, thou God of hosts ; show the light of thy countenance, and we shall be whole.

8 Thou hast brought a vine out of Egypt ; thou hast cast out the heathen, and planted it.

9 Thou madest room for it ; and when it had taken root, it filled the land.

10 The hills were covered with the shadow of it, and the boughs thereof were like the goodly cedar-trees.

11 She stretched out her branches unto the sea, and her boughs unto the river.

12 Why hast thou then broken down her hedge, that all they that go by pluck off her grapes?

13 The wild boar out of the wood doth root it up, and the wild beasts of the field devour it.

14 Turn thee again, thou God of hosts, look down from heaven, behold, and visit this vine ;

15 And the place of the vineyard that thy right hand hath planted, and the branch that thou madest so strong for thyself.

16 It is burnt with fire, and cut down ; and they shall perish at the rebuke of thy countenance.

17 Let thy hand be upon the man of thy right hand, and upon the son of man, whom thou madest so strong for thine own self.

18 And so will not we go back from thee : O let us live, and we shall call upon thy Name.

19 Turn us again, O LORD God of hosts ; show the light of thy countenance, and we shall be whole.

1892

PSALM 80. *Qui regis Israel.*

HEAR, O thou Shepherd of Israel, thou that leadest Joseph like a sheep : show thyself also, thou that sittest upon the Cherubim.

2 Before Ephraim, Benjamin, and Manasses : stir up thy strength, and come and help us.

3 Turn us again, O God : show the light of thy countenance, and we shall be whole.

4 O LORD God of hosts : how long wilt thou be angry with thy people that prayeth?

5 Thou feedest them with the bread of tears : and givest them plenteousness of tears to drink.

6 Thou hast made us a very strife unto our neighbours : and our enemies laugh us to scorn.

7 Turn us again, thou God of hosts : show the light of thy countenance, and we shall be whole.

8 Thou hast brought a vine out of Egypt : thou hast cast out the heathen, and planted it.

9 Thou madest room for it : and when it had taken root, it filled the land.

10 The hills were covered with the shadow of it : and the boughs thereof were like the goodly cedar-trees.

11 She stretched out her branches unto the sea : and her boughs unto the river.

12 Why hast thou then broken down her hedge : that all they that go by pluck off her grapes?

13 The wild boar out of the wood doth root it up : and the wild beasts of the field devour it.

14 Turn thee again, thou God of hosts, look down from heaven : behold, and visit this vine ;

15 And the place of the vineyard that thy right hand hath planted : and the branch that thou madest so strong for thyself.

16 It is burnt with fire, and cut down : and they shall perish at the rebuke of thy countenance.

17 Let thy hand be upon the man of thy right hand : and upon the son of man, whom thou madest so strong for thine own self.

18 And so will not we go back from thee : O let us live, and we shall call upon thy Name.

19 Turn us again, O LORD God of hosts : show the light of thy countenance, and we shall be whole.

[20]"Cherubims" prior to 1793.

1928

Psalm 80. *Qui regis Israel.*

HEAR, O thou Shepherd of Israel, thou that leadest
Joseph like a flock; * show thyself also, thou that sittest
upon the Cherubim.
2 Before Ephraim, Benjamin, and Manasseh, * stir
up thy strength, and come and help us.
3 Turn us again, O God; * show the light of thy
countenance, and we shall be whole.
4 O LORD God of hosts, * how long wilt thou be
angry with thy people that prayeth?
5 Thou feedest them with the bread of tears, * and
givest them plenteousness of tears to drink.
6 Thou hast made us a very strife unto our neighbours, * and our enemies laugh us to scorn.
7 Turn us again, thou God of hosts; * show the
light of thy countenance, and we shall be whole.
8 Thou hast brought a vine out of Egypt; * thou
hast cast out the heathen, and planted it.
9 Thou madest room for it; * and when it had
taken root, it filled the land.
10 The hills were covered with the shadow of it, *
and the boughs thereof were like the goodly cedar-
trees.
11 She stretched out her branches unto the sea, *
and her boughs unto the River.
12 Why hast thou then broken down her hedge, *
that all they that go by pluck off her grapes?
13 The wild boar out of the wood doth root it up, *
and the wild beasts of the field devour it.
14 Turn thee again, thou God of hosts, look down
from heaven, * behold, and visit this vine;
15 And the place of the vineyard that thy right
hand hath planted, * and the branch that thou madest
so strong for thyself.
16 It is burnt with fire, and cut down; * and they
shall perish at the rebuke of thy countenance.
17 Let thy hand be upon the man of thy right
hand, * and upon the son of man, whom thou madest
so strong for thine own self.
18 And so will not we go back from thee: * O let us
live, and we shall call upon thy Name.
19 Turn us again, O LORD God of hosts; * show the
light of thy countenance, and we shall be whole.

1979

80 *Qui regis Israel*

1 Hear, O Shepherd of Israel, leading Joseph like a flock; *
shine forth, you that are enthroned upon the cherubim.

2 In the presence of Ephraim, Benjamin, and Manasseh, *
stir up your strength and come to help us.

3 Restore us, O God of hosts; *
show the light of your countenance, and we shall be saved.

4 O LORD God of hosts, *
how long will you be angered
despite the prayers of your people?

5 You have fed them with the bread of tears; *
you have given them bowls of tears to drink.

6 You have made us the derision of our neighbors, *
and our enemies laugh us to scorn.

7 Restore us, O God of hosts; *
show the light of your countenance, and we shall be saved.

8 You have brought a vine out of Egypt; *
you cast out the nations and planted it.

9 You prepared the ground for it; *
it took root and filled the land.

10 The mountains were covered by its shadow *
and the towering cedar trees by its boughs.

11 You stretched out its tendrils to the Sea *
and its branches to the River.

12 Why have you broken down its wall, *
so that all who pass by pluck off its grapes?

13 The wild boar of the forest has ravaged it, *
and the beasts of the field have grazed upon it.

14 Turn now, O God of hosts, look down from heaven;
behold and tend this vine; *
preserve what your right hand has planted.

15 They burn it with fire like rubbish; *
at the rebuke of your countenance let them perish.

16 Let your hand be upon the man of your right hand, *
the son of man you have made so strong for yourself.

17 And so will we never turn away from you; *
give us life, that we may call upon your Name.

18 Restore us, O LORD God of hosts; *
show the light of your countenance, and we shall be saved.

Psalm lxxxi. *Exultate Deo.*

SING we merrily unto God our strength ; make a cheerful noise unto the God of Jacob.

2 Take the psalm, bring hither the tabret, the merry harp with the lute.

3 Blow up the trumpet in the new-moon, even in the time appointed, and upon our solemn feast-day.

4 For this was made a statute for Israel, and a law of the God of Jacob.

5 This he ordained in Joseph for a testimony, when he came out of the land of Egypt, and had heard a strange language.

6 I eased his shoulder from the burden, and his hands were delivered from making the pots.

7 Thou calledst upon me in troubles, and I delivered thee ; and heard thee what time as the storm fell upon thee.

8 I proved thee also at the waters of strife.

9 Hear, O my people ; and I will assure thee, O Israel, if thou wilt hearken unto me,

10 There shall no strange god be in thee, neither shalt thou worship any other god.

11 I and the LORD thy God, who brought thee out of the land of Egypt : open thy mouth wide, and I shall fill it.

12 But my people would not hear my voice ; and Israel would not obey me ;

13 So I gave them up into their own hearts' lusts, and let them follow their own imaginations.

14 O that my people would have hearkened unto me! for if Israel had walked in my ways,

15 I should soon have put down their enemies, and turned my hand against their adversaries.

16 The haters of the LORD should have been found liars ; but their time should have endured for ever.

17 He should have fed them also with the finest wheat-flour ; and with honey out of the stony rock should I have satisfied thee.

PSALM 81. *Exultate Deo.*

SING we merrily unto God our strength : make a cheerful noise unto the God of Jacob.

2 Take the psalm, bring hither the tabret : the merry harp with the lute.

3 Blow up the trumpet in the new moon : even in the time appointed, and upon our solemn feast-day.

4 For this was made a statute for Israel : and a law of the God of Jacob.

5 This he ordained in Joseph for a testimony : when he came out of the land of Egypt, and had heard a strange language.

6 I eased his shoulder from the burden : and his hands were delivered from making the pots.

7 Thou callèdst upon me in troubles, and I delivered thee : and heard thee what time as the storm fell upon thee.

8 I proved thee also : at the waters of strife.

9 Hear, O my people, and I will assure thee, O Israel : if thou wilt hearken unto me,

10 There shall no strange god be in thee : neither shalt thou worship any other god.

11 I and the LORD thy God, who brought thee out of the land of Egypt : open thy mouth wide, and I shall fill it.

12 But my people would not hear my voice : and Israel would not obey me ;

13 So I gave them up into their own hearts' lusts : and let them follow their own imaginations.

14 O that my people would have hearkened unto me : for if Israel had walked in my ways,

15 I should soon have put down their enemies : and turned my hand against their adversaries.

16 The haters of the LORD should have been found liars : but their time should have endured for ever.

17 He should have fed them also with the finest wheat-flour : and with honey out of the stony rock should I have satisfied thee.

The Psalter

346, 347

Evening Prayer.

Psalm lxxxii. *Deus stetit.*

GOD standeth in the congregation of princes ; he is a Judge among gods.

Evening Prayer.

PSALM 82. *Deus stetit.*

GOD standeth in the congregation of princes : he is a Judge among gods.

Psalm 81. *Exultate Deo.*

SING we merrily unto God our strength; * make a cheerful noise unto the God of Jacob.

2 Take the psalm, bring hither the tabret, * the merry harp with the lute.

3 Blow up the trumpet in the new moon, * even in the time appointed, and upon our solemn feast-day.

4 For this was made a statute for Israel, * and a law of the God of Jacob.

5 This he ordained in Joseph for a testimony, * when he came out of the land of Egypt, and had heard a strange language.

6 I eased his shoulder from the burden, * and his hands were delivered from making the pots.

7 Thou calledst upon me in troubles, and I delivered thee; * and heard thee what time as the storm fell upon thee.

8 I proved thee also * at the waters of strife.

9 Hear, O my people; and I will assure thee, O Israel, * if thou wilt hearken unto me,

10 There shall no strange god be in thee, * neither shalt thou worship any other god.

11 I and the LORD thy God, who brought thee out of the land of Egypt: * open thy mouth wide, and I shall fill it.

12 But my people would not hear my voice; * and Israel would not obey me;

13 So I gave them up into their own hearts' lusts, * and let them follow their own imaginations.

14 O that my people would have hearkened unto me! * for if Israel had walked in my ways,

15 I should soon have put down their enemies, * and turned my hand against their adversaries.

16 The haters of the LORD should have submitted themselves unto him; * but their time should have endured for ever.

17 I would have fed them also with the finest wheat-flour; * and with honey out of the stony rock would I have satisfied thee.

Evening Prayer.

Psalm 82. *Deus stetit.*

GOD standeth in the congregation of princes; * he is a Judge among gods.

81 *Exultate Deo*

1 Sing with joy to God our strength *
and raise a loud shout to the God of Jacob.

2 Raise a song and sound the timbrel, *
the merry harp, and the lyre.

3 Blow the ram's-horn at the new moon, *
and at the full moon, the day of our feast.

4 For this is a statute for Israel, *
a law of the God of Jacob.

5 He laid it as a solemn charge upon Joseph, *
when he came out of the land of Egypt.

6 I heard an unfamiliar voice saying, *
"I eased his shoulder from the burden;
his hands were set free from bearing the load."

7 You called on me in trouble, and I saved you; *
I answered you from the secret place of thunder
and tested you at the waters of Meribah.

8 Hear, O my people, and I will admonish you: *
O Israel, if you would but listen to me!

9 There shall be no strange god among you; *
you shall not worship a foreign god.

10 I am the LORD your God,
who brought you out of the land of Egypt and said, *
"Open your mouth wide, and I will fill it."

11 And yet my people did not hear my voice, *
and Israel would not obey me.

12 So I gave them over to the stubbornness of their hearts, *
to follow their own devices.

13 Oh, that my people would listen to me! *
that Israel would walk in my ways!

14 I should soon subdue their enemies *
and turn my hand against their foes.

15 Those who hate the LORD would cringe before him, *
and their punishment would last for ever.

16 But Israel would I feed with the finest wheat *
and satisfy him with honey from the rock

Sixteenth Day: Evening Prayer

82 *Deus stetit*

1 God takes his stand in the council of heaven; *
he gives judgment in the midst of the gods:

2 How long will ye give wrong judgment, and accept the persons of the ungodly?

3 Defend the poor and fatherless ; see that such as are in need and necessity have right.

4 Deliver the outcast and poor ; save them from the hand of the ungodly.

5 They will not be learned, nor understand, but walk on still in darkness : all the foundations of the earth are out of course.

6 I have said, Ye are gods, and ye are all the children of the Most Highest.

7 But ye shall die like men, and fall like one of the princes.

8 Arise, O God, and judge thou the earth ; for thou shalt take all heathen to thine inheritance.

Psalm lxxxiii. *Deus, quis similis?*

HOLD not thy tongue, O God, keep not still silence : refrain not thyself, O God.

2 For lo, thine enemies make a murmuring ; and they that hate thee have lift up their head.

3 They have imagined craftily against thy people, and taken counsel against thy secret ones.

4 They have said, Come, and let us root them out, that they be no more a people, and that the name of Israel may be no more in remembrance.

5 For they have cast their heads together with one consent, and are confederate against thee :

6 The tabernacles of the Edomites, and the Ishmaelites ;[21] the Moabites, and Hagarenes ;[22]

7 Gebal, and Ammon, and Amalek ; the Philistines, with them that dwell at Tyre.

8 Assur also is joined with them ; and have holpen the children of Lot.

9 But do thou to them as unto the Midianites ;[23] unto Sisera, and unto Jabin at the brook of Kison ;

10 Who perished at Endor, and became as the dung of the earth.

11 Make them and their princes like Oreb and Zeb ; yea, make all their princes like as Zeba and Salmana ;

12 Who say, Let us take to ourselves the houses of God in possession.

---

[21]"Ismaelites" in the English book.

[22]"Hagarens" prior to 1793.

[23]"Madianites" until 1822.

2 How long will ye give wrong judgment : and accept the persons of the ungodly?

3 Defend the poor and fatherless : see that such as are in need and necessity have right.

4 Deliver the outcast and poor : save them from the hand of the ungodly.

5 They will not be learned, nor understand, but walk on still in darkness : all the foundations of the earth are out of course.

6 I have said, Ye are gods : and ye are all the children of the Most Highest.

7 But ye shall die like men : and fall like one of the princes.

8 Arise, O God, and judge thou the earth : for thou shalt take all heathen to thine inheritance.

PSALM 83. *Deus, quis similis?*

HOLD not thy tongue, O God, keep not still silence : refrain not thyself, O God.

2 For lo, thine enemies make a murmuring : and they that hate thee have lift up their head.

3 They have imagined craftily against thy people : and taken counsel against thy secret ones.

4 They have said, Come, and let us root them out, that they be no more a people : and that the name of Israel may be no more in remembrance.

5 For they have cast their heads together with one consent : and are confederate against thee :

6 The tabernacles of the Edomites, and the Ishmaelites : the Moabites, and Hagarenes ;

7 Gebal, and Ammon, and Amalek : the Philistines, with them that dwell at Tyre.

8 Assur also is joined with them : and have holpen the children of Lot.

9 But do thou to them as unto the Madianites[1] : unto Sisera, and unto Jabin at the brook of Kison ;

10 Who perished at Endor : and became as the dung of the earth.

11 Make them and their princes like Oreb and Zeb : yea, make all their princes like as Zeba and Salmana ;

12 Who say, Let us take to ourselves : the houses of God in possession.

---

[1]*sic.*

1928

2 How long will ye give wrong judgment, * and accept the persons of the ungodly?

3 Defend the poor and fatherless; * see that such as are in need and necessity have right.

4 Deliver the outcast and poor; * save them from the hand of the ungodly.

5 They know not, neither do they understand, but walk on still in darkness: * all the foundations of the earth are out of course.

6 I have said, Ye are gods, * and ye are all the children of the Most Highest.

7 But ye shall die like men, * and fall like one of the princes.

8 Arise, O God, and judge thou the earth; * for thou shalt take all nations to thine inheritance.

Psalm 83. *Deus, quis similis?*

HOLD not thy tongue, O God, keep not still silence: * refrain not thyself, O God.

2 For lo, thine enemies make a murmuring; * and they that hate thee have lift up their head.

3 They have imagined craftily against thy people, * and taken counsel against thy secret ones.

4 They have said, Come, and let us root them out, that they be no more a people, * and that the name of Israel may be no more in remembrance.

5 For they have cast their heads together with one consent, * and are confederate against thee:

6 The tabernacles of the Edomites, and the Ishmaelites; * the Moabites, and Hagarenes;

7 Gebal, and Ammon, and Amalek; * the Philistines, with them that dwell at Tyre.

8 Assyria also is joined with them; * they have holpen the children of Lot.

9 But do thou to them as unto the Midianites; * unto Sisera, and unto Jabin at the brook of Kishon;

10 Who perished at Endor, * and became as the dung of the earth.

11 Make them and their princes like Oreb and Zeëb; * yea, make all their princes like as Zebah and Zalmunna;

12 Who say, Let us take to ourselves * the houses of God in possession.

1979

2 “How long will you judge unjustly, *
and show favor to the wicked?

3 Save the weak and the orphan; *
defend the humble and needy;

4 Rescue the weak and the poor; *
deliver them from the power of the wicked.

5 They do not know, neither do they understand;
they go about in darkness; *
all the foundations of the earth are shaken.

6 Now I say to you, ‘You are gods, *
and all of you children of the Most High; *

7 Nevertheless, you shall die like mortals, *
and fall like any prince.’”

8 Arise, O God, and rule the earth, *
for you shall take all nations for your own.

83 *Deus, quis similis?*

1 O God, do not be silent; *
do not keep still nor hold your peace, O God;

2 For your enemies are in tumult, *
and those who hate you have lifted up their heads.

3 They take secret counsel against your people *
and plot against those whom you protect.

4 They have said, “Come, let us wipe them out from among the nations; *
let the name of Israel be remembered no more.”

5 They have conspired together; *
they have made an alliance against you:

6 The tents of Edom and the Ishmaelites; *
the Moabites and the Hagarenes;

7 Gebal, and Ammon, and Amalek; *
the Philistines and those who dwell in Tyre.

8 The Assyrians also have joined them, *
and have come to help the people of Lot.

9 Do to them as you did to Midian, *
to Sisera, and to Jabin at the river of Kishon:

10 They were destroyed at Endor; *
they became like dung upon the ground.

11 Make their leaders like Oreb and Zeëb, *
and all their commanders like Zebah and Zalmunna,

12 Who said, “Let us take for ourselves *
the fields of God as our possession.”

13 O my God, make them like unto a wheel, and as the stubble before the wind ;

14 Like as the fire that burneth up the wood, and as the flame that consumeth the mountains.

15 Persecute them even so with thy tempest, and make them afraid with thy storm.

16 Make their faces ashamed, O LORD, that they may seek thy Name.

17 Let them be confounded and vexed ever more and more ; let them be put to shame, and perish.

18 And they shall know that thou, whose Name is JEHOVAH, art only the Most Highest over all the earth.

13 O my God, make them like unto a wheel : and as the stubble before the wind ;

14 Like as the fire that burneth up the wood : and as the flame that consumeth the mountains ;

15 Persecute them even so with thy tempest : and make them afraid with thy storm.

16 Make their faces ashamed, O LORD : that they may seek thy Name.

17 Let them be confounded and vexed ever more and more : let them be put to shame, and perish.

18 And they shall know that thou, whose Name is JEHOVAH : art only the Most Highest over all the earth.

Psalm lxxxiv. *Quam dilecta!*

O HOW amiable are thy dwellings, thou LORD of hosts!

2 My soul hath a desire and longing to enter into the courts of the LORD ; my heart and my flesh rejoice in the living God.

3 Yea, the sparrow hath found her an house, and the swallow a nest, where she may lay her young ; even thy altars, O LORD of hosts, my King and my God.

4 Blessed are they that dwell in thy house ; they will be alway praising thee.

5 Blessed is the man whose strength is in thee ; in whose heart are thy ways.

6 Who going through the vale of misery use it for a well ; and the pools are filled with water.

7 They will go from strength to strength, and unto the God of gods appeareth every one of them in Sion.

8 O LORD God of hosts, hear my prayer ; hearken, O God of Jacob.

9 Behold, O God our defender, and look upon the face of thine Anointed.

10 For one day in thy courts is better than a thousand.

11 I had rather be a door-keeper in the house of my God, than to dwell in the tents of ungodliness.

12 For the LORD God is a light and defence ; the LORD will give grace and worship ; and no good thing shall he withhold from them that live a godly life.

PSALM 84. *Quam dilecta!*

O HOW amiable are thy dwellings : thou LORD of hosts!

2 My soul hath a desire and longing to enter into the courts of the LORD : my heart and my flesh rejoice in the living God.

3 Yea, the sparrow hath found her an house, and the swallow a nest, where she may lay her young : even thy altars, O LORD of hosts, my King and my God.

4 Blessed are they that dwell in thy house : they will be alway praising thee.

5 Blessed is the man whose strength is in thee : in whose heart are thy ways.

6 Who going through the vale of misery use it for a well : and the pools are filled with water.

7 They will go from strength to strength : and unto the God of gods appeareth every one of them in Sion.

8 O LORD God of hosts, hear my prayer : hearken, O God of Jacob.

9 Behold, O God our defender : and look upon the face of thine anointed.

10 For one day in thy courts : is better than a thousand.

11 I had rather be a door-keeper in the house of my God : than to dwell in the tents of ungodliness.

12 For the LORD God is a light and defence : the LORD will give grace and worship, and no good thing shall he withhold from them that live a godly life.

1928

13 O my God, make them like unto the whiling dust, * and as the stubble before the wind;

14 Like as the fire that burneth up the forest, * and as the flame that consumeth the mountains;

15 Pursue them even so with thy tempest, * and make them afraid with thy storm.

16 Make their faces ashamed, O LORD, * that they may seek thy Name.

17 Let them be confounded and vexed ever more and more; * let them be put to shame, and perish.

18 And they shall know that thou, whose Name is JEHOVAH, * art only the Most Highest over all the earth.

Psalm 84. *Quam dilecta!*

O HOW amiable are thy dwellings, * thou LORD of hosts!

2 My soul hath a desire and longing to enter into the courts of the LORD; * my heart and my flesh rejoice in the living God.

3 Yea, the sparrow hath found her an house, and the swallow a nest, where she may lay here young; * even thy altars, O LORD of hosts, my King and my God.

4 Blessed are they that dwell in thy house; * they will be alway praising thee.

5 Blessed is the man whose strength is in thee; * in whose heart are thy ways.

6 Who going through the vale of misery use it for a well; * and the pools are filled with water.

7 They will go from strength to strength, * and unto the God of gods appeareth every one of them in Sion.

8 O LORD God of hosts, hear my prayer; * hearken, O God of Jacob.

9 Behold, O God our defender, * and look upon the face of thine anointed.

10 For one day in thy courts * is better than a thousand.

11 I had rather be a door-keeper in the house of my God, * than to dwell in the tents of ungodliness.

12 For the LORD God is a light and defence; * the LORD will give grace and worship; and no good thing shall he withhold from them that live a godly life.

1979

13 O my God, make them like whirling dust *
and like chaff before the wind;

14 Like fire that burns down a forest, *
like the flame that sets mountains ablaze.

15 Drive them with your tempest *
and terrify them with your storm;

16 Cover their faces with shame, O LORD, *
that they may seek your Name.

17 Let them be disgraced and terrified for ever; *
let them be put to confusion and perish.

18 Let them know that you, whose Name is YAHWEH, *
you alone are the Most High over all the earth.

84 *Quam dilecta!*

1 How dear to me is your dwelling, O LORD of hosts! *
My soul has a desire and longing for the courts of the LORD;
my heart and my flesh rejoice in the living God.

2 The sparrow has found her a house
and the swallow a nest where she may lay her young; *
by the side of your altars, O LORD of hosts,
my King and my God.

3 Happy are they who dwell in your house! *
they will always be praising you.

4 Happy are the people whose strength is in you! *
whose hearts are set on the pilgrims' way.

5 Those who go through the desolate valley will find it a place of springs, *
for the early rains have covered it with pools of water.

6 They will climb from height to height, *
and the God of gods will reveal himself in Zion.

7 LORD God of hosts, hear my prayer; *
hearken, O God of Jacob.

8 Behold our defender, O God; *
and look upon the face of your Anointed.

9 For one day in your courts is better than a thousand in my own room, *
and to stand at the threshold of the house of my God
than to dwell in the tents of the wicked.

10 For the LORD God is both sun and shield; *
he will give grace and glory;

11 No good thing will the LORD withhold *
from those who walk with integrity.

13 O LORD God of hosts, blessed is the man that putteth his trust in thee.

Psalm lxxxv. *Benedixisti, Domine.*

LORD, thou art become gracious unto thy land; thou hast turned away the captivity of Jacob.

2 Thou hast forgiven the offence of thy people, and covered all their sins.

3 Thou hast taken away all thy displeasure, and turned thyself from thy wrathful indignation.

4 Turn us then, O God our Saviour, and let thine anger cease from us.

5 Wilt thou be displeased at us for ever? and wilt thou stretch out thy wrath from one generation to another?

6 Wilt thou not turn again, and quicken us, that thy people may rejoice in thee?

7 Show us thy mercy, O LORD, and grant us thy salvation.

8 I will hearken what the LORD God will say concerning me; for he shall speak peace unto his people, and to his saints, that they turn not again.

9 For his salvation is nigh them that fear him; that glory may dwell in our land.

10 Mercy and truth are met together: righteousness and peace have kissed each other.

11 Truth shall flourish out of the earth, and righteousness hath looked down from heaven.

12 Yea, the LORD shall show loving-kindness; and our land shall give her increase.

13 Righteousness shall go before him; and he shall direct his going in the way.

THE SEVENTEENTH DAY.

Morning Prayer.

Psalm lxxxvi. *Inclina, Domine.*

BOW down thine ear, O LORD, and hear me; for I am poor, and in misery.

2 Preserve thou my soul, for I am holy: my God, save thy servant that putteth his trust in thee.

3 Be merciful unto me, O LORD; for I will call daily upon thee.

13 O LORD God of hosts: blessed is the man that putteth his trust in thee.

Psalm 85. *Benedixisti, Domine.*

LORD, thou art become gracious unto thy land: thou hast turned away the captivity of Jacob.

2 Thou hast forgiven the offence of thy people: and covered all their sins.

3 Thou hast taken away all thy displeasure: and turned thyself from thy wrathful indignation.

4 Turn us then, O God our Saviour: and let thine anger cease from us.

5 Wilt thou be displeased at us for ever: and wilt thou stretch out thy wrath from one generation to another?

6 Wilt thou not turn again, and quicken us: that thy people may rejoice in thee?

7 Show us thy mercy, O LORD: and grant us thy salvation.

8 I will hearken what the LORD God will say concerning me: for he shall speak peace unto his people, and to his saints, that they turn not again.

9 For his salvation is nigh them that fear him: that glory may dwell in our land.

10 Mercy and truth are met together: righteousness and peace have kissed each other.

11 Truth shall flourish out of the earth: and righteousness hath looked down from heaven.

12 Yea, the LORD shall show loving-kindness: and our land shall give her increase.

13 Righteousness shall go before him: and he shall direct his going in the way.

THE SEVENTEENTH DAY.

Morning Prayer.

Psalm 86. *Inclina, Domine.*

BOW down thine ear, O LORD, and hear me: for I am poor, and in misery.

2 Preserve thou my soul, for I am holy: my God, save thy servant that putteth his trust in thee.

3 Be merciful unto me, O LORD: for I will call daily upon thee.

13 O LORD God of hosts, * blessed is the man that
putteth his trust in thee.

Psalm 85. *Benedixisti, Domine.*

LORD, thou art become gracious unto thy land; *
thou hast turned away the captivity of Jacob.
2 Thou hast forgiven the offence of thy people, *
and covered all their sins.
3 Thou hast taken away all thy displeasure, * and
turned thyself from thy wrathful indignation.
4 Turn us then, O God our Saviour, * and let thine
anger cease from us.
5 Wilt thou be displeased at us for ever? * and wilt
thou stretch out thy wrath from one generation to
another?
6 Wilt thou not turn again, and quicken us, * that
thy people may rejoice in thee?
7 Show us thy mercy, O LORD, * and grant us thy
salvation.
8 I will hearken what the LORD God will say; * for
he shall speak peace unto his people, and to his saints,
that they turn not again unto foolishness.
9 For his salvation is nigh them that fear him; *
that glory may dwell in our land.
10 Mercy and truth are met together: * righteousness and peace have kissed each other.
11 Truth shall flourish out of the earth, * and righteousness hath looked down from heaven.
12 Yea, the LORD shall show loving-kindness; * and
our land shall give her increase.
13 Righteousness shall go before him, * and shall
direct his going in the way.

The Seventeenth Day.

Morning Prayer.

Psalm 86. *Inclina, Domine.*

BOW down thine ear, O LORD, and hear me; * for I
am poor, and in misery.
2 Preserve thou my soul, for I am holy: * my God,
save thy servant that putteth his trust in thee.
3 Be merciful unto me, O LORD; * for I will call
daily upon thee.

12 O LORD of hosts, *
happy are they who put their trust in you!

85 *Benedixisti, Domine*

1 You have been gracious to your land, O LORD, *
you have restored the good fortune of Jacob.

2 You have forgiven the iniquity of your people *
and blotted out all their sins.

3 You have withdrawn all your fury *
and turned yourself from your wrathful indignation.

4 Restore us then, O God our Savior; *
let your anger depart from us.

5 Will you be displeased with us for ever? *
will you prolong your anger from age to age?

6 Will you not give us life again, *
that your people may rejoice in you?

7 Show us your mercy, O LORD, *
and grant us your salvation.

8 I will listen to what the LORD God is saying, *
for he is speaking peace to his faithful people
and to those who turn their hearts to him.

9 Truly, his salvation is very near to those who fear him, *
that his glory may dwell in our land.

10 Mercy and truth have met together; *
righteousness and peace have kissed each other.

11 Truth shall spring up from the earth, *
and righteousness shall look down from heaven.

12 The LORD will indeed grant prosperity, *
and our land will yield its increase.

13 Righteousness shall go before him, *
and peace shall be a pathway for his feet.

Seventeenth Day: Morning Prayer

86 *Inclina, Domine*

1 Bow down your ear, O LORD, and answer me, *
for I am poor and in misery.

2 Keep watch over my life, for I am faithful; *
save your servant who puts his trust in you.

3 Be merciful to me, O LORD, for you are my God; *
I call upon you all the day long.

4 Comfort the soul of thy servant ; for unto thee, O Lord, do I lift up my soul.

5 For thou, Lord, art good and gracious, and of great mercy unto all them that call upon thee.

6 Give ear, LORD, unto my prayer, and ponder the voice of my humble desires.

7 In the time of my trouble I will call upon thee ; for thou hearest me.

8 Among the gods there is none like unto thee, O Lord ; there is not one that can do as thou doest.

9 All nations whom thou hast made shall come and worship thee, O Lord ; and shall glorify thy Name.

10 For thou art great, and doest wondrous things : thou art God alone.

11 Teach me thy way, O LORD, and I will walk in thy truth : O knit my heart unto thee, that I may fear thy Name.

12 I will thank thee, O Lord my God, with all my heart ; and will praise thy Name for evermore.

13 For great is thy mercy toward me ; and thou hast delivered my soul from the nethermost hell.

14 O God, the proud are risen against me ; and the congregations of naughty men have sought after my soul, and have not set thee before their eyes.

15 But thou, O Lord God, art full of compassion and mercy, long-suffering, plenteous in goodness and truth.

16 O turn thee then unto me, and have mercy upon me ; give thy strength unto thy servant, and help the son of thine handmaid.

17 Show some token upon me for good ; that they who hate me may see it, and be ashamed, because thou, LORD, hast holpen me, and comforted me.

4 Comfort the soul of thy servant : for unto thee, O Lord, do I lift up my soul.

5 For thou, Lord, art good and gracious : and of great mercy unto all them that call upon thee.

6 Give ear, LORD, unto my prayer : and ponder the voice of my humble desires.

7 In the time of my trouble I will call upon thee : for thou hearest me.

8 Among the gods there is none like unto thee, O Lord : there is not one that can do as thou doest.

9 All nations whom thou hast made shall come and worship thee, O Lord : and shall glorify thy Name.

10 For thou art great, and doest wondrous things : thou art God alone.

11 Teach me thy way, O LORD, and I will walk in thy truth : O knit my heart unto thee, that I may fear thy Name.

12 I will thank thee, O Lord my God, with all my heart : and will praise thy Name for evermore.

13 For great is thy mercy toward me : and thou hast delivered my soul from the nethermost hell.

14 O God, the proud are risen against me : and the congregations of naughty men have sought after my soul, and have not set thee before their eyes.

15 But thou, O Lord God, art full of compassion and mercy : long-suffering, plenteous in goodness and truth.

16 O turn thee then unto me, and have mercy upon me : give thy strength unto thy servant, and help the son of thine handmaid.

17 Show some token upon me for good ; that they who hate me may see it, and be ashamed : because thou, LORD, hast holpen me, and comforted me.

Psalm lxxxvii. *Fundamenta ejus.*

HER foundations are upon the holy hills : the LORD loveth the gates of Sion more than all the dwellings of Jacob.

2 Very excellent things are spoken of thee, thou city of God.

3 I will think upon Rahab and Babylon, with them that know me.

PSALM 87. *Fundamenta ejus.*

HER foundations are upon the holy hills : the LORD loveth the gates of Sion more than all the dwellings of Jacob.

2 Very excellent things are spoken of thee : thou city of God.

3 I will think upon Rahab and Babylon : with them that know me.

1928

4 Comfort the soul of thy servant; * for unto thee, O Lord, do I lift up my soul.

5 For thou, Lord, art good and gracious, * and of great mercy unto all them that call upon thee.

6 Give ear, LORD, unto my prayer, * and ponder the voice of my humble desires.

7 In the time of my trouble I will call upon thee; * for thou hearest me.

8 Among the gods there is none like unto thee, O Lord; * there is not one that can do as thou doest.

9 All nations whom thou hast made shall come and worship thee, O Lord; * and shall glorify thy Name.

10 For thou art great, and doest wondrous things: * thou art God alone.

11 Teach me thy way, O LORD, and I will walk in thy truth: * O knit my heart unto thee, that I may fear thy Name.

12 I will thank thee, O Lord my God, with all my heart; * and will praise thy Name for evermore.

13 For great is thy mercy toward me; * and thou hast delivered my soul from the nethermost hell.

14 O God, the proud are risen against me; * and the congregations of violent men have sought after my soul, and have not set thee before their eyes.

15 But thou, O Lord God, art full of compassion and mercy, * long-suffering, plenteous in goodness and truth.

16 O turn thee then unto me, and have mercy upon me; * give thy strength unto thy servant, and help the son of thine handmaid.

17 Show some token upon me for good; that they who hate me may see it, and be ashamed, * because thou, LORD, hast holpen me, and comforted me.

1979

4 Gladden the soul of your servant, *
for to you O LORD, I lift up my soul.

5 For you, O LORD, are good and forgiving, *
and great is your love toward all who call upon you.

6 Give ear, O LORD, to my prayer, *
and attend to the voice of my supplications.

7 In the time of my trouble I will call upon you, *
for you will answer me.

8 Among the gods there is none like you, O LORD, *
nor anything like your works.

9 All nations you have made will come and worship you, O LORD, *
and glorify your Name.

10 For you are great;
you do wondrous things; *
and you alone are God.

11 Teach me your way, O LORD,
and I will walk in your truth; *
knit my heart to you that I may fear your Name.

12 I will thank you, O LORD my God, with all my heart, *
and glorify your Name for evermore.

13 For great is your love toward me; *
you have delivered me from the nethermost Pit.

14 The arrogant rise up against me, O God,
and a band of violent men seeks my life; *
they have not set you before their eyes.

15 But you, O LORD, are gracious and full of compassion, *
slow to anger, and full of kindness and truth.

16 Turn to me and have mercy upon me; *
give your strength to your servant;
and save the child of your handmaid.

17 Show me a sign of your favor,
so that those who hate me may see it and be ashamed; *
because you, O LORD, have helped me and comforted me.

Psalm 87. *Fundamenta ejus.*

HER foundations are upon the holy hills: * the LORD loveth the gates of Sion more than all the dwellings of Jacob.

2 Very excellent things are spoken of thee, * thou city of God.

3 I will make mention of Egypt and Babylon, * among them that know me.

87 *Fundamenta ejus*

1 On the holy mountain stands the city he has founded; *
the LORD loves the gates of Zion
more than all the dwellings of Jacob.

2 Glorious things are spoken of you, *
O city of our God.

3 I count Egypt and Babylon among those who know me; *
behold Philistia, Tyre, and Ethiopia:
in Zion were they born.

1789-1871

4 Behold, ye the Philistines also ; and they of Tyre, with the Morians ; lo, there was he born.
5 And, of Sion it shall be reported that he was born in her ; and the Most High shall stablish her.
6 The LORD shall rehearse it, when he writeth up the people, that he was born there.
7 The singers also and trumpeters shall he rehearse : All my fresh springs shall be in thee.

Psalm lxxxviii. *Domine, Deus.*

O LORD God of my salvation, I have cried day and night before thee : O let my prayer enter into thy presence, incline thine ear unto my calling ;
2 For my soul is full of trouble, and my life draweth nigh unto hell.
3 I am counted as one of them that go down into the pit, and I am even as a man that hath no strength ;
4 Free among the dead, like unto them that are wounded, and lie in the grave, who are out of remembrance, and are cut away from thy hand.
5 Thou hast laid me in the lowest pit, in a place of darkness, and in the deep.
6 Thine indignation lieth hard upon me, and thou hast vexed me with all thy storms.
7 Thou hast put away mine acquaintance far from me, and made me to be abhorred of them.
8 I am so fast in prison that I cannot get forth.
9 My sight faileth for very trouble ; LORD, I have called daily upon thee, I have stretched forth my hands unto thee.
10 Dost thou show wonders among the dead? or shall the dead rise up again, and praise thee?
11 Shall thy loving-kindness be showed in the grave? or thy faithfulness in destruction?
12 Shall thy wondrous works be known in the dark? and thy righteousness in the land where all things are forgotten?
13 Unto thee have I cried, O LORD ; and early shall my prayer come before thee.
14 LORD, why abhorrest thou my soul, and hidest thou thy face from me?
15 I am in misery, and like unto him that is at the point to die ; even from my youth up thy terrors have I suffered with a troubled mind.

1892

4 Behold, yea the Philistines also : and they of Tyre, with the Morians ; lo, there was he born.
5 And of Sion it shall be reported that he was born in her : and the Most High shall stablish her.
6 The LORD shall rehearse it, when he writeth up the people : that he was born there.
7 The singers also and trumpeters shall he rehearse : All my fresh springs are in thee.

PSALM 88. *Domine, Deus.*

O LORD God of my salvation, I have cried day and night before thee : O let my prayer enter into thy presence, incline thine ear unto my calling ;
2 For my soul is full of trouble : and my life draweth nigh unto hell.
3 I am counted as one of them that go down into the pit : and I have been even as a man that hath no strength.
4 Free among the dead, like unto them that are wounded, and lie in the grave : who are out of remembrance, and are cut away from thy hand.
5 Thou hast laid me in the lowest pit : in a place of darkness, and in the deep.
6 Thine indignation lieth hard upon me : and thou hast vexed me with all thy storms.
7 Thou hast put away mine acquaintance far from me : and made me to be abhorred of them.
8 I am so fast in prison : that I cannot get forth.
9 My sight faileth for very trouble : LORD, I have called daily upon thee, I have stretched forth my hands unto thee.
10 Dost thou show wonders among the dead : or shall the dead rise up again, and praise thee?
11 Shall thy loving-kindness be showed in the grave : or thy faithfulness in destruction?
12 Shall thy wondrous works be known in the dark : and thy righteousness in the land where all things are forgotten?
13 Unto thee have I cried, O LORD : and early shall my prayer come before thee.
14 LORD, why abhorrest thou my soul : and hidest thou thy face from me?
15 I am in misery, and like unto him that is at the point to die : even from my youth up, thy terrors have I suffered with a troubled mind.

4 Behold, Philistia also; and Tyre, with Ethiopia; * lo, in Sion were they born.

5 Yea, of Sion it shall be reported, this one and that one were born in her; * and the Most High shall stablish her.

6 The LORD shall record it, when he writeth up the peoples; * lo, in Sion were they born.

7 The singers also and trumpeters shall make answer: * All my fresh springs are in thee.

Psalm 88. *Domine, Deus.*

O LORD God of my salvation, I have cried day and night before thee: * O let my prayer enter into thy presence, incline thine ear unto my calling;

2 For my soul is full of trouble, * and my life draweth nigh unto the grave.

3 I am counted as one of them that go down into the pit, * and I am even as a man that hath no strength;

4 Cast off among the dead, like unto them that are slain, and lie in the grave, * who are out of remembrance, and are cut away from thy hand.

5 Thou hast laid me in the lowest pit, * in a place of darkness, and in the deep.

6 Thine indignation lieth hard upon me, * and thou hast vexed me with all thy storms.

7 Thou hast put away mine acquaintance far from me, * and made me to be abhorred of them.

8 I am so fast in prison * that I cannot get forth.

9 My sight faileth for very trouble; * LORD, I have called daily upon thee, I have stretched forth my hands unto thee.

10 Dost thou show wonders among the dead? * or shall the dead rise up again, and praise thee?

11 Shall thy loving-kindness be showed in the grave? * or thy faithfulness in destruction?

12 Shall thy wondrous works be known in the dark? * and thy righteousness in the land where all things are forgotten?

13 Unto thee have I cried, O LORD; * and early shall my prayer come before thee.

14 LORD, why abhorrest thou my soul, * and hidest thou thy face from me?

15 I am in misery, and like unto him that is at the point to die; * even from my youth up, thy terrors have I suffered with a troubled mind.

4 Of Zion it shall be said, "Everyone was born in her, *
and the Most High himself shall sustain her."

5 The LORD will record as he enrolls the peoples, *
"These also were born there."

6 The singers and the dancers will say, *
"All my fresh springs are in you."

88 *Domine, Deus*

1 O LORD, my God, my Savior, *
by day and night I cry to you.

2 Let my prayer enter into your presence; *
incline your ear to my lamentation.

3 For I am full of trouble; *
my life is at the brink of the grave.

4 I am counted among those who go down to the Pit; *
I have become like one who has no strength;

5 Lost among the dead, *
like the slain who lie in the grave,

6 Whom you remember no more, *
for they are cut off from your hand.

7 You have laid me in the depths of the Pit, *
in dark places, and in the abyss.

8 Your anger weighs upon me heavily, *
and all your great waves overwhelm me.

9 You have put my friends far from me;
you have made me to be abhorred by them; *
I am in prison and cannot get free.

10 My sight has failed me because of trouble; *
LORD, I have called upon you daily;
I have stretched out my hands to you.

11 Do you work wonders for the dead? *
will those who have died stand up and give you thanks?

12 Will your loving-kindness be declared in the grave? *
your faithfulness in the land of destruction?

13 Will your wonders be known in the dark? *
or your righteousness in the country where all is forgotten?

14 But as for me, O LORD, I cry to you for help; *
in the morning my prayer comes before you.

15 LORD, why have you rejected me? *
why have you hidden your face from me?

16 Thy wrathful displeasure goeth over me, and the fear of thee hath undone me.

17 They came round about me daily like water, and compassed me together on every side.

18 My lovers and friends hast thou put away from me, and hid mine acquaintance out of my sight.

Evening Prayer.

Psalm lxxxix. *Misericordias Domini.*

MY song shall be alway of the loving-kindness of the LORD ; with my mouth will I ever be showing thy truth from one generation to another.

2 For I have said, Mercy shall be set up for ever ; thy truth shalt thou establish in the heavens.

3 I have made a covenant with my chosen ; I have sworn unto David my servant :

4 Thy seed will I establish for ever, and set up thy throne from one generation to another.

5 O LORD, the very heavens shall praise thy wondrous works ; and thy truth in the congregation of the saints.

6 For who is he among the clouds, that shall be compared unto the LORD?

7 And what is he among the gods, that shall be like unto the LORD?

8 God is very greatly to be feared in the council of the saints, and to be had in reverence of all them that are round about him.

9 O LORD God of hosts, who is like unto thee? thy truth, most mighty LORD, is on every side.

10 Thou rulest the raging of the sea ; thou stillest the waves thereof when they arise.

11 Thou hast subdued Egypt, and destroyed it ; thou hast scattered thine enemies abroad with thy mighty arm.

12 The heavens are thine, the earth also is thine ; thou hast laid the foundation of the round world, and all that therein is.

13 Thou hast made the north and the south ; Tabor and Hermon shall rejoice in thy Name.

14 Thou hast a mighty arm ; strong is thy hand, and high is thy right hand.

16 Thy wrathful displeasure goeth over me : and the fear of thee hath undone me.

17 They came round about me daily like water : and compassed me together on every side.

18 My lovers and friends hast thou put away from me : and hid mine acquaintance out of my sight.

Evening Prayer.

PSALM 89. *Misericordias Domini.*

MY song shall be alway of the loving-kindness of the LORD : with my mouth will I ever be showing thy truth from one generation to another.

2 For I have said, Mercy shall be set up for ever : thy truth shalt thou stablish in the heavens.

3 I have made a covenant with my chosen : I have sworn unto David my servant :

4 Thy seed will I stablish for ever : and set up thy throne from one generation to another.

5 O LORD, the very heavens shall praise thy wondrous works : and thy truth in the congregation of the saints.

6 For who is he among the clouds : that shall be compared unto the LORD?

7 And what is he among the gods : that shall be like unto the LORD?

8 God is very greatly to be feared in the council of the saints : and to be had in reverence of all them that are round about him.

9 O Lord God of hosts, who is like unto thee : thy truth, most mighty LORD, is on every side.

10 Thou rulest the raging of the sea : thou stillest the waves thereof when they arise.

11 Thou hast subdued Egypt, and destroyed it : thou hast scattered thine enemies abroad with thy mighty arm.

12 The heavens are thine, the earth also is thine : thou hast laid the foundation of the round world, and all that therein is.

13 Thou hast made the north and the south : Tabor and Hermon shall rejoice in thy Name.

14 Thou hast a mighty arm : strong is thy hand, and high is thy right hand.

16 Thy wrathful displeasure goeth over me, * and the fear of thee hath undone me.
17 They came round about me daily like water, * and compassed me together on every side.
18 My lovers and friends hast thou put away from me, * and hid mine acquaintance out of my sight.

Evening Prayer.

Psalm 89. *Misericordias Domini.*

MY song shall be alway of the loving-kindness of the Lord; * with my mouth will I ever be showing thy truth from one generation to another.
2 For I have said, Mercy shall be set up for ever; * thy truth shalt thou stablish in the heavens.
3 I have made a covenant with my chosen; * I have sworn unto David my servant:
4 Thy seed will I stablish for ever, * and set up thy throne from one generation to another.
5 O Lord, the very heavens shall praise thy wondrous works; * and thy truth in the congregation of the saints.
6 For who is he among the clouds, * that shall be compared unto the Lord?
7 And what is he among the gods, * that shall be like unto the Lord?
8 God is very greatly to be feared in the council of the saints, * and to be had in reverence of all them that are round about him.
9 O Lord God of hosts, who is like unto thee? * thy truth, most mighty Lord, is on every side.
10 Thou rulest the raging of the sea; * thou stillest the waves thereof when they arise.
11 Thou hast subdued Egypt, and destroyed it; * thou hast scattered thine enemies abroad with thy mighty arm.
12 The heavens are thine, the earth also is thine; * thou hast laid the foundation of the round world, and all that therein is.
13 Thou hast made the north and the south; * Tabor and Hermon shall rejoice in thy Name.
14 Thou hast a mighty arm; * strong is thy hand, and high is thy right hand.

16 Ever since my youth, I have been wretched and at the point of death; *
I have borne your terrors with a troubled mind.

17 Your blazing anger has swept over me; *
your terrors have destroyed me;

18 They surround me all day long like a flood; *
they encompass me on every side.

19 My friend and my neighbor you have put away from me, *
and darkness is my only companion.

Seventeenth Day: Evening Prayer

89

Part I *Misericordias Domini*

1 Your love, O Lord, for ever will I sing; *
from age to age my mouth will proclaim your faithfulness.

2 For I am persuaded that your love is established for ever; *
you have set your faithfulness firmly in the heavens.

3 "I have made a covenant with my chosen one; *
I have sworn an oath to David my servant:

4 'I will establish your line for ever, *
and preserve your throne for all generations.'"

5 The heavens bear witness to your wonders, O Lord, *
and to your faithfulness in the assembly of the holy ones;

6 For who in the skies can be compared to the Lord? *
who is like the Lord among the gods?

7 God is much to be feared in the council of the holy ones, *
great and terrible to all those round about him.

8 Who is like you, Lord God of hosts? *
O mighty Lord, your faithfulness is all around you.

9 You rule the raging of the sea *
and still the surging of its waves.

10 You have crushed Rahab of the deep with a deadly wound; *
you have scattered your enemies with your mighty arm.

11 Yours are the heavens; the earth also is yours; *
you laid the foundations of the world and all that is in it.

12 You have made the north and the south; *
Tabor and Hermon rejoice in your Name.

13 You have a mighty arm; *
strong is your hand and high is your right hand.

14 Righteousness and justice are the foundations of your throne; *
love and truth go before your face.

15 Righteousness and equity are the habitation of thy seat; mercy and truth shall go before thy face.

16 Blessed is the people, O LORD, that can rejoice in thee; they shall walk in the light of thy countenance.

17 Their delight shall be daily in thy Name; and in thy righteousness shall they make their boast.

18 For thou art the glory of their strength, and in thy loving-kindness thou shalt lift up our horns.

19 For the LORD is our defence; the Holy One of Israel is our King.

20 Thou spakest sometime in visions unto thy saints, and saidst, I have laid help upon one that is mighty, I have exalted One chosen out of the people.

21 I have found David my servant; with my holy oil have I anointed him.

22 My hand shall hold him fast, and my arm shall strengthen him.

23 The enemy shall not be able to do him violence; the son of wickedness shall not hurt him.

24 I will smite down his foes before his face, and plague them that hate him.

25 My truth also and my mercy shall be with him; and in my Name shall his horn be exalted.

26 I will set his dominion also in the sea, and his right hand in the floods.

27 He shall call me, Thou art my Father, my God, and my strong salvation.

28 And I will make him my First-born, higher than the kings of the earth.

29 My mercy will I keep for him for evermore, and my covenant shall stand fast with him.

30 His seed also will I make to endure for ever, and his throne as the days of heaven.

31 But if his children forsake my law, and walk not in my judgments;

32 If they break my statutes, and keep not my commandments; I will visit their offences with the rod, and their sin with scourges.

33 Nevertheless, my loving-kindness will I not utterly take from him, nor suffer my truth to fail.

34 My covenant will I not break, nor alter the thing that is gone out of my lips: I have sworn once by my holiness, that I will not fail David.

15 Righteousness and equity are the habitation of thy seat: mercy and truth shall go before thy face.

16 Blessed is the people, O LORD, that can rejoice in thee: they shall walk in the light of thy countenance.

17 Their delight shall be daily in thy Name: and in thy righteousness shall they make their boast.

18 For thou art the glory of their strength: and in thy loving-kindness thou shalt lift up our horns.

19 For the LORD is our defence: the Holy One of Israel is our King.

20 Thou spakest sometime in visions unto thy saints, and saidst: I have laid help upon one that is mighty, I have exalted one chosen out of the people.

21 I have found David my servant: with my holy oil have I anointed him.

22 My hand shall hold him fast: and my arm shall strengthen him.

23 The enemy shall not be able to do him violence: the son of wickedness shall not hurt him.

24 I will smite down his foes before his face: and plague them that hate him.

25 My truth also and my mercy shall be with him: and in my Name shall his horn be exalted.

26 I will set his dominion also in the sea: and his right hand in the floods.

27 He shall call me, Thou art my Father: my God, and my strong salvation.

28 And I will make him my firstborn: higher than the kings of the earth.

29 My mercy will I keep for him for evermore: and my covenant shall stand fast with him.

30 His seed also will I make to endure for ever: and his throne as the days of heaven.

31 But if his children forsake my law: and walk not in my judgments;

32 If they break my statutes, and keep not my commandments: I will visit their offences with the rod, and their sin with scourges.

33 Nevertheless, my loving-kindness will I not utterly take from him: nor suffer my truth to fail.

34 My covenant will I not break, nor alter the thing that is gone out of my lips: I have sworn once by my holiness, that I will not fail David.

15 Righteousness and equity are the habitation of
thy seat; * mercy and truth shall go before thy face.
16 Blessed is the people, O LORD, that can rejoice
in thee; * they shall walk in the light of thy countenance.
17 Their delight shall be daily in thy Name; * and
in thy righteousness shall they make their boast.
18 For thou art the glory of their strength, * and in
thy loving-kindness thou shalt lift up our horns.
19 For the LORD is our defence; * the Holy One of
Israel is our King.
20 Thou spakest sometime in visions unto thy
saints, and saidst, * I have laid help upon one that is
mighty, I have exalted one chosen out of the people.
21 I have found David my servant; * with my holy
oil have I anointed him.
22 My hand shall hold him fast, * and my arm shall
strengthen him.
23 The enemy shall not be able to do him
violence; * the son of wickedness shall not hurt him.
24 I will smite down his foes before his face, * and
plague them that hate him.
25 My truth also and my mercy shall be with him; *
and in my Name shall his horn be exalted.
26 I will set his dominion also in the sea, * and his
right hand in the floods.
27 He shall call me, Thou art my Father, * my
God, and my strong salvation.
28 And I will make him my firstborn, * higher than
the kings of the earth.
29 My mercy will I keep for him for evermore, *
and my covenant shall stand fast with him.
30 His seed also will I make to endure for ever, *
and his throne as the days of heaven.
31 But if his children forsake my law, * and walk
not in my judgments;
32 If they break my statutes, and keep not my
commandments; * I will visit their offences with the
rod, and their sin with scourges.
33 Nevertheless, my loving-kindness will I not
utterly take from him, * nor suffer my truth to fail.
34 My covenant will I not break, nor alter the thing
that is gone out of my lips: * I have sworn once by my
holiness, that I will not fail David.

15 Happy are the people who know the festal shout! *
they walk, O LORD, in the light of your presence.

16 They rejoice daily in your Name; *
they are jubilant in your righteousness.

17 For you are the glory of their strength, *
and by your favor our might is exalted.

18 Truly, the LORD is our ruler; *
the Holy One of Israel is our King.

Psalm 89: Part II *Tunc locutus es*

19 You spoke once in a vision and said to your faithful people: *
"I have set the crown upon a warrior
and have exalted one chosen out of the people.

20 I have found David my servant; *
with my holy oil have I anointed him.

21 My hand will hold him fast *
and my arm will make him strong.

22 No enemy shall deceive him, *
nor any wicked man bring him down.

23 I will crush his foes before him *
and strike down those who hate him.

24 My faithfulness and love shall be with him, *
and he shall be victorious through my Name.

25 I shall make his dominion extend *
from the Great Sea to the River.

26 He will say to me, 'You are my Father, *
my God, and the rock of my salvation.'

27 I will make him my firstborn *
and higher than the kings of the earth.

28 I will keep my love for him for ever, *
and my covenant will stand firm for him.

29 I will establish his line for ever *
and his throne as the days of heaven."

30 "If his children forsake my law *
and do not walk according to my judgments;

31 If they break my statutes *
and do not keep my commandments;

32 I will punish their transgressions with a rod *
and their iniquities with the lash;

33 But I will not take my love from him, *
nor let my faithfulness prove false.

34 I will not break my covenant, *
nor change what has gone out of my lips.

1789-1871

35 His seed shall endure for ever, and his seat is like as the sun before me.

36 He shall stand fast for evermore as the moon, and as the faithful witness in heaven.

37 But thou hast abhorred and forsaken thine Anointed, and art displeased at him.

38 Thou hast broken the covenant of thy servant, and cast his crown to the ground.

39 Thou hast overthrown all his hedges, and broken down his strongholds.

40 All they that go by spoil him, and he is become a reproach to his neighbours.

41 Thou hast set up the right hand of his enemies, and made all his adversaries to rejoice.

42 Thou hast taken away the edge of his sword, and givest him not victory in the battle.

43 Thou hast put out his glory, and cast his throne down to the ground.

44 The days of his youth hast thou shortened, and covered him with dishonour.

45 LORD, how long wilt thou hide thyself? for ever? and shall thy wrath burn like fire?

46 O remember how short my time is ; wherefore hast thou made all men for nought?

47 What man is he that liveth, and shall not see death? and shall he deliver his soul from the hand of hell?

48 Lord, where are thy old loving-kindnesses, which thou swarest unto David in thy truth?

49 Remember, Lord, the rebuke that thy servants have, and how I do bear in my bosom the rebukes of many people ;

50 Wherewith thine enemies have blasphemed thee, and slandered the footsteps of thine Anointed. Praised be the LORD for evermore. Amen, and Amen.

1892

35 His seed shall endure for ever : and his seat is like as the sun before me.

36 He shall stand fast for evermore as the moon : and as the faithful witness in heaven.

37 But thou hast abhorred and forsaken thine anointed : and art displeased at him.

38 Thou hast broken the covenant of thy servant : and cast his crown to the ground.

39 Thou hast overthrown all his hedges : and broken down his strongholds.

40 All they that go by spoil him : and he is become a reproach to his neighbours.

41 Thou hast set up the right hand of his enemies : and made all his adversaries to rejoice.

42 Thou hast taken away the edge of his sword : and givest him not victory in the battle.

43 Thou hast put out his glory : and cast his throne down to the ground.

44 The days of his youth hast thou shortened : and covered him with dishonour.

45 LORD, how long will thou hide thyself, for ever : and shall thy wrath burn like fire?

46 O remember how short my time is : wherefore hast thou made all men for nought?

47 What man is he that liveth, and shall not see death : and shall he deliver his soul from the land of hell?

48 Lord, where are thy old loving-kindnesses : which thou swarest unto David in thy truth?

49 Remember, Lord, the rebuke that thy servants have : and how I do bear in my bosom the rebukes of many people ;

50 Wherewith thine enemies have blasphemed thee, and slandered the footsteps of thine anointed : Praised be the LORD for evermore. Amen, and Amen.

1928

35 His seed shall endure for ever, * and his throne is like as the sun before me.

36 He shall stand fast for evermore as the moon, * and as the faithful witness in heaven.

37 But thou hast abhorred and forsaken thine anointed, * and art displeased at him.

38 Thou hast broken the covenant of thy servant, * and cast his crown to the ground.

39 Thou hast overthrown all his hedges, * and broken down his strongholds.

40 All they that go by spoil him, * and he is become a reproach to his neighbours.

41 Thou hast set up the right hand of his enemies, * and made all his adversaries to rejoice.

42 Thou hast taken away the edge of his sword, * and givest him not victory in the battle.

43 Thou hast put out his glory, * and cast his throne down to the ground.

44 The days of his youth hast thou shortened, * and covered him with dishonour.

45 LORD, how long wilt thou hide thyself? for ever? * and shall thy wrath burn like fire?

46 O remember how short my time is; * wherefore hast thou made all men for nought?

47 What man is he that liveth, and shall not see death? * and shall he deliver his soul from the power of the grave?

48 Lord, where are thy old loving-kindnesses, * which thou swarest unto David in thy truth?

49 Remember, Lord, the rebuke that thy servants have, * and how I do bear in my bosom the rebukes of many people;

50 Wherewith thine enemies have blasphemed thee, * and slandered the footsteps of thine anointed.

51 Praised be the LORD for evermore. * Amen, and Amen.

1979

35 Once for all I have sworn by my holiness: *
'I will not lie to David.

36 His line shall endure for ever *
and his throne as the sun before me;

37 It shall stand fast for evermore like the moon, *
the abiding witness in the sky.'"

38 But you have cast off and rejected your anointed; *
you have become enraged at him.

39 You have broken your covenant with your servant, *
defiled his crown, and hurled it to the ground.

40 You have breached all his walls *
and laid his strongholds in ruins.

41 All who pass by despoil him; *
he has become the scorn of his neighbors.

42 You have exalted the right hand of his foes *
and made all his enemies rejoice.

43 You have turned back the edge of his sword *
and have not sustained him in battle.

44 You have put an end to his splendor *
and cast his throne to the ground.

45 You have cut short the days of his youth *
and have covered him with shame.

46 How long will you hide yourself, O LORD?
will you hide yourself for ever? *
how long will your anger burn like fire?

47 Remember, LORD, how short life is, *
how frail you have made all flesh.

48 Who can live and not see death? *
who can save himself from the power of the grave?

49 Where, Lord, are your loving-kindnesses of old, *
which you promised David in your faithfulness?

50 Remember, Lord, how your servant is mocked, *
how I carry in my bosom the taunts of many peoples,

51 The taunts your enemies have hurled, O LORD, *
which they hurled at the heels of your anointed.

52 Blessed be the LORD for evermore! *
Amen, I say, Amen.

THE EIGHTEENTH DAY.

Morning Prayer.

Psalm xc. *Domine, refugium.*

LORD, thou hast been our refuge, from one generation to another.

2 Before the mountains were brought forth, or ever the earth and the world were made, thou art God from everlasting, and world without end.

3 Thou turnest man to destruction ; again thou sayest, Come again, ye children of men.

4 For a thousand years in thy sight are but as yesterday ; seeing that is past, and as a watch in the night.

5 As soon as thou scatterest them they are even as a sleep ; and fade away suddenly like the grass.

6 In the morning it is green, and groweth up ; but in the evening it is cut down, dried up, and withered.

7 For we consume away in thy displeasure, and are afraid at thy wrathful indignation.

8 Thou hast set our misdeeds before thee ; and our secret sins in the light of thy countenance.

9 For when thou art angry all our days are gone : we bring our years to an end, as it were a tale that is told.

10 The days of our age are threescore years and ten ; and though men be so strong that they come to fourscore years, yet is their strength then but labour and sorrow ; so soon passeth it away, and we are gone.

11 But who regardeth the power of thy wrath? for even thereafter as a man feareth, so is thy displeasure.

12 So teach us to number our days, that we may apply our hearts unto wisdom.

13 Turn thee again, O LORD, at the last, and be gracious unto thy servants.

14 O satisfy us with thy mercy, and that soon : so shall we rejoice and be glad all the days of our life.

15 Comfort us again now after the time that thou hast plagued us ; and for the years wherein we have suffered adversity.

16 Show thy servants thy work, and their children thy glory.

17 And the glorious Majesty of the LORD our God be upon us : prosper thou the work of our hands upon us ; O prosper thou our handy-work.

THE EIGHTEENTH DAY.

Morning Prayer.

PSALM 90. *Domine, refugium.*

LORD, thou hast been our refuge : from one generation to another.

2 Before the mountains were brought forth, or ever the earth and the world were made : thou art God from everlasting, and world without end.

3 Thou turnest man to destruction : again thou sayest, Come again, ye children of men.

4 For a thousand years in thy sight are but as yesterday : seeing that is past as a watch in the night.

5 As soon as thou scatterest them they are even as a sleep : and fade away suddenly like the grass.

6 In the morning it is green, and groweth up : but in the evening it is cut down, dried up, and withered.

7 For we consume away in thy displeasure : and are afraid at thy wrathful indignation.

8 Thou hast set our misdeeds before thee : and our secret sins in the light of thy countenance.

9 For when thou art angry all our days are gone : we bring our years to an end, as it were a tale that is told.

10 The days of our age are threescore years and ten ; and though men be so strong that they come to fourscore years : yet is their strength then but labour and sorrow ; so soon passeth it away, and we are gone.

11 But who regardeth the power of thy wrath : for even thereafter as a man feareth, so is thy displeasure.

12 O teach us to number our days : that we may apply our hearts unto wisdom.

13 Turn thee again, O LORD, at the last : and be gracious unto thy servants.

14 O satisfy us with thy mercy, and that soon : so shall we rejoice and be glad all the days of our life.

15 Comfort us again now after the time that thou hast plagued us : and for the years wherein we have suffered adversity.

16 Show thy servants thy work : and their children thy glory.

17 And the glorious majesty of the LORD our God be upon us : prosper thou the work of our hands upon us ; O prosper thou our handy-work.

BOOK IV.

The Eighteenth Day.

Morning Prayer.

Psalm 90. *Domine, refugium.*

LORD, thou hast been our refuge, * from one generation to another.

2 Before the mountains were brought forth, or ever the earth and the world were made, * thou art God from everlasting, and world without end.

3 Thou turnest man to destruction; * again thou sayest, Come again, ye children of men.

4 For a thousand years in thy sight are but as yesterday when it is past, * and as a watch in the night.

5 As soon as thou scatterest them they are even as a sleep; * and fade away suddenly like the grass.

6 In the morning it is green, and groweth up; * but in the evening it is cut down, dried up, and withered.

7 For we consume away in thy displeasure, * and are afraid at thy wrathful indignation.

8 Thou hast set our misdeeds before thee; * and our secret sins in the light of thy countenance.

9 For when thou art angry all our days are gone: * we bring our years to an end, as it were a tale that is told.

10 The days of our age are threescore years and ten; and though men be so strong that they come to fourscore years, * yet is their strength then but labour and sorrow; so soon passeth it away, and we are gone.

11 But who regarded the power of thy wrath? * or feareth aright thy indignation?

12 So teach us to number our days, * that we may apply our hearts unto wisdom.

13 Turn thee again, O LORD, at the last, * and be gracious unto thy servants.

14 O satisfy us with thy mercy, and that soon: * so shall we rejoice and be glad all the days of our life.

15 Comfort us again now after the time that thou hast plagued us; * and for the years wherein we have suffered adversity.

16 Show thy servants thy work, * and their children thy glory.

17 And the glorious majesty of the LORD our God be upon us: * prosper thou the work of our hands upon us; O prosper thou our handy-work.

Book Four

Eighteenth Day: Morning Prayer

90 *Domine, refugium*

1 Lord, you have been our refuge *
from one generation to another.

2 Before the mountains were brought forth,
or the land and the earth were born, *
from age to age you are God.

3 You turn us back to the dust and say, *
"Go back, O child of earth."

4 For a thousand years in your sight are like yesterday
when it is past *
and like a watch in the night.

5 You sweep us away like a dream; *
we fade away suddenly like the grass.

6 In the morning it is green and flourishes; *
in the evening it is dried up and withered.

7 For we consume away in your displeasure; *
we are afraid because of your wrathful indignation.

8 Our iniquities you have set before you, *
and our secret sins in the light of your countenance.

9 When you are angry, all our days are gone; *
we bring our years to an end like a sigh.

10 The span of our life is seventy years,
perhaps in strength even eighty; *
yet the sum of them is but labor and sorrow,
for they pass away quickly and we are gone.

11 Who regards the power of your wrath? *
who rightly fears your indignation?

12 So teach us to number our days *
that we may apply our hearts to wisdom.

13 Return, O LORD; how long will you tarry? *
be gracious to your servants.

14 Satisfy us by your loving-kindness in the morning; *
so shall we rejoice and be glad all the days of our life.

15 Make us glad by the measure of the days that you afflicted us *
and the years in which we suffered adversity.

16 Show your servant your works *
and your splendor to their children.

17 May the graciousness of the LORD our God be upon us; *
prosper the work of our hands;
prosper our handiwork.

Psalm xci. *Qui habitat.*

WHOSO dwelleth under the defence of the Most High, shall abide under the shadow of the Almighty.

2 I will say unto the LORD, Thou art my hope, and my stronghold ; my God, in him will I trust.

3 For he shall deliver thee from the snare of the hunter, and from the noisome pestilence.

4 He shall defend thee under his wings, and thou shalt be safe under his feathers ; his faithfulness and truth shall be thy shield and buckler.

5 Thou shalt not be afraid for any terror by night, nor for the arrow that flieth by day ;

6 For the pestilence that walketh in darkness, nor for the sickness that destroyeth in the noon-day.

7 A thousand shall fall beside thee, and ten thousand at thy right hand ; but it shall not come nigh thee.

8 Yea, with thine eyes shalt thou behold, and see the reward of the ungodly.

9 For thou, LORD, art my hope ; thou hast set thine house of defence very high.

10 There shall no evil happen unto thee, neither shall any plague come nigh thy dwelling.

11 For he shall give his angels charge over thee, to keep thee in all thy ways.

12 They shall bear thee in their hands, that thou hurt not thy foot against a stone.

13 Thou shalt go upon the lion and adder : the young lion and the dragon shalt thou tread under thy feet.

14 Because he hath set his love upon me, therefore will I deliver him ; I will set him up, because he hath known my Name.

15 He shall call upon me, and I will hear him ; yea, I am with him in trouble ; I will deliver him, and bring him to honour.

16 With long life will I satisfy him, and show him my salvation.

PSALM 91. *Qui habitat.*

WHOSO dwelleth under the defence of the Most High : shall abide under the shadow of the Almighty.

2 I will say unto the LORD, Thou art my hope, and my stronghold : my God, in him will I trust.

3 For he shall deliver thee from the snare of the hunter : and from the noisome pestilence.

4 He shall defend thee under his wings, and thou shalt be safe under his feathers : his faithfulness and truth shall be thy shield and buckler.

5 Thou shalt not be afraid for any terror by night : nor for the arrow that flieth by day ;

6 For the pestilence that walketh in darkness : nor for the sickness that destroyeth in the noon-day.

7 A thousand shall fall beside thee, and ten thousand at thy right hand : but it shall not come nigh thee.

8 Yea, with thine eyes shalt thou behold : and see the reward of the ungodly.

9 For thou, LORD, art my hope : thou hast set thine house of defence very high.

10 There shall no evil happen unto thee : neither shall any plague come nigh thy dwelling.

11 For he shall give his angels charge over thee : to keep thee in all thy ways.

12 They shall bear thee in their hands : that thou hurt not thy foot against a stone.

13 Thou shalt go upon the lion and adder : the young lion and the dragon shalt thou tread under thy feet.

14 Because he hath set his love upon me, therefore will I deliver him : I will set him up, because he hath known my Name.

15 He shall call upon me, and I will hear him : yea, I am with him in trouble ; I will deliver him, and bring him to honour.

16 With long life will I satisfy him : and show him my salvation.

Psalm 91. *Qui habitat.*

WHOSO dwelleth under the defence of the Most High, * shall abide under the shadow of the Almighty.

2 I will say unto the LORD, Thou art my hope, and my stronghold; * my God, in him will I trust.

3 For he shall deliver thee from the snare of the hunter, * and from the noisome pestilence.

4 He shall defend thee under his wings, and thou shalt be safe under his feathers; * his faithfulness and truth shall be thy shield and buckler.

5 Thou shalt not be afraid for any terror by night, * nor for the arrow that flieth by day;

6 For the pestilence that walketh in darkness, * nor for the sickness that destroyeth in the noon-day.

7 A thousand shall fall beside thee, and ten thousand at thy right hand; * but it shall not come nigh thee.

8 Yea, with thine eyes shalt thou behold, * and see the reward of the ungodly.

9 For thou, LORD, art my hope; * thou hast set thine house of defence very high.

10 There shall no evil happen unto thee, * neither shall any plague come nigh thy dwelling.

11 For he shall give his angels charge over thee, * to keep thee in all thy ways.

12 They shall bear thee in their hands, * that thou hurt not thy foot against a stone.

13 Thou shalt go upon the lion and adder: * the young lion and the dragon shalt thou tread under thy feet.

14 Because he hath set his love upon me, therefore will I deliver him; * I will set him up, because he hath known my Name.

15 He shall call upon me, and I will hear him; * yea, I am with him in trouble; I will deliver him, and bring him to honour.

16 With long life will I satisfy him, * and show him my salvation.

91 *Qui habitat*

1 He who dwells in the shelter of the Most High, *
abides under the shadow of the Almighty.

2 He shall say to the LORD,
"You are my refuge and my stronghold, *
my God in whom I put my trust."

3 He shall deliver you from the snare of the hunter *
and from the deadly pestilence.

4 He shall cover you with his pinions,
and you shall find refuge under his wings; *
his faithfulness shall be a shield and buckler.

5 You shall not be afraid of any terror by night, *
nor of the arrow that flies by day;

6 Of the plague that stalks in the darkness, *
nor of the sickness that lays waste at mid-day.

7 A thousand shall fall at your side
and ten thousand at your right hand, *
but it shall not come near you.

8 Your eyes have only to behold *
to see the reward of the wicked.

9 Because you have made the LORD your refuge, *
and the Most High your habitation,

10 There shall no evil happen to you, *
neither shall any plague come near your dwelling.

11 For he shall give his angels charge over you, *
to keep you in all your ways.

12 They shall bear you in their hands, *
lest you dash your foot against a stone.

13 You shall tread upon the lion and adder; *
you shall trample the young lion and the serpent under your feet.

14 Because he is bound to me in love,
therefore will I deliver him; *
I will protect him, because he knows my Name.

15 He shall call upon me, and I will answer him; *
I am with him in trouble;
I will rescue him and bring him to honor.

16 With long life will I satisfy him, *
and show him my salvation.

Psalm xcii. *Bonum est confiteri.*

IT is a good thing to give thanks unto the LORD, and to sing praises unto thy Name, O Most Highest ;

2 To tell of thy loving-kindness early in the morning, and of thy truth in the night season ;

3 Upon an instrument of ten strings, and upon the lute ; upon a loud instrument, and upon the harp.

4 For thou, LORD, hast made me glad through thy works ; and I will rejoice in giving praise for the operations of thy hands.

5 O LORD, how glorious are thy works! thy thoughts are very deep.

6 An unwise man doth not well consider this, and a fool doth not understand it.

7 When the ungodly are green as the grass, and when all the workers of wickedness do flourish, then shall they be destroyed for ever ; but thou, LORD, art the Most Highest for evermore.

8 For lo, thine enemies, O LORD, lo, thine enemies shall perish ; and all the workers of wickedness shall be destroyed.

9 But my horn shall be exalted like the horn of an unicorn ; for I am anointed with fresh oil.

10 Mine eye also shall see his lust of mine enemies, and mine ear shall hear his desire of the wicked that arise up against me.

11 The righteous shall flourish like a palm-tree, and shall spread abroad like a cedar in Libanus.

12 Such as are planted in the house of the LORD, shall flourish in the courts of the house of our God.

13 They also shall bring forth more fruit in their age, and shall be fat and well-liking ;

14 That they may show how true the LORD my strength is, and that there is no unrighteousness in him.

Evening Prayer.

Psalm xciii. *Dominus regnavit.*

THE LORD is King, and hath put on glorious apparel ; the LORD hath put on his apparel, and girded himself with strength.

2 He hath made the round world so sure, that it cannot be moved.

PSALM 92. *Bonum est confiteri.*

IT is a good thing to give thanks unto the LORD : and to sing praises unto thy Name, O Most Highest ;

2 To tell of thy loving-kindness early in the morning : and of thy truth in the night season ;

3 Upon an instrument of ten strings, and upon the lute : upon a loud instrument, and upon the harp.

4 For thou, LORD, hast made me glad through thy works : and I will rejoice in giving praise for the operations of thy hands.

5 O LORD, how glorious are thy works : thy thoughts are very deep.

6 An unwise man doth not well consider this : and a fool doth not understand it.

7 When the ungodly are green as the grass, and when all the workers of wickedness do flourish : then shall they be destroyed for ever ; but thou, LORD, art the most Highest for evermore.

8 For lo, thine enemies, O LORD, lo, thine enemies shall perish : and all the workers of wickedness shall be destroyed.

9 But my horn shall be exalted like the horn of an unicorn : for I am anointed with fresh oil.

10 Mine eye also shall see his lust of mine enemies : and mine ear shall hear his desire of the wicked that arise up against me.

11 The righteous shall flourish like a palm-tree : and shall spread abroad like a cedar in Libanus.

12 Such as are planted in the house of the LORD : shall flourish in the courts of the house of our God.

13 They also shall bring forth more fruit in their age : and shall be fat and well-liking ;

14 That they may show how true the LORD my strength is : and that there is no unrighteousness in him.

Evening Prayer.

PSALM 93. *Dominus regnavit.*

THE LORD is King, and hath put on glorious apparel : the LORD hath put on his apparel, and girded himself with strength.

2 He hath made the round world so sure : that it cannot be moved.

1928

Psalm 92. *Bonum est confiteri.*

IT is a good thing to give thanks unto the LORD, * and to sing praises unto thy Name, O Most Highest;

2 To tell of thy loving-kindness early in the morning, * and of thy truth in the night season;

3 Upon an instrument of ten strings, and upon the lute; * upon a loud instrument, and upon the harp.

4 For thou, LORD, hast made me glad through thy works; * and I will rejoice in giving praise for the operations of thy hands.

5 O LORD, how glorious are thy works! * thy thoughts are very deep.

6 An unwise man doth not well consider this, * and a fool doth not understand it.

7 When the ungodly are green as the grass, and when all the workers of wickedness do flourish, * then shall they be destroyed for ever; but thou, LORD, art the Most Highest for evermore.

8 For lo, thine enemies, O LORD, lo, thine enemies shall perish; * and all the workers of wickedness shall be destroyed.

9 But my horn shall be exalted like the horn of an unicorn; * for I am anointed with fresh oil.

10 Mine eye also shall see his lust of mine enemies, * and mine ear shall hear his desire of the wicked that arise up against me.

11 The righteous shall flourish like a palm-tree, * and shall spread abroad like a cedar in Lebanon.

12 Such as are planted in the house of the LORD, * shall flourish in the courts of the house of our God.

13 They also shall bring forth more fruit in their age, * and shall be fat and well-liking;

14 That they may show how true the LORD my strength is, * and that there is no unrighteousness in him.

Evening Prayer.

Psalm 93. *Dominus regnavit.*

THE LORD is King, and hath put on glorious apparel; * the LORD hath put on his apparel, and girded himself with strength.

2 He hath made the round world so sure, * that it cannot be moved.

1979

92 *Bonum est confiteri*

1 It is a good thing to give thanks to the LORD, *
and to sing praises to your Name, O Most High;

2 To tell of your loving-kindness early in the morning *
and of your faithfulness in the night season;

3 On the psaltery, and on the lyre, *
and to the melody of the harp.

4 For you have made me glad by your acts, O LORD; *
and I shout for joy because of the works of your hands.

5 LORD, how great are your works! *
your thoughts are very deep.

6 The dullard does not know,
nor does the fool understand, *
that though the wicked grow like weeds,
and all the workers of iniquity flourish,

7 They flourish only to be destroyed for ever; *
but you, O LORD, are exalted for evermore.

8 For lo, your enemies, O LORD,
lo, your enemies shall perish, *
and all the workers of iniquity shall be scattered.

9 But my horn you have exalted like the horns of wild bulls; *
I am anointed with fresh oil.

10 My eyes also gloat over my enemies, *
and my ears rejoice to hear the doom of the wicked who rise up against me.

11 The righteous shall flourish like a palm tree, *
and shall spread abroad like a cedar of Lebanon.

12 Those who are planted in the house of the LORD *
shall flourish in the courts of our God;

13 They shall sill bear fruit in old age; *
they shall be green and succulent;

14 That they may show how upright the LORD is, *
my Rock, in whom there is no fault.

Eighteenth Day: Evening Prayer

93 *Dominus regnavit*

1 The LORD is King;
he has put on splendid apparel; *
the LORD has put on his apparel
and girded himself with strength.

2 He has made the whole world so sure *
that it cannot be moved;

3 Ever since the world began hath thy seat been prepared : thou art from everlasting.

4 The floods are risen, O LORD, the floods have lift up their voice ; the floods lift up their waves.

5 The waves of the sea are mighty, and rage horribly ; but yet the LORD, who dwelleth on high, is mightier.

6 Thy testimonies, O LORD, are very sure : holiness becometh thine house for ever.

3 Ever since the world began, hath thy seat been prepared : thou art from everlasting.

4 The floods are risen, O LORD, the floods have lift up their voice : the floods lift up their waves.

5 The waves of the sea are mighty, and rage horribly : but yet the LORD, who dwelleth on high, is mightier.

6 Thy testimonies, O LORD, are very sure : holiness becometh thine house for ever.

Psalm xciv. *Deus ultionum.*

O LORD God, to whom vengeance belongeth, thou God, to whom vengeance belongeth, show thyself.

2 Arise, thou Judge of the world, and reward the proud after their deserving.

3 LORD, how long shall the ungodly, how long shall the ungodly triumph?

4 How long shall all wicked doers speak so disdainfully, and make such proud boasting?

5 They smite down thy people, O LORD, and trouble thine heritage.

6 They murder the widow and the stranger, and put the fatherless to death.

7 And yet they say, Tush, the LORD shall not see, neither shall the God of Jacob regard it.

8 Take heed, ye unwise among the people : O ye fools, when will ye understand?

9 He that planted the ear, shall he not hear? or he that made the eye, shall he not see?

10 Or he that nurtureth the heathen, it is he that teacheth man knowledge ; shall not he punish?

11 The LORD knoweth the thoughts of man, that they are but vain.

12 Blessed is the man whom thou chastenest, O LORD, and teachest him in thy law ;

13 That thou mayest give him patience in time of adversity, until the pit be digged up for the ungodly.

14 For the LORD will not fail his people ; neither will he forsake his inheritance.

15 Until righteousness turn again unto judgment : all such as are true in heart shall follow it.

PSALM 94. *Deus ultionum.*

O LORD God, to whom vengeance belongeth : thou God, to whom vengeance belongeth, show thyself.

2 Arise, thou Judge of the world : and reward the proud after their deserving.

3 LORD, how long shall the ungodly : how long shall the ungodly triumph?

4 How long shall all wicked doers speak so disdainfully : and make such proud boasting?

5 They smite down thy people, O LORD : and trouble thine heritage.

6 They murder the widow and the stranger : and put the fatherless to death.

7 And yet they say, Tush, the LORD shall not see : neither shall the God of Jacob regard it.

8 Take heed, ye unwise among the people : O ye fools, when will ye understand?

9 He that planted the ear, shall he not hear? : or he that made the eye, shall he not see?

10 Or he that nurtureth the heathen : it is he that teacheth man knowledge ; shall not he punish?

11 The LORD knoweth the thoughts of man : that they are but vain.

12 Blessed is the man whom thou chastenest, O LORD : and teachest him in thy law ;

13 That thou mayest give him patience in time of adversity : until the pit be digged up for the ungodly.

14 For the LORD will not fail his people : neither will he forsake his inheritance.

15 Until righteousness turn again unto judgment : all such as are true in heart shall follow it.

1928

3 Ever since the world began, hath thy seat been prepared: * thou art from everlasting.

4 The floods are risen, O LORD, the floods have lift up their voice; * the floods lift up their waves.

5 The waves of the sea are mighty, and rage horribly; * but yet the LORD, who dwelleth on high, is mightier.

6 Thy testimonies, O LORD, are very sure: * holiness becometh thine house for ever.

1979

3 Ever since the world began, your throne has been established; *
you are from everlasting.

4 The waters have lifted up, O LORD,
the waters have lifted up their voice; *
the waters have lifted up their pounding waves.

5 Mightier than the sound of many waters,
mightier than the breakers of the sea, *
mightier is the LORD who dwells on high.

6 Your testimonies are very sure, *
and holiness adorns your house, O LORD
for ever and for evermore.

1928

Psalm 94. *Deus ultionum.*

O LORD God, to whom vengeance belongeth, * thou God, to whom vengeance belongeth, show thyself.

2 Arise, thou Judge of the world, * and reward the proud after their deserving.

3 LORD, how long shall the ungodly, * how long shall the ungodly triumph?

4 How long shall all wicked doers speak so disdainfully, * and make such proud boasting?

5 They smite down thy people, O LORD, * and trouble thine heritage.

6 They murder the widow and the stranger, * and put the fatherless to death.

7 And yet they say, Tush, the LORD shall not see, * neither shall the God of Jacob regard it.

8 Take heed, ye unwise among the people: * O ye fools, when will ye understand?

9 He that planted the ear, shall he not hear? * or he that made the eye, shall he not see?

10 Or he that instructeth the heathen, * it is he that teacheth man knowledge; shall not he punish?

11 The LORD knoweth the thoughts of man, * that they are but vain.

12 Blessed is the man whom thou chastenest, O LORD, * and teachest him in thy law;

13 That thou mayest give him patience in time of adversity, * until the pit be digged up for the ungodly.

14 For the LORD will not fail his people; * neither will he forsake his inheritance;

15 Until righteousness turn again unto judgment: * all such as are true in heart shall follow it.

1979

94 *Deus ultionum*

1 O LORD God of vengeance, *
O God of vengeance, show yourself.

2 Rise up, O Judge of the world; *
give the arrogant their just deserts.

3 How long shall the wicked, O LORD, *
how long shall the wicked triumph?

4 They bluster in their insolence; *
all evildoers are full of boasting.

5 They crush your people, O LORD, *
and afflict your chosen nation.

6 They murder the widow and the stranger *
and put the orphans to death.

7 Yet they say, "The LORD does not see, *
the God of Jacob takes no notice."

8 Consider well, you dullards among the people; *
when will you fools understand?

9 He that planted the ear, does he not hear? *
he that formed the eye, does he not see?

10 He who admonishes the nations, will he not punish? *
he who teaches all the world, has he no knowledge?

11 The LORD knows our human thoughts; *
how like a puff of wind they are.

12 Happy are they whom you instruct, O Lord! *
whom you teach out of your law;

13 To give them rest in evil days, *
until a pit is dug for the wicked.

14 For the LORD will not abandon his people, *
nor will he forsake his own.

15 For judgment will again be just, *
and all the true of heart will follow it.

1789-1871

16 Who will rise up with me against the wicked? or who will take my part against the evil doers?
17 If the LORD had not helped me, it had not failed, but my soul had been put to silence.
18 But when I said, My foot hath slipped; thy mercy, O LORD, held me up.
19 In the multitude of the sorrows that I had in my heart, thy comforts have refreshed my soul.
20 Wilt thou have any thing to do with the stool of wickedness, which imagineth mischief as a law?
21 They gather them together against the soul of the righteous, and condemn the innocent blood.
22 But the LORD is my refuge, and my God is the strength of my confidence.
23 He shall recompense them their wickedness, and destroy them in their own malice; yea, the LORD our God shall destroy them.

THE NINETEENTH DAY.

Morning Prayer.

Psalm xcv. *Venite, exultemus.*

O COME, let us sing unto the LORD; let us heartily rejoice in the strength of our salvation.
2 Let us come before his presence with thanksgiving; and show ourselves glad in him with psalms.
3 For the LORD is a great God; and a great King above all gods.
4 In his hand are all the corners of the earth; and the strength of the hills is his also.
5 The sea is his, and he made it; and his hands prepared the dry land.
6 O come, let us worship and fall down, and kneel before the LORD our Maker.
7 For he is the Lord our God; and we are the people of his pasture, and the sheep of his hand.
8 To-day if ye will hear his voice, harden not your hearts as in the provocation, and as in the day of temptation in the wilderness;
9 When your fathers tempted me, proved me, and saw my works.

1892

16 Who will rise up with me against the wicked: or who will take my part against the evil doers?
17 If the LORD had not helped me: it had not failed, but my soul had been put to silence.
18 But when I said, My foot hath slipt: thy mercy, O LORD, held me up.
19 In the multitude of the sorrows that I had in my heart: thy comforts have refreshed my soul.
20 Wilt thou have any thing to do with the stool of wickedness: which imagineth mischief as a law?
21 They gather them together against the soul of the righteous: and condemn the innocent blood.
22 But the LORD is my refuge: and my God is the strength of my confidence.
23 He shall recompense them their wickedness, and destroy them in their own malice: yea, the LORD our God shall destroy them.

THE NINETEENTH DAY.

Morning Prayer.

PSALM 95. *Venite, exultemus.*

O COME, let us sing unto the LORD: let us heartily rejoice in the strength of our salvation.
2 Let us come before his presence with thanksgiving: and show ourselves glad in him with psalms.
3 For the LORD is a great God: and a great King above all gods.
4 In his hand are all the corners of the earth: and the strength of the hills is his also.
5 The sea is his, and he made it: and his hands prepared the dry land.
6 O come, let us worship and fall down: and kneel before the LORD our Maker.
7 For he is the Lord our God: and we are the people of his pasture, and the sheep of his hand.
8 To-day if ye will hear his voice, harden not your hearts: as in the provocation, and as in the day of temptation in the wilderness;
9 When your fathers tempted me: proved me, and saw my works.

1928

16 Who will rise up with me against the wicked? * or who will take my part against the evil doers?

17 If the LORD had not helped me, * it had not failed, but my soul had been put to silence.

18 But when I said, My foot hath slipt; * thy mercy, O LORD, held me up.

19 In the multitude of the sorrows that I had in my heart, * thy comforts have refreshed my soul.

20 Wilt thou have any thing to do with the throne of wickedness, * which imagineth mischief as a law?

21 They gather them together against the soul of the righteous, * and condemn the innocent blood.

22 But the LORD is my refuge, * and my God is the strength of my confidence.

23 He shall recompense them their wickedness, and destroy them in their own malice; * yea, the LORD our God shall destroy them.

The Nineteenth Day.

Morning Prayer.

Psalm 95. *Venite, exultemus.*

O COME, let us sing unto the LORD; * let us heartily rejoice in the strength of our salvation.

2 Let us come before his presence with thanksgiving; * and show ourselves glad in him with psalms.

3 For the LORD is a great God; * and a great King above all gods.

4 In his hand are all the corners of the earth; * and the strength of the hills is his also.

5 The sea is his, and he made it; * and his hands prepared the dry land.

6 O come, let us worship and fall down, * and kneel before the LORD our Maker.

7 For he is the Lord our God; * and we are the people of his pasture, and the sheep of his hand.

8 To-day if ye will hear his voice, harden not your hearts * as in the provocation, and as in the day of temptation in the wilderness;

9 When your fathers tempted me, * proved me, and saw my works.

1979

16 Who rose up for me against the wicked? *
who took my part against the evildoers?

17 If the LORD had not come to my help, *
I should soon have dwelt in the land of silence.

18 As often as I said, "My foot has slipped," *
your love, O LORD, upheld me.

19 When many cares fill my mind, *
your consolations cheer my soul.

20 Can a corrupt tribunal have any part with you, *
one which frames evil into law?

21 They conspire against the life of the just *
and condemn the innocent to death.

22 But the LORD has become my stronghold, *
and my God the rock of my trust.

23 He will turn their wickedness back upon them
and destroy them in their own malice; *
the LORD our God will destroy them.

Nineteenth Day: Morning Prayer

95 *Venite, exultemus*

1 Come, let us sing to the LORD; *
let us shout for joy to the Rock of our salvation.

2 Let us come before his presence with thanksgiving *
and raise a loud shout to him with psalms.

3 For the LORD is a great God, *
and a great King above all gods.

4 In his hand are the caverns of the earth, *
and the heights of the hills are his also.

5 The sea is his, for he made it, *
and his hands have molded the dry land.

6 Come, let us bow down, and bend the knee, *
and kneel before the LORD our Maker.

7 For he is our God,
and we are people of his pasture and the sheep of his hand. *
Oh, that today you would hearken to his voice!

8 Harden not your hearts,
as your forebears did in the wilderness, *
at Meribah, and on that day at Massah,
when they tempted me.

9 They put me to the test, *
though they had seen my works.

1789-1871

10 Forty years long was I grieved with this generation, and said, It is a people that do err in their hearts, for they have not known my ways :
11 Unto whom I sware in my wrath, that they should not enter into my rest.

Psalm xcvi. *Cantate Domino.*

O SING unto the LORD a new song ; sing unto the LORD, all the whole earth.
2 Sing unto the LORD, and praise his Name ; be telling of his salvation from day to day.
3 Declare his honour unto the heathen, and his wonders unto all people.
4 For the LORD is great, and cannot worthily be praised ; he is more to be feared than all gods.
5 As for all the gods of the heathen, they are but idols ; but it is the LORD that made the heavens.
6 Glory and worship are before him ; power and honour are in his sanctuary.
7 Ascribe unto the LORD, O ye kindreds of the people, ascribe unto the LORD worship and power.
8 Ascribe unto the LORD the honour due unto his Name ; bring presents, and come into his courts.
9 O worship the LORD in the beauty of holiness ; let the whole earth stand in awe of him.
10 Tell it out among the heathen, that the LORD is King, and that it is he who hath made the round world so fast that it cannot be moved ; and how that he shall judge the people righteously.
11 Let the heavens rejoice, and let the earth be glad ; let the sea make a noise, and all that therein is.
12 Let the field be joyful, and all that is in it ; then shall all the trees of the wood rejoice before the LORD.
13 For he cometh, for he cometh to judge the earth ; and with righteousness to judge the world, and the people with his truth.

Psalm xcvii. *Dominus regnavit.*

THE LORD is King, the earth may be glad thereof ; yea, the multitude of the isles may be glad thereof.
2 Clouds and darkness are round about him : righteousness and judgment are the habitation of his seat.

1892

10 Forty years long was I grieved with this generation, and said : It is a people that do err in their hearts, for they have not known my ways :
11 Unto whom I sware in my wrath : that they should not enter into my rest.

PSALM 96. *Cantate Domino.*

O SING unto the LORD a new song : sing unto the LORD, all the whole earth.
2 Sing unto the LORD, and praise his Name : be telling of his salvation from day to day.
3 Declare his honour unto the heathen : and his wonders unto all people.
4 For the LORD is great, and cannot worthily be praised : he is more to be feared than all gods.
5 As for all the gods of the heathen, they are but idols : but it is the LORD that made the heavens.
6 Glory and worship are before him : power and honour are in his sanctuary.
7 Ascribe unto the LORD, O ye kindreds of the people : ascribe unto the LORD worship and power.
8 Ascribe unto the LORD the honour due unto his Name : bring presents, and come into his courts.
9 O worship the LORD in the beauty of holiness : let the whole earth stand in awe of him.
10 Tell it out among the heathen, that the LORD is King : and that it is he who hath made the round world so fast that it cannot be moved ; and how that he shall judge the people righteously.
11 Let the heavens rejoice, and let the earth be glad : let the sea make a noise, and all that therein is.
12 Let the field be joyful, and all that is in it : then shall all the trees of the wood rejoice before the LORD.
13 For he cometh, for he cometh to judge the earth : and with righteousness to judge the world, and the people with his truth.

PSALM 97. *Dominus regnavit.*

THE LORD is King, the earth may be glad thereof : yea, the multitude of the isles may be glad thereof.
2 Clouds and darkness are round about him : righteousness and judgment are the habitation of his seat.

10 Forty years long was I grieved with this generation, and said, * It is a people that do err in their hearts, for they have not known my ways:

11 Unto whom I sware in my wrath, * that they should not enter into my rest.

Psalm 96. *Cantate Domino.*

O SING unto the LORD a new song; * sing unto the LORD, all the whole earth.

2 Sing unto the LORD, and praise his Name; * be telling of his salvation from day to day.

3 Declare his honour unto the heathen, * and his wonders unto all peoples.

4 For the LORD is great, and cannot worthily be praised; * he is more to be feared than all gods.

5 As for all the gods of the heathen, they are but idols; * but it is the LORD that made the heavens.

6 Glory and worship are before him; * power and honour are in his sanctuary.

7 Ascribe unto the LORD, O ye kindreds of the peoples, * ascribe unto the LORD worship and power.

8 Ascribe unto the LORD the honour due unto his Name; * bring presents, and come into his courts.

9 O worship the LORD in the beauty of holiness; * let the whole earth stand in awe of him.

10 Tell it out among the heathen, that the LORD is King, and that it is he who hath made the round world so fast that it cannot be moved; * and how that he shall judge the peoples righteously.

11 Let the heavens rejoice, and let the earth be glad; * let the sea make a noise, and all that therein is.

12 Let the field be joyful, and all that is in it; * then shall all the trees of the wood rejoice before the LORD.

13 For he cometh, for he cometh to judge the earth; * and with righteousness to judge the world, and the peoples with his truth.

Psalm 97. *Dominus regnavit.*

THE LORD is King, the earth may be glad thereof; * yea, the multitude of the isles may be glad thereof.

2 Clouds and darkness are round about him: * righteousness and judgment are the habitation of his seat.

10 Forty years long I detested that generation and said, *
"This people are wayward in their hearts;
they do not know my ways."

11 So I swore in my wrath, *
"They shall not enter into my rest."

96 *Cantate Domino*

1 Sing to the LORD a new song; *
sing to the LORD, all the whole earth.

2 Sing to the LORD and bless his Name; *
proclaim the good news of his salvation from day to day.

3 Declare his glory among the nations *
and his wonders among all peoples.

4 For great is the LORD and greatly to be praised; *
he is more to be feared than all gods.

5 As for all the gods of the nations, they are but idols; *
but it is the LORD who made the heavens.

6 Oh, the majesty and magnificence of his presence! *
Oh, the power and splendor of his sanctuary!

7 Ascribe to the LORD, you families of the peoples; *
ascribe to the LORD honor and power.

8 Ascribe to the LORD the honor due his Name; *
bring offerings and come into his courts.

9 Worship the LORD in the beauty of holiness; *
let the whole earth tremble before him.

10 Tell it out among the nations: "The LORD is King! *
he has made the world so firm that it cannot be moved;
he will judge the peoples with equity."

11 Let the heavens rejoice, and let the earth be glad;
let the sea thunder and all that is in it; *
let the field be joyful and all that is therein.

12 Then shall all the trees of the wood shout for joy
before the LORD when he comes, *
when he comes to judge the earth.

13 He will judge the world with righteousness *
and the peoples with his truth.

97 *Dominus regnavit*

1 The LORD is King;
let the earth rejoice; *
let the multitude of the isles be glad.

2 Clouds and darkness are round about him, *
righteousness and justice are the foundations of his throne.

3 There shall go a fire before him, and burn up his enemies on every side.
4 His lightnings gave shine unto the world : the earth saw it, and was afraid.
5 The hills melted like wax at the presence of the LORD ; at the presence of the Lord of the whole earth.
6 The heavens have declared his righteousness, and all the people have seen his glory.
7 Confounded be all they that worship carved images, and that delight in vain gods : worship him, all ye gods.
8 Sion heard of it, and rejoiced ; and the daughters of Judah were glad, because of thy judgments, O LORD.
9 For thou, LORD, art higher than all that are in the earth : thou art exalted far above all gods.
10 O ye that love the LORD, see that ye hate the thing which is evil : the Lord preserveth the souls of his saints ; he shall deliver them from the hand of the ungodly.
11 There is sprung up a light for the righteous, and joyful gladness for such as are true-hearted.
12 Rejoice in the LORD, ye righteous ; and give thanks for a remembrance of his holiness.

3 There shall go a fire before him : and burn up his enemies on every side.
4 His lightnings gave shine unto the world : the earth saw it, and was afraid.
5 The hills melted like wax at the presence of the LORD : at the presence of the Lord of the whole earth.
6 The heavens have declared his righteousness : and all the people have seen his glory.
7 Confounded be all they that worship carved images, and that delight in vain gods : worship him, all ye gods.
8 Sion heard of it, and rejoiced : and the daughters of Judah were glad, because of thy judgments, O LORD.
9 For thou, LORD, art higher than all that are in the earth : thou art exalted far above all gods.
10 O ye that love the LORD, see that ye hate the thing which is evil : the Lord preserveth the souls of his saints ; he shall deliver them from the hand of the ungodly.
11 There is sprung up a light for the righteous : and joyful gladness for such as are true-hearted.
12 Rejoice in the LORD, ye righteous : and give thanks for a remembrance of his holiness.

Evening Prayer.

Psalm xcviii. *Cantate Domino.*

O SING unto the LORD a new song ; for he hath done marvellous things.
2 With his own right hand, and with his holy arm, hath he gotten himself the victory.
3 The LORD declared his salvation ; his righteousness hath he openly showed in the sight of the heathen.
4 He hath remembered his mercy and truth toward the house of Israel ; and all the ends of the world have seen the salvation of our God.
5 Show yourselves joyful unto the LORD, all ye lands ; sing, rejoice, and give thanks.
6 Praise the LORD upon the harp ; sing to the harp with a psalm of thanksgiving.
7 With trumpets also and shawms, O show yourselves joyful before the LORD, the King.

Evening Prayer.

PSALM 98. *Cantate Domino.*

O SING unto the LORD a new song : for he hath done marvellous things.
2 With his own right hand, and with his holy arm : hath he gotten himself the victory.
3 The LORD declared his salvation : his righteousness hath he openly showed in the sight of the heathen.
4 He hath remembered his mercy and truth toward the house of Israel : and all the ends of the world have seen the salvation of our God.
5 Show yourselves joyful unto the LORD, all ye lands : sing, rejoice, and give thanks.
6 Praise the LORD upon the harp : sing to the harp with a psalm of thanksgiving.
7 With trumpets also and shawms : O show yourselves joyful before the LORD, the King.

1928

3 There shall go a fire before him, * and burn up his enemies on every side.

4 His lightnings gave shine unto the world: * the earth saw it, and was afraid.

5 The hills melted like wax at the presence of the LORD; * at the presence of the Lord of the whole earth.

6 The heavens have declared his righteousness, * and all the peoples have seen his glory.

7 Confounded be all they that worship carved images, and that delight in vain gods: * worship him, all ye gods.

8 Sion heard of it, and rejoiced; and the daughters of Judah were glad, * because of thy judgments, O LORD.

9 For thou, LORD, art higher than all that are in the earth: * thou art exalted far above all gods.

10 O ye that love the LORD, see that ye hate the thing which is evil: * the Lord preserveth the souls of his saints; he shall deliver them from the hand of the ungodly.

11 There is sprung up a light for the righteous, * and joyful gladness for such as are true-hearted.

12 Rejoice in the LORD, ye righteous; * and give thanks for a remembrance of his holiness.

Evening Prayer.

Psalm 98. *Cantate Domino.*

O SING unto the LORD a new song; * for he hath done marvellous things.

2 With his own right hand, and with his holy arm, * hath he gotten himself the victory.

3 The LORD declared his salvation; * his righteousness hath he openly showed in the sight of the heathen.

4 He hath remembered his mercy and truth toward the house of Israel; * and all the ends of the world have seen the salvation of our God.

5 Show yourselves joyful unto the LORD, all ye lands; * sing, rejoice, and give thanks.

6 Praise the LORD upon the harp; * sing to the harp with a psalm of thanksgiving.

7 With trumpets also and shawms, * O show yourselves joyful before the LORD, the King.

1979

3 A fire goes before him *
and burns up his enemies on every side.

4 His lightnings light up the world; *
the earth sees it and is afraid.

5 The mountains melt like wax at the presence of the LORD, *
at the presence of the Lord of the whole earth.

6 The heavens declare his righteousness, *
and all the peoples see his glory.

7 Confounded be all who worship carved images
and delight in false gods! *
Bow down before him, all you gods.

8 Zion hears and is glad, and the cities of Judah rejoice, *
because of your judgments, O LORD.

9 For you are the LORD,
most high over all the earth; *
you are exalted far above all gods.

10 The LORD loves those who hate evil; *
he preserves the lives of his saints
and delivers them from the hand of the wicked.

11 Light has sprung up for the righteous, *
and joyful gladness for those who are truehearted.

12 Rejoice in the LORD, you righteous, *
and give thanks to his holy Name.

Nineteenth Day: Evening Prayer

98 *Cantate Domino*

1 Sing to the LORD a new song, *
for he has done marvelous things.

2 With his right hand and his holy arm *
has he won for himself the victory.

3 The LORD has made known his victory; *
his righteousness has he openly shown in the sight of the nations.

4 He remembers his mercy and faithfulness to the house of Israel, *
and all the ends of the earth have seen the victory of our God.

5 Shout with joy to the LORD, all you lands *
lift up your voice, rejoice, and sing.

6 Sing to the LORD with the harp, *
with the harp and the voice of song

7 With trumpets and the sound of the horn *
shout with joy before the King, the LORD.

1789-1871	1892
8 Let the sea make a noise, and all that therein is ; the round world, and they that dwell therein.	8 Let the sea make a noise, and all that therein is : the round world, and they that dwell therein.
9 Let the floods clap their hands, and let the hills be joyful together before the LORD ; for he is come to judge the earth.	9 Let the floods clap their hands, and let the hills be joyful together before the LORD : for he is come to judge the earth.
10 With righteousness shall he judge the world, and the people with equity.	10 With righteousness shall he judge the world : and the people with equity.
Psalm xcix. *Dominus regnavit.*	PSALM 99. *Dominus regnavit.*
THE LORD is King, be the people never so impatient ; he sitteth between the Cherubim,[24] be the earth never so unquiet.	THE LORD is King, be the people never so impatient : he sitteth between the Cherubim, be the earth never so unquiet.
2 The LORD is great in Sion, and high above all people.	2 The LORD is great in Sion : and high above all people.
3 They shall give thanks unto thy Name, which is great, wonderful, and holy.	3 They shall give thanks unto thy Name : which is great, wonderful, and holy.
4 The King's power loveth judgment ; thou hast prepared equity, thou hast executed judgment and righteousness in Jacob.	4 The King's power loveth judgment ; thou hast prepared equity : thou hast executed judgment and righteousness in Jacob.
5 O magnify the LORD our God, and fall down before his footstool ; for he is holy.	5 O magnify the LORD our God : and fall down before his footstool ; for he is holy.
6 Moses and Aaron among his priests, and Samuel among such as call upon his Name : these called upon the LORD, and he heard them.	6 Moses and Aaron among his priests, and Samuel among such as call upon his Name : these called upon the LORD, and he heard them.
7 He spake unto them out of the cloudy pillar ; for they kept his testimonies, and the law that he gave them.	7 He spake unto them out of the cloudy pillar : for they kept his testimonies, and the law that he gave them.
8 Thou heardest them, O LORD our God ; thou forgavest them, O God, and punishedst their own inventions.	8 Thou heardest them, O LORD our God : thou forgavest them, O God, and punishedst their own inventions.
9 O magnify the LORD our God, and worship him upon his holy hill ; for the LORD our God is holy.	9 O magnify the LORD our God, and worship him upon his holy hill : for the LORD our God is holy.
Psalm c. *Jubilate Deo.*	PSALM 100. *Jubilate Deo.*
O BE[25] joyful in the LORD, all ye lands : serve the LORD with gladness, and come before his presence with a song.	O BE joyful in the LORD, all ye lands : serve the LORD with gladness, and come before his presence with a song.

[24]"Cherubims" prior to 1793.

[25]"O be ye" from 1822 until 1871.

1928

8 Let the sea make a noise, and all that therein is; * the round world, and they that dwell therein.

9 Let the floods clap their hands, and let the hills be joyful together before the LORD; * for he is come to judge the earth.

10 With righteousness shall he judge the world, * and the peoples with equity.

Psalm 99. *Dominus regnavit.*

THE LORD is King, be the people never so impatient; * he sitteth between the Cherubim, be the earth never so unquiet.

2 The LORD is great in Sion, * and high above all people.

3 They shall give thanks unto thy Name, * which is great, wonderful, and holy.

4 The King's power loveth judgment; thou hast prepared equity, * thou hast executed judgment and righteousness in Jacob.

5 O magnify the LORD our God, and fall down before his footstool; * for he is holy.

6 Moses and Aaron among his priests, and Samuel among such as call upon his Name: * these called upon the LORD, and he heard them.

7 He spake unto them out of the cloudy pillar; * for they kept his testimonies, and the law that he gave them.

8 Thou heardest them, O LORD our God; * thou forgavest them, O God, though thou didst punish their wicked doings.

9 O magnify the LORD our God, and worship him upon his holy hill; * for the LORD our God is holy.

Psalm 100. *Jubilate Deo.*

O BE joyful in the LORD, all ye lands: * serve the LORD with gladness, and come before his presence with a song.

1979

8 Let the sea make a noise and all that is in it, *
the lands and those who dwell therein.

9 Let the rivers clap their hands, *
and let the hills ring out with joy before the LORD,
when he comes to judge the earth.

10 In righteousness shall he judge the world *
and the peoples with equity.

99 *Dominus regnavit*

1 The LORD is King;
let the people tremble; *
he is enthroned upon the cherubim;
let the earth shake.

2 The LORD is great is Zion; *
he is high above all peoples.

3 Let them confess his Name, which is great and awesome; *
he is the Holy One.

4 "O mighty King, lover of justice,
you have established equity; *
you have executed justice and righteousness in Jacob."

5 Proclaim the greatness of the LORD our God
and fall down before his footstool; *
he is the Holy One.

6 Moses and Aaron among his priests,
and Samuel among those who call upon his Name, *
they called upon the LORD, and he answered them.

7 He spoke to them out of the pillar of cloud; *
they kept his testimonies and the decree that he gave them.

8 "O LORD our God, you answered them indeed; *
you were a God who forgave them,
yet punished them for their evil deeds."

9 Proclaim the greatness of the LORD our God
and worship him upon his holy hill; *
for the LORD our God is the Holy One.

100 *Jubilate Deo*

1 Be joyful in the LORD, all you lands; *
serve the LORD with gladness
and come before his presence with a song.

2 Be ye sure that the LORD he is God ; it is he that hath made us, and not we ourselves ; we are his people, and the sheep of his pasture.

3 O go your way into his gates with thanksgiving, and into his courts with praise ; be thankful unto him, and speak good of his Name.

4 For the LORD is gracious, his mercy is everlasting ; and his truth endureth from generation to generation.

2 Be ye sure that the LORD he is God ; it is he that hath made us, and not we ourselves : we are his people, and the sheep of his pasture.

3 O go your way into his gates with thanksgiving, and into his courts with praise : be thankful unto him, and speak good of his Name.

4 For the LORD is gracious, his mercy is everlasting : and his truth endureth from generation to generation.

Psalm ci. *Misericordiam et judicium.*

MY song shall be of mercy and judgment ; unto thee, O LORD, will I sing.

2 O let me have understanding in the way of godliness!

3 When wilt thou come unto me? I will walk in my house with a perfect heart.

4 I will take no wicked thing in hand ; I hate the sins of unfaithfulness ; there shall no such cleave unto me.

5 A froward heart shall depart from me ; I will not know a wicked person.

6 Whoso privily slandereth his neighbour, him will I destroy.

7 Whoso hath also a proud look and high stomach, I will not suffer him.

8 Mine eyes look upon such as are faithful in the land, that they may dwell with me.

9 Whoso leadeth a godly life, he shall be my servant.

10 There shall no deceitful person dwell in my house ; he that telleth lies shall not tarry in my sight.

11 I shall soon destroy all the ungodly that are in the land ; that I may root out all wicked doers from the city of the LORD.

PSALM 101. *Misericordiam et judicium.*

MY song shall be of mercy and judgment : unto thee, O LORD, will I sing.

2 O let me have understanding : in the way of godliness!

3 When wilt thou come unto me : I will walk in my house with a perfect heart.

4 I will take no wicked thing in hand ; I hate the sins of unfaithfulness : there shall no such cleave unto me.

5 A froward heart shall depart from me : I will not know a wicked person.

6 Whoso privily slandereth his neighbour : him will I destroy.

7 Whoso hath also a proud look and high stomach : I will not suffer him.

8 Mine eyes look upon such as are faithful in the land : that they may dwell with me.

9 Whoso leadeth a godly life : he shall be my servant.

10 There shall no deceitful person dwell in my house : he that telleth lies shall not tarry in my sight.

11 I shall soon destroy all the ungodly that are in the land : that I may root out all wicked doers from the city of the LORD.

THE TWENTIETH DAY.

Morning Prayer.

Psalm cii. *Domine, exaudi.*

HEAR my prayer, O LORD, and let my crying come unto thee.

2 Hide not thy face from me in the time of my trouble ; incline thine ear unto me when I call ; O hear me, and that right soon.

3 For my days are consumed away like smoke, and my bones are burnt up as it were a firebrand.

THE TWENTIETH DAY.

Morning Prayer.

PSALM 102. *Domine, exaudi.*

HEAR my prayer, O LORD : and let my crying come unto thee.

2 Hide not thy face from me in the time of my trouble : incline thine ear unto me when I call ; O hear me, and that right soon.

3 For my days are consumed away like smoke : and my bones are burnt up as it were a firebrand.

2 Be ye sure that the LORD he is God; it is he that hath made us, and not we ourselves; * we are his people, and the sheep of his pasture.

3 O go your way into his gates with thanksgiving, and into his courts with praise; * be thankful unto him, and speak good of his Name.

4 For the LORD is gracious, his mercy is everlasting; * and his truth endureth from generation to generation.

Psalm 101. *Misericordiam et judicium.*

MY song shall be of mercy and judgment; * unto thee, O LORD, will I sing.

2 O let me have understanding * in the way of godliness!

3 When wilt thou come unto me? * I will walk in my house with a perfect heart.

4 I will take no wicked thing in hand; I hate the sins of unfaithfulness; * there shall no such cleave unto me.

5 A froward heart shall depart from me; * I will not know a wicked person.

6 Whoso privily slandereth his neighbour, * him will I destroy.

7 Whoso hath also a haughty look and a proud heart, * I will not suffer him.

8 Mine eyes look upon such as are faithful in the land, * that they may dwell with me.

9 Whoso leadeth a godly life, * he shall be my servant.

10 There shall no deceitful person dwell in my house; * he that telleth lies shall not tarry in my sight.

11 I shall soon destroy all the ungodly that are in the land; * that I may root out all wicked doers from the city of the LORD.

The Twentieth Day.

Morning Prayer.

Psalm 102. *Domine, exaudi.*

HEAR my prayer, O LORD, * and let my crying come unto thee.

2 Hide not thy face from me in the time of my trouble; * incline thine ear unto me when I call; O hear me, and that right soon.

3 For my days are consumed away like smoke, * and my bones are burnt up as it were a firebrand.

2 Know this: The LORD himself is God; *
he himself has made us, and we are his;
we are his people and the sheep of his pasture.

3 Enter his gates with thanksgiving;
go into his courts with praise; *
give thanks to him and call upon his Name.

4 For the LORD is good;
his mercy is everlasting; *
and his faithfulness endures from age to age.

101 *Misericordiam et judicium*

1 I will sing of mercy and justice; *
to you, O LORD, will I sing praises.

2 I will strive to follow a blameless course;
oh, when will you come to me? *
I will walk with sincerity of heart within my house.

3 I will set no worthless thing before my eyes; *
I hate the doers of evil deeds;
they shall not remain with me.

4 A crooked heart shall be far from me; *
I will not know evil.

5 Those who in secret slander their neighbors I will destroy; *
those who have a haughty look and a proud heart I cannot abide.

6 My eyes are upon the faithful in the land, that they may dwell with me, *
and only those who lead a blameless life shall be my servants.

7 Those who act deceitfully shall not dwell in my house, *
and those who tell lies shall not continue in my sight.

8 I will soon destroy all the wicked in the land, *
that I may root out all evildoers from the city of the LORD.

Twentieth Day: Morning Prayer

102 *Domine, exaudi*

1 LORD, hear my prayer, and let my cry come before you; *
hide not your face from me in the day of my trouble.

2 Incline your ear to me; *
when I call, make haste to answer me,

3 For my days drift away like smoke, *
and my bones are hot as burning coals.

4 My heart is smitten like grass and withered, *
so that I forget to eat my bread.

1789-1871

4 My heart is smitten down, and withered like grass ; so that I forget to eat my bread.

5 For the voice of my groaning, my bones will scarce cleave to my flesh.

6 I am become like a pelican in the wilderness, and like an owl that is in the desert.

7 I have watched, and am even as it were a sparrow, that sitteth alone upon the house-top.

8 Mine enemies revile me all the day long ; and they that are mad upon me are sworn together against me.

9 For I have eaten ashes as it were bread, and mingled my drink with weeping ;

10 And that, because of thine indignation and wrath ; for thou hast taken me up, and cast me down.

11 My days are gone like a shadow, and I am withered like grass.

12 But thou, O LORD, shalt endure for ever, and thy remembrance throughout all generations.

13 Thou shalt arise, and have mercy upon Sion ; for it is time that thou have mercy upon her, yea, the time is come.

14 And why? thy servants think upon her stones, and it pitieth them to see her in the dust.

15 The heathen shall fear thy Name, O LORD ; and all the kings of the earth thy Majesty ;

16 When the LORD shall build up Sion, and when his glory shall appear ;

17 When he turneth him unto the prayer of the poor destitute, and despiseth not their desire.

18 This shall be written for those that come after, and the people which shall be born shall praise the LORD.

19 For he hath looked down from his sanctuary ; out of the heaven did the LORD behold the earth ;

20 That he might hear the mourning[26] of such as are in captivity, and deliver the children appointed unto death ;

21 That they may declare the Name of the LORD in Sion, and his worship at Jerusalem ;

22 When the peoples are gathered together, and the kingdoms also, to serve the LORD.

23 He brought down my strength in my journey, and shortened my days.

24 But I said, O my God, take me not away in the midst of mine age ; as for thy years, they endure throughout all generations.

1892

4 My heart is smitten down, and withered like grass : so that I forget to eat my bread.

5 For the voice of my groaning : my bones will scarce cleave to my flesh.

6 I am become like a pelican in the wilderness : and like an owl that is in the desert.

7 I have watched, and am even as it were a sparrow : that sitteth alone upon the housetop.

8 Mine enemies revile me all the day long : and they that are mad upon me are sworn together against me.

9 For I have eaten ashes as it were bread : and mingled my drink with weeping ;

10 And that, because of thine indignation and wrath : for thou hast taken me up, and cast me down.

11 My days are gone like a shadow : and I am withered like grass.

12 But thou, O LORD, shalt endure for ever : and thy remembrance throughout all generations.

13 Thou shalt arise, and have mercy upon Sion : for it is time that thou have mercy upon her, yea, the time is come.

14 And why? thy servants think upon her stones : and it pitieth them to see her in the dust.

15 The heathen shall fear thy Name, O LORD : and all the kings of the earth thy majesty ;

16 When the LORD shall build up Sion : and when his glory shall appear ;

17 When he turneth him unto the prayer of the poor destitute : and despiseth not their desire.

18 This shall be written for those that come after : and the people which shall be born shall praise the LORD.

19 For he hath looked down from his sanctuary : out of the heaven did the LORD behold the earth ;

20 That he might hear the mournings of such as are in captivity : and deliver the children appointed unto death ;

21 That they may declare the Name of the LORD in Sion : and his worship at Jerusalem ;

22 When the people are gathered together : and the kingdoms also, to serve the LORD.

23 He brought down my strength in my journey : and shortened my days.

24 But I said, O my God, take me not away in the midst of mine age : as for thy years, they endure throughout all generations.

[26] "mourning" prior to 1793.

1928

4 My heart is smitten down, and withered like grass; * so that I forget to eat my bread.

5 For the voice of my groaning, * my bones will scarce cleave to my flesh.

6 I am become like a pelican in the wilderness, * and like an owl that is in the desert.

7 I have watched, and am even as it were a sparrow, * that sitteth alone upon the housetop.

8 Mine enemies revile me all the day long; * and they that are mad upon me are sworn together against me.

9 For I have eaten ashes as it were bread, * and mingled my drink with weeping;

10 And that, because of thine indignation and wrath; * for thou hast taken me up, and cast me down.

11 My days are gone like a shadow, * and I am withered like grass.

12 But thou, O LORD, shalt endure for ever, * and thy remembrance throughout all generations

13 Thou shalt arise, and have mercy upon Sion; * for it is time that thou have mercy upon her, yea, the time is come.

14 And why? thy servants think upon her stones, * and it pitieth them to see her in the dust.

15 The nations shall fear thy Name, O LORD; * and all the kings of the earth thy majesty;

16 When the LORD shall build up Sion, * and when his glory shall appear;

17 When he turneth him unto the prayer of the poor destitute, * and despiseth not their desire.

18 This shall be written for those that come after, * and the people which shall be born shall praise the LORD.

19 For he hath looked down from his sanctuary; * out of the heaven did the LORD behold the earth;

20 That he might hear the mournings of such as are in captivity, * and deliver them that are appointed unto death;

21 That they may declare the Name of the LORD in Sion, * and his worship at Jerusalem;

22 When the peoples are gathered together, * and the kingdoms also, to serve the LORD.

23 He brought down my strength in my journey, * and shortened my days.

24 But I said, O my God, take me not away in the midst of mine age; * as for thy years, they endure throughout all generations.

1979

5 Because of the voice of my groaning *
I am but skin and bones.

6 I have become like a vulture in the wilderness, *
like an owl among the ruins.

7 I lie awake and groan; *
I am like a sparrow, lonely on a house-top.

8 My enemies revile me all day long, *
and those who scoff at me have taken an oath against me.

9 For I have eaten ashes for bread *
and mingled my drink with weeping.

10 Because of your indignation and wrath *
you have lifted me up and thrown me away.

11 My days pass away like a shadow, *
and I wither like the grass.

12 But you, O LORD, endure for ever, *
and your Name from age to age.

13 You will arise and have compassion on Zion,
for it is time to have mercy upon her; *
indeed, the appointed time has come.

14 For your servants love her very rubble, *
and are moved to pity even for her dust.

15 The nations shall fear your Name, O LORD, *
and all the kings of the earth your glory.

16 For the LORD will build up Zion, *
and his glory will appear.

17 He will look with favor on the prayer of the homeless; *
he will not despise their plea.

18 Let this be written for a future generation, *
so that a people yet unborn may praise the LORD.

19 For the LORD looked down from his holy place on high; *
from the heavens he beheld the earth;

20 That he might hear the groan of the captive *
and set free those condemned to die;

21 That they may declare in Zion the Name of the LORD, *
and his praise in Jerusalem;

22 When the peoples are gathered together, *
and the kingdoms also, to serve the LORD.

23 He has brought down my strength before my time; *
he has shortened the number of my days;

24 And I said, "O my God,
do not take me away in the midst of my days; *
your years endure throughout all generations.

25 Thou, Lord, in the beginning hast laid the foundation of the earth, and the heavens are the work of thy hands.

26 They shall perish, but thou shalt endure: they all shall wax old as doth a garment;

27 And as a vesture shalt thou change them, and they shall be changed; but thou art the same, and thy years shall not fail.

28 The children of thy servants shall continue, and their seed shall stand fast in thy sight.

Psalm ciii. *Benedic, anima mea.*

PRAISE the LORD, O my soul; and all that is within me, praise his holy Name.

2 Praise the LORD, O my soul, and forget not all his benefits:

3 Who forgiveth all thy sin, and healeth all thine infirmities;

4 Who saveth thy life from destruction, and crowneth thee with mercy and loving-kindness;

5 Who satisfieth thy mouth with good things, making thee young and lusty as an eagle.

6 The LORD executeth righteousness and judgment for all them that are oppressed with wrong.

7 He showed his ways unto Moses, his works unto the children of Israel.

8 The LORD is full of compassion and mercy, long-suffering, and of great goodness.

9 He will not alway be chiding; neither keepeth he his anger for ever.

10 He hath not dealt with us after our sins; nor rewarded us according to our wickednesses.

11 For look how high the heaven is in comparison of the earth; so great is his mercy also toward them that fear him.

12 Look how wide also the east is from the west; so far hath he set our sins from us.

13 Yea, like as a father pitieth his own children; even so is the LORD merciful unto them that fear him.

14 For he knoweth whereof we are made; he remembereth that we are but dust.

15 The days of man are but as grass; for he flourisheth as a flower of the field.

25 Thou, Lord, in the beginning hast laid the foundation of the earth: and the heavens are the work of thy hands.

26 They shall perish, but thou shalt endure: they all shall wax old as doth a garment;

27 And as a vesture shalt thou change them, and they shall be changed: but thou art the same, and thy years shall not fail.

28 The children of thy servants shall continue: and their seed shall stand fast in thy sight.

PSALM 103. *Benedic, anima mea.*

PRAISE the LORD, O my soul: and all that is within me, praise his holy Name.

2 Praise the LORD, O my soul: and forget not all his benefits:

3 Who forgiveth all thy sin: and healeth all thine infirmities;

4 Who saveth thy life from destruction: and crowneth thee with mercy and loving-kindness;

5 Who satisfieth thy mouth with good things: making thee young and lusty as an eagle.

6 The LORD executeth righteousness and judgment: for all them that are oppressed with wrong.

7 He showed his ways unto Moses: his works unto the children of Israel.

8 The LORD is full of compassion and mercy: long-suffering, and of great goodness.

9 He will not alway be chiding: neither keepeth he his anger for ever.

10 He hath not dealt with us after our sins: nor rewarded us according to our wickednesses.

11 For look how high the heaven is in comparison of the earth: so great is his mercy also toward them that fear him.

12 Look how wide also the east is from the west: so far hath he set our sins from us.

13 Yea, like as a father pitieth his own children: even so is the LORD merciful unto them that fear him.

14 For he knoweth whereof we are made: he remembereth that we are but dust.

15 The days of man are but as grass: for he flourisheth as a flower of the field.

1928

25 Thou, Lord, in the beginning hast laid the foundation of the earth, * and the heavens are the work of
thy hands.
26 They shall perish, but thou shalt endure: * they
all shall wax old as doth a garment;
27 And as a vesture shalt thou change them, and
they shall be changed; * but thou art the same, and thy
years shall not fail.
28 The children of thy servants shall continue, *
and their seed shall stand fast in thy sight.

1979

25 In the beginning, O LORD, you laid the foundations of the earth. *
and the heavens are the work of your hands;

26 They shall perish, but you will endure;
they all shall wear out like a garment; *
as clothing you will change them,
and they shall be changed;

27 But you are always the same, *
and your years will never end.

28 The children of your servants shall continue, *
and their offspring shall stand fast in your sight."

1928

Psalm 103. *Benedic, anima mea.*

PRAISE the LORD, O my soul; * and all that is within
me, praise his holy Name.
2 Praise the LORD, O my soul, * and forget not all
his benefits:
3 Who forgiveth all thy sin, * and healeth all thine
infirmities;
4 Who saveth thy life from destruction, * and
crowneth thee with mercy and loving-kindness;
5 Who satisfieth thy mouth with good things, *
making thee young and lusty as an eagle.
6 The LORD executeth righteousness and judgment * for all them that are oppressed with wrong.
7 He showed his ways unto Moses, * his works
unto the children of Israel.
8 The LORD is full of compassion and mercy, *
long-suffering, and of great goodness.
9 He will not alway be chiding; * neither keepeth
he his anger for ever.
10 He hath not dealt with us after our sins; * nor
rewarded us according to our wickednesses.
11 For look how high the heaven is in comparison
of the earth; * so great is his mercy also toward them
that fear him.
12 Look how wide also the east is from the west; *
so far hath he set our sins from us.
13 Yea, like as a father pitieth his own children; *
even so is the LORD merciful unto them that fear him.
14 For he knoweth whereof we are made; * he
remembereth that we are but dust.
15 The days of man are but as grass; * for he
flourisheth as a flower of the field.

1979

103 *Benedic, anima mea*

1 Bless the LORD, O my soul, *
and all that is within me, bless his holy Name.

2 Bless the LORD, O my soul, *
and forget not all his benefits.

3 He forgives all your sins *
and heals all your infirmities;

4 He redeems your life from the grave *
and crowns you with mercy and loving-kindness;

5 He satisfies you with good things, *
and your youth is renewed like an eagle's.

6 The LORD executes righteousness *
and judgment for all who are oppressed.

7 He made his ways known to Moses *
and his works to the children of Israel.

8 The LORD is full of compassion and mercy, *
slow to anger and of great kindness.

9 He will not always accuse us, *
nor will he keep his anger for ever.

10 He has not dealt with us according to our sins, *
nor rewarded us according to our wickedness.

11 For as the heavens are high above the earth, *
so is his mercy great upon those who fear him.

12 As far as the east is from the west, *
so far has he removed our sins from us.

13 As a father cares for his children, *
so does the LORD care for those who fear him.

14 For he himself knows whereof we are made; *
he remembers that we are but dust.

15 Our days are like the grass; *
we flourish like a flower of the field;

1789-1871

16 For as soon as the wind goeth over it, it is gone ; and the place thereof shall know it no more.

17 But the merciful goodness of the LORD endureth for ever and ever upon them that fear him ; and his righteousness upon children's children ;

18 Even upon such as keep his covenant, and think upon his commandments to do them.

19 The LORD hath prepared his seat in heaven, and his kingdom ruleth over all.

20 O praise the LORD, ye angels of his, ye that excel in strength ; ye that fulfil his commandment, and hearken unto the voice of his word.[27]

21 O praise the LORD, all ye his hosts ; ye servants of his that do his pleasure.

22 O speak good of the LORD, all ye works of his, in all places of his dominion : praise thou the LORD, O my soul.

1892

16 For as soon as the wind goeth over it, it is gone : and the place thereof shall know it no more.

17 But the merciful goodness of the LORD endureth for ever and ever upon them that fear him : and his righteousness upon children's children ;

18 Even upon such as keep his covenant : and think upon his commandments to do them.

19 The LORD hath prepared his seat in heaven : and his kingdom ruleth over all.

20 O praise the LORD, ye angels of his, ye that excel in strength : ye that fulfil his commandment, and hearken unto the voice of his words.

21 O praise the LORD, all ye his hosts : ye servants of his that do his pleasure.

22 O speak good of the LORD, all ye works of his, in all places of his dominion : praise thou the LORD, O my soul.

1789-1871

Evening Prayer.

Psalm civ. *Benedic, anima mea.*

PRAISE the LORD, O my soul : O LORD my God, thou art become exceeding glorious ; thou art clothed with majesty and honour.

2 Thou deckest thyself with light as it were with a garment, and spreadest out the heavens like a curtain.

3 Who layeth the beams of his chambers in the waters, and maketh the clouds his chariot, and walketh upon the wings of the wind.

4 He maketh his angels spirits, and his ministers a flaming fire.

5 He laid the foundations of the earth, that it never should move at any time.

6 Thou coveredst it with the deep like as with a garment ; the waters stand in the hills.

7 At thy rebuke they flee ; at the voice of thy thunder they are afraid.

8 They go up as high as the hills, and down to the valleys beneath ; even unto the place which thou hast appointed for them.

9 Thou hast set them their bounds, which they shall not pass, neither turn again to cover the earth.

10 He sendeth the springs into the rivers, which run among the hills.

1892

Evening Prayer.

PSALM 104. *Benedic, anima mea.*

PRAISE the LORD, O my soul : O LORD my God, thou art become exceeding glorious ; thou art clothed with majesty and honour.

2 Thou deckest thyself with light as it were with a garment : and spreadest out the heavens like a curtain.

3 Who layeth the beams of his chambers in the waters : and maketh the clouds his chariot, and walketh upon the wings of the wind.

4 He maketh his angels spirits : and his ministers a flaming fire.

5 He laid the foundations of the earth : that it never should move at any time.

6 Thou coveredst it with the deep like as with a garment : the waters stand in the hills.

7 At thy rebuke they flee : at the voice of thy thunder they are afraid.

8 They go up as high as the hills, and down to the valleys beneath : even unto the place which thou hast appointed for them.

9 Thou hast set them their bounds, which they shall not pass : neither turn again to cover the earth.

10 He sendeth the springs into the rivers : which run among the hills.

[27] "words" prior to 1845.

16 For as soon as the wind goeth over it, it is
gone; * and the place thereof shall know it no more.
17 But the merciful goodness of the LORD endureth
for ever and ever upon them that fear him; * and his
righteousness upon children's children;
18 Even upon such as keep his covenant, * and
think upon his commandments to do them.
19 The LORD hath prepared his seat in heaven, *
and his kingdom ruleth over all.
20 O praise the LORD, ye angels of his, ye that excel
in strength; * ye that fulfil his commandment, and
hearken unto the voice of his word.
21 O praise the LORD, all ye his hosts; * ye servants
of his that do his pleasure.
22 O speak good of the LORD, all ye works of his, in
all places of his dominion: * praise thou the LORD, O
my soul.

16 When the wind goes over it, it is gone, *
and its place shall know it no more.

17 But the merciful goodness of the LORD endures for ever
on those who fear him, *
and his righteousness on children's children;

18 On those who keep his covenant *
and remember his commandments and do them.

19 The LORD has set his throne in heaven, *
and his kingship has dominion over all.

20 Bless the LORD, you angels of his,
you mighty ones who do his bidding, *
and hearken to the voice of his word.

21 Bless the LORD, all you his hosts, *
you ministers of his who do his will.

22 Bless the LORD, all you works of his,
in all places of his dominion; *
bless the LORD, O my soul.

Evening Prayer.

Psalm 104. *Benedic, anima mea.*

PRAISE the LORD, O my soul: * O LORD my God,
thou art become exceeding glorious; thou art clothed
with majesty and honour.
2 Thou deckest thyself with light as it were with a
garment, * and spreadest out the heavens like a
curtain.
3 Who layeth the beams of his chambers in the
waters, * and maketh the clouds his chariot, and
walketh upon the wings of the wind.
4 He maketh his angels winds, * and his ministers a
flaming fire.
5 He laid the foundations of the earth, * that it
never should move at any time.
6 Thou coveredst it with the deep like as with a
garment; * the waters stand above the hills.
7 At thy rebuke they flee; * at the voice of thy
thunder they haste away.
8 They go up as high as the hills, and down to the
valleys beneath; * even unto the place which thou hast
appointed for them.
9 Thou hast set them their bounds, which they
shall not pass, * neither turn again to cover the earth.
10 He sendeth the springs into the rivers, * which
run among the hills.

Twentieth Day: Evening Prayer

104 *Benedic, anima mea*

1 Bless the LORD, O my soul; *
O LORD my God, how excellent is your greatness!
you are clothed with majesty and splendor.

2 You wrap yourself with light as with a cloak *
and spread out the heavens like a curtain.

3 You lay the beams of your chambers in the waters above; *
you make the clouds your chariot;
you ride on the wings of the wind.

4 You make the winds your messengers *
and flames of fire your servants.

5 You have set the earth upon its foundations, *
so that it never shall move at any time.

6 You covered it with the Deep as with a mantle; *
the waters stood higher than the mountains.

7 At your rebuke they fled; *
at the voice of your thunder they hastened away.

8 They went up into the hills and down to the valleys beneath, *
to the places you had appointed for them.

9 You set the limits that they should not pass; *
they shall not again cover the earth.

10 You send the springs into the valleys; *
they flow between the mountains.

1789-1871	1892
11 All the beasts[28] of the field drink thereof, and the wild asses quench their thirst.	11 All beasts of the field drink thereof : and the wild asses quench their thirst.
12 Beside them shall the fowls of the air have their habitation, and sing among the branches.	12 Beside them shall the fowls of the air have their habitation : and sing among the branches.
13 He watereth the hills from above ; the earth is filled with the fruit of thy works.	13 He watereth the hills from above : the earth is filled with the fruit of thy works.
14 He bringeth forth grass for the cattle, and green herb for the service of men ;	14 He bringeth forth grass for the cattle : and green herb for the service of men ;
15 That he may bring food out of the earth, and wine that maketh glad the heart of man ; and oil to make him a cheerful countenance, and bread to strengthen man's heart.	15 That he may bring food out of the earth, and wine that maketh glad the heart of man : and oil to make him a cheerful countenance, and bread to strengthen man's heart.
16 The trees of the LORD also are full of sap ; even the cedars of Libanus which he hath planted ;	16 The trees of the LORD also are full of sap : even the cedars of Libanus which he hath planted ;
17 Wherein the birds make their nests ; and the fir-trees are a dwelling for the stork.	17 Wherein the birds make their nests : and the fir-trees are a dwelling for the stork.
18 The high hills are a refuge for the wild goats ; and so are the stony rocks for the conies.	18 The high hills are a refuge for the wild goats : and so are the stony rocks for the conies.
19 He appointed the moon for certain seasons, and the sun knoweth his going down.	19 He appointed the moon for certain seasons : and the sun knoweth his going down.
20 Thou makest darkness that it may be night ; wherein all the beasts of the forest[29] do move.	20 Thou makest darkness that it may be night : wherein all the beasts of the forest do move.
21 The lions, roaring after their prey, do seek their meat from God.	21 The lions, roaring after their prey : do seek their meat from God.
22 The sun ariseth, and they get them away together, and lay them down in their dens.	22 The sun ariseth, and they get them away together : and lay them down in their dens.
23 Man goeth forth to his work, and to his labour, until the evening.	23 Man goeth forth to his work, and to his labour : until the evening.
24 O LORD, how manifold are thy works! in wisdom hast thou made them all ; the earth is full of thy riches.	24 O LORD, how manifold are thy works : in wisdom hast thou made them all ; the earth is full of thy riches.
25 So is the great and wide sea also ; wherein are things creeping innumerable, both small and great beasts.	25 So is the great and wide sea also : wherein are things creeping innumerable, both small and great beasts.
26 There go the ships, and there is that Leviathan, whom thou hast made to take his pastime therein.	26 There go the ships, and there is that leviathan : whom thou hast made to take his pastime therein.
27 These wait all upon thee, that thou mayest give them meat in due season.	27 These wait all upon thee : that thou mayest give them meat in due season.
28 When thou givest it them, they gather it ; and when thou openest thy hand, they are filled with good.	28 When thou givest it them, they gather it : and when thou openest thy hand, they are filled with good.
29 When thou hidest thy face, they are troubled : when thou takest away their breath, they die, and are turned again to their dust.	29 When thou hidest thy face, they are troubled : when thou takest away their breath, they die, and are turned again to their dust.

[28]"All beasts" prior to 1822.

[29]"forests" from 1845 until 1871.

1928

11 All beasts of the field drink thereof, * and the wild asses quench their thirst.

12 Beside them shall the fowls of the air have their habitation, * and sing among the branches.

13 He watereth the hills from above; * the earth is filled with the fruit of thy works.

14 He bringeth forth grass for the cattle, * and green herb for the service of men;

15 That he may bring food out of the earth, and wine that maketh glad the heart of man; * and oil to make him a cheerful countenance, and bread to strengthen man's heart.

16 The trees of the LORD also are full of sap; * even the cedars of Lebanon which he hath planted;

17 Wherein the birds make their nests; * and the fir-trees are a dwelling for the stork.

18 The high hills are a refuge for the wild goats; * and so are the stony rocks for the conies.

19 He appointed the moon for certain seasons, * and the sun knoweth his going down.

20 Thou makest darkness that it may be night; * wherein all the beasts of the forest do move.

21 The lions, roaring after their prey, * do seek their meat from God.

22 The sun ariseth, and they get them away together, * and lay them down in their dens.

23 Man goeth forth to his work, and to his labour, * until the evening.

24 O LORD, how manifold are thy works! * in wisdom hast thou made them all; the earth is full of thy riches.

25 So is the great and wide sea also; * wherein are things creeping innumerable, both small and great beasts.

26 There go the ships, and there is that leviathan, * whom thou hast made to take his pastime therein.

27 These wait all upon thee, * that thou mayest give them meat in due season.

28 When thou givest it them, they gather it; * and when thou openest thy hand, they are filled with good.

29 When thou hidest thy face, they are troubled: * when thou takest away their breath, they die, and are turned again to their dust.

1979

11 All the beasts of the field drink their fill from them, *
and the wild asses quench their thirst.

12 Beside them the birds of the air make their nests *
and sing among the branches.

13 You water the mountains from your dwelling on high; *
the earth is fully satisfied by the fruit of your works.

14 You make grass grow for flocks and herds *
and plants to serve mankind;

15 That they may bring forth food from the earth, *
and wine to gladden our hearts,

16 Oil to make a cheerful countenance, *
and bread to strengthen the heart.

17 The trees of the LORD are full of sap, *
the cedars of Lebanon which he planted,

18 In which the birds build their nests, *
and in whose tops the stork makes his dwelling.

19 The high hills are a refuge for the mountain goats, *
and the stony cliffs for the rock badgers.

20 You appointed the moon to mark the seasons, *
and the sun knows the time of its setting.

21 You make darkness that it may be night, *
in which all the beasts of the forest prowl.

22 The lions roar after their prey *
and seek their food from God.

23 The sun rises, and they slip away *
and lay themselves down in their dens.

24 Man goes forth to his work *
and to his labor until the evening.

25 O LORD, how manifold are your works! *
in wisdom you have made them all;
the earth is full of your creatures.

26 Yonder is the great and wide sea
with its living things too many to number, *
creatures both small and great.

27 There move the ships,
and there is that Leviathan, *
which you have made for the sport of it.

28 All of them look to you *
to give them their food in due season.

29 You give it to them; they gather it; *
you open your hand, and they are filled with good things.

30 When thou lettest thy breath go forth, they shall be made ; and thou shalt renew the face of the earth.
31 The glorious Majesty of the LORD shall endure for ever ; the LORD shall rejoice in his works.
32 The earth shall tremble at the look of him ; if he do but touch the hills, they shall smoke.
33 I will sing unto the LORD as long as I live ; I will praise my God while I have my being.
34 And so shall my words please him : my joy shall be in the LORD.
35 As for sinners, they shall be consumed out of the earth, and the ungodly shall come to an end. Praise thou the LORD, O my soul. Praise the LORD.

THE TWENTY-FIRST DAY.

Morning Prayer.

Psalm cv. *Confitemini Domino.*

O GIVE thanks unto the LORD, and call upon his Name ; tell the people what things he hath done.
2 O let your songs be of him, and praise him ; and let your talking be of all his wondrous works.
3 Rejoice in his holy Name ; let the heart of them rejoice that seek the LORD.
4 Seek the LORD and his strength ; seek his face evermore.
5 Remember the marvellous works that he hath done ; his wonders, and the judgments of his mouth ;
6 O ye seed of Abraham his servant, ye children of Jacob his chosen.
7 He is the LORD our God ; his judgments are in all the world.
8 He hath been alway mindful of his covenant and promise, that he made to a thousand generations ;
9 Even the covenant that he made with Abraham ; and the oath that he sware unto Isaac ;
10 And appointed the same unto Jacob for a law, and to Israel for an everlasting testament ;

30 When thou lettest thy breath go forth, they shall be made : and thou shalt renew the face of the earth.
31 The glorious majesty of the LORD shall endure for ever : the LORD shall rejoice in his works.
32 The earth shall tremble at the look of him : if he do but touch the hills, they shall smoke.
33 I will sing unto the LORD as long as I live : I will praise my God while I have my being.
34 And so shall my words please him : my joy shall be in the LORD.
35 As for sinners, they shall be consumed out of the earth, and the ungodly shall come to an end : Praise thou the LORD, O my soul. Praise the LORD.

THE TWENTY-FIRST DAY.

Morning Prayer.

PSALM 105. *Confitemini Domino.*

O GIVE thanks unto the LORD, and call upon his Name : tell the people what things he hath done.
2 O let your songs be of him, and praise him : and let your talking be of all his wondrous works.
3 Rejoice in his holy Name : let the heart of them rejoice that seek the LORD.
4 Seek the LORD and his strength : seek his face evermore.
5 Remember the marvellous works that he hath done : his wonders, and the judgments of his mouth ;
6 O ye seed of Abraham his servant : ye children of Jacob his chosen.
7 He is the LORD our God : his judgments are in all the world.
8 He hath been alway mindful of his covenant and promise : that he made to a thousand generations ;
9 Even the covenant that he made with Abraham : and the oath that he sware unto Isaac ;
10 And appointed the same unto Jacob for a law : and to Israel for an everlasting testament ;

30 When thou lettest thy breath go forth, they shall
be made; * and thou shalt renew the face of the earth.
31 The glorious majesty of the LORD shall endure
for ever; * the LORD shall rejoice in his works.
32 The earth shall tremble at the look of him; * if
he do but touch the hills, they shall smoke.
33 I will sing unto the LORD as long as I live; * I will
praise my God while I have my being.
34 And so shall my words please him: * my joy shall
be in the LORD.
35 As for sinners, they shall be consumed out of
the earth, * and the ungodly shall come to an end.
36 Praise thou the LORD, O my soul. * Praise the
LORD.

The Twenty-first Day.

Morning Prayer.

Psalm 105. *Confitemini Domino.*

O GIVE thanks unto the LORD, and call upon his
Name; * tell the people what things he hath done.
2 O let your songs be of him, and praise him; * and
let your talking be of all his wondrous works.
3 Rejoice in his holy Name; * let the heart of them
rejoice that seek the LORD.
4 Seek the LORD and his strength; * seek his face
evermore.
5 Remember the marvellous works that he hath
done; * his wonders, and the judgments of his mouth;
6 O ye seed of Abraham his servant, * ye children
of Jacob his chosen.
7 He is the LORD our God; * his judgments are in
all the world.
8 He hath been alway mindful of his covenant and
promise, * that he made to a thousand generations;
9 Even the covenant that he made with Abraham; * and the oath that he sware unto Isaac;
10 And appointed the same unto Jacob for a law, *
and to Israel for an everlasting testament;

30 You hide your face, and they are terrified; *
you take away their breath,
and they die and return to their dust.

31 You sent forth your Spirit, and they are created; *
and so you renew the face of the earth.

32 May the glory of the LORD endure for ever; *
may the LORD rejoice in all his works.

33 He looks at the earth and it trembles; *
he touches the mountains and they smoke.

34 I will sing to the LORD as long as I live; *
I will praise my God while I have my being.

35 May these words of mine please him; *
I will rejoice in the LORD.

36 Let sinners be consumed out of the earth, *
and the wicked be no more.

37 Bless the LORD, O my soul. *
Hallelujah!

Twenty-first Day: Morning Prayer

105

Part I *Confitemini Domino*

1 Give thanks to the LORD and call upon his Name; *
make known his deeds among the peoples.

2 Sing to him, sing praises to him, *
and speak of all his marvelous works.

3 Glory in his holy Name; *
let the hearts of those who seek the LORD rejoice.

4 Search for the LORD and his strength; *
continually seek his face.

5 Remember the marvels he has done, *
his wonders and the judgements of his mouth,

6 O offspring of Abraham his servant, *
O children of Jacob his chosen.

7 He is the LORD our God; *
his judgments prevail in all the world.

8 He has always been mindful of his covenant, *
the promise he made for a thousand generations:

9 The covenant he made with Abraham, *
the oath that he swore to Isaac,

10 Which he established as a statute for Jacob, *
and everlasting covenant for Israel,

1789-1871

11 Saying, Unto thee will I give the land of Canaan, the lot of your inheritance :

12 When there were yet but a few of them, and they strangers in the land ;

13 What time as they went from one nation to another, from one kingdom to another people ;

14 He suffered no man to do them wrong, but reproved even kings for their sakes ;

15 Touch not mine Anointed, and do my prophets no harm.

16 Moreover, he called for a dearth upon the land, and destroyed all the provision of bread.

17 But he had sent a man before them, even Joseph, who was sold to be a bond-servant ;

18 Whose feet they hurt in the stocks ; the iron entered into his soul ;

19 Until the time came that his cause was known : the word of the LORD tried him.

20 The king sent, and delivered him ; the prince of the people let him go free.

21 He made him lord also of his house, and ruler of all his substance ;

22 That he might inform his princes after his will, and teach his senators wisdom.

23 Israel also came into Egypt, and Jacob was a stranger in the land of Ham.

24 And he increased his people exceedingly, and made them stronger than their enemies ;

25 Whose heart turned so, that they hated his people, and dealt untruly with his servants.

26 Then sent he Moses his servant, and Aaron whom he had chosen.

27 And these showed his tokens among them, and wonders in the land of Ham.

28 He sent darkness, and it was dark ; and they were not obedient unto his word.

29 He turned their waters into blood, and slew their fish.

30 Their land brought forth frogs ; yea, even in their kings' chambers.

1892

11 Saying, Unto thee will I give the land of Canaan : the lot of your inheritance :

12 When there were yet but a few of them : and they strangers in the land ;

13 What time as they went from one nation to another : from one kingdom to another people ;

14 He suffered no man to do them wrong : but reproved even kings for their sakes ;

15 Touch not mine anointed : and do my prophets no harm.

16 Moreover, he called for a dearth upon the land : and destroyed all the provision of bread.

17 But he had sent a man before them : even Joseph, who was sold to be a bond-servant ;

18 Whose feet they hurt in the stocks : the iron entered into his soul ;

19 Until the time came that his cause was known : the word of the LORD tried him.

20 The king sent, and delivered him : the prince of the people let him go free.

21 He made him lord also of his house : and ruler of all his substance ;

22 That he might inform his princes after his will : and teach his senators wisdom.

23 Israel also came into Egypt : and Jacob was a stranger in the land of Ham.

24 And he increased his people exceedingly : and made them stronger than their enemies ;

25 Whose heart turned so, that they hated his people : and dealt untruly with his servants.

26 Then sent he Moses his servant : and Aaron whom he had chosen.

27 And these showed his tokens among them : and wonders in the land of Ham.

28 He sent darkness, and it was dark : and they were not obedient unto his word.

29 He turned their waters into blood : and slew their fish.

30 Their land brought forth frogs : yea, even in their kings' chambers.

1928

11 Saying, Unto thee will I give the land of Canaan, * the lot of your inheritance:

12 When there were yet but a few of them, * and they strangers in the land;

13 What time as they went from one nation to another, * from one kingdom to another people;

14 He suffered no man to do them wrong, * but reproved even kings for their sakes;

15 Touch not mine anointed, * and do my prophets no harm.

16 Moreover, he called for a dearth upon the land, * and destroyed all the provision of bread.

17 But he had sent a man before them, * even Joseph, who was sold to be a bond-servant;

18 Whose feet they hurt in the stocks; * the iron entered into his soul;

19 Until the time came that his cause was known: * the word of the LORD tried him.

20 The king sent, and delivered him; * the prince of the people let him go free.

21 He made him lord also of his house, * and ruler of all his substance;

22 That he might inform his princes after his will, * and teach his senators wisdom.

23 Israel also came into Egypt, * and Jacob was a stranger in the land of Ham.

24 And he increased his people exceedingly, * and made them stronger than their enemies;

25 Whose heart turned so, that they hated his people, * and dealt untruly with his servants.

26 Then sent he Moses his servant, * and Aaron whom he had chosen.

27 And these showed his tokens among them, * and wonders in the land of Ham.

28 He sent darkness, and it was dark; * and they were not obedient unto his word.

29 He turned their waters into blood, * and slew their fish.

30 Their land brought forth frogs; * yea, even in their kings' chambers.

1979

11 Saying, "To you will I give the land of Canaan *
to be your allotted inheritance."

12 When they were few in number, *
of little account, and sojourners in the land,

13 Wandering from nation to nation *
and from one kingdom to another,

14 He let no one oppress them *
and rebuked kings for their sake,

15 Saying, "Do not touch my anointed *
and do my prophets no harm."

16 Then he called for a famine in the land *
and destroyed the supply of bread.

17 He sent a man before them, *
Joseph, who was sold as a slave.

18 They bruised his feet in fetters; *
his neck they put in an iron collar.

19 Until his prediction came to pass, *
the word of the LORD tested him.

20 The king sent and released him; *
the ruler of the peoples set him free.

21 He set him as a master over his household, *
as a ruler over all his possessions.

22 To instruct his princes according to his will *
and to teach his elders wisdom.

Psalm 105: Part II *Et intravit Israel*

23 Israel came into Egypt, *
and Jacob became a sojourner in the land of Ham.

24 The LORD made his people exceedingly fruitful; *
he made them stronger than their enemies;

25 Whose heart he turned, so that they hated his people, *
and dealt unjustly with his servants.

26 He sent Moses his servant, *
and Aaron whom he had chosen.

27 They worked his signs among them, *
and portents in the land of Ham.

28 He sent darkness, and it grew dark; *
but the Egyptians rebelled against his words.

29 He turned their waters into blood *
and caused their fish to die.

30 Their land was overrun by frogs, *
in the very chambers of their kings.

31 He spake the word, and there came all manner of flies, and lice in all their quarters.
32 He gave them hailstones for rain ; and flames of fire in their land.
33 He smote their vines also and fig-trees ; and destroyed the trees that were in their coasts.
34 He spake the word, and the grasshoppers came, and caterpillars innumerable, and did eat up all the grass in their land, and devoured the fruit of their ground.
35 He smote all the firstborn in their land ; even the chief of all their strength.
36 He brought them forth also with silver and gold ; there was not one feeble person among their tribes.
37 Egypt was glad at their departing ; for they were afraid of them.
38 He spread out a cloud to be a covering ; and fire to give light in the night-season.
39 At their desire he brought quails ; and he filled them with the bread of heaven.
40 He opened the rock of stone, and the waters flowed out, so that rivers ran in the dry places.
41 For why? he remembered his holy promise ; and Abraham his servant.
42 And he brought forth his people with joy, and his chosen with gladness ;
43 And gave them the lands of the heathen ; and they took the labours of the people in possession ;
44 That they might keep his statutes, and observe his laws.

31 He spake the word, and there came all manner of flies : and lice in all their quarters.
32 He gave them hailstones for rain : and flames of fire in their land.
33 He smote their vines also and fig-trees : and destroyed the trees that were in their coasts.
34 He spake the word, and the grasshoppers came, and caterpillars innumerable : and did eat up all the grass in their land, and devoured the fruit of their ground.
35 He smote all the firstborn in their land : even the chief of all their strength.
36 He brought them forth also with silver and gold : there was not one feeble person among their tribes.
37 Egypt was glad at their departing : for they were afraid of them.
38 He spread out a cloud to be a covering : and fire to give light in the night season.
39 At their desire he brought quails : and he filled them with the bread of heaven.
40 He opened the rock of stone, and the waters flowed out : so that rivers ran in the dry places.
41 For why? he remembered his holy promise : and Abraham his servant.
42 And he brought forth his people with joy : and his chosen with gladness ;
43 And gave them the lands of the heathen : and they took the labours of the people in possession ;
44 That they might keep his statutes : and observe his laws.

Evening Prayer.

Psalm cvi. *Confitemini Domino.*

O GIVE thanks unto the LORD ; for he is gracious, and his mercy endureth for ever.
2 Who can express the noble acts of the LORD, or show forth all his praise?
3 Blessed are they that alway keep judgment, and do righteousness.

Evening Prayer.

PSALM 106. *Confitemini Domino.*

O GIVE thanks unto the LORD, for he is gracious : and his mercy endureth for ever.
2 Who can express the noble acts of the LORD : or show forth all his praise?
3 Blessed are they that alway keep judgment : and do righteousness.

1928

31 He spake the word, and there came all manner of flies, * and lice in all their quarters.

32 He gave them hailstones for rain; * and flames of fire in their land.

33 He smote their vines also and fig-trees; * and destroyed the trees that were in their coasts.

34 He spake the word, and the grasshoppers came, and caterpillars innumerable, * and did eat up all the grass in their land, and devoured the fruit of their ground.

35 He smote all the firstborn in their land; * even the chief of all their strength.

36 He brought them forth also with silver and gold; * there was not one feeble person among their tribes.

37 Egypt was glad at their departing; * for they were afraid of them.

38 He spread out a cloud to be a covering, * and fire to give light in the night season.

39 At their desire he brought quails; * and he filled them with the bread of heaven.

40 He opened the rock of stone, and the waters flowed out, * so that rivers ran in the dry places.

41 For why? he remembered his holy promise; * and Abraham his servant.

42 And he brought forth his people with joy, * and his chosen with gladness;

43 And gave them the lands of the heathen; * and they took the labours of the people in possession;

44 That they might keep his statutes, * and observe his laws.

Evening Prayer.

Psalm 106. *Confitemini Domino.*

O GIVE thanks unto the LORD; for he is gracious, * and his mercy endureth for ever.

2 Who can express the noble acts of the LORD, * or show forth all his praise?

3 Blessed are they that alway keep judgment, * and do righteousness.

1979

31 He spoke, and there came swarms of insects *
and gnats within all their borders.

32 He gave them hailstones instead of rain, *
and flames of fire throughout their land.

33 He blasted their vines and their fig trees *
and shattered every tree in their country.

34 He spoke, and the locust came, *
and young locusts without number,

35 Which ate up all the green plants in their land *
and devoured the fruit of their soil.

36 He struck down the firstborn of their land, *
the firstfruits of all their strength.

37 He led out his people with silver and gold; *
in all their tribes there was not one that stumbled.

38 Egypt was glad of their going, *
because they were afraid of them.

39 He spread out a cloud for a covering *
and a fire to give light in the night season.

40 They asked, and quails appeared, *
and he satisfied them with bread from heaven.

41 He opened the rock, and water flowed, *
so the river ran in the dry places.

42 For God remembered his holy word *
and Abraham his servant.

43 So he led forth his people with gladness, *
his chosen with shouts of joy.

44 He gave his people the lands of the nations, *
and they took the fruit of others' toil,

45 That they might keep his statutes *
and observe his laws.
Hallelujah!

Twenty-first Day: Evening Prayer

106

Part I *Confitemini Domino*

1 Hallelujah!
Give thanks to the LORD, for he is good, *
for his mercy endures for ever.

2 Who can declare the mighty acts of the LORD *
or show forth all his praise?

3 Happy are those who act with justice *
and always do what is right!

1789-1871

4 Remember me, O LORD, according to the favour that thou bearest unto thy people ; O visit me with thy salvation ;

5 That I may see the felicity of thy chosen, and rejoice in the gladness of thy people, and give thanks with thine inheritance.

6 We have sinned with our fathers ; we have done amiss, and dealt wickedly.

7 Our fathers regarded not thy wonders in Egypt, neither kept they thy great goodness in remembrance ; but were disobedient at the sea, even at the Red Sea.

8 Nevertheless, he helped them for his Name's sake, that he might make his power to be known.

9 He rebuked the Red Sea also, and it was dried up ; so he led them through the deep, as through a wilderness.

10 And he saved them from the adversary's hand, and delivered them from the hand of the enemy.

11 As for those that troubled them, the waters overwhelmed them ; there was not one of them left.

12 Then believed they his words, and sang praise unto him.

13 But within a while they forgat his works, and would not abide his counsel.

14 But lust came upon them in the wilderness, and they tempted God in the desert.

15 And he gave them their desire, and sent leanness withal into their soul.

16 They angered Moses also in the tents, and Aaron the saint of the LORD.

17 So the earth opened, and swallowed up Dathan, and covered the congregation of Abiram.

18 And the fire was kindled in their company ; the flame burnt up the ungodly.

19 They made a calf in Horeb, and worshipped the molten image.

20 Thus they turned their glory into the similitude of a calf that eateth hay.

21 And they forgat God their Saviour, who had done so great things in Egypt ;

1892

4 Remember me, O LORD, according to the favour that thou bearest unto thy people : O visit me with thy salvation ;

5 That I may see the felicity of thy chosen : and rejoice in the gladness of thy people, and give thanks with thine inheritance.

6 We have sinned with our fathers : we have done amiss, and dealt wickedly.

7 Our fathers regarded not thy wonders in Egypt, neither kept they thy great goodness in remembrance : but were disobedient at the sea, even at the Red Sea.

8 Nevertheless, he helped them for his Name's sake : that he might make his power to be known.

9 He rebuked the Red Sea also, and it was dried up : so he led them through the deep, as through a wilderness.

10 And he saved them from the adversary's hand : and delivered them from the hand of the enemy.

11 As for those that troubled them, the waters overwhelmed them : there was not one of them left.

12 Then believed they his words : and sang praise unto him.

13 But within a while they forgat his works : and would not abide his counsel.

14 But lust came upon them in the wilderness : and they tempted God in the desert.

15 And he gave them their desire : and sent leanness withal into their soul.

16 They angered Moses also in the tents : and Aaron the saint of the LORD.

17 So the earth opened, and swallowed up Dathan : and covered the congregation of Abiram.

18 And the fire was kindled in their company : the flame burnt up the ungodly.

19 They made a calf in Horeb : and worshipped the molten image.

20 Thus they turned their glory : into the similitude of a calf that eateth hay.

21 And they forgat God their Saviour : who had done so great things in Egypt ;

4 Remember me, O LORD, according to the favour that thou bearest unto thy people; * O visit me with thy salvation;

5 That I may see the felicity of thy chosen, * and rejoice in the gladness of thy people, and give thanks with thine inheritance.

6 We have sinned with our fathers; * we have done amiss, and dealt wickedly.

7 Our fathers regarded not thy wonders in Egypt, neither kept they thy great goodness in remembrance; * but were disobedient at the sea, even at the Red Sea.

8 Nevertheless, he helped them for his Name's sake, * that he might make his power to be known.

9 He rebuked the Red Sea also, and it was dried up; * so he led them through the deep, as through a wilderness.

10 And he saved them from the adversary's hand, * and delivered them from the hand of the enemy.

11 As for those that troubled them, the waters overwhelmed them; * there was not one of them left.

12 Then believed they his words, * and sang praise unto him.

13 But within a while they forgat his works, * and would not abide his counsel.

14 But lust came upon them in the wilderness, * and they tempted God in the desert.

15 And he gave them their desire, * and sent leanness withal into their soul.

16 They angered Moses also in the tents, * and Aaron the saint of the LORD.

17 So the earth opened, and swallowed up Dathan, * and covered the congregation of Abiram.

18 And the fire was kindled in their company; * the flame burnt up the ungodly.

19 They made a calf in Horeb, * and worshipped the molten image.

20 Thus they turned their glory * into the similitude of a calf that eateth hay.

21 And they forgat God their Saviour, * who had done so great things in Egypt;

4 Remember me, O LORD, with the favor you have for your people, *
and visit me with your saving help;

5 That I may see the prosperity of your elect
and be glad with the gladness of your people, *
that I may glory with your inheritance.

6 We have sinned as our forebears did; *
we have done wrong and dealt wickedly.

7 In Egypt they did not consider your marvelous works,
nor remember the abundance of your love; *
they defied the Most High at the Red Sea.

8 But he saved them for his Name's sake, *
to make his power known.

9 He rebuked the Red Sea, and it dried up, *
and he led them through the deep as through a desert.

10 He saved them from the hand of those who hated them *
and redeemed them from the hand of the enemy.

11 The waters covered their oppressors; *
not one of them was left.

12 Then they believed his words *
and sang him songs of praise.

13 But they soon forgot his deeds *
and did not wait for his counsel.

14 A craving seized them in the wilderness, *
and they put God to the test in the desert.

15 He gave them what they asked, *
but sent leanness into their soul.

16 They envied Moses in the camp, *
and Aaron, the holy one of the LORD.

17 The earth opened and swallowed Dathan *
and covered the company of Abiram.

18 fire blazed up against their company, *
and flames devoured the wicked.

Psalm 106: Part II *Et fecerunt vitulum*

19 Israel made a bull-calf at Horeb *
and worshiped a molten image;

20 And so they exchanged their Glory *
for the image of an ox that feeds on grass.

21 They forgot God their Savior, *
who had done great things in Egypt,

22 Wondrous works in the land of Ham; and fearful things by the Red Sea.

23 So he said he would have destroyed them, had not Moses his chosen stood before him in the gap, to turn away his wrathful indignation, lest he should destroy them.

24 Yea, they thought scorn of that pleasant land, and gave no credence unto his word;

25 But murmured in their tents, and hearkened not unto the voice of the LORD.

26 Then lift he up his hand against them, to overthrow them in the wilderness;

27 To cast out their seed among the nations, and to scatter them in the lands.

28 They joined themselves unto Baal-peor, and ate the offerings of the dead.

29 Thus they provoked him to anger with their own inventions; and the plague was great among them.

30 Then stood up Phinees, and prayed; and so the plague ceased.

31 And that was counted unto him for righteousness, among all posterities for evermore.

32 They angered him also at the waters of strife, so that he punished Moses for their sakes;

33 Because they provoked his spirit, so that he spake unadvisedly with his lips.

34 Neither destroyed they the heathen, as the LORD commanded them;

35 But were mingled among the heathen, and learned their works.

36 Insomuch that they worshipped their idols, which turned to their own decay; yea, they offered their sons and their daughters unto devils;

37 And shed innocent blood, even the blood of their sons and of their daughters, whom they offered unto the idols of Canaan; and the land was defiled with blood.

38 Thus were they stained with their own works, and went a whoring with their own inventions.

39 Therefore was the wrath of the LORD kindled against his people, insomuch that he abhorred his own inheritance.

40 And he gave them over into the hand of the heathen; and they that hated them were lords over them.

22 Wondrous works in the land of Ham: and fearful things by the Red Sea.

23 So he said he would have destroyed them, had not Moses his chosen stood before him in the gap: to turn away his wrathful indignation, lest he should destroy them.

24 Yea, they thought scorn of that pleasant land: and gave no credence unto his word;

25 But murmured in their tents: and hearkened not unto the voice of the LORD.

26 Then lift he up his hand against them: to overthrow them in the wilderness;

27 To cast out their seed among the nations: and to scatter them in the lands.

28 They joined themselves unto Baal-peor: and ate the offerings of the dead.

29 Thus they provoked him to anger with their own inventions: and the plague was great among them.

30 Then stood up Phinees, and prayed: and so the plague ceased.

31 And that was counted unto him for righteousness: among all posterities for evermore.

32 They angered him also at the waters of strife: so that he punished Moses for their sakes;

33 Because they provoked his spirit: so that he spake unadvisedly with his lips.

34 Neither destroyed they the heathen: as the LORD commanded them;

35 But were mingled among the heathen: and learned their works.

36 Insomuch that they worshipped their idols, which turned to their own decay: yea, they offered their sons and their daughters unto devils;

37 And shed innocent blood, even the blood of their sons and of their daughters: whom they offered unto the idols of Canaan; and the land was defiled with blood.

38 Thus were they stained with their own works: and went a whoring with their own inventions.

39 Therefore was the wrath of the LORD kindled against his people: insomuch that he abhorred his own inheritance.

40 And he gave them over into the hand of the heathen: and they that hated them were lords over them.

1928

22 Wondrous works in the land of Ham; * and fearful things by the Red Sea.

23 So he said he would have destroyed them, had not Moses his chosen stood before him in the gap, * to turn away his wrathful indignation, lest he should destroy them.

24 Yea, they thought scorn of that pleasant land, * and gave no credence unto his word;

25 But murmured in their tents, * and hearkened not unto the voice of the LORD.

26 Then lift he up his hand against them, * to overthrow them in the wilderness;

27 To cast out their seed among the nations, * and to scatter them in the lands.

28 They joined themselves unto Baal-peor, * and ate the offerings of the dead.

29 Thus they provoked him to anger with their own inventions; * and the plague was great among them.

30 Then stood up Phinehas, and interposed; * and so the plague ceased.

31 And that was counted unto him for righteousness, * among all posterities for evermore.

32 They angered him also at the waters of strife, * so that he punished Moses for their sakes;

33 Because they provoked his spirit, * so that he spake unadvisedly with his lips.

34 Neither destroyed they the heathen, * as the LORD commanded them;

35 But were mingled among the heathen, * and learned their works.

36 Insomuch that they worshipped their idols, which became a snare unto them; * yea, they offered their sons and their daughters unto devils;

37 And shed innocent blood, even the blood of their sons and of their daughters, * whom they offered unto the idols of Canaan; and the land was defiled with blood.

38 Thus were they stained with their own works, * and went a whoring with their own invention.

39 Therefore was the wrath of the LORD kindled against his people, * insomuch that he abhorred his own inheritance.

40 And he gave them over into the hand of the heathen; * and they that hated them were lords over them.

1979

22 Wonderful deeds in the land of Ham, *
and fearful things at the Red Sea.

23 So he would have destroyed them,
had not Moses his chosen stood before him in the breach, *
to turn away his wrath from consuming them.

24 They refused the pleasant land *
and would not believe his promise.

25 They grumbled in their tents *
and would not listen to the voice of the LORD.

26 So he lifted his hand against them, *
to overthrow them in the wilderness,

27 To cast out their seed among the nations, *
and to scatter them throughout the lands.

28 They joined themselves to Baal-Peor *
and ate sacrifices offered to the dead.

29 They provoked him to anger with their actions, *
and a plague broke out among them.

30 Then Phinehas stood up and interceded, *
and the plague came to an end.

31 This was reckoned to him as righteousness *
throughout all generations for ever.

32 Again they provoked his anger at the waters of Meribah, *
so that he punished Moses because of them;

33 For they so embittered his spirit *
that he spoke rash words with his lips.

34 They did not destroy the peoples *
as the LORD had commanded them.

35 They intermingled with the heathen *
and learned their pagan ways,

36 So that they worshiped their idols, *
which became a snare to them.

37 They sacrificed their sons *
and their daughters to evil spirits.

38 They shed innocent blood,
the blood of their sons and daughters, *
which they offered to the idols of Canaan,
and the land was defiled with blood.

39 Thus they were polluted by their actions *
and went whoring in their evil deeds.

40 Therefore the wrath of the LORD was kindled against his people *
and he abhorred his inheritance.

41 Their enemies oppressed them, and had them in subjection.
42 Many a time did he deliver them ; but they rebelled against him with their own inventions, and were brought down in their wickedness.
43 Nevertheless, when he saw their adversity, he heard their complaint.
44 He thought upon his covenant, and pitied them, according unto the multitude of his mercies ; yea, he made all those that led them away captive to pity them.
45 Deliver us, O LORD our God, and gather us from among the heathen ; that we may give thanks unto thy holy Name, and make our boast of thy praise.
46 Blessed be the LORD God of Israel, from everlasting, and world without end ; and let all the people say, Amen.

41 Their enemies oppressed them : and had them in subjection.
42 Many a time did he deliver them : but they rebelled against him with their own inventions, and were brought down in their wickedness.
43 Nevertheless, when he saw their adversity : he heard their complaint.
44 He thought upon his covenant, and pitied them, according unto the multitude of his mercies : yea, he made all those that led them away captive to pity them.
45 Deliver us, O LORD our God, and gather us from among the heathen : that we may give thanks unto thy holy Name, and make our boast of thy praise.
46 Blessed be the LORD God of Israel, from everlasting, and world without end : And let all the people say, Amen.

THE TWENTY-SECOND DAY.

Morning Prayer.

Psalm cvii. *Confitemini Domino.*

O GIVE thanks unto the LORD ; for he is gracious, and his mercy endureth for ever.
2 Let them give thanks whom the LORD hath redeemed, and delivered from the hand of the enemy ;
3 And gathered them out of the lands, from the east, and from the west ; from the north, and from the south.
4 They went astray in the wilderness out of the way, and found no city to dwell in.
5 Hungry and thirsty, their soul fainted in them.
6 So they cried unto the LORD in their trouble, and he delivered them from their distress.
7 He led them forth by the right way, that they might go to the city where they dwelt.

THE TWENTY-SECOND DAY.

Morning Prayer.

PSALM 107. *Confitemini Domino.*

O GIVE thanks unto the LORD, for he is gracious : and his mercy endureth for ever.
2 Let them give thanks whom the LORD hath redeemed : and delivered from the hand of the enemy ;
3 And gathered them out of the lands, from the east, and from the west : from the north, and from the south.
4 They went astray in the wilderness out of the way : and found no city to dwell in.
5 Hungry and thirsty : their soul fainted in them.
6 So they cried unto the LORD in their trouble : and he delivered them from their distress.
7 He led them forth by the right way : that they might go to the city where they dwelt.

41 Their enemies oppressed them, * and had them in subjection.

42 Many a time did he deliver them; * but they rebelled against him with their own inventions, and were brought down in their wickedness.

43 Nevertheless, when he saw their adversity, * he heard their complaint.

44 He thought upon his covenant, and pitied them, according unto the multitude of his mercies; * yea, he made all those that led them away captive to pity them.

45 Deliver us, O LORD our God, and gather us from among the heathen; * that we may give thanks unto thy holy Name, and make our boast of thy praise.

46 Blessed be the LORD God of Israel, from everlasting, and world without end; * And let all the people say, Amen.

BOOK V.

The Twenty-second Day.

Morning Prayer.

Psalm 107. *Confitemini Domino.*

O GIVE thanks unto the LORD, for he is gracious, * and his mercy endureth for ever.

2 Let them give thanks whom the LORD hath redeemed, * and delivered from the hand of the enemy;

3 And gathered them out of the lands, from the east, and from the west; * from the north, and from the south.

4 They went astray in the wilderness out of the way, * and found no city to dwell in.

5 Hungry and thirsty, * their soul fainted in them.

6 So they cried unto the LORD in their trouble, * and he delivered them from their distress.

7 He led them forth by the right way, * that they might go to the city where they dwelt.

41 He gave them over to the hand of the heathen, *
and those who hated them ruled over them.

42 Their enemies oppressed them, *
and they were humbled under their hand.

43 Many a time did he deliver them,
but they rebelled through their own devices, *
and were brought down in their iniquity.

44 Nevertheless, he saw their distress, *
when he heard their lamentation.

45 He remembered his covenant with them *
and relented in accordance with his great mercy.

46 He caused them to be pitied *
by those who held them captive.

47 Save us, O LORD our God,
and gather us from among the nations, *
that we may give thanks to your holy Name
and glory in your praise.

48 Blessed be the LORD, the God of Israel,
from everlasting and to everlasting; *
and let all the people say, "Amen!"
Hallelujah!

Book Five

Twenty-second Day: Morning Prayer

107

Part I *Confitemini Domino*

1 Give thanks to the LORD, for he is good, *
and his mercy endures for ever.

2 Let all those whom the LORD has redeemed proclaim *
that he redeemed them from the hand of the foe.

3 He gathered them out of the lands; *
from the east and from the west,
from the north and from the south.

4 Some wandered in desert wastes; *
they found no way to a city where they might dwell.

5 They were hungry and thirsty; *
their spirits languished within them.

6 They they cried to the LORD in their trouble, *
and he delivered them from their distress.

7 He put their feet on a straight path *
to go to a city where they might dwell.

1789-1871

8 O that men would therefore praise the LORD for his goodness ; and declare the wonders that he doeth for the children of men!

9 For he satisfieth the empty soul, and filleth the hungry soul with goodness.

10 Such as sit in darkness, and in the shadow of death, being fast bound in misery and iron ;

11 Because they rebelled against the words of the Lord, and lightly regarded the counsel of the Most Highest ;

12 He also brought down their heart through heaviness : they fell down, and there was none to help them.

13 So when they cried unto the LORD in their trouble, he delivered them out of their distress.

14 For he brought them out of darkness, and out of the shadow of death, and brake their bonds in sunder.

15 O that men would therefore praise the LORD for his goodness ; and declare the wonders that he doeth for the children of men!

16 For he hath broken the gates of brass, and smitten the bars of iron in sunder.

17 Foolish men are plagued for their offence, and because of their wickedness.

18 Their soul abhorred all manner of meat, and they were even hard at death's door.

19 So when they cried unto the LORD in their trouble, he delivered them out of their distress.

20 He sent his word, and healed them ; and they were saved from their destruction.

21 O that men would therefore praise the LORD for his goodness ; and declare the wonders that he doeth for the children of men!

22 That they would offer unto him the sacrifice of thanksgiving, and tell out his works with gladness!

23 They that go down to the sea in ships, and occupy their business in great waters ;

24 These men see the works of the LORD, and his wonders in the deep.

25 For at his word the stormy wind ariseth, which lifteth up the waves thereof.

26 They are carried up to the heaven, and down again to the deep ; their soul melteth away because of the trouble.

27 They reel to and fro, and stagger like a drunken man, and are at their wits'[30] end.

28 So when they cry unto the LORD in their trouble, he delivereth them out of their distress.

1892

8 O that men would therefore praise the LORD for his goodness : and declare the wonders that he doeth for the children of men!

9 For he satisfieth the empty soul : and filleth the hungry soul with goodness.

10 Such as sit in darkness, and in the shadow of death : being fast bound in misery and iron ;

11 Because they rebelled against the words of the Lord : and lightly regarded the counsel of the Most Highest ;

12 He also brought down their heart through heaviness : they fell down, and there was none to help them.

13 So when they cried unto the LORD in their trouble : he delivered them out of their distress.

14 For he brought them out of darkness, and out of the shadow of death : and brake their bonds in sunder.

15 O that men would therefore praise the LORD for his goodness : and declare the wonders that he doeth for the children of men!

16 For he hath broken the gates of brass : and smitten the bars of iron in sunder.

17 Foolish men are plagued for their offence : and because of their wickedness.

18 Their soul abhorred all manner of meat : and they were even hard at death's door.

19 So when they cried unto the LORD in their trouble : he delivered them out of their distress.

20 He sent his word, and healed them : and they were saved from their destruction.

21 O that men would therefore praise the LORD for his goodness : and declare the wonders that he doeth for the children of men!

22 That they would offer unto him the sacrifice of thanksgiving : and tell out his works with gladness!

23 They that go down to the sea in ships : and occupy their business in great waters ;

24 These men see the works of the LORD : and his wonders in the deep.

25 For at his word the stormy wind ariseth : which lifteth up the waves thereof.

26 They are carried up to the heaven, and down again to the deep : their soul melteth away because of the trouble.

27 They reel to and fro, and stagger like a drunken man : and are at their wit's end.

28 So when they cry unto the LORD in their trouble : he delivereth them out of their distress.

[30] "wits" prior to 1793 ; wit's until 1871.

1928

8 O that men would therefore praise the LORD for his goodness; * and declare the wonders that he doeth for the children of men!

9 For he satisfieth the empty soul, * and filleth the hungry soul with goodness.

10 Such as sit in darkness, and in the shadow of death, * being fast bound in misery and iron;

11 Because they rebelled against the words of the Lord, * and lightly regarded the counsel of the Most Highest;

12 He also brought down their heart through heaviness: * they fell down, and there was none to help them.

13 So when they cried unto the LORD in their trouble, * he delivered them out of their distress.

14 For he brought them out of darkness, and out of the shadow of death, * and brake their bonds in sunder.

15 O that men would therefore praise the LORD for his goodness; * and declare the wonders that he doeth for the children of men!

16 For he hath broken the gates of brass, * and smitten the bars of iron in sunder.

17 Foolish men are plagued for their offence, * and because of their wickedness.

18 Their soul abhorred all manner of meat, * and they were even hard at death's door.

19 So when they cried unto the LORD in their trouble, * he delivered them out of their distress.

20 He sent his word, and healed them; * and they were saved from their destruction.

21 O that men would therefore praise the LORD for his goodness; * and declare the wonders that he doeth for the children of men!

22 That they would offer unto him the sacrifice of thanksgiving, * and tell out his works with gladness!

23 They that go down to the sea in ships, * and occupy their business in great waters;

24 These men see the works of the LORD, * and his wonders in the deep.

25 For at his word the stormy wind ariseth, * which lifteth up the waves thereof.

26 They are carried up to the heaven, and down again to the deep; * their soul melteth away because of the trouble.

27 They reel to and fro, and stagger like a drunken man, * and are at their wit's end.

28 So when they cry unto the LORD in their trouble, * he delivereth them out of their distress.

1979

8 Let them give thanks to the LORD for his mercy *
and the wonders he does for his children.

9 For he satisfies the thirsty *
and fills the hungry with good things.

10 Some sat in darkness and deep gloom, *
bound fast in misery and iron;

11 Because they rebelled against the words of God *
and despised the counsel of the Most High.

12 So he humbled their spirits with hard labor; *
they stumbled, and there was none to help.

13 Then they cried to the LORD in their trouble, *
and he delivered them from their distress.

14 He led them out of darkness and deep gloom *
and broke their bonds asunder.

15 Let them give thanks to the LORD for his mercy *
and the wonders he does for his children.

16 For he shatters the doors of bronze *
and breaks in two the iron bars.

17 Some were fools and took to rebellious ways; *
they were afflicted because of their sins.

18 They abhorred all manner of food *
and drew near to death's door.

19 Then they cried to the LORD in their trouble, *
and he delivered them from their distress.

20 He sent forth his word and healed them *
and saved them from the grave.

21 Let them give thanks to the LORD for his mercy *
and the wonders he does for his children.

22 Let them offer a sacrifice of thanksgiving *
and tell of his acts with shouts of joy.

23 Some went down to the sea in ships *
and plied their trade in deep waters;

24 They beheld the works of the LORD *
and his wonders in the deep.

25 Then he spoke, and a stormy wind arose, *
which tossed high the waves of the sea.

26 They mounted up to the heavens and fell back to the depths; *
their hearts melted because of their peril.

27 They reeled and staggered like drunkards *
and were at their wits' end.

28 Then they cried to the LORD in their trouble, *
and he delivered them from their distress.

29 For he maketh the storm to cease, so that the waves thereof are still.
30 Then are they glad, because they are at rest ; and so he bringeth them unto the haven where they would be.
31 O that men would therefore praise the LORD for his goodness ; and declare the wonders that he doeth for the children of men!
32 That they would exalt him also in the congregation of the people, and praise him in the seat of the elders!
33 Who turneth the floods into a wilderness, and drieth up the water-springs.
34 A fruitful land maketh he barren, for the wickedness of them that dwell therein.
35 Again, he maketh the wilderness a standing water, and water-springs of a dry ground.
36 And there he setteth the hungry, that they may build them a city to dwell in ;
37 That they may sow their land, and plant vineyards, to yield them fruits of increase.
38 He blesseth them, so that they multiply exceedingly ; and suffereth not their cattle to decrease.
39 And again, when they are minished and brought low through oppression, through any plague or trouble ;
40 Though he suffer them to be evil-entreated through tyrants, and let them wander out of the way in the wilderness ;
41 Yet helpeth he the poor out of misery, and maketh him households like a flock of sheep.
42 The righteous will consider this, and rejoice ; and the mouth of all wickedness shall be stopped.
43 Whoso is wise, will ponder these things ; and they shall understand the loving-kindness of the LORD.

29 For he maketh the storm to cease : so that the waves thereof are still.
30 Then are they glad, because they are at rest : and so he bringeth them unto the haven where they would be.
31 O that men would therefore praise the LORD for his goodness : and declare the wonders that he doeth for the children of men!
32 That they would exalt him also in the congregation of the people : and praise him in the seat of the elders!
33 Who turneth the floods into a wilderness : and drieth up the water-springs.
34 A fruitful land maketh he barren : for the wickedness of them that dwell therein.
35 Again, he maketh the wilderness a standing water : and water-springs of a dry ground.
36 And there he setteth the hungry : that they may build them a city to dwell in ;
37 That they may sow their land, and plant vineyards : to yield them fruits of increase.
38 He blesseth them, so that they multiply exceedingly : and suffereth not their cattle to decrease.
39 And again, when they are minished and brought low : through oppression, through any plague or trouble ;
40 Though he suffer them to be evil entreated through tyrants : and let them wander out of the way in the wilderness ;
41 Yet helpeth he the poor out of misery : and maketh him households like a flock of sheep.
42 The righteous will consider this, and rejoice : and the mouth of all wickedness shall be stopped.
43 Whoso is wise, will ponder these things : and they shall understand the loving-kindness of the LORD.

Evening Prayer.

Psalm cviii. *Paratum cor meum.*

O GOD, my heart is ready, my heart is ready ; I will sing, and give praise with the best member that I have.
2 Awake, thou lute and harp ; I myself will awake right early.
3 I will give thanks unto thee, O LORD, among the people ; I will sing praises unto thee among the nations.

Evening Prayer.

PSALM 108. *Paratum cor meum.*

O GOD, my heart is ready, my heart is ready : I will sing, and give praise with the best member that I have.
2 Awake, thou lute and harp : I myself will awake right early.
3 I will give thanks unto thee, O LORD, among the people : I will sing praises unto thee among the nations.

29 For he maketh the storm to cease, * so that the waves thereof are still.
30 Then are they glad, because they are at rest; * and so he bringeth them unto the haven where they would be.
31 O that men would therefore praise the LORD for his goodness; * and declare the wonders that he doeth for the children of men!
32 That they would exalt him also in the congregation of the people, * and praise him in the seat of the elders!

33 He turneth the floods into a wilderness, * and drieth up the water-springs.
34 A fruitful land maketh he barren, * for the wickedness of them that dwell therein.
35 Again, he maketh the wilderness a standing water, * and water-springs of a dry ground.
36 And there he setteth the hungry, * that they may build them a city to dwell in;
37 That they may sow their land, and plant vineyards, * to yield them fruits of increase.
38 He blesseth them, so that they multiply exceedingly; * and suffereth not their cattle to decrease.
39 And again, when they are minished and brought low * through oppression, through any plague or trouble;
40 Though he suffer them to be evil entreated through tyrants, * and let them wander out of the way in the wilderness;
41 Yet helpeth he the poor out of misery, * and maketh him households like a flock of sheep.
42 The righteous will consider this, and rejoice; * and the mouth of all wickedness shall be stopped.
43 Whoso is wise, will ponder these things; * and they shall understand the loving-kindness of the LORD.

Evening Prayer.

Psalm 108. *Paratum cor meum.*

O GOD, my heart is ready, my heart is ready; * I will sing, and give praise with the best member that I have.
2 Awake, thou lute and harp; * I myself will awake right early.
3 I will give thanks unto thee, O LORD, among the peoples; * I will sing praises unto thee among the nations.

29 He stilled the storm to a whisper *
and quieted the waves of the sea.

30 Then were they glad because of the calm, *
and he brought them to the harbor they were bound for.

31 Let them give thanks to the LORD for his mercy *
and the wonders he does for his children.

32 Let them exalt him in the congregation of the people *
and praise him in the council of the elders.

Psalm 107: Part II *Posuit flumina*

33 The LORD changed rivers into deserts, *
and water-springs into thirsty ground.

34 A fruitful land into salt flats, *
because of the wickedness of those who dwell there.

35 He changed deserts into pools of water *
and dry land into water-springs.

36 He settled the hungry there, *
and they founded a city to dwell in.

37 They sowed fields, and planted vineyards, *
and brought in a fruitful harvest.

38 He blessed them, so that they increased greatly; *
he did not let their herds decrease.

39 Yet when they were diminished and brought low, *
through stress of adversity and sorrow,

40 (He pours contempt on princes *
and makes them wander in trackless wastes)

41 He lifted up the poor out of misery *
and multiplied their families like flocks of sheep.

42 The upright will see this and rejoice, *
and all wickedness will shut its mouth.

43 Whoever is wise will ponder these things, *
and consider well the mercies of the LORD.

Twenty-second Day: Evening Prayer

108 *Paratum cor meum*

1 My heart is firmly fixed, O God, my heart is fixed; *
I will sing and make melody.

2 Wake up, my spirit;
awake, lute and harp; *
I myself will waken the dawn.

3 I will confess you among the peoples, O LORD; *
I will sing praises to you among the nations.

4 For thy mercy is greater than the heavens, and thy truth reacheth unto the clouds.
5 Set up thyself, O God, above the heavens, and thy glory above all the earth ;
6 That thy beloved may be delivered : let thy right hand save them, and hear thou me.
7 God hath spoken in his holiness ; I will rejoice therefore, and divide Sichem, and mete out the valley of Succoth.
8 Gilead is mine, and Manasses is mine ; Ephraim also is the strength of my head ;
9 Judah is my law-giver ; Moab is my wash-pot ; over Edom will I cast out my shoe ; upon Philistia will I triumph.
10 Who will lead me into the strong city? and who will bring me into Edom?
11 Hast not thou forsaken us, O God? and wilt not thou, O God, go forth with our hosts?
12 O help us against the enemy : for vain is the help of man.
13 Through God we shall do great acts ; and it is he that shall tread down our enemies.

4 For thy mercy is greater than the heavens : and thy truth reacheth unto the clouds.
5 Set up thyself, O God, above the heavens : and thy glory above all the earth ;
6 That thy beloved may be delivered : let thy right hand save them, and hear thou me.
7 God hath spoken in his holiness : I will rejoice therefore, and divide Sichem, and mete out the valley of Succoth.
8 Gilead is mine, and Manasses is mine : Ephraim also is the strength of my head ;
9 Judah is my lawgiver ; Moab is my wash-pot : over Edom will I cast out my shoe ; upon Philistia will I triumph.
10 Who will lead me into the strong city.? : and who will bring me into Edom?
11 Hast not thou forsaken us, O God : and wilt not thou, O God, go forth with our hosts?
12 O help us against the enemy : for vain is the help of man.
13 Through God we shall do great acts : and it is he that shall tread down our enemies.

Psalm cix. *Deus, laudum.*[31]

HOLD not thy tongue, O God of my praise ; for the mouth of the ungodly, yea, the mouth of the deceitful is opened upon me.
2 And they have spoken against me with false tongues ; they compassed me about also with words of hatred, and fought against me without a cause.
3 For the love that I had unto them, lo, they take now my contrary part ; but I give myself unto prayer.
4 Thus have they rewarded me evil for good, and hatred for my good-will.
5 Set thou an ungodly man to be ruler over him, and let Satan stand at his right hand.
6 When sentence is given upon him, let him be condemned ; and let his prayer be turned into sin.
7 Let his days be few ; and let another take his office.
8 Let his children be fatherless, and his wife a widow.

PSALM 109. *Deus, laudem.*

HOLD not thy tongue, O God of my praise : for the mouth of the ungodly, yea, the mouth of the deceitful is opened upon me.
2 And they have spoken against me with false tongues : they compassed me about also with words of hatred, and fought against me without a cause.
3 For the love that I had unto them, lo, they take now my contrary part : but I give myself unto prayer.
4 Thus have they rewarded me evil for good : and hatred for my goodwill.
5 Set thou an ungodly man to be ruler over him : and let Satan stand at his right hand.
6 When sentence is given upon him, let him be condemned : and let his prayer be turned into sin.
7 Let his days be few : and let another take his office.
8 Let his children be fatherless : and his wife a widow.

[31] *sic.*

4 For thy mercy is greater than the heavens, * and thy truth reacheth unto the clouds.
5 Set up thyself, O God, above the heavens, * and thy glory above all the earth;
6 That thy beloved may be delivered: * let thy right hand save them, and hear thou me.

7 God hath spoken in his holiness; * I will rejoice therefore, and divide Shechem, and mete out the valley of Succoth.
8 Gilead is mine, and Manasseh is mine; * Ephraim also is the strength of my head; Judah is my lawgiver;
9 Moab is my wash-pot; over Edom will I cast out my shoe; * upon Philistia will I triumph.
10 Who will lead me into the strong city? * and who will bring me into Edom?
11 Hast not thou forsaken us, O God? * and wilt not thou, O God, go forth with our hosts?
12 O help us against the enemy: * for vain is the help of man.
13 Through God we shall do great acts; * and it is he that shall tread down our enemies.

Psalm 109. *Deus, laudem.*

HOLD not thy tongue, O God of my praise; * for the mouth of the ungodly, yea, the mouth of the deceitful is opened upon me.
2 And they have spoken against me with false tongues; * they compassed me about also with words of hatred, and fought against me without a cause.
3 For the love that I had unto them, lo, they take now my contrary part; * but I give myself unto prayer.
4 Thus have they rewarded me evil for good, * and hatred for my good will.

5 Set thou an ungodly man to be ruler over him, * and let an adversary stand at his right hand.
6 When sentence is given upon him, let him be condemned; * and let his prayer be turned into sin.
7 Let his days be few; * and let another take his office.
8 Let his children be fatherless, * and his wife a widow.

4 For your loving-kindness is greater than the heavens, *
and your faithfulness reaches to the clouds.

5 Exalt yourself above the heavens, O God, *
and your glory over all the earth.

6 So that those who are dear to you may be delivered, *
save with your right hand and answer me.

7 God spoke from his holy place and said, *
"I will exult and parcel out Shechem;
I will divide the valley of Succoth.

8 Gilead is mine and Manasseh is mine; *
Ephraim is my helmet and Judah my scepter.

9 Moab is my washbasin,
on Edom I throw down my sandal to claim it, *
and over Philistia will I shout in triumph."

10 Who will lead me into the strong city? *
who will bring me into Edom?

11 Have you not cast us off, O God? *
you no longer go out, O God, with our armies.

12 Grant us your help against the enemy, *
for vain is the help of man.

13 With God we will do valiant deeds, *
and he shall tread our enemies under foot.

109 *Deus, laudem*

1 Hold not your tongue, O God of my praise; *
for the mouth of the wicked,
for the mouth of the deceitful, is opened against me.

2 They speak to me with a lying tongue; *
they encompass me with hateful words
and fight against me without a cause.

3 Despite my love, they accuse me; *
but as for me, I pray for them.

4 They repay evil for good, *
and hatred for my love.

5 Set a wicked man against him, *
and let an accuser stand at his right hand.

6 When he is judged, let him be found guilty, *
and let his appeal be in vain.

7 Let his days be few, *
and let another take his office.

8 Let his children be fatherless, *
and his wife become a widow.

1789-1871

9 Let his children be vagabonds, and beg their bread ; let them seek it also out of desolate places.

10 Let the extortioner consume all that he hath ; and let the stranger spoil his labour.

11 Let there be no man to pity him, nor to have compassion upon his fatherless children.

12 Let his posterity be destroyed ; and in the next generation let his name be clean put out.

13 Let the wickedness of his fathers be had in remembrance in the sight of the LORD ; and let not the sin of his mother be done away.

14 Let them alway be before the LORD, that he may root out the memorial of them from off the earth ;

15 And that, because his mind was not to do good ; but persecuted the poor helpless man, that he might slay him that was vexed at the heart.

16 His delight was in cursing, and it shall happen unto him ; he loved not blessing, therefore shall it be far from him.

17 He clothed himself with cursing like as with a raiment, and it shall come into his bowels like water, and like oil into his bones.

18 Let it be unto him as the cloak that he hath upon him, and as the girdle that he is always[32] girded withal.

19 Let it thus happen from the LORD unto mine enemies, and to those that speak evil against my soul.

20 But deal thou with me, O LORD God, according unto thy Name ; for sweet is thy mercy.

21 O deliver me, for I am helpless and poor, and my heart is wounded within me.

22 I go hence like the shadow that departeth, and am driven away as the grasshopper.

23 My knees are weak through fasting ; my flesh is dried up for want of fatness.

24 I became also a reproach unto them : they that looked upon me shaked their heads.

25 Help me, O LORD my God ; O save me according to thy mercy ;

26 And they shall know how that this is thy hand, and that thou, LORD, hast done it.

1892

9 Let his children be vagabonds, and beg their bread : let them seek it also out of desolate places.

10 Let the extortioner consume all that he hath : and let the stranger spoil his labour.

11 Let there be no man to pity him : nor to have compassion upon his fatherless children.

12 Let his posterity be destroyed : and in the next generation let his name be clean put out.

13 Let the wickedness of his fathers be had in remembrance in the sight of the LORD : and let not the sin of his mother be done away.

14 Let them alway be before the LORD : that he may root out the memorial of them from off the earth ;

15 And that, because his mind was not to do good : but persecuted the poor helpless man, that he might slay him that was vexed at the heart.

16 His delight was in cursing, and it shall happen unto him : he loved not blessing, therefore shall it be far from him.

17 He clothed himself with cursing like as with a raiment : and it shall come into his bowels like water, and like oil into his bones.

18 Let it be unto him as the cloak that he hath upon him : and as the girdle that he is alway girded withal.

19 Let it thus happen from the LORD unto mine enemies : and to those that speak evil against my soul.

20 But deal thou with me, O LORD God, according unto thy Name : for sweet is thy mercy.

21 O deliver me, for I am helpless and poor : and my heart is wounded within me.

22 I go hence like the shadow that departeth : and am driven away as the grasshopper.

23 My knees are weak through fasting : my flesh is dried up for want of fatness.

24 I became also a reproach unto them : they that looked upon me shaked their heads.

25 Help me, O LORD my God : O save me according to thy mercy ;

26 And they shall know how that this is thy hand : and that thou, LORD, hast done it.

[32] "alway" prior to 1822.

9 Let his children be vagabonds, and beg their bread; * let them seek it also out of desolate places.

10 Let the extortioner consume all that he hath; * and let the stranger spoil his labour.

11 Let there be no man to pity him, * nor to have compassion upon his fatherless children.

12 Let his posterity be destroyed; * and in the next generation let his name be clean put out.

13 Let the wickedness of his fathers be had in remembrance in the sight of the LORD; * and let not the sin of his mother be done away.

14 Let them alway be before the LORD, * that he may root out the memorial of them from off the earth;

15 And that, because his mind was not to do good; * but persecuted the poor helpless man, that he might slay him that was vexed at the heart.

16 His delight was in cursing, and it shall happen unto him; * he loved not blessing, therefore shall it be far from him.

17 He clothed himself with cursing like as with a raiment, * and it shall come into his bowels like water, and like oil into his bones.

18 Let it be unto him as the cloak that he hath upon him, * and as the girdle that he is alway girded withal.

19 Let it thus happen from the LORD unto mine enemies, * and to those that speak evil against my soul.

20 But deal thou with me, O LORD God, according unto thy Name; * for sweet is thy mercy.

21 O deliver me, for I am helpless and poor, * and my heart is wounded within me.

22 I go hence like the shadow that departeth, * and am driven away as the grasshopper.

23 My knees are weak through fasting; * my flesh is dried up for want of fatness.

24 I am become also a reproach unto them: * they that look upon me shake their heads.

25 Help me, O LORD my God; * O save me according to thy mercy;

26 And they shall know how that this is thy hand, * and that thou, LORD, hast done it.

9 Let his children be waifs and beggars; *
let them be driven from the ruins of their homes.

10 Let the creditor seize everything he has; *
let strangers plunder his grains.

11 Let there be no one to show him kindness, *
and none to pity his fatherless children.

12 Let his descendants be destroyed, *
and his name be blotted out in the next generation.

13 Let the wickedness of his fathers be remembered before
the LORD, *
and his mother's sin not be blotted out;

14 Let their sin be always before the LORD; *
but let him root out their names from the earth;

15 Because he did not remember to show mercy, *
but persecuted the poor and needy
and sought to kill the brokenhearted.

16 He love cursing,
let it come upon him; *
he took no delight in blessing,
let it depart from him.

17 He put on cursing like a garment, *
let it soak into his body like water
and into his bones like oil;

18 Let it be to him like the cloak which he
wraps around himself, *
and like the belt that he wears continually.

19 Let this be the recompense from the LORD to my accusers, *
and to those who speak evil against me.

20 But you, O Lord my GOD,
oh, deal with me according to your Name; *
for your tender mercy's sake, deliver me.

21 For I am poor and needy, *
and my heart is wounded within me.

22 I have faded away like a shadow when it lengthens; *
I am shaken off like a locust.

23 My knees are weak through fasting, *
and my flesh is wasted and gaunt.

24 I have become a reproach to them; *
they see and shake their heads.

25 Help me, O LORD my God; *
save me for your mercy's sake.

26 Let them know that this is your hand, *
that you, O LORD, have done it.

27 Though they curse, yet bless thou ; and let them be confounded that rise up against me ; but let thy servant rejoice.

28 Let mine adversaries be clothed with shame ; and let them cover themselves with their own confusion, as with a cloak.

29 As for me, I will give great thanks unto the LORD with my mouth, and praise him among the multitude ;

30 For he shall stand at the right hand of the poor, to save his soul from unrighteous judges.

27 Though they curse, yet bless thou : and let them be confounded that rise up against me ; but let thy servant rejoice.

28 Let mine adversaries be clothed with shame : and let them cover themselves with their own confusion, as with a cloak.

29 As for me, I will give great thanks unto the LORD with my mouth : and praise him among the multitude ;

30 For he shall stand at the right hand of the poor : to save his soul from unrighteous judges.

THE TWENTY-THIRD DAY.

Morning Prayer.

Psalm cx. *Dixit Dominus.*

THE LORD said unto my Lord, Sit thou on my right hand, until I make thine enemies thy footstool.

2 The LORD shall send the rod of thy power out of Sion : be thou ruler, even in the midst among thine enemies.

3 In the day of thy power shall thy people offer thee free-will offerings with an holy worship : the dew of thy birth is of the womb of the morning.

4 The LORD sware, and will not repent, Thou art a Priest for ever after the order of Melchizedech.

5 The Lord upon thy right hand shall wound even kings in the day of his wrath.

6 He shall judge among the heathen ; he shall fill the places with the dead bodies, and smite in sunder the heads over divers countries.

7 He shall drink of the brook in the way ; therefore shall he lift up his head.

THE TWENTY-THIRD DAY.

Morning Prayer.

PSALM 110. *Dixit Dominus.*

THE LORD said unto my Lord : Sit thou on my right hand, until I make thine enemies thy footstool.

2 The LORD shall send the rod of thy power out of Sion : be thou ruler, even in the midst among thine enemies.

3 In the day of thy power shall thy people offer thee free-will offerings with an holy worship : the dew of thy birth is of the womb of the morning.

4 The LORD sware, and will not repent : Thou art a Priest for ever after the order of Melchizedech.

5 The Lord upon thy right hand : shall wound even kings in the day of his wrath.

6 He shall judge among the heathen : he shall fill the places with the dead bodies, and smite in sunder the heads over divers countries.

7 He shall drink of the brook in the way : therefore shall he lift up his head.

Psalm cxi. *Confitebor tibi.*

I WILL give thanks unto the LORD with my whole heart, secretly among the faithful, and in the congregation.

2 The works of the LORD are great, sought out of all them that have pleasure therein.

3 His work is worthy to be praised and had in honour, and his righteousness endureth for ever.

4 The merciful and gracious LORD hath so done his marvellous works, that they ought to be had in remembrance.

5 He hath given meat unto them that fear him ; he shall ever be mindful of his covenant.

PSALM 111. *Confitebor tibi.*

I WILL give thanks unto the LORD with my whole heart : secretly among the faithful, and in the congregation.

2 The works of the LORD are great : sought out of all them that have pleasure therein.

3 His work is worthy to be praised and had in honour : righteousness endureth for ever.

4 The merciful and gracious LORD hath so done his marvellous works : that they ought to be had in remembrance.

5 He hath given meat unto them that fear him : he shall ever be mindful of his covenant.

27 Though they curse, yet bless thou; * and let them be confounded that rise up against me; but let thy servant rejoice.

28 Let mine adversaries be clothed with shame; * and let them cover themselves with their own confusion, as with a cloak.

29 As for me, I will give great thanks unto the LORD with my mouth, * and praise him among the multitude;

30 For he shall stand at the right hand of the poor, * to save his soul from unrighteous judges.

27 They may curse, but you will bless; *
let those who rise up against me be put to shame,
and your servant will rejoice.

28 Let my accusers be clothed with disgrace *
and wrap themselves in their shame as in a cloak.

29 I will give great thanks to the LORD with my mouth; *
in the midst of the multitude will I praise him;

30 Because he stands ar the right hand of the needy, *
to save his life from those who would condemn him.

The Twenty-third Day.
Morning Prayer.
Psalm 110. *Dixit Dominus.*

THE LORD said unto my Lord, * Sit thou on my right hand, until I make thine enemies thy footstool.

2 The LORD shall send the rod of thy power out of Sion: * be thou ruler, even in the midst among thine enemies.

3 In the day of thy power shall thy people offer themselves willingly with an holy worship: * thy young men come to thee as dew from the womb of the morning.

4 The LORD sware, and will not repent, * Thou art a Priest for ever after the order of Melchizedek.

5 The Lord upon thy right hand * shall wound even kings in the day of his wrath.

6 He shall judge among the heathen; * he shall fill the places with the dead bodies, and smite in sunder the heads over divers countries.

7 He shall drink of the brook in the way; * therefore shall he lift up his head.

Twenty-third Day: Morning Prayer

110 *Dixit Dominus*

1 The LORD said to my Lord, "Sit at my right hand, *
until I make your enemies your footstool."

2 The LORD will send the scepter of your power out of Zion, *
saying "Rule over your enemies round about you.

3 Princely state has been yours from the day of your birth; *
in the beauty of holiness have I begotten you,
like dew from the womb of the morning."

4 The LORD has sworn and he will not recant: *
"You are a priest for ever after the order of Melchizedek."

5 The Lord who is at your right hand
will smite kings in the day of his wrath; *
he will rule over the nations.

6 He will heap high the corpses; *
he will smash heads over the wide earth.

7 He will drink from the brook beside the road; *
therefore he will lift high his head.

Psalm 111. *Confitebor tibi.*

I WILL give thanks unto the LORD with my whole heart, * secretly among the faithful, and in the congregation.

2 The works of the LORD are great, * sought out of all them that have pleasure therein.

3 His work is worthy to be praised and had in honour, * righteousness endureth for ever.

4 The merciful and gracious LORD hath so done his marvellous works, * that they ought to be had in remembrance.

5 He hath given meat unto them that fear him; * he shall ever be mindful of his covenant.

111 *Confitebor tibi*

1 Hallelujah!
I will give thanks to the LORD with my whole heart, *
in the assembly of the upright, in the congregation.

2 Great are the deeds of the LORD! *
they are studied by all who delight in them.

3 His work is full of majesty and splendor, *
and his righteousness endures for ever.

4 He makes his marvelous works to be remembered; *
the LORD is gracious and full of compassion.

5 He gives food to those who fear him; *
he is ever mindful of his covenant.

1789-1871

6 He hath showed his people the power of his works, that he may give them the heritage of the heathen.

7 The works of his hands are verity and judgment ; all his commandments are true.

8 They stand fast for ever and ever, and are done in truth and equity.

9 He sent redemption unto his people ; he hath commanded his covenant for ever ; holy and reverend is his Name.

10 The fear of the LORD is the beginning of wisdom ; a good understanding have all they that do thereafter ; the praise or it endureth for ever.

Psalm cxii. *Beatus vir.*

BLESSED is the man that feareth the LORD ; he hath great delight in his commandments.

2 His seed shall be mighty upon earth ; the generation of the faithful shall be blessed.

3 Riches and plenteousness shall be in his house ; and his righteousness endureth for ever.

4 Unto the godly there ariseth up light in the darkness ; he is merciful, loving, and righteous.

5 A good man is merciful, and lendeth ; and will guide his words with discretion.

6 For he shall never be moved : and the righteous shall be had in everlasting remembrance.

7 He will not be afraid of any evil tidings ; for his heart standeth fast, and believeth in the LORD.

8 His heart is stablished,[33] and will not shrink, until he see his desire upon his enemies.

9 He hath dispersed abroad, and given to the poor, and his righteousness remaineth for ever ; his horn shall be exalted with honour.

10 The ungodly shall see it, and it shall grieve him ; he shall gnash with his teeth, and consume away ; the desire of the ungodly shall perish.

1892

6 He hath showed his people the power of his works : that he may give them the heritage of the heathen.

7 The works of his hands are verity and judgment : all his commandments are true.

8 They stand fast for ever and ever : and are done in truth and equity.

9 He sent redemption unto his people : he hath commanded his covenant for ever ; holy and reverend is his Name.

10 The fear of the LORD is the beginning of wisdom : a good understanding have all they that do thereafter ; the praise of it endureth for ever.

PSALM 112. *Beatus vir.*

BLESSED is the man that feareth the LORD : he hath great delight in his commandments.

2 His seed shall be mighty upon earth : the generation of the faithful shall be blessed.

3 Riches and plenteousness shall be in his house : and his righteousness endureth for ever.

4 Unto the godly there ariseth up light in the darkness : he is merciful, loving, and righteous.

5 A good man is merciful, and lendeth : and will guide his words with discretion.

6 For he shall never be moved : and the righteous shall be had in everlasting remembrance.

7 He will not be afraid of any evil tidings : for his heart standeth fast, and believeth in the LORD.

8 His heart is stablished, and will not shrink : until he see his desire upon his enemies.

9 He hath dispersed abroad, and given to the poor : and his righteousness remaineth for ever ; his horn shall be exalted with honour.

10 The ungodly shall see it, and it shall grieve him : he shall gnash with his teeth, and consume away ; the desire of the ungodly shall perish.

[33]"established" in the English book.

6 He hath showed his people the power of his works, * that he may give them the heritage of the heathen.

7 The works of his hands are verity and judgment; * all his commandments are true.

8 They stand fast for ever and ever, * and are done in truth and equity.

9 He sent redemption unto his people; * he hath commanded his covenant for ever; holy and reverend is his Name.

10 The fear of the LORD is the beginning of wisdom; * a good understanding have all they that do thereafter; his praise endureth for ever.

6 He has shown his people the power of his works *
in giving them the lands of the nations.

7 The works of his hands are faithfulness and justice; *
all his commandments are sure.

8 They stand fast for ever and ever, *
because they are done in truth and equity.

9 He sent redemption to his people;
he commanded his covenant for ever; *
holy and awesome is his Name.

10 The fear of the LORD is the beginning of wisdom; *
those who act accordingly have a good understanding;
his praise endures for ever.

Psalm 112. *Beatus vir.*

BLESSED is the man that feareth the LORD; * he hath great delight in his commandments.

2 His seed shall be mighty upon earth; * the generation of the faithful shall be blessed.

3 Riches and plenteousness shall be in his house; * and his righteousness endureth for ever.

4 Unto the godly there ariseth up light in the darkness; * he is merciful, loving, and righteous.

5 A good man is merciful, and lendeth; * and will guide his words with discretion.

6 For he shall never be moved: * and the righteous shall be had in everlasting remembrance.

7 He will not be afraid of any evil tidings; * for his heart standeth fast, and believeth in the LORD.

8 His heart is stablished, and will not shrink, * until he see his desire upon his enemies.

9 He hath dispersed abroad, and given to the poor, * and his righteousness remaineth for ever; his horn shall be exalted with honour.

10 The ungodly shall see it, and it shall grieve him; * he shall gnash with his teeth, and consume away; the desire of the ungodly shall perish.

112 *Beatus vir*

1 Hallelujah!
Happy are they who fear the Lord *
and have great delight in his commandments!

2 Their descendants will be mighty in the land; *
the generation of the upright will be blessed.

3 Wealth and riches will be in their house, *
and their righteousness will last for ever.

4 Light shines in the darkness for the upright; *
the righteous are merciful and full of compassion.

5 It is good for them to be generous in lending *
and to manage their affairs with justice.

6 For they will never be shaken; *
the righteous will be kept in everlasting remembrance.

7 They will not be afraid of any evil rumors; *
their heart is right;
they put their trust in the Lord.

8 Their heart is established and will not shrink, *
until they see their desire upon their enemies.

9 They have given freely to the poor, *
and their righteousness stands fast for ever;
they will hold up their head with honor.

10 The wicked will see it and be angry;
they will gnash their teeth and pine away; *
the desires of the wicked will perish.

Psalm cxiii. *Laudate, pueri.*

PRAISE the LORD, ye servants ; O praise the Name of the LORD.

2 Blessed be the Name of the LORD from this time forth for evermore.

3 The LORD'S Name is praised from the rising up of the sun unto the going down of the same.

4 The LORD is high above all heathen, and his glory above the heavens.

5 Who is like unto the LORD our God, that hath his dwelling so high, and yet humbleth himself to behold the things that are in heaven and earth!

6 He taketh up the simple out of the dust, and lifteth the poor out of the mire ;

7 That he may set him with the princes, even with the princes of his people.

8 He maketh the barren woman to keep house, and to be a joyful mother of children.

PSALM 113. *Laudate, pueri.*

PRAISE the LORD, ye servants : O praise the Name of the LORD.

2 Blessed be the Name of the LORD : from this time forth for evermore.

3 The LORD'S Name is praised : from the rising up of the sun unto the going down of the same

4 The LORD is high above all heathen : and his glory above the heavens.

5 Who is like unto the LORD our God, that hath his dwelling so high : and yet humbleth himself to behold the things that are in heaven and earth!

6 He taketh up the simple out of the dust : and lifteth the poor out of the mire ;

7 That he may set him with the princes : even with the princes of his people.

8 He maketh the barren woman to keep house : and to be a joyful mother of children.

Evening Prayer.

Psalm cxiv. *In exitu Israel.*

WHEN Israel came out of Egypt, and the house of Jacob from among the strange people,

2 Judah was his sanctuary, and Israel his dominion.

3 The sea saw that, and fled ; Jordan was driven back.

4 The mountains skipped like rams, and the little hills like young sheep.

5 What aileth thee, O thou sea, that thou fleddest? and thou Jordan, that thou wast driven back?

6 Ye mountains, that ye skipped like rams? and ye little hills, like young sheep.

7 Tremble, thou earth, at the presence of the Lord ; at the presence of the God of Jacob ;

8 Who turned the hard rock into a standing water, and the flint-stone into a springing well.

Evening Prayer.

PSALM 114. *In exitu Israel.*

WHEN Israel came out of Egypt : and the house of Jacob from among the strange people,

2 Judah was his sanctuary : and Israel his dominion.

3 The sea saw that, and fled : Jordan was driven back.

4 The mountains skipped like rams : and the little hills like young sheep.

5 What aileth thee, O thou sea, that thou fleddest : and thou Jordan, that thou wast driven back?

6 Ye mountains, that ye skipped like rams : and ye little hills, like young sheep?

7 Tremble, thou earth, at the presence of the Lord : at the presence of the God of Jacob ;

8 Who turned the hard rock into a standing water : and the flint-stone into a springing well.

Psalm 113. *Laudate, pueri.*

PRAISE the LORD, ye servants; * O praise the Name of the LORD.
2 Blessed be the Name of the LORD * from this time forth for evermore.
3 The LORD'S Name is praised * from the rising up of the sun unto the going down of the same
4 The LORD is high above all nations, * and his glory above the heavens.
5 Who is like unto the LORD our God, that hath his dwelling so high, * and yet humbleth himself to behold the things that are in heaven and earth!
6 He taketh up the simple out of the dust, * and lifteth the poor out of the mire;
7 That he may set him with the princes, * even with the princes of his people.
8 He maketh the barren woman to keep house, * and to be a joyful mother of children.

113 *Laudata, pueri*

1 Hallelujah!
Give praise, you servants of the LORD; *
praise the Name of the LORD.

2 Let the Name of the LORD be blessed, *
from this time forth for evermore.

3 From the rising of the sun to its going down *
let the Name of the LORD be praised.

4 The LORD is high above all nations, *
and his glory above the heavens.

5 Who is like the LORD our God, who sits enthroned on high, *
but stoops to behold the heavens and the earth?

6 He takes up the weak out of the dust *
and lifts up the poor from the ashes.

7 He sets them with the princes, *
with the princes of his people.

8 He makes the woman of a childless house *
to be a joyful mother of children.

Evening Prayer.

Psalm 114. *In exitu Israel.*

WHEN Israel came out of Egypt, * and the house of Jacob from among the strange people,
2 Judah was his sanctuary, * and Israel his dominion.
3 The sea saw that, and fled; * Jordan was driven back.
4 The mountains skipped like rams, * and the little hills like young sheep.
5 What aileth thee, O thou sea, that thou fleddest? * and thou Jordan, that thou wast driven back?
6 Ye mountains, that ye skipped like rams? * and ye little hills, like young sheep?
7 Tremble, thou earth, at the presence of the Lord: * at the presence of the God of Jacob;
8 Who turned the hard rock into a standing water, * and the flint-stone into a springing well.

Twenty-third Day: Evening Prayer

114 *In exitu Israel*

1 Hallelujah!
When Israel came out of Egypt, *
the house of Jacob from a people of strange speech,

2 Judah became God's sanctuary *
and Israel his dominion.

3 The sea beheld it and fled; *
Jordan turned and went back.

4 The mountains skipped like rams, *
and the little hills like young sheep.

5 What ailed you, O sea, that you fled? *
O Jordan, that you turned back?

6 You mountains, that you skipped like rams? *
you little hills like young sheep?

7 Tremble, O earth, at the presence of the Lord, *
at the presence of the God of Jacob,

8 Who turned the hard rock into a pool of water *
and flint-stone into a flowing spring.

Psalm cxv. *Non nobis, Domine.*

NOT unto us, O LORD, not unto us, but unto thy Name give the praise ; for thy loving mercy, and for thy truth's sake.

2 Wherefore shall the heathen say, Where is now their God?

3 As for our God, he is in heaven : he hath done whatsoever pleased him.

4 Their idols are silver and gold, even the work of men's hands.

5 They have mouths, and speak not ; eyes have they, and see not.

6 They have ears, and hear not ; noses have they, and smell not.

7 They have hands, and handle not ; feet have they, and walk not ; neither speak they through their throat.

8 They that make them are like unto them ; and so are all such as put their trust in them.

9 But thou, house of Israel, trust thou in the LORD ; he is their succour and defence.

10 Ye house of Aaron, put your trust in the LORD ; he is their helper and defender.

11 Ye that fear the LORD, put your trust in the LORD ; he is their helper and defender.

12 The LORD hath been mindful of us, and he shall bless us ; even he shall bless the house of Israel, he shall bless the house of Aaron.

13 He shall bless them that fear the LORD, both small and great.

14 The LORD shall increase you more and more, you and your children.

15 Ye are the blessed of the LORD, who made heaven and earth.

16 All the whole heavens are the LORD'S ; the earth hath he given to the children of men.

17 The dead praise not thee, O LORD, neither all they that go down into silence.

18 But we will praise the LORD, from this time forth for evermore. Praise the LORD.

PSALM 115. *Non nobis, Domine.*

NOT unto us, O LORD, not unto us, but unto thy Name give the praise : for thy loving mercy, and for thy truth's sake.

2 Wherefore shall the heathen say : Where is now their God?

3 As for our God, he is in heaven : he hath done whatsoever pleased him.

4 Their idols are silver and gold : even the work of men's hands.

5 They have mouths, and speak not : eyes have they, and see not.

6 They have ears, and hear not : noses have they, and smell not.

7 They have hands, and handle not ; feet have they, and walk not : neither speak they through their throat.

8 They that make them are like unto them : and so are all such as put their trust in them.

9 But thou, house of Israel, trust thou in the LORD : he is their succour and defence.

10 Ye house of Aaron, put your trust in the LORD : he is their helper and defender.

11 Ye that fear the LORD, put your trust in the LORD : he is their helper and defender.

12 The LORD hath been mindful of us, and he shall bless us : even he shall bless the house of Israel, he shall bless the house of Aaron.

13 He shall bless them that fear the LORD : both small and great.

14 The LORD shall increase you more and more : you and your children.

15 Ye are the blessed of the LORD : who made heaven and earth.

16 All the whole heavens are the LORD'S : the earth hath he given to the children of men.

17 The dead praise not thee, O LORD : neither all they that go down into silence.

18 But we will praise the LORD : from this time forth for evermore. Praise the LORD.

Psalm 115. *Non nobis, Domine.*

NOT unto us, O LORD, not unto us, but unto thy Name give the praise; * for thy loving mercy, and for thy truth's sake.

2 Wherefore shall the heathen say, * Where is now their God?

3 As for our God, he is in heaven: * he hath done whatsoever pleased him.

4 Their idols are silver and gold, * even the work of men's hands.

5 They have mouths, and speak not; * eyes have they, and see not.

6 They have ears, and hear not; * noses have they, and smell not.

7 They have hands, and handle not; feet have they, and walk not; * neither speak they through their throat.

8 They that make them are like unto them; * and so are all such as put their trust in them.

9 But thou, house of Israel, trust thou in the LORD; * he is their helper and defender.

10 Ye house of Aaron, put your trust in the LORD; * he is their helper and defender.

11 Ye that fear the LORD, put your trust in the LORD; * he is their helper and defender.

12 The LORD hath been mindful of us, and he shall bless us; * even he shall bless the house of Israel, he shall bless the house of Aaron.

13 He shall bless them that fear the LORD, * both small and great.

14 The LORD shall increase you more and more, * you and your children.

15 Ye are the blessed of the LORD, * who made heaven and earth.

16 All the whole heavens are the LORD'S; * the earth hath he given to the children of men.

17 The dead praise not thee, O LORD, * neither all they that go down into silence.

18 But we will praise the LORD, * from this time forth for evermore. Praise the LORD.

115 *Non nobis, Domine*

1 Not to us, O LORD, not to us,
but to your Name give glory; *
because of your love and because of your faithfulness.

2 Why should the heathen say, *
"Where then is their God?"

3 Our God is in heaven; *
whatever he wills to do he does.

4 Their idols are silver and gold, *
the work of human hands.

5 They have mouths, but they cannot speak; *
eyes have they, but they cannot see;

6 They have ears, but they cannot hear; *
noses, but they cannot smell;

7 They have hands, but they cannot feel;
feet, but they cannot walk; *
they make no sound with their throat.

8 Those who make them are like them, *
and so are all who put their trust in them.

9 O Israel, trust in the LORD; *
he is their help and their shield.

10 O house of Aaron, trust in the LORD; *
he is their help and their shield.

11 You who fear the LORD, trust in the LORD; *
he is their help and their shield.

12 The LORD has been mindful of us, and he will bless us; *
he will bless the house of Israel;
he will bless the house of Aaron;

13 He will bless those who fear the LORD, *
both small and great together.

14 May the LORD increase you more and more, *
you and your children after you.

15 May you be blessed by the LORD, *
the maker of heaven and earth.

16 The heaven of heavens is the LORD'S, *
but he entrusted the earth to its peoples.

17 The dead do not praise the LORD, *
nor all those who go down into silence;

18 But we will bless the LORD, *
from this time forth for evermore.
Hallelujah!

THE TWENTY-FOURTH DAY.

Morning Prayer.

Psalm cxvi. *Dilexi, quoniam.*

I AM well pleased that the LORD hath heard the voice of my prayer ;

2 That he hath inclined his ear unto me ; therefore will I call upon him as long as I live.

3 The snare of death compassed me round about, and the pains of hell gat hold upon me.

4 I shall find trouble and heaviness and I will call upon the Name of the LORD ; O LORD, I beseech thee, deliver my soul.

5 Gracious is the LORD, and righteous ; yea, our God is merciful.

6 The LORD preserveth the simple : I was in misery, and he helped me.

7 Turn again then unto thy rest, O my soul ; for the LORD hath rewarded thee.

8 And why? thou hast delivered my soul from death, mine eyes from tears, and my feet from falling.

9 I will walk before the LORD in the land of the living.

10 I believed, and therefore will I speak ; but I was sore troubled : I said in my haste, All men are liars.

11 What reward shall I give unto the LORD for all the benefits that he hath done unto me?

12 I will receive the cup of salvation, and call upon the Name of the LORD.

13 I will pay my vows now in the presence of all his people : right dear in the sight of the LORD is the death of his saints.

14 Behold, O LORD, how that I am thy servant ; I am thy servant, and the son of thy[34] handmaid ; thou hast broken my bonds in sunder.

15 I will offer to thee the sacrifice of thanksgiving, and will call upon the Name of the LORD.

16 I will pay my vows unto the LORD, in the sight of all his people, in the courts of the LORD'S house ; even in the midst of thee, O Jerusalem. Praise the LORD.

THE TWENTY-FOURTH DAY.

Morning Prayer.

PSALM 116. *Dilexi, quoniam.*

I AM well pleased : that the LORD hath heard the voice of my prayer ;

2 That he hath inclined his ear unto me : therefore will I call upon him as long as I live.

3 The snare of death compassed me round about : and the pains of hell gat hold upon me.

4 I shall find trouble and heaviness, and will call upon the Name of the LORD : O LORD, I beseech thee, deliver my soul.

5 Gracious is the LORD, and righteous : yea, our God is merciful.

6 The LORD preserveth the simple : I was in misery, and he helped me.

7 Turn again then unto thy rest, O my soul : for the LORD hath rewarded thee.

8 And why? thou hast delivered my soul from death : mine eyes from tears, and my feet from falling.

9 I will walk before the LORD : in the land of the living.

10 I believed, and therefore will I speak ; but I was sore troubled : I said in my haste, All men are liars.

11 What reward shall I give unto the LORD : for all the benefits that he hath done unto me?

12 I will receive the cup of salvation : and call upon the Name of the LORD.

13 I will pay my vows now in the presence of all his people : right dear in the sight of the LORD is the death of his saints.

14 Behold, O LORD, how that I am thy servant : I am thy servant, and the son of thine handmaid ; thou hast broken my bonds in sunder.

15 I will offer to thee the sacrifice of thanksgiving : and will call upon the Name of the LORD.

16 I will pay my vows unto the LORD, in the sight of all his people : in the courts of the LORD'S house, even in the midst of thee, O Jerusalem. Praise the LORD.

[34]"thine" prior to 1793.

1928

The Twenty-fourth Day.

Morning Prayer.

Psalm 116. *Dilexi, quoniam.*

MY delight is in the LORD; * because he hath heard
the voice of my prayer;
2 Because he hath inclined his ear unto me; *
therefore will I call upon him as long as I live.
3 The snare of death compassed me round about, *
and the pains of hell gat hold upon me.
4 I found trouble and heaviness; then called I upon
the Name of the LORD; * O LORD, I beseech thee,
deliver my soul.
5 Gracious is the LORD, and righteous; * yea, our
God is merciful.
6 The LORD preserveth the simple: * I was in
misery, and he helped me.
7 Turn again then unto thy rest, O my soul; * for
the LORD hath rewarded thee.
8 And why? thou hast delivered my soul from
death, * mine eyes from tears, and my feet from falling.
9 I will walk before the LORD * in the land of the
living.
10 I believed, and therefore will I speak; but I was
sore troubled: * I said in my haste, All men are liars.
11 What reward shall I give unto the LORD * for all
the benefits that he hath done unto me?
12 I will receive the cup of salvation, * and call
upon the Name of the LORD.
13 I will pay my vows now in the presence of all his
people: * right dear in the sight of the LORD is the
death of his saints.
14 Behold, O LORD, how that I am thy servant; * I
am thy servant, and the son of thine handmaid; thou
hast broken my bonds in sunder.
15 I will offer to thee the sacrifice of thanksgiving, * and will call upon the Name of the LORD.
16 I will pay my vows unto the LORD, in the sight of
all his people, * in the courts of the LORD'S house; even
in the midst of thee, O Jerusalem. Praise the LORD.

1979

Twenty-fourth Day: Morning Prayer

116 *Dilexi, quoniam*

1 I love the LORD, because he has heard the voice of my supplication, *
because he has inclined his ear to me whenever I called upon him.

2 The cords of death entangled me;
the grip of the grave took hold of me; *
I came to grief and sorrow.

3 Then I called upon the Name of the LORD: *
"O LORD, I pray you, save my life."

4 Gracious is the LORD and righteous; *
our God is full of compassion.

5 The LORD watches over the innocent; *
I was brought very low, and he helped me.

6 Turn again to your rest, O my soul, *
for the LORD has treated you well.

7 For you have rescued my life from death, *
my eyes from tears, and my feet from stumbling.

8 I will walk in the presence of the LORD *
in the land of the living.

9 I believed, even when I said,
"I have been brought very low." *
In my distress I said, "No one can be trusted."

10 How shall I repay the LORD *
for all the good things he has done for me?

11 I will lift up the cup of salvation *
and call upon the Name of the LORD.

12 I will fulfill my vows to the LORD *
in the presence of all his people.

13 Precious in the sight of the LORD *
is the death of his servants.

14 O LORD, I am your servant; *
I am your servant and the child of your handmaid;
you have freed me from my bonds.

15 I will offer you the sacrifice of thanksgiving *
and call upon the Name of the LORD.

16 I will fulfill my vows to the LORD *
in the presence of all his people,

17 In the courts of the LORD'S house, *
in the midst of you, O Jerusalem.
Hallelujah!

Psalm cxvii. *Laudate Dominum.*

O PRAISE the LORD, all ye heathen ; praise him, all ye nations.

2 For his merciful kindness is ever more and more towards us ; and the truth of the LORD endureth for ever. Praise the LORD.

Psalm cxviii. *Confitemini Domino.*

O GIVE thanks unto the LORD, for he is gracious ; because his mercy endureth for ever.

2 Let Israel now confess that he is gracious, and that his mercy endureth for ever.

3 Let the house of Aaron now confess, that his mercy endureth for ever.

4 Yea, let them now that fear the LORD confess, that his mercy endureth for ever.

5 I called upon the LORD in trouble ; and the LORD heard me at large.

6 The LORD is on my side ; I will not fear what man doeth unto me.

7 The LORD taketh my part with them that help me ; therefore shall I see my desire upon mine enemies.

8 It is better to trust in the LORD, than to put any confidence in man.

9 It is better to trust in the LORD, than to put any confidence in princes.

10 All nations compassed me round about ; but in the Name of the LORD will I destroy them.

11 They kept me in on every side, they kept me in, I say, on every side ; but in the Name of the LORD will I destroy them.

12 They came about me like bees, and are extinct even as the fire among the thorns ; for in the Name of the LORD I will destroy them.

13 Thou hast thrust sore at me, that I might fall ; but the LORD was my help.

14 The LORD is my strength, and my song ; and is become my salvation.

15 The voice of joy and health is in the dwellings of the righteous ; the right hand of the LORD bringeth mighty things to pass.

PSALM 117. *Laudate Dominum.*

O PRAISE the LORD, all ye heathen : praise him, all ye nations.

2 For his merciful kindness is ever more and more toward us : and the truth of the LORD endureth for ever. Praise the LORD.

PSALM 118. *Confitemini Domino.*

O GIVE thanks unto the LORD, for he is gracious : because his mercy endureth for ever.

2 Let Israel now confess that he is gracious : and that his mercy endureth for ever.

3 Let the house of Aaron now confess : that his mercy endureth for ever.

4 Yea, let them now that fear the LORD confess : that his mercy endureth for ever.

5 I called upon the LORD in trouble : and the LORD heard me at large.

6 The LORD is on my side : I will not fear what man doeth unto me.

7 The LORD taketh my part with them that help me : therefore shall I see my desire upon mine enemies.

8 It is better to trust in the LORD : than to put any confidence in man.

9 It is better to trust in the LORD : than to put any confidence in princes.

10 All nations compassed me round about : but in the Name of the LORD will I destroy them.

11 They kept me in on every side, they kept me in, I say, on every side : but in the Name of the LORD will I destroy them.

12 They came about me like bees, and are extinct even as the fire among the thorns : for in the Name of the LORD I will destroy them.

13 Thou hast thrust sore at me, that I might fall : but the LORD was my help.

14 The LORD is my strength, and my song : and is become my salvation.

15 The voice of joy and health is in the dwellings of the righteous : the right hand of the LORD bringeth mighty things to pass.

Psalm 117. *Laudate Dominum.*

O PRAISE the LORD, all ye nations; * praise him, all ye peoples.

2 For his merciful kindness is ever more and more toward us; * and the truth of the LORD endureth for ever. Praise the LORD.

Psalm 118. *Confitemini Domino.*

O GIVE thanks unto the LORD, for he is gracious; * because his mercy endureth for ever.

2 Let Israel now confess that he is gracious, * and that his mercy endureth for ever.

3 Let the house of Aaron now confess, * that his mercy endureth for ever.

4 Yea, let them now that fear the LORD confess, * that his mercy endureth for ever.

5 I called upon the LORD in trouble; * and the LORD heard me at large.

6 The LORD is on my side; * I will not fear what man doeth unto me.

7 The LORD taketh my part with them that help me; * therefore shall I see my desire upon mine enemies.

8 It is better to trust in the LORD, * than to put any confidence in man.

9 It is better to trust in the LORD, * than to put any confidence in princes.

10 All nations compassed me round about; * but in the Name of the LORD will I destroy them.

11 They kept me in on every side, they kept me in, I say, on every side; * but in the Name of the LORD will I destroy them.

12 They came about me like bees, and are extinct even as the fire among the thorns; * for in the Name of the LORD I will destroy them.

13 Thou hast thrust sore at me, that I might fall; * but the LORD was my help.

14 The LORD is my strength, and my song; * and is become my salvation.

15 The voice of joy and health is in the dwellings of the righteous; * the right hand of the LORD bringeth mighty things to pass.

117 *Laudate Dominum*

1 Praise the LORD, all you nations; *
laud him, all you peoples.

2 For his loving-kindness toward us is great, *
and the faithfulness of the LORD endures for ever.
Hallelujah!

118 *Confitemini Domino*

1 Give thanks to the LORD, for he is good; *
his mercy endures for ever.

2 Let Israel now proclaim, *
"His mercy endures for ever."

3 Let the house of Aaron now proclaim, *
"His mercy endures for ever."

4 Let those who fear the LORD now proclaim, *
"His mercy endures for ever."

5 I called to the LORD in my distress; *
the LORD answered by setting me free.

6 The LORD is at my side, therefore I will not fear; *
what can anyone do to me?

7 The LORD is at my side to help me; *
I will triumph over those who hate me.

8 It is better to rely on the LORD *
than to put any trust in flesh.

9 It is better to rely on the LORD *
than to put any trust in rulers.

10 All the ungodly encompass me; *
in the name of the LORD I will repel them.

11 They hem me in, they hem me in on every side; *
in the name of the LORD I will repel them.

12 They swarm about me like bees;
they blaze like a fire of thorns; *
in the name of the LORD I will repel them.

13 I was pressed so hard that I almost fell, *
but the LORD came to my help.

14 The LORD is my strength and my song, *
and he has become my salvation.

15 There is a sound of exultation and victory *
in the tents of the righteous:

1789-1871

16 The right hand of the LORD hath the pre-
eminence ; the right hand of the LORD bringeth mighty
things to pass.
17 I shall not die, but live, and declare the works of
the LORD.
18 The LORD hath chastened and corrected me ;
but he hath not given me over unto death.
19 Open me the gates of righteousness, that I may
go into them, and give thanks unto the LORD.
20 This is the gate of the LORD, the righteous shall
enter into it.
21 I will thank thee ; for thou hast heard me, and
art become my salvation.
22 The same stone which the builders refused, is
become the head-stone in the corner.
23 This is the LORD'S doing, and it is marvellous in
our eyes.
24 This is the day which the LORD hath made ; we
will rejoice and be glad in it.
25 Help me now, O LORD : O LORD, send us now
prosperity.
26 Blessed be he that cometh in the Name of the
LORD : we have wished you good luck, ye that are of
the house of the LORD.
27 God is the LORD, who hath showed us light :
bind the sacrifice with cords, yea, even unto the horns
of the altar.
28 Thou art my God, and I will thank thee ; thou
art my God, and I will praise thee.
29 O give thanks unto the LORD ; for he is gracious,
and his mercy endureth for ever.

1892

16 The right hand of the LORD hath the pre-
eminence : the right hand of the LORD bringeth mighty
things to pass.
17 I shall not die, but live : and declare the works
of the LORD.
18 The LORD hath chastened and corrected me :
but he hath not given me over unto death.
19 Open me the gates of righteousness : that I may
go into them, and give thanks unto the LORD.
20 This is the gate of the LORD : the righteous shall
enter into it.
21 I will thank thee, for thou hast heard me : and
art become my salvation.
22 The same stone which the builders refused : is
become the head-stone in the corner.
23 This is the LORD'S doing : and it is marvellous in
our eyes.
24 This is the day which the LORD hath made : we
will rejoice and be glad in it.
25 Help me now, O LORD : O LORD, send us now
prosperity.
26 Blessed be he that cometh in the Name of the
LORD : we have wished you good luck, ye that are of
the house of the LORD.
27 God is the LORD, who hath showed us light :
bind the sacrifice with cords, yea, even unto the horns
of the altar.
28 Thou art my God, and I will thank thee : thou
art my God, and I will praise thee.
29 O give thanks unto the LORD, for he is gracious :
and his mercy endureth for ever.

1789-1871

Evening Prayer.

Psalm cxix. *Beati immaculati.*

BLESSED are those that are undefiled in the way, and
walk in the law of the LORD.
2 Blessed are they that keep his testimonies, and
seek him with their whole heart.
3 Even they who do no wickedness, and walk in his
ways.

1892

Evening Prayer.

PSALM 119. *Beati immaculati.*

BLESSED are those that are undefiled in the way : and
walk in the law of the LORD.
2 Blessed are they that keep his testimonies : and
seek him with their whole heart.
3 For they who do no wickedness : walk in his ways.

16 The right hand of the LORD hath the pre-eminence; * the right hand of the LORD bringeth mighty things to pass.

17 I shall not die, but live, * and declare the works of the LORD.

18 The LORD hath chastened and corrected me; * but he hath not given me over unto death.

19 Open me the gates of righteousness, * that I may go into them, and give thanks unto the LORD.

20 This is the gate of the LORD, * the righteous shall enter into it.

21 I will thank thee; for thou hast heard me, * and art become my salvation.

22 The same stone which the builders refused, * is become the head-stone in the corner.

23 This is the LORD'S doing, * and it is marvellous in our eyes.

24 This is the day which the LORD hath made; * we will rejoice and be glad in it.

25 Help me now, O LORD: * O LORD, send us now prosperity.

26 Blessed be he that cometh in the Name of the LORD: * we have wished you good luck, we that are of the house of the LORD.

27 God is the LORD, who hath showed us light: * bind the sacrifice with cords, yea, even unto the horns of the altar.

28 Thou art my God, and I will thank thee; * thou art my God, and I will praise thee.

29 O give thanks unto the LORD; for he is gracious, * and his mercy endureth for ever.

Evening Prayer.

Psalm 119. I. *Beati immaculati.*

BLESSED are those that are undefiled in the way, * and walk in the law of the LORD.

2 Blessed are they that keep his testimonies, * and seek him with their whole heart;

3 Even they who do no wickedness, * and walk in his ways.

16 "The right hand of the LORD has triumphed! *
the right hand of the LORD is exalted!
the right hand of the LORD has triumphed!"

17 I shall not die, but live, *
and declare the works of the LORD.

18 The LORD has punished me sorely, *
but he did not hand me over to death.

19 Open for me the gates of righteousness; *
I will enter them;
I will offer thanks to the LORD.

20 "This is the gate of the LORD; *
he who is righteous may enter."

21 I will give thanks to you, for you answered me *
and have become my salvation.

22 The same stone which the builders rejected *
has become the chief cornerstone.

23 This is the LORD'S doing, *
and it is marvelous in our eyes.

24 On this day the LORD has acted; *
we will rejoice and be glad in it.

25 Hosannah, LORD, hosannah! *
LORD, send us now success.

26 Blessed is he who comes in the name of the Lord; *
we bless you from the house of the LORD.

27 God is the LORD; he has shined upon us; *
form a procession with branches up to the horns of the altar.

28 "You are my God, and I will thank you; *
you are my God, and I will exalt you."

29 Give thanks to the LORD, for he is good; *
his mercy endures for ever.

Twenty-fourth Day: Evening Prayer

119

Aleph *Beati immaculati*

1 Happy are they whose way is blameless, *
who walk in the law of the LORD!

2 Happy are they who observe his decrees *
and seek him with all their hearts!

3 Who never do any wrong, *
but always walk in his ways.

4 Thou hast charged that we shall diligently keep thy commandments.
5 O that my ways were made so direct, that I might keep thy statutes!
6 So shall I not be confounded, while I have respect unto all thy commandments.
7 I will thank thee with an unfeigned heart, when I shall have learned the judgments of thy righteousness.
8 I will keep thy ceremonies; O forsake me not utterly.

4 Thou hast charged : that we shall diligently keep thy commandments.
5 O that my ways were made so direct : that I might keep thy statutes!
6 So shall I not be confounded : while I have respect unto all thy commandments.
7 I will thank thee with an unfeigned heart : when I shall have learned the judgments of thy righteousness.
8 I will keep thy ceremonies : O forsake me not utterly.

In quo corriget?[35]

WHEREWITHAL shall a young man cleanse his way? even by ruling himself after thy word.
2 With my whole heart have I sought thee; O let me not go wrong out of thy commandments!
3 Thy words have I hid within my heart, that I should not sin against thee.
4 Blessed art thou, O LORD; O teach me thy statutes.
5 With my lips have I been telling of all the judgments of thy mouth.
6 I have had as great delight in the way of thy testimonies, as in all manner of riches.
7 I will talk of thy commandments, and have respect unto thy ways.
8 My delight shall be in thy statutes, and I will not forget thy word.

In quo corrigit?

WHEREWITHAL shall a young man cleanse his way : even by ruling himself after thy word.
10 With my whole heart have I sought thee : O let me not go wrong out of thy commandments.
11 Thy words have I hid within my heart : that I should not sin against thee.
12 Blessed art thou, O LORD : O teach me thy statutes.
13 With my lips have I been telling : of all the judgments of thy mouth.
14 I have had as great delight in the way of thy testimonies : as in all manner of riches.
15 I will talk of thy commandments : and have respect unto thy ways.
16 My delight shall be in thy statutes : and I will not forget thy word.

Retribue servo tuo.

O DO well unto thy servant; that I may live, and keep thy word.
2 Open thou mine eyes; that I may see the wondrous things of thy law.
3 I am a stranger upon earth; O hide not thy commandments from me!
4 My soul breaketh out for the very fervent desire that it hath alway unto thy judgments.
5 Thou hast rebuked the proud; and cursed are they that do err from thy commandments.
6 O turn from me shame and rebuke; for I have kept thy testimonies.

Retribue servo tuo.

O DO well unto thy servant : that I may live, and keep thy word.
18 Open thou mine eyes : that I may see the wondrous things of thy law.
19 I am a stranger upon earth : O hide not thy commandments from me.
20 My soul breaketh out for the very fervent desire : that it hath alway unto thy judgments.
21 Thou hast rebuked the proud : and cursed are they that do err from thy commandments.
22 O turn from me shame and rebuke : for I have kept thy testimonies.

[35] *sic.*

4 Thou hast charged * that we shall diligently keep thy commandments.

5 O that my ways were made so direct, * that I might keep thy statutes!

6 So shall I not be confounded, * while I have respect unto all thy commandments.

7 I will thank thee with an unfeigned heart, * when I shall have learned the judgments of thy righteousness.

8 I will keep thy statutes; * O forsake me not utterly.

II. *In quo corrigit?*

WHEREWITHAL shall a young man cleanse his way? * even by ruling himself after thy word.

10 With my whole heart have I sought thee; * O let me not go wrong out of thy commandments.

11 Thy word have I hid within my heart, * that I should not sin against thee.

12 Blessed art thou, O LORD; * O teach me thy statutes.

13 With my lips have I been telling * of all the judgments of thy mouth.

14 I have had as great delight in the way of thy testimonies, * as in all manner of riches.

15 I will talk of thy commandments, * and have respect unto thy ways.

16 My delight shall be in thy statutes, * and I will not forget thy word.

III. *Retribue servo tuo.*

O DO well unto thy servant; * that I may live, and keep thy word.

18 Open thou mine eyes; * that I may see the wondrous things of thy law.

19 I am a stranger upon earth; * O hide not thy commandments from me.

20 My soul breaketh out for the very fervent desire * that it hath alway unto thy judgments.

21 Thou hast rebuked the proud; * and cursed are they that do err from thy commandments.

22 O turn from me shame and rebuke; * for I have kept thy testimonies.

4 You laid down your commandments, *
that we should fully keep them.

5 Oh, that my ways were made so direct *
that I might keep your statutes!

6 Then I should not be put to shame, *
when I regard all your commandments.

7 I will thank you with an unfeigned heart, *
when I have learned your righteous judgments.

8 I will keep your statutes; *
do not utterly forsake me.

Beth *In quo corrigit?*

9 How shall a young man cleanse his way? *
By keeping to your words.

10 With my whole heart I seek you; *
let me not stray from your commandments.

11 I treasure your promise in my heart, *
that I may not sin against you.

12 Blessed are you, O LORD; *
instruct me in your statutes.

13 With my lips will I recite *
all the judgments of your mouth.

14 I have taken greater delight in the way of your decrees *
than in all manner of riches.

15 I will meditate on your commandments *
and give attention to your ways.

16 My delight is in your statutes; *
I will not forget your word.

Gimel *Rebtribue servo tuo*

17 Deal bountifully with your servant, *
that I may live and keep your word.

18 Open my eyes, that I may see *
the wonders of your law.

19 I am a stranger here on earth; *
do not hide your commandments from me.

20 My soul is consumed at all times *
with longing for your judgments.

21 You have rebuked the insolent; *
cursed are they who stray from your commandments!

22 Turn from me shame and rebuke, *
for I have kept your decrees.

1789-1871

7 Princes also did sit and speak against me ; but thy servant is occupied in thy statutes.
8 For thy testimonies are my delight, and my counsellors.

1892

23 Princes also did sit and speak against me : but thy servant is occupied in thy statutes.
24 For thy testimonies are my delight : and my counsellors.

1789-1871

Adhæsit pavimento.

MY soul cleaveth to the dust ; O quicken thou me, according to thy word.
2 I have acknowledged my ways, and thou heardest me : O teach me thy statutes!
3 Make me to understand the way of thy commandments ; and so shall I talk of thy wondrous works.
4 My soul melteth away for very heaviness ; comfort thou me according unto thy word.
5 Take from me the way of lying, and cause thou me to make much of thy law.
6 I have chosen the way of truth, and thy judgments have I laid before me.
7 I have stuck unto thy testimonies ; O LORD, confound me not!
8 I will run the way of thy commandments, when thou hast set my heart at liberty.

1892

Adhæsit pavimento.

MY soul cleaveth to the dust : O quicken thou me, according to thy word.
26 I have acknowledged my ways, and thou heardest me : O teach me thy statutes.
27 Make me to understand the way of thy commandments : and so shall I talk of thy wondrous works.
28 My soul melteth away for very heaviness : comfort thou me according unto thy word.
29 Take from me the way of lying : and cause thou me to make much of thy law.
30 I have chosen the way of truth : and thy judgments have I laid before me.
31 I have stuck unto thy testimonies : O LORD, confound me not.
32 I will run the way of thy commandments : when thou hast set my heart at liberty.

1789-1871

THE TWENTY-FIFTH DAY.

Morning Prayer.

Legem pone.

TEACH me, O LORD, the way of thy statutes, and I shall keep it unto the end.
2 Give me understanding, and I shall keep thy law ; yea, I shall keep it with my whole heart.
3 Make me to go in the path of thy commandments ; for therein is my desire.
4 Incline mine heart unto thy testimonies, and not to covetousness.
5 O turn away mine eyes, lest they behold vanity ; and quicken thou me in thy way.
6 O stablish thy word in thy servant, that I may fear thee.
7 Take away the rebuke that I am afraid of ; for thy judgments are good.
8 Behold, my delight is in thy commandments ; O quicken me in thy righteousness.

1892

THE TWENTY-FIFTH DAY.

Morning Prayer.

Legem pone.

TEACH me, O LORD, the way of thy statutes : and I shall keep it unto the end.
34 Give me understanding, and I shall keep thy law : yea, I shall keep it with my whole heart.
35 Make me to go in the path of thy commandments : for therein is my desire.
36 Incline my heart unto thy testimonies : and not to covetousness.
37 O turn away mine eyes, lest they behold vanity : and quicken thou me in thy way.
38 O stablish thy word in thy servant : that I may fear thee.
39 Take away the rebuke that I am afraid of : for thy judgments are good.
40 Behold, my delight is in thy commandments : O quicken me in thy righteousness.

1928

23 Princes also did sit and speak against me; * but
thy servant is occupied in thy statutes.
24 For thy testimonies are my delight, * and my
counsellors.

IV. *Adhæsit pavimento.*

MY soul cleaveth to the dust; * O quicken thou me,
according to thy word.
26 I have acknowledged my ways, and thou
heardest me: * O teach me thy statutes.
27 Make me to understand the way of thy
commandments; * and so shall I talk of thy wondrous
works.
28 My soul melteth away for very heaviness; *
comfort thou me according unto thy word.
29 Take from me the way of lying, * and cause
thou me to make much of thy law.
30 I have chosen the way of truth, * and thy judgments have I laid before me.
31 I have stuck unto thy testimonies; * O LORD,
confound me not.
32 I will run the way of thy commandments, *
when thou hast set my heart at liberty.

The Twenty-fifth Day.

Morning Prayer.

V. *Legem pone.*

TEACH me, O LORD, the way of thy statutes, * and I
shall keep it unto the end.
34 Give me understanding, and I shall keep thy
law; * yea, I shall keep it with my whole heart.
35 Make me to go in the path of thy commandments; * for therein is my desire.
36 Incline my heart unto thy testimonies, * and not
to covetousness.
37 O turn away mine eyes, lest they behold
vanity; * and quicken thou me in thy way.
38 O stablish thy word in thy servant, * that I may
fear thee.
39 Take away the rebuke that I am afraid of; * for
thy judgments are good.
40 Behold, my delight is in thy commandments; *
O quicken me in thy righteousness.

1979

23 Even though rulers sit and plot against me, *
I will meditate on your statutes.

24 For your decrees are my delight, *
and they are my counselors.

Daleth *Adhæsit pavimento*

25 My soul cleaves to the dust; *
give me life according to your word.

26 I have confessed my ways, and you answered me; *
instruct me in your statutes.

27 Make me understand the way of your commandments, *
that I may meditate on your marvelous works.

28 My soul melts away for sorrow; *
strengthen me according to your word.

29 Take from me the way of lying; *
let me find grace through your law.

30 I have chosen the way of faithfulness; *
I have set your judgments before me.

31 I hold fast to your decrees; *
O LORD, let me not be put to shame.

32 I will run the way of your commandments, *
for you have set my heart at liberty.

Twenty-fifth Day: Morning Prayer

He *Legem pone*

33 Teach me, O LORD, the way of your statutes, *
and I shall keep it to the end.

34 Give me understanding, and I shall keep your law; *
I shall keep it with all my heart.

35 Make me go in the path of your commandments, *
for that is my desire.

36 Incline my heart to your decrees *
and not to unjust gain.

37 Turn my eyes from watching what is worthless; *
give me life in your ways.

38 Fulfill your promise to your servant, *
which you make to those who fear you.

39 Turn away the reproach which I dread, *
because your judgments are good.

40 Behold, I long for your commandments; *
in your righteousness preserve my life.

Et veniat super me.

LET thy loving mercy come also unto me, O LORD, even thy salvation, according unto thy word.

2 So shall I make answer unto my blasphemers ; for my trust is in thy word.

3 O take not the word of thy truth utterly out of my mouth ; for my hope is in thy judgments.

4 So shall I alway keep thy law ; yea, for ever and ever.

5 And I will walk at liberty ; for I seek thy commandments.

6 I will speak of thy testimonies also, even before kings, and will not be ashamed.

7 And my delight shall be in thy commandments, which I have loved.

8 My hands also will I lift up unto thy commandments, which I have loved ; and my study shall be in thy statutes.

Et veniat super me.

LET thy loving mercy come also unto me, O LORD : even thy salvation, according unto thy word.

42 So shall I make answer unto my blasphemers : for my trust is in thy word.

43 O take not the word of thy truth utterly out of my mouth : for my hope is in thy judgments.

44 So shall I alway keep thy law : yea, for ever and ever.

45 And I will walk at liberty : for I seek thy commandments.

46 I will speak of thy testimonies also, even before kings : and will not be ashamed.

47 And my delight shall be in thy commandments : which I have loved.

48 My hands also will I lift up unto thy commandments, which I have loved : and my study shall be in thy statutes.

Memor esto servi tui.

O THINK upon thy servant, as concerning thy word, wherein thou hast caused me to put my trust.

2 The same is my comfort in my trouble ; for thy word hath quickened me.

3 The proud have had me exceedingly in derision ; yet have I not shrinked from thy law.

4 For I remembered thine everlasting judgments, O LORD, and received comfort.

5 I am horribly afraid, for the ungodly that forsake thy law.

6 Thy statutes have been my songs, in the house of my pilgrimage.

7 I have thought upon thy Name, O LORD, in the night-season, and have kept thy law.

8 This I had, because I kept thy commandments.

Memor esto verbi tui.

O THINK upon thy servant, as concerning thy word : wherein thou hast caused me to put my trust.

50 The same is my comfort in my trouble : for thy word hath quickened me.

51 The proud have had me exceedingly in derision : yet have I not shrinked from thy law.

52 For I remembered thine everlasting judgments, O LORD : and received comfort.

53 I am horribly afraid : for the ungodly that forsake thy law.

54 Thy statutes have been my songs : in the house of my pilgrimage.

55 I have thought upon thy Name, O LORD, in the night season : and have kept thy law.

56 This I had : because I kept thy commandments.

Portio mea, Domine.

THOU art my portion, O LORD ; I have promised to keep thy law.

2 I made my humble petition in thy presence with my whole heart ; O be merciful unto me, according to thy word.

Portio mea, Domine.

THOU art my portion, O LORD : I have promised to keep thy law.

58 I made my humble petition in thy presence with my whole heart : O be merciful unto me, according to thy word.

1928

VI. *Et veniat super me.*

LET thy loving mercy come also unto me, O LORD, *
even thy salvation, according unto thy word.
42 So shall I make answer unto my blasphemers; *
for my trust is in thy word.
43 O take not the word of thy truth utterly out of
my mouth; * for my hope is in thy judgments.
44 So shall I alway keep thy law; * yea, for ever and
ever.
45 And I will walk at liberty; * for I seek thy
commandments.
46 I will speak of thy testimonies also, even before
kings, * and will not be ashamed.
47 And my delight shall be in thy commandments, * which I have loved.
48 My hands also will I lift up unto thy commandments, which I have loved; * and my study shall be in
thy statutes.

VII. *Memor esto verbi tui.*

O THINK upon thy servant, as concerning thy
word, * wherein thou hast caused me to put my trust.
50 The same is my comfort in my trouble; * for thy
word hath quickened me.
51 The proud have had me exceedingly in derision; * yet have I not shrinked from thy law.
52 For I remembered thine everlasting judgments,
O LORD, * and received comfort.
53 I am horribly afraid, * for the ungodly that
forsake thy law.
54 Thy statutes have been my songs, * in the house
of my pilgrimage.
55 I have thought upon thy Name, O LORD, in the
night season, * and have kept thy law.
56 This I had, * because I kept thy commandments.

VIII. *Portio mea, Domine.*

THOU art my portion, O LORD; * I have promised to
keep thy law.
58 I made my humble petition in thy presence with
my whole heart; * O be merciful unto me, according to
thy word.

1979

Waw *Et veniat super me*

41 Let your loving-kindness come to me, O LORD, *
and your salvation, according to your promise.

42 Then shall I have a word for those who taunt me, *
because I trust in your words.

43 Do not take the word of truth out of my mouth, *
for my hope is in your judgments.

44 I shall continue to keep your law; *
I shall keep it for ever and ever.

45 I will walk at liberty, *
because I study your commandments.

46 I will tell of your decrees before kings *
and will not be ashamed.

47 I delight in your commandments, *
which I have always loved.

48 I will lift up my hands to your commandments, *
and I will meditate on your statutes.

Zayin *Memor esto verbo tui*

49 Remember your word to your servant, *
because you have given me hope.

50 This is my comfort in my trouble, *
that your promise gives me life.

51 The proud have derided me cruelly, *
but I have not turned from your law.

52 When I remember your judgments of old, *
O LORD, I take great comfort.

53 I am filled with a burning rage, *
because of the wicked who forsake your law.

54 Your statutes have been like songs to me *
wherever I have lived as a stranger.

55 I remember your Name in the night, O LORD, *
and dwell upon your law.

56 This is how it has been with me, *
because I have kept your commandments.

Heth *Portio mea, Domine*

57 You only are my portion, O LORD; *
I have promised to keep your words.

58 I entreat you with all my heart, *
be merciful to me according to your promise.

3 I called mine own ways to remembrance, and turned my feet unto thy testimonies.

4 I made haste, and prolonged not the time, to keep thy commandments.

5 The congregations of the ungodly have robbed me ; but I have not forgotten thy law.

6 At midnight I will rise to give thanks unto thee, because of thy righteous judgments.

7 I am a companion of all them that fear thee, and keep thy commandments.

8 The earth, O LORD, is full of thy mercy : O teach me thy statutes!

Bonitatem fecisti.

O LORD, thou hast dealt graciously with thy servant, according unto thy word.

2 O learn me true understanding and knowledge ; for I have believed thy commandments.

3 Before I was troubled, I went wrong ; but now have I kept thy word.

4 Thou art good and gracious ; O teach me thy statutes!

5 The proud have imagined a lie against me ; but I will keep thy commandments with my whole heart.

6 Their heart is as fat as brawn ; but my delight hath been in thy law.

7 It is good for me that I have been in trouble ; that I may learn thy statutes.

8 The law of thy mouth is dearer unto me than thousands of gold and silver.

Evening Prayer.

Manus tuæ fecerunt me.

THY hands have made me and fashioned me : O give me understanding, that I may learn thy commandments.

2 They that fear thee will be glad when they see me ; because I have put my trust in thy word.

3 I'know, O LORD, that thy judgments are right, and that thou of very faithfulness hast caused me to be troubled.

4 O let thy merciful kindness be my comfort, according to thy word unto thy servant.

59 I called mine own ways to remembrance : and turned my feet unto thy testimonies.

60 I made haste, and prolonged not the time : to keep thy commandments.

61 The congregations of the ungodly have robbed me : but I have not forgotten thy law.

62 At midnight I will rise to give thanks unto thee : because of thy righteous judgments.

63 I am a companion of all them that fear thee : and keep thy commandments.

64 The earth, O LORD, is full of thy mercy : O teach me thy statutes.

Bonitatem fecisti.

O LORD, thou hast dealt graciously with thy servant : according unto thy word.

66 O learn me true understanding and knowledge : for I have believed thy commandments.

67 Before I was troubled, I went wrong : but now have I kept thy word.

68 Thou art good and gracious : O teach me thy statutes.

69 The proud have imagined a lie against me : but I will keep thy commandments with my whole heart.

70 Their heart is as fat as brawn : but my delight hath been in thy law.

71 It is good for me that I have been in trouble : that I may learn thy statutes.

72 The law of thy mouth is dearer unto me : than thousands of gold and silver.

Evening Prayer.

Manus tuæ fecerunt me.

THY hands have made me and fashioned me : O give me understanding, that I may learn thy commandments.

74 They that fear thee will be glad when they see me : because I have put my trust in thy word.

75 I know, O LORD, that thy judgments are right : and that thou of very faithfulness hast caused me to be troubled.

76 O let thy merciful kindness be my comfort : according to thy word unto thy servant.

1928

59 I called mine own ways to remembrance, * and
turned my feet unto thy testimonies.
60 I made haste, and prolonged not the time, * to
keep thy commandments.
61 The snares of the ungodly have compassed me
about; * but I have not forgotten thy law.
62 At midnight I will rise to give thanks unto
thee, * because of thy righteous judgments.
63 I am a companion of all them that fear thee, *
and keep thy commandments.
64 The earth, O LORD, is full of thy mercy: * O
teach me thy statutes.

IX. *Bonitatem fecisti.*

O LORD, thou hast dealt graciously with thy
servant, * according unto thy word.
66 O teach me true understanding and knowledge; * for I have believed thy commandments.
67 Before I was troubled, I went wrong; * but now
have I kept thy word.
68 Thou art good and gracious; * O teach me thy
statutes.
69 The proud have imagined a lie against me; * but
I will keep thy commandments with my whole heart.
70 Their heart is as fat as brawn; * but my delight
hath been in thy law.
71 It is good for me that I have been in trouble; *
that I may learn thy statutes.
72 The law of thy mouth is dearer unto me * than
thousands of gold and silver.

Evening Prayer.

X. *Manus tuæ fecerunt me.*

THY hands have made me and fashioned me: * O give
me understanding, that I may learn thy commandments.
74 They that fear thee will be glad when they see
me; * because I have put my trust in thy word.
75 I know, O LORD, that thy judgments are right, *
and that thou of very faithfulness hast caused me to be
troubled.
76 O let thy merciful kindness be my comfort, *
according to thy word unto thy servant.

1979

59 I have considered my ways *
and turned my feet toward your decrees.

60 I hasten and do not tarry *
to keep your commandments.

61 Though the cords of the wicked entangle me, *
I do not forget your law.

62 At midnight I will rise to give you thanks, *
because of your righteous judgments.

63 I am a companion of all who fear you *
and of those who keep your commandments.

64 The earth, O LORD, is full of your love; *
instruct me in your statutes.

Teth *Bonitatem fecisti*

65 O LORD, you have dealt graciously with your servant, *
according to your word.

66 Teach me discernment and knowledge, *
for I have believed in your commandments.

67 Before I was afflicted I went astray, *
but now I keep your word.

68 You are good and you bring forth good; *
instruct me in your statutes.

69 The proud have smeared me with lies, *
but I will keep your commandments with my whole heart.

70 Their heart is gross and fat, *
but my delight is in your law.

71 It is good for me that I have been afflicted, *
that I might learn your statutes.

72 The law of your mouth is dearer to me *
than thousands in gold and silver.

Twenty-fifth Day: Evening Prayer

Yodh *Manus tuæ fecerunt me*

73 Your hands have made me and fashioned me; *
give me understanding, that I may learn your commandments.

74 Those who fear you will be glad when they see me, *
because I trust in your word.

75 I know, O LORD, that your judgments are right *
and that in faithfulness you have afflicted me.

76 Let your loving-kindness be my comfort, *
as you have promised to your servant.

5 O let thy loving mercies come unto me, that I may live ; for thy law is my delight.
6 Let the proud be confounded, for they go wickedly about to destroy me ; but I will be occupied in thy commandments.
7 Let such as fear thee, and have known thy testimonies, be turned unto me.
8 O let my heart be sound in thy statutes, that I be not ashamed.

77 O let thy loving mercies come unto me, that I may live : for thy law is my delight.
78 Let the proud be confounded, for they go wickedly about to destroy me : but I will be occupied in thy commandments.
79 Let such as fear thee, and have known thy testimonies : be turned unto me.
80 O let my heart be sound in thy statutes : that I be not ashamed.

Defecit anima mea.

MY soul hath longed for thy salvation, and I have a good hope because of thy word.
2 Mine eyes long sore for thy word ; saying, O when wilt thou comfort me?
3 For I am become like a bottle in the smoke ; yet do I not forget thy statutes.
4 How many are the days of thy servant? when wilt thou be avenged of them that persecute me?
5 The proud have digged pits for me, which are not after thy law.
6 All thy commandments are true : they persecute me falsely ; O be thou my help.
7 They had almost made an end of me upon earth ; but I forsook not thy commandments.
8 O quicken me after thy loving-kindness ; and so shall I keep the testimonies of thy mouth.

Defecit anima mea.

MY soul hath longed for thy salvation : and I have a good hope because of thy word.
82 Mine eyes long sore for thy word : saying, O when wilt thou comfort me?
83 For I am become like a bottle in the smoke : yet do I not forget thy statutes.
84 How many are the days of thy servant : when wilt thou be avenged of them that persecute me?
85 The proud have digged pits for me : which are not after thy law.
86 All thy commandments are true : they persecute me falsely ; O be thou my help.
87 They had almost made an end of me upon earth : but I forsook not thy commandments.
88 O quicken me after thy loving-kindness : and so shall I keep the testimonies of thy mouth.

In æternum, Domine.

O LORD, thy word endureth for ever in heaven.
2 Thy truth also remaineth from one generation to another ; thou hast laid the foundation of the earth, and it abideth.
3 They continue this day according to thine ordinance ; for all things serve thee.
4 If my delight had not been in thy law, I should have perished in my trouble.
5 I will never forget thy commandments ; for with them thou hast quickened me.
6 I am thine : O save me, for I have sought thy commandments.

In æternum, Domine.

O LORD, thy word : endureth for ever in heaven.
90 Thy truth also remaineth from one generation to another : thou hast laid the foundation of the earth, and it abideth.
91 They continue this day according to thine ordinance : for all things serve thee.
92 If my delight had not been in thy law : I should have perished in my trouble.
93 I will never forget thy commandments : for with them thou hast quickened me.
94 I am thine, O save me : for I have sought thy commandments.

1928

77 O let thy loving mercies come unto me, that I may live; * for thy law is my delight.

78 Let the proud be confounded, for they go wickedly about to destroy me; * but I will be occupied in thy commandments.

79 Let such as fear thee, and have known thy testimonies, * be turned unto me.

80 O let my heart be sound in thy statutes, * that I be not ashamed.

XI. *Defecit anima mea.*

MY soul hath longed for thy salvation, * and I have a good hope because of thy word.

82 Mine eyes long sore for thy word; * saying, O when wilt thou comfort me?

83 For I am become like a bottle in the smoke; * yet do I not forget thy statutes.

84 How many are the days of thy servant? * when wilt thou be avenged of them that persecute me?

85 The proud have digged pits for me, * which are not after thy law.

86 All thy commandments are true: * they persecute me falsely; O be thou my help.

87 They had almost made an end of me upon earth; * but I forsook not thy commandments.

88 O quicken me after thy loving-kindness; * and so shall I keep the testimonies of thy mouth.

XII. *In æternum, Domine.*

O LORD, thy word * endureth for ever in heaven.

90 Thy truth also remaineth from one generation to another; * thou hast laid the foundation of the earth, and it abideth.

91 They continue this day according to thine ordinance; * for all things serve thee.

92 If my delight had not been in thy law, * I should have perished in my trouble.

93 I will never forget thy commandments; * for with them thou hast quickened me.

94 I am thine: O save me, * for I have sought thy commandments.

1979

77 Let your compassion come to me, that I may live, *
for your law is my delight.

78 Let the arrogant be put to shame, for they wrong me with lies; *
but I will meditate on your commandments.

79 Let those who fear you turn to me, *
and also those who know your decrees.

80 Let my heart be sound in your statutes, *
that I may not be put to shame.

Kaph *Defecit in salutare*

81 My soul has longed for your salvation; *
I have put my hope in your word.

82 My eyes have failed from watching for your promise, *
and I say, "When will you comfort me?"

83 I have become like a leather flask in the smoke, *
but I have not forgotten your statutes.

84 How much longer must I wait? *
when will you give judgment against those who persecute me?

85 The proud have dug pits for me; *
they do not keep your law.

86 All your commandments are true; *
help me, for they persecute me with lies.

87 They had almost made an end of me on earth, *
but I have not forsaken your commandments.

88 In your loving-kindness, revive me, *
that I may keep the decrees of your mouth.

Lamedh *In æternnum, Domine*

89 O LORD, your word is everlasting; *
it stands firm in the heavens.

90 Your faithfulness remains from one generation to another; *
you established the earth, and it abides.

91 By your decree these continue to this day, *
for all things are your servants.

92 If my delight had not been in your law, *
I should have perished in my affliction.

93 I will never forget your commandments, *
because by them you give me life.

94 I am yours; oh, that you would save me! *
for I study your commandments.

7 The ungodly laid wait for me, to destroy me ; but I will consider thy testimonies.
8 I see that all things come to an end ; but thy commandment is exceeding broad.

Quomodo dilexi!

LORD, what love have I unto thy law! all the day long is my study in it.
2 Thou, through thy commandments, hast made me wiser than mine enemies ; for they are ever with me.
3 I have more understanding than my teachers ; for thy testimonies are my study.
4 I am wiser than the aged ; because I keep thy commandments.
5 I have refrained my feet from every evil way, that I may keep thy word.
6 I have not shrunk from thy judgments ; for thou teachest me.
7 O how sweet are thy words unto my throat ; yea, sweeter than honey unto my mouth!
8 Through thy commandments I get understanding : therefore I hate all evil ways.

THE TWENTY-SIXTH DAY.

Morning Prayer.

Lucerna pedibus meis.

THY word is a lantern unto my feet, and a light unto my paths.
2 I have sworn, and am stedfastly purposed, to keep thy righteous judgments.
3 I am troubled above measure : quicken me, O LORD, according to thy word.
4 Let the free-will offerings of my mouth please thee, O LORD ; and teach me thy judgments.
5 My soul is alway in my hand ; yet do I not forget thy law.
6 The ungodly have laid a snare for me ; but yet I swerved not from thy commandments.
7 Thy testimonies have I claimed as mine heritage for ever ; and why? they are the very joy of my heart.
8 I have applied my heart to fulfil thy statutes alway, even unto the end.

95 The ungodly laid wait for me, to destroy me : but I will consider thy testimonies.
96 I see that all things come to an end : but thy commandment is exceeding broad.

Quomodo dilexi!

LORD, what love have I unto thy law : all the day long is my study in it.
98 Thou, through thy commandments, hast made me wiser than mine enemies : for they are ever with me.
99 I have more understanding than my teachers : for thy testimonies are my study.
100 I am wiser than the aged : because I keep thy commandments.
101 I have refrained my feet from every evil way : that I may keep thy word.
102 I have not shrunk from thy judgments : for thou teachest me.
103 O how sweet are thy words unto my throat : yea, sweeter than honey unto my mouth!
104 Through thy commandments I get understanding : therefore I hate all evil ways.

THE TWENTY-SIXTH DAY.

Morning Prayer.

Lucerna pedibus meis.

THY word is a lantern unto my feet : and a light unto my paths.
106 I have sworn, and am stedfastly purposed : to keep thy righteous judgments.
107 I am troubled above measure : quicken me, O LORD, according to thy word.
108 Let the free-will offerings of my mouth please thee, O LORD : and teach me thy judgments.
109 My soul is alway in my hand : yet do I not forget thy law.
110 The ungodly have laid a snare for me : but yet I swerved not from thy commandments.
111 Thy testimonies have I claimed as mine heritage for ever : and why? they are the very joy of my heart.
112 I have applied my heart to fulfil thy statutes alway : even unto the end.

95 The ungodly laid wait for me, to destroy me; *
but I will consider thy testimonies.
96 I see that all things come to an end; * but thy
commandment is exceeding broad.

95 Though the wicked lie in wait for me to destroy me, *
I will apply my mind to your decrees.

96 I see that all things come to an end, *
but your commandment has no bounds.

XIII. *Quomodo dilexi!*

LORD, what love have I unto thy law! * all the day
long is my study in it.
98 Thou, through thy commandments, hast made
me wiser than mine enemies; * for they are ever with
me.
99 I have more understanding than my teachers; *
for thy testimonies are my study.
100 I am wiser than the aged; * because I keep thy
commandments.
101 I have refrained my feet from every evil way, *
that I may keep thy word.
102 I have not shrunk from thy judgments; * for
thou teachest me.
103 O how sweet are thy words unto my throat; *
yea, sweeter than honey unto my mouth!
104 Through thy commandments I get understanding: * therefore I hate all evil ways.

Mem *Quomodo dilexi!*

97 Oh, how I love your law! *
all the day long it is in my mind.

98 Your commandment has made me wiser than my enemies, *
and it is always with me.

99 I have more understanding than all my teachers, *
for your decrees are my study.

100 I am wiser than the elders, *
because I observe your commandments.

101 I restrain my feet from every evil way, *
that I may keep your word.

102 I do not shrink from your judgments, *
because you yourself have taught me.

103 How sweet are your words to my taste! *
they are sweeter than honey to my mouth.

104 Through your commandments I gain understanding; *
therefore I hate every lying way.

The Twenty-sixth Day.

Morning Prayer.

XIV. *Lucerna pedibus meis.*

THY word is a lantern unto my feet, * and a light unto
my paths.
106 I have sworn, and am stedfastly purposed, * to
keep thy righteous judgments.
107 I am troubled above measure: * quicken me, O
LORD, according to thy word.
108 Let the free-will offerings of my mouth please
thee, O LORD; * and teach me thy judgments.
109 My soul is alway in my hand; * yet do I not
forget thy law.
110 The ungodly have laid a snare for me; * but yet
I swerved not from thy commandments.
111 Thy testimonies have I claimed as mine
heritage for ever; * and why? they are the very joy of
my heart.
112 I have applied my heart to fulfil thy statutes
alway, * even unto the end.

Twenty-sixth Day: Morning Prayer

Nun *Lucerna pedibus meis*

105 Your word is lantern to my feet *
and a light upon my path.

106 I have sworn and am determined *
to keep your righteous judgments.

107 I am deeply troubled; *
preserve my life, O LORD, according to your word.

108 Accept, O LORD, the willing tribute of my lips, *
and teach me your judgments.

109 My life is always in my hand, *
yet I do not forget your law.

110 The wicked have set a trap for me, *
but I have not strayed from your commandments.

111 Your decrees are my inheritance for ever; *
truly, they are the joy of my heart.

112 I have applied my heart to fulfill your statutes *
for ever and to the end.

1789-1871

Iniquos odio habui.

I HATE them that imagine evil things ; but thy law do I love.

2 Thou art my defence and shield ; and my trust is in thy word.

3 Away from me, ye wicked ; I will keep the commandments of my God.

4 O stablish me according to thy word, that I may live ; and let me not be disappointed of my hope.

5 Hold thou me up, and I shall be safe ; yea, my delight shall be ever in thy statutes.

6 Thou hast trodden down all them that depart from thy statutes ; for they imagine but deceit.

7 Thou puttest away all the ungodly of the earth like dross ; therefore I love thy testimonies.

8 My flesh trembleth for fear of thee ; and I am afraid of thy judgments.

1892

Iniquos odio habui.

I HATE them that imagine evil things : but thy law do I love.

114 Thou art my defence and shield : and my trust is in thy word.

115 Away from me, ye wicked : I will keep the commandments of my God.

116 O stablish me according to thy word, that I may live : and let me not be disappointed of my hope.

117 Hold thou me up, and I shall be safe : yea, my delight shall be ever in thy statutes.

118 Thou hast trodden down all them that depart from thy statutes : for they imagine but deceit.

119 Thou puttest away all the ungodly of the earth like dross : therefore I love thy testimonies.

120 My flesh trembleth for fear of thee : and I am afraid of thy judgments.

1789-1871

Feci judicium.

I DEAL with the thing that is lawful and right ; O give me not over unto mine oppressors!

2 Make thou thy servant to delight in that which is good, that the proud do me no wrong.

3 Mine eyes are wasted away with looking for thy health, and for the word of thy righteousness.

4 O deal with thy servant according unto thy loving mercy, and teach me thy statutes.

5 I am thy servant ; O grant me understanding, that I may know thy testimonies.

6 It is time for thee, LORD, to lay to thine hand ; for they have destroyed thy law.

7 For I love thy commandments above gold and precious stones.

8 Therefore hold I straight all thy commandments ; and all false ways I utterly abhor.

1892

Feci judicium.

I DEAL with the thing that is lawful and right : O give me not over unto mine oppressors.

122 Make thou thy servant to delight in that which is good : that the proud do me no wrong.

123 Mine eyes are wasted away with looking for thy health : and for the word of thy righteousness.

124 O deal with thy servant according unto thy loving mercy : and teach me thy statutes.

125 I am thy servant ; O grant me understanding : that I may know thy testimonies.

126 It is time for thee, LORD, to lay to thine hand : for they have destroyed thy law.

127 For I love thy commandments : above gold and precious stones.

128 Therefore hold I straight all thy commandments : and all false ways I utterly abhor.

1789-1871

Mirabilia.

THY testimonies are wonderful ; therefore doth my soul keep them.

2 When thy word goeth forth, it giveth light and understanding unto the simple.

1892

Mirabilia.

THY testimonies are wonderful : therefore doth my soul keep them.

130 When thy word goeth forth : it giveth light and understanding unto the simple.

XV. *Iniquos odio habui.*

I HATE them that imagine evil things; * but thy law do I love.

114 Thou art my defence and shield; * and my trust is in thy word.

115 Away from me, ye wicked; * I will keep the commandments of my God.

116 O stablish me according to thy word, that I may live; * and let me not be disappointed of my hope.

117 Hold thou me up, and I shall be safe; * yea, my delight shall be ever in thy statutes.

118 Thou hast trodden down all them that depart from thy statutes; * for they imagine but deceit.

119 Thou puttest away all the ungodly of the earth like dross; * therefore I love thy testimonies.

120 My flesh trembleth for fear of thee; * and I am afraid of thy judgments.

Samekh *Iniquos odio habui*

113 I hate those who have a divided heart, *
but your law do I love.

114 You are my refuge and shield; *
my hope is in your word.

115 Away from me, you wicked! *
I will keep the commandments of my God.

116 Sustain me according to your promise, that I may live, *
and let me not be disappointed in my hope.

117 Hold me up, and I shall be safe, *
and my delight shall be ever in your statutes.

118 You spurn all who stray from your statutes; *
their deceitfulness is in vain.

119 In your sight all the wicked of the earth are but dross; *
therefore I love your decrees.

120 My flesh trembles with dread of you; *
I am afraid of your judgments.

XVI. *Feci judicium.*

I DEAL with the thing that is lawful and right; * O give me not over unto mine oppressors.

122 Make thou thy servant to delight in that which is good, * that the proud do me no wrong.

123 Mine eyes are wasted away with looking for thy health, * and for the word of thy righteousness.

124 O deal with thy servant according unto thy loving mercy, * and teach me thy statutes.

125 I am thy servant; O grant me understanding, * that I may know thy testimonies.

126 It is time for thee, LORD, to lay to thine hand; * for they have destroyed thy law.

127 For I love thy commandments * above gold and precious stones.

128 Therefore hold I straight all thy commandments; * and all false ways I utterly abhor.

Ayin *Feci judicium*

121 I have done what is just and right; *
do not deliver me to my oppressors.

122 Be surety for your servant's good; *
let not the proud oppress me.

123 My eyes have failed from watching for your salvation *
and for your righteous promise.

124 Deal with your servant according to your loving-kindness *
and teach me your statutes.

125 I am your servant; grant me understanding, *
that I may know your decrees.

126 It is time for you to act, O LORD, *
for they have broken your law.

127 Truly, I love your commandments *
more than gold and precious stones.

128 I hold all your commandments to be right for me; *
all paths of falsehood I abhor.

XVII. *Mirabilia.*

THY testimonies are wonderful; * therefore doth my soul keep them.

130 When thy word goeth forth, * it giveth light and understanding unto the simple.

Pe *Mirabilia*

129 Your decrees are wonderful; *
therefore I obey them with all my heart.

130 When your word goes forth it gives light; *
it gives understanding to the simple.

1789-1871

3 I opened my mouth, and drew in my breath ; for my delight was in thy commandments.
4 O look thou upon me, and be merciful unto me, as thou usest to do unto those that love thy Name.
5 Order my steps in thy word ; and so shall no wickedness have dominion over me.
6 O deliver me from the wrongful dealings of men ; and so shall I keep thy commandments.
7 Show the light of thy countenance upon thy servant, and teach me thy statutes.
8 Mine eyes gush out with water, because men keep not thy law.

1892

131 I opened my mouth, and drew in my breath : for my delight was in thy commandments.
132 O look thou upon me, and be merciful unto me : as thou usest to do unto those that love thy Name.
133 Order my steps in thy word : and so shall no wickedness have dominion over me.
134 O deliver me from the wrongful dealings of men : and so shall I keep thy commandments.
135 Show the light of thy countenance upon thy servant : and teach me thy statutes.
136 Mine eyes gush out with water : because men keep not thy law.

1789-1871

Justus es, Domine.

RIGHTEOUS art thou, O LORD ; and true is thy judgment.
2 The testimonies that thou hast commanded are exceeding righteous and true.
3 My zeal hath even consumed me ; because mine enemies have forgotten thy words.
4 Thy word is tried to the uttermost, and thy servant loveth it.
5 I am small and of no reputation ; yet do I not forget thy commandments.
6 Thy righteousness is an everlasting righteousness, and thy law is the truth.
7 Trouble and heaviness have taken hold upon me ; yet is my delight in thy commandments.
8 The righteousness of thy testimonies is everlasting : O grant me understanding, and I shall live.

1892

Justus es, Domine.

RIGHTEOUS art thou O LORD : and true is thy judgment.
138 The testimonies that thou hast commanded : are exceeding righteous and true.
139 My zeal hath even consumed me : because mine enemies have forgotten thy words.
140 Thy word is tried to the uttermost : and thy servant loveth it.
141 I am small and of no reputation : yet do I not forget thy commandments.
142 Thy righteousness is an everlasting righteousness : and thy law is the truth.
143 Trouble and heaviness have taken hold upon me : yet is my delight in thy commandments.
144 The righteousness of thy testimonies is everlasting : O grant me understanding, and I shall live.

1789-1871

Evening Prayer.

Clamavi in toto corde meo.

I CALL with my whole heart ; hear me, O LORD ; I will keep thy statutes.
2 Yea, even unto thee do I call ; help me, and I shall keep thy testimonies.
3 Early in the morning do I cry unto thee ; for in thy word is my trust.
4 Mine eyes prevent the night watches ; that I might be occupied in thy words.

1892

Evening Prayer.

Clamavi in toto corde meo.

I CALL with my whole heart : hear me, O LORD, I will keep thy statutes.
146 Yea, even unto thee do I call : help me, and I shall keep thy testimonies.
147 Early in the morning do I cry unto thee : for in thy word is my trust.
148 Mine eyes prevent the night watches : that I might be occupied in thy words.

131 I opened my mouth, and drew in my breath; *
for my delight was in thy commandments.
132 O look thou upon me, and be merciful unto
me, * as thou usest to do unto those that love thy
Name.
133 Order my steps in thy word; * and so shall no
wickedness have dominion over me.
134 O deliver me from the wrongful dealings of
men; * and so shall I keep thy commandments.
135 Show the light of thy countenance upon thy
servant, * and teach me thy statutes.
136 Mine eyes gush out with water, * because men
keep not thy law.

XVIII. *Justus es, Domine.*

RIGHTEOUS art thou, O LORD; * and true are thy
judgments.
138 The testimonies that thou hast commanded *
are exceeding righteous and true.
139 My zeal hath even consumed me; * because
mine enemies have forgotten thy words.
140 Thy word is tried to the uttermost, * and thy
servant loveth it.
141 I am small and of no reputation; * yet do I not
forget thy commandments.
142 Thy righteousness is an everlasting righteousness, * and thy law is the truth.
143 Trouble and heaviness have taken hold upon
me; * yet is my delight in thy commandments.
144 The righteousness of thy testimonies is everlasting: * O grant me understanding, and I shall live.

Evening Prayer.

XIX. *Clamavi in toto corde meo.*

I CALL with my whole heart; * hear me, O LORD; I
will keep thy statutes.
146 Yea, even unto thee do I call; * help me, and I
shall keep thy testimonies.
147 Early in the morning do I cry unto thee; * for
in thy word is my trust.
148 Mine eyes prevent the night watches; * that I
might be occupied in thy word.

131 I open my mouth and pant; *
I long for your commandments.

132 Turn to me in mercy, *
as you always do to those who love your Name.

133 Steady my footsteps in your word; *
let no iniquity have dominion over me.

134 Rescue me from those who oppress me, *
and I will keep your commandments.

135 Let your countenance shine upon your servant *
and teach me your statutes.

136 My eyes shed streams of tears, *
because people do not keep your law.

Sadhe *Justus es, Domine*

137 You are righteous, O LORD, *
and upright are your judgments.

138 You have issued your decrees *
with justice and in perfect faithfulness.

139 My indignation has consumed me, *
because my enemies forget your words.

140 Your word has been tested to the uttermost, *
and your servant holds it dear.

141 I am small and of little account, *
yet I do not forget your commandments.

142 Your justice is an everlasting justice *
and your law is the truth.

143 Trouble and distress have come upon me, *
yet your commandments are my delight.

144 The righteousness of your decrees is everlasting; *
grant me understanding, that I may live.

Twenty-sixth Day: Evening Prayer

Qoph *Clamavi in toto corde meo*

145 I call with my whole heart; *
answer me, O LORD, that I may keep your statutes.

146 I call to you;
oh, that you would save me! *
I will keep your decrees.

147 Early in the morning I cry out to you, *
for in your word is my trust.

148 My eyes are open in the night watches, *
that I may meditate upon your promise.

1789-1871

5 Hear my voice, O LORD, according unto thy loving-kindness ; quicken me, according as thou art wont.
6 They draw nigh that of malice persecute me, and are far from thy law.
7 Be thou nigh at hand, O LORD ; for all thy commandments are true.
8 As concerning thy testimonies, I have known long since, that thou hast grounded them for ever.

1892

149 Hear my voice, O LORD, according unto thy loving-kindness : quicken me, according as thou art wont.
150 They draw nigh that of malice persecute me : and are far from thy law.
151 Be thou nigh at hand, O LORD : for all thy commandments are true.
152 As concerning thy testimonies, I have known long since : that thou hast grounded them for ever.

1789-1871

Vide humilitatem.

O CONSIDER mine adversity, and deliver me, for I do not forget thy law.
2 Avenge thou my cause, and deliver me ; quicken me according to thy word.
3 Health is far from the ungodly ; for they regard not thy statutes.
4 Great is thy mercy, O LORD ; quicken me, as thou art wont.
5 Many there are that trouble me, and persecute me ; yet do I not swerve from thy testimonies.
6 It grieveth me when I see the transgressors ; because they keep not thy law.
7 Consider, O LORD, how I love thy commandments ; O quicken me, according to thy loving-kindness.
8 Thy word is true from everlasting ; all the judgments of thy righteousness endure for evermore.

1892

Vide humilitatem.

O CONSIDER mine adversity, and deliver me : for I do not forget thy law.
154 Avenge thou my cause, and deliver me : quicken me according to thy word.
155 Health is far from the ungodly : for they regard not thy statutes.
156 Great is thy mercy, O LORD : quicken me, as thou art wont.
157 Many there are that trouble me, and persecute me : yet do I not swerve from thy testimonies.
158 It grieveth me when I see the transgressors : because they keep not thy law.
159 Consider, O LORD, how I love thy commandments : O quicken me, according to thy loving-kindness.
160 Thy word is true from everlasting : all the judgments of thy righteousness endure for evermore.

1789-1871

Principes persecuti sunt.

PRINCES have persecuted me without a cause ; but my heart standeth in awe of thy word.
2 I am as glad of thy word, as one that findeth great spoils.
3 As for lies, I hate and abhor them ; but thy law do I love.
4 Seven times a day do I praise thee ; because of thy righteous judgments.
5 Great is the peace that they have who love thy law ; and they are not offended at it.
6 LORD, I have looked for thy saving health, and done after thy commandments.
7 My soul hath kept thy testimonies, and loved them exceedingly.

1892

Principes persecuti sunt.

PRINCES have persecuted me without a cause : but my heart standeth in awe of thy word.
162 I am as glad of thy word : as one that findeth great spoils.
163 As for lies, I hate and abhor them : but thy law do I love.
164 Seven times a day do I praise thee : because of thy righteous judgments.
165 Great is the peace that they have who love thy law : and they are not offended at it.
166 LORD, I have looked for thy saving health : and done after thy commandments.
167 My soul hath kept thy testimonies : and loved them exceedingly.

149 Hear my voice, O LORD, according unto thy loving-kindness; * quicken me, according to thy judgments.
150 They draw nigh that of malice persecute me, * and are far from thy law.
151 Be thou nigh at hand, O LORD; * for all thy commandments are true.
152 As concerning thy testimonies, I have known long since, * that thou hast grounded them for ever.

149 Hear my voice, O LORD, according to your loving-kindness; *
according to your judgments, give me life.

150 They draw near who in malice persecute me; *
they are very far from your law.

151 You, O LORD, are near at hand, *
and all your commandments are true.

152 Long have I known from your decrees *
that you have established them for ever.

XX. *Vide humilitatem.*

O CONSIDER mine adversity, and deliver me, * for I do not forget thy law.
154 Avenge thou my cause, and deliver me; * quicken me according to thy word.
155 Health is far from the ungodly; * for they regard not thy statutes.
156 Great is thy mercy, O LORD; * quicken me, as thou art wont.
157 Many there are that trouble me, and persecute me; * yet do I not swerve from thy testimonies.
158 It grieveth me when I see the transgressors; * because they keep not thy law.
159 Consider, O LORD, how I love thy commandments; * O quicken me, according to thy loving-kindness.
160 Thy word is true from everlasting; * all the judgments of thy righteousness endure for evermore.

Resh *Vide humilitatem*

153 Behold my affliction and deliver me, *
for I do not forget your law.

154 Plead my cause and redeem me; *
according to your promise, give me life.

155 Deliverance is far from the wicked, *
for they do not study your statutes.

156 Great is your compassion, O LORD; *
preserve my life, according to your judgments.

157 There are many who persecute and oppress me, *
yet I have not swerved from your decrees.

158 I look with loathing at the faithless, *
for they have not kept your word.

159 See how I love your commandments! *
O LORD, in your mercy, preserve me.

160 The heart of your word is truth; *
all your righteous judgments endure for evermore.

XXI. *Principes persecuti sunt.*

PRINCES have persecuted me without a cause; * but my heart standeth in awe of thy word.
162 I am as glad of thy word, * as one that findeth great spoils.
163 As for lies, I hate and abhor them; * but thy law do I love.
164 Seven times a day do I praise thee; * because of thy righteous judgments.
165 Great is the peace that they have who love thy law; * and they have none occasion of stumbling.
166 LORD, I have looked for thy saving health, * and done after thy commandments.
167 My soul hath kept thy testimonies, * and loved them exceedingly.

Shin *Principes persecuti sunt*

161 Rulers have persecuted me without a cause, *
but my heart stands in awe of your word.

162 I am as glad because of your promise *
as one who finds great spoils.

163 As for lies, I hate and abhor them, *
but your law is my love.

164 Seven times a day do I praise you, *
because of your righteous judgments.

165 Great peace have they who love your law; *
for them there is no stumbling block.

166 I have hoped for your salvation, O LORD, *
and I have fulfilled your commandments.

167 I have kept your decrees *
and I have loved them deeply.

8 I have kept thy commandments and testimonies ; for all my ways are before thee.

Appropinquet deprecatio.

LET my complaint come before thee, O LORD ; give me understanding according to thy word.

2 Let my supplication come before thee ; deliver me according to thy word.

3 My lips shall speak of thy praise, when thou hast taught me thy statutes.

4 Yea, my tongue shall sing of thy word ; for all thy commandments are righteous.

5 Let thine hand help me ; for I have chosen thy commandments.

6 I have longed for thy saving health, O LORD ; and in thy law is my delight.

7 O let my soul live, and it shall praise thee ; and thy judgments shall help me.

8 I have gone astray like a sheep that is lost ; O seek thy servant, for I do not forget thy commandments.

THE TWENTY-SEVENTH DAY.

Morning Prayer.

Psalm cxx. *Ad Dominum.*

WHEN I was in trouble, I called upon the LORD, and he heard me.

2 Deliver my soul, O LORD, from lying lips, and from a deceitful tongue.

3 What reward shall be given or done unto thee, thou false tongue? even mighty and sharp arrows, with hot burning coals.

4 Woe is me, that I am constrained to dwell with Mesech, and to have my habitation among the tents of Kedar!

5 My soul hath long dwelt among them that are enemies unto peace.

6 I labour for peace ; but when I speak unto them thereof, they make them ready to battle.

168 I have kept thy commandments and testimonies : for all my ways are before thee.

Appropinquet deprecatio.

LET my complaint come before thee, O LORD : give me understanding according to thy word.

170 Let my supplication come before thee : deliver me according to thy word.

171 My lips shall speak of thy praise : when thou hast taught me thy statutes.

172 Yea, my tongue shall sing of thy word : for all thy commandments are righteous.

173 Let thine hand help me : for I have chosen thy commandments.

174 I have longed for thy saving health, O LORD : and in thy law is my delight.

175 O let my soul live, and it shall praise thee : and thy judgments shall help me.

176 I have gone astray like a sheep that is lost : O seek thy servant, for I do not forget thy commandments.

THE TWENTY-SEVENTH DAY.

Morning Prayer.

PSALM 120. *Ad Dominum.*

WHEN I was in trouble, I called upon the LORD : and he heard me.

2 Deliver my soul, O LORD, from lying lips : and from a deceitful tongue.

3 What reward shall be given or done unto thee, thou false tongue : even mighty and sharp arrows, with hot burning coals.

4 Woe is me, that I am constrained to dwell with Mesech : and to have my habitation among the tents of Kedar!

5 My soul hath long dwelt among them : that are enemies unto peace.

6 I labour for peace ; but when I speak unto them thereof : they make them ready to battle.

168 I have kept thy commandments and testimonies; * for all my ways are before thee.

168 I have kept your commandments and decrees, *
for all my ways are before you.

XXII. *Appropinquet deprecatio.*

LET my complaint come before thee, O LORD; * give me understanding according to thy word.

170 Let my supplication come before thee; * deliver me according to thy word.

171 My lips shall speak of thy praise, * when thou hast taught me thy statutes.

172 Yea, my tongue shall sing of thy word; * for all thy commandments are righteous.

173 Let thine hand help me; * for I have chosen thy commandments.

174 I have longed for thy saving health, O LORD; * and in thy law is my delight.

175 O let my soul live, and it shall praise thee; * and thy judgments shall help me.

176 I have gone astray like a sheep that is lost; * O seek thy servant, for I do not forget thy commandments.

Taw *Appropinquet deprecatio*

169 Let my cry come before you, O LORD; *
give me understanding, according to your word.

170 Let my supplication come before you; *
deliver me, according to your promise.

171 My lips shall pour forth your praise, *
when you teach me your statutes.

172 My tongue shall sing of your promise, *
for all your commandments are righteous.

173 Let your hand be ready to help me, *
for I have chosen your commandments.

174 I long for your salvation, O LORD, *
and your law is my delight.

175 Let me live, and I will praise you, *
and let your judgments help me.

176 I have gone astray like a sheep that is lost; *
search for your servant,
for I do not forget your commandments.

The Twenty-seventh Day.

Morning Prayer.

Psalm 120. *Ad Dominum.*

WHEN I was in trouble, I called upon the LORD, * and he heard me.

2 Deliver my soul, O LORD, from lying lips, * and from a deceitful tongue.

3 What reward shall be given or done unto thee, thou false tongue? * even mighty and sharp arrows, with hot burning coals.

4 Woe is me, that I am constrained to dwell with Meshech, * and to have my habitation among the tents of Kedar!

5 My soul hath long dwelt among them * that are enemies unto peace.

6 I labour for peace; but when I speak unto them thereof, * they make them ready to battle.

Twenty-seventh Day: Morning Prayer

120 *Ad Dominum*

1 When I was in trouble, I called to the LORD; *
I called to the LORD, and he answered me.

2 Deliver me, O LORD, from lying lips *
and from the deceitful tongue.

3 What shall be done to you, and what more besides, *
O you deceitful tongue?

4 The sharpened arrows of a warrior, *
along with hot glowing coals.

5 How hateful it is that I must lodge in Meshech *
and dwell among the tents of Kedar!

6 Too long have I had to live *
among the enemies of peace.

7 I am on the side of peace, *
but when I speak of it, they are for war.

Psalm cxxi. *Levavi oculos meos.*[36]

I WILL lift up mine eyes unto the hills, from whence cometh my help.

2 My help cometh even from the LORD, who hath made heaven and earth.

3 He will not suffer thy foot to be moved; and he that keepeth thee will not sleep.

4 Behold, he that keepeth Israel shall neither slumber nor sleep.

5 The LORD himself is thy keeper; the LORD is thy defence upon thy right hand;

6 So that the sun shall not burn thee by day, neither the moon by night.

7 The LORD shall preserve thee from all evil; yea, it is even he that shall keep thy soul.

8 The LORD shall preserve thy going out, and thy coming in, from this time forth for evermore.

PSALM 121. *Levavi oculos.*

I WILL lift up mine eyes unto the hills : from whence cometh my help.

2 My help cometh even from the LORD : who hath made heaven and earth.

3 He will not suffer thy foot to be moved : and he that keepeth thee will not sleep.

4 Behold, he that keepeth Israel : shall neither slumber nor sleep.

5 The LORD himself is thy keeper : the LORD is thy defence upon thy right hand;

6 So that the sun shall not burn thee by day : neither the moon by night.

7 The LORD shall preserve thee from all evil : yea, it is even he that shall keep thy soul.

8 The LORD shall preserve thy going out, and thy coming in : from this time forth for evermore.

Psalm cxxii. *Lætatus sum.*

I WAS glad when they said unto me, We will go into the house of the LORD.

2 Our feet shall stand in thy gates, O Jerusalem.

3 Jerusalem is built as a city that is at unity in itself.

4 For thither the tribes go up, even the tribes of the LORD, to testify unto Israel, to give thanks unto the Name of the LORD.

5 For there is the seat of judgment, even the seat of the house of David.

6 O pray for the peace of Jerusalem; they shall prosper that love thee.

7 Peace be within thy walls, and plenteousness within thy palaces.

8 For my brethren and companions' sakes, I will wish thee prosperity.

9 Yea, because of the house of the LORD our God, I will seek to do thee good.

PSALM 122. *Lætatus sum.*

I WAS glad when they said unto me : We will go into the house of the LORD.

2 Our feet shall stand in thy gates : O Jerusalem.

3 Jerusalem is built as a city : that is at unity in itself.

4 For thither the tribes go up, even the tribes of the LORD : to testify unto Israel, to give thanks unto the Name of the LORD.

5 For there is the seat of judgment : even the seat of the house of David.

6 O pray for the peace of Jerusalem : they shall prosper that love thee.

7 Peace be within thy walls : and plenteousness within thy palaces.

8 For my brethren and companions' sakes : I will wish thee prosperity.

9 Yea, because of the house of the LORD our God : I will seek to do thee good.

[36] *Levavi oculos* until 1871.

Psalm 121. *Levavi oculos.*

I WILL lift up mine eyes unto the hills; * from whence cometh my help?

2 My help cometh even from the LORD, * who hath made heaven and earth.

3 He will not suffer thy foot to be moved; * and he that keepeth thee will not sleep.

4 Behold, he that keepeth Israel * shall neither slumber nor sleep.

5 The LORD himself is thy keeper; * the LORD is thy defence upon thy right hand;

6 So that the sun shall not burn thee by day, * neither the moon by night.

7 The LORD shall preserve thee from all evil; * yea, it is even he that shall keep thy soul.

8 The LORD shall preserve thy going out, and thy coming in, * from this time forth for evermore.

121 *Levavi oculos*

1 I lift up my eyes to the hills; *
from where is my help to come?

2 My help comes from the LORD, *
the maker of heaven and earth.

3 He will not let your foot be moved *
and he who watches over you will not fall asleep.

4 Behold, he who keeps watch over Israel *
shall neither slumber nor sleep;

5 The LORD himself watches over you; *
the LORD is your shade at your right hand,

6 So that the sun shall not strike you by day, *
nor the moon by night.

7 The LORD shall preserve you from all evil; *
it is he who shall keep you safe.

8 The LORD shall watch over your going out and
your coming in, *
from this time forth for evermore.

Psalm 122. *Lætatus sum.*

I WAS glad when they said unto me, * We will go into the house of the LORD.

2 Our feet shall stand in thy gates, * O Jerusalem.

3 Jerusalem is built as a city * that is at unity in itself.

4 For thither the tribes go up, even the tribes of the LORD, * to testify unto Israel, to give thanks unto the Name of the LORD.

5 For there is the seat of judgment, * even the seat of the house of David.

6 O pray for the peace of Jerusalem; * they shall prosper that love thee.

7 Peace be within thy walls, * and plenteousness within thy palaces.

8 For my brethren and companions' sakes, * I will wish thee prosperity.

9 Yea, because of the house of the LORD our God, * I will seek to do thee good.

122 *Lætatus sum*

1 I was glad when they said to me, *
"Let us go to the house of the LORD."

2 Now our feet are standing *
within your gates, O Jerusalem.

3 Jerusalem is built as a city *
that is at unity with itself;

4 To which the tribes go up,
the tribes of the LORD, *
the assembly of Israel,
to praise the Name of the LORD.

5 For there are the thrones of judgment, *
the thrones of the house of David.

6 Pray for the peace of Jerusalem: *
"May they prosper who love you.

7 Peace be within your walls *
and quietness within your towers.

8 For my brethren and companions' sake, *
I pray for your prosperity,

9 Because of the house of the LORD our God, *
I will seek to do you good."

Psalm cxxiii. *Ad te levavi oculos meos.*

UNTO thee lift I up mine eyes, O Thou that dwellest in the heavens.

2 Behold, even as the eyes of servants look unto the hand of their masters, and as the eyes of a maiden unto the hand of her mistress, even so our eyes wait upon the LORD our God, until he have mercy upon us.

3 Have mercy upon us, O LORD, have mercy upon us ; for we are utterly despised.

4 Our soul is filled with the scornful reproof of the wealthy, and with the despitefulness of the proud.

PSALM 123. *Ad te levavi oculos meos.*

UNTO thee lift I up mine eyes : O thou that dwellest in the heavens.

2 Behold, even as the eyes of servants look unto the hand of their masters, and as the eyes of a maiden unto the hand of her mistress : even so our eyes wait upon the LORD our God, until he have mercy upon us.

3 Have mercy upon us, O LORD, have mercy upon us : for we are utterly despised.

4 Our soul is filled with the scornful reproof of the wealthy : and with the despitefulness of the proud.

Psalm cxxiv. *Nisi quia Dominus.*

IF the LORD himself had not been on our side, now may Israel say ; if the LORD himself had not been on our side, when men rose up against us ;

2 They had swallowed us up quick ; when they were so wrathfully displeased at us.

3 Yea, the waters had drowned us, and the stream had gone over our soul.

4 The deep waters of the proud had gone even over our soul.

5 But praised be the LORD, who hath not given us over for a prey unto their teeth.

6 Our soul is escaped even as a bird out of the snare of the fowler ; the snare is broken, and we are delivered.

7 Our help standeth in the Name of the LORD, who hath made heaven and earth.

PSALM 124. *Nisi quia Dominus.*

IF the LORD himself had not been on our side, now may Israel say : if the LORD himself had not been on our side, when men rose up against us ;

2 They had swallowed us up quick : when they were so wrathfully displeased at us.

3 Yea, the waters had drowned us : and the stream had gone over our soul.

4 The deep waters of the proud : had gone even over our soul.

5 But praised be the LORD : who hath not given us over for a prey unto their teeth.

6 Our soul is escaped even as a bird out of the snare of the fowler : the snare is broken, and we are delivered.

7 Our help standeth in the Name of the LORD : who hath made heaven and earth.

Psalm cxxv. *Qui confidunt.*

THEY that put their trust in the LORD shall be even as the Mount Sion, which may not be removed, but standeth fast for ever.

2 The hills stand about Jerusalem ; even so standeth the LORD round about his people, from this time forth for evermore.

3 For the rod of the ungodly cometh not into the lot of the righteous ; lest the righteous put their hand unto wickedness.

PSALM 125. *Qui confidunt.*

THEY that put their trust in the LORD shall be even as the mount Sion : which may not be removed, but standeth fast for ever.

2 The hills stand about Jerusalem : even so standeth the LORD round about his people, from this time forth for evermore.

3 For the rod of the ungodly cometh not into the lot of the righteous : lest the righteous put their hand unto wickedness.

1928 | 1979

Psalm 123. *Ad te levavi oculos meos.*

UNTO thee lift I up mine eyes, * O thou that dwellest in the heavens.

2 Behold, even as the eyes of servants look unto the hand of their masters, and as the eyes of a maiden unto the hand of her mistress, * even so our eyes wait upon the LORD our God, until he have mercy upon us.

3 Have mercy upon us, O LORD, have mercy upon us; * for we are utterly despised.

4 Our soul is filled with the scornful reproof of the wealthy, * and with the despitefulness of the proud.

123 *Ad te levavi oculos meos*

1 To you I lift up my eyes, *
to you enthroned in the heavens.

2 As the eyes of servants look to the hand of their masters, *
and the eyes of a maid to the hand of her mistress,

3 So our eyes look to the LORD our God, *
until he show us his mercy.

4 Have mercy upon us, O LORD, have mercy, *
for we have had more than enough of contempt,

5 Too much of the scorn of the indolent rich, *
and of the derision of the proud.

Psalm 124. *Nisi quia Dominus.*

IF the LORD himself had not been on our side, now may Israel say; * if the LORD himself had not been on our side, when men rose up against us;

2 They had swallowed us up alive; * when they were so wrathfully displeased at us.

3 Yea, the waters had drowned us, * and the stream had gone over our soul.

4 The deep waters of the proud * had gone even over our soul.

5 But praised be the LORD, * who hath not given us over for a prey unto their teeth.

6 Our soul is escaped even as a bird out of the snare of the fowler; * the snare is broken, and we are delivered.

7 Our help standeth in the Name of the LORD, * who hath made heaven and earth.

124 *Nisi quia Dominus*

1 If the LORD had not been on our side, *
let Israel now say;

2 If the LORD had not been on our side, *
when enemies rose up against us;

3 Then would they have swallowed us up alive *
in their fierce anger toward us;

4 Then would the waters have overwhelmed us *
and the torrent gone over us;

5 Then would the raging waters *
have gone right over us.

6 Blessed be the LORD! *
he has not given us over to be a prey for their teeth.

7 We have escaped like a bird from the snare of the fowler; *
the snare is broken, and we have escaped.

8 Our help is in the Name of the LORD, *
the maker of heaven and earth.

Psalm 125. *Qui confidunt.*

THEY that put their trust in the LORD shall be even as the mount Sion, * which may not be removed, but standeth fast for ever.

2 The hills stand about Jerusalem; * even so standeth the LORD round about his people, from this time forth for evermore.

3 For the sceptre of the ungodly shall not abide upon the lot of the righteous; * lest the righteous put their hand unto wickedness.

125 *Qui confidunt*

1 Those who trust in the LORD are like Mount Zion, *
which cannot be moved, but stands fast for ever.

2 The hills stand about Jerusalem; *
so does the LORD stand round about his people,
from this time forth for evermore.

3 The scepter of the wicked shall not hold sway over the land allotted to the just, *
so that the just shall not put their hands to evil.

1789-1871	1892
4 Do well, O LORD, unto those that are good and true of heart.	4 Do well, O LORD : unto those that are good and true of heart.
5 As for such as turn back unto their own wickedness, the LORD shall lead them forth with the evil doers ; but peace shall be upon Israel.	5 As for such as turn back unto their own wickedness : the LORD shall lead them forth with the evil doers ; but peace shall be upon Israel.
Evening Prayer.	**Evening Prayer.**
Psalm cxxvi. *In convertendo.*	PSALM 126. *In convertendo.*
WHEN the LORD turned again the captivity of Sion, then were we like unto them that dream.	WHEN the LORD turned again the captivity of Sion : then were we like unto them that dream.
2 Then was our mouth filled with laughter, and our tongue with joy.	2 Then was our mouth filled with laughter : and our tongue with joy.
3 Then said they among the heathen, The LORD hath done great things for them.	3 Then said they among the heathen : The LORD hath done great things for them.
4 Yea, the LORD hath done great things for us already ; whereof we rejoice.	4 Yea, the LORD hath done great things for us already : whereof we rejoice.
5 Turn our captivity, O LORD, as the rivers in the south.	5 Turn our captivity, O LORD : as the rivers in the south.
6 They that sow in tears shall reap in joy.	6 They that sow in tears : shall reap in joy.
7 He that now goeth on his way weeping, and beareth forth good seed, shall doubtless come again with joy, and bring his sheaves with him.	7 He that now goeth on his way weeping, and beareth forth good seed : shall doubtless come again with joy, and bring his sheaves with him.
Psalm cxxvii. *Nisi Dominus.*	PSALM 127. *Nisi Dominus.*
EXCEPT the LORD build the house, their labour is but lost that build it.	EXCEPT the LORD build the house : their labour is but lost that build it.
2 Except the LORD keep the city, the watchman waketh but in vain.	2 Except the LORD keep the city : the watchman waketh but in vain.
3 It is but lost labour that ye haste to rise up early, and so late take rest, and eat the bread of carefulness ; for so he giveth his beloved sleep.	3 It is but lost labour that ye haste to rise up early, and so late take rest, and eat the bread of carefulness : for so he giveth his beloved sleep.
4 Lo, children, and the fruit of the womb, are an heritage and gift that cometh of the LORD.	4 Lo, children, and the fruit of the womb : are an heritage and gift that cometh of the LORD.
5 Like as the arrows in the hand of the giant, even so are the young children.	5 Like as the arrows in the hand of the giant : even so are the young children.
6 Happy is the man that hath his quiver full of them ; they shall not be ashamed when they speak with their enemies in the gate.	6 Happy is the man that hath his quiver full of them : they shall not be ashamed when they speak with their enemies in the gate.

4 Do well, O LORD, * unto those that are good and true of heart.

5 As for such as turn back unto their own wickedness, * the LORD shall lead them forth with the evil doers; but peace shall be upon Israel.

Evening Prayer.

Psalm 126. *In convertendo.*

WHEN the LORD turned again the captivity of Sion, * then were we like unto them that dream.

2 Then was our mouth filled with laughter, * and our tongue with joy.

3 Then said they among the heathen, * The LORD hath done great things for them.

4 Yea, the LORD hath done great things for us already; * whereof we rejoice.

5 Turn our captivity, O LORD, * as the rivers in the south.

6 They that sow in tears * shall reap in joy.

7 He that now goeth on his way weeping, and beareth forth good seed, * shall doubtless come again with joy, and bring his sheaves with him.

Psalm 127. *Nisi Dominus.*

EXCEPT the LORD build the house, * their labour is but lost that build it.

2 Except the LORD keep the city, * the watchman waketh but in vain.

3 It is but lost labour that ye haste to rise up early, and so late take rest, and eat the bread of carefulness; * for so he giveth his beloved sleep.

4 Lo, children, and the fruit of the womb, * are an heritage and gift that cometh of the LORD.

5 Like as the arrows in the hand of the giant, * even so are the young children.

6 Happy is the man that hath his quiver full of them; * they shall not be ashamed when they speak with their enemies in the gate.

4 Show your goodness, O LORD, to those who are good *
and to those who are true of heart.

5 As for those who turn aside to crooked ways,
the LORD will lead them away with the evildoers; *
but peace be upon Israel.

Twenty-seventh Day: Evening Prayer

126 *In convertendo*

1 When the LORD restored the fortunes of Zion, *
then were we like those who dream.

2 Then was our mouth filled with laughter, *
and our tongue with shouts of joy.

3 Then they said among the nations, *
"The LORD has done great things for them."

4 The LORD has done great things for us, *
and we are glad indeed.

5 Restore our fortunes, O LORD, *
like the watercourses of the Negev.

6 Those who sowed with tears *
will reap with songs of joy.

7 Those who go out weeping, carrying the seed, *
will come again with joy, shouldering their sheaves.

127 *Nisi Dominus*

1 Unless the LORD builds the house, *
their labor is in vain who build it.

2 Unless the LORD watches over the city, *
in vain the watchman keeps his vigil.

3 It is in vain that you rise so early and go to bed so late; *
vain, too, to eat the bread of toil,
for he gives to his beloved sleep.

4 Children are a heritage from the LORD, *
and the fruit of the womb is a gift.

5 Like arrows in the hand of a warrior *
are the children of one's youth.

6 Happy is the man who has his quiver full of them! *
he shall not be put to shame
when he contends with his enemies in the gate.

Psalm cxxviii. *Beati omnes.*

BLESSED are all they that fear the LORD, and walk in his ways.

2 For thou shalt eat the labour[37] of thine hands : O well is thee, and happy shalt thou be!

3 Thy wife shall be as the fruitful vine upon the walls of thine house.

4 Thy children like the olive-branches round about thy table.

5 Lo, thus shall the man be blessed that feareth the LORD.

6 The LORD from out of Sion shall so bless thee, that thou shalt see Jerusalem in prosperity all thy life long ;

7 Yea, that thou shalt see thy children's children, and peace upon Israel.

PSALM 128. *Beati omnes.*

BLESSED are all they that fear the LORD : and walk in his ways.

2 For thou shalt eat the labours of thine hands : O well is thee, and happy shalt thou be.

3 Thy wife shall be as the fruitful vine : upon the walls of thine house.

4 Thy children like the olive-branches : round about thy table.

5 Lo, thus shall the man be blessed : that feareth the LORD.

6 The LORD from out of Sion shall so bless thee : that thou shalt see Jerusalem in prosperity all thy life long ;

7 Yea, that thou shalt see thy children's children : and peace upor Israel.

Psalm cxxix. *Sæpe expugnaverunt.*

MANY a time have they fought against me from my youth up, may Israel now say :

2 Yea, many a time have they vexed me from my youth up ; but they have not prevailed against me.

3 The plowers plowed upon my back, and made long furrows.

4 But the righteous LORD hath hewn the snares of the ungodly in pieces.

5 Let them be confounded and turned backward, as many as have evil will at Sion.

6 Let them be even as the grass upon the housetops, which withereth afore it be plucked up ;

7 Whereof the mower filleth not his hand, neither he that bindeth up the sheaves his bosom.

8 So that they who go by say not so much as, The LORD prosper you ; we wish you good luck in the Name of the LORD.

PSALM 129. *Sæpe expugnaverunt.*

MANY a time have they fought against me from my youth up : may Israel now say ;

2 Yea, many a time have they vexed me from my youth up : but they have not prevailed against me.

3 The plowers plowed upon my back : and made long furrows.

4 But the righteous LORD : hath hewn the snares of the ungodly in pieces.

5 Let them be confounded and turned backward : as many as have evil will at Sion.

6 Let them be even as the grass growing upon the housetops : which withereth afore it be plucked up ;

7 Whereof the mower filleth not his hand : neither he that bindeth up the sheaves his bosom.

8 So that they who go by say not so much as, The LORD prosper you : we wish you good luck in the Name of the LORD.

Psalm cxxx. *De profundis.*

OUT of the deep have I called unto thee, O LORD ; Lord, hear my voice.

2 O let thine ears consider well the voice of my complaint.

PSALM 130. *De profundis.*

OUT of the deep have I called unto thee, O LORD : Lord, hear my voice.

2 O let thine ears consider well : the voice of my complaint.

[37] "labours" in the English book.

Psalm 128. *Beati omnes.*

BLESSED are all they that fear the LORD, * and walk in his ways.

2 For thou shalt eat the labours of thine hands: * O well is thee, and happy shalt thou be.

3 Thy wife shall be as the fruitful vine * upon the walls of thine house;

4 Thy children like the olive-branches * round about thy table.

5 Lo, thus shall the man be blessed * that feareth the LORD.

6 The LORD from out of Sion shall so bless thee, * that thou shalt see Jerusalem in prosperity all thy life long;

7 Yea, that thou shalt see thy children's children, * and peace upon Israel.

128 *Beati omnes*

1 Happy are they all who fear the LORD, *
and who follow in his ways!

2 You shall eat the fruit of your labor; *
happiness and prosperity shall be yours.

3 Your wife shall be like a fruitful vine within your house, *
your children like olive shoots round about your table.

4 The man who fears the LORD *
shall thus indeed be blessed.

5 The LORD bless you from Zion, *
and may you see the prosperity of Jerusalem all the days of your life.

6 May you live to see your children's children; *
may peace be upon Israel.

Psalm 129. *Sæpe expugnaverunt.*

MANY a time have they fought against me from my youth up, * may Israel now say;

2 Yea, many a time have they vexed me from my youth up; * but they have not prevailed against me.

3 The plowers plowed upon my back, * and made long furrows.

4 But the righteous LORD * hath hewn the snares of the ungodly in pieces.

5 Let them be confounded and turned backward, * as many as have evil will at Sion.

6 Let them be even as the grass upon the house-tops, * which withereth afore it be grown up;

7 Whereof the mower filleth not his hand, * neither he that bindeth up the sheaves his bosom.

8 So that they who go by say not so much as, The LORD prosper you; * we wish you good luck in the Name of the LORD.

129 *Sæpe expugnaverunt*

1 "Greatly have they oppressed me since my youth," *
let Israel now say;

2 "Greatly have they oppressed me since my youth, *
but they have not prevailed against me."

3 The plowmen plowed upon my back *
and made their furrows long.

4 The LORD, the Righteous One, *
has cut the cords of the wicked.

5 Let them be put to shame and thrown back, *
all those who are enemies of Zion.

6 Let them be like grass upon the housetops, *
which withers before it can be plucked;

7 Which does not fill the hand of the reaper, *
nor the bosom of him who binds the sheaves;

8 So that those who go by say not so much as,
"The LORD prosper you. *
We wish you well in the Name of the LORD."

Psalm 130. *De profundis.*

OUT of the deep have I called unto thee, O LORD; * Lord, hear my voice.

2 O let thine ears consider well * the voice of my complaint.

130 *De profundis*

1 Out of the depth have I called to you, O LORD;
LORD, hear my voice; *
let your ears consider well the voice of my supplication.

2 If you, LORD, were to note what is done amiss, *
O Lord, who could stand?

3 If thou, LORD, wilt be extreme to mark what is done amiss, O Lord, who may abide it?
4 For there is mercy with thee; therefore shalt thou be feared.
5 I look for the LORD; my soul doth wait for him; in his word is my trust.
6 My soul fleeth unto the Lord before the morning watch; I say, before the morning watch.
7 O Israel, trust in the LORD; for with the LORD there is mercy, and with him is plenteous redemption.
8 And he shall redeem Israel from all his sins.

Psalm cxxxi. *Domine, non est.*

LORD, I am not high-minded; I have no proud looks.
2 I do not exercise myself in great matters which are too high for me.
3 But I refrain my soul, and keep it low, like as a child that is weaned from his mother: yea, my soul is even as a weaned child.
4 O Israel, trust in the LORD from this time forth for evermore.

THE TWENTY-EIGHTH DAY.

Morning Prayer.

Psalm cxxxii. *Memento, Domine.*

LORD, remember David, and all his trouble:
2 How he sware unto the LORD, and vowed a vow unto the Almighty God of Jacob;
3 I will not come within the tabernacle of mine house, nor climb up into my bed;
4 I will not suffer mine eyes to sleep, nor mine eyelids to slumber; neither the temples of my head to take any rest;
5 Until I find out a place for the temple of the LORD; an habitation for the mighty God of Jacob.
6 Lo, we heard the same at Ephrata, and found it in the wood.
7 We will go into his tabernacle, and fall low on our knees before his footstool.
8 Arise, O LORD, into thy resting-place; thou, and the ark of thy strength.

3 If thou, LORD, wilt be extreme to mark what is done amiss: O Lord, who may abide it?
4 For there is mercy with thee: therefore shalt thou be feared.
5 I look for the LORD; my soul doth wait for him: in his word is my trust.
6 My soul fleeth unto the Lord: before the morning watch, I say, before the morning watch.
7 O Israel, trust in the LORD, for with the LORD there is mercy: and with him is plenteous redemption.
8 And he shall redeem Israel: from all his sins.

PSALM 131. *Domine, non est.*

LORD, I am not high-minded: I have no proud looks.
2 I do not exercise myself in great matters: which are too high for me.
3 But I refrain my soul, and keep it low, like as a child that is weaned from his mother: yea, my soul is even as a weaned child.
4 O Israel, trust in the LORD: from this time forth for evermore.

THE TWENTY-EIGHTH DAY.

Morning Prayer.

PSALM 132. *Memento, Domine.*

LORD, remember David: and all his trouble:
2 How he sware unto the LORD: and vowed a vow unto the Almighty God of Jacob:
3 I will not come within the tabernacle of mine house: nor climb up into my bed;
4 I will not suffer mine eyes to sleep, nor mine eyelids to slumber: neither the temples of my head to take any rest;
5 Until I find out a place for the temple of the LORD: an habitation for the Mighty God of Jacob.
6 Lo, we heard the same at Ephrata: and found it in the wood.
7 We will go into his tabernacle: and fall low on our knees before his footstool.
8 Arise, O LORD, into thy resting-place: thou, and the ark of thy strength.

1928

3 If thou, LORD, wilt be extreme to mark what is
done amiss, * O Lord, who may abide it?
4 For there is mercy with thee; * therefore shalt
thou be feared.
5 I look for the LORD; my soul doth wait for him; *
in his word is my trust.
6 My soul fleeth unto the Lord before the morning
watch; * I say, before the morning watch.
7 O Israel, trust in the LORD; for with the LORD
there is mercy, * and with him is plenteous redemption.
8 And he shall redeem Israel * from all his sins.

Psalm 131. *Domine, non est.*

LORD, I am not high-minded; * I have no proud
looks.
2 I do not exercise myself in great matters * which
are too high for me.
3 But I refrain my soul, and keep it low, like as a
child that is weaned from his mother: * yea, my soul is
even as a weaned child.
4 O Israel, trust in the LORD * from this time forth
for evermore.

The Twenty-eighth Day.

Morning Prayer.

Psalm 132. *Memento, Domine.*

LORD, remember David, * and all his trouble:
2 How he sware unto the LORD, * and vowed a
vow unto the Almighty God of Jacob:
3 I will not come within the tabernacle of mine
house, * nor climb up into my bed;
4 I will not suffer mine eyes to sleep, nor mine
eyelids to slumber; * neither the temples of my head to
take any rest;
5 Until I find out a place for the temple of the
LORD; * an habitation for the Mighty God of Jacob.
6 Lo, we heard the same at Ephratah, * and found
it in the wood.
7 We will go into his tabernacle, * and fall low on
our knees before his footstool.
8 Arise, O LORD, into thy resting-place; * thou, and
the ark of thy strength.

1979

3 For there is forgiveness with you; *
therefore you shall be feared.

4 I wait for the LORD; my soul waits for him; *
in his word is my hope.

5 My soul waits for the LORD,
more than watchmen for the morning, *
more than watchmen for the morning.

6 O Israel, wait for the LORD, *
for with the LORD there is mercy;

7 With him there is plenteous redemption, *
and he shall redeem Israel from all their sins.

131 *Domine, non est*

1 O LORD, I am not proud; *
I have no haughty looks.

2 I do not occupy myself with great matters, *
or with things that are too hard for me.

3 But I still my soul and make it quiet,
like a child upon its mother's breast; *
my soul is quieted within me.

4 O Israel, wait upon the LORD, *
from this time forth for evermore.

Twenty-eighth Day: Morning Prayer

132 *Memento, Domine*

1 LORD, remember David, *
and all the hardships he endured;

2 How he swore an oath to the LORD *
and vowed a vow to the Mighty One of Jacob:

3 "I will not come under the roof of my house, *
nor climb up into my bed;

4 I will not allow my eyes to sleep, *
nor let my eyelids slumber;

5 Until I find a place for the LORD, *
a dwelling for the Mighty One of Jacob."

6 "The ark! We heart it was in Ephratah; *
we found it in the fields of Jearim.

7 Let us go to God's dwelling place; *
let us fall upon our knees before his footstool."

8 Arise, O LORD, into your resting-place, *
you and the ark of your strength.

9 Let thy priests be clothed with righteousness ; and let thy saints sing with joyfulness.
10 For thy servant David's sake, turn not away the face of thine Anointed.
11 The LORD hath made a faithful oath unto David, and he shall not shrink from it ;
12 Of the fruit of thy body shall I set upon thy seat.
13 If thy children will keep my covenant, and my testimonies that I shall learn them ; their children also shall sit upon thy throne for evermore.
14 For the LORD hath chosen Sion to be an habitation for himself ; he hath longed for her.
15 This shall be my rest for ever : here will I dwell, for I have a delight therein.
16 I will bless her victuals with increase, and will satisfy her poor with bread.
17 I will deck her priests with health, and her saints shall rejoice and sing.
18 There shall I make the horn of David to flourish : I have ordained a lantern for mine Anointed.
19 As for his enemies, I shall clothe them with shame ; but upon himself shall his crown flourish.

9 Let thy priests be clothed with righteousness : and let thy saints sing with joyfulness.
10 For thy servant David's sake : turn not away the presence of thine anointed.
11 The LORD hath made a faithful oath unto David : and he shall not shrink from it :
12 Of the fruit of thy body : shall I set upon thy seat.
13 If thy children will keep my covenant, and my testimonies that I shall learn them : their children also shall sit upon thy seat for evermore.
14 For the LORD hath chosen Sion to be an habitation for himself : he hath longed for her.
15 This shall be my rest for ever : here will I dwell, for I have a delight therein.
16 I will bless her victuals with increase : and will satisfy her poor with bread.
17 I will deck her priests with health : and her saints shall rejoice and sing.
18 There shall I make the horn of David to flourish : I have ordained a lantern for mine anointed.
19 As for his enemies, I shall clothe them with shame : but upon himself shall his crown flourish.

Psalm cxxxiii. *Ecce, quam bonum!*

BEHOLD, how good and joyful a thing it is, brethren, to dwell together in unity!
2 It is like the precious ointment upon the head, that ran down unto the beard, even unto Aaron's beard, and went down to the skirts of his clothing.
3 Like as the dew of Hermon, which fell upon the hill of Sion.
4 For there the LORD promised his blessing, and life for evermore.

PSALM 133. *Ecce, quam bonum!*

BEHOLD, how good and joyful a thing it is : brethren[2] to dwell together in unity!
2 It is like the precious ointment upon the head, that ran down unto the beard : even unto Aaron's beard, and went down to the skirts of his clothing.
3 Like as the dew of Hermon : which fell upon the hill of Sion.
4 For there the LORD promised his blessing : and life for evermore.

Psalm cxxxiv. *Ecce nunc.*

BEHOLD now, praise the LORD, all ye servants of the LORD ;

PSALM 134. *Ecce nunc.*

BEHOLD now, praise the LORD : all ye servants of the LORD ;

[2] *sic*

9 Let thy priests be clothed with righteousness; *
and let thy saints sing with joyfulness.
10 For thy servant David's sake, * turn not away
the face of thine anointed.
11 The LORD hath made a faithful oath unto
David, * and he shall not shrink from it:
12 Of the fruit of thy body * shall I set upon thy
throne.
13 If thy children will keep my covenant, and my
testimonies that I shall teach them; * their children
also shall sit upon thy throne for evermore.
14 For the LORD hath chosen Sion to be an habitation for himself; * he hath longed for her.
15 This shall be my rest for ever: * here will I dwell,
for I have a delight therein.
16 I will bless her victuals with increase, * and will
satisfy her poor with bread.
17 I will deck her priests with health, * and her
saints shall rejoice and sing.
18 There shall I make the horn of David to
flourish: * I have ordained a lantern for mine anointed.
19 As for his enemies, I shall clothe them with
shame; * but upon himself shall his crown flourish.

9 Let your priests be clothed with righteousness; *
let your faithful people sing with joy.

10 For your servant David's sake, *
do not turn away the face of your Anointed.

11 The LORD has sworn an oath to David; *
in truth, he will not break it:

12 "A son, the fruit of your body *
will I set upon your throne.

13 If your children keep my covenant
and my testimonies that I shall teach them, *
their children will sit upon your throne for evermore."

14 For the LORD has chosen Zion; *
he has desired her for his habitation:

15 "This shall be my resting-place for ever; *
here will I dwell, for I delight in her.

16 I will surely bless her provisions, *
and satisfy her poor with bread.

17 I will clothe her priests with salvation, *
and her faithful people will rejoice and sing.

18 There will I make the horn of David flourish; *
I have prepared a lamp for my Anointed.

19 As for his enemies, I will clothe them with shame; *
but as for him, his crown will shine."

Psalm 133. *Ecce, quam bonum!*

BEHOLD, how good and joyful a thing it is, * for
brethren to dwell together in unity!
2 It is like the precious oil upon the head, that ran
down unto the beard, * even unto Aaron's beard, and
went down to the skirts of his clothing.
3 Like as the dew of Hermon, * which fell upon the
hill of Sion.
4 For there the LORD promised his blessing, * and
life for evermore.

133 *Ecce, quam bonum!*

1 Oh, how good and pleasant it is, *
when brethren live together in unity!

2 It is like fine oil upon the head *
that runs down upon the beard,

3 Upon the beard of Aaron, *
and runs down upon the collar of his robe.

4 It is like the dew of Hermon *
that falls upon the hills of Zion.

5 For there the LORD has ordained the blessing: *
life for evermore.

Psalm 134. *Ecce nunc.*

BEHOLD now, praise the LORD, * all ye servants of
the LORD;

134 *Ecce nunc*

1 Behold now, bless the LORD, all you servants of the LORD, *
you that stand by night in the house of the LORD.

2 Ye that by night stand in the house of the LORD, even in the courts of the house of our God.
3 Lift up your hands in the sanctuary, and praise the LORD.
4 The LORD, that made heaven and earth, give thee blessing out of Sion.

Psalm cxxxv. *Laudate Nomen.*

O PRAISE the LORD, laud ye the Name of the LORD ; praise it, O ye servants of the LORD ;
2 Ye that stand in the house of the LORD, in the courts of the house of our God.
3 O praise the LORD, for the LORD is gracious ; O sing praises unto his Name, for it is lovely.
4 For why? the LORD hath chosen Jacob unto himself, and Israel for his own possession.
5 For I know that the LORD is great, and that our Lord is above all gods.
6 Whatsoever the LORD pleased, that did he in heaven, and in earth ; and in the sea,[38] and in all deep places.
7 He bringeth forth the clouds from the ends of the world, and sendeth forth lightnings with the rain, bringing the winds out of his treasures.
8 He smote the firstborn of Egypt, both of man and beast.
9 He hath sent tokens and wonders into the midst of thee, O thou land of Egypt ; upon Pharaoh, and all his servants.
10 He smote divers nations, and slew mighty kings ;
11 Sehon, king of the Amorites ; and Og, the king of Basan ; and all the kingdoms of Canaan ;
12 And gave their land to be an heritage, even an heritage unto Israel his people.
13 Thy Name, O LORD, endureth for ever ; so doth thy memorial, O LORD, from one generation to another.
14 For the LORD will avenge his people, and be gracious unto his servants.
15 As for the images of the heathen, they are but silver and gold ; the works of men's hands.
16 They have mouths, and speak not ; eyes have they, but they see not.

2 Ye that by night stand in the house of the LORD : even in the courts of the house of our God.
3 Lift up your hands in the sanctuary : and praise the LORD.
4 The LORD that made heaven and earth : give thee blessing out of Sion.

PSALM 135. *Laudate Nomen.*

O PRAISE the LORD, laud ye the Name of the LORD : praise it, O ye servants of the LORD ;
2 Ye that stand in the house of the LORD : in the courts of the house of our God.
3 O praise the LORD, for the LORD is gracious : O sing praises unto his Name, for it is lovely.
4 For why? the LORD hath chosen Jacob unto himself : and Israel for his own possession.
5 For I know that the LORD is great : and that our Lord is above all gods.
6 Whatsoever the LORD pleased, that did he in heaven, and in earth : and in the sea, and in all deep places.
7 He bringeth forth the clouds from the ends of the world : and sendeth forth lightnings with the rain, bringing the winds out of his treasures.
8 He smote the firstborn of Egypt : both of man and beast.
9 He hath sent tokens and wonders into the midst of thee, O thou land of Egypt : upon Pharaoh, and all his servants.
10 He smote divers nations : and slew mighty kings ;
11 Sehon, king of the Amorites ; and Og, the king of Basan : and all the kingdoms of Canaan ;
12 And gave their land to be an heritage : even an heritage unto Israel his people.
13 Thy Name, O LORD, endureth for ever : so doth thy memorial, O LORD, from one generation to another.
14 For the LORD will avenge his people : and be gracious unto his servants.
15 As for the images of the heathen, they are but silver and gold : the work of men's hands.
16 They have mouths, and speak not : eyes have they, but they see not.

[38] "and" added in 1871.

2 Ye that by night stand in the house of the LORD, * even in the courts of the house of our God.
3 Lift up your hands in the sanctuary, * and praise the LORD.
4 The LORD that made heaven and earth * give thee blessing out of Sion.

Psalm 135. *Laudate Nomen.*

O PRAISE the LORD, laud ye the Name of the LORD; * praise it, O ye servants of the LORD;
2 Ye that stand in the house of the LORD, * in the courts of the house of our God.
3 O praise the LORD, for the LORD is gracious; * O sing praises unto his Name, for it is lovely.
4 For why? the LORD hath chosen Jacob unto himself, * and Israel for his own possession.
5 For I know that the LORD is great, * and that our Lord is above all gods.
6 Whatsoever the LORD pleased, that did he in heaven, and in earth; * and in the sea, and in all deep places.
7 He bringeth forth the clouds from the ends of the world, * and sendeth forth lightnings with the rain, bringing the winds out of his treasuries.
8 He smote the firstborn of Egypt, * both of man and beast.
9 He hath sent tokens and wonders into the midst of thee, O thou land of Egypt; * upon Pharaoh, and all his servants.
10 He smote divers nations, * and slew mighty kings;
11 Sihon, king of the Amorites; and Og, the king of Bashan; * and all the kingdoms of Canaan;
12 And gave their land to be an heritage, * even an heritage unto Israel his people.
13 Thy Name, O LORD, endureth for ever; * so doth thy memorial, O LORD, from one generation to another.
14 For the LORD will avenge his people, * and be gracious unto his servants.
15 As for the images of the heathen, they are but silver and gold; * the work of men's hands.
16 They have mouths, and speak not; * eyes have they, but they see not.

2 Lift up your hands in the holy place and bless the LORD; *
the LORD who made heaven and earth bless
you out of Zion.

135 *Laudate nomen*

1 Hallelujah!
Praise the Name of the LORD; *
give praise, you servants of the LORD,

2 You who stand in the house of the LORD, *
in the courts of the house of our God.

3 Praise the LORD, for the LORD is good; *
sing praises to his Name, for it is lovely.

4 For the LORD has chosen Jacob for himself *
and Israel for his own possession.

5 For I know that the LORD is great, *
and that our Lord is above all gods.

6 The LORD does whatever pleases him, in heaven and on earth, *
in the seas and all the deeps.

7 He brings up rain clouds from the ends of the earth; *
he sends out lightning with the rain,
and brings the winds out of his storehouse.

8 It was he who struck down the firstborn of Egypt, *
the firstborn both of man and beast.

9 He sent signs and wonders into the midst of you, O Egypt, *
against Pharaoh and all his servants.

10 He overthrew many nations *
and put mighty kings to death:

11 Sihon, king of the Amorites,
and Og, the king of Bashan, *
and all the kingdoms of Canaan.

12 He gave their land to be an inheritance, *
an inheritance for Israel his people.

13 O LORD, your Name is everlasting; *
your renown, O LORD, endures from age to age.

14 For the LORD gives his people justice *
and shows compassion to his servants.

15 The idols of the heathen are silver and gold, *
the work of human hands.

16 They have mouths, but they cannot speak; *
eyes have they, but they cannot see.

17 They have ears, and yet they hear not ; neither is there any breath in their mouths.

18 They that make them are like unto them ; and so are all they that put their trust in them.

19 Praise the LORD, ye house of Israel ; praise the LORD, ye house of Aaron.

20 Praise the LORD, ye house of Levi ; ye that fear the LORD, praise the LORD.

21 Praised be the LORD out of Sion, who dwelleth at Jerusalem.

Evening Prayer.

Psalm cxxxvi. *Confitemini Domino.*

O GIVE thanks unto the LORD, for he is gracious : and his mercy endureth for ever.

2 O give thanks unto the God of all gods : for his mercy endureth for ever.

3 O thank the Lord of all lords : for his mercy endureth for ever.

4 Who only doeth great wonders : for his mercy endureth for ever.

5 Who by his excellent wisdom made the heavens : for his mercy endureth for ever.

6 Who laid out the earth above the waters : for his mercy endureth for ever.

7 Who hath made great lights : for his mercy endureth for ever :

8 The sun to rule the day : for his mercy endureth for ever :

9 The moon and the stars to govern the night : for his mercy endureth for ever.

10 Who smote Egypt, with their first-born : for his mercy endureth for ever :

11 And brought out Israel from among them : for his mercy endureth for ever :

12 With a mighty hand and stretched-out arm : for his mercy endureth for ever.

13 Who divided the Red Sea in two parts : for his mercy endureth for ever :

17 They have ears, and yet they hear not : neither is there any breath in their mouths.

18 They that make them are like unto them : and so are all they that put their trust in them.

19 Praise the LORD, ye house of Israel : praise the LORD, ye house of Aaron.

20 Praise the LORD, ye house of Levi : ye that fear the LORD, praise the LORD.

21 Praised be the LORD out of Sion : who dwelleth at Jerusalem.

Evening Prayer.

PSALM 136. *Confitemini.*

O GIVE thanks unto the LORD, for he is gracious : and his mercy endureth for ever.

2 O give thanks unto the God of all gods : for his mercy endureth for ever.

3 O thank the Lord of all lords : for his mercy endureth for ever.

4 Who only doeth great wonders : for his mercy endureth for ever.

5 Who by his excellent wisdom made the heavens : for his mercy endureth for ever.

6 Who laid out the earth above the waters : for his mercy endureth for ever.

7 Who hath made great lights : for his mercy endureth for ever :

8 The sun to rule the day : for his mercy endureth for ever ;

9 The moon and the stars to govern the night : for his mercy endureth for ever.

10 Who smote Egypt, with their firstborn : for his mercy endureth for ever ;

11 And brought out Israel from among them : for his mercy endureth for ever ;

12 With a mighty hand and stretched-out arm : for his mercy endureth for ever.

13 Who divided the Red Sea in two parts : for his mercy endureth for ever ;

17 They have ears, and yet they hear not; * neither
is there any breath in their mouths.
18 They that make them are like unto them; * and
so are all they that put their trust in them.
19 Praise the LORD, ye house of Israel; * praise the
LORD, ye house of Aaron.
20 Praise the LORD, ye house of Levi; * ye that fear
the LORD, praise the LORD.
21 Praised be the LORD out of Sion, * who dwelleth
at Jerusalem.

Evening Prayer.

Psalm 136. *Confitemini.*

O GIVE thanks unto the LORD, for he is gracious: *
and his mercy endureth for ever.
2 O give thanks unto the God of all gods: * for his
mercy endureth for ever.
3 O thank the Lord of all lords: * for his mercy
endureth for ever.
4 Who only doeth great wonders: * for his mercy
endureth for ever.
5 Who by his excellent wisdom made the heavens: * for his mercy endureth for ever.
6 Who laid out the earth above the waters: * for his
mercy endureth for ever.
7 Who hath made great lights: * for his mercy
endureth for ever:
8 The sun to rule the day: * for his mercy endureth
for ever;
9 The moon and the stars to govern the night: * for
his mercy endureth for ever.
10 Who smote Egypt, with their firstborn: * for his
mercy endureth for ever;
11 And brought out Israel from among them: * for
his mercy endureth for ever;
12 With a mighty hand and stretched-out arm: *
for his mercy endureth for ever.
13 Who divided the Red Sea in two parts: * for his
mercy endureth for ever;

17 They have ears, but they cannot hear; *
neither is there any breath in their mouth.

18 Those who make them are like them, *
and so are all who put their trust in them.

19 Bless the LORD, O house of Israel; *
O house of Aaron, bless the LORD.

20 Bless the LORD, O house of Levi; *
you who fear the LORD, bless the LORD.

21 Blessed be the LORD out of Zion, *
who dwells in Jerusalem.
Hallelujah!

Twenty-eighth Day: Evening Prayer

136 *Confitemini*

1 Give thanks to the LORD, for he is good, *
for his mercy endures for ever.

2 Give thanks to the God of gods, *
for his mercy endures for ever.

3 Give thanks to the Lord of lords, *
for his mercy endures for ever.

4 Who only does great wonders, *
for his mercy endures for ever;

5 Who by wisdom made the heavens, *
for his mercy endures for ever;

6 Who spread out the earth upon the waters, *
for his mercy endures for ever;

7 Who created great lights, *
for his mercy endures for ever;

8 The sun to rule the day, *
for his mercy endures for ever;

9 The moon and the stars to govern the night, *
for his mercy endures for ever.

10 Who struck down the firstborn of Egypt, *
for his mercy endures for ever;

11 And brought out Israel from among them, *
for his mercy endures for ever;

12 With a mighty hand and a stretched-out arm, *
for his mercy endures for ever;

13 Who divided the Red Sea in two, *
for his mercy endures for ever;

14 And made Israel to go through the midst of it : for his mercy endureth for ever.
15 But as for Pharaoh and his host, he overthrew them in the Red Sea : for his mercy endureth for ever.
16 Who led his people through the wilderness : for his mercy endureth for ever.
17 Who smote great kings : for his mercy endureth for ever :
18 Yea, and slew mighty kings : for his mercy endureth for ever :
19 Sehon, king of the Amorites : for his mercy endureth for ever :
20 And Og, the king of Basan : for his mercy endureth for ever :
21 And gave away their land for an heritage : for his mercy endureth for ever :
22 Even for an heritage unto Israel, his servant : for his mercy endureth for ever :
23 Who remembered us when we were in trouble : for his mercy endureth for ever.
24 And hath delivered us from our enemies : for his mercy endureth for ever.
25 Who giveth food to all flesh : for his mercy endureth for ever.
26 O give thanks unto the God of heaven : for his mercy endureth for ever.
27 O give thanks unto the Lord of lords : for his mercy endureth for ever.

Psalm cxxxvii. *Super flumina.*

BY the waters of Babylon we sat down and wept, when we remembered thee, O Sion.
2 As for our harps, we hanged them up upon the trees that are therein.
3 For they that led us away captive, required of us then a song, and melody in our heaviness : Sing us one of the songs of Sion.
4 How shall we sing the LORD'S song in a strange land?
5 If I forget thee, O Jerusalem, let my right hand forget her cunning.

14 And made Israel to go through the midst of it : for his mercy endureth for ever.
15 But as for Pharaoh and his host, he overthrew them in the Red Sea : for his mercy endureth for ever.
16 Who led his people through the wilderness : for his mercy endureth for ever.
17 Who smote great kings : for his mercy endureth for ever ;
18 Yea, and slew mighty kings : for his mercy endureth for ever ;
19 Sehon, king of the Amorites : for his mercy endureth for ever ;
20 And Og, the king of Basan : for his mercy endureth for ever ;
21 And gave away their land for an heritage : for his mercy endureth for ever ;
22 Even for an heritage unto Israel his servant : for his mercy endureth for ever.
23 Who remembered us when we were in trouble : for his mercy endureth for ever ;
24 And hath delivered us from our enemies : for his mercy endureth for ever.
25 Who giveth food to all flesh : for his mercy endureth for ever.
26 O give thanks unto the God of heaven : for his mercy endureth for ever.
27 O give thanks unto the Lord of lords : for his mercy endureth for ever.

PSALM 137. *Super flumina.*

BY the waters of Babylon we sat down and wept : when we remembered thee, O Sion.
2 As for our harps, we hanged them up : upon the trees that are therein.
3 For they that led us away captive, required of us then a song, and melody in our heaviness : Sing us one of the songs of Sion.
4 How shall we sing the LORD'S song : in a strange land?
5 If I forget thee, O Jerusalem : let my right hand forget her cunning.

1928

14 And made Israel to go through the midst of it: *
for his mercy endureth for ever.
15 But as for Pharaoh and his host, he overthrew
them in the Red Sea: * for his mercy endureth for ever.
16 Who led his people through the wilderness: * for
his mercy endureth for ever.
17 Who smote great kings: * for his mercy
endureth for ever;
18 Yea, and slew mighty kings: * for his mercy
endureth for ever;
19 Sihon, king of the Amorites: * for his mercy
endureth for ever;
20 And Og, the king of Bashan: * for his mercy
endureth for ever;
21 And gave away their land for an heritage: * for
his mercy endureth for ever;
22 Even for an heritage unto Israel his servant: *
for his mercy endureth for ever.
23 Who remembered us when we were in
trouble: * for his mercy endureth for ever;
24 And hath delivered us from our enemies: * for
his mercy endureth for ever.
25 Who giveth food to all flesh: * for his mercy
endureth for ever.
26 O give thanks unto the God of heaven: * for his
mercy endureth for ever.
27 O give thanks unto the Lord of lords: * for his
mercy endureth for ever.

Psalm 137. *Super flumina.*

BY the waters of Babylon we sat down and wept, *
when we remembered thee, O Sion.
2 As for our harps, we hanged them up * upon the
trees that are therein.
3 For they that led us away captive, required of us
then a song, and melody in our heaviness: * Sing us
one of the songs of Sion.
4 How shall we sing the LORD'S song * in a strange
land?
5 If I forget thee, O Jerusalem, * let my right hand
forget her cunning.

1979

14 And made Israel to pass through the midst of it, *
for his mercy endures for ever;

15 But swept Pharaoh and his army into the Red Sea, *
for his mercy endures for ever;

16 Who led his people through the wilderness, *
for his mercy endures for ever.

17 Who struck down great kings, *
for his mercy endures for ever;

18 And slew mighty kings, *
for his mercy endures for ever;

19 Sihon, king of the Amorites, *
for his mercy endures for ever;

20 And Og, the king of Bashan, *
for his mercy endures for ever;

21 And gave away their lands for an inheritance, *
for his mercy endures for ever;

22 An inheritance for Israel his servant, *
for his mercy endures for ever.

23 Who remembered us in our low estate, *
for his mercy endures for ever;

24 And delivered us from our enemies, *
for his mercy endures for ever;

25 Who gives food to all creatures, *
for his mercy endures for ever.

26 Give thanks to the God of heaven, *
for his mercy endures for ever.

137 *Super flumina*

1 By the waters of Babylon we sat down and wept, *
when we remembered you, O Zion.

2 As for our harps, we hung them up *
on the trees in the midst of that land.

3 For those who led us away captive asked us for a song,
and our oppressors called for mirth: *
"Sing us one of the songs of Zion."

4 How shall we sing the LORD'S song *
upon an alien soil?

5 If I forget you, O Jerusalem, *
let my right hand forget its skill.

1789-1871

6 If I do not remember thee, let my tongue cleave to the roof of my mouth ; yea, if I prefer not Jerusalem in my mirth.

7 Remember the children of Edom, O LORD, in the day of Jerusalem ; how they said, Down with it, down with it, even to the ground.

8 O daughter of Babylon, wasted with misery ; yea, happy shall he be that rewardeth thee as thou hast served us.

9 Blessed shall he be that taketh thy children, and throweth them against the stones.

Psalm cxxxviii. *Confitebor tibi.*

I WILL give thanks unto thee, O Lord, with my whole heart ; even before the gods will I sing praise unto thee.

2 I will worship toward thy holy temple, and praise thy Name, because of thy loving-kindness and truth ; for thou hast magnified thy Name, and thy Word, above all things.

3 When I called upon thee, thou heardest me ; and enduedst my soul with much strength.

4 All the kings of the earth shall praise thee, O LORD ; for they have heard the words of thy mouth.

5 Yea, they shall sing of the ways of the LORD, that great is the glory of the LORD.

6 For though the LORD be high, yet hath he respect unto the lowly ; as for the proud, he beholdeth them afar off.

7 Though I walk in the midst of trouble, yet shalt thou refresh me ; thou shalt stretch forth thy hand upon the furiousness of mine enemies, and thy right hand shall save me.

8 The LORD shall make good his loving-kindness toward me ; yea, thy mercy, O LORD, endureth for ever ; despise not then the works of thine own hands.

1892

6 If I do not remember thee, let my tongue cleave to the roof of my mouth : yea, if I prefer not Jerusalem in my mirth.

7 Remember the children of Edom, O LORD, in the day of Jerusalem : how they said, Down with it, down with it, even to the ground.

8 O daughter of Babylon, wasted with misery : yea, happy shall he be that rewardeth thee as thou hast served us.

9 Blessed shall he be that taketh thy children : and throweth them against the stones.

PSALM 138. *Confitebor tibi.*

I WILL give thanks unto thee, O Lord, with my whole heart : even before the gods will I sing praise unto thee.

2 I will worship toward thy holy temple, and praise thy Name, because of thy loving-kindness and truth : for thou hast magnified thy Name, and thy word, above all things.

3 When I called upon thee, thou heardest me : and enduedst my soul with much strength.

4 All the kings of the earth shall praise thee, O LORD : for they have heard the words of thy mouth.

5 Yea, they shall sing in[3] the ways of the LORD : that great is the glory of the LORD.

6 For though the LORD be high, yet hath he respect unto the lowly : as for the proud, he beholdeth them afar off.

7 Though I walk in the midst of trouble, yet shalt thou refresh me : thou shalt stretch forth thy hand upon the furiousness of mine enemies, and thy right hand shall save me.

8 The LORD shall make good his loving-kindness toward me : yea, thy mercy, O LORD, endureth for ever ; despise not then the works of thine own hands.

[3] *sic*

6 If I do not remember thee, let my tongue cleave to the roof of my mouth; * yea, if I prefer not Jerusalem above my chief joy.

7 Remember the children of Edom, O LORD, in the day of Jerusalem; * how they said, Down with it, down with it, even to the ground.

8 O daughter of Babylon, wasted with misery; * yea, happy shall he be that rewardeth thee as thou hast served us.

9 Blessed shall he be that taketh thy children, * and throweth them against the stones.

6 Let my tongue cleave to the roof of my mouth
if I do not remember you, *
if I do not set Jerusalem above my highest joy.

7 Remember the day of Jerusalem, O LORD,
against the people of Edom, *
who said, "Down with it! down with it!
even to the ground!"

8 O Daughter of Babylon, doomed to destruction, *
happy the one who pays you back
for what you have done to us!

9 Happy shall he be who takes you little ones, *
and dashes them against the rock!

Psalm 138. *Confitebor tibi.*

I WILL give thanks unto thee, O Lord, with my whole heart; * even before the gods will I sing praise unto thee.

2 I will worship toward thy holy temple, and praise thy Name, because of thy loving-kindness and truth; * for thou hast magnified thy Name, and thy word, above all things.

3 When I called upon thee, thou heardest me; * and enduedst my soul with much strength.

4 All the kings of the earth shall praise thee, O LORD; * for they have heard the words of thy mouth.

5 Yea, they shall sing of the ways of the LORD, * that great is the glory of the LORD.

6 For though the LORD be high, yet hath he respect unto the lowly; * as for the proud, he beholdeth them afar off.

7 Though I walk in the midst of trouble, yet shalt thou refresh me; * thou shalt stretch forth thy hand upon the furiousness of mine enemies, and thy right hand shall save me.

8 The LORD shall make good his loving-kindness toward me; * yea, thy mercy, O LORD, endureth for ever; despise not then the works of thine own hands.

138 *Confitebor tibi*

1 I will give thanks to you, O LORD, with my whole heart; *
before the gods I will sing your praise.

2 I will bow down toward your holy temple
and praise your Name, *
because of your love and faithfulness;

3 For you have glorified your Name *
and your word above all things.

4 When I called, you answered me; *
you increased my strength within me.

5 All the kings of the earth will praise you, O LORD, *
when they have heard the words of your mouth.

6 They will sing of the ways of the LORD, *
that great is the glory of the LORD.

7 Though the LORD be high, he cares for the lowly; *
he perceives the haughty from afar.

8 Though I walk in the midst of trouble, you keep me safe; *
you stretch forth your hand against the fury of my enemies;
your right hand shall save me.

9 The LORD will make good his purpose for me; *
O LORD, your love endures for ever;
do not abandon the works of your hands.

THE TWENTY-NINTH DAY.

Morning Prayer.

Psalm cxxxix. *Domine, probasti.*

O LORD, thou hast searched me out, and known me. thou knowest my down-sitting, and mine up-rising; thou understandest my thoughts long before.

2 Thou art about my path, and about my bed; and spiest out all my ways.

3 For lo, there is not a word in my tongue, but thou, O LORD, knowest it altogether.

4 Thou hast fashioned me behind and before, and laid thine hand upon me.

5 Such knowledge is too wonderful and excellent for me; I cannot attain unto it.

6 Whither shall I go then from thy Spirit? or whither shall I go then from thy presence?

7 If I climb up into heaven, thou art there; if I go down to hell, thou art there also.

8 If I take the wings of the morning, and remain in the uttermost parts of the sea;

9 Even there also shall thy hand lead me, and thy right hand shall hold me.

10 If I say, Peradventure the darkness shall cover me; then shall my night be turned to day.

11 Yea, the darkness is no darkness with thee, but the night is as clear as the day; the darkness and light to thee are both alike.

12 For my reins are thine; thou hast covered me in my mother's womb.

13 I will give thanks unto thee, for I am fearfully and wonderfully made: marvellous are thy works, and that my soul knoweth right well.

14 My bones are not hid from thee, though I be made secretly, and fashioned beneath in the earth.

15 Thine eyes did see my substance, yet being imperfect; and in thy book were all my members written;

16 Which day by day were fashioned, when as yet there was none of them.

17 How dear are thy counsels unto me, O God; O how great is the sum of them!

THE TWENTY-NINTH DAY.

Morning Prayer.

PSALM 139. *Domine, probasti.*

O LORD, thou hast searched me out, and known me.: thou knowest my down-sitting, and mine up-rising; thou understandest my thoughts long before.

2 Thou art about my path, and about my bed: and spiest out all my ways.

3 For lo, there is not a word in my tongue: but thou, O LORD, knowest it altogether.

4 Thou hast fashioned me behind and before: and laid thine hand upon me.

5 Such knowledge is too wonderful and excellent for me: I cannot attain unto it.

6 Whither shall I go then from thy Spirit: or whither shall I go then from thy presence?

7 If I climb up into heaven, thou art there: if I go down to hell, thou art there also.

8 If I take the wings of the morning: and remain in the uttermost parts of the sea;

9 Even there also shall thy hand lead me: and thy right hand shall hold me.

10 If I say, Peradventure the darkness shall cover me: then shall my night be turned to day.

11 Yea, the darkness is no darkness with thee, but the night is as clear as the day: the darkness and light to thee are both alike.

12 For my reins are thine: thou hast covered me in my mother's womb.

13 I will give thanks unto thee, for I am fearfully and wonderfully made: marvellous are thy works, and that my soul knoweth right well.

14 My bones are not hid from thee: though I be made secretly, and fashioned beneath in the earth.

15 Thine eyes did see my substance, yet being imperfect: and in thy book were all my members written;

16 Which day by day were fashioned: when as yet there was none of them.

17 How dear are thy counsels unto me, O God: O how great is the sum of them!

The Twenty-ninth Day.

Morning Prayer.

Psalm 139. *Domine, probasti.*

O LORD, thou hast searched me out, and known
me. * Thou knowest my down-sitting, and mine up-
rising; thou understandest my thoughts long before.
2 Thou art about my path, and about my bed; *
and art acquainted with all my ways.
3 For lo, there is not a word in my tongue, * but
thou, O LORD, knowest it altogether.
4 Thou hast beset me behind and before, * and laid
thine hand upon me.
5 Such knowledge is too wonderful and excellent
for me; * I cannot attain unto it.
6 Whither shall I go then from thy Spirit? * or
whither shall I go then from thy presence?
7 If I climb up into heaven, thou art there; * if I go
down to hell, thou art there also.
8 If I take the wings of the morning, * and remain
in the uttermost parts of the sea;
9 Even there also shall thy hand lead me, * and thy
right hand shall hold me.
10 If I say, Peradventure the darkness shall cover
me; * then shall my night be turned to day.
11 Yea, the darkness is no darkness with thee, but
the night is as clear as the day; * the darkness and light
to thee are both alike.
12 For my reins are thine; * thou hast covered me
in my mother's womb.
13 I will give thanks unto thee, for I am fearfully
and wonderfully made: * marvellous are thy works, and
that my soul knoweth right well.
14 My bones are not hid from thee, * though I be
made secretly, and fashioned beneath in the earth.
15 Thine eyes did see my substance, yet being
imperfect; * and in thy book were all my members written;
16 Which day by day were fashioned, * when as yet
there was none of them.

17 How dear are thy counsels unto me, O God; *
O how great is the sum of them!

Twenty-ninth Day: Morning Prayer

139 *Domine, probasti*

1 LORD, you have searched me out and known me; *
you know my sitting down and my rising up;
you discern my thoughts from afar.

2 You trace my journeys and my resting-places *
and are acquainted with all my ways.

3 Indeed, there is not a word on my lips, *
but you, O LORD, know it altogether.

4 You press upon me behind and before *
and lay your hand upon me.

5 Such knowledge is too wonderful for me; *
it is so high that I cannot attain to it.

6 Where can I go then from your Spirit? *
where can I flee from your presence?

7 If I climb up to heaven, you are there; *
if I make the grave my bed, you are there also.

8 If I take the wings of the morning *
and dwell in the uttermost parts of the sea,

9 Even there your hand will lead me *
and your right hand hold me fast.

10 If I say, "Surely the darkness will cover me, *
and the light around me turn to night,"

11 Darkness is not dark to you;
the night is as bright as the day; *
darkness and light to you are both alike.

12 For you yourself created my inmost parts; *
you knit me together in my mother's womb.

13 I will thank you because I am marvelously made; *
your works are wonderful, and I know it well.

14 My body was not hidden from you, *
while I was being made in secret
and woven in the depths of the earth.

15 Your eyes beheld my limbs, yet unfinished in the womb;
all of them were written in your book; *
they were fashioned day by day,
when as yet there was none of them.

16 How deep I find your thoughts, O God! *
how great is the sum of them!

17 If I were to count them, they would be more in number
than the sand; *
to count them all, my life span would need to
be like yours.

1789-1871

18 If I tell them, they are more in number than the sand : when I wake up, I am present with thee.
19 Wilt thou not slay the wicked, O God? Depart from me, ye blood-thirsty men.
20 For they speak unrighteously against thee ; and thine enemies take thy Name in vain.
21 Do not I hate them, O LORD, that hate thee? and am not I grieved with those that rise up against thee?
22 Yea, I hate them right sore ; even as though they were mine enemies.
23 Try me, O God, and seek the ground of my heart ; prove me, and examine my thoughts.
24 Look well if there be any way of wickedness in me ; and lead me in the way everlasting.

Psalm cxl. *Eripe me, Domine.*

DELIVER me, O LORD, from the evil man ; and preserve me from the wicked man ;
2 Who imagine mischief in their hearts, and stir up strife all the day long.
3 They have sharpened their tongues like a serpent ; adder's poison is under their lips.
4 Keep me, O LORD, from the hands of the ungodly ; preserve me from the wicked men, who are purposed to overthrow my goings.
5 The proud have laid a snare for me, and spread a net abroad with cords ; yea, and set traps in my way.
6 I said unto the LORD, Thou art my God, hear the voice of my prayers, O LORD.
7 O LORD God, thou strength of my health ; thou hast covered my head in the day of battle.
8 Let not the ungodly have his desire, O LORD ; let not his mischievous imagination prosper, lest they be too proud.
9 Let the mischief of their own lips fall upon the head of them that compass me about.
10 Let hot burning coals fall upon them ; let them be cast into the fire, and into the pit, that they never rise up again.
11 A man full of words shall not prosper upon the earth : evil shall hunt the wicked person to overthrow him.
12 Sure I am that the LORD will avenge the poor, and maintain the cause of the helpless.
13 The righteous also shall give thanks unto thy Name ; and the just shall continue in thy sight.

1892

18 If I tell them, they are more in number than the sand : when I wake up, I am present with thee.
19 Wilt thou not slay the wicked, O God : Depart from me, ye blood-thirsty men.
20 For they speak unrighteously against thee : and thine enemies take thy Name in vain.
21 Do not I hate them, O LORD, that hate thee : and am not I grieved with those that rise up against thee?
22 Yea, I hate them right sore : even as though they were mine enemies.
23 Try me, O God, and seek the ground of my heart : prove me, and examine my thoughts.
24 Look well if there be any way of wickedness in me : and lead me in the way everlasting.

PSALM 140. *Eripe me, Domine.*

DELIVER me, O LORD, from the evil man : and preserve me from the wicked man ;
2 Who imagine mischief in their hearts : and stir up strife all the day long.
3 They have sharpened their tongues like a serpent : adder's poison is under their lips.
4 Keep me, O LORD, from the hands of the ungodly : preserve me from the wicked men, who are purposed to overthrow my goings.
5 The proud have laid a snare for me, and spread a net abroad with cords : yea, and set traps in my way.
6 I said unto the LORD, Thou art my God : hear the voice of my prayers, O LORD.
7 O LORD God, thou strength of my health : thou hast covered my head in the day of battle.
8 Let not the ungodly have his desire, O LORD : let not his mischievous imagination prosper, lest they be too proud.
9 Let the mischief of their own lips fall upon the head of them : that compass me about.
10 Let hot burning coals fall upon them : let them be cast into the fire, and into the pit, that they never rise up again.
11 A man full of words shall not prosper upon the earth : evil shall hunt the wicked person to overthrow him.
12 Sure I am that the LORD will avenge the poor : and maintain the cause of the helpless.
13 The righteous also shall give thanks unto thy Name : and the just shall continue in thy sight.

1928

18 If I tell them, they are more in number than the sand: * when I wake up, I am present with thee.

19 Wilt thou not slay the wicked, O God? * Depart from me, ye blood-thirsty men.

20 For they speak unrighteously against thee; * and thine enemies take thy Name in vain.

21 Do not I hate them, O LORD, that hate thee? * and am not I grieved with those that rise up against thee?

22 Yea, I hate them right sore; * even as though they were mine enemies.

23 Try me, O God, and seek the ground of my heart; * prove me, and examine my thoughts.

24 Look well if there be any way of wickedness in me; * and lead me in the way everlasting.

Psalm 140. *Eripe me, Domine.*

DELIVER me, O LORD, from the evil man; * and preserve me from the wicked man;

2 Who imagine mischief in their hearts, * and stir up strife all the day long.

3 They have sharpened their tongues like a serpent; * adder's poison is under their lips.

4 Keep me, O LORD, from the hands of the ungodly; * preserve me from the wicked men, who are purposed to overthrow my goings.

5 The proud have laid a snare for me, and spread a net abroad with cords; * yea, and set traps in my way.

6 I said unto the LORD, Thou art my God, * hear the voice of my prayers, O LORD.

7 O LORD God, thou strength of my health; * thou hast covered my head in the day of battle.

8 Let not the ungodly have his desire, O LORD; * let not his mischievous imagination prosper, lest they be too proud.

9 Let the mischief of their own lips fall upon the head of them * that compass me about.

10 Let hot burning coals fall upon them; * let them be cast into the fire, and into the pit, that they never rise up again.

11 A man full of words shall not prosper upon the earth: * evil shall hunt the wicked person to overthrow him.

12 Sure I am that the LORD will avenge the poor, * and maintain the cause of the helpless.

13 The righteous also shall give thanks unto thy Name; * and the just shall continue in thy sight.

1979

18 Oh, that you would slay the wicked, O God! *
You that thirst for blood, depart from me.

19 They speak despitefully against you; *
your enemies take your Name in vain.

20 Do I not hate those, O LORD, who hate you? *
and do I not loathe those who rise up against you?

21 I hate them with a perfect hatred; *
they have become my own enemies.

22 Search me out, O God, and know my heart; *
try me and know my restless thoughts.

23 Look well whether there be any wickedness in me *
and lead me in the way that is everlasting.

140 *Eripe me, Domine*

1 Deliver me, O LORD, from evildoers; *
protect me from the violent,

2 Who devise evil in their hearts *
and stir up strife all day long.

3 They have sharpened their tongues like a serpent; *
adder's poison is under their lips.

4 Keep me, O LORD, from the hands of the wicked; *
protect me from the violent,
who are determined to trip me up.

5 The proud have hidden a snare for me
and stretched out a net of cords; *
they have set traps for me along the path.

6 I have said to the LORD, "You are my God; *
listen, O LORD, to my supplication.

7 O Lord GOD, the strength of my salvation, *
you have covered my head in the day of battle.

8 Do not grant the desires of the wicked, O LORD, *
nor let their evil plans prosper.

9 Let not those who surround me lift up their heads; *
let the evil of their lips overwhelm them.

10 Let hot burning coals fall upon them; *
let them be cast into the mire, never to rise up again."

11 A slanderer shall not be established on the earth, *
and evil shall hunt down the lawless.

12 I know that the LORD will maintain the cause of the poor *
and render justice to the needy.

13 Surely, the righteous will give thanks to your Name, *
and the upright shall continue in your sight.

Psalm cxli. *Domine, clamavi.*

LORD, I call upon thee; haste thee unto me, and consider my voice, when I cry unto thee.

2 Let my prayer be set forth in thy sight as the incense; and let the lifting up of my hands be an evening sacrifice.

3 Set a watch, O LORD, before my mouth, and keep the door of my lips.

4 O let not mine heart be inclined to any evil thing; let me not be occupied in ungodly works with the men that work wickedness, lest I eat of such things as please them.

5 Let the righteous rather smite me friendly, and reprove me.

6 But let not their precious balms break my head; yea, I will pray yet against their wickedness.

7 Let their judges be overthrown in stony places, that they may hear my words; for they are sweet.

8 Our bones lie scattered before the pit, like as when one breaketh and heweth wood upon the earth.

9 But mine eyes look unto thee, O LORD God; in thee is my trust; O cast not out my soul.

10 Keep me from the snare that they have laid for me, and from the traps of the wicked doers.

11 Let the ungodly fall into their own nets together, and let me ever escape them.

Evening Prayer.

PSALM 141. *Domine, clamavi.*

LORD, I call upon thee, haste thee unto me: and consider my voice, when I cry unto thee.

2 Let my prayer be set forth in thy sight as the incense: and let the lifting up of my hands be an evening sacrifice.

3 Set a watch, O LORD, before my mouth: and keep the door of my lips.

4 O let not mine heart be inclined to any evil thing: let me not be occupied in ungodly works with the men that work wickedness, lest I eat of such things as please them.

5 Let the righteous rather smite me friendly: and reprove me.

6 But let not their precious balms break my head: yea, I will pray yet against their wickedness.

7 Let their judges be overthrown in stony places: that they may hear my words; for they are sweet.

8 Our bones lie scattered before the pit: like as when one breaketh and heweth wood upon the earth.

9 But mine eyes look unto thee, O LORD God: in thee is my trust; O cast not out my soul.

10 Keep me from the snare that they have laid for me: and from the traps of the wicked doers.

11 Let the ungodly fall into their own nets together: and let me ever escape them.

Evening Prayer.

Psalm cxlii. *Voce mea ad Dominum.*

I CRIED unto the LORD with my voice; yea, even unto the LORD did I make my supplication.

2 I poured out my complaints before him, and showed him of my trouble.

3 When my spirit was in heaviness, thou knewest my path; in the way wherein I walked, have they privily laid a snare for me.

4 I looked also upon my right hand, and saw there was no man that would know me.

5 I had no place to flee unto, and no man cared for my soul.

6 I cried unto thee, O LORD, and said, Thou art my hope, and my portion in the land of the living.

PSALM 142. *Voce mea ad Dominum.*

I CRIED unto the LORD with my voice: yea, even unto the LORD did I make my supplication.

2 I poured out my complaints before him: and showed him of my trouble.

3 When my spirit was in heaviness, thou knewest my path: in the way wherein I walked, have they privily laid a snare for me.

4 I looked also upon my right hand: and saw there was no man that would know me.

5 I had no place to flee unto: and no man cared for my soul.

6 I cried unto thee, O LORD, and said: Thou art my hope, and my portion in the land of the living.

Evening Prayer.

Psalm 141. *Domine, clamavi.*

LORD, I call upon thee; haste thee unto me, * and consider my voice, when I cry unto thee.

2 Let my prayer be set forth in thy sight as the incense; * and let the lifting up of my hands be an evening sacrifice.

3 Set a watch, O LORD, before my mouth, * and keep the door of my lips.

4 O let not mine heart be inclined to any evil thing; * let me not be occupied in ungodly works with the men that work wickedness, neither let me eat of such things as please them.

5 Let the righteous rather smite me friendly, and reprove me; * yea, let not my head refuse their precious balms.

6 As for the ungodly, * I will pray yet against their wickedness.

7 Let their judges be overthrown in stony places, * that they may hear my words; for they are sweet.

8 Our bones lie scattered before the pit, * like as when one breaketh and heweth wood upon the earth.

9 But mine eyes look unto thee, O LORD God; * in thee is my trust; O cast not out my soul.

10 Keep me from the snare that they have laid for me, * and from the traps of the wicked doers.

11 Let the ungodly fall into their own nets together, * and let me ever escape them.

Psalm 142. *Voce mea ad Dominum.*

I CRIED unto the LORD with my voice; * yea, even unto the LORD did I make my supplication.

2 I poured out my complaints before him, * and showed him of my trouble.

3 When my spirit was in heaviness, thou knewest my path; * in the way wherein I walked, have they privily laid a snare for me.

4 I looked also upon my right hand, * and saw there was no man that would know me.

5 I had no place to flee unto, * and no man cared for my soul.

6 I cried unto thee, O LORD, and said, * Thou art my hope, and my portion in the land of the living.

Twenty-ninth Day: Evening Prayer

141 *Domine, clamavi*

1 O LORD, I call to you; come to me quickly; *
hear my voice when I cry to you.

2 Let my prayer be set forth in your sight as incense, *
the lifting up of my hands as the evening sacrifice.

3 Set a watch before my mouth, O LORD,
and guard the door of my lips; *
let not my heart incline to any evil thing.

4 Let me not be occupied in wickedness with evildoers, *
nor eat of their choice foods.

5 Let the righteous smite me in friendly rebuke;
let not the oil of the unrighteous anoint my head; *
for my prayer is continually against their wicked deeds.

6 Let their rulers be overthrown in stony places, *
that they may know my words are true.

7 As when a plowman turns over the earth in furrows, *
let their bones be scattered at the mouth of the grave.

8 But my eyes are turned to you, Lord GOD; *
in you I take refuge;
do not strip me of my life.

9 Protect me from the snare which they have laid for me *
and from the traps of the evildoers.

10 Let the wicked fall into their own nets, *
while I myself escape.

142 *Voce me ad Dominum*

1 I cry to the LORD with my voice; *
to the LORD I make loud supplication.

2 I pour out my complaint before him *
and tell him all my trouble.

3 When my spirit languishes within me, you know my path; *
in the way wherein I walk they have hidden a trap for me.

4 I look to my right hand and find no one who knows me; *
I have no place to flee to, and no one cares for me.

5 I cry out to you, O LORD; *
I say, "You are my refuge,
my portion in the land of the living."

6 Listen to my cry for help, for I have been brought very low; *
save me from those who pursue me,
for they are too strong for me.

7 Consider my complaint ; for I am brought very low.
8 O deliver me from my persecutors ; for they are too strong for me.
9 Bring my soul out of prison, that I may give thanks unto thy Name ; which thing if thou wilt grant me, then shall the righteous resort unto my company.

Psalm cxliii. *Domine, exaudi.*

HEAR my prayer, O LORD, and consider my desire ; hearken unto me for thy truth and righteousness' sake.
2 And enter not into judgment with thy servant ; for in thy sight shall no man living be justified.
3 For the enemy hath persecuted my soul ; he hath smitten my life down to the ground ; he hath laid me in the darkness, as the men that have been long dead.
4 Therefore is my spirit vexed within me, and my heart within me is desolate.
5 Yet do I remember the time past ; I muse upon all thy works ; yea, I exercise myself in the works of thy hands.
6 I stretch forth my hands unto thee ; my soul gaspeth unto thee as a thirsty land.
7 Hear me, O LORD, and that soon ; for my spirit waxeth faint : hide not thy face from me, lest I be like unto them that go down into the pit.
8 O let me hear thy loving-kindness betimes in the morning ; for in thee is my trust : show thou me the way that I should walk in ; for I lift up my soul unto thee.
9 Deliver me, O LORD, from mine enemies ; for I flee unto thee to hide me.
10 Teach me to do the thing that pleaseth thee ; for thou art my God : let thy loving Spirit lead me forth into the land of righteousness.
11 Quicken me, O LORD, for thy Name's sake ; and for thy righteousness' sake bring my soul out of trouble.
12 And of thy goodness slay mine enemies, and destroy all them that vex my soul ; for I am thy servant.

7 Consider my complaint : for I am brought very low.
8 O deliver me from my persecutors : for thy are too strong for me.
9 Bring my soul out of prison, that I may give thanks unto thy Name : which thing if thou wilt grant me, then shall the righteous resort unto my company.

PSALM 143. *Domine, exaudi.*

HEAR my prayer, O LORD, and consider my desire : hearken unto me for thy truth and righteousness' sake.
2 And enter not into judgment with thy servant : for in thy sight shall no man living be justified.
3 For the enemy hath persecuted my soul ; he hath smitten my life down to the ground : he hath laid me in the darkness, as the men that have been long dead.
4 Therefore is my spirit vexed within me : and my heart within me is desolate.
5 Yet do I remember the time past ; I muse upon all thy works : yea, I exercise myself in the works of thy hands.
6 I stretch forth my hands unto thee : my soul gaspeth unto thee as a thirsty land.
7 Hear me, O LORD, and that soon, for my spirit waxeth faint : hide not thy face from me, lest I be like unto them that go down into the pit.
8 O let me hear thy loving-kindness betimes in the morning, for in thee is my trust : show thou me the way that I should walk in, for I lift up my soul unto thee.
9 Deliver me, O LORD, from mine enemies : for I flee unto thee to hide me.
10 Teach me to do the thing that pleaseth thee ; for thou art my God : let thy loving Spirit lead me forth into the land of righteousness.
11 Quicken me, O LORD, for thy Name's sake : and for thy righteousness' sake bring my soul out of trouble.
12 And of thy goodness slay mine enemies : and destroy all them that vex my soul ; for I am thy servant.

7 Consider my complaint; * for I am brought very low.
8 O deliver me from my persecutors; * for thy are too strong for me.
9 Bring my soul out of prison, that I may give thanks unto thy Name; * which thing if thou wilt grant me, then shall the righteous resort unto my company.

7 Bring me out of prison, that I may give thanks to your Name; *
when you have dealt bountifully with me,
the righteous will gather around me.

Psalm 143. *Domine, exaudi.*

HEAR my prayer, O LORD, and consider my desire; * hearken unto me for thy truth and righteousness' sake.
2 And enter not into judgment with thy servant; * for in thy sight shall no man living be justified.
3 For the enemy hath persecuted my soul; he hath smitten my life down to the ground; * he hath laid me in the darkness, as the men that have been long dead.
4 Therefore is my spirit vexed within me, * and my heart within me is desolate.
5 Yet do I remember the time past; I muse upon all thy works; * yea, I exercise myself in the works of thy hands.
6 I stretch forth my hands unto thee; * my soul gaspeth unto thee as a thirsty land.
7 Hear me, O LORD, and that soon; for my spirit waxeth faint: * hide not thy face from me, lest I be like unto them that go down into the pit.
8 O let me hear thy loving-kindness betimes in the morning; for in thee is my trust: * show thou me the way that I should walk in; for I lift up my soul unto thee.
9 Deliver me, O LORD, from mine enemies; * for I flee unto thee to hide me.
10 Teach me to do the thing that pleaseth thee; for thou art my God: * let thy loving Spirit lead me forth into the land of righteousness.
11 Quicken me, O LORD, for thy Name's sake; * and for thy righteousness' sake bring my soul out of trouble.
12 And of thy goodness slay mine enemies, * and destroy all them that vex my soul; for I am thy servant.

143 *Domine, exaudi*

1 LORD, hear my prayer,
and in your faithfulness heed my supplications; *
answer me in your righteousness.

2 Enter not into judgment with your servant, *
for in your sight shall no one living be justified.

3 For my enemy has sought my life;
he has crushed me to the ground; *
he has made me live in dark places like those who are long dead.

4 My spirit faints within me; *
my heart within me is desolate.

5 I remember the time past;
I muse upon all your deeds; *
I consider the works of your hands.

6 I spread out my hands to you; *
my soul gasps to you like a thirsty land.

7 O LORD, make haste to answer me; my spirit fails me; *
do not hide your face from me
or I shall be like those who go down to the Pit.

8 Let me hear of your loving-kindness in the morning,
for I put my trust in you; *
show me the road that I must walk,
for I lift up my soul to you.

9 Deliver me from my enemies, O LORD, *
for I flee to you for refuge.

10 Teach me to do what pleases you, for you are my God; *
let your good Spirit lead me on level ground.

11 Revive me, O LORD, for your Name's sake; *
for your righteousness' sake, bring me out of trouble.

12 Of your goodness, destroy my enemies
and bring all my foes to naught, *
for truly I am your servant.

THE THIRTIETH DAY.

Morning Prayer.

Psalm cxliv. *Benedictus Dominus.*

BLESSED be the LORD my strength, who teacheth my hands to war, and my fingers to fight:

2 My hope and my fortress, my castle and deliverer, my defender in whom I trust; who subdueth my people that is under me.

3 LORD, what is man that thou hast such respect unto him! or the son of man, that thou so regardest him!

4 Man is like a thing of nought; his time passeth away like a shadow.

5 Bow thy heavens, O LORD, and come down; touch the mountains, and they shall smoke.

6 Cast forth thy lightning, and tear them; shoot out thine arrows, and consume them.

7 Send down thine hand from above; deliver me, and take me out of the great waters, from the hand of strange children;

8 Whose mouth talketh of vanity, and their right hand is a right hand of wickedness.

9 I will sing a new song unto thee, O God; and sing praises unto thee upon a ten-stringed lute.

10 Thou hast given victory unto kings, and hast delivered David thy servant from the peril of the sword.

11 Save me, and deliver me from the hand of strange children, whose mouth talketh of vanity, and their right hand is a right hand of iniquity:

12 That our sons may grow up as the young plants, and that our daughters may be as the polished corners of the temple:

13 That our garners may be full and plenteous with all manner of store; that our sheep may bring forth thousands, and ten thousands in our streets:

14 That our oxen may be strong to labour; that there be no decay, no leading into captivity, and no complaining in our streets.

15 Happy are the people that are in such a case; yea, blessed are the people who have the LORD for their God.

THE THIRTIETH DAY.

Morning Prayer.

PSALM 144. *Benedictus Dominus.*

BLESSED be the LORD my strength: who teacheth my hands to war, and my fingers to fight:

2 My hope and my fortress, my castle and deliverer, my defender in whom I trust: who subdueth my people that is under me.

3 LORD, what is man, that thou hast such respect unto him: or the son of man, that thou so regardest him?

4 Man is like a thing of nought: his time passeth away like a shadow.

5 Bow thy heavens, O LORD, and come down: touch the mountains, and they shall smoke.

6 Cast forth thy lightning, and tear them: shoot out thine arrows, and consume them.

7 Send down thine hand from above: deliver me, and take me out of the great waters, from the hand of strange children;

8 Whose mouth talketh of vanity: and their right hand is a right hand of wickedness.

9 I will sing a new song unto thee, O God: and sing praises unto thee upon a ten-stringed lute.

10 Thou hast given victory unto kings: and hast delivered David thy servant from the peril of the sword.

11 Save me, and deliver me from the hand of strange children: whose mouth talketh of vanity, and their right hand is a right hand of iniquity:

12 That our sons may grow up as the young plants: and that our daughters may be as the polished corners of the temple;

13 That our garners may be full and plenteous with all manner of store: that our sheep may bring forth thousands, and ten thousands in our streets;

14 That our oxen may be strong to labour, that there be no decay: no leading into captivity, and no complaining in our streets.

15 Happy are the people that are in such a case: yea, blessed are the people who have the LORD for their God.

The Thirtieth Day.

Morning Prayer.

Psalm 144. *Benedictus Dominus.*

BLESSED be the LORD my strength, * who teacheth my hands to war, and my fingers to fight:

2 My hope and my fortress, my castle and deliverer, my defender in whom I trust; * who subdueth my people that is under me.

3 LORD, what is man that thou hast such respect unto him? * or the son of man, that thou so regardest him?

4 Man is like a thing of nought; * his time passeth away like a shadow.

5 Bow thy heavens, O LORD, and come down; * touch the mountains, and they shall smoke.

6 Cast forth thy lightning, and tear them; * shoot out thine arrows, and consume them.

7 Send down thine hand from above; * deliver me, and take me out of the great waters, from the hand of strangers;

8 Whose mouth talketh of vanity, * and their right hand is a right hand of wickedness.

9 I will sing a new song unto thee, O God; * and sing praises unto thee upon a ten-stringed lute.

10 Thou hast given victory unto kings, * and hast delivered David thy servant from the peril of the sword.

11 Save me, and deliver me from the hand of strangers, * whose mouth talketh of vanity, and their right hand is a right hand of iniquity:

12 That our sons may grow up as the young plants, * and that our daughters may be as the polished corners of the temple;

13 That our garners may be full and plenteous with all manner of store; * that our sheep may bring forth thousands, and ten thousands in our fields;

14 That our oxen may be strong to labour; that there be no decay, * no leading into captivity, and no complaining in our streets.

15 Happy are the people that are in such a case; * yea, blessed are the people who have the LORD for their God.

Thirtieth Day: Morning Prayer

144 *Benedictus Dominus*

1 Blessed be the LORD my rock! *
who trains my hands to fight and my fingers to battle;

2 My help and my fortress, my stronghold and my deliverer, *
my shield in whom I trust,
who subdues the peoples under me.

3 O LORD, what are we that you should care for us? *
mere mortals that you should think of us?

4 We are like a puff of wind; *
our days are like a passing shadow.

5 Bow your heavens, O LORD, and come down; *
touch the mountains, and they shall smoke.

6 Hurl the lightning and scatter them; *
shoot out your arrows and rout them.

7 Stretch out your hand from on high; *
rescue me and deliver me from the great waters,
from the hand of foreign peoples,

8 Whose mouths speak deceitfully *
and whose right hand is raised in falsehood.

9 O God, I will sing to you a new song; *
I will play to you on a ten-stringed lyre.

10 You give victory to kings *
and have rescued David your servant.

11 Rescue me from the hurtful sword *
and deliver me from the hand of foreign peoples,

12 Whose mouths speak deceitfully *
and whose right hand is raised in falsehood.

13 May our sons be like plants well nurtured from their youth, *
and our daughters like sculptured corners of a palace.

14 May our barns be filled to overflowing with all manner of crops; *
may the flocks in our pastures increase by thousands and tens of thousands;
may our cattle be fat and sleek.

15 May there be no breaching of the walls, no going into exile, *
no wailing in the public squares.

16 Happy are the people of whom this is so! *
happy are the people whose God is the LORD!

Psalm cxlv. *Exaltabo te, Deus.*

I WILL magnify thee, O God, my King ; and I will praise thy Name for ever and ever.

2 Every day will I give thanks unto thee ; and praise thy Name for ever and ever.

3 Great is the LORD, and marvellous worthy to be praised ; there is no end of his greatness.

4 One generation shall praise thy works unto another, and declare thy power.

5 As for me, I will be talking of thy worship, thy glory, thy praise, and wondrous works ;

6 So that men shall speak of the might of thy marvellous acts ; and I will also tell of thy greatness.

7 The memorial of thine abundant kindness shall be showed ; and men shall sing of thy righteousness.

8 The LORD is gracious and merciful ; long-suffering, and of great goodness.

9 The LORD is loving unto every man ; and his mercy is over all his works.

10 All thy works praise thee, O LORD ; and thy saints give thanks unto thee.

11 They show the glory of thy kingdom, and talk of thy power ;

12 That thy power, thy glory, and mightiness of thy kingdom, might be known unto men.

13 Thy kingdom is an everlasting kingdom, and thy dominion endureth throughout all ages.

14 The LORD upholdeth all such as fall, and lifteth up all those that are down.

15 The eyes of all wait upon thee, O Lord ; and thou givest them their meat in due season.

16 Thou openest thine hand, and fillest all things living with plenteousness.

17 The LORD is righteous in all his ways, and holy in all his works.

18 The LORD is nigh unto all them that call upon him ; yea, all such as call upon him faithfully.

19 He will fulfil the desire of them that fear him ; he also will hear their cry, and will help them.

20 The LORD preserveth all them that love him ; but scattereth abroad all the ungodly.

PSALM 145. *Exaltabo te, Deus.*

I WILL magnify thee, O God, my King : and I will praise thy Name for ever and ever.

2 Every day will I give thanks unto thee : and praise thy Name for ever and ever.

3 Great is the LORD, and marvellous worthy to be praised : there is no end of his greatness.

4 One generation shall praise thy works unto another : and declare thy power.

5 As for me, I will be talking of thy worship : thy glory, thy praise, and wondrous works ;

6 So that men shall speak of the might of thy marvellous acts : and I will also tell of thy greatness.

7 The memorial of thine abundant kindness shall be showed : and men shall sing of thy righteousness.

8 The LORD is gracious and merciful : long-suffering, and of great goodness.

9 The LORD is loving unto every man : and his mercy is over all his works.

10 All thy works praise thee, O LORD : and thy saints give thanks unto thee.

11 They show the glory of thy kingdom : and talk of thy power ;

12 That thy power, thy glory, and mightiness of thy kingdom : might be known unto men.

13 Thy kingdom is an everlasting kingdom : and thy dominion endureth throughout all ages.

14 The LORD upholdeth all such as fall : and lifteth up all those that are down.

15 The eyes of all wait upon thee, O Lord : and thou givest them their meat in due season.

16 Thou openest thine hand : and fillest all things living with plenteousness.

17 The LORD is righteous in all his ways : and holy in all his works.

18 The LORD is nigh unto all them that call upon him : yea, all such as call upon him faithfully.

19 He will fulfil the desire of them that fear him : he also will hear their cry, and will help them.

20 The LORD preserveth all them that love him : but scattereth abroad all the ungodly.

Psalm 145. *Exaltabo te, Deus.*

I WILL magnify thee, O God, my King; * and I will praise thy Name for ever and ever.

2 Every day will I give thanks unto thee; * and praise thy Name for ever and ever.

3 Great is the LORD, and marvellous worthy to be praised; * there is no end of his greatness.

4 One generation shall praise thy works unto another, * and declare thy power.

5 As for me, I will be talking of thy worship, * thy glory, thy praise, and wondrous works;

6 So that men shall speak of the might of thy marvellous acts; * and I will also tell of thy greatness.

7 The memorial of thine abundant kindness shall be showed; * and men shall sing of thy righteousness.

8 The LORD is gracious and merciful; * long-suffering, and of great goodness.

9 The LORD is loving unto every man; * and his mercy is over all his works.

10 All thy works praise thee, O LORD; * and thy saints give thanks unto thee.

11 They show the glory of thy kingdom, * and talk of thy power;

12 That thy power, thy glory, and mightiness of thy kingdom, * might be known unto men.

13 Thy kingdom is an everlasting kingdom, * and thy dominion endureth throughout all ages.

14 The LORD upholdeth all such as fall, * and lifteth up all those that are down.

15 The eyes of all wait upon thee, O Lord; * and thou givest them their meat in due season.

16 Thou openest thine hand, * and fillest all things living with plenteousness.

17 The LORD is righteous in all his ways, * and holy in all his works.

18 The LORD is nigh unto all them that call upon him; * yea, all such as call upon him faithfully.

19 He will fulfil the desire of them that fear him; * he also will hear their cry, and will help them.

20 The LORD preserveth all them that love him; * but scattereth abroad all the ungodly.

145 *Exaltabo te, Deus*

1 I will exalt you, O God my King, *
and bless your Name for ever and ever.

2 Every day will I bless you *
and praise your Name for ever and ever.

3 Great is the LORD and greatly to be praised; *
there is no end to his greatness.

4 One generation shall praise your works to another *
and shall declare your power.

5 I will ponder the glorious splendor of your majesty *
and all your marvelous works.

6 They shall speak of the might of your wondrous acts, *
and I will tell of your greatness.

7 They shall publish the remembrance of your great goodness; *
they shall sing of your righteous deeds.

8 The LORD is gracious and full of compassion, *
slow to anger and of great kindness.

9 The LORD is loving to everyone *
and his compassion is over all his works.

10 All your works praise you, O LORD, *
and your faithful servants bless you.

11 They make known the glory of your kingdom *
and speak of your power;

12 That the peoples may know of your power *
and the glorious splendor of your kingdom.

13 Your kingdom is an everlasting kingdom; *
your dominion endures throughout all ages.

14 The LORD is faithful in all his words *
and merciful in all his deeds.

15 The LORD upholds all those who fall; *
he lifts up those who are bowed down.

16 The eyes of all wait upon you, O LORD, *
and you give them their food in due season.

17 You open wide your hand *
and satisfy the needs of every living creature.

18 The LORD is righteous in all his ways *
and loving in all his works.

19 The LORD is near to those who call upon him, *
to all who call upon him faithfully.

20 He fulfills the desire of those who fear him; *
he hears their cry and helps them.

21 My mouth shall speak the praise of the LORD ; and let all flesh give thanks unto his holy Name for ever and ever.

21 My mouth shall speak the praise of the LORD : and let all flesh give thanks unto his holy Name for ever and ever.

Psalm cxlvi. *Lauda, anima mea.*

PRAISE the LORD, O my soul : while I live, will I praise the LORD ; yea, as long as I have any being, I will sing praises unto my God.
2 O put not your trust in princes, nor in any child of man ; for there is no help in them.
3 For when the breath of man goeth forth, he shall turn again to his earth, and then all his thoughts perish.
4 Blessed is he that hath the God of Jacob for his help, and whose hope is in the LORD his God :
5 Who made heaven and earth, the sea, and all that therein is ; who keepeth his promise for ever ;
6 Who helpeth them to right that suffer wrong ; who feedeth the hungry.
7 The LORD looseth men out of prison ; the LORD giveth sight to the blind.
8 The LORD helpeth them that are fallen ; the LORD careth for the righteous.
9 The LORD careth for the strangers ; he defendeth the fatherless and widow : as for the way of the ungodly, he turneth it upside down.
10 The LORD thy God, O Sion, shall be King for evermore, and throughout all generations.

PSALM 146. *Lauda, anima mea.*

PRAISE the LORD, O my soul ; while I live, will I praise the LORD : yea, as long as I have any being, I will sing praises unto my God.
2 O put not your trust in princes, nor in any child of man : for there is no help in them.
3 For when the breath of man goeth forth, he shall turn again to his earth : and then all his thoughts perish.
4 Blessed is he that hath the God of Jacob for his help : and whose hope is in the LORD his God :
5 Who made heaven and earth, the sea, and all that therein is : who keepeth his promise for ever ;
6 Who helpeth them to right that suffer wrong : who feedeth the hungry.
7 The LORD looseth men out of prison : the LORD giveth sight to the blind.
8 The LORD helpeth them that are fallen : the LORD careth for the righteous.
9 The LORD careth for the strangers ; he defendeth the fatherless and widow : as for the way of the ungodly, he turneth it upside down.
10 The LORD thy God, O Sion, shall be King for evermore : and throughout all generations.

Evening Prayer.

Psalm cxlvii. *Laudate Dominum.*

O PRAISE the LORD, for it is a good thing to sing praises unto our God ; yea, a joyful and pleasant thing it is to be thankful.
2 The LORD doth build up Jerusalem, and gather together the outcasts of Israel.
3 He healeth those that are broken in heart, and giveth medicine to heal their sickness.
4 He telleth the number of the stars, and calleth them all by their names.

Evening Prayer.

PSALM 147. *Laudate Dominum.*

O PRAISE the LORD, for it is a good thing to sing praises unto our God : yea, a joyful and pleasant thing it is to be thankful.
2 The LORD doth build up Jerusalem : and gather together the outcasts of Israel.
3 He healeth those that are broken in heart : and giveth medicine to heal their sickness.
4 He telleth the number of the stars : and calleth them all by their names.

21 My mouth shall speak the praise of the LORD; * and let all flesh give thanks unto his holy Name for ever and ever.

21 The LORD preserves all those who love him, *
but he destroys all the wicked.

22 My mouth shall speak the praise of the LORD; *
let all flesh bless his holy Name for ever and ever.

Psalm 146. *Lauda, anima mea.*

PRAISE the LORD, O my soul: while I live, will I praise the LORD; * yea, as long as I have any being, I will sing praises unto my God.
2 O put not your trust in princes, nor in any child of man; * for there is no help in them.
3 For when the breath of man goeth forth, he shall turn again to his earth, * and then all his thoughts perish.
4 Blessed is he that hath the God of Jacob for his help, * and whose hope is in the LORD his God:
5 Who made heaven and earth, the sea, and all that therein is; * who keepeth his promise for ever;
6 Who helpeth them to right that suffer wrong; * who feedeth the hungry.
7 The LORD looseth men out of prison; * the LORD giveth sight to the blind.
8 The LORD helpeth them that are fallen; * the LORD careth for the righteous.
9 The LORD careth for the strangers; he defendeth the fatherless and widow: * as for the way of the ungodly, he turneth it upside down.
10 The LORD thy God, O Sion, shall be King for evermore, * and throughout all generations.

146 *Lauda, anima mea*

1 Hallelujah!
Praise the LORD, O my soul! *
I will praise the LORD as long as I live;
I will sing praises to my God while I have my being.

2 Put not your trust in rulers, nor in any child of earth, *
for there is no help in them.

3 When they breathe their last, they return to earth, *
and in that day their thoughts perish.

4 Happy are they who have the God of Jacob for their help! *
whose hope is in the LORD their God;

5 Who made heaven and earth, the seas, and all that is in them; *
who keeps his promise for ever;

6 Who gives justice to those who are oppressed, *
and food to those who hunger.

7 The LORD sets the prisoners free;
the LORD opens the eyes of the blind; *
the LORD lifts up those who are bowed down;

8 The LORD loves the righteous;
the LORD cares for the stranger; *
he sustains the orphan and widow,
but frustrates the way of the wicked.

9 The LORD shall reign for ever, *
your God, O Zion, throughout all generations.
Hallelujah!

Evening Prayer.

Psalm 147. *Laudate Dominum.*

O PRAISE the LORD, for it is a good thing to sing praises unto our God; * yea, a joyful and pleasant thing it is to be thankful.
2 The LORD doth build up Jerusalem, * and gather together the outcasts of Israel.
3 He healeth those that are broken in heart, * and giveth medicine to heal their sickness.
4 He telleth the number of the stars, * and calleth them all by their names.

Thirtieth Day: Evening Prayer

147 *Laudate Dominum*

1 Hallelujah!
How good it is to sing praises to our God! *
how pleasant it is to honor him with praise!

2 The LORD rebuilds Jerusalem; *
he gathers the exiles of Israel.

3 He heals the brokenhearted *
and binds up their wounds.

4 He counts the number of the stars *
and calls them all by their names.

5 Great is our Lord, and great is his power ; yea, and his wisdom is infinite.

6 The LORD setteth up the meek, and bringeth the ungodly down to the ground.

7 O sing unto the LORD with thanksgiving ; sing praises upon the harp unto our God :

8 Who covereth the heaven with clouds, and prepareth rain for the earth ; and maketh the grass to grow upon the mountains, and herb for the use of men ;

9 Who giveth fodder unto the cattle, and feedeth the young ravens that call upon him.

10 He hath no pleasure in the strength of an horse ; neither delighteth he in any man's legs.

11 But the LORD'S delight is in them that fear him, and put their trust in his mercy.

12 Praise the LORD, O Jerusalem ; praise thy God, O Sion.

13 For he hath made fast the bars of thy gates, and hath blessed thy children within thee.

14 He maketh peace in thy borders, and filleth thee with the flour of wheat.

15 He sendeth forth his commandment upon earth, and his word runneth very swiftly.

16 He giveth snow like wool, and scattereth the hoarfrost like ashes.

17 He casteth forth his ice like morsels : who is able to abide his frost?

18 He sendeth out his word, and melteth them : he bloweth with his wind, and the waters flow.

19 He showeth his word unto Jacob, his statutes and ordinances unto Israel.

20 He hath not dealt so with any nation ; neither have the heathen knowledge of his laws.

5 Great is our Lord, and great is his power : yea, and his wisdom is infinite.

6 The LORD setteth up the meek : and bringeth the ungodly down to the ground.

7 O sing unto the LORD with thanksgiving : sing praises upon the harp unto our God :

8 Who covereth the heaven with clouds, and prepareth rain for the earth : and maketh the grass to grow upon the mountains, and herb for the use of men ;

9 Who giveth fodder unto the cattle : and feedeth the young ravens that call upon him.

10 He hath no pleasure in the strength of an horse : neither delighteth he in any man's legs.

11 But the LORD'S delight is in them that fear him : and put their trust in his mercy.

12 Praise the LORD, O Jerusalem : praise thy God, O Sion.

13 For he hath made fast the bars of thy gates : and hath blessed thy children within thee.

14 He maketh peace in thy borders : and filleth thee with the flour of wheat.

15 He sendeth forth his commandment upon earth : and his word runneth very swiftly.

16 He giveth snow like wool : and scattereth the hoar-frost like ashes.

17 He casteth forth his ice like morsels : who is able to abide his frost?

18 He sendeth out his word, and melteth them : he bloweth with his wind, and the waters flow.

19 He showeth his word unto Jacob : his statutes and ordinances unto Israel.

20 He hath not dealt so with any nation : neither have the heathen knowledge of his laws.

Psalm cxlviii. *Laudate Dominum.*

O PRAISE the LORD of heaven : praise him in the height.

2 Praise him, all ye angels of his : praise him, all his hosts.[39]

PSALM 148. *Laudate Dominum.*

O PRAISE the LORD of heaven : praise him in the height.

2 Praise him, all ye angels of his : praise him, all his host.

[39]"host" prior to 1822.

5 Great is our Lord, and great is his power; * yea,
and his wisdom is infinite.
6 The LORD setteth up the meek, * and bringeth
the ungodly down to the ground.
7 O sing unto the LORD with thanksgiving; * sing
praises upon the harp unto our God:
8 Who covereth the heaven with clouds, and
prepareth rain for the earth; * and maketh the grass to
grow upon the mountains, and herb for the use of men;
9 Who giveth fodder unto the cattle, * and feedeth
the young ravens that call upon him.
10 He hath no pleasure in the strength of an
horse; * neither delighteth he in any man's legs.
11 But the LORD'S delight is in them that fear
him, * and put their trust in his mercy.
12 Praise the LORD, O Jerusalem; * praise thy God,
O Sion.
13 For he hath made fast the bars of thy gates, *
and hath blessed thy children within thee.
14 He maketh peace in thy borders, * and filleth
thee with the flour of wheat.
15 He sendeth forth his commandment upon
earth, * and his word runneth very swiftly.
16 He giveth snow like wool, * and scattereth the
hoarfrost like ashes.
17 He casteth forth his ice like morsels: * who is
able to abide his frost?
18 He sendeth out his word, and melteth them: *
he bloweth with his wind, and the waters flow.
19 He showeth his word unto Jacob, * his statutes
and ordinances unto Israel.
20 He hath not dealt so with any nation; * neither
have the heathen knowledge of his laws.

5 Great is our LORD and mighty in power; *
there is no limit to his wisdom.

6 The LORD lifts up the lowly, *
but casts the wicked to the ground.

7 Sing to the LORD with thanksgiving; *
make music to our God upon the harp.

8 He covers the heavens with clouds *
and prepares rain for the earth;

9 He makes grass to grow upon the mountains *
and green plants to serve mankind.

10 He provides food for flocks and herds *
and for the young ravens when they cry.

11 He is not impressed by the might of a horse; *
he has no pleasure in the strength of a man;

12 But the LORD has pleasure in those who fear him, *
in those who await his gracious favor.

13 Worship the LORD, O Jerusalem; *
praise your God, O Zion;

14 For he has strengthened the bars of your gates; *
he has blessed your children within you.

15 He has established peace on your borders; *
he satisfies you with the finest wheat.

16 He sends out his command to the earth, *
and his word runs very swiftly.

17 He gives snow like wool; *
he scatters hoarfrost like ashes.

18 He scatters his hail like bread crumbs; *
who can stand against his cold?

19 He sends forth his word and melts them; *
he blows with his wind, and the waters flow.

20 He declares his word to Jacob, *
his statutes and his judgments to Israel.

21 He has not done so to any other nation; *
to them he has not revealed his judgments.
Hallelujah!

Psalm 148. *Laudate Dominum.*

O PRAISE the LORD from the heavens: * praise him
in the heights.
2 Praise him, all ye angels of his: * praise him, all
his host.

148 *Laudate Dominum*

1 Hallelujah!
Praise the LORD from the heavens; *
praise him in the heights.

2 Praise him, all you angels of his; *
praise him, all his host.

1789-1871

3 Praise him, sun and moon : praise him, all ye stars and light.

4 Praise him, all ye heavens, and ye waters that are above the heavens.

5 Let them praise the Name of the LORD : for he spake the word, and they were made ; he commanded, and they were created.

6 He hath made them fast for ever and ever : he hath given them a law which shall not be broken.

7 Praise the LORD upon earth, ye dragons and all deeps :

8 Fire and hail, snow and vapours, wind and storm, fulfilling his word :

9 Mountains and all hills ; fruitful trees and all cedars :

10 Beasts and all cattle ; worms and feathered fowls :

11 Kings of the earth, and all people ; princes, and all judges of the world :

12 Young men and maidens, old men and children, praise the Name of the LORD : for his Name only is excellent, and his praise above heaven and earth.

13 He shall exalt the horn of his people : all his saints shall praise him ; even the children of Israel, even the people that serveth him.

1892

3 Praise him, sun and moon : praise him, all ye stars and light.

4 Praise him, all ye heavens : and ye waters that are above the heavens.

5 Let them praise the Name of the LORD : for he spake the word, and they were made ; he commanded, and they were created.

6 He hath made them fast for ever and ever : he hath given them a law which shall not be broken.

7 Praise the LORD upon earth : ye dragons and all deeps ;

8 Fire and hail, snow and vapours : wind and storm, fulfilling his word ;

9 Mountains and all hills : fruitful trees and all cedars ;

10 Beasts and all cattle : worms and feathered fowls ;

11 Kings of the earth, and all people : princes, and all judges of the world ;

12 Young men and maidens, old men and children, praise the Name of the LORD : for his Name only is excellent, and his praise above heaven and earth.

13 He shall exalt the horn of his people ; all his saints shall praise him : even the children of Israel, even the people that serveth him.

1789-1871

Psalm cxlix. *Cantate Domino.*

O SING unto the LORD a new song ; let the congregation of saints praise him.

2 Let Israel rejoice in him that made him, and let the children of Sion be joyful in their King.

3 Let them praise his Name in the dance : let them sing praises unto him with tabret and harp.

4 For the LORD hath pleasure in his people, and helpeth the meek-hearted.

5 Let the saints be joyful with glory ; let them rejoice in their beds.

6 Let the praises of God be in their mouth ; and a two-edged sword in their hands ;

1892

PSALM 149. *Cantate Domino.*

O SING unto the LORD a new song : let the congregation of saints praise him.

2 Let Israel rejoice in him that made him : and let the children of Sion be joyful in their King.

3 Let them praise his Name in the dance : let them sing praises unto him with tabret and harp.

4 For the LORD hath pleasure in his people : and helpeth the meek-hearted.

5 Let the saints be joyful with glory : let them rejoice in their beds.

6 Let the praises of God be in their mouth : and a two-edged sword in their hands ;

3 Praise him, sun and moon: * praise him, all ye
stars and light.
4 Praise him, all ye heavens, * and ye waters that
are above the heavens.
5 Let them praise the Name of the LORD: * for he
spake the word, and they were made; he commanded,
and they were created.
6 He hath made them fast for ever and ever: * he
hath given them a law which shall not be broken.
7 Praise the LORD from the earth, * ye dragons and
all deeps;
8 Fire and hail, snow and vapours, * wind and
storm, fulfilling his word;
9 Mountains and all hills; * fruitful trees and all
cedars;
10 Beasts and all cattle; * creeping things and flying
fowls;
11 Kings of the earth, and all peoples; * princes,
and all judges of the world;
12 Young men and maidens, old men and children,
praise the Name of the LORD: * for his Name only is
excellent, and his praise above heaven and earth.
13 He shall exalt the horn of his people: all his
saints shall praise him; * even the children of Israel,
even the people that serveth him.

3 Praise him, sun and moon; *
praise him, all you shining stars.

4 Praise him, heaven of heavens, *
and you waters above the heavens.

5 Let them praise the Name of the LORD; *
for he commanded, and they were created.

6 He made them stand fast for ever and ever; *
he gave them a law which shall not pass away.

7 Praise the LORD from the earth, *
you sea-monsters and all deeps;

8 Fire and hail, snow and fog, *
tempestuous wind, doing his will;

9 Mountains and all hills, *
fruit trees and all cedars;

10 Wild beast and all cattle, *
creeping things and wingèd birds;

11 Kings of the earth and all peoples, *
princes and all rulers of the world;

12 Young men and maidens, *
old and young together.

13 Let them praise the Name of the LORD, *
for his Name only is exalted,
his splendor is over earth and heaven.

14 He has raised up strength for his people
and praise for all his loyal servants, *
the children of Israel, a people who are near him.
Hallelujah!

Psalm 149. *Cantate Domino.*

O SING unto the LORD a new song; * let the congregation of saints praise him.
2 Let Israel rejoice in him that made him, * and let
the children of Sion be joyful in their King.
3 Let them praise his Name in the dance: * let
them sing praises unto him with tabret and harp.
4 For the LORD hath pleasure in his people, * and
helpeth the meek-hearted.
5 Let the saints be joyful with glory; * let them
rejoice in their beds.
6 Let the praises of God be in their mouth: * and a
two-edged sword in their hands;

149 *Cantate Domino*

1 Hallelujah!
Sing to the LORD a new song; *
sing his praise in the congregation of the faithful.

2 Let Israel rejoice in his Maker; *
let the children of Zion be joyful in their King.

3 Let them praise his Name in the dance; *
let them sing praise to him with timbrel and harp.

4 For the LORD takes pleasure in his people *
and adorns the poor with victory.

5 Let the faithful rejoice in triumph; *
let them be joyful on their beds.

6 Let the praises of God be in their throat *
and a two-edged sword in their hand;

7 To be avenged of the heathen, and to rebuke the people ;
8 To bind their kings in chains, and their nobles with links of iron.
9 That they may be avenged of them ; as it is written, Such honour have all his saints.

7 To be avenged of the heathen : and to rebuke the people ;
8 To bind their kings in chains : and their nobles with links of iron ;
9 That they may be avenged of them, as it is written : Such honour have all his saints.

Psalm cl. *Laudate Dominum.*

O PRAISE God in his holiness : praise him in the firmament of his power.
2 Praise him in his noble acts : praise him according to his excellent greatness.
3 Praise him in the sound of the trumpet : praise him upon the lute and harp.
4 Praise him in the cymbals and dances : praise him upon the strings and pipe.
5 Praise him upon the well-tuned cymbals : praise him upon the loud cymbals.
6 Let every thing that hath breath praise the LORD.

THE END OF THE PSALTER.

PSALM 150. *Laudate Dominum.*

O PRAISE God in his holiness : praise him in the firmament of his power.
2 Praise him in his noble acts : praise him according to his excellent greatness.
3 Praise him in the sound of the trumpet : praise him upon the lute and harp.
4 Praise him in the cymbals and dances : praise him upon the strings and pipe.
5 Praise him upon the well-tuned cymbals : praise him upon the loud cymbals.
6 Let every thing that hath breath : praise the LORD.

THE END OF THE PSALTER.

1928

7 To be avenged of the nations, * and to rebuke the peoples;
8 To bind their kings in chains, * and their nobles with links of iron;
9 To execute judgment upon them; as it is written, * Such honour have all his saints.

Psalm 150. *Laudate Dominum.*

O PRAISE God in his sanctuary: * praise him in the firmament of his power.
2 Praise him in his noble acts: * praise him according to his excellent greatness.
3 Praise him in the sound of the trumpet: * praise him upon the lute and harp.
4 Praise him in the timbrels and dances: * praise him upon the strings and pipe.
5 Praise him upon the well-tuned cymbals: * praise him upon the loud cymbals.
6 Let every thing that hath breath * praise the LORD.

The End of the Psalter.

1979

7 To wreak vengeance on the nations *
and punishment on the peoples;

8 To bind their kings in chains *
and their nobles with links of iron;

9 To inflict on them the judgment decreed; *
this is glory for all his faithful people.
Hallelujah!

150 *Laudate Dominum*

1 Hallelujah!
Praise God in his holy temple; *
praise him in the firmament of his power.

2 Praise him for his mighty acts; *
praise him for his excellent greatness.

3 Praise him with the blast of the ram's-horn; *
praise him with lyre and harp.

4 Praise him with timbrel and dance; *
praise him with strings and pipe.

5 Praise him with resounding cymbals; *
praise him with loud-clanging cymbals.

6 Let everything that has breath *
praise the LORD.
Hallelujah!

Texts and Documents

The student of the 1979 prayer book is fortunate to have access to twenty-nine volumes of *Prayer Book Studies*, which document both the textual development and the rationale of the revised rites. The four commission *Reports* of leading up to the 1928 book are also widely available in secular libraries. However, such resources are not readily accessible for study of previous revisions. Thus this volume concludes with a selection of eighteenth and nineteenth century texts and documents.

The selection which follows is designed primarily for group discussion in the classroom, and the texts are accordingly not deprived the slightly provocative edge which marks them upon occasion. They are selected to provide first-hand acquaintance with foundational documents, particularly of the eighteenth century, and also to give the flavor of the church life and discourse in which revision took place. As might be expected in a volume of this kind, the documents are collected with only the key points in liturgical life in mind, and thus the selection does not purport to be a full documentary history of the liturgy.

The eighteenth century documents are for the most part familiar to students of Episcopal Church history, although I have added a few which are less well known, including a hitherto unpublished Seabury manuscript. This document provides liturgical information and some of the flavor of Connecticut church life, and also provides insights into the spirituality of the new Church's first bishop.

The documents of the nineteenth century center on two men who have come to be commemorated in our liturgical calendar for their contributions to many aspects of Episcopal Church life.

The documents relating the William Augustus Muhlenberg's Memorial reveal how the Church's struggle for identity and mission served as well as a catalyst for liturgical revision. Although it bore little fruit in its own day, the Memorial introduced into our discourse what has become a permanent concern with liturgy, ministry and church reunion.

The largest single selection is the entire text of William Huntington Reed's "Revision of the American Common Prayer" of 1881, a work which forcefully took up Muhlenberg's concerns and added others no less important. Although superseded in some respects, in many ways this article remains the Magna Carta of liturgical revision in the Episcopal Church. The article will receive detailed examination in the third volume of the present work, but it should be noted here that the issues it raises and the methods by which those issues are treated are still very much with the Church. Huntington's work is also useful in that it summarizes the state of liturgical learning in his day, and quotes and puts into context a host of other documents in the way that only a contemporary witness can.

The *Book of Offices* unsuccessfully proposed in 1889 was, among other things, the first of three attempts to bring Episcopalians noonday prayer and compline. It also sought to provide for other occasions not supplied in the principal service book. Some of its collects are reproduced here to illustrate the liturgical expression of the religious temper of this country the end of the Gilded Age. Nacent "Muscular Christianity" and an intense concern with personal purity here find voice, but do so along with pointed expressions of a new social morality.

The selection concludes with a linking document, the 1913 "California" resolution of General Convention which began that modern work of revision which can be studied in the more readily available resources.

1. The Concordat between Samuel Seabury and the Scottish Bishops

In the Name of the holy and undivided Trinity, Father, Son, and Holy Ghost, One God blessed for ever; Amen:—

The wise and gracious Providence of this mercifull God, having put it into the hearts of the Christians of the Episcopal persuasion in Connecticut in North America, to desire that the Blessings of a free, valid and purely Ecclesiastical Episcopacy, might be communicated to them, and a Church regularly formed in that part of the western world upon the most antient, and primitive Model: And application having been made for this purpose, by the Reverend Dr. Samuel Seabury, Presbyter in Connecticut, to the Right Reverend the Bishops of the Church in Scotland: The said Bishops having taken this proposal into their serious Consideration, most heartily concurred to promote and encourage the same, as far as lay in their power; and accordingly began the pious and good work recommended to them, by complying with the request of the Clergy in Connecticut, and advancing the said Dr. Samuel Seabury to the high Order of the Episcopate; At the same time earnestly praying that this Work of the Lord thus happily begun might prosper in his hands, till it should please the great and glorious Head of the Church, to increase the number of Bishops in America, and send forth more such Labourers into that part of his Harvest. —Animated with this pious hope, and earnestly desirous to establish a Bond of peace, and holy Communion, between the two Churches, the Bishops of the Church in Scotland, whose names are underwritten, having had full and free Conference with Bishop Seabury, after his Consecration and Advancement as aforesaid, agreed with him on the following Articles, which are to serve as a Concordate, or Bond of Union, between the Catholic remainder of the antient Church of Scotland, and the now rising church in the State of Connecticut.

Art. I. They agree in thankfully receiving, and humbly and heartily embracing the whole Doctrine of the Gospel, as revealed and set forth in the holy Scriptures: and it is their earnest and in the holy Scriptures: and it is their earnest and common Faith, once delivered to the Saints, and happily preserved in the Church of Christ, thru his divine power and protection, who promised that the Gates of Hell should never prevail against it.

Art. II. They agree in believing this Church to be the mystical Body of Christ, of which he alone is the Head, and supreme Governour, and that under him, the chief Ministers, or Managers of the Affairs of this spiritual Society, are those called Bishops, whose Exercise of their sacred Office being independent of all Lay powers, it follows of consequence, that their spiritual Authority and Jurisdiction cannot be affected by any Lay-Deprivation.

Art. III. They agree in declaring that the Episcopal Church in Connecticut is to be in full Communion with the Episcopal Church in Scotland, it being their sincere Resolution to put matters on such a footing, as that the Members of both Churches may with freedom and safety communicate with either, when their Occasions call them from the one Country to the other: Only taking Care when in Scotland not to hold Communion in sacred Offices with those persons, who under pretence of Ordination by an English, or Irish bishop, do, or shall take upon them, to officiate as Clergymen in any part of the National Church of Scotland, and whom the Scottish Bishops cannot help looking upon, as schismatical Intruders, designed only to answer worldly purposes, and uncommissioned Disturbers of the poor Remains of that once flourishing Church, which both their predecessors and they, have, under many Difficulties, laboured to preserve pure and uncorrupted to future Ages.

Art. IV. With a view to the salutary purpose mentioned in the preceding Article, they agree in desiring that there may be as near a Conformity in Worship, and Discipline established between the two Churches as is consistent with the different Circumstances and Customs of Nations: And in order to avoid any bad effects that might otherwise arise from political Differences, they hereby express their earnest Wish and firm Intention to observe such prudent Generality in their public Prayers, with respect to these points, as shall appear most agreeable to Apostolic Rules, and the practice of the primitive Church.

Art. V. As the Celebration of the holy Eucharist, or the Administration of the Sacrament of the Body and Blood of Christ, is the principal Bond of Union among Christians, as well as the most Solemn Act of Worship in the Christian Church, the Bishops aforesaid agree in desiring that there may be as little Variance here as possible. And tho' the Scottish Bishops are very far from prescribing to their Brethren in this matter, they cannot help ardently wishing that Bishop Seabury would endeavour all he can consistently with peace and prudence, to make the Celebration of this venerable Mystery conformable to the most primitive Doctrine and practice in that respect: Which is the pattern the Church of Scotland has copied after in her Communion Office, and which it has been the Wish of some of the most eminent Divines of the Church of England that she also had more closely followed, than she seems to have done since she gave up her first reformed Liturgy used in the Reign of King Edward VI.; between which, and the form used in the Church of Scotland, there is no Difference in any point, which the primitive Church reckoned essential to the right Ministration of the holy Eucharist. — In this capital Article therefore of the Eucharistic Service, in which the Scottish Bishops so earnestly wish for as much Unity as possible, Bishop Seabury also agrees to take a serious View of the Communion Office recommended by them, and if found agreeable to the genuine Standards of Antiquity, to give his Sanction to it, and by gentle Methods of Argument and Persuasion, to endeavour, as they have done, to introduce it by degrees into practice without the Compulsion of Authority on the one side, or the prejudice of former Custom on the other.

Art. VI. It is also hereby agreed and resolved upon for the better answering the purposes of this Concordate, that a brotherly fellowship be henceforth maintained between the Episcopal Churches in Scotland and Connecticut, and such a mutual Intercourse of Ecclesiastical Correspondence carried on, when Opportunity offers, or necessity requires as may tend to the Support, and Edification of both Churches.

ART. VII. The Bishops aforesaid do hereby jointly declare, in the most solemn manner, that in the whole of this Transaction, they have nothing else in view, but the Glory of God, and the good of his Church; And being thus pure and upright in their Intentions, they cannot but hope, that all whom it may concern, will put the most fair and candid construction on their Conduct, and take no Offence at their feeble, but sincere Endeavours to promote what they believe to be the Cause of Truth, and of the common Salvation.

In Testimony of their Love to which, and in mutual good Faith and Confidence, they have for themselves, and their Successors in Office cheerfully put their Names and Seals to these presents at Aberdeen this fifteenth day of November, in the year of our Lord, one thousand, seven hundred, and eighty-four.

ROBERT KILGOUR,
BISHOP & PRIMUS. [SEAL.]
ARTHUR PETRIE, BISHOP. [SEAL.]
JOHN SKINNER, JR., BISHOP. [SEAL.]
SAMUEL SEABURY, BISHOP. [SEAL.]

2. Bishop Seabury's "Injunction" of August 12, 1785

SAMUEL, by divine permission, Bishop of the Episcopal Church in the State of Connecticut, to the Clergy of the said Church, GREETING:

IT having pleased almighty GOD, that the late *British* Colony of Connecticut should become a free, sovereign and independent State, as it now is, some alterations in the Liturgy and Offices of our Church are necessary to be made, to accommodate them to the civil Constitution of the country in which we live; for the peace, security and prosperity of which, both as good subjects and faithful Christians, it is our duty constantly to pray—WE, the Bishop aforesaid, have thought fit, by and with the advice and assistance of such of our Clergy as we have had opportunity of consulting, to issue this *Injunction,* hereby authorizing and requiring YOU, and every one of You, the Presbyters and Deacons of the Church above mentioned, in the celebration of Divine Service, to make the following alterations in the Liturgy and Offices of our Church, *viz.:*

I. In the suffrages after the Creed, in morning and evening Prayer, instead of *O Lord save the King,* You are to read, *O Lord save the Church;* to which the congregation are to make the accustomed response, *And mercifully hear us,* &c.

II. The prayer for the King, in the morning and evening service, to be left out; and the prayer for the Royal Family to be thus altered; *Almighty God, the fountain of all goodness, we humbly beseech thee to bless the* Governor *and* Rulers *of this State; endue them with thy Holy Spirit;*—and so on as it now stands.

III. In the Litany the 15, 16, 17, 18th petitions to be omitted, and the petition for Bishops, Priests, and Deacons, immediately to follow that for the universal Church. The 20, and 21st petitions to be thus read, *That it may please thee to endue the* Governor *and* Rulers *of this State, with grace, wisdom and understanding. That it may please thee to bless and keep the Judges and inferior Magistrates, giving them grace to execute justice and to maintain truth.* To both which the usual response—*We beseech thee to hear us, good Lord,*—is to be made by the congregation.

IV. In the prayer for the whole state of Christ's Church, the part relating to Rulers and Ministers is to be thus altered—*We beseech thee also to save and defend all Christian Kings, Princes, and Governors; and grant that they, and all that are put in authority, may truly and impartially minister justice, to the punishment of wickedness and vice, and to the maintenance of true religion and virtue. Give grace, O heavenly Father, to all Bishops, Priests, and Deacons, that they may*—and so on, as it now stands.

V. The prayers for the King that stand before the Nicene Creed in the Communion service, to be omitted.

VI. In the answer in the Catechism to the question—What is thy duty towards thy neighbour? for—*to honor and obey the King*—substitute, *to honor and obey my civil Rulers, and to submit myself,* &c.

VII. That during every session of the Great and General Court, or Assembly, you do use the following collect, in its proper place, both in morning and evening prayer.

"Most gracious God, we humbly beseech thee, as for this State in general, so especially for the great and general Court at this time assembled: That thou wouldst be pleased to direct and prosper all their consultations to the advancement of thy glory, and the good of thy church, the safety, honor, and the welfare of thy people; that all things may be so ordered and settled by their endeavours, upon the best and surest foundations, that peace and happiness, truth and justice, religion and piety may be established among us for all generations. These and all other necessaries for them, for us, and thy whole church, we humbly beg in the name and mediation of Jesus Christ our most blessed Lord and Saviour. Amen."

VIII. That you discontinue the observation of the fifth of November, the thirtieth of January, the twenty-ninth of May, and the twenty-fifth of October.

Commending you, Reverend Brethren, your congregations, and labours in the Gospel, to the grace, protections, and blessing of Almighty God, We remain your affectionate brother and servant in Christ Jesus, our Lord.

Done at New London,
August 12th, 1785

3. Seabury's Communion Office

The
Communion-Office,
OR ORDER
FOR THE ADMINISTRATION
OF THE
HOLY EUCHARIST
OR
SUPPER OF THE LORD.
WITH
PRIVATE DEVOTIONS.

Recommended to the Episcopal Congregations in *Connecticut*,

By the Right Reverend
BISHOP SEABURY.

NEW-LONDON:
Printed by T. Green, m,dcc,lxxxvi.

THE
Communion-office.

¶ *The Exhortation.*

DEARLY beloved in the Lord, ye that mind to come to the holy Communion of the body and blood of our Saviour Christ, must consider how St. Paul exhorteth all persons diligently to try and examine themselves, before they presume to eat of that bread, and drink of that cup. For as the benefit is great, if with a true penitent heart and lively faith we receive that holy sacrament, (for then we spiritually eat the flesh of Christ, and drink his blood; then we dwell in Christ, and Christ in us; we are one with Christ, and Christ with us;) so is the danger great, if we receive the same unworthily, not considering the Lord's body; for then we are guilty of the body and blood of Christ our Saviour; we kindle God's wrath against us, and bring his judgments upon us. Judge therefore yourselves, brethren, that ye be not judged of the Lord; repent you truly for your sins past; have a lively and stedfast faith in Christ our Saviour; amend your lives, and be in perfect charity with all men: so shall ye be meet partakers of those holy mysteries. And, above all things, ye must give most humble and hearty thanks to God the Father, the Son, and the Holy Ghost, for the redemption of the world, by the death and passion of our Saviour Christ, both God and man, who did humble himself even to the death upon the cross for us miserable sinners, who lay in darkness and the shadow of death, that he might make us the children of God, and exalt us to everlasting life. And to the end that we should always remember the exceeding great love of our Master and only Saviour Jesus Christ thus dying for us, and the innumerable benefits which by his precious bloodshedding he hath obtained to us, he hath instituted and ordained holy mysteries, as pledges of his love, and for a continual remembrance of his death, to our great and endless comfort. To him, therefore, with the Father, and the Holy Ghost, let us give (as we are most bounded) continual thanks, submitting ourselves wholly to his holy will and pleasure, and studying to serve him in true holiness and righteousness all the days of our life. *Amen.*

¶ *Then the Priest, or Deacon, shall say,*

Let us present our offerings to the Lord with reverence and Godly fear.

¶ *Then the Priest shall begin the offertory, saying one or more of these sentences following, as he thinketh most convenient in his discretion.*

IN process of time it came to pass, that Cain brought of the fruit of the ground an offering unto the Lord. And Abel, he also brought of the firstlings of his flock, and of the fat thereof. And the Lord had respect unto Abel, and to his offering: but unto Cain and to his offering he had not respect. *Gen.* iv. 3, 4.

Speak unto the children of Israel, that they

bring me an offering: of every man that giveth it willingly with his heart, ye shall take my offering. *Exod.* xxv. 2.

Ye shall not appear before the Lord empty. Every man shall give as he is able, according to the blessing of the Lord your God which he hath given you. *Deut.* xvi. 16, 17.

Give unto the Lord the glory due unto his name: bring an offering, and come into his courts. *Psal.* xcvi. 8.

Lay not up for yourselves treasures upon earth, where moth and rust doth corrupt, and where thieves break through and steal: but lay up for yourselves treasures in heaven, where neither moth nor rust doth corrupt, and where thieves do not break through nor steal. *Math.* vi. 19, 20.

Not every one that saith unto me, Lord, Lord, shall enter into the kingdom of heaven: but he that doth the will of my Father which is in heaven. *Math.* vii. 21.

Jesus sat over against the treasury, and beheld how the people cast money into it: and many that were rich cast in much. And there came a certain poor widow, and she threw in two mites, which make a farthing. And he called unto him his disciples, and saith unto them, Verily I say unto you, that this poor widow hath cast more in, than all they which have cast into the treasury. For all they did cast in of their abundance: but she of her want did cast in all that she had, even all her living. *Mark* xii. 41, 42, 43, 44.

Who goeth a warfare at any time of his own charge? who planteth a vineyard, and eateth not of the fruit thereof? or who feedeth a flock, and eateth not of the milk of the flock? 1 *Cor.* ix. 7.

If we have sown unto you spiritual things, is it a great matter if we should reap your carnal things? 1 *Cor.* ix. 11.

Do ye not know, that they which minister about holy things, live of the sacrifice? and they which wait at the altar, are partakers with the altar? Even so hath the Lord ordained, that they who preach the gospel, should live of the gospel. 1 *Cor.* ix. 13, 14.

He that soweth sparingly, shall reap also sparingly: and he who soweth bountifully, shall reap also bountifully. Every man according as he purposeth in his heart, so let him give; not grudgingly, or of necessity: for God loveth a cheerful giver. 2 *Cor.* ix. 6, 7.

Let him that is taught in the word, communicate unto him that teacheth, in all good things. Be not deceived; God is not mocked: for whatsoever a man soweth, that shall he also reap. *Gal.* vi. 6, 7.

Charge them that are rich in this world, that they be not high-minded, nor trust in uncertain riches, but in the living God, who giveth us richly all things to enjoy: That they do good, that they be rich in good works, ready to distribute, willing to communicate; laying up in store for themselves a good foundation against the time to come, that they may lay hold on eternal life. 1 *Tim.* vi. 17, 18, 19.

God is not unrighteous, to forget your work and labour of love, which ye have shewed toward his name, in that ye have ministered to the saints, and do minister. *Heb.* vi. 10.

To do good, and to communicate, forget not; for with such sacrifices God is well pleased. *Heb.* xiii. 16.

¶ *While the Priest distinctly pronounceth some or all of these sentences for the offertory, the Deacon, or (if no such be present) some other fit person, shall receive the devotions of the people, in a bason provided for the purpose. And when all have offered, he shall reverently bring, and deliver it to the Priest; who shall humbly present it before the Lord, and set it upon the holy table, saying,*

BLESSED be thou, O Lord God, for ever and ever. Thine, O Lord, is the greatness, and the glory, and the victory, and the majesty; for all that is in the heaven and in the earth is thine: thine is the kingdom, O Lord, and thou art exalted as head above all: both riches and honour come of thee, and of thine own do we give unto thee. *Amen.*

¶ *And the Priest shall then offer up, and place the bread and wine prepared for the sacrament upon the Lord's table, putting a little pure water into the cup: and shall say,*

The Lord be with you.
Answer. And with thy spirit.
Priest. Lift up your hearts.
Answer. We lift them up unto the Lord.
Priest. Let us give thanks unto our Lord, God.
Answer. It is meet and right so to do.
Priest. It is very meet, right, and our bounden duty, that we should at all times, and in all places, give thanks unto thee O Lord, * [holy Father,] Almighty, everlasting God.

* *These words* (holy Father) *must be omitted on Trinity Sunday.*

¶ *Here shall follow the proper preface, according to the time, if there be any especially appointed; or else immediately shall follow,*

Therefore with angels and archangels *&c.*

¶ *Proper Prefaces*

¶ *Upon Christmas-day, and seven days after.*

BECAUSE thou didst give Jesus Christ thine only Son, to be born * [as on this day] for us, who, by the operation of the Holy Ghost, was made very man of the substance of the blessed Virgin Mary his mother, and that without spot of sin, to make us clean from all sin. Therefore with angels, *&c.*

* *During the seven days after Christmas, say,* as at this time.

¶ *Upon Easter-day, and seven days after.*

BUT chiefly are we bound to praise thee, for the glorious resurrection of thy Son Jesus Christ our Lord: For he is the very Paschal Lamb, which was offered for us, and hath taken away the sin of the world; who by his death hath destroyed death, and by his rising to life again, hath restored to us everlasting life. Therefore with angels, *&c.*

¶ *Upon Ascension-day, and seven days after.*

THROUGH thy most dearly beloved Son, Jesus Christ our Lord: who, after his most glorious resurrection, manifestly appeared to all his apostles, and in their sight ascended up into heaven, to prepare a place for us; that where he is, thither might we also ascend, and reign with him in glory. Therefore with angels and archangels, *&c.*

¶ *Upon Whitsunday, and six days after.*

THROUGH Jesus Christ our Lord; according to whose most true promise the Holy Ghost came down * [as on this day] from heaven, with a sudden great sound, as it had been a mighty wind, in the likeness of fiery tongues, lighting upon the apostles, to teach them, and to lead them to all truth, giving them both the gift of divers languages, and also boldness with fervent zeal constantly to preach to gospel unto all nations, whereby we are brought out of darkness and error into the clear light and true knowledge of thee, and of thy Son Jesus Christ. Therefore angels, *&c.*

* *During the six days after Whitsunday, say* as at this time.

¶ *Upon the feast of Trinity only.*

WHO art one God, one Lord; not one only person, but three persons in one substance. For that which we believe of the glory of the Father, the same we believe of the Son, and of the Holy Ghost, without any difference of inequality. Therefore with angels, *&c.*

¶ *After which prefaces shall follow immediately this doxology.*

THEREFORE with angels and archangels, and with all the company of heaven, we laud and magnify thy glorious name, evermore praising thee, and saying, Holy holy, holy Lord God of hosts, heaven and earth are full of thy glory. Glory be to thee, O Lord most high. *Amen..*

¶ *Then the Priest standing at such a part of the holy table as he may with the most ease and decency use both his hands, and shall say the prayer of consecration, as followeth.*

ALL glory be to thee, Almighty God, our heavenly Father, for that thou of thy tender mercy didst give thy only Son Jesus Christ to suffer death upon the cross for our redemption; who made there (by his one oblation of himself once offered) a full, perfect, and sufficient sacrifice, oblation, and satisfaction, for the sins of the whole world; and did institute, and in his holy gospel command us to continue a perpetual memory of that his precious death and sacrifice until his coming again. For, in the night that he was betrayed,

(*a*) he took bread; and when he had given thanks (*b*) he brake it, and gave [it] to his disciples, saying, Take, eat, (*c*) THIS IS MY BODY, which is given for you: DO this in remembrance of me. Likewise after supper (*d*) he took the cup; and when he had given thanks, he gave it to them, saying, Drink ye all of this, for (*e*) THIS IS MY BLOOD, of the new testament, which is shed for you, and for many, for the remission of sins: DO this as oft as ye shall drink it in remembrance of me.

(a) Here the Priest is to take the paten into his hands:
(b) And here to break the bread:
(c) And here to lay his hands upon all the bread.
(d) Here he is to take the cup into his hand:
(e) And here to lay his hand upon every vessel (be it chalice or flagon) in which there is any wine to be consecrated.

The Oblation.

WHEREFORE, O Lord and heavenly Father, according to the institution of thy dearly beloved Son our Saviour Jesus Christ, we thy humble servants do celebrate and make here before thy divine majesty, with these thy holy gifts, WHICH WE NOW OFFER UNTO THEE, the memorial thy Son hath commanded us to make; having in remembrance his blessed passion, and precious death, his mighty resurrection, and glorious ascension; rendering unto thee most hearty thanks for the innumerable benefits procured unto us by the same.

The Invocation.

And we most humbly beseech thee, O merciful Father to hear us, and of thy almighty goodness vouchsafe to bless and sanctify, with thy word and Holy Spirit, these thy gifts and creatures of bread and wine, that they may become the body and blood of thy most dearly beloved Son. And we earnestly desire thy fatherly goodness, mercifully to accept this our sacrifice of praise and thanksgiving, most humbly beseeching thee to grant, that by the merits and death of thy Son Jesus Christ, and through faith in his blood, we (and all thy whole church) may obtain remission of our sins, and all other benefits of his passion. And here we offer and present unto thee, O Lord, ourselves, our souls and bodies, to be a reasonable, holy and lively sacrifice unto thee, humbly beseeching thee, that we and all others who shall be partakers of this holy Communion, may worthily receive the most precious body and blood of thy Son Jesus Christ, be filled with thy grace and heavenly benediction, and made one body with him, that he may dwell in them and they in him. And although we are unworthy, through our manifold sins, to offer unto thee any sacrifice; yet we beseech thee to accept this our bounden duty and service, not weighing our merits, but pardoning our offences, through Jesus Christ our Lord: by whom, and with whom, in the unity of the Holy Ghost, all honour and glory be unto thee, O Father Almighty, world without end. *Amen.*

¶ *Let us pray for the whole state of Christ's Church.*[1]

ALMIGHTY and everliving God, who by thy holy Apostle hast taught us to make prayers and supplications, and to give thanks for all men; We humbly beseech thee most mercifully to accept our alms and oblations, and to receive these our prayers, which we offer unto thy divine majesty; beseeching thee to inspire continually the universal church with the spirit of truth, unity and concord; and grant that all they who do confess thy holy name, may agree in the truth of thy holy word and live in unity and godly love. We beseech thee also to save and defend all Christian Kings, Princes, and Governors; and grant that they, and all who are in authority, may truly and impartially minister justice to the punishment of wickedness and vice, and to the maintenance of thy true religion and virtue. Give grace, O heavenly Father, to all Bishops, Priests, and Deacons, that they may both by their life and doctrine set forth thy true and lively word, and rightly and duly administer thy holy sacraments: and to all thy people give thy heavenly grace, that with meek heart, and due reverence, they may hear and receive thy holy word, truly serving thee in holiness and righteousness all the days of their life. And we commend especially to thy merciful goodness the congregation here assembled in thy name, to celebrate the commemoration of the most precious death and sacrifice of thy Son and our Saviour Jesus Christ. And we most humbly beseech thee of thy goodness, O Lord, to comfort and succour all those who in this transitory life are in trouble, sorrow, need, sickness, or any other adversity. And we also bless thy holy name for all thy servants, who, having finished their course in faith, do now rest from their labours: yielding unto thee most high praise and hearty thanks, for the wonderful goodness and virtue declared in all thy saints, who have been the choice vessels of thy grace, and the lights of the world in their several generations: most humbly beseeching thee to give us grace to follow the example of their stedfastness in thy faith, and obedience to thy holy commandments, that at the day of the general resurrection, we and all they who are of the mystical body of thy Son, may be set on his right hand, and hear that his most joyful voice, Come, ye blessed of my father, inherit the kingdom prepared for you from the foundation of the world. Grant this, O Father, for Jesus Christ's sake, our only Mediator and Advocate. *Amen.*

As our Saviour Christ hath commanded and taught us, we are bold to say,

OUR Father who art in heaven, Hallowed be thy name. Thy kingdom come. Thy will be done in earth as it is in heaven. Give us this day our daily bread. And forgive us our trespasses, as we forgive them that trespass against us. And lead us not into temptation; but deliver us from evil. For thine is the kingdom, and the power and glory, forever and ever. *Amen.*

¶ *Then shall the Priest say to them that come to receive the holy Communion, this invitation.*

YE that do truly and earnestly repent you of your sins, and are in love and charity with your neighbours, and intend to lead a new life, following the commandments of God, and walking from henceforth in his holy ways: Draw near with faith and take this holy sacrament to your comfort; and make your humble confession to Almighty God.

¶ *Then shall this general confession be made, by the people, along with the Priest; all humbly kneeling upon their knees.*

ALMIGHTY God, Father of our Lord Jesus Christ, maker of all things, judge of all men; We acknowledge and bewail our manifold sins and wickedness, which we from time to time most grieviously have committed, by thought, word, and deed, against thy divine Majesty; provoking most justly thy wrath and indignation against us. We do earnestly repent, and are heartily sorry for these our misdoings; the remembrance of them is grievous unto us; the burden of them is intolerable. Have mercy upon us, have mercy upon us, most merciful Father; for thy Son our Lord Jesus Christ's sake, forgive us all that is past; and grant, that we may ever hereafter serve and please thee, in newness of life, to the honour and glory of thy name, through Jesus Christ our Lord. *Amen.*

¶ *Then shall the Priest, or the Bishop, (being present,) stand up, and turning himself to the people, pronounce the absolution as followeth.*

ALMIGHTY God our heavenly Father, who, of his great mercy, hath promised forgiveness of sins to all them that with hearty repentance and true faith turn unto him; Have mercy upon you; pardon and deliver you from all your sins; confirm and strengthen you in all goodness; and bring you to everlasting life, through Jesus Christ our Lord. *Amen.*

¶ *Then shall the Priest say,*

Hear what comfortable words our Saviour Christ saith unto all that truly turn to him:

COME unto me, all ye that labour, and are heavy laden, and I will refresh you. *Matth.* ix. 28.

Private ejaculation.

Refresh, O Lord, thy servant wearied with the burden of sin.

God so loved the world, that he gave his only begotten Son, that whosoever believeth in him, should not perish, but have everlasting life. *John* iii. 16.

Private ejaculation.

Lord, I believe in thy Son Jesus Christ, and let this faith purify me from all iniquity.

Hear also what St. Paul saith.
This is a faithful saying, and worthy of all acceptation, that Christ Jesus came into the world to save sinners. 1 *Tim.* i. 15.

Private ejaculation.

I embrace with all thankfulness that salvation that Jesus has brought into the world.

Hear also what St. John saith.
If any man sin, we have an advocate with the Father, Jesus Christ the righteous: and he is the propitiation for our sins. 1 *John* ii. 1, 2.

Private ejaculation.

Intercede for me, O blessed Jesu! that my sins may be pardoned, through the merits of thy death.

¶ *Then shall the Priest, turning him to the altar, kneel down, and say, in the name of all them that shall communicate, this collect of humble access to the holy Communion, as followeth.*

WE do not presume to come to this thy holy table, O merciful Lord, trusting in our own righteousness, but in thy manifold and great mercies. We are not worthy so much as to gather up the crumbs under thy table: But thou art the same Lord, whose property is always to have mercy. Grant us therefore, gracious Lord, so to eat the flesh of thy dear Son Jesus Christ, and to drink his blood, that our sinful bodies may be made clean by his most sacred body, and our souls washed through his most precious blood, and that we may evermore dwell in him, and he in us. *Amen.*

¶ *Then shall the Bishop, if he be present, or else the Priest that celebrateth, first receive the communion in both kinds himself, and next deliver it to other Bishops, Presbyters, and Deacons, (if there be any present,) and after to the people in due order, all humbly kneeling. And when he receiveth himself, or delivereth the sacrament of the body of Christ to others, he shall say,*

THE body of our Lord Jesus Christ, which was given for thee, preserve thy soul and body unto everlasting life.

¶ *Here the person receiving shall say,* Amen.

¶ *And when the Priest receiveth the cup himself, or delivereth it to others, he shall say,*

THE blood of our Lord Jesus Christ, which was shed for thee, preserve thy soul and body unto everlasting life.

¶ *Here the person receiving shall say,* Amen.

¶ *If the consecrated bread or wine be all spent before all have communicated, the Priest is to consecrate more, according to the form before prescribed, beginning at the words,* All glory be to thee, *&c. and ending with the words,* that they may become the body and blood of thy most dearly beloved. Son.

¶ *When all have communicated, he that celebrates shall go to the Lord's table, and cover with a fair linen cloth that which remaineth of the consecrated elements, and then say,*

Having now received the precious body and blood of Christ, let us give thanks to our Lord God, who hath graciously vouchsafed to admit us to the participation of his holy mysteries: and let us beg of him grace to perform our vows, and to persevere in our good resolutions; that being made holy, we may obtain everlasting life, through the merits of the all-sufficient sacrifice of our Lord and Saviour Jesus Christ.[2]

¶ *Then the Priest shall say this collect of thanksgiving, as followeth.*

ALMIGHTY and everliving God, we most heartily thank thee, for that thou dost vouchsafe to feed us, who have duly received these holy mysteries, with the spiritual food of the most precious body and blood of thy Son our Saviour Jesus Christ; and doth assure us thereby of thy favour and goodness towards us, and that we are very members incorporate in the mystical body of thy Son, which is the blessed company of all faithful people, and are also heirs through hope of thy everlasting kingdom, by the merits of his most precious death and passion. We now most humbly beseech thee, O heavenly Father, so to assist us with thy grace and Holy Spirit, that we may continue in that holy communion and fellowship, and do all such good works as thou hast commanded us to walk in, through Jesus Christ our Lord; to whom, with Thee and the Holy Ghost, be all honour and glory, world without end. *Amen.*

¶ *Then shall be said or sung,* Gloria in excelsis, *as followeth.*

GLORY be to God on high, and in earth peace, good will toward men. We praise thee, we bless the, we worship thee, we glorify thee, we give thanks to thee, for thy great glory, O Lord God, heavenly King, God the Father Almighty; and to Thee, O God, the only begotten Son Jesu Christ; and to Thee, O God, the Holy Ghost.

O Lord, the only begotten Son Jesus Christ; O Lord God, Lamb of God, Son of the Father, who takest away the sins of the world, have mercy upon us. Thou that takest away the sins of the world, receive our prayer. Thou that sittest at the right hand of God the Father, have mercy upon us.

For thou only art holy, thou only art the Lord, thou only, O Christ, with the Holy Ghost, art most high in the glory of God the Father. *Amen.*

¶ *Then the Priest, or Bishop, if he be present, shall let them depart, with this blessing.*

THE peace of God, which passeth all understanding, keep your hearts and minds in the knowledge and love of God, and of his Son Jesus Christ our Lord: and the blessing of God Almighty, the Father, the Son, and the Holy Ghost be amongst you, and remain with you always. *Amen.*

THE END

Private Devotions for the Altar

BLESSED Jesus! Saviour of the world! who hast called me to the participation of these thy holy mysteries, accept my humble approach to thy sacred table, increase my faith, settle my devotion, fix my contemplation on thy powerful mercy; and while with my mouth I receive the sacred symbols of thy body and blood, may they be the means of heavenly nourishment to prepare my body and soul for that everlasting life which thou hast purchased by thy merits, and promised to bestow on all who believe in and depend on thee. *Amen.*

Prayer to God.

O Gracious and merciful God, Thou supreme Being, Father, Word and Holy Ghost, look down from heaven, the throne of thy essential glory, upon me thy unworthy creature, with the eyes of thy covenanted mercy and compassion; O Lord my God, I disclaim all merit, I renounce all righteousness of my own, either inherent in my nature, or acquired by my own industry: And I fly for refuge, for pardon and sa[n]ctification, to the righteousness of thy Christ: For his sake, for the sake of the blessed Jesus, the Son of thy covenanted love, whom Thou hast set forth to be a propitiation for fallen man, and in whom alone Thou art well pleased, have mercy upon me, receive my prayers, pardon my infirmities, strengthen my weak resolutions, guide my steps to thy holy altar, and there feed me with the meat which perisheth not, but endureth to everlasting life. *Amen.*

After Receiving.

BLESSED Jesus! Thou hast now blest me with the food of thy own merciful institution, and, in humble faith of thy gracious promise, I have bowed myself at thy table, to receive the precious pledges of thy dying love; O may thy presence go with me from this happy participation of thy goodness, that when I return to the necessary labours and employments of the miserable world, I may be enabled by thy grace to obey thy commandments, and conducted by thy watchful care through all trials, till, according to thy divine wisdom, I have finished my course here with joy, that so I may depart out of this world in peace, and in a stedfast dependence on thy merits, O blessed Jesus, in whose prevailing words I shut up all my imperfect wishes, saying,

Our Father, &c. Amen.

---

4. A Burial office for Infants

who depart this life before they have polluted their baptism by actual sin. By Bishop Seabury.[3]

The Priest going before the corpse into the churchyard; either into the church or the grave, shall say.[4]

All flesh is grass, and all its glory like the flower of the field. The grass withereth, the flower fadeth when the wind of Jehovah bloweth upon it. *Isaiah xl.* 6, 7.

Suffer little children to come unto me. *Matt.* xix. 14.

Whosoever cometh to me, said the blessed Jesus, I will in no wise cast out. *John* vi. 37.

I am the resurrection and the life. *John* xi. 25.

Precious in the sight of the Lord is the death of his saints. *Psa.* cxvi. 15.

Blessed therefore are the dead who die in the Lord. *Rev.* xiv. 13.

They are taken away from the evil to come. *Isaiah* lvii. 1.

Coming to the grave shall be said or sung,

Glory be to the Father, &c.

As it was in the beginning, &c.

While the corpse is made ready for interment shall be said by the Priest, or sung,

Man that is born of a woman hath but a short time to live, and is full of misery. He cometh up and is cut down like a flower; he fleeth as it were a shadow, and never continueth in one stay.

In the midst of life we are in death. Of whom may we seek for succour, but of thee, O Lord, who for our sins art justly displeased?

Yet, O Lord God most holy, O Lord most mighty, O holy and most merciful Saviour, deliver us not into the bitter pains of eternal death.

Thou knowest, Lord, the secrets of our hearts. Shut not thy merciful ears to our prayers; but spare us, Lord most holy, O God most mighty, O holy and merciful Saviour, thou most worthy Judge eternal, suffer us not at our last hour for any pains of death to fall from thee.

While earth is cast on the body, the Priest shall say,

In the name of the most holy and undivided Trinity, Father, Son, and Holy Ghost, in whose likeness man was created, we commit this body to the ground; earth to earth; ashes to ashes; dust to dust; in sure and certain hope of the resurrection to eternal life through our Lord Jesus Christ, who is the resurrection and the life; who at his second coming shall change this vile body, according to his most gracious promise, by raising it from the dead, and transforming it into the likeness of his own glorified body, according to the mighty working whereby he is able to subdue all things to himself.

Lord of life and glory, Jesus, eternal Son of God, have mercy on us, and hear the prayer of thine own appointment.

Our Father, &c.

O Almighty God, who through thine only begotten Son Jesus Christ, hast overcome death and opened unto us the gate of everlasting life, mercifullly grant, that as this deceased infant hath been baptized into the death of thy beloved Son Jesus Christ, and thereby made his disciple, and the heir of eternal glory, and now at thy command hath gone out of this mortal life before *he* hath done good or evil; the garment of *his* regeneration remaining pure and unspotted, and *his* soul having already found admission, through the merit of the Redeemer, into thy paradise, so *his* body may have a happy passage through the grave and gate of death to a joyful resurrection at the last day, and may then be made partaker of everlasting glory, through Him who died, and was buried, and rose again for us, Jesus Christ thy Son, our Lord and Saviour. *Amen.*

Glory to the Father, &c.
As it was in the beginning, &c.

Almighty God with whom do live the spirits of those who depart hence in the Lord, and with whom the souls of the faithful, after they are delivered from the burden of the flesh, are in joy and felicity! we give thee hearty thanks for all the gracious dispensations of thy wise Providence! And we beseech thee, by this and every other instance of daily mortality, to teach us who are yet alive to consider how frail and uncertain our condition is; that seriously numbering our days, we may earnestly apply ourselves to attain thy heavenly promises, and at the tremendous appearing of the great God, even our Saviour Jesus Christ, may with all those who have departed hence in Him, have our perfect consummation and bliss, both in body and soul, in thy eternal and everlasting glory, through the same Jesus Christ our Lord. *Amen.*

Our deceased infants who have been baptized into the death of Jesus Christ, shall all be delivered from the hand of the enemy, the great destroyer death, and shall return to their own border, thy heavenly kingdom, O God; for this is the will of the Father, that of all that he hath given to the Son, he shall lose nothing, but should raise it up again at the last day.

The grace of our Lord Jesus Christ, and the love of God, and the fellowship of the Holy Ghost, be with us all ever more. *Amen.*

---

5. Bishop Seabury's liturgical *vade-mecum*

from a manuscript in the Saint Mark's Library of the General Theological Seminary, New York.

Occasional Prayers

and

Offices.

List of Communicants[5]

Mr Jonathan Starr. *
Mr Charles Jeffery. *
Mr Jonathan Starr Jr. *
M^{rs}. Mary Starr.
Mrs Palms. *
Mrs Sarah Wilson. *
Mrs Goddard. *
Mrs Cheney. *
Mrs Ann Jeffery. *
Mrs Elisth Winthrop *—
Mrs Sarah Deshon *
Mrs Rebecka Mumford.
Mrs Elisth Saltonstall *
Miss Abigail Starr.
Sappho Servant of Mrs. Stewart. *
Mrs Weeks.

N.B. Mrs Mumford has not communicated since Xrmass 1786.

[a second column]
Miss Maria Seabury. *
Mrs Elisth. Starr.
Mrs Rebecca Truman.
Mrs Mary Constant.
Mrs Amelia Allen.
Miss Frances Stewart. *
Mrs Grace Chew. *
* Mrs Hopewell Saltonstall Xrmass
M^{rs} ~~God~~ Goddard 1787.
Mrs Violetta R. Taylor *
Miss Sarah Billings *
Mr Ichabod Powers, Jr. *
Mrs Powers, * on
Quinqua. Sunday 1788.
Mrs Pool 2.3 Lent.
Mrs Lament Billings
Mr Eben^{r}. Goddard.
Mrs Shoseel *
Mr Jared Starr.
Mrs Aib^{l} Starr *
* Dead.—Removed

D^{r}. Samuel Seabury. *
Mrs Frances Seabury.
M^{r} Ch^{as}. Nicol Taylor. *
M^{rs} ~~M^{rs}~~ Sarah Luke. *
Mr Henry Truman.
Mr Edward Seabury. *
Mr Charles Seabury
Ichabod, Servant to
Capt. Deshon.
Rose, Servant to
Capt. Froud.
Mrs Naomi Edgecomb.
M^{r}. Jesse Edgecomb *
M^{rs}. Thos. Lelln Ju^{r}.
Sam ____ a free black. *
Mrs Sarah Coil.
Mr Thos Allen. *
Miss Goddard [illegible mark]
M^{rs}. Mary Cheny
M^{rs} M^{c}.Carty *
[a second column]
Mrs Ruth Harvy
Miss Deborah Harvy *
M^{rs}. Lucy Marten *
Miss Polly Truman
Miss Ann Hazard
Mr Ebenor Holt
Mr Ebenor Holt Junr.
Mrs Sarah Wheat
Mrs Martha Jackson
Mrs Elizth. Hazard *
Mr Hom Heymas
Mr Edward Hallam
Mrs Mary Hallam
Mr Hart Leech
Mrs Ann Seabury—
Mrs Mumford—
Caesar a black
Susan _____
Margaret _____
Celia _____

Occasional Prayers to be used in Churches

The following Prayer was used at New London during the prevalence of The Dysentery in the year 1787.

O Almighty Lord God, the Creator of all things, the Lord of life & death, of sickness & health; Regard our supplications, we humbly beseech Thee: And, as Thou hast thought proper to visit our sins by great sickness & mortality, in the midst of thy judgment, O Lord, remember thy mercy: Have pity upon us miserable sinners, & withdraw from us the grievous sickness with which we are afflicted. May this thy fatherly correction have its due influence upon us, by leading us to consider how frail & uncertain our life is; That so we may apply our hearts unto that heavenly wisdom which in the end will bring us to everlasting life, through Jesus Christ our Lord. Amen.

¶ *For a sick person who desires the Prayers of the Church.*

O lord, look down from heaven, we humbly beseech Thee, behold, visit, & relieve thy sick servant for whom our prayers are desired: Look upon him in mercy; comfort him with the sense of thy goodness; preserve him from the temptations of the enemy; give him patience under his affliction, &, in thy good time restore him ~~him~~ to health, & enable him, by thy grace, to lead the residue of his life in thy fear & to thy glory: Or else give him grace so to take thy visitation, that, after this painful life ended, he may dwell with Thee in life everlasting, through Jesus Christ our Lord. Amen.

¶ *For a sick Child.*

Almighty God, & merciful Father, to whom alone belong the issues of life & death: Look down from heaven, we humbly beseech Thee, with the eyes of mercy, upon the sick Child for whom our prayers are desired: Visit him, O Lord, with thy salvation; deliver him in thy good appointed time from his bodily pain, & save his soul for thy mercies sake; that if it shall be thy good pleasure to prolong his days here on earth, he may live to Thee, & be an instrumen[t] of thy glory, by serving Thee faithfully, & doing good in his generation: Or else receive him into those heavenly habitations, where the souls of them that sleep in the Lord Jesus enjoy perpetual rest & felicity. Grant this, O Lord, for thy mercies sake, in the same Thy Son our Lord Jesus Christ. Amen.

¶ *For a person bound to Sea.*

O Eternal God, who alone spreadest out the heavens, & rulest the raging of the Sea; who hast compassed the waters with bounds untill day & night come to an end: Be pleased to receive into thy almighty & most gracious protection, the person of thy servant for whom our prayers are desired; Preserve him from the dangers of the Sea, & from the violence of enemies; & grant that he may return in health & safety to enjoy the blessings of the land, with the fruits of his labours; &, with a thankful remembrance of thy mercies, to praise & glorify thy holy name, through Jesus Christ our Lord. Amen.

¶ *For a person under Affliction.*

O Merciful God, & heavenly Father, who hast taught us in thy Holy Word, that Thou dost not willingly afflict, or grieve the children of men: Look with pity, we beseech Thee, upon the sorrows of thy servant for whom our prayers are desired: In thy goodness Thou hast thought best to visit him with trouble, & to bring distress upon him. Remember him, O Lord, in mercy; sanctify thy fatherly correction to him; endue his soul with patience under his affliction, & with resignation to thy blessed will; comfort him with a sense of thy goodness; lift up the light of thy countenance upon him, and give him peace, through Jesus Christ our Lord. Amen.

A Form of Consecrating Churches, Chapels, and Church Yards, or Places of Burial.

¶ *When the Bishop & Clergy (two at least being present) have entered the Church in their habits, as they walk up to the Altar, they shall repeat the 24th Psalm, the Bishop beginning, & the Clergy answering, Verse by Verse.*

The earth is the Lord's and all that therein is: the compass of the world, and they that dwell therein.

For he hath founded it upon the seas: and prepared it upon it upon the floods.

Who shall ascend into the hill of the Lord: or who shall rise upon in his holy place?

Even he that hath clean hands, and pure heart: and that hath not lifted up his mind unto vanity, nor sworn to deceive his neighbour.

He shall receive the blessing from the Lord: and righteousness from the God of his salvation.

This is the generation of them that seek him: even of them that seek thy face, O Jacob.

Lift up your heads, O ye gates, and be ye lift up, ye everlasting doors: and the King of glory shall come in.

Who is this King of glory: it is the Lord strong and mighty, even the Lord mighty in battle.

Lift up your heads, O ye gates, and be ye lift up, ye everlasting doors: and the King of glory shall come in.

Who is the King of glory: even the Lord of hosts, he is the King of glory.

Glory be to the Father, &c:

As it was in the beginning &c. Amen.

¶ *When the Bishop is seated in the Chancel, the instrument of Dedication shall be presented to him by the Founder, or some proper persons, which he shall cause his Register, or one appointed for the purpose, to read. Then the Bishop shall lay the instrument on the Holy Table; and standing at the north side, shall turn to the Congregation and say,*

Dearly beloved in the Lord; forasmuch as devout and holy men, as well under the Law as under the Gospel, moved either by the secret inspiration of the Blessed Spirit, or by the express command of God, or by their own reason, & sense of the natural decency of things, have erected houses for the public worship of God, and separated them from all profane and common uses, in order to fill men's minds with greater reverence for his glorious Majesty, and to affect their hearts with more devotion and humility in his service; which pious works have been approved and graciously accepted by our Heavenly Father: Let us not doubt but that he will also favorably approve this our godly purpose of setting apart this Place in solemn manner to the performance of the Several Offices of our religious worship; and let us faithfully and devoutly beg his blessing on this our undertaking, and say, humbly kneeling on our knees—

¶ *Then all kneeling the Bishop and Clergy shall say the Lord's Prayer.*

Our Father who art in heaven, Hallowed be thy Name; Thy kingdom come; Thy will be done in earth, as it is in heaven: Give us this day our daily bread; And forgive us our trespasses, as we forgive them that trespass against us; And lead us not into temptation; But deliver us from evil; for thine is the kingdom, & the power, & the glory, for ever & ever. Amen.

¶ *Then the Bishop still kneeling shall say this Prayer following.*

O Eternal God, mighty in power, O Majesty incomprehensible, whom the Heaven of Heavens cannot contain, much less the walls of Temples made with hands; and who yet hast been graciously pleased to promise thy especial presence in whatever place even two or three of thy faithful servants shall assemble in thy name, to offer up their supplications and their praises to Thee; vouchsafe, O Lord, to be now present with us, who are gathered here together to Consecrate this Place, with its sacred utensils & furniture[6] with great humility & readiness of heart, to the honour of thy great Name; for celebrating thy Holy Sacraments; for offering our prayers & thanksgivings to thy glorious Majesty; for blessing thy people in thy Name, & for performing all other Holy Ordinances & religious duties. Accept, O Lord, this service at our hands, & bless it with such success as may tend most to thy glory, & the furtherance of our happiness, through Jesus Christ our Lord & Saviour. Amen.

¶ *The Bishop shall then stand up & say these Collects.*

Regard, O Lord, the supplications of thy Servants; and grant that whosoever shall be dedicated to Thee in this House by Baptism, may be washed & sanctified with the Holy Ghost, delivered from thy wrath, received into the ark of Christs Church, & ever remain in the number of thy faithful & elect children.

Grant O Lord, that they who in this Place shall renew the promise & vow which they made, or which was made by their sureties in their name, at their baptism, & thereupon shall be confirmed by the laying of the hands of the Bishop, may continue thine forever; & being preserved in the unity of thy Church, may daily increase in thy Holy Spirit more & more, untill they come to thine everlasting kingdom. Amen.[7]

Grant, O Lord, that whosoever shall receive in this Place the Blessed Sacrament of the Body & Blood of Christ thy Son, may come to that Holy Ordinance with a true penitent heart, lively faith, & perfect charity; & being filled with thy grace & heavenly benediction, may, to their great & endless comfort, obtain remission of their sins, & all other benefits of his passion. Amen.[8]

Grant, O Lord, that by the Holy Word which shall be redde & preached within this House, the hearers thereof may both perceive & know what things they ought to do, & may have grace & power obediently to fulfil the same.

Grant, O Lord, that whosoever shall be joined together in this Place in the holy bands of Matrimony, may faithfully perform & keep the vow & covenant betwixt them made, & may live according to thy laws & remain in perfect love & peace together unto their lives end.

Grant, O Lord, Thou who art the Lord of life & death, of health & sickness, that such as are sick, afflicted, or distressed, in mind, body, or estate, & shall desire the prayers of the Congregation which shall assemble in this Place, that Thou wilt be pleased in mercy to hear the prayers of thy servant for all such, granting them patience under their sufferings, & a happy issue out of all their afflictions. Amen.[9]

Grant, O Lord, that all such as have, though thy mercy, been preserved in the great danger of child-birth, & shall come to this place, according to their bounden duty, to give Thee thanks for the same, may, through thy help, both faithfully live, & walk according to thy will in this life present, & also be partakers of everlasting glory in the life to come.

Grant, O God, that all such offenders as, by godly discipline, shall be sent to this place, to give Thee glory by a public confession of their crimes, may, by thine infinite grace, come to a true sense of their sin & danger, & from their heart repent them truly of all their offences against Thee & their neighbour; & that all others may thereby be warned to flee from the wrath to come. Amen.[10]

Grant, O Lord, that all who enter into this place, may seriously consider, that this is the House of God—an House of Prayer, & of Divine Worship; & that they may behave themselves in it with that devotion, reverence; & humility, which are due to thy fix this divine Majesty. Amen.[11]

Grant, O God, we beseech Thee, that whosoever shall draw near unto Thee in this place, to confess their sins unto Thee, to give Thee thanks for thy great benefits, to set forth thy most worthy praise, to hear thy most Holy Word, to commemorate the death & sacrifice of thy Son, & to ask such things as are requisite & necessary as well for the body as the soul, may do it with that steadfastness of faith, that seriousness of attention, & devout affection of mind, that Thou mayest accept their bounden duty & service, & vouchsafe unto them whatever else in thine infinite mercy thou shalt see to be most expedient for them. And this we beg for Jesus Christs ~~his~~ sake, our blessed Lord & Saviour. Amen.

We also bless thy name, O God almighty, that it hath pleased Thee to put it into the hearts of thy servants, the members of this Congregation, to erect this House to the honour & worship of thy divine Majesty. Regard, O Lord, the piety of their intention, & accept the liberality of all who have contributed to it. Bless, O Lord, them, their families and their substance. Remember them concerning this; wipe not out this kindness which they have shewed for the House of their God, & the Offices thereof. And as Thou, O Lord, didst by thy grace, inspire them with the design of building this House, & hast, by thy good providence, enabled them to complete it in great beauty and elegance, & hast excited them, by the Holy Spirit, to dedicate it, this day, to Thee, to be an House of Prayer & holy Worship, & an acknowledgment of thy sovereignty & goodness: We beseech Thee, to keep it ever under thy gracious & almighty pròtection; preserve it from the rage of the elements, from the violence of enemies, & from the profanation of wicked & ungodly men, that it may long continue a monument of thy goodness & of the liberality and devotion of its pious founders: And grant that all they who shall enjoy the benefit of this their good work, may shew forth their thankfulness by making a right use of it to the glory of thy blessed name, through Jesus Christ our Lord. Amen.

¶ *The the Service of the day shall be redde by one of the Priests—the Minister of the Place if present.*

¶ *Proper Psalms, Lxxxiv. cxxii. cxxxii.*

¶ *First Lesson, i Kings chap. viii. from ver. 22 to 62.*

¶ *Second Lesson, Heb. Chap. x. from ver 19 to 26.*

¶ *After the Litany, let the Bishop proceed to the Communion Service, & then, instead of the Collect for the Day, shall be redde this Following.*

O most glorious Lord God, we acknowledge that we are not worthy to offer unto Thee anything belonging to us; yet we beseech Thee, out of thine infinite goodness, graciously to accept the Dedication of this Place to thy worship & service, & to prosper this our religious undertaking: Receive the prayers & intercession of us & all other thy servants, who either now or hereafter entering into this thy House, shall serve Thee with reverence & godly fear: Affect us with an awful apprehension of thy Heavenly Majesty, & with a deep sense of our own unworthiness, that so approaching thy Sanctuary with lowliness & devotion, & bringing with us our clean thoughts, pure hearts, bodies undefiled, and minds sanctified, we may be an acceptable people in thy sight through Jesus Christ our Lord. Amen.

The Epistle, i Cor xi. 17.

Now in this that I declare unto you, I praise you not, that you come together, not for the better, but for the worse. For first of all, when ye come together in the Church, I hear that there be divisions among you; & I partly believe it. For there must be also heresies among you, that they which are approved may be made manifest among you. When ye come together therefore into one place, this is not to eat the Lords Supper. For in eating every one taketh before other, his own Supper; & one is hungry, & another is drunken. What, have ye not houses to eat & to drink in? or despise ye the Church of God, & shame them that have not? What shall I say to you? shall I praise you in this? I praise you not.

The Gospel, John ii. 13.

And the Jews passover was at hand, & Jesus went up to Jerusalem, & found in the temple those that sold oxen, & sheep, & doves, & the changers of money sitting. And when he had made a scourge of small cords, he drove them all out of the temple, & the sheep, & the oxen; & poured out the changers money, & overthrew the tables; & said unto them that sold doves, Take these things hence; make not my Fathers house an house of merchandise. And his disciples remembered that it was written, The zeal of thine house hath eaten me up.

¶ *After the Nicene Creed, the Bishop shall proceed to the Administration of the Holy Eucharist, concluding with the Blessing. When there is a Church Yard, or Burying-Place to be consecrated, after the usual service of the day, let the Bishop, Clergy, & People go into the ground to be consecrated, & let the Bishop say,*

O God, who hast taught us in thy Holy Word, that there is a difference between the spirit of a beast that goeth downward to the earth, & the spirit of a man which ascendeth up to God who gave it; & likewise hast instructed us by the example of thy devout servants, to set apart peculiar places, wherein the bodies of thy Saints may be committed to the ground, in sure & certain hope of the resurrection to eternal life: Accept, we beseech Thee, this pious & charitable work of ours, in separating & consecrating this portion of ground, where they may rest in peace, & be preserved from all indignities: And give us all grace, that, by the frequent instance of mortality which we behold, we may learn, & seriously consider, how frail & uncertain our condition here on earth is; & may so number our days as to apply our hearts unto wisdom; that in the midst of life thinking upon death, & daily preparing ourselves for the judgment that is to follow, we may have our part in the Resurrection, with him, who died for our sins & rose again for our justification, & now liveth & reigneth with Thee & the Holy Ghost, one God, world without end. Amen.

2 Cor. xiii. 14

The Grace of our Lord Jesus Christ, & the Love of God, & the Fellowship of the Holy Ghost, be with us all evermore. Amen.

Copy of the Deed of Dedication,
at the Consecration of St. James' Church in
New London.

At a meeting of the church-Wardens, Vestrymen, & Parishioners of St. James' Church in the City of New London, on the seventeenth day of September, 1787, it was unanimously resolved & voted, That,

As Almighty God had been pleased to put it into their hearts to build a New Church for the Celebration of his Worship according to the Liturgy of the Church of England, accommodated to the Civil Constitution of this State, & had in the course of his good Providence enabled them to complete it according to the best of their ability; It was their full purpose & earnest desire, that the said New Church, to be called St. James' Church, be dedicated to the Worship & Service of Almighty God, according to the Liturgy of the Church of England aforesaid —We, therefore, the Church-Wardens, Vestrymen, & Parishioners of the said Church, DO, for us, & our successors, dedicate, appropriate, give & grant this said Church by us erected, unto Almighty God, our heavenly King & Father, to be Consecrated & used to his Worship & Service according to the Liturgy aforesaid—divesting ourselves of all right & title, & desclaiming all authority to employ it hereafter to any common or profane use. And we the Church-Wardens, Vestrymen, & Parishioners aforesaid, do further resolve and vote, that the two Church-Wardens, Mess[r]. Jonathan Starr, & Rosewell Saltonstall, do, in our name & behalf, sign & seal this instrument of Dedication, & do acquaint the Right Reverend Dr. Seabury, our Diocesan Bishop therewith, & request, that he would consecrate the said New Church to Almighty God, & set it apart, to be forever hereafter employed in his Worship & Service, —Promising, as far as in us lies, to take care of the repairs of said Church—that it may be kept, together with its furniture, sacred utensils, & books, in a decent state for the celebration of divine service. And also, that we will as God shall enable us, endeavour always to procure & support a Minister in Priests Orders, to celebrate Gods holy Worship according to the Liturgy aforesaid. In witness whereof We the said Church-wardens have hereunto set our hands & seals, the day & year above written.
Signed

Jon[a] StarrJu[r.] (LS.)
Ros. Saltonstall (LS)

Signed
in the presence of
Gabriel Se[illegible]re Ju[r.]
Rosewell Saltonstall Ju[r].

(L.S.)
Be it known to all whom it may concern, That on the 20th day of September, 1787, the above instrument of Dedication was presented unto us, the Bishop of Connecticut, at the Holy Table, by M[r] Jonathan Starr Junior, the Senior Church-warden, & openly redde before the Congregation there assembled. And that in consequence therefor the said New Church, called

St. James' Church, was, on that day, duly Consecrated, & set apart for the Worship & Service of Almighty God forever. In Witness whereof, We have hereunto affixed our Episcopal Seal, the day & year above written, And in the fourth year of our Consecration.

> *This Collect was, by direction of the Bp of Connecticut, redde in all the Churches in his Diocese on Ashwednesday, & on the Sundays in Lent, 1789, after the Collect, We beseech thee, O Father, in the Morning, & before the Prayer for all Conditions of Men, in the Afternoon—on account of the Insects which, for several years had destroyed the Wheat.*

O Almighty God, by whose providence the whole Creation is sustained and fed: We are taught by thy holy Word that thou dost not willingly afflict the children of men; but that thy judgments are intended to bring them to repentance, and ~~to~~ a due sense of their dependence on Thee, that thou mayest ~~shew~~ have mercy upon them. In thy wisdom, ~~O God~~, thou hast thought good to cut short the produce of the earth, and frustrate the hope of the husbandman by devouring Insects—Justly do we deserve this punishment, for we have sinned against Thee. We acknowledge our wickedness, O God, and we implore thy mercy. Give us, we beseech thee, unfeigned repentance for all our errors and sins, and accept the contrition of our hearts: Remove thy chastisement from us, and bless the labour of our hands, that our land may yield her increase, and we thy servants may rejoice in ~~the comfort of~~ thy loving-kindness. Hear us, O heavenly Father, and have mercy on us miserable sinners, for the merits sake of thy Son, Jesus Christ, our Mediator and Redeemer. Amen.

Consecration of the Holy Eucharist.

All glory be to thee, Almighty God, our heavenly Father, for that thou * * *

[In the same hand, but very weak]

> Extract from Dr Thos Wilson's (late Lord Bishop of Sodor & Man) Directions & Devotions in the Communion Service, Third 8vo. Edit. of his works Vol. II. p 112.

Most merciful God, the Father of our Lord Jesus Christ, look graciously on the gifts now lying before Thee; & send down thy Holy Spirit on this Sacrifice, that He may make this bread & this wine the body & blood of thy Christ, that all they who partake of them may be confirmed in godliness—may have remission of their sins —may be delivered from the devil & his wiles —may be filled with the Holy Ghost—may be worthy of thy Christ, & obtain everlasting Life;—Thou, O Lord, Almighty, being reconciled unto them, through the same Jesus Christ our Lord. Amen.

> Extract from the Sacra Privata of the same. Third 8vo Edit. of his Works, Vol II. p. 226, 227.

Immediately after the Consecration (I suppose by the English office).

We offer unto Thee, our King, & our God, this Bread & this Cup.

We give Thee thanks for these, & for all thy mercies; Beseeching Thee to send down thy Holy Spirit upon this Sacrifice, that he may make this Bread the Body of thy Christ, & this Cup ~~this Cup~~ the Blood of thy Christ. And that all we who are partakers thereof, may thereby obtain remission of our sins, & all other benefits of his passion.

And, together with us, remember, O God, for good, the whole mystical body of thy Son; that such as are yet alive may finish their course with joy; & that we, with all such as are dead in the Lord, may rest in hope, & rise in glory, for thy Sons sake, whose death we now commemorate. Amen.

May I atone Thee, O God, by offering to Thee the pure & unbloody Sacrifice which Thou hast ordained by Jesus Christ. Amen.

From page 477.[12]

—And when I shall not be able to pray for myself, the good Lord favourably hear the prayers of his Church for me.

Grant that the sins which I have committed in this world may not be imputed unto me; but that escaping the gates of Hell, I may dwell in the regions of light, with Abraham, & Isaac, & Jacob, untill the day of the general resurrection, & that I may hear those joyful words of thy Son — Come ye blessed &c.

From page 484.[13]

Vouchsafe my soul a place of rest in the Paradise of God, with all thy blessed Saints, & my body a part in the blessed resurrection.

Extract from Mr. R. Nelsons life of Bp Bull, page 475.

Mr. Nelson having observed that Mrs. Bull had been lately laid "in that silent retirement she had provided for herself (viz: next to her husband) till the last trump shall summon them both to judgment", he adds, "And the Lord grant unto them, that they may find mercy of the Lord in that day". 2 Tim. 1.19

At the opening of a Court of Justice[14]

Remember no[t, O] Lord our offences, &c.: Liturgy

O Lord, we beseech thee mercifully hear our prayers, &c. } Commination.

O God, who art the author of peace &c: }

O Lord, our heavenly Father &c.
} Morning Prayer

The Prayer for the President.
The Prayer for all conditions of men.

This Collect.

Almighty God, who upholdest & governest all things in heaven & on earth; Hear the humble supplications which we make before thy divine Majesty in behalf of the Court now opened for the administration of Justice to thy People. Let thy wisdom guide & direct all their determination; that impartiality & truth being the directors of all their proceeding, they may promote the peace, order, & happiness of Civil Society: and that we & all thy People being in constant safety under the protection of thy good providence, may, under the impartial administration of just & equal laws, lead godly & quiet lives in this world; & by thy mercy, obtain everlasting life in the world to come, through Jesus Christ our Lord & Saviour. Amen.

General Thanksgiving.
Alm. God, the fountain of all wisdom &c:
Post-Communion.
The Lords Prayer & Blessing.

At the supreme Court New London
September 1795.

Enter not into judgment &c: Ps cxliii. 2
If we say we have no sin &c: i John i. 8,9
Collect for Ashwednesday
Almighty & everlasting God &c:
Lords Prayer
Our Father &c:
Collect for ~~Peace Grace~~ Peace,
Morning Prayer
O God, from whom &c:
Collect for ~~Aid Against Perils~~ Grace.
O Lord, our heavenly Father &c:

Prayer for the President & all in authority

O Lord, our heavenly Father, the high & mighty &c:

Prayer for the people & government of the U. States.

O Almighty & everlasting God, we make our supplications to thy divine majesty, humbly imploring thy protection & blessing on the people & government of the United States of America, & especially on the people & government of this State in which we live—entreating thy favour & gracious goodness towards them. Particularly we make our prayers to thee in behalf of the ~~(Supreme)~~ Court ~~of this State,~~ by thy good providence, now assembled for the administration of justice to thy people. Look with favour, O God, on the Judges of the Court, ~~& all~~ the subordinate officers belonging to it & on all concerned in the administration of justice in it. Direct them by thy grace in whatever business shall come before them; & grant that all their decisions may be grounded on the principles of truth & integrity: So that peace & happiness, justice & righteousness, religion & piety may flourish among us for all generations: And that thy people being secure, through the protection of equal laws & the administration of impartial justice, may joyfully serve thee in all godly quietness, & may live in peace & unity with each other, & in peace & friendship with all mankind. Hear us, we beseech thee, O God, for the sake of Jesus Christ, our Redeemer & Saviour. Amen.

Prayer for all conditions of men.

O God, the Creator & Preserver of all Mankind &c:

General Thanksgiving.

Almighty God, Father of all mercies &c:

2 Cor. xiii. 14

The Grace of our Lord Jesus Christ &c:

Amen.

[The rest is in a second hand.]

Churches consecrated by
Bishop Seabury—Connecticut:

S^{t}. Pauls Church Norwalk —
S^{t}. James's Church New London
Sepr. 20. 1789
Christ Church Norwich Landing
S^{t}. John's church Stratfield [sic]
Trinity Church New Town Sepr. 19. 1793
S^{t}. John's church New Milford
Sepr. 25. 1793
Christ's Church Westbury. Novr. 18. 1794.
Church. Taskaway June 8. 1795
S^{t}. Stephen's Church, East Haddam,
Octr. 18. 1795
S^{t}. Matthews Church, Plimouth
Octr. 20. 1795
S^{t}. Mark's Church. Harrington
Octr. 22. 1795

This record is made from an entry on a loose piece of Paper, written ~~by and signed~~ and attested and signed in the following Words. The above is a list of churches which [have] been consecrated in Connecticut by. Samuel Bp of Conn: & Rhode Island.

Churches consecrated by Bishop Jarvis—
S^{t}. John's Church, Waterbury
Novr. 1st. 1797
S^{t}. Peter's Church, Plymouth
Novr. 2. 1797—
Family Church Fairfield
Octr. 18. 1798—
S^{t}. James's Church, Derby.
Nov^{r}: 20. 1799.
S^{t}. James's Church Danbury. Oct: 6th 1802
— Chh— Hartford. Novr. 11th. 1802

[There follow forty-three blank leaves. From the back, with the book held inverted, begins a collection of music in Seabury's hand. The first section is a selection of hymn tunes in two parts. For each Seabury gives a melody (usually in tenor clef) and a bass line. No notation for realizing the bass is included. The tunes are, as Seabury cites them, The 100th Psalm, Wells, Bray, Plymouth., Bangor, Mear, S. Martins, Wantage, Newbury, First Psalm, 102 Psalm, Paringdon, Portsmouth, Wirksworth, Newcastle, Little Marlborough, 46th Psalm, S. Helens, 149th Psalm or Hanover, and 136th Psalm or Bethesda. The liturgical music includes both text and music. "Chaunts," given with Seabury's titles, include Venite exultemus, Cantate Domino, Magnificat, Benedictus, Jubilate Deo, Nunc dimittis, Deus misereatur (words only). and Benedicite omnia opera. No composers are indicated for the hymns or chants.

---

6. Changes in the English Book proposed at a Convention, September 7th & 8th, 1785, in Boston

At a Convention of Clergymen and Lay Deputies of the Episcopal Church of the States of Massachusetts, Rhode Island, and Hew Hampshire, held at Boston, Sept. 7 and 8, 1785.

Present.

Rev. Edward Bass, Rector of St. Paul's Church, Newburyport.

Rev. Wm. Willard Wheeler, Rector of the united Churches of Scituate, Marshfield, Braintree, and Bridgewater.

Rev. Nathaniel Fisher, Rector of St. Peter's Church, Salem.

Rev. Samuel Parker, Rector of Trinity Church, Boston.

Hon. Tristram Dalton, Esq., Deputy of St. Paul's Church, Newburyport.

Stephen Greenleaf, Esq., and Mrs. Benjamin Greene, Deputies of Trinity Church, Boston.

Thomas Ivers, Esq., and Mrs. James Sherman, Deputies of Christ Church, Boston.

Dr. Charles Stockbridge, Deputy of Scituate, Marshfield, and Bridgewater.

Rev. Wm. Willard Wheeler, Deputy of Braintree.

Mr. Woodward Abraham, Deputy of Marblehead.

Mr. Joshua Kingsbury, Deputy of Dedham.

Mr. Joseph Aspinwall, Deputy of Stoughton.

Mr. John Bours, Deputy of Trinity Church, Newport, Rhode Island.

Mr. John Usher, Deputy of Bristol, R.I.

Dr. Francis Borland, Deputy of Queen's Chapel, Portsmouth, N.H.

Voted, Rev. Edward Bass, President of this Convention.

Voted, Rev. Nathaniel Fisher, Secretary.

Voted, That the Clergy and Laity now assembled shall deliberate in one body, but shall vote separately, and the concurrence of both orders shall be necessary to give validity to every measure.

Voted, That the Convention take into consideration the revival of the Liturgy and offices of the Church, as contained in the Book of Common Prayer, and make such alterations as may be necessary; and that the omissions and alterations, agreed upon by a Committee of Convocation, held at Middletown, in Connecticut, August 3, 1785, as contained in paper No. 1, serve as a basis for our present proceedings.

The Convention then proceeded to a revisal of the State Prayers, in the Book of Common Prayer, and came to the following resolutions, as a substitute for the State Prayers.

That in the Suffrage after the Creed, in morning and evening prayer, instead of, "O Lord save the King," it be read, O Lord save the Church, to which the congregations are to make the accustomed response, "and mercifully hear us," &c.

That the prayer for the King, in morning and evening service, be left out; and the prayer for the Royal Family be thus altered,—Almighty God, the fountain of all goodness, we humbly beseech thee to bless the Governor and Council of this Commonwealth, endue them with thy Holy Spirit, and so on, as it now stands.

That in the Litany, the 15th, 16th, 17th and 18th petitions be omitted, and petition for Bishops, Priests, and Deacons, immediately follow that for the universal Church; the 20th and 21st petition be thus read,—that it may please thee to endue the Governor and Council of this common wealth with grace and wisdom, and understanding; that it may please thee to bless and keep the Judges and subordinate Magistrates, giving them grace to execute justice, and to maintain truth:—to both which, the usual response, "we beseech thee to hear us, good Lord," is to be made by the congregation.

That in the prayer for the whole state of Christ's church Militant, the part relating to Rulers and Ministers, be thus altered:—We beseech thee also to save and defend, all Christian Kings, Princes, and Governors, and grant that they, and all that are in authority, may truly and impartially minister justice to the punishment of wickedness and vice, and to the maintenance of thy true religion and virtue; give grace, O Heavenly Father, to all Bishops, Priests, and Deacons, that they may,—and so on, as it now stands.

That the prayers for the King, that stand before the Nicene Creed, in the Communion Service, be omitted.

That the Answer in the Catechism, to the question, "What is thy duty towards thy neighbour," for, "to honor and obey the King," be substituted, to honor and obey my civil rulers, to submit myself, &c.

That during every session of the General Court, the following Collect be used in its proper place:—Most Gracious God we humbly beseech thee, as for this Commonwealth in general, so especially for the General Court at this time assembled, that thou wouldest be pleased to direct and prosper all their consultations, to the advancement of thy glory, the good of thy Church, the safety, honor and welfare of thy people; that all things may be so ordered and settled, by their endeavors, upon the best and surest foundations, that peace and happiness, truth and justice, religion and piety, may be established among us, for all generations;—these, and all other necessaries, for them, for us, and thy whole Church, we humbly beg, in the name and mediation of Jesus Christ, our most blessed Lord and Saviour. Amen.

That the observation of 5th November, 30th January, 29th May, and 25th October, be discontinued.

In the other parts of the Liturgy and offices of the Church, they came to the following resolutions:

That in the Te Deum, the sentence following this, "when thou tookedst upon thee to deliver man," be thus altered, thou didst humble thyself to be born of a pure virgin.

That the Article in the Apostles' Creed, "He descended into Hell," be omitted.

That the Creed commonly called the Creed of St. Athanasius, be wholly disused.

That it be left discretionary with the Minister, Wardens, and Vestry, of each particular Church, or congregation, to omit or use the Nicene Creed, as they shall severally choose.

That the response after the suffrage, "give peace in our time, O Lord," be thus altered, "and make all nations to rejoice in thy loving kindness, O God."

That the Lord's Prayer after the Apostles' Creed, and also what is usually called the shorter Litany, or the petitions, "Lord have mercy upon us, Christ have mercy," &c. be omitted, or left out. That the petitions in the Litany, from, "O Christ hear us," inclusive, to the prayer beginning, "O God, merciful Father," and from the end of that prayer including the response, "O Lord arise, help us, and deliver us, for thy name's sake," as far as the suffrage, "From our enemies defend us, O Christ," exclusive, be also omitted.

That the Lord's Prayer, at the beginning of the Communion Service, be omitted; and that the Gloria Patri be repeated only at the last of the Psalms, read at morning and evening service, when more than one, or that it be repeated but once in reading the Psalms.

The Prayer for the Clergy and people, in morning and evening service, to be thus read, Almighty and everlasting God, from whom alone every good and perfect gift doth come, send down upon all bishops and Pastors, and the congregations committed to their charge, the

508, 509

healthful Spirit of thy grace, &c.

That in the first warning, for the Celebration of the Holy Communion, the word, "damnation," following these words, "increase your," be read, condemnation; and the two paragraphs after these words, "or else come not to that holy table," be omitted, and the following one be read, And if there be any of you, who by these means cannot quiet their own conscience, &c. The words "learned and discreet," epithets given to ministers, &c. be also omitted.

That in the Exhortation at the Communion, the paragraph concerning the danger of receiving the same unworthily, be thus altered:—So is the danger great, if we receive the same unworthily, not considering the Lord's Body, for then we are guilty of the Body and Blood of Christ our Saviour, we eat and drink judgment to ourselves, kindling God's wrath against us, and provoking him to afflict us with divers diseases, and sundry kinds of death.

That it be left discretionary with the Minister, whether the words, "The body of our Lord Jesus Christ," &c., be repeated to each communicant separately, when the bread is given, or whether it shall be repeated but once, for all then present at the Altar—and the same also at giving the cup; and if the latter is adopted, that the plural be then used, instead of the singular.

That at the Baptism of Infants, parents may be admitted Sponsors, with one or other persons, if a suitable one can be procured,—if not, the parents alone, in their own persons, or by their proxies.

In the first address to the people at the Baptismal Office, the words, "All men are conceived and born of sin," be omitted, and the words, "our Saviour Christ," follow "for as much as."

That the words, "release him of his sins," in the address to the Sponsors, be omitted; that when the child or person is baptized in church, instead of repeating the Creed, the priest may say, Dost thou believe all the articles of the Christian faith, as contained in the Apostles' Creed? to which the answer shall be, I do, and, by God's help, I will instruct this child in that faith; the following question to be thus altered, Wilt thou have this child to be baptized in that faith? The usual response to follow; the last demand and response to be omitted.

That the sign of the Cross may be omitted, if particularly desired by the Sponsors.

In the last prayer, the following alterations to be made: "That it hath pleased thee, by the holy baptism, to regenerate this infant or person," the word, "Vulgar tongue," in the Exhortation or charge to the Sponsors, be omitted; and the words, "if opportunity presents," be added at the end of the Charge.

At the Burial of the Dead, the Commitment of the body to the ground, to be thus altered: For as much as it hath pleased almighty God, to take out of this mortal life, the soul of our brother (or sister), here departed, we therefore commit his (or her) body to the ground, earth to earth, ashes to ashes, dust to dust, looking for the resurrection of the body, and the life of the world to come, through our Lord Jesus Christ, who shall change our vile body that it may be like unto his glorious body, according to the mighty working, whereby he is able to subdue all things unto himself.

The prayer following the Lord's Prayer, to be omitted; and after the word, "beginning of the world," in the last prayer, be added this paragraph: SO that we, with all those that are departed in the true faith of thy holy name, may then have our perfect consummation and bliss, both in body and soul, in thy eternal and everlasting glory, through Jesus Christ our Lord, grant this, &c.

That the office of churching of Women, be omitted, excepting the introduction, the latter part of which shall be read: You shall therefore join in giving hearty thanks to God; and the Collect, which shall be thus altered: O Almighty God, we give thee humble thanks, for thy great mercy vouchsafed to this woman, thy servant, who now desires to offer up her praises and thanksgivings to thee; and grant, &c.

The second paragraph in the Introduction to the Commination Service, to be thus read: instead whereof, it is thought good at this time, in the presence of you all, should be read the general sentences of God's cursing against impenitent sinners, gathered out of the seven and twentieth chapter of Deuteronomy and other places of Scripture:—the remainder of this paragraph, with the Rubrick, that "the people shall answer and say, Amen," to the Curses, to be omitted.

That the Absolution, in the office of Visitation of the Sick, be expunged, and the Absolution used in the Communion Service, be substituted in its stead, if necessary.

That the Introduction to the Marriage Service, containing the reasons why matrimony was ordained, be omitted, from the words, "holy matrimony," to "therefore, if any man can shew any just cause," &c.

That the words, "plight and give thee my troth," be altered to pledge thee my truth; that the words, "with my body I thee worship, and with all my worldly goods I thee endow," in giving the ring, be omitted.

That it be left discretionary with the Minister, whether the Collect for the day be read more than once in the morning service, and also whether the Communion Service shall be read in the Reading Desk or in the Altar.

Voted, That it be recommended to the several Churches in these States, immediately to make the omission, and adopt the alterations contained in the printed paper No. 1, and agreed upon by this Convention, as a substitute for the State Prayer, in the Book of Common Prayer, and that using the other alterations be postponed till after the time to which this Convention shall be adjourned, in order that it may be seen, how far the other States will conform to said alterations.

Voted, That it is the opinion of the this Convention, that it is not necessary nor convenient to send a Delegate or Delegatees to the General Convention, to be holden at Philadelphia on the Tuesday preceding the Feast of St. Michael, but that a copy of the proceedings of this Convention be communicated, by a Committee to be hereafter chosen, to the President or some member of said Convention, to be communicated to said Body, and also to the Bishop or clergy of Connecticut, previous to the Convention to held at New Haven, to be communicated to them, requesting a speedy communication of each of their proceedings to said Committee.

Voted, That said Committee furnish all the Churches in the three States not represented here, and those whose members are absent, with a copy of the alterations in the Liturgy, agreed upon by this Convention, and request of them a return of their actings thereon, to this Convention, at their adjournment.

Voted, Rev. Mr. Parker, Thomas Ivers, Esq., and Mr. Benjamin Greene, be said Committee, with a power to employ a Clerk to assist them.

Voted, That the Rev. Mr. Bass and Mr. Fisher be a Committee to form a Collect, to be inserted among the occasional prayers for the case of persons who have lost their friends, for persons sick, and for persons bound to sea, and report at the adjournment.

Voted, That this Convention be adjourned to October 26th, and in case the Committee shall not then have received the returns from the Conventions at New Haven and Philadelphia, that they be authorized to adjourn said Convention, to such future day as they shall judge best, and notify the members of the same.

In consequence of the preceding votes of Convention, attested copies of the proposed alterations in the Liturgy and Offices of the Church, were transmitted to the Churches and Clergymen.

One to the Right Rev. Bishop Seabury, New London, Con.
" Rev. Bela Hubband, New Haven, Con.
" Rev. Benjamin Moore, New York.
" Rev. William White, D.D., Philadelphia.
" St. Paul's Church, Newburyport, Mass.

" Trinity Church, Boston, Mass.
" Christ Church, " "
" St. Peter's Church, Salem, Mass.
" United Churches at Scituate and Marshfield.
" Christ Church, Braintree, Mass.
" Church, Marblehead, Mass.
" Church, Falmouth, Mass.
" Trinity Church, Newport, R.I.
" St. Michael's Church, Bristol, R.I.
" Church, Providence, R.I.
" Church, Narragansett, R.I.
" Queen's Chapel, Portsmouth, N.H.
" Church, Claremont, N.H.
" Church, Holderness, N.H.

---

7. Changes in the English Book agreed upon in the First General Convention, 1785

Alterations agreed on and confirmed in Convention, for rendering the Liturgy conformable to the principles of the American Revolution, and the constitutions of the several states.

1st. That in the suffrages after the Creed, instead of *O Lord, save the King,* be said, *O Lord, bless and preserve these United States.*

2nd. That the prayer for the Royal family, in the morning and evening service, be omitted.

3rd. That in the Litany the 15th, 16th, 17th, and 18th, petitions be omitted, and that instead of the 20th and 21st petitions, be substituted the following—*That it may please Thee to endue the Congress of these United States, and all others in authority, legislative, executive, and judicial, with grace, wisdom and understanding, to execute justice and to maintain truth.*

4th. That when the Litany is not said, the *prayer for the high court of Parliament* be thus altered—"*Most gracious God, we humbly beseech thee, as for these United States in general, so especially for their delegates in Congress, that thou wouldest be pleased to direct and prosper all their consultations to the advancement of thy glory, the good of thy Church, the safety, honour and welfare of thy people, that all things may be so ordered and settled by their endeavors upon the best and surest foundations, that peace and happiness, truth and justice, religion and piety, may be established among us for all generations,*" &c. to the end: then the prayer for the king's majesty, altered as follows: viz.—

A Prayer for our Civil Rulers.

O Lord, Our heavenly Father, the high and mighty Ruler of the universe, who dost from thy Throne, behold all the Dwellers upon Earth; we most heartily beseech thee, with thy Favour to behold all in Authority, legislative, executive and judicial in these United States; and so replenish them with the Grace of thy holy Spirit, that they may alway incline to thy will and walk in thy way. Endue them plenteously with heavenly Gifts, grant them in Health and Wealth long to live and, that after this Life, they may attain everlasting Joy and Felicity, through Jesus Christ our Lord. Amen.

5th. That the 1st Collect for the King in the Communion Service be omitted; and that the second be altered as follows—instead of "*the hearts of Kings are in thy rule and governance,*" be said—"*That the hearts of all Rulers are in thy governance,*" &c; and instead of the words—"*heart of George thy servant,*" insert,—"*so to direct the Rulers of these states, that in all their thoughts, &c.*" changing the singular pronouns to the plural.

[No sixth paragraph survives.]

7th That in the answer in the Catechism to the question—"*What is thy duty towards thy neighbour?*" for "*to honour and obey the king,*" be substituted—"*to honour and obey my civil rulers, to submit myself, &c.*"

8th. That instead of the observation of the 5th of November, the 30th of January, the 29th of May, and the 25th of October, the following service be used on the 4th of July, being the Anniversary of Independence.

9th. That in the Forms of Prayer to be used at Sea, in the Prayer "O *eternal God, &c.*" instead of these Words—"*unto our most gracious Sovereign Lord King George and his Kingdomes,*" be inserted the Words—"*to the United States of America,*" and that instead of the Word —"*Island*" be inserted the Word "*Country;*" and in the collect "O *Almighty God, the Sovereign Commander,*" be omitted the Words—"*the Honour of our Sovereign,*" and the Words "*the honour of our Country*" instead.

Service for the 4th of July.

With the sentences before Morning and Evening Prayer.

The Lord has been mindful of us, and he shall bless us, he shall bless them that fear him, both small and great. O that men would therefore praise the Lord, for his goodness, and declare the wonders that he doeth for the children of men.

Hymn, instead of the Venite.

My song shall be alway of the loving kindness of the Lord: with my mouth will I ever be showing forth his truth from one generation to another. *Psal.* 89. 1.

The merciful and gracious Lord hath so done his marvellous works: that they ought to be had in remembrance. *Psal.* 111. 4

Who can express the noble acts of the Lord: or show forth all his praise. *Psal.* 106.2

The works of the Lord are great: sought out of all them that have pleasure therein. *Psal.* 111. 2.

For he will not alway be chiding: neither keepeth he his anger for ever. *Psal.* 103. 9.

He hath not dealt with us after our sins: nor rewarded us according to our wickedness. *Verse* 10.

For look how high the heaven is in comparison of the earth: so great is his mercy also toward them that fear him. *Verse* 11.

Yea, like as a father pitieth his own children: even so is the Lord merciful unto them that fear him. *Verse* 13.

Thou, O God, hast proved us: thou also hast tried us, like as silver is tried. *Psal.* 66. 9.

Thou didst remember us in our low estate, and redeem us from our enemies: for thy mercy endureth for ever. *Psal.* 136. 23,24.

Proper Psalms, 118, except v. 10,11,12,13, 22,23, to conclude with v. 24.

1. Lesson Deut. 8 2. Lesson Thess. 5. v. 12,—23 both inclusive.

Collect for the day.

Almighty God, who hast in all ages showed forth thy power and mercy in the wonderful preservation of thy church, and in the protection of every nation and people professing thy holy and eternal truth, and putting their sure trust in thee; we yield thee our unfeigned thanks and praise for all thy public mercies, and more especially for that signal and wonderful manifestation of thy providence which we commemorate this day; wherefore not unto us, O Lord, not unto us, but unto thy Name be ascribed all honour and glory, in all churches of the Saints, from generation to generation, through Jesus Christ our Lord. *Amen.*

A Thanksgiving for the day, to be said after the General Thanksgiving.

O God, whose Name is excellent in all the earth, and thy glory above the heavens; who as on this day didst inspire and direct the hearts of our delegates in Congress, to lay the perpetual foundations of peace, liberty, and safety; we bless and adore thy glorious Majesty, for this thy loving kindness and providence. And we humbly pray that the devout sense of this signal mercy may renew and increase in us a spirit of love and thankfulness to thee its only Author, a spirit of peaceable submission to the laws and government of our country, and a spirit of fervent zeal for our holy religion, which thou hast preserved and secured to us and to our posterity. May we improve these inestimable blessings for the advancement of religion, liberty, and science throughout this land, till the wilderness and solitary place be made glad through us, and the desert rejoice and blossom as the rose. This we beg through the merits of Jesus Christ our Saviour. *Amen.*

---

8. Changes in the English Book proposed by the First General Convention, 1785

Alterations in the Book of Common Prayer and Administration of the Sacraments, and other Rites and Ceremonies of the Church, according to the use of the Church of England, proposed and recommended to the Protestant Episcopal Church in the United States of America.

The Order for Morning and Evening service, Daily through the Year.

1st. The following Sentences of Scripture, are ordered to be prefixed to the usual Sentences, viz.—

The Lord is in his Holy Temple; let all the Earth keep Silence before Him. *Hab.* ii. 20.

From the Rising of the Sun to the going down of the Same, my Name shall be great among the Gentiles; and in every Place Incense shall be offered unto my Name, and a pure Offering: for my Name shall be great among the Heathen, saith the Lord of Hosts. Malachi.

Where two or three are gathered together in my Name, there am I in the midst of them. St. Matthew.

The Sacrifices of God are a broken Spirit, &c., with one or two more of the other Sentences. But this is to stand next after the Sentence, "Where two or three."

2d. That the Rubric preceding the Absolution, be altered thus—"A *declaration to be made by the Minister alone, standing, concerning the forgiveness of sins.*"

3d. That in the Lord's prayer, the word "*who*" be substituted in lieu of "*which*;" and that "*those who trespass*" stand instead of "*them that trespass.*"

4th. That the "Gloria Patri" be omitted after the "O *come let us sing, &c.*" and in every other place, where, by the present Rubric it is ordered to be inserted, to "the end of the" reading psalms; when, shall be said or sung "*Gloria Patri, &c.*" or, "*Glory be to God on high, and in earth peace and good will towards men, &c.*" at the discretion of the Minister.

5th. That in the "Te Deum" instead of "*honourable*" it be "*adorable, true, and only son;*" and instead of "*didst not abhor the Virgins' womb;*" "*didst humble thyself to be born of a pure Virgin.*"

6th. That until a proper selection of Psalms be made, each Minister be allowed to use such as he may chuse.

7th. That the same liberty be allowed, respecting the lessons.

8th. That the article in "the Apostles creed" "*He descended into hell*" be omitted.

9th. That the *Athanasian* and the *Nicene* creeds be entirely omitted.

10th. That after the response "*and with thy spirit,*" all be omitted to the words "O *Lord show thy mercy upon us;*" which the *Minister shall pronounce, still kneeling.*

11th. That in the suffrage "*make thy chosen people joyful,*" the word "*chosen*" be omitted; and also the following suffrages, to "O *God, make clean our hearts within us.*"

12th. That the Rubric after these words "*and take not thy Holy Spirit from us,*" be omitted. Then the two collects to be said: in the collect for grace, the words "*be ordered,*" to be omitted; and the word "*be*" inserted, instead of, "*to do alway that is.*"

13th. In the collect "*for the Clergy and People,*" read—"*Almighty and everlasting God, send down upon all Bishops and other Pastors and the Congregations committed, &c,*" to the end.

14th. That after reading all the Psalms and not at the end of each, *Gloria Patri* or the *Gloria in Excelsis Deo* shall be used at the Discretion of the Minister.

15th. That the Lord's prayer after the Litany, and the subsequent Rubric be omitted.

16th. That the short Litany be read as follows—"*Son of God, we beseech thee to hear us. Son of God, we beseech thee to hear us. O Lamb of God, that takest away the sins of the world, Grant us thy peace. O Christ, hear us. O Christ, hear us. Lord, have mercy upon us and deal not with us according to our sins, neither reward us according to iniquities.*" After which, omit the words—"*Let us pray.*"

17th. That the *Gloria Patri*, after *O Lord arise, &c.* be omitted; as also "*Let us pray,*" after "*we put our trust in thee.*"

18th. That in the following prayer, instead of "*righteously have deserved,*" it be "*justly have deserved.*"

19th. That in the 1st. warning for the Communion, the word "*damnation,*" following these words "*increase your, &c.*" be read "*condemnation;*" and the two paragraphs after these words "*or else come not to that holy table,*" be omitted; and the following one be read, *and if there be any of you, who by these means, cannot quiet their conscience, &c.* The words "*learned and discreet,*" epithets given to the ministers, to be also omitted.

20th. In the exhortation to the communion, let it run thus—"*For as the benefit is great, &c. to drink his blood, so is the danger great, if we receive the same unworthily. Judge therefore yourselves, &c.*"

21st. That in the rubric preceding the absolution, instead of "*pronounce this absolution,*" it be—"*Then shall the minister stand up, and turning himself to the people say, &c.*"

22d. That in the baptism of infants, parents may be admitted as sponsors.

23d. That the minister, in speaking to the Sponsors, after these words "*vouchsafe to release him,*" say—"*release him from sin.*" In the second prayer, instead of "*remission of his sins,*" read —"*remission of sin.*"

24th. That the questions addressed to the sponsors, and answers, instead of the present Form, be as follows—"*the sinful desires of the flesh.*"

25th. "*Dost thou believe the articles of the christian faith, as contained in the Apostle's creed, and wilt thou endeavour to have this child instructed accordingly?*" Answer: "*I do believe them, and, by God's help, will endeavour so to do.*"

Wilt thou endeavour to have him brought up in the fear of God, and to obey God's holy will and commandments? Answer "*I will, by God's assistance.*"

26th. That the sign of the cross may be omitted, if particularly desired by the Sponsors or Parents, and the prayer to be thus altered (by the direction of a short rubric) "*We receive this child into the congregation of Christ's flock; and pray that hereafter he may never be ashamed, &c.*" to the end.

27th. That the address—"*seeing now dearly beloved, &c.*" be omitted.

28th. That the prayer after the Lord's prayer, be thus changed—"*We yield thee hearty thanks, &c.*" to "*receive this Infant as thine own child by baptism, and to incorporate him, &c.*"

29th. That in the following exhortation, to words "*to renounce the devil and all his works,*" and in the charge to the Sponsors, the words "*vulgar tongue*" be omitted.

30th. That the forms of private baptism and of confirmation, be made conformable to these alterations.

31st. That in the exhortation before matrimony, all between these words "*holy matrimony,*" and "*therefore if any man, &c.*" be omitted.

32d. That the words "*I plight thee my troth*" be omitted in both places; and also the words—"*with my body I thee worship;*" and also —"*pledged their troth either to other.*"

33d. That all after the blessing be omitted.

34th. In the burial service, instead of the two Psalms, take the following verses of both—viz. Ps. 39, Verses 6,7,8,9,12,13, and Psalm 90, to v.

13. In the rubric, the words "*unbaptized or*" to be omitted.

For the Declaration and form of interment, beginning—"Forasmuch as &c." insert the following—viz. "*Forasmuch as it hath pleased Almighty God, in his wise Providence, to take out of this world the soul of our deceased brother (sister) lying now before us; We therefore commit his (her) body to the ground, earth to earth, ashes to ashes, dust to dust;* (thus at sea—*to the deep to be turned into corruption) looking for the general resurrection in the last day, and the life of the world to come, thro' our Lord Jesus Christ; at whose second coming in glorious Majesty, to judge the world, the earth and the sea shall give up their dead; and the corruptible bodies of those who sleep in him shall be changed, and made like unto his own glorious body, according to the mighty working, whereby he is able to subdue all things unto Himself.*"

In the sentence "*I heard a voice, &c.*" insert "*who*" for "*which.*"

The prayer following the Lord's prayer to be omitted. In the next collect, leave out the words "*as our hope is, this our brother doth.*" For "*them that,*" insert "*those who.*"

35th. In the visitation of the sick, instead of the absolution as it now stands, insert the declaration of forgiveness which is appointed for the communion service; or, either of the collects, which are taken from the Commination office, and appropriated to Ash Wednesday, may be used.

In the Psalm, omit the 3d, 6th, 8th, 9th, and 11th verses. In the Commendatory prayer, for "*miserable and naughty,*" say "*vain and miserable.*" Strike out the word "*purged.*"

In the prayer "*for persons troubled in mind,*" omit all that stands between the words "*afflicted servant,*" and "*his soul is full,*" &c. and instead thereof say "*afflicted servant, whose soul is full of trouble,*" and strike out the particle "*but,*" and proceed, "*O merciful God,*" &c.

36th. A form of Prayer and visitation of Prisoners for notorious crimes, and especially persons under sentence of death, being much wanted, the form entitled "Prayers for persons under sentence of death, agreed upon in a synod of the archbishops and bishops, and the rest of the clergy of Ireland, at Dublin, in the year 1711," as it now stands in the book of Common Prayer of the church of Ireland, is agreed upon, and ordered to be adopted, with the following alterations, viz:

For the absolution, take the same declaration of forgiveness, or either of the collects above directed for the visitation of the sick. The short collect "*O Saviour of the world,*" &c. to be left out; and for the word "*frailness,*" say "*frailty.*"

37th. In the Catechism, besides the alteration respecting the civil Powers, alter as follows: viz. "What is your name? N.M. When did you receive this name? I received it in Baptism, whereby I became a member of the christian church. what was promised for you in baptism? That I should be instructed to believe the christian faith, as contained in the Apostle's Creed, and to obey God's holy will, and keep his commandments.

Dost thou think thou art bound to believe all the articles of the christian faith, as contained in this creed, and to obey God's holy will and keep his commandments?" "Yes verily," &c.

Instead of the words "*verily, and indeed taken,*" say—"*spiritually taken.*"

Answer to question "*How many Sacraments?*" "*Two, Baptism and the Lord's Supper.*"

38th. Instead of a particular Service for the churching of women, and psalms, the following *special prayer* is to be introduced, after the General Thanksgiving; viz. This to be said, when any woman desires to return thanks, &c. "O Almighty God, we give thee most humble and hearty thanks, for that thou hast been graciously pleased to preserve this woman, thy servant, through the great pains and perils of childbirth. Incline her, we beseech thee, to show forth her thankfulness, for this thy great mercy, not only with her lips, but by a holy and virtuous life. Be pleased O God, so to establish her health, that she may lead the remainder of her days to thy honour and glory, through Jesus Christ, our Lord. Amen."

39th. The *Commination office* for Ash Wednesday to be discontinued, as it is considered rather as a discouragement to sincere Christians from coming to church on that day, than an encouragement, and therefore the three collects, the first beginning—"*O Lord, we beseech thee,*"—2d, "*O most mighty God,*"—3d, "*turn us, O Good Lord,*" shall be continued among the occasional prayer; and used after the collect on Ash Wednesday, and on such other occasions as the minister shall think fit.

Table of Holy Days.

The following Days are to be kept Holy by this Ch'h. Viz.

All the Sundays in the year in the Order enumerated in the Table of Proper Lessons with their respective Services.

Christmas
Circumcision
Epiphany
Easter Day, Monday and Tuesday
Ascension Day
Whitsunday, Monday and Tuesday

The following Days are to be observed as Days of Fasting Viz,

Good Friday and Ashwednesday

The following Days are to be observed as Days of Thanksgiving Viz, The 4th of July in Commemoration of American independence, and the first Thursday in November as a Day of Gen'l Thanksgiving.

[then follow the Articles of Religion]

9. Changes in the Proposed Book agreed on by the Maryland Convention, Annapolis, April 4, 1786

The Convention then took into serious consideration the Book of Common Prayer and administration of the Sacraments, &c., as recommended by the General Convention at Philadelphia, for the future use of the Protestant Episcopal Church in these United States; and although they could have wished that the book had been published in time enough for every member to have had a deliberate consideration and perusal of it, before the meeting of this Convention, yet nevertheless, having examined and considered it, with all the attention and care that the time of their sitting would admit, they do approve and ratify the same, as far as their powers extend, and recommend it to the use of the several churches in this State as soon as the congregations can be supplied with a sufficient number of books—proposing to the General Convention that shall meet in Philadelphia in June next, that in the future editions of the Common Prayer Book, the following additions, alterations or amendments be ordered, viz: that after the Apostles' Creed be added—'OR THIS,' inserted the Nicene Creed; so that both be not read on the same day. That in the first article of religion, the words 'true God' as applied to the Son, be changed into the words 'Eternal God.' That at the end of the first article, to the words 'Father and Son' be added the words 'very and eternal God,' as applied to the Holy Spirit, the same being in the original article. That in the Consecration Prayer, in the Holy Sacrament, after the words 'until his coming again,' and before the words 'our Saviour Jesus Christ's holy institution,' be inserted the following paragraph instead of that which now stands, viz: 'Hear us O merciful Father, we most humbly beseech thee, and of thy Almighty goodness vouchsafe so to bless and sanctify these thy creatures of bread and wine, that we receiving them according to thy Son.' And that in the baptismal office, a rubric be inserted, allowing the Minister, when many children are to be baptized at the same time, after dipping or sprinkling each child, pronouncing the words 'I baptize thee,' &c., and making the sign of the cross on the forehead, to return the child to the sponsors and say what follows for the whole number of children thus baptized, viz: 'We receive these children into the congregation of Christ's flock, and have signed them with the sign of the cross, in token,' &c.

10. Action of the New Jersey Convention with regard to the Proposed Book, May 19th, 1786

To the General Convention of the Protestant Episcopal Church in the United States of America, to be held in the city of Philadelphia in June next.

The Memorial of the Convention of the Said Church in New Jersey, now held in the city of Perth Amboy,

Respectfully showeth,

That your memorialists have unanimously approved of the alterations in liturgy, as they appear in the New Prayer Book, to render it consistent with the American revolution, and constitutions of the respective States as made and concluded on by the late General Convention of the said church, held at Philadelphia, in September and October last, they being satisfactory and agreeable to their wish.

They have also approved of their plan for obtaining consecration of Bishops, and pursuant to their recommendation, have appointed a committee to correspond with the English Bishops for that purpose.

They have also with great pleasure considered their address to the Archbishops and Bishops of the Church of England, which your memorialists are of the opinion was properly calculated to obtain the end proposed.

But it is with the greatest concern they are constrained to remark, that the other proceeding of the said Convention, in their opinion, have an undoubted tendency to prolong, if not entirely prevent, the obtaining of the Prayer thereof. In this opinion your memorialists conceive they are supported by the answer of the said venerable Bishops, with a copy of which they have been favored during their sitting at this place; for which reason, among others, they did not ratify, but disapproved of the other parts of the proceedings of the said General Convention.

Your memorialists do not question the right of every National or independent church to make such alterations from time to time, in the mode of its publick worship, as upon mature consideration may be found expedient; but they doubt the right of any order or orders of men, in an Episcopal Church without a bishop, to make any alterations not warranted by immediate necessity, especially such as not only go to the mode of worship but also to its doctrines. Wherefore your memorialists cannot forbear remarking, that, in their opinion, all unnecessary alterations must be unreasonable and impolitic, and will prove highly detrimental to the Church in General.

Your memorialists cannot approve of the said late General Convention having published in the manner they have, the new Book of Common Prayer, as altered, with the psalms and kalendar transposed and changed by their committee, without their revision and express approbation; but since they have done so, and if it was proper to have been considered, your memorialists have to regret that the same was not sooner published, that they might have been enabled to have declared the sentiments of their constituents as well as their own. The prejudices and prepossessions of mankind in favor of old customs, especially in religious matters are generally so strong as to require great delicacy and caution in the introduction of any alterations or innovations, although manifestly for the better; which was also one reason, why they could not at this time ratify the alterations so unnecessarily made. And they are very apprehensive that until alterations can be made consistent with the customs of the primitive church, and with the rules of the Church of England, from which it is our boast to have descended, a ratification of them would create great uneasiness in the minds of many members of the church, and in great probability cause dissentions and schisms. Although they may not disapprove of all the alterations made in the said new book, yet thy have to regret the unreasonableness and irregularity of them.

Your memorialists having an anxious desire of cementing, perpetuating and extending the union so happily begun in the Church, with all deference and submission, humbly request and entreat the said General Convention now soon to meet, that they will revise the proceedings of the said late convention, and their aforesaid committee, and remove every cause that may have excited any jealousy and fear, that the Episcopal Church in the United States of America have any intention or desire essentially to depart, either in doctrine or discipline, from the Church of England; but, on the contrary, to convince the world that it is their wish and intention to maintain the doctrines of the gospel, as now held by the church of England, and to adhere to the liturgy of the said church, as far as shall be consistent with the American revolution and the constitutions of the respective states: thereby removing every obstacle in the way of obtaining the consecration of such, and so many persons to the Episcopal character, as shall render our ecclesiastical government complete; and secure to the Episcopalians in America, and to their descendants, a succession of that necessary order. And they will use all means in their power to promote and perpetuate harmony and unanimity among ourselves, and with the said Church of England, as a mother or sister church, and with every Protestant Church in the universe.

By order of the Convention,
ABRAHAM BEACH, President
Perth Amboy, May 19, 1786.

11. Changes in the Proposed Book put forward by the Pennsylvania Convention, May 27, 1786

The Convention having examined the Book of Common Prayer, as revised and proposed by the General Convention of September and October last, instruct their deputies to the ensuing General Convention to propose the following amendments:—*First,* That in the Morning Prayer, the Nicene Creed be inserted after the Apostles' Creed, with the words, 'Or this,' between them, with a rubric, requiring that the Nicene be used on the following festivals, viz: on Christmas-day, the Epiphany, Easter-day, Ascension-day, Whitsunday, and Trinity Sunday. *Second,* That, in the Consecration Prayer, in the office of the Holy Sacrament, after the words, 'until his coming again,' and before the words 'according to thy Son our Saviour Jesus Christ's holy institution,' be inserted the following paragraph, instead of that now used: 'Hear us, O merciful Father, we most humbly beseech thee; and of thy almighty goodness, vouchsafe so to bless and sanctify these thy creatures of bread and wine, that we receiving them.' *Third,* That, in the communion service, where the Nicene Creed stood, there be a rubric, requiring the use of one of the Creeds, as in the Morning Prayer, when the two services shall not have been used at the same time, or in connection. *Fourth,* That, in all the offices of Baptism, the articles of the Apostles' Creed be distinctly repeated, and this question and answer inserted in the baptism of infants: Q. Wilt thou endeavor, that the child now presented to be baptized, may be instructed in this faith? A. I will. *Fifth,* That, in the burial service, the beginning of the omitted prayer be retained to these words, 'Joy and felicity' with the addition of a thanksgiving to Almighty God for the good examples of all righteous persons departed, like that in the conclusion of the prayer for Christ's Church militant. *Sixth,* That the first, fifth, and eleventh of the new articles be omitted, and the first, second, fourth, fifth, fourteenth, twenty-second, twenty-sixth, and thirtieth of the old Articles be retained. *Seventh,* That, the fourth article of the new be entitled 'Of the Creeds'; and the Nicene be recognized therein with the Apostles. *Eighth, That, the ninth of the old articles be retained as far as the word 'damnation'; and the said word to be changed to 'condemnation'. Ninth,* That, the seventeenth of the old articles be retained, with the following alteration: omit the words, 'to life,' and these, 'secret to us' with what follows to the words, 'in due season',—inclusively; inserting instead thereof 'to admit to the inestimable privileges of the Gospel dispensation all those Gentiles, as well as Jews, who should believe in his Son Jesus Christ.' After the word 'calling' insert 'of God'. End at these words 'everlasting felicity'. *Tenth,* That, the thirty-fifth article of the old book be retained, so far as it refers to the homilies, as containing godly and wholesome doctrine. *Eleventh,* That, instead of the old thirty-seventh article, there be a new one, declaratory of our allegiance to the civil authority in these states, and the obedience due to the magistrates thereof.

12. Changes in the Proposed Book put forward by the Virginia Convention, Richmond, 1786

Monday, May 29, 1786.

The Convention having met according to adjournment,

Mr. Page, from the Committee appointed to consider the report of the Select Committee, so far as relates to the Articles of Religion, reported, That they had gone through the business to them referred, and come to several resolutions thereon, which were read, and ordered to be referred to a Committee of the Whole Convention.

The Convention having, according to order, resolved itself into a Committee of the Whole Convention on the report above referred—after some time spent therein, Mr. President resumed the Chair, and the Hon. Mr. Blair reported, That the said Committee had, according to order, gone through the business to them referred, and made some amendments therein, which were read, and, when further amended, agreed to, as followeth:—

Resolved, That the first article of Religion be agreed to.

In the second article, lines 13th and 14th, strike out the words *was never any,* and insert, *there is no.*

Resolved, That such part of the second article as related to the books commonly called Apocryphal, ought to be expunged.

Resolved, That the third article be agreed to.

In the fourth article after the word *creed* insert, *as contained in the Book of Common Prayer recommended by the late General Convention.*

Resolved, That the fifth and sixth Articles be agreed to.

In the 7th article strike out the words

justified by faith only, in the seventh line, and inset *thus justified by faith.*

Resolved, That the 8th, 9th, and 10th articles be agreed to.

Resolved, That the eleventh article on predestination be omitted.

Resolved, That the 12th, 13th, and 14th articles be agreed to.

In the 15th article strike out the words, *as by an instrument*, in the seventh line.

Resolved, That the 18th, 19th and 20th articles be agreed to.

On a motion Resolved, That the Convention will to-morrow proceed by ballot to the appointment of deputies to the next General Convention.

On a motion Resolved, That the Committee appointed to draw up instructions for the deputies to the General Convention be directed, among other things, to instruct them to move for such alterations in the book of Common Prayer and Articles of Religion as shall be agreed to by this Convention, as fit to be proposed to the General Convention.

Resolved, That the order of the day for the Convention to resolve itself into a Committee of the Whole Convention on the report of the Select Committee, be put off until to-morrow.

The Convention adjourned till to-morrow, 10 o'clock.

Tuesday, May 30, 1786.

On a motion, Ordered, That the thanks of this Convention be given to the late deputies who attended the General Convention held at Phila for their diligent attention to the interests of the Church, and faithful discharge of the duties of their appointment.

Mr. Wormeley, from the Committee appointed to draw up instructions for the deputies of the next General Convention, presented a draught of such instructions, which were read, and, with some amendments, agreed to as followeth:—

Gentlemen,—You are instructed to move for such alterations in the Book of Common Prayer and Articles of Religion as shall be agreed upon by this Convention as fit to be proposed to the General Convention.

We consider the Protestant Episcopal Church in America as an incorporate Society, and therefore unity in doctrine and worship its characteristic: Conformably to this, you will not carp at expression, nor carry your objections to unessential points; guarding against schisms by all possible means, and giving our Church every benefit and strength it can acquire from union.

It is superfluous to observe to you, that the sooner our Church can have the benefit of Episcopal superintendence, the nearer it will approach to perfection; and to recommend to your attention the aid of this necessary character.

On the same day the following resolution was also adopted:—

Resolved, That the Book of Common Prayer as recommended by the late General Convention be approved, ratified and used, except the rubric before the Communion Service, and such alterations of the Arts. as are referred to the consideration of the next General Convention; and that the Psalms be used as heretofore until a sufficient number of the new books can be procured.

13. Changes in the Proposed Book put forward by the South Carolina Convention, May 31st, 1786

The Convention resumed the consideration of the Report of the Committee for revising the Liturgy of the Church of England; which being read, is as follows:

The Committee appointed to examine the alteration of the Liturgy, as set forth by the

General Convention held in Philadelphia; Report,

That the punctuation throughout be critically attended to.

The first introductory sentence to be adopted, and expunge the rest. And after reading the *first*, proceed to the Apostles' creed, and there leave out the word *again*, between the words *rose* and *from*. But if the whole of the introductory sentences as they now stand, should be approved, the words, *God is*, instead of *He is*, to be used in the concluding one. At the conclusion of the address to the congregation, after the word *saying*, omit the words *after me*. The Declaration to remain as in the original absolution, only expunging the word *power*. The Lord's Prayer to be transposed after the words in the Litany, *neither reward us after our Iniquities*. The sentences after the Lord's Prayer to be expunged, except the *two first;* and the *Venite* to conclude with the *Gloria Patri*. In the *Te Deum*, instead of *pure Virgin*, read *the Blessed*, and add the word *most*, between *thy* and *precious blood*. And instead of *as our Trust*, read *for our Trust*. The *Benedictus* to be omitted. After the *Jubilate* expunge the sentences, *O Lord bless &c.* and *mercifully hear, &c.* Before the Litany add to the Rubric in Italics, to correspond with our mode of praying for the sick. When the prayers of the congregation are desired for a sick person or persons, the Minister shall say, *The prayers of this Congregation are desired for, &c.* In the Litany expunge after *others in authority*, the words *Legislative, Executive and Judicial*. Instead of *women in childbirth*, read *all women through the Perils of childbirth*. Use the words *young children*, before *all sick persons;* with an asterisk * of accommodation, when any body particularly desires the prayers of the congregation, and to be printed as in the *prayer for all conditions of men*. In the last response immediately before the prayer, *We humbly beseech thee*, instead of *as we*, read, *for we do put &c.*

Evening Service. The first sentence and Belief as in the Morning Service. The *Magnificat* and *Nunc Dimittis* to be omitted. The *Gloria Patri* to be used at the conclusion of *Deus miseratur*. Then proceed to the vesicles before the Lord's Prayer, *The Lord be with you*, and go on with the Lord's Prayer, &c. till you come to *bless and preserve these states*, which omit, but use all the rest, and then begin the prayers with the Collect for the Day, as in the old form, 3d Collect. The Collect in the old Liturgy to be retained. The Prayer for fair weather, to be altered as follows: *O Almighty and Merciful God, although we for our Iniquities have worthily deserved a plague of rain and waters, yet of thy bountiful goodness, send us, we beseech thee, such favourable weather, &c.*

Communion Service. Part of the Rubrick at the conclusion of this Service (as now printed) to be transposed, and make it the first rubric at the beginning of the Service. Expunge the word *and*, before *if any of the Consecrated*. In the exhortation, *Dearly beloved in the Lord*, instead of *Guilty of the blood, &c.* use a Colon after unworthily, and read thus; *for thereby we profane the Body and Blood, &c.*

Public Baptism. In the four petitions for the Child's sanctification, read thus: *O! merciful God grant that all carnal affections may die in this child, and that all things, &c.* The third wholly approved of. The fourth, omit the words *by our office and ministry*. These alterations will apply to Baptism of such as are of Riper Years. In the consecration of the water, instead of *therein*, read *therewith* (in Italics). In Rubrick, expunge, *and warily*.

Catechism. Make this alteration in explication of the Lord's Prayer. Instead of words *Ghostly and Bodily*, read *dangers spiritual and temporal;* and expunge, *from our Ghostly enemy*. To preserve the analogy in the answer, *of what is the outward visible sign or form in Baptism*, read, *water wherewith*, instead of water whereis.

Confirmation. Omit the word *Ghostly*.

Matrimony. After the words, *Dearly beloved* in the Exhortation, read as follows, *the holy Estate of Matrimony instituted of God, is not by any to be entered into unadvisedly or lightly, but reverently and discreetly, in the fear of God. I therefore require and charge, &c.* till you come to the word *coupled,* which read *united otherwise than God's word doth allow, their marriage is not lawful.* Expunge the Rubrick, between the mutual stipulation of the Man and Woman. For if the man with his right hand takes the woman by her right hand, they have consequently a mutual hold on each other. On putting the ring on the woman's finger, say, *with this Ring I thee wed, In the Name of the Father, and of the Son and of the Holy Ghost.*

BURIAL. That the Lesson is not printed at large; recommend that it be.

Expunge in the Interment, *lying before us.* Quere? Whether the words, *as our Hope is this our Brother doth,* is not a typographical omission.

FOURTH OF JULY. Expunge the words in the Collect, *all Churches of the Saints.*

SERVICE AT SEA. Last Collect; instead of, *in our lives,* read thus, *such as may appear by an humble, holy and obedient life, before thee all our days.*

ART. 1. Expunge the word *both,* before *visible;* ditto after *man's nature* read thus, *by humbling himself to be born of the blessed Virgin, and thereby became God and Man in one Christ.*

ART. 2. At the conclusion, omit the word *of,* and read *was never doubted in the Church.*

ART. 3. Add the words *through and,* after mankind.

ART. 16. Instead of *Christian men,* read *Christians.*

Signed,

HENRY PURCELL,
Rector of St. Michael's.

EDWARD ELLINGTON.
Rector of St. James', Goose-Creek.

ROBERT SMITH.

The report being gone through, and the alterations suggested being approved, the Deputies to the General Convention are desired to use their endeavours to get them adopted, at the next meeting, on the 3d Thursday in June.

On motion, Resolved, that the Liturgy, as altered by the Convention held in Philadelphia in September last, be used in the Protestant Episcopal Church in this State, on Sunday next, being Whitsunday.

14. Action of the New York Convention with regard to the Proposed Book, June 14th, 1786

Resolved, That (out of respect to the English Bishops and because the minds of the people are not yet sufficiently informed) the consideration of the Book of Common Prayer with the proposed alterations be deferred to a future day.

15. Changes in the Proposed Book suggested by the English Bishops, June, 1786

To the Committee of the General Convention at Philadelphia, The Rev. Dr. White, President, The Rev. Dr. Smith, The Rev. Mr. Provoost, The Hon. James Duane, Samuel Powell, and Richard Peters, Esqrs.

MR. PRESIDENT AND GENTLEMEN:

INFLUENCED by the same sentiments of fraternal regard, expressed by the Archbishops and Bishops in their answer to your address, we desire you to be persuaded, that if we have not yet been able to comply with your request, the delay has proceeded from no tardiness on our part. The only cause of it has been the uncertainty in which we were left by receiving your address, unaccompanied by those communications with regard to your Liturgy, Articles and Ecclesiastical Constitution, without the knowledge of which we could not presume to apply to the Legislature for such powers as were necessary to the completion of your wishes. The Journal of your Convention, and the first part of your Liturgy, did not reach us till more than two months after our receipt of your address; and we were not in possession of the remaining part of it, and of your articles until the last day of April. The whole of your communications was then, with as little delay as possible, taken into consideration at a meeting of the Archbishops and fifteen of the Bishops, being all who were then in London and able to attend; and it was impossible not to observe with concern, that if the essential doctrines of our common faith were retained, less respect, however, was paid to our Liturgy than its own excellence, and your declared attachment to it, had led us to expect; not to mention a variety of verbal alterations, of the necessity or propriety of which we are by no means satisfied, we saw with grief that two of the Confessions of our Christian faith, respectable for their antiquity, have been entirely laid aside; and that even in that called the Apostles' Creed, an article is omitted which was thought necessary to be inserted, with a view to a particular heresy, in a very early age of the Church, and has ever since had the venerable sanction of universal reception. Nevertheless, as a proof of the sincere desire which we feel to continue in spiritual communion with the members of your Church in America, and to complete the Orders of your Ministry, and trusting that the communications which we shall make to you, on the subject of these and some other alterations, will have their desired effect, we have, even under these circumstances, prepared a Bill for conveying to us the powers necessary for this purpose. It will in a few days be presented to Parliament, and we have the best reasons to hope that it will receive the assent of the Legislature. This Bill will enable the Archbishops and Bishops to give Episcopal consecration to the persons who shall be recommended, without requiring from them any oaths or subscriptions inconsistent with the situation in which the late Revolution has placed them; upon condition that the full satisfaction of the sufficiency of the persons recommended, which you offer us in your address, be given to Archbishops and Bishops. You will doubtless receive it as a mark both of our friendly disposition toward you, and of our desire to avoid all delay on this occasion, that we have taken this earliest opportunity of conveying to you this intelligence, and that we proceed (as supposing ourselves invested with that power which for your sakes we have requested) to state to you particularly the several heads upon which that satisfaction which you offer will be accepted, and the mode in which it may be given. The anxiety which is shown by the Church of England to prevent the intrusion of unqualified persons into even the inferior offices of our Ministry, confirms our own sentiments, and points it out to be our duty, very earnestly to require the most decisive proofs of the qualifications of those who may be offered for admission to that Order to which the superintendence of those offices is committed. At our several Ordinations of a Deacon and a Priest, the candidate submits himself to the examination of the bishop as to his proficiency in learning; he gives the proper security of his soundness in the Faith by the subscriptions which are made previously necessary; he is required to bring testimonials of his virtuous conversation during the three preceding years; and that no mode of inquiry may be omitted, public notice of his offering himself to be ordained is given in the Parish church where he resides or ministers, and the people are solemnly called upon to declare if they know any impediment, for the which he ought not to be admitted. At the time of Ordination, too, the same solemn call is made on the congregations then present.

Examination, subscription, and testimonials

are not indeed repeated at the consecration of an English bishop, because the person to be consecrated has added to the securities given at his former Ordinations, that sanction which arises from his having constantly lived and exercised his ministry under the eyes and observation of his country. But the objects of our present consideration are very differently circumstanced; their sufficiency in learning, the soundness of their faith, and the purity of their manners, are not matters of notoriety here. Means, therefore, must be found to satisfy the Archbishop who consecrates, and the Bishops who present them, that, in the words of our Church, "they be apt and meet for their learning and godly conversation, to exercise their ministry duly to the honour of God and the edifying of his Church, and to be wholesome examples and patterns to the flock of Christ."

With regard to the first qualification, sufficiency in good learning, we apprehend that the subjecting a person, who is to be admitted to the office of a Bishop in the church, to that examination which is required previous to the ordination of Priests and Deacons, might lessen that reverend estimation which ought never to be separated from the Episcopal character: we therefore do not require any further satisfaction on this point, that will be given to us by the forms of testimonials in the annexed paper, fully trusting that those who sign them will be well aware, how greatly incompetence in this respect must lessen the weight and authority of the bishop and affect the credit of the Episcopal Church.

Under the second head, that of subscription, our desire is to require that subscription only to be repeated, which you have already been called upon to make by the Tenth Article of your Ecclesiastical Constitution: but we should forget the duty which we owe to our own Church, and act inconsistently with that sincere regard which we bear to yours, if we were not explicit in declaring, that, after the disposition we have shown to comply with the prayer of your address, we think it now incumbent upon you to use your utmost exertions also for the removal of any stumbling-block of offence which may possibly prove an obstacle to the success of it. We therefore most earnestly exhort you, that previously to the time of your making such subscription, you restore to its integrity the Apostles' Creed, in which you have omitted an article, merely, as it seems, from misapprehension of the sense in which it is understood by our Church; nor can we help adding, that we hope you will think it but a decent proof of the attachment which you profess to the services of our Liturgy, to give to the other two Creeds a place in your Book of Common Prayer, even though the use of them should be left discretional. We should be inexcusable, too, if, at the time when you are requesting the establishment of Bishops in your church, we did not strongly represent to you that the Eighth Article of your Ecclesiastical Constitution appears to us to be a degradation of the Clerical, and still more of the Episcopal character. We persuade ourselves, that in your ensuing Convention some alteration will be thought necessary in this article, before this reaches you; or, it not, that due attention will be given to it in consequence of our representation.

On the third and last head, which respects purity of manners, the reputation of the Church, both in England and America, and the interest of our common Christianity is so deeply concerned in it, that we feel it our indispensable duty to provide, on this subject, the most effectual securities. It is presumed, that the same previous public notice of the intention of the person to be consecrated, will be given in the Church where he resides in America, for the same reasons, and therefore nearly in the same form with that used in England before our Ordinations. The call upon the persons present at the time of consecration, must be deemed of little use before a congregation composed of those to whom the person to be consecrated is unknown. The testimonials signed by persons living in England admit of reference and examination, and the characters of those who give them are subject to scrutiny, and in cases of criminal deceit to punishment. In proportion as these circumstances are less applicable to testimonials from America, those testimonials must be more explicit, and supported by a greater number of signatures. We therefore think it necessary that the several persons, candidates for Episcopal consecration, should bring us, both a testimonial from the General Convention of the Protestant Episcopal Church, with as many signatures as can be obtained, and a more particular one, from the respective Conventions in those States which recommend them. It will appear from the tenor of the letters testimonial used in England, a form of which is annexed, that the ministers who sign them bear testimony to the qualifications of the candidates on their own personal knowledge. Such a testimony is not to be expected from the members of the General Convention of the Episcopal Church in America on this occasion. We think it sufficient, therefore, that they declare they know no impediment, but believe the person to be consecrated is of a virtuous life and sound faith. We have sent you such a form as appears to us proper to be used for that purpose. More specific declarations must be made by members of the Convention each State from which the persons offered for consecration are respectively recommended; their personal knowledge of them there can be no doubt of; we trust, therefore, they will have no objection to the adoption of the form of a testimonial which is annexed, and drawn upon the same principles, and containing the same attestations of person knowledge with that above mentioned, as acquired previously to our Ordinations. We trust we shall receive these testimonials signed by such a majority in each Convention that recommend, as to leave no doubt of the fitness of the candidates upon the minds of those whose consciences are concerned in the consecration of them.

Thus much we have thought it right to communicate to you, without reserve, at present, intending to give you further information as soon as we are able. In the mean time, we pray God to direct your counsels in this very weighty matter, and are,

Mr. President and gentlemen,

Your affectionate Brethren,

J. CANTUAR

W. EBOR.

---

16. Changes in the Proposed Book adopted by the General Convention at Wilmington, October 11th, 1786

An Act of the General Convention of Clerical and Lay Deputies of the Protestant Episcopal Church, in the States of New York, New Jersey, Pennsylvanian, Delaware, and South Carolina, held at Wilmington, in the State of Delaware, on Wednesday, the 11th of October, 1786.

WHEREAS, at a General Convention of clerical and Lay Deputies of the Protestant Episcopal church in sundry of the United States of America, viz., New York, New Jersey, Pennsylvania, Delaware, Maryland, Virginia, and South Carolina, holden at the City of Philadelphia, on the Tuesday before the Feast of St. Michael, in the year of our Lord, 1785, and divers subsequent days, it was agreed and declared, that "The Book of Common Prayer and Administration of the Sacraments and other Rites and Ceremonies of the Church, according to the use of the Church of England," should be continued to be used by this Church, as the same was altered by the said Convention, in a certain instrument of writing, passed by their authority, intituled "Alterations of the Liturgy of the Protestant Episcopal Church in the United States of

America, in order to render the same conformable to the American Revolution and the Constitutions of the respective States." And it was further agreed and declared, that the Book of Common Prayer and Administration of the Sacraments and other rites and Ceremonies of the Church, according to the use of the Church of England, as altered by an instrument of writing passed under the authority of the aforesaid Convention, intituled, "Alterations in the Book of Common Prayer and Administration of the Sacraments and other Rites and Ceremonies of the Church, according to the use of the Church of England, proposed and recommended to the Protestant Episcopal Church in the United States of America, should be used in this Church, when the same should have been ratified by the conventions which had respectively sent deputies to the said General Convention." And thereupon the said Convention, anxious to complete their Episcopal system by means of the Church of England, did transcribe and transmit an address to the Most Reverend and Right Revered the Archbishops of Canterbury and York, and the Bishops of the Church of England, earnestly entreating that venerable body to confer the Episcopal character on such persons as should be recommended by this Church in the several States so represented.

And whereas the Clerical and Lay Deputies of this Church have received the most friendly and affectionate letters, in answer to the said address, from the said Archbishops and Bishops, opening a fair prospect of the success of their said application, but at the same time earnestly exhorting this Convention to use their utmost exertions for the removal of certain objections by them made, against some parts of the alterations in the Book of Common Prayer and Rites and Ceremonies of this Church last mentioned. In pursuance whereof, this present General Convention hath been called and is now assembled: and being sincerely desirous to give every satisfaction to their Lordships which will be consistent with the union and general content of this Church they represent, and declaring their steadfast resolution to maintain the same essential Articles of Faith and Discipline with the church of England:

Now, therefore, the said Deputies do hereby determine and declare:

First,—That in the Creed commonly called the Apostles' Creed, these words, "He descended into Hell," shall be and continue a part of that Creed.

Secondly,—That the Nicene Creed shall also be inserted in the said Book of Common Prayer, immediately after the Apostles' Creed, prefaced with the Rubrick (or this).

And whereas,—In consequence of the objections expressed by their Lordships to the alterations in the Book of Common Prayer last mentioned, the Conventions in some of the States represented in this General Convention had suspended the ratification and use of the said Book of Common Prayer, by reason whereof it will be improper that persons to be consecrated or ordained as Bishops, Priest, or Deacons respectively, should subscribed the declaration contained in the Tenth Article of the of the General Ecclesiastical Constitution, without some modification:

Therefore it is hereby determined and declared,

Thirdly,—That the second clause so to be subscribed by a Bishop, Priest, or Deacon of this Church, in any of the States which have not already ratified or used the last-mentioned Book of Common Prayer, shall be in the words following: "And I do solemnly engage to conform to the doctrine and worship of the Protestant Episcopal Church, according to the use of the Church of England, as the same is altered by the General Convention, in a certain instrument of writing passed by their authority, intituled, 'Alterations of the Liturgy of the Protestant Episcopal Church in the United States of America, in order to render the same conformable to the American Revolution and the Constitution of the respective States,' until the new Book of Common Prayer, recommended by the General Convention, shall be ratified or used in the State in which I am—(Bishop, or Deacon, as the case may be)—by the authority of the Convention thereof. And I do further solemnly engage, that when the said New Book of Common Prayer shall be ratified or used by the authority of the Convention in the State for which I am consecrated a Bishop—(or ordained a Priest or Deacon)—I will conform to the doctrines and worship of the Protestant Episcopal Church, as settled and determined in the last-mentioned Book of Common Prayer and administration of the Sacraments, set forth by the General Convention of the Protestant Episcopal Church in the United States."

And it is hereby further determined and declared,

That these words in the Preface to the new proposed Book of Common Prayer, viz., "In the Creed commonly called 'the Apostles' Creed,' one clause is omitted, as being of uncertain meaning, and"—together with the note referred to in that place, be from henceforth no part of the Preface to the said proposed Book of Common Prayer.

And it hereby further determined and declared,

That the Fourth Article of Religion in the new proposed Book of Common Prayer, be altered to render it conformable to the adoption of the Nicene Creed, as follows: "Of the Creeds. The two Creeds, namely, that commonly called the Apostles' Creed and the Nicene Creed, ought to be received and believed, because they," etc., etc.

Done in General Convention, at Wilmington, in the State of Delaware, the day and year first aforesaid.

17. Alterations Proposed at the General Convention of 1826, at the request of Bishop Hobart

The House of Bishops, deeply solicitous to preserve unimpaired the Liturgy of the Church, and yet desirous to remove the reasons alleged from the supposed length of the service, for the omission of some of its parts, and particularly for the omission of that part of the communion office, which is commonly called the *Ante-*Communion office, do *unanimously* propose to the House of Clerical and Lay Deputies, the following resolutions, to be submitted to the several State Conventions, in order to be acted upon at the next General Convention, agreeably to the Eighth Art. of the Constitution.

1. Resolved,—That in "The Order how the Psalter is appointed to be read," the following be added the fourth paragraph "or any other psalm or psalms, except in those days in which proper psalms are appointed:" so that the whole paragraph will read as follows: "The minister, instead of reading from the Psalter as divided for daily Morning and Evening Prayer may read one of the selections set out by this Church, or any other psalm or psalms, except in those days in which 'proper psalms' are appointed."

2. Resolved,—That in "The order how the rest of the holy Scripture is appointed to be read," the following be inserted after the fifth paragraph: "The minister may, at his discretion, instead of the entire lessons, read suitable portions thereof, not less than fifteen verses. And on other days than Sundays and holy days, in those places where morning and evening prayer is not daily used, he may read other portions of the Old and New Testaments, instead of the prescribed lessons; it being recommended that, unless circumstances render it inexpedient, on the

stated prayer days of Wednesdays and Fridays, the lessons for those days, or for one of the intervening days be read."

The Bishops in the use of the office of confirmation, finding that the preface is frequently not suited to the age and character of those who are presented for this holy ordinance, unanimously propose the following resolution:

3. Resolved,—that after the present preface in the office of Confirmation, the following be inserted, to be used instead of the former, at the discretion of the Bishop: "It appears from holy Scripture, that the Apostles laid their hands on those who were baptized; and this ordinance, styled by the apostle Paul, the 'laying on of hands,' and ranked by him among the principles of the doctrine of Christ, has been retained in the Church, under the name of *Confirmation*; and is very convenient, and proper to be observed, to the end that persons being sufficiently instructed in what they promised, or what was promised for them in their baptism, and being in other respects, duly qualified, may themselves, with their own mouth and consent, openly before the Church, ratify and confirm the same, and also promise, that by the grace of God, they will evermore endeavour themselves faithfully to observe such things as they, by their own confession, have assented unto."

And to correct the injurious misapprehension, as to the meaning of certain terms, in the first collect of the office of confirmation, the Bishops *unanimously* propose the following resolution:

4. Resolved,—That after the first collect in the office of Confirmation, the following be inserted, to be used at the discretion of the bishop, instead of the first collect, "Almighty and everliving God, who hast vouchsafed, in baptism, to regenerate these thy Servants, by water and the Holy Ghost; thus giving them a title to all the blessings of thy covenant of grace and mercy, in thy Son Jesus Christ, and now dost graciously confirm unto them, ratifying the promises then made, all their holy privileges; grant unto them, we beseech thee, O Lord, the renewing of the Holy Ghost; strengthen them with the power of this divine Comforter; and daily increase in them thy manifold gifts of grace, the spirit of wisdom and understanding, the spirit of counsel and ghostly strength, the spirit of knowledge and true godliness, and fill them, O Lord, with the spirit of thy holy fear, now and forever. *Amen.*"

And whereas, in the opinion of the Bishops, there is no doubt as to the obligation of ministers to say, on all Sundays and other holy days, that part of the communion office which is commonly called the ante-communion, yet as the practice of some of the clergy is not conformable to this construction of the rubric on this point, the House of Bishops propose the following resolution:

5. Resolved,—That the following be adopted as a substitute for the first sentence in the rubric, immediately after the communion office:

"On all Sundays and other holy days, shall be said, all that is appointed at the Communion, unto the end of the Gospel, concluding divine Service, in all cases when there is a Sermon or Communion, when there is not, with the blessing."

18. The Muhlenberg Memorial

1853

TO THE BISHOPS OF THE PROTESTANT EPISCOPAL CHURCH, IN COUNCIL ASSEMBLED:

RIGHT REVEREND FATHERS:—

The undersigned, presbyters of the Church of which you have the oversight, venture to approach your venerable body with an expression of sentiment, which their estimate of your office in relation to the times does not permit them to withhold. In so doing, they have confidence in your readiness to appreciate their motives and their aims. The actual posture of our Church with reference to the great moral and social necessities of the day, presents to the mind of the undersigned a subject of grave and anxious thought. Did they suppose that this was confined to themselves, they would not feel warranted in submitting it to your attention; but they believe it to be participated in by many of their brethren, who may not have seen the expediency of declaring their views, or at least a mature season for such a course.

The divided and distracted state of our American Protestant Christianity, the new and subtle forms of unbelief adapting themselves with the fatal success to the spirit of the age, the consolidated forces of Romanism bearing with renewed skill and activity against the Protestant faith, and as more or less the consequence of these, the utter ignorance of the Gospel among so large a portion of the lower classes of our population, making a heathen world in our midst, are among the considerations which induce your memorialists to present the inquiry whether the period has not arrived for the adoption of measures, to meet these exigencies of the times, more comprehensive than any yet provided for by our present ecclesiastical system: in other words, whether the Protestant Episcopal Church, with only her present canonical means and appliances, her fixed and invariable modes of public worship, and her traditional customs and usages, is competent to the work of preaching and dispensing the Gospel to all sorts and conditions of men, and so adequate to do the work of the Lord in this land and in this age? This question, your petitioners, for their own part, and in consonance with many thoughtful minds among us, believe must be answered in the negative. Their memorial proceeds on the assumption that our Church, confined to the exercise of her present system, is not sufficient to the great purposes above-mentioned—that a wider door must be opened for admission to the Gospel ministry, than that through which her candidates for holy orders are now obliged to enter. Besides such candidates among her own members, it is believed that men can be found among the other bodies of Christians around us, who would gladly receive ordination at your hands, could they obtain it, without that entire surrender which would now be required of them, of *all* the liberty in public worship to which they have been accustomed—men, who could not bring themselves to conform in all particulars to our prescriptions and customs, but yet sound in the faith, and who having the gifts of preachers and pastors, would be able ministers of the New Testament. With deference it is asked, ought such an accession to your means, in executing your high commission, "Go into all the world and preach the Gospel to every creature," be refused, for the sake of conformity in matters recognized in the preface to the Book of Common Prayer as unessentials? Dare we pray the Lord of the harvest, to send forth laborers into the harvest, while we reject all laborers but those of one peculiar type? The extension of orders to the class of men contemplated (with whatever safeguards, not infringing on evangelical freedom, which your wisdom might deem expedient) appears to your petitioners to be a subject supremely worthy of your deliberations.

In addition to the prospect of the immediate good which would thus be opened, an important step would be taken toward the effecting of a Church unity in the Protestant Christendom of our land. To become a central bond of union among Christians, who, though differing in name, yet hold to the one Faith, the one Lord, and the one Baptism, and who need only such a bond to be drawn together in closer and more primitive fellowship, is here believed to be the peculiar province and high privilege of your venerable body as a College of CATHOLIC AND APOSTOLIC BISHOPS *as such*.

This leads your petitioners to declare the ultimate design of their memorial—which is to submit the practicability, under your auspices, of some ecclesiastical system, broader and more comprehensive than that which you now administer, surrounding and including the Protestant Episcopal Church as it now is, leaving that Church untouched, identical with that Church in all its great principles, yet providing for as much freedom in opinion, discipline, and worship, as is compatible with the essential faith and order of the Gospel. To define and act upon such a system, it is believed, must sooner or later be the work of an American Catholic Episcopate.

In justice to themselves on this occasion, your memorialists beg leave to remark that, although aware that the foregoing views are not confined to their own small number, they have no reason to suppose that any other parties contemplate a public expression of them, like the present. Having therefore undertaken it, they trust that they have not laid themselves open to the charge of unwarranted intrusion. They find their warrant in the prayer now offered up by all our congregations, "that the comfortable Gospel of Christ may be truly preached, truly received, and truly followed, in all places, to the breaking down of the kingdom of Sin, Satan, and Death." Convinced that, for the attainment of these blessed ends, there must be some greater concert of action among Protestant Christians, than any which yet exists, and believing that with you, Right Reverend Fathers, it rests to take the first measures tending thereto, your petitioners could not do less than humbly submit their memorial to such consideration as in your wisdom you may see fit to give it. Praying that it may not be dismissed without reference to a Commission, and assuring you, Right Reverend Fathers, of our dutiful veneration and esteem.

We are,

Most Respectfully,

Your Brethren and Servants
in the Gospel of Christ,

W. A. Muhlenberg,
C. F. Cruse,
Philip Berry,
Edward Harwood
G. T. Bedell,
Henry Gregory,
Alex. H. Vinton,
M. A. De Wolfe Howe,
S. H. Turner,
S. R. Johnson,
C. W. Andrews,
F. E. Lawrence,
and others.

New York, *October 14th,* 1853.

Concurring in the main purport of the above memorial, and believing that the necessities of the times call for some special efforts to promote unity among Christian, and to enlarge for that and other great ends the efficiency of the Protestant Episcopal church, but not being able to adopt certain suggestions of the memorial, the undersigned most heartily join in the prayer that the subject may be referred to a Commission of your Venerable Body.

John Henry Hobart
A. Cleveland Coxe,
Ed. Y. Higbee,
Francis Vinton,
Isaac G. Hubbard,
and others.

---

19. An Exposition of the Memorial

of Sundry Presbyters
of the Protestant Episcopal Church; Presented
to the House of Bishops, During the General
Convention of Said Church, 1853.

By One of the Memorialists
[Wm. A. Muhlenberg]

* * * We are not asking how far others possess that divine note of an evangelical church—the preaching of the Gospel to the poor—but how far we possess it ourselves. No other answer can be made than the confession that we are miserably wanting.

By common consent the memorial is sustained in that the P. E. Church does not dispense the Gospel to all sorts and conditions of men, in the measure (for this must be meant) which is due from a branch of the Catholic Church of Christ.

And now what is the cause? Where does the fault lie? Evidently it must lie either in the Church's system or in the administration of that system; or it may be distributed between both—in what proportions need not just now be said. The fault cannot be wholly in the administration of our system, for that would argue a greater degree of incompetency or lukewarmness in our clergy and laity than could be shown to exist. Our clergy, taken as a whole, no one charges with want either of ability or of zeal. Their labours will compare with those of any body of clergy in the land. * * *

[Our Church] is not equipped for availing herself of opportunities as they occur. She is encumbered by her own apparatus. She is like David in Saul's armor, but not like him expert in using the sling and the stone. She proceeds warily and according to rule; hence she fails to be "instant in season and out of season" in doing the Master's work. Thus there is fault in her modes and methods themselves, not simply the application of them. In asserting this the memorial does not more than give bent to what is extensively felt and acknowledged among us. Many of the best friends of the church, alive to all her excellences, are beginning to see that she is too purely a conservative body—that she is deficient in flexibility and in the power of adaptation to time and circumstances—that her way of proceeding is too much one and the same on all occasions, at all times and with all kinds of persons.

This unaccommodativeness of the church might be shown in various respects. We see it most strikingly in the character of her fixed public services. Excellent and beyond compare as these services are, evidently they are calculated only for devout and well-ordered congregations. They are suited to those who are accustomed to them—or, to express the fact more definitely, the services of the church are adapted only to "assemblies of the faithful." In truth, they were made for no other. The Prayer Book, throughout, is constructed on the hypothesis of the sincere faith and piety of the worshipper. This underlies all the parts of it. From the Baptismal office in which the infant avows itself a Christian, to the Burial rite in which every one is interred "in the sure and certain hope of a resurrection to eternal life"[15] they all suppose true believing people. they were not composed for any other sort of people. but, unhappily, the world is full of other sort of people; the church is in the midst of other sort of people; she has them on every side of her, yet she can never proceed to preach the Gospel to them, except on the violent presumption that they are what they are not—seeing the first thing she does, of whatever description be the hearers, is to address them as believers, and exhort them to unite in a service designed for such and such alone.

Preaching the gospel is one thing,[16] Divine worship is another. The former is to prepare men for the latter. The church reverses the order in every case in which the Christian character of the assembly may not be fairly presumed, and the fixed order being always to begin with the prescribed acts of worship. She thus makes no provision for preaching, apart from acts of worship. The two are not necessarily conjoined.[17] There may be occasions for the one, or the other, or for both. So it was in the beginning. The Apostles proclaimed the Gospel in the courts of the temple, in the synagogues, in the streets, wherever they could get hearers, for the purpose of making converts to their doctrine; the converts met in places and companies of their own for prayer, for the breaking of bread, and the several acts of Christian worship. So it should be still, if the church means to deal at all with ignorant, unconverted, unbaptized men—that is, if she means to make aggression on the world. She would then find occasions for preaching the Gospel, that might, or might not, be connected with formal acts of worship. As she ignores such occasions by not taking them into account, she ignores her aggressive office.[18]

Again, our mode of worship with its "decent pomp," with its chaste and sober forms couched in general terms, leaving the worshippers to make the particular applications, from time to time, for themselves, with its condensed and classic style (as especially in the collects) commends itself, we must own, rather to persons of cultivated or, at least of somewhat regulated minds.[19] People of ordinary cast, not used to keeping their emotions under restraint, sympathize more readily with more spontaneous worship, appreciate more diffusive language in prayer, and desire the specific expression of what they feel at the time. Hence there seems to them more of reality and freshness in the devotions of "the meeting" than of the church. They think the minister prays more from the heart when he utters himself *impromptu,* than when he reads from a book. They can, indeed, be taught better. But we must take men as they are; at any rate, when we begin with them we must take them as they are. We must accommodate ourselves to them—we must lead them on by degrees. After all we shall never wholly eradicate the feeling in question from the popular mind. In fact it comes of the essential subjectivity of Protestantism; and if our church will make no provision for it, if she will treat it only as a vulgar prejudice not to be indulged, then, so far, it is her fault that she does not reach more extensively the Protestant mind and heart. For the vulgar prejudice, however, we continually do make allowance. What is more common than for one, priding himself on being a good churchman, nevertheless to be quite content that his domestics, or other dependents, should be "dissenters?" While he repairs to church, he reckons it quite in order that they should go to "meeting," where, he allows, the prayers, the preaching, and the ways in general are more congenial with their tastes and feelings, and so, on the whole, more edifying. On no account would he cross the threshold of a "dissenting" place of worship himself, yet he has no fear that the souls of his servants, of whom, as *paterfamilias,* he has the charge, are in any jeopardy, though they worship nowhere else. This being so, might we not suspect that possibly something is to be learned from the meeting? It may be part of our orthodoxy to believe that every thing is wrong there, and that every thing is and must be right in the Church. Still the meeting outnumbers the Church. To be sure, we may recollect that it is a little flock, to which the Lord has promised the kingdom; not, however, without some misgivings whether just that be the little flock which includes so many more of the rich than of the poor in its fold. * * *

Further, trying the system by its fruits, as the church has failed in preaching for the people, so she has failed in songs for the people. Neither is this a minor failure. Singing in metre is ever the delight of the masses moved by religion. The hymn in the church answers to the ballad in the nation. The chorales of Luther did as much for the Reformation as his preaching. Not to cite from history the many instances in point, what would Methodism, at its rise, have done without its hymnody? What would it do now? * * * The Evangelical movement was also marked by a new out-pouring of hymns and melodies which have been the means of cherishing the divine affections in the hearts of thousands from that day to this. Meanwhile the legitimate parochial psalmody kept on, from generation to generation, in the doggerel of Sternhold and Hopkins, or in the somewhat improved rhymes of Tate and Brady, sung to the tunes approved by the parish clerk. * * * It is a healthful sign of late years that the use of hymns has now become much more common in the English congregations. In this respect their freedom is much larger than ours. Every congregation may have a book of its own. The church in this country has evinced a remarkable disaffection to hymns. Until the year 1808 the whole of the authorized number was 27, it was then enlarged to 56. In 1826 the present 208, not until after considerable opposition, were admitted (of which it is relevant to remark in passing, a large number are the compositions of non-Episcopalians), but with the retention of that most extraordinary rubric which forbids their use on any occasion when one of the psalms in metre is not also sung. This operates to the entire exclusion of hymns whenever the order for morning or evening prayer is alone used, although of that order the psalms make so large a part. Hence, in churches in which there is the daily service, not a song of praise is heard except on Sundays and holy days, in which a Jew as well as a Christian might not join. Whence this jealousy of evangelical devotion, and a form of it, in which, as has been said, the common people especially delight? Is it a sign that ours is a church for the common people?

* * * And then in the matter of public worship, much might be done by setting forth shorter services and a larger variety of them—by allowing a discretionary use of parts of the Prayer-Book, and also, within certain limits, the use of free prayer.[20] It is easy to suggest measures by which the Church's adaptability and popular efficiency might be increased, but not so easy, it must be confessed, to anticipate a sufficient agreement in regard to them to secure their adoption. * * *

The following seems to be the least amount of *desiderata* in the morning and evening prayer—

1. Liberty to begin at the confession or the Lord's prayer—

2. Double the number of the present ten selections of psalms; or permission to use any portion of the psalter instead of the psalms for the day—

3. A variety of canticles in scripture words; some of them from the New Testament, to be used in place of the *Venite,* and after the lessons, according to the several seasons of the church year and at the discretion of the minister—

4. A revision of the calendar to adapt the lessons to the church year—

5. A collection of prayers, thanksgivings, and litanies, any of which might be used together with the present prayers after the Creed, or in the place of any of them.

Should any one think that these would be large changes in the prayer-book, let him observe to what part of it they are confined. Let him observe that they do not touch the Liturgy—the liturgy proper—that is, the communion office. In that I have to speak of no changes—for two reasons—

First. The office already admits of all the variety that is desirable, by reason of the places which occur in the course of it, for the introduction of variable matter. Thus immediately before it, in compliance with ancient usage, an *Introit* may be sung, taken from any of the psalms or other parts of scripture. Before the sermon there may be an anthem, psalm, or hymn. After the sermon the minister may pray *ad libitum,*[21] and again a psalm, hymn, or anthem may be used. The same after the offertory. Before the final blessing, prayers from any part of the Book are in place. All this is sanctioned by usage, which thus allows devotions of the most diversified character, suitable to times and seasons, to be interwoven with the communion service, without touching its fixed parts. In the form of scriptural anthems, expressly allowed by the House of Bishops, it may be enriched and illustrated with any amount of treasures from Holy Writ.

The other reason why nothing in regard to this office has been suggested, is a profound reverence for it as the most perfect work of the kind on earth. It is the Liturgy of liturgies. It is worthy, so far as any human composition can be worthy, of the great mystery of our faith which it enshrines. Laden with the precious truths of Redemption, clothed in the richest yet simplest language, combining the Law and the Gospel, presenting a yearly round of chosen words from Evangelists and Apostles, uttering now the deepest supplications of sinners suing for mercy, and now the seraphic strains of worshippers mingling with the company of Heaven, beginning and ending with the Lord's prayer, this wonderful service is a grand and complete summary of the whole of our Religion. The church which has this as the centre and heart of her worship, might on that account alone prove herself a true branch of the Church of the Redeemer. Her children will never know how much they owe to it, how invaluable a treasure, next only to God's own word it is, until they find what a blessed means it will have been of preparing them for the Communion service of the saints in Heaven. A pious veneration, let it be said—has checked any thoughts but those of affection for this crowning glory of the Prayer Book. * * *

[The Memorial was presented at the time of the General Convention which met in New York, in October of 1853. The House of Bishops referred the Memorial to a committee of five, later six, members of the House. The committee's first action was to survey certain members of the Church, in order, according to its chairman,

> *first*, to ascertain as far as possible how far the more enlightened and influential of our people were prepared to sanction any change; *secondly*, to gain for the Commissioners the aid of those who were best qualified to afford it, and who occupied various positions; and *thirdly*, to present, not only to churchmen, but to others, subjects which merit more consideration than they have yet received.

Record of who the Bishops deemed to be the more enlightened and influential people were does not survive, and all of the responses received by the committee are not preserved. Bishop Potter published some of them in his *Memorial Papers* (1857).]

20. From the "Circular and Questions"

issued by the Bishops in response to the Memorial

* * *

6. Is our present system of family, Sunday School, and catechetical instruction and training chargeable with any serious defects? If yea, please state them; suggest your opinion respecting the proper remedy.

7. Ought or ought not our parish churches in large towns to be opened more frequently on the Lord's day; and to different congregations at different hours?

8. What can be done for the religious instruction of boys when they leave the Sunday School?

9. Do the laymen and laywomen of our congregations co-operate sufficiently with the pastor in the work of winning souls? How can that co-operation be safely increased?

10. How can a spirit of true brotherly intercourse among our members be promoted?

11. Ought not young men to be seen in our churches in much larger number? Please to suggest means.

12. How can the proper influence of our Church over men engrossed in business be secured?

13. By what specific means can we increase adequately the pecuniary contributions of Churchmen to the work of evangelizing our own land, and the world at large? Do we instruct our people sufficiently on the dangers and responsibilities involved in the possession of property?

II.

1. Could changes be advantageously made in our Liturgical services?

(a.) By lengthening, shortening, or dividing?

(b.) By adapting the lessons, anthem, &c., better to the different ecclesiastical seasons?

(c.) By a larger number of special services and prayers for special occasions?

(d.) By a larger discretion in the use of hymns, and other sacred music?

(e.) By services specially fitted for missionary work at home or abroad?

(f.) By allowing the authorities of each Diocese larger liberty?

* * *

3. Ought the conditions now imposed on candidates, who have been licensed or ordained in other Protestant communions, be relaxed?

(a.) As to term of time?

(b.) Degree of conformity to the worship, discipline, &c., of the P. E. Church?

4. Are any facts known to you indicating a preference, on the part of ministers of other Protestant bodies, for Episcopal ordination, if it were in their power?

5. Are there any facts known to you indicating on the part of the members of such bodies, a disposition to make any sacrifices of sectarian feeling for the sake of restoring unity?

6. Are our Liturgical services, and the discretion accorded to our several Dioceses, as free as they were in the early church?

7. Ought the Church to make better provision for training teachers, nurses, &c?

8. Ought it to afford its female members who have leisure and inclination for benevolent labours, any more systematic means of pursuing them, than exist at present?

21. From the Report of the Bishops' Committee.

* * * Our liturgical services, be it remembered, were framed with a special view to the wants of a worshipping people. They were provided with a direct reference to organized parish Churches. They were intended to furnish two or more daily services to a population already won to the church. But our actual mission is to many, in truth, to a large majority not yet conciliated to the Church, and, for the most part, strangers to her forms of worship. We have to seek those who have not been gathered into organized parishes,—who do not recognize in us any claim to spiritual oversight over them. We have to labour in places where very much of our work is outside of that contemplated in the plan of our offices, and in the prevalent methods of our preaching. * * *

In seeking to modify or adapt our forms of worship to the actual wants and condition of a very large portion of our population, we do but act upon a principle distinctly recognized in our own and our Mother church. In the preface to the Book of Common Prayer it is declared "that in every Church, whatever cannot be clearly determined to belong to doctrine may be referred to discipline; and therefore by common consent and authority may be altered, abridged, enlarged, amended or otherwise disposed of, as may seem most convenient for the edification of the people, according to the various exigencies of times and occasions." It is also affirmed in the same preface, that the Church of England having made various reviews and changes—her aim hath been "to do that which according to her best understanding, might most tend to the preservation of peace and unity in the Church; the procuring of reverence, and the exciting of piety and devotion in the worship of God; and finally the cutting off occasion from them that seek occasion of cavil or quarrel against her Liturgy." * * *

[A long section follows exhorting priests to better prepared, more popular preaching, preaching which treats a greater variety of life's experiences.]

These remarks point to the expediency, not to say necessity, of a corresponding variety, to some extent, in our Liturgical services. It is the general voice of our communion, that in adjusting the length of our public services, more regard should be had to the physical ability of both minister and people; and this is especially important in those parts of our country where the heats of summer are long-continued and debilitating, rendering mental exertion burdensome, and even perilous to health. More attention also seems to be demanded to the degree of Liturgical culture among the people, and a more economical use of our clerical force. By the arrangements which the Commission would recommend, it is believed that, in most of our established congregations, three services may be had on Sunday, and several during the week, without overburdening the strength and ability of the minister. * * *

It has been the purpose of the Commission, however, so far as their present labours go, to leave the Prayer Book untouched: they have also doubted how far the consideration of such proposed alterations would fall within the duty assigned to them; and, at all events, they felt that, if any alterations of the Prayer Book were proposed, the House of Deputies would be entitled to take part in the preliminary discussion connected with them, and that much more time ought to be devoted to the work than they have been able to command. They have concluded, therefore, to commend this subject to the General Convention, to be disposed of as in its wisdom it may judge to be most expedient. They have many valuable papers, embodying the results of much labour and learning, and of a very extended experience, which will be at the service of a committee, should the Convention decide to appoint one.

After much reflection, the Commission have come to the unanimous conclusion that some of the most material of the improvements which are loudly called for, and which commend themselves to our own judgment, might be attained without legislation.

There is nothing in the Rubrics or Canons which requires that, when the Holy Communion is administered, it should be preceded, immediately or otherwise, by the office for daily Prayer. The practice rests merely on usage, and there are occasions when, for want of physical ability on the part of the minister, or from the very large number of persons communicating, or for other reasons, it would be right that the liberty, which the law does not withhold, of omitting the Daily Prayer should be exercised. To secure this, nothing more would be needed, it is thought, than a declarative resolution of this House. The same discretion seems allowable, in respect to the time of using the Litany, and the Ante-Communion Office. Canon XLVII., of 1832, already provides for special services, to be set forth by Bishops in their own Dioceses; and the Commission have concluded that, by exercising the power thus given, provision could be made for those local necessities which result from peculiarities in the character of the population, or in the circumstances under which the Church is to be extended. * * * The effect of this amendment would be to enable particular dioceses under the direction of the ecclesiastical authority of the same, during such seasons as Passion Week, Christmas, and the like, to substitute Lessons, Anthem, or Canticles more appropriate to the occasions, and also to bring the provision of this Canon into harmony with those of Canon XLVII. (1832).

The House of Clerical and Lay Deputies having requested * * * this House in 1853 to consider the propriety of setting forth a form of prayer for the increase of the Holy Ministry, according to the command of Christ, "Pray ye the Lord of the harvest that He would send forth laborers into his harvest," and a resolution to the same effect of the Bishop of Pennsylvania in this House having been referred to the Commission, and several propositions having been made for the adoption of other occasional Prayer and Thanksgivings, the Commission have thought that it might be proper to offer for consideration the following forms:—

1. A Prayer for Unity.
2. A Prayer for the Increase of the Ministry.
3. A Prayer for Missions and Missionaries.
4. A Prayer for the Young, to be used on occasions of Catechizing and the like.
5. A Prayer for a Person about to be exposed to special danger.
6. A Prayer in time of public calamities, dangers, or difficulties.
7. A Thanksgiving for deliverance of a person from any peril.
8. A Prayer for deliverance from public calamities and dangers.
9. A Thanksgiving for the recovery of a sick child.

A PRAYER FOR UNITY.

O God, the Father of our Lord Jesus Christ, our only Saviour, the Prince of Peace, give us grace seriously to lay to heart the great dangers we are in by our unhappy divisions. Take away all hatred and prejudice, and whatever else may hinder us from godly union and concord: that, as there is but one body, and one Spirit, and one hope of our calling, one Lord, one faith, one baptism, on God and Father of us all; so we may henceforth be all of one heart and one soul, united in the holy bond of truth, of faith and charity, and may with one mind and one mouth glorify thee: through Jesus Christ our Lord. Amen.

A PRAYER FOR THE INCREASE OF THE MINISTRY.

O Almighty God, who hast in thy holy church committed to the hands of men the ministry of reconciliation, to gather together a great flock in all parts of the world, to the eternal praise of thy holy name; we humbly beseech thee that thou wilt put it into the hearts of many faithful men to seek this sacred ministry, appointed for the salvation of mankind; that so thy church may rejoice in a due supply of true and faithful pastors, and the bounds of thy blessed kingdom may be enlarged: through Jesus Christ our Lord. Amen.

A PRAYER FOR MISSIONS AND MISSIONARIES.

O Lord, who didst come to seek and to save the lost, and to whom all power is given in heaven and in earth, hear, we beseech thee, the prayers of thy church for those who, at thy command, go forth to preach the gospel to every creature. Preserve them from all dangers to which they may be exposed; from perils by land and perils by water; from the deadly pestilence; from the violence of the persecutor; from doubt and impatience; from discouragement and discord; and from all the devices of the powers of darkness. And while they plant and water, send thou, O Lord, the increase; gather in the multitude of the heathen; convert, in Christian lands, such as neglect so great salvation; so that thy name may be glorified, and thy kingdom come, O gracious Saviour of the world, to whom, with the Father, and the Holy Ghost, be honour and glory, world without end. Amen.

A PRAYER FOR THE YOUNG AT CATECHISINGS OR IN SUNDAY SCHOOLS.

Almighty Father, who hast promised that they who seek early thy heavenly wisdom, shall early find it, and find it more precious than all the treasures of this world, send down on these thy children the grace and blessing of thy Holy Spirit; that they, being trained up in the nurture and admonition of the Lord, may choose and love thy way, and depart from it no more for ever; and that, when thou makest up thy jewels in thy glorious kingdom, these children may be there, and may be thine; all of which we ask for the sake of thy holy child Jesus, our only Saviour and Redeemer. Amen.

A PRAYER FOR A PERSON EXPOSED TO ANY SPECIAL PERIL.

Almighty God, the Saviour of all men, we humbly commend to thy tender care and sure protection in *his* danger, thy *servant* for whom our prayers are desired. Let thy fatherly hand, we beseech thee, be over *him;* let thy holy angels have charge of *him*; with thy loving-kindness defend *him*, as with a shield: and either bring *him* out of *his* peril in safety, with a heart to show forth thy praises for ever, or else sustain *him* with that glorious hope by which alone thy servants can have victory in suffering and in death, through the sole merits of Jesus Christ our Lord. Amen.

A PRAYER IN TIME OF PUBLIC CALAMITIES, DANGERS, OR DIFFICULTIES.

O most mighty God!...King of kings, and Lord of lords, without whose care the watchman waketh but in vain, we implore, in this our time of need, thy succour and blessing in behalf of our rulers and magistrates, and of all the people of this land (*or*, of this commonwealth, *or*, of this community). Remember not our many and great transgressions; turn from us the judgments which we feel (*or*, fear); and give us wisdom to discern, and courage to attempt, and faithfulness to do, and patience to endure, whatsoever shall be well-pleasing in thy sight; that so thy chastenings may yield the peaceable fruits of righteousness, and that at the last we may rejoice in thy salvation, through Jesus Christ our Lord. Amen.

A THANKSGIVING FOR A PERSON DELIVERED FROM ANY PERIL.

O God, most mighty and most gracious, by whom the hairs of our heads are all numbered, we give thee hearty thanks that thou hast delivered from *his* great peril thy servant, who now desireth that the thanksgiving of many on *his* behalf may redound to thy glory. Write on *his* mind the perpetual remembrance of thy preserving mercy; save *him* from the hardness of an ungrateful heart, and grant that all *his* future days, and all that thou hast graciously continued to *him*, may be consecrated to thee and to thy blessed service, through Jesus Christ our Lord. Amen.

A THANKSGIVING FOR DELIVERANCE FROM PUBLIC CALAMITIES.

O eternal God, the shield of our help, beneath whose sovereign defence thy people dwell in safety, we bless and praise, we laud and magnify thy glorious name for all thy goodness to the people of this land (*or*, of this commonwealth, *or*, of this community), and especially for our merciful deliverance from those calamities which of late we suffered (*or*, dreaded). Inspire our souls with grateful love; lift up our voices in songs of thankfulness; and so pour out upon us thy Holy Spirit, that we may be humble and watchful in our prosperity, patient and steadfast in our afflictions, and always enjoy the blessed confidence of that people whose God is the Lord; all which we ask through Jesus Christ, our Mediator and Redeemer, to whom, with the Father and the Holy Ghost, be all honour and glory, praise and dominion, now and for ever. Amen.

A THANKSGIVING FOR THE RECOVERY OF A SICK CHILD.

Almighty Father, who at the prayers of thy servants, Elijah and Elisha, didst gladden the hearts of two pious mothers by restoring them their dead, and who, by thy Son Jesus Christ, didst raise to health and life the children of many sorrowing parents, accept, we beseech thee, the thanks of thy *servants* who *call* upon us to join our praises with their own for the deliverance of their dear child from sickness and the grave. May that recovered child be ever thine; and may the hearts of all to whom *he* is precious, so burn at the remembrance of thy goodness, that they may hold no thank-offering too costly to show forth thy praise, and may present themselves, a living sacrifice, holy and acceptable unto thee, through the merits of Jesus Christ our Saviour. Amen.

22. Action of the House of Bishops

in response to the Memorial, 1856

Whereas, The use of the Book of Common Prayer, as regulated by custom, has special reference to established parish Churches and to a population already incorporated with the Church; and whereas, our actual work is, or should be, among many not yet connected with our congregations, or where there are no established parishes, or where said parishes are yet in their infancy:

And whereas, There are or may be in different Dioceses, peculiar emergencies arising out of the character or condition of certain portions of the population which demand some special services;

And whereas, The Book of Common Prayer should be so used as most effectually to cherish true devotion and set forth the gospel and work of Christ, and contribute to the extension of his kingdom among men;

And whereas, The House of Bishops have heretofore expressed opinions as to usages which may be allowed under existing Rubrics and Canons: Therefore,

Resolved, as the opinion of the Bishops,

1. That the Order of the Morning Prayer, the Litany, and the Communion Service, being separate offices, may, as in former times, be used separately under the advice of the Bishop of the Diocese.

2. That on special occasions, or at extraordinary services not otherwise provided for, ministers may, at their discretion, use such parts of the Book of Common Prayer, and such lesson or lessons from Holy Scripture, as shall in their judgment tend most to edification.

3. That the Bishops of the several Dioceses may provide such special services as, in their judgment, shall be required by the peculiar spiritual necessities of any class or portion of the population within said Dioceses: provided that such services shall not take the place of the services or offices of the Book of Common Prayer in congregations capable of its use.

4. That in view of the desirableness of union amongst Christians, and as a pledge of willingness to communicate and receive information tending to that end, and in order to conference, if occasion or opportunity should occur, this House will appoint, by ballot, a committee of five Bishops, as an organ of communication or conference with such Christian bodies or individuals as may desire it, to be entitled the *Commission on Church Unity.*

5. That in making the above appointment, it is clearly understood that the Commission is clothed with no authority to mature plans of union with other Christian bodies, or to propound expositions of doctrine and discipline.

23. Alterations proposed by the General Convention of 1880.

Resolved, That the ratification of the Book of Common Prayer be amended so as to read as follows, and that such proposed amendment be made known to the several Diocesan Conventions, in order that it may be adopted in the next General Convention according to Article 8 of the Constitution:

The Ratification of the Book of Common Prayer.

By the Bishops, the Clergy, and the Laity of the Protestant Episcopal Church in the United States of America, in General Convention assembled.

The General Convention of this Church,

having heretofore, to wit, on the sixteenth day of October, A.D. 1789, set forth and established a Book of Common Prayer and Administration of the Sacraments and other Rites and Ceremonies of the Church, and thereby established the said book and declared it to be the Liturgy of this Church, and required that it be received as such by all the members of the same, and be in used from and after the first day of October, A.D. 1790; the same book is hereby ratified and confirmed, and ordered to be the use of this Church from this time forth.

But note, however, that on days other than Sunday, Christmas Day, the Epiphany, Ash-Wednesday, Good Friday, and Ascension Day, it shall suffice if the minister begin Morning or Evening Prayer at the General Confession, or the Lord's Prayer preceded by one or more of the sentences appointed at the beginning of Morning and Evening Prayer, and end after the Collect for Grace, or the Collect for Aid against Perils, with 2. Cor. xiii. 14, using so much of the Lessons appointed for the day, and so much of the Psalter, as he shall judge to be for edification.

And note also, that on any day when Morning and Evening Prayer have been duly said, or are to be said, and upon days other than those first afore mentioned, it shall suffice when need may require, if a Sermon or Lecture be preceded by at least the Lord's Prayer and one or more Collects found in this book, provided that no prayers not set forth in said book, or otherwise authorized by this Church, shall be used before or after such sermon or lecture.

And note also, that on any day the Morning Prayer, the Litany, or the Order for the Administration of the Lord's Supper, may be used as a separate and independent service, provided that no one of these services shall be disused habitually.

24. Revision of the American Common Prayer[22]

William Reed Huntington
The American Church Review, Vol. XXXIII. No. 2, April, 1881

The revision of long established formularies of public worship is, as it ought to be, a matter compassed about with obstacles many and great. A wise doubtfulness prompts conservative minds to throw every mover for change upon the defensive, when liturgical interests are at stake. So many men are born into the world with a native disposition to tamper with and tinker all settled things, and so many more become persuaded, as time goes on, of a personal "mission" to pull down and re-make whatever has been once built up, esteeming life a failure unless they have contrived to build each his own monument upon a clearing, that lovers of the old ways are sometimes compelled in sheer self-defence, to put on the appearance of being more obstinately set against change than they really are. It ought not to be absolutely impossible to alter a national hand-book of worship (which is what any manual calling itself a Common Prayer must aspire to become) but it is well that it should be all but impossible to do so. Logically it might seem as if the possession of a power to make involved a continuance of power to re-make; and so it does, to a certain extent, but only to a certain extent. Living organisms cannot be remodelled with the same freedom as dead matter. A solemnity hangs about the moment of birth that attaches to no other crisis in a man's life until death comes. Similarly there are certain features which the founders of institutions, the first makers of organic law, imprint lastingly upon their work. We may destroy the living thing so brought to birth; to kill is always possible; but only by very gradual and plastic methods can we hope in any measure to reconstruct the actual embodiment of life once achieved. The men of 1789 had us in their power, even as the men of 1549 had both them and us. In every creative epoch many things are settled by which unborn generations will be bound.[23]

It may be urged that this is an argument against adopting liturgies in the first instance as vehicles of worship; and such undoubtedly it is in so far as immobility ought in such matters to be reckoned at disadvantage. But we are bound to take into account the gain which comes with immobility as well as the drawbacks. We must consider how large a proportion of the reverence which the great institutes of human life exact from us is due to the fixity of the things themselves. Mount Blanc loses nothing of its hold upon our reverence because we always find it in the same place. Men like to feel that there is something in the world stronger than the individual will, stronger simply because it expresses the settled common sense of many as to what is fitting and right in contrast with the whim of one. Lawyers, as a class, are almost as conservative as ecclesiastics, and for the very reason that they also are charged with the custody of established forms which it is important that men should reverence. Laws affecting the tenure of property, the binding force of contracts, the stability of the marriage relation, not only cannot be lightly altered, the very phraseology in which they are couched must be carefully handled, for fear lest with the passing away of the form something of the substance go also.

Moreover the affections of men fasten themselves very tenaciously to such a trellis as a liturgy affords. The love for "the old words and the old tunes" against which all innovators in hymnody, however deserving, have to do battle, asserts itself under the form of love for the old prayers with ten fold vehemence. An immense fund of latent heat smoulders under the maxim "Let the ancient customs prevail;" and few of the victories achieved by the Papacy are so startling as those that have resulted in the displacement of the liturgical uses of local Churches, that of Paris for example, by the Roman rite.

But true principles, as we are often reminded, become falsehoods when shoved across the line of proper measure. The very cycles of the astronomers have an end, and the clockwork of the most ancient heavens, or at least our reading of it, calls, from time to time, for readjustment. So long as man continues fallible his best intended workmanship will occasionally demand such alteration for the better as, within the limits already pointed out, may be possible.

Many signs of the times suggest that the hour for a fresh review of the Anglican formularies of worship is nigh at hand. Some of these tokens are written on a sky broad enough to cover the whole English-speaking race, others of them are visible chiefly within our own national horizon. With respect to the English book, Cardwell[24] writing in 1840 and Freeman[25] in 1855, considered revision, however desirable in the abstract, to be a thing utterly out of reach, not within the circle, as the parliamentary phrase now runs, of "practical politics."

But it may be fairly questioned whether these high authorities, were they living to-day, would not concur in the judgment of a more recent writer when he says,—in language which, *mutatis mutandis,* applies to our own case. "The most weighty plea in favor of timely inquiry into the subject is that the process of Revision is actually going on piecemeal, and with no very intelligent survey of the bearings as a preliminary to any one instalment. The New Lectionary of 1871, the Shortened Services Act, the debates in the Convocation of Canterbury on rubrical amendments, none of them marked by any sufficient care of knowledge, and all fraught with at least the possibility of serious consequence, are examples of formal and recognized inroads on the Act of Uniformity; which such practical, though unauthorized additions to the scanty group of Anglican formularies as the Three Hours' Devotion, Harvest Thanksgivings, Public Institution of Incumbents, Ordination of Readers and Deaconesses and Children's Services prove incontestably that the narrow limits of the Common Prayer Book are no longer adequate for the spiritual needs of the Church of England....

"It is evident then that contented acquiescence with the old state of things already belongs in the past, and that a return to it is impossible. We must perforce advance, for good or ill, in the path of Revision, and cannot even materially slacken the pace nor defer the crisis. One choice, however, is left in our power, and that is the most important of all, namely the direction which Revision shall take—that of conservative and recuperative addition, or that of further evisceration, ceremonial or devotional."[26]

A measure looking in the direction towards which this reviewer points was actually passed by the General Convention of our own Church at its late session in October, 1880.

The wording of the Resolution referred to was as follows:

"*Resolved:* That a Joint Committee, to consist of seven Bishops, seven Presbyters and seven Laymen be appointed to consider and report to the next General Convention, whether, in view of the fact that this Church is soon to enter upon the second century of its organized existence in this country, the changed conditions of the national life do not demand certain alterations in the Book of Common Prayer in the direction of liturgical enrichment and increased flexibility of use."[27]

In the present article the writer proposes to inquire, in connection with this measure, (1.) What motives may fairly be supposed to have actuated the Convention in allowing so important an initiatory step to be taken.

(2.) What measure of authority was conferred on and what scope given to the Joint Committee then constituted.

(3.) What reasons exist for considering the present a happy moment to attempt liturgical revision, within certain limits, should such a thing be determined upon.

(4.) What serious difficulties and obstacles are likely to be encountered in Committee, in Convention, and in the Church at large.

(5.) What particular improvements and adjustments of our existing system would be, in point of fact, best worth the effort necessary to secure them.

I.

MOTIVES.

The interpretation of motives, difficult enough in the case of individuals, becomes mere guess-work when the action under analysis is that of a large body of men. Which one of many considerations urged upon the Convention carried with it the supreme weight of persuasion in this particular instance it is impossible to say. Two or three arguments, however, from their frequent re-appearance in the debate, may fairly be judged to have exercised a controlling influence. One of these was hinted at in the language of the resolution itself, namely, the call for revision that has grown out of "the changed conditions of the national life." Shrewd and far-seeing as were William White and his coadjutors in their forecast of nineteenth century needs made from the standpoint of the Peace of Versailles, they would have been more than human had they succeeded in anticipating all the civil and ecclesiastical consequences destined to flow from that memorable event. Certainly it ought not to be held strange that this "new America" of ours, with its enormously multiplied territory, its conglomerate of races, its novel forms of association, its multiplicity of industries not dreamed of a generation ago, should have demands to make in respect to a better adaptation of ancient formularies to present wants, such as thoughtful people count both reasonable and cogent. That a Prayer-Book revised primarily for the use of a half-proscribed Church planted here and there along a sparsely inhabited sea-coast, should serve as amply as it does the purposes of a population now swollen from four millions to fifty, and covering the whole breadth of the continent, is marvel enough; to assert for the book entire adequacy to meet these altered circumstances is a mistake. "New time, new favors and new joys," so a familiar hymn affirms, "do a new song require." We have conceded the principle so far as psalmody is concerned, why not apply it to the service of prayer as well as to that of praise, and in addition to our new hymns secure also such new intercessions and new thanksgivings as the needs of to-day suggest.

The reverence in the resolution to the approaching completion of the century has since been playfully characterized as a bit of "sentimentalism."[28] The criticism would be entirely just if the mere recurrence of the centennial anniversary were the point chiefly emphasized. But when a century closes as this one of ours has done with a great social revolution whereby "all estates of men" have been more or less affected, the proposal to signalize entrance upon a fresh stretch of national life by making devotional preparation for it is something better than a pretty conceit; there is a serious reasonableness in it.[29]

Every revision of the Common Prayer of the Church of England, and there have been four of them since Edward's first book was put in print, has taken place at some important era of transition in the national life: and conversely it may be said that every civil crisis, with a single exception, has left its mark upon the formularies.

To one who argues that because we in this country are evidently entering upon a new phase of the national life we ought similarly to re-enforce and re-adjust our service-book, it is no sufficient reply to urge the severance effected here between Church and State. The fact that ours is a non-established Church does not make her wholly unresponsive to the shocks of change that touch the civil fabric. In so far as a political renewal alters the social grading of society, bringing in education, for instance, where before it was not, or suddenly developing new forms of industrial activity, the Church, whether established or not, is in duty bound to take cognizance of the fresh field of duty thus suddenly thrust upon her, and to prepare herself accordingly.

In the Preface added to the English Prayer-Book at the Restoration, and commonly attributed to Sanderson, "that staid and well-weighed man," and Hammond called him, there occurs a sentence which, both on account of its embodying in few words the whole philosophy of liturgical revision and because of a certain practical bearing presently to be pointed out, it is worth while in spite of its familiarity, to quote;—

"The particular forms of Divine worship, and the rites and ceremonies appointed to be used therein, being things in their own nature indifferent and alterable and so acknowledged; it is but reasonable, that upon weighty and important considerations, according to the various exigency to times and occasions, such changes and alterations should be made therein, as to those that are in place of authority should from time to time seem either necessary or expedient."

Contemporaneously with this utterance there came into the Prayer Book, as a direct consequence of the enormous enlargement of the naval and commercial marine that had taken place under the Commonwealth, the "Forms of Prayer to be used at Sea." Here was a wise and right-minded recognition of a new want that had sprung up with a new time, a want which jealousy of the Puritans who had built up the naval supremacy did not prevent the Caroline bishops from meeting. But the change that passed on England during five years of Cromwell was as nothing compared with the transformation of America under ninety-five years of the federal constitution. Take a single illustration. The year of 1789, the date of the Ratification of the American Prayer Book, saw sea-island cotton first planted in the United States and it was about that time that upland cotton also began to be cultivated for home and foreign use. As the effect of this scarcely noticed experiment there straightway sprang up an industry, North and South, which has been to our country almost what her shipping interest is to Great Britain. Bishop White and his associates were not to blame for failure to provide bread that all this unanticipated multitude of toilers should eat. And yet a failure there had been. No one who has not labored at the task of trying to commend the Church of the Prayer-Book to the working class, as it is represented in our large manufacturing towns, can know how lamentable that failure is. We gather in the rich and the poor, but the great middle class that makes the staple and the strength of American society stands aloof.

Nowhere in this country, for instance, has the Church had a better opportunity to show what it could do for American people than in the city of Lowell, where cotton spinning had its first large development. It was a virgin soil: the Episcopal Church, as rarely happens, was earliest on the ground: and, not only so, but it enjoyed for some years, the friendly protection of the proprietors of the new settlement, almost a religious monopoly,—was, in fact, an ecclesiastical preserve. Moreover this beginning antedated the Irish occupation by many years, at least so far as skilled labor was concerned, for during a considerable period the operatives in the mills were of native New England stock, the best possible material to be made over into churchmen and churchwomen. And yet notwithstanding all this, and notwithstanding the patient and unintermitted toil through more than fifty years of perhaps the most laborious parish priest on the American clergy list, the Episcopal Church has to-day but a comparatively slender hold upon the affections and loyalty of the people of this largest of the manufacturing cities of New England.

A similar failure to "reach the masses," betrays itself in Worcester and Fall River, the two cities of like character that come next in order of population, for in the former of these last named places only about two per cent of the inhabitants have affiliations of any sort with the Episcopal Church.

It was considerations of this sort, backed perhaps by memories of the ringing appeal sounded three years before at Boston by the Bishop of Connecticut, that moved the Convention to interpret as something better than a bit of sentimentalism, the invitation to look the times in the face, and give the new century its infant baptism.

But besides all this there pressed upon the mind of Bishops and Deputies a cumulative argument of a wholly different sort. The demand for revision seemed to be closing in upon the Church on converging lines. It was plain that, before long, hands of change must necessarily be laid upon certain semi-detached portions of the Prayer-Book. There was the new Lectionary, for example, that would presently be knocking for hospitable reception within the covers, and the old Easter tables, as they now stand, could not, if was observed, last very much longer. A new book, in the publisher's sense of that term, would soon have to be made. The sanctity of stereotype plates must be disturbed. Moreover, here was an admirable opportunity to settle the wrangle, now of nine years standing, over the best way of bringing to pass shortened services for week-day use. Add to this the fact that the intrinsic weakness of the driblet method of revision[30] had been made so abundantly plain that even its former friends wisely refrained from all attempt to urge it, and our summing up of probable motives becomes approximately complete.

II.

AUTHORITY AND SCOPE.

As to the measure of authority conferred on, and scope allowed to the Committee of Twenty-one, it is possible to speak with more definiteness.

A precisian might of course, were he so disposed, take up the ground that the report of the Committee when made ought to be monosyllabic, "Yes" or "No." The wording of the resolution admits of such a construction beyond a doubt; the Joint Committee was requested to consider and report whether etc. etc. But no one who listened to the debate on the resolution could have been left in uncertainty as to the real *animus* of the measure. The thing intended to be authorized was an experimental review, with implied reference to a limited revision at some time future, in case the fruits of the review should commend themselves to the mind of the Church.

A distinction must be drawn between revision and review. Revision implies review as an antecedent step, but review is by no means necessarily followed by revision. The English book was reviewed and revised in 1662; it was reviewed but not revised in 1689. Review is tentative and advisory; revision is authoritative and final. In the present instance not an atom of power to effect binding change has been conveyed. No authority has been given to anybody to touch a line or a letter of the Prayer-Book save in the way of suggestion and recommendation. Responsible action has been held wholly in reserve.

Moreover even the pathway of review was most scrupulously hedged. Applying to the resolution the legal maxim *expressio unius est exclusio alterius,* one sees at a glance that doctrinal change is a matter left wholly on one side. The two points to which the Committee is instructed to bend all its studies are "liturgical enrichment" and "increased flexibility of use." Whatsoever is more than these is irrelevant. Accurate distinguishment between such "enrichments" as have and such as have not a doctrinal bearing is, no doubt, a delicate point, and must be set down among the difficulties to be encountered. As such it will be considered further on. For the present the fact to be noted is that the authorized reviewers are both in honor and in duty bound to keep themselves absolutely clear of controversial bias. The movement is not a movement to alter in any slightest respect the dogmatic teaching of the Church, not a movement to unsettle the foundations, not a movement towards disowning or repudiating our past, but simply and only an endeavor to make the Common Prayer, if possible (and we are far from being sure, as yet, that it is possible), a better thing of its kind, more comprehensive, more elastic, more readily responsive to the demands of all occasions and the needs of "all sorts and conditions of men." Some who are deeply persuaded that only by doctrinal revision in one direction or another can the Prayer-Book be made thoroughly to commend itself to the heart and mind of the American people will esteem the measure of change above indicated not worth the effort indispensable to the attainment of it. Be it so; other some there are who do think the attempt well-advised and who are willing to waive their own pet notions as to possible doctrinal improvements of the book for the sake of securing a *consensus* upon certain great practical improvements which come within the range of things attainable.

Certain it is that any attempt of a body of reviewers like this to disturb, even by "shadowed hint," the existing doctrinal settlement under which we are living together, would be resented by the whole Church.

There are divines among us who in the interest of a more sharply defined orthodoxy are conscientiously bent upon securing the reintroduction among our formularies of the so-called Athanasian Creed.

There are others who consider that a more damaging blow at the catholicity of our dogmatic position as a Church could scarcely be dealt.

Again, there are theologians who account the Prayer-Book to be so thoroughly saturated in all its parts which the sacramental idea, that they would account it not only a piece of far-seeing statesmanship, but also a perfectly safe procedure to allow those who chose to do so to thank God after a child's baptism for the simple fact that he had thereby been "grafted into the body of Christ's Church."

But over against these a much larger number who think nothing of the sort, and who would put up with the liturgical shortcomings of the Prayer-Book, and go without "enrichments" for a thousand years, rather than see the single word "regenerate" dropped out of the post-baptismal office.

Sensible men not a few are to be found who hold that the incoming tide of host-worship with which, as thy conceive, our reformed Church is threatened can never be stayed unless some carefully contrived definition inserted in the Prayer-Book shall make impossible this subtle and refined species of idolatry. But men no whit less sensible laugh them in the face, pointing to the "black rubric" and its history as evidence that between the admitted doctrine of the real presence and the disallowed tenet of transubstantiation no impervious barrier of words can possibly be run.

These illustrations of probable divergence in opinion, in case the field of doctrine were once entered, might be multiplied. The re-translation of the Nicene Creed and the more accurate punctuation of its sentences; the rendering of the word Sabbath in the Fourth Commandment into its English equivalent of Rest; the abolition of the curious misnomer under which we go on calling XXXVIII Articles XXXIX; the removal from the Catechism, or else the conversion into mother English of that sad *crux infantum* the answer to the question, "What desirest thou of God in this prayer?"[31] are a few examples of less importance than those previously cited; and yet, in the case of the least of them, it is most unlikely that the advocates of change would have the show of hands in their favor, so sensitive is the mind of the Church to anything that looks in the least degree like tampering with the standards of weight and measure of the shekels of the sanctuary.

On the other hand, there are certain manifest and palpable instances of inaccuracy and, more rarely, infelicity of diction which the reviewers might very properly take occasion to amend even though such alterations could not be classified by a strict constructionist under either of the two heads "enrichment" and "flexibility." In the masterly Report of the Rev. Dr. T. W. Coit to the Joint Committee appointed by the Convention of 1841 to prepare a Standard Prayer-Book,[32] a document of classical rank, there is more than one intimation of the hope that future reviewers would be given a larger liberty in this direction than he had himself enjoyed. He chafed, and naturally enough, under the necessity of reprinting in a "standard" book, evident and acknowledged solecisms and blunders. "We wanted," he says, "to correct one ungrammatical clause in the Consecration Prayer of the Communion Service. It is in the last sentence but one, at its close. It should be, not that he may dwell in them and they in him, but, that he may dwell in us and we in him.[33] The prayer is made up out of two or three others; and anyone who will examine the parts put together, will easily see how the thing was overlooked. A much greater error was overlooked elsewhere; showing that our American compilers were not sufficiently aware of the necessity which requires that the Prayer-Book should always be consistent with itself. I allude to something in the office for the Private Baptism of Children. Suppose a Clergyman to avail himself of the license given in the Rubrics after the certification. He will then be made to talk thus: "As the Holy Gospel doth witness to our comfort, on this wise—Dost thou in the name of this child," etc.[34]

Other cases of evident inaccuracy, besides those referred to by this eminent critic, might be cited, even from the latest Standard Prayer-Book, that of 1871. It is hard, for instance, to imagine even the veriest martinet in such matters objecting to the redress of a great wrong done on page 36 of the volume mentioned, where the prayer "to be used at the meetings of Convention" is entered under the general heading "For malefactors after condemnation." Our ecclesiastical legislators have doubtless, like the rest of us "erred and strayed" more than once, but to deal out to them such harsh measure as this is cruel.

A strange uncertainty would seem from the Rubric to exist with reference to the limits of the Litany. On page 554 of the Standard Prayer-Book, the words "Here endeth the Litany," occur immediately after the prayer "We humbly beseech Thee, O Father," while on page 31 the same statement is placed immediately after the minor benediction.

These are not faults for which it could ever be worth while to revise a Prayer-Book, but they are blemishes of which the revisers of a Prayer-Book ought to take note.

It is a graver matter to speak of infelicities of diction in a book so justly famous as the Prayer-Book for its pure and wholesome English. Wordsworth's curse on

> One who would peep and botanize
> Upon his mother's grave

seems, in the judgment of many, fairly earned by the critic, who ever he may be, who ventures to suggest that in any slightest instance the language of the formularies might have been more happily phrased. But there are spots on the sun. In the prayer already referred to, that for use "at the meetings of Convention" the petition, "We beseech thee to be *present* with the council of thy Church here assembled in thy name and *presence*," does seem open to the charge of tautology if nothing worse.

It would be well if wherever the word occurs in the Prayer-Book in connection with Deity the anthropomorphic plural "ears" could be replaced by the symbolic singular "ear."

Considering also the great evil of having in a formulary of worship too many things that have to be laboriously explained, it might be well if in the Litany the adjective "sudden," which ever since Hooker's day has given perpetual occasion for cavil, where to yield to "untimely," or some like word more suggestive than "sudden" of the thought clumsily expressed in the "Chapel Liturgy" by the awkward phrase "death unprepared for."[35]

It must be again remarked that these are not points for the sake of which word-fanciers would be justified in disturbing an existing order of things; they are simply instances of lesser improvements that might very properly accompany larger ones, should larger ones ever be seriously undertaken.

With so many pegs upon which controversies might be hung, staring us in the face, can we think of it as at all likely that any considerable number of churchmen assembled in committee (to say nothing of Convention) will be able to agree upon a common line of action with reference to an amendment of the formularies?

That is the very point at issue, and how it is to be decided only the event can show. Certainly in the roll of the victories of charity, a favorable result, were it achieved, would stand exceeding high.

This reflection naturally leads up to the enquiry whether there is any special reason to consider the present a happy moment to attempt within the limits already defined a revision of the Prayer-Book.

III.

TIMELINESS.

The argument for timeliness has been, in part, already stated. A revision will be timely, if the times imperatively demand it; and the main reasons for thinking that they do are before the reader. Something, however, is still left to be said in evidence that the movement now begun is opportune,—not rudely thrust upon the Church. "To everything," saith the preacher, "there is a season, and a time to every purpose under heaven," and among the categories that follow this statement, we find reckoned what answers to liturgical enrichment, for "there is," he observes, "a time to build up."

Fifty years ago, a persuasive argument against attempting to amend the Prayer-Book, either in text or rubrics, might have been based upon the lack of hands competent to undertake so delicate a task. Raw material well adapted to edification was lying about in blocks, but skilled workmen were scarce. This can hardly be said to-day. Simultaneously with the beginning of the Oxford movement there naturally sprang up a fresh interest in liturgical studies, an interest which has gone on deepening and widening until in volume and momentum the stream has now probably reached its outer limit. The convincing citation, "There were giants in those days," with which a late bishop of one of the New England dioceses used to enforce his major premise that wisdom died with Cranmer and his colleagues, no longer satisfies. Probably no period of corresponding length in the whole range of English Church history has shown itself so rich in the fruits of liturgical study as the fifty years that have elapsed since the introduction into the English Parliament of the first Reform Bill.[36] This particular historical landmark is mentioned on account of the close connection of cause and effect between it and remarkable movement set on foot by Newman, Pusey, Keble and Froude. To be sure, one of the earliest utterances in the Tracts ran in these words: "Attempts are making to get the Liturgy altered. My dear brethren, I beseech you consider with me whether you ought not to resist the alteration of even one jot or tittle of it."[37]

And yet, notwithstanding this disclaimer, one of the main impulses that lay behind the whole movement represented by the Tracts was an earnest desire to quicken the life of the Church of England in the region of worship. In the *Table of the Tracts, showing their arrangement according to Subjects,* the "Liturgical" section comes first.

The present writer acknowledges but a very limited sympathy with the doctrinal motives and aims of either the earlier or the later Tractarians. But let us, above all things, be fair. With whatever prepossessions one looks back upon it, the ground traversed by the Church of England during the past fifty years cannot be otherwise regarded than as a field sown with mingled tares and wheat. Individuals will differ in judgment as to the proportion in which these two products of a common soil have co-existed, but even those who have most stoutly opposed themselves to the Oxford movement, as a whole, are fain to credit it with, at least, this one good result, the rescue of the usages of worship from slovenliness and torpor, and the establishment of a better standard of what is seemly, reverent and beautiful in the public service of Almighty God. Not that there have not been, even in this respect, grave errors in the direction of excess; the statement ventured is simply this, that, up to a certain point, all Churchmen agree in admitting a genuine and wholesome improvement in the popular estimate of what public worship, as such, ought to be. An immense amount of devout study has been given, during the period mentioned, by many able men to liturgical subjects, and it would be strange indeed if fifty years of searching criticism had not resulted in the detection of some few points in which formularies originally compiled to meet the needs of the sixteenth century might be better adapted to the requirements of the twentieth. Or to put the same point in another way, has not all this searching into the mines of buried treasure, all this getting together of quarried stone (with possibly a certain surplusage of stubble) been so much labor lost, if there is never to come the recognition of a ripe moment for the Church to avail itself of the results achieved. Are the studious toils of a Palmer, a Maskell, a Neale, a

Scudamore and a Bright to go for nothing except in so far as they have been contributory to our fund of ecclesiological lore? If so, the contempt often expressed for ritual and liturgical studies by students busy with other lines of research would seem to be not wholly undeserved.

A good opportunity is now before the Church to give answer as to whether this form of investigation is or is not anything better than a species of sacred antiquarianism. Liturgiology as an aspirant for recognition among the useful sciences may be said at the present moment to be waiting for the verdict. To be sure it can be asserted for liturgiology that to those who love it is a study that proves itself, like poetry, "its own exceeding great reward." It is not worth while to dispute this point. Liturgiology pursued for its own sake may not be the loftiest of studies, but this, at least, can be said for it that it is a not less respectable object of pursuit than many another speciality the devotees of which look down upon the liturgiologist with self-complacent scorn as a mere chiffonier. The forms which Christian worship has taken on in successive generations and among peoples of various blood are certainly as well worthy of analysis and classification, as are the *flora* and *fauna* of Patagonia or New Zealand. But while the Patagonian naturalist secures recognition and is decorated, every jaunty man of letters feels at liberty to scoff at the liturgiologist as a laborious trifler.[38]

Moreover, remembering that in favorite studies, as in crops, there rules a principle of rotation, fashion affecting even staid divines with its subtle influence, we may look to see presently a decline of interest in this particular department of enquiry. Especially may serious men be expected to turn their attention in other directions, should it be found that a *Non possumus* awaits every effort to make the fruits of their labor available for the nourishment of the Church's daily life. So then, instead of deferring action until liturgical knowledge shall have become more widely spread, and available liturgical material more abundant, we shall, if we are wise, perceive that only by moving promptly will it be possible in this case, to take the tide at the full. Never again will opportunity be more ripe.

Another evidence of timeliness is supplied by the present pacific condition of the Church. Previous movements towards liturgical revision have been of a more or less partisan and acrimonious temper. Now for the first time we seem to be taking up this subject without the expression of a fear from any quarter that if changes are made this or that party will get the advantage of some other. The peculiar conditions that ensure this unwonted truce of God are not likely to last forever, nor is it perhaps wholly desirable that they should do so; what is desirable, and very desirable, is that we should avail ourselves of the lull to accomplish certain changes for the better, which in ordinary times the prevalent heat of friction makes impossible. The Joint Committee of Twenty-one is confidently believed to contain within itself every shade of color known to belong to the Anglican spectrum; if white light should be found to emerge, three years hence, as a result of the Committee's labors, it will be said, and truly, that never before in our history could such a blending of the rays possibly have taken place.

Still another consideration properly included under the general head of timeliness is said to have been urged with much force in the House of Bishops when the "enrichment" resolution was under discussion.

Up to the present time the Episcopal Church of this country has stood easily at the head in the matter of providing for the people a dignified and beautiful order of divine service. In fact, there has been, until lately, no one to compete. But all this is changing. Ours are no longer the only congregations in which common prayer is to be found. It is true that thus far the attempts at imitation have been rather grotesque than formidable, but such, until recently, have also been, in the judgment of foreign critics, all of our American endeavors after art. We are to consider what apt learners our quick-witted countrymen have shown themselves to be, in so much that even Christmas Day once the *bête noire* of Puritan legislators has come to be accounted almost a national festival, and well shall be convinced that our primacy in the field of liturgics is not an absolutely assured position. This argument is open to the criticism that it seems to lower and cheapen the whole subject by representing Anglican religion in a mendicant attitude bidding for the favor of the great American public, and vexed that others, fellow-suppliants, have stolen a good formula of appeal. Nevertheless there is a certain amount of reasonableness in this way of putting the thing. Certainly with those who reckon the liturgical mode of worship among the notes of the Church, the argument is one that ought to have marked influence; while with those who, not so persuaded, nevertheless view with pleased interest the general spread of a liturgical taste among the people of this country, seeing in it a token of better things to come, a harbinger of larger agreements than we have yet attained to, and of an approaching "consolation of Israel" once not thought possible,—even with such the argument ought not to be wholly powerless.[39]

The fact that the Convocations of Canterbury and York have taken in hand and carried through a revision of the rubrics of the Prayer-Book will seem to those who hold that our Church ought to advance *pari passu* with the Church of England, and no faster, another evidence of the timeliness of the American movement. Under the title of *The Convocation Prayer-Book,* there has lately appeared in England an edition of the Prayer-Book so printed as to show how the book would read were the recommendations of York and Canterbury to go into effect. It is true that the consent of Parliament must be secured before the altered rubrics can have the force of law; but whatever may come of the rubrics recommended, the existence of the book containing them is evidence enough of a wide-spread conviction among the English Clergy that change is needed.

Indeed never has this point been more powerfully put in the fewest possible words than by the brilliant, and no less logical than brilliant Bishop of Peterborough in a recent speech in the Upper House of Convocation.[40] "If the Church of England wants absolute peace, she should have definite rubrics."

It is true he goes on to say that in his judgment the dangers of carrying the question of rubrical revision into Parliament are greater than the evil of letting it alone, but it is to be remembered that we in this country are hampered with no Parliamentary entanglements and are free to do of our own motion, and in a quiet, orderly way, that which the Church of England can only do at the risk of something very like revolution.

But this matter of the rubrics and their susceptibility of improvement will come up later on. It seemed proper to refer to it, if no more, under the head of timeliness. If nothing else in the way of change be opportune at the present moment, it is an easy task to show that the rubrics, as they stand, cry aloud for a revision.

IV.

OBSTACLES AND DIFFICULTIES.

The obstacles to be encountered by any Committee undertaking so to carry forward a review of the Prayer-Book that revision may eventually result, are of two sorts; there are the inherent difficulties of the work itself, such, for instance, as that of matching the literary style of the sixteenth century writers, and there is the wholesome dread of a change for the worse which is sure to assert itself in many quarters the moment definite propositions shall have reached a point at which the "yeas and nays" are likely to be called.

Beginning then with the inherent difficulties, and taking them in the inverse order of arduousness, we see at once how hard it must be to secure unity and self-consistency in the revision of a book so complicated as the Common Prayer. It is like remodelling an old house. We think it a very easy matter, something that can be done in one's head, but the mistake is discovered when the new door designed to give symmetry to this room is found to have spoiled the looks of that, when the enlargement of the library turns out to have overtaxed the heating energy of the fire-place, and the ingenious staircase, instead of ending where it was expected to end, brings up against an intractable brick wall. Just such perils as these will beset anybody who ventures to disturb the adjustments of "the Prayer-Book as it is" and to introduce desirable additions. But domestic architecture is not given up on account of the patient carefulness the practice of it demands, neither need Liturgical Revision be despaired of because it requires of the men who undertake it a like wisdom in looking before and after.

The really formidable barrier to revision, so far as what have been called the "inherent difficulties" are concerned, is reached when we touch style. How to handle without harming the sentences in which English religion phrased itself when the English language was fresher and more fluent than it can ever be again is a serious question. The hands that seek to "enrich" may well be cautioned to take heed lest they despoil. It is to be remembered, however, in the way of reassurance that the alterations most likely to find favor with the reviewers are such as will enrich by restoring lost excellencies, rather than by introducing forms fashioned on a modern anvil.

The most sensitive critic should not, on the score of taste, find fault with the replacement in the Evening Prayer of the *Magnificat* and the *Nunc Dimittis,* nor of bringing back a few of the Versicles that in the English book follow the Lord's Prayer, nor yet of our being allowed to say "Lighten our darkness, we beseech thee, O Lord," rather than "O Lord, our Heavenly Father, by whose Almighty power we have been preserved this day." Objections to these alterations may be readily imagined, but it would be necessary to base them on other grounds than those of literary fastidiousness. In the case of enrichments like these no one could raise the cry that the faultless English of the Prayer-Book had been marred.

But what shall be said of the composition of entirely new services and offices if it should be judged expedient to give admission to any such? How can we be sure that such modern additions to the edifice would be sufficiently in keeping with the general tone of the older architecture? It might be held to be an adequate answer to these questions to reply that if the living Church cannot now trust herself to speak out through her formularies in her natural voice as she did venture to do in the seventeenth century and eighteenth, it must be that she has fallen into that stage of decrepitude where the natural voice is uncertain.

But, really, what ought to be said is this,—that if the same canons of style that ruled the sixteenth century writers are studied and obeyed, there is no reason in the world why a result equally satisfactory with the one then attained should not be reached now. There is nothing supernatural about the English of the Prayer-Book. Cranmer and his associates were not inspired. The prose style of the nineteenth century may not be as good as that of the sixteenth but, at is best, it is vastly superior to the eighteenth, and of this last there are already no inconsiderable specimens in the American Book of Common Prayer. The Office for the Visitation of Prisoners, for example, is so redolent of the times of the Georges, when it was composed, that it might be appropriately enough interleaved with prints out of Hogarth. A bit of Palladian architecture in a Gothic church is not more easily recognized. Many worse things might happen to the Prayer-Book than that the nineteenth century should leave its impress upon the pages.

In fact, it is just as possible, if men will only

think so, to use our language with effect for any good purpose to-day as it was three hundred years ago. All that is necessary is a willingness to submit to the same restrictions, and those mostly moral, that controlled the old writers; and our work, though not identical with theirs, will have the proper similarity. True, a modern author may not be able to reproduce, without a palpable betrayal of affectation and mannerism, the precise characteristics of a bygone style. Chattertons are not numerous. It is easier to secure for the brass andirons and mahogany dining chairs of our own manufacture the look of those that belonged to our grandfathers than it is to catch the tones of voices long dead; and just as good judgment dictates the wisdom of repeating the honest and thorough workmanship of the old cabinet-makers in place of slavishly imitating their patterns, so it will be well if the compilers of devotional forms for modern use seek to say what they have to say with sixteenth century simplicity rather than in sixteenth century speech. In letters, as in conduct, the supreme charm of style is the absence of self-consciousness. "Say in plain words the thing you mean, and say it as if you meant it," is good advice to any seeker after rhetorical excellence, be he young or old. The Reformers, that is to say, the men who Englished the Prayer-Book, in seeking to meet the devotional needs of the people of their own time do not seem to have been at pains to tie themselves to the diction of a previous generation. They dared to "call a spade a spade" whenever and wherever the tool came into use, and they have their reward in the permanence of their work. Sweetnesses and prettinesses they banished altogether. Indeed, in those days it seems not to have occurred to people that such things had anything to do with religion. It was not that they did not know how to talk in the sweet way,—never has sentimentalism been more rife in general literature than then, but they would not talk in that way, the stern traditions of Holy Church throughout all the world forbade. Religion, was a most serious thing to their minds, and they would speak of it most seriously or not at all.

Never since language began to be used have severity and tenderness been more marvelously blended than in the older portions of the English Prayer-Book.

This effect is largely due to an almost entire abstention on the part of the writers from figurative language, or at least from all imagery that is not readily recognized as Scriptural. Bread and beef are what men demand for a steady diet. Sweetmeats are well enough now and then, but only now and then.

It is the failure to observe this plain canon of style that has made shipwreck of many an attempt to construct liturgies *de novo.* Ambitious framers of forms of worship seem almost invariably to forget that there may be such a thing as a too exquisite prayer, an altogether too "eloquent address to the throne of grace." The longest and fullest supplicatory portion of the Prayer-Book, the Litany, does not contain, from the first sentence to the last,[41] one single figurative expression, it is literally plain English from the beginning to end; but could language be framed more intense, more satisfying, more likely to endure?

Scriptural metaphor, whether because it comes to us with the stamp of authority or on account of some subtle intrinsic excellence, it may be difficult to say, does not pall upon the taste. And yet even this is used sparingly in the Prayer-Book, some of the most striking exceptions to the general rule being afforded by the collects for the first and third Sundays in Advent, the collects for the Epiphany and Easter Even, and the opening prayer in the Baptismal Office. All these are instances of strictly Scriptural metaphor, and moreover it is to be kept in mind that they are designed for occasional, not constant use. In the orders for daily Morning, and Evening Prayer, the "lost sheep" of the General Confession and the "dew" of God's blessing in the Collect for Clergy and People are almost the sole, if not the sole cases of evident metaphor, and these again are Scriptural. When in Jeremy Taylor's prayer, introduced by the American revisers into the Order for the Visitation of the Sick, we come upon the comparison of human life to a "vale of misery" we feel that somehow we have struck a new current in the atmosphere; for the moment, it is the rhetorician who speaks and no longer the earnest seeker after God.

Besides this freedom from figures of speech, we notice in the style of Prayer-Book English a careful avoidance of whatever looks like a metaphysical abstraction. The aim is ever to present God and divine things as realities rather than as mere concepts or notions of the mind. So far as the writer remembers, not a single prayer in the whole book begins with that formula so dear to the makers of extemporary forms of devotion, "O Thou." On the contrary the approach to the Divine Majesty is almost always made with a reference to some attribute or characteristic that links Deity to man and man's affairs; it is "O God, the Protector of all that trust in thee," or "almighty and everlasting God who of thy tender love towards mankind," or "Lord of all power and might, who art the author and giver of all good things."

Cardinal Newman in one of his theological works written before his departure from the Church of England, has a powerful passage bearing upon this point. He is criticizing the evangelicals for their one-sided way of setting forth what it must mean to "preach the Gospel." No less a person than Leigh Richmond is the object of his strictures.

"A remarkable contrast between our Church's and this false view of religion," he says, "is afforded in the respective modes of treating a death bed in the Visitation of the sick, in a popular modern work, the Dairyman's Daughter. The latter runs thus: My dear friend, do you not FEEL *that you are supported?* The Lord deals very gently with me, she replied. Are not His promises *very precious to you?* They are all yea and amen in Christ Jesus. * * * Do you experience any *doubts or temptations* on the subject of your eternal safety? No sir; the Lord deals very gently with me and gives me peace. What are your *views* of the dark valley of death now that you are passing through it? *It is not dark.* Now, if it be said that such questions and answers are not only in their place innocent but natural and beautiful, I answer that this is not the point, but this, viz., they are evidently intended whatever their merits as a pattern of *what deathbed examinations should be.* Such is the Visitation of the Sick in the nineteenth century. Now let us listen to the nervous and stern tone of the sixteenth. In the Prayer-Book the Minister is instructed to say to the person visited,—Forasmuch as after this life there is an account to be given to the *Righteous Judge,* * * * I require you to examine yourself and your estate both toward God and man. Therefore I shall rehearse to you the *Articles of our Faith,* that you may know whether you do believe as a Christian man should or no. * * * 'Then shall the Minister examine whether he repent him truly of his sins, and be in *charity* with all the world; exhorting him to forgive from the bottom of his heart all persons who have offended him, and if he hath offended any other to *ask their forgiveness,* and where he hath done injury or wrong to any man that he *make amends* to the utmost of his power.' * * * Such is the contrast between the dreamy talk of modern Protestantism, and 'holy fear's stern glow' in the Church Catholic."[42]

In this striking, though perhaps somewhat unnecessarily harsh way, Newman brings out a point which is unquestionably true, namely, that the language of the Prayer-Book is of the sort which it is just now the fashion to call realistic, that is, a language conversant with great facts rather than with phases of feeling and moods of mind;—which after all is only another way of saying that it is a Book of *Common* Prayer and not a manual for the furtherance of spiritual introspection.

These, then, are the characteristics of the Prayer-Book style; it is simple, straightforward, unmetaphorical, realistic. Seriously it looks almost like a studied insult alike to the scholarship and to the religion of our day, to say that these are excellencies attainable no longer. That revisers venturing upon additions to the Prayer-Book would be found to set the face as a flint against any slightest approach to sentimentality is true. But why assume that the men do not exist who are capable of such a measure of self-control? Grant that there are whole volumes of devotional matter, original and compiled, which one may ransack without finding a single form that is not either prolix, wishy-washy or superfluous;—it does not follow that if the Prayer-Book is to be enriched, the enrichments must necessarily come from such sources. Moreover it is to be remembered that there is another vice of style to be shunned in liturgical composition quite as carefully as sentimentality, namely, jejuneness. We cannot escape being sentimental simply by being dull. Feeling must not be denied its place in prayer for fear that it may not prove itself a duly chastened feeling. There ought to be a heart of fire underneath the calm surface of every formulary or worship. Flame and smoke are out of place; but a liturgy should glow throughout. Coldness, pure and simple, has no place in devotion.

Over and above the intrinsic difficulties in the way of revision growing out of the delicate nature of the work itself, obstacles of a different sort are certain to be encountered. In so large a body of men as the Joint Committee of the two Houses, entire and cordial agreement is almost too much to be expected; and then even supposing a unanimous report be submitted, what is likely to follow? Why this,—if the changes proposed are few, the cry will be raised, It surely is not worth while to alter the Prayer-Book for the sake of so insignificant a gain; whereas if the changes proposed are considerable, the counter cry will be sounded, This is revolution.

Then there is the anxious question, How will it look to the English? What will be the effect on the Concordat, if we touch the Prayer-Book? To be sure, the Concordat does not seem to weigh very heavily on the shoulders of the other party, as indeed there is no reason why it should. Convocation does not much disturb itself as to the view General Convention is likely to take of its sayings and doings, and even disestablishment might proceed without our being called into consultation. And yet the *Concordat* difficulty will have to be reckoned with; and the dire spectre of a possible disowning of us by our mother the Church of England will have to be laid, before any alterations in the Book of Common Prayer will be accounted by some among us perfectly safe.

But it is scarcely worth while to go on gratuitously suggesting opposition arguments. They will be sure to present themselves unsolicited in due time. For the present it is enough to add that if the movement for liturgical revision has not in it enough toughness of fibre to enable it to survive rigorous attack, it does not deserve success.

V.

DESIDERATA.

Under the head of liturgical enrichment ought to be classed whatever alteration would really serve to enhance the beauty, majesty or fitness of accepted formularies of worship. Excision may, under conceivable circumstances, be enrichment. James Wyatt undoubtedly imagined that he was improving the English cathedrals when he white-washed their interiors, added composition pinnacles to the west towers of Durham, and re-arranged the ancient monuments of Salisbury; but an important part of the enrichment accomplished by our nineteenth-century restorers has lain simply in the undoing of what Wyatt did.

Again, substitution may be enrichment, as in the case where a wooden spire built upon a stone tower is taken down to be replaced by honest work. It would be an enrichment if in St. George's Chapel, the central shrine of British royalty, the sham insignia now overhanging the stalls of the kings of the garter were to give room to genuine armor. Not merely then by addition but possibly in some instances, by both subtraction and substitution, we may find "the Prayer-Book as it is" open to improvement.

Before, however, entering upon any criticism of the formularies in detail, it is important to draw a distinction between two very different things, namely the structure of a liturgical office and the contents of it. By structure should be understood the skeleton or frame that makes the groundwork of any given office, by contents the actual liturgical material employed in filling out the office to its proper contour.

The offices of the Roman Breviary, for example, continue, for the most part, identical in structure from day to day, the year through; but they vary in contents. For an illustration nearer home, take our own *Order for Daily Morning Prayer.* The structure of it is as follows: —1. Sentences, 2. Exhortation, 3. Confession, 4. Absolution, 5. Lord's Prayer, 6. Versicles, 7. Invitatory Psalm, 8. The Psalms for the day, 9. Lection, 10. Anthem or Canticle, 11. Lection, 12. Anthem or Canticle, 13. Creed, 14. Versicles, 15. Collect for the day, 16. Stated Collects and Prayers, 17. Benediction.

Now it is evident that without departing by a hair's breadth from the lines of this framework, an indefinite number of services might by a process of substitution be put together, each one of which would in outward appearance differ widely from every other one. The identical skeleton, that is to say, might be so variously clothed upon that no two of its embodiments would be alike. But is it desirable to run very much after variety of such a sort in a book of prayer designed for common use? Most assuredly, No. To jeopard the supreme *desideratum* in a people's manual of worship, simplicity: to make it any harder than it now is for the average "stranger in the Church" to find the places, would be on the part of revisionists, an unpardonable blunder.

There are, however, a few points at which the Morning Prayer might advantageously be enriched, and no risk run. It would surely add nothing to the difficulty of finding the places, if for one-half of the present opening sentences there were to be substituted sentences appropriate to special days and seasons of the ecclesiastical year. We should in this way be enabled to give the key-note of the morning's worship at the very outset. Having once departed, as in the case of our first two sentences, from the English precedent of putting only penitential verses of Scripture to this use, there is no reason why we should not carry out still more fully in our selection the principle of appropriateness. The sentences displaced need not be lost, for they might still stand as now, at the opening of the Evening Prayer.

Passing on to the declarations of absolution there is an opportunity to simplify the arrangement by omitting the alternate form borrowed from the Order for the Administration of the Lord's Supper, where only it properly belongs. This, however, is a change likely to be resisted on doctrinal grounds, and need not be urged.

Coming to the *Venite,* we find another opportunity to accentuate the Christian Year. It may be said that the rubric, as it is already written, allows for the substitution of special anthems on the greater festivals and fasts. This is true; but by giving the anthem for Easter a place of honor, while relegating anthems for the other great days to an unnoticed spot between the Selections and the Psalter, the American compilers did practically discriminate in favor of Easter and against the rest. The real needs of the case would be more wisely met, if the permission to omit *Venite* now attached to "the nineteenth day of the month" were to be extended to Ash Wednesday and Good Friday, and special New Testament anthems analogous to the Easter one were to be inserted along with the respective Collects, Epistles and Gospels, for

Christmas Day and Whitsunday.

By this change, we should put each of the three great festivals of the year into possession of an invitatory anthem of its own; and we should obviate on the fasting days, by the simple expedient of omission, the futile efforts of Choir-master and organist to transform *Venite* from a cry of joy into a moan of grief.

This brings us to the Psalter. Here we have an opportunity to correct the palpable blunder by which it has come about that the greatest of the penitential psalms, the fifty-first, has no place assigned it among the proper psalms either for Ash-Wednesday or for Good Friday.[43] It would also be well to make optional, if not obligatory, the use of "proper psalms" on days other than those already provided with them; *e.g.* Advent Sunday, the Epiphany, Easter Even, Trinity Sunday, and All Saints' Day.[44] There would be a still larger gain in the direction of "flexibility of use," as well as a great economy of valuable space, if instead of reprinting some thirty of the Psalms of David under the name of Selections, we were to provide for allowing "select" Psalms to be announced by number in the same manner that "proper" Psalms are now announced. Instead of only the ten selections we now have, there might then be made available twenty or thirty groups of Psalms at absolutely no sacrifice of room. It has been objected to this proposal that the same difficulty which now attaches to the finding of the "proper Psalms" on great days would embarrass congregations whenever "select Psalms" were given out; but this is fairly met by the counter consideration that if our people were to be educated in the use of select Psalms into a more facile handling of the Psalter it would be just so much gained for days when the "proper Psalms" must of necessity be found and read. The services, that is to say, would run all the more smoothly on the great days, after congregations had become habituated, on ordinary days, to picking out the Psalms by number.

Another step in the line of simplification, and one which it is in order to mention here, would be the removal from the Morning Prayer of *Gloria in Excelsis*, seeing that it is never, or almost never, sung at the end of the Psalms unless at Evening Prayer. As to the expediency of restoring what has been lost of *Benedictus* after the second lesson, the present writer offers no opinion. There are some who warmly advocate the replacement, and there is, unquestionably, much to be said in favor of it. It is unlikely that any doctrinal motive dictated the abbreviation.

Pausing a moment at the Creeds for the insertion of a better title than "*Or this*" before the confession of Nicæa, we pass to the versicles that follow.

Here again it would be enrichment to restore the words of the English book, although the task of finding an equally melodious equivalent for *O Lord, save the Queen* might not be easy.

Happily the other versicles are such as no civil revolution can make obsolete. It will never be amiss to pray.

Endue thy Ministers with righteousness.

Answer.—*And make thy chosen people joyful.*

These are all the alterations for which the present Morning Prayer considered as a form of Divine Service for Sundays would seem to call. It will be observed that they are far from being of a radical character, that they affect the structure of the office not at all, and touch the contents of it but slightly. The case is altered when we come to the Order for Evening Prayer. Here there is a demand, not indeed for any structural change, but for very decided enrichment by substitution. The wording of the office is altogether too exact an echo of what has been said only a few hours before in Morning Prayer. It betokens a poverty of resources that does not really exist, when we allow ourselves thus to exhort, confess, absolve, intercede, and give thanks in the very same phrases at three in the afternoon that were on our lips at eleven in the morning.

Doubtless liturgical worship owes a good measure of its charm to the subtle power of repetition; but the principle is one that must be handled and applied with the most delicate tact, or virtue goes out of it. We must distinguish between similarity and sameness. The ordered recurrence of accents is what makes the rhythm of verse; but for all that, there is a difference between poetry and sing-song, just as there is a difference between melody and monotony. Moreover the taste of mankind undergoes change as to the sorts of repetition which it is disposed to tolerate. No modern poet of standing would venture, for instance, to employ identical epithets to the extent that Homer does, making Aurora "rosy-fingered" every time she appears upon the scene, and Juno as invariably "ox-eyed." People were pleased with it then, they would not be pleased with it now. It is possible in liturgics so to employ the principle of repetition that no wearying sense of sameness will be conveyed, and again it is possible so to mismanage it as to transform worship into something little better than a "slow mechanic exercise." Mere iteration, as such, is barren of spiritual power, witness the endless saying over of *Kyrie Eleison* in the Oriental service-books, a species of vain repetition which a liturgical writer of high intelligence rightly characterizes as "unmeaning, if not profane."[45] Now the common popular criticism upon the Evening Prayer of the Church is that it repeats too slavishly the wording of the Morning Prayer. If this is an unjust criticism we ought not to let ourselves be troubled by it. On the other hand, if it is a just criticism, it will be much wiser of us to heed than to stifle the voice that tells us the truth. It might seem to be straining a point, were one to venture to explain the present very noticeable disinclination of churchmen to attend a second service on Sunday, by connecting it with the particular infelicity in question; but that the excuse We have said all this once to-day; why say it again? may possibly have something, even if not much, to do with the staying at home is certainly a fair conjecture.

Without altering at all the structure of the Evening Prayer, it would be perfectly possible so to re-fill or reclothe that formulary as to give it the one thing needful which now it lacks, —freshness. In such a process the *Magnificat* and the *Nunc Dimittis* would play an important part; as would also certain "ancient collects" of which we have heard much of late.[46] Failing this, the next best thing (and the thing, it may be added, much more likely to be done, considering what a tough resistant is old usage) would be the provision of an alternate and optional form of Evening Prayer, to be used either in lieu of, or as supplementary to the existing office. In the framing of such a *Later Evensong* a larger freedom would be possible than the refilling of a form the main lines of which were already fixed. Still, the first plan would be better, if only it could be brought within the range of things possible.

Next to Evening Prayer in the order of the Table of Contents comes The Litany. Here there is no call for enrichment,[47] though increased flexibility of use might be secured for this venerable form of intercessory prayer by prefixing to it the following rubric abridged from a similar one proposed in The Convocation Prayer-Book.

"A *General Supplication, to be sung or said on Sundays, Wednesdays and Fridays, and on the Rogation Days, after the third collect at Morning or Evening Prayer, or before the Administration of the Holy Communion; or as a separate Service.*

NOTE. *The Litany may be omitted altogether on Christmas Day, Easter Day and Whitsunday.*"

In connection with the Morning and Evening Service there is another important question that imperatively demands discussion, namely, week-day worship. The movement for "shortened services," so called, has shared the usual fate of all efforts at bettering the life of the Church, in being from the outset of its course widely and seriously misunderstood. The impression has gone abroad, and to-day holds possession of many otherwise well-informed people, that a large and growing party in the Episcopal Church has openly declared itself wearied out with overmuch prayer and praise. Were such indeed the fact, the scandal would be grave; but the real truth about the matter is that the promoters of shortened services, instead of seeking to diminish, are really eager to see multiplied the amount of worship rendered in our Churches. "Shorted services" is a phrase of English not American origin, and has won its way here by dint of euphony rather than of fitness. Readjusted services, though a more clumsy, would be a less misdirecting term. In the matter of Sunday worship, the liberty now generally conceded of using separately the Morning Prayer, the Litany and the Holy Communion is all that need be asked. Whether these services, or at least two of them, do not in themselves admit of a certain measure of improvement is a point that has already been considered, but there certainly is no need of shortening them, whatever else it may be thought well to do. When what a Boston worthy once termed "a holy alacrity" is observed, on the part of both minister and singers, even the aggregated services of Morning Prayer, Litany and "Ante-Communion," together with a sermon five-and-twenty minutes long, can easily be brought within the compass of an hour and a half,—a measure of time not unreasonably large to be given to the principal occasion of worship on the Lord's Day. As for the Evening Prayer,—there certainly ought to be no call for the shortening of that on Sundays; for it would be scarcely decent or proper to devote to such a service anything less than the half hour the existing office demands.

What the advocates of shortened services really desire to see furthered is an increase in the frequency of opportunities for worship during the week, their conviction being that if the Church were to authorize brief services for morning and evening use, such as would not occupy much more time than family prayers ordinarily do, the attendance might be secured of many who, at present, put aside the whole question of going to Church on week-days as impracticable. Supposing it could be proved that such a provision would work to the discouragement of family prayer, it would plainly be wrong to advocate it; no priesthood is more sacred than that which comes with fatherhood. But we must face the fact that in our modern American life family prayer, like sundry other wholesome habits, has fallen largely into disuse. If the Church can, in any measure, supplement the deficiencies of the household, and help to supply to individuals a blessing they would gladly enjoy at their own homes, if they might, it is her plain duty to do so. Moreover, many a Minister who single-handed cannot now prudently undertake a daily service, as that is commonly understood, would acknowledge himself equal to the less extended requirement.

Not a few careful and friendly observers of the practical work of the Anglican religion have been reluctantly led to consider the daily service, as an institution, only meagrely successful. Looking at the matter historically we find no reason to wonder at such a conclusion.

Our existing usage (or more correctly, perhaps, *non-usage*), dates from the Reformation period. The English Church and nation of that day had grown up familiar with the spectacle of a very large body of clerics, secular and regular, whose daily occupation may be said to have been the pursuit of religion.[48] The religion pursued consisted chiefly in the saying of prayers, and very thoroughly, so far at least as the consumption of time was concerned, were the prayers said. What more natural than that, under such circumstances, and with such associations, the compilers of a common Prayer-Book for the people should have failed to see any good reason for discriminating between the amount of service proper to the Lord's Day and the amount that might be reasonably expected on other days? Theoretically they were right, all time belongs to God and He is as appropriately worshipped on Tuesdays and Thursdays as on Sundays. And yet as a result of their making no such discrimination, we have the daily service on our hands,—a comparative, even if not an utter failure. We may lament the fact, but a fact it is, that in spite of all its improved appliances for securing leisure, the world is busier than ever it was; and there will always be those who will insist that the command to labor on six days is as imperative as the injunction to rest upon the seventh. As a consequence of all this accelerated business, and of the diminution in the number of persons officially set apart for prayer, the unabridged service of the Church fails to command a week-day attendance. We have no "clerks" nowadays to fill the choir. The only clerks known to modern times are busy at their desks.

It may be urged in reply to this, that the practical working of the daily service ought to be kept a secondary consideration, and that its main purpose is symbolical, or representative; the priest kneeling in his place, day by day, as a witness that the people, though unable personally to be present, do, in heart and mind, approve of a daily morning and evening sacrifice of prayer. This conception of the daily service as a vicarious thing has a certain mystical beauty about it, but if it is to be adopted as the Church's own let us, at least, clear ourselves of inconsistency by striking out the word "common" from before the word "prayer" in characterizing our book.

What is really needed for daily use in our parishes is a short form of worship specially framed for the purpose. If they could be employed without offence to the Protestant ear (and they are good English-Reformation words) Week-Day Matins and Week-Day Evensong would not be ill chosen names for such services. The frame-work of these Lesser Orders for Morning and Evening Prayer, as they might also be called were the other titles found obnoxious, ought to be modelled upon the lines of the existing daily offices, though with a careful avoidance of identity in contents. There should be, for instance, as unvarying elements, the reading of the lessons for the day, the use of the collect for the day, and the saying or singing of the psalms for the day. Another constant would be the Lord's Prayer; but aside from these the *Lesser Order* need have nothing in common with the Order as we have it now. There might be, for example, after the manner of the old service books, an invitatory opening with versicles and responses, or if the present mode of opening by sentences were preferred, specially chosen sentences, different from those with which the Sunday worship has made us familiar could be employed. Moreover, the anthems or canticles and the prayers, with the exception of the two just mentioned, ought also to be distinctive, and, in the technical sense of the word, *proper* to week day use.

Again, it would serve very powerfully and appropriately to emphasize the pivot points in the ritual year if this same principle were to be applied to Saints' days, and we were to have special *Holy-day Matins* and *Holy-day Evensong,* there still being required, on the greater festivals and fasts, the normal Morning and Evening Prayer proper to the Lord's Day.[49]

The argument in favor of thus specializing the services for week-days and holy days, in preference to following the only method heretofore thought possible, namely, that of shortening the Lord's Day Order, rests on two grounds. In the first place permissions to skip and omit are of themselves objectionable in a book of devotions. They have an uncomely look. Our American Common Prayer boasts too many disfigurements of this sort already.

Such a rubric as *The Minister may, at his discretion, omit all that follows to etc.*, puts one in mind of the finger-post pointing out the short cut to weary travellers. It is inopportune thus to hint at exhaustion as the probable concomitant of worship. That each form should have an integrity of its own, should as "a separate whole" be either said complete, or left unsaid, is better liturgical philosophy than any "shortened services act" can show.

In the second place, a certain amount of variety would be secured by the proposed method which under the existing system we miss. There is of course, such a danger as that of providing too much liturgical variety. Amateur makers of Prayer-Books almost invariably fall into this slough. Hymn books, as is well known, often destroy their own usefulness by including too many hymns; and Prayer-Books may do the same by having too many prayers.[50]

To transgress in the compiling of formularies material than the mind of an habitual worshipper is likely to assimilate is to misread human nature. But here, as elsewhere, there is a just mean. Cranmer and his colleagues in the work of revision jumped at one bound from a scheme which provided a distinctive set of services for every day in the year to a scheme that assigned one stereotyped form to all days.

Now nothing would be more unwise than any attempt to restore the methods of the Breviary, with its complicated and artificial forms of devotion; but so far to imitate the Breviary as to provide within limits for a recognition of man's innate love of change would be wisdom. By having a distinctive service for week-days, and a distinctive service for holy days, we might add just that little increment to the Church's power of traction that in many instances would avail to change "I cannot go to church this morning" into "I cannot stay away."

It will be urged as a counter-argument to these considerations that the thing is impossible, that such a measure of enrichment is entirely in excess of anything the Church has expressed a wish to have, and that for reviewers to propose a plan so sweeping would be suicide. Doubtless this might be a sufficient answer to anybody who imagined that by a bare majority vote of two successive General Conventions new formularies of daily worship could be forced upon the Church. But suppose such formularies were to be made *optional;* suppose there were to be given to Parishes the choice between these three things viz.: (*a*) the normal Morning Prayer; (*b*) a shortened form of the normal Morning Prayer; and (*c*) such a special order as has been sketched,—what then? Would the Church's liberty be impaired? On the contrary, would not the borders of that liberty have been most wisely and safely widened by the steady hand of law?

This is perhaps the right point at which to call attention to the present state of the "shortened services" controversy, for wearisome as the story has become by frequent repetition, the *nexus* between it and the subject in hand is too important to be left out of sight.

In the General Convention of 1877, where the topic under its American aspects was for the first time thoroughly discussed, the two Houses came to a dead lock. The deputies on the one hand, almost to a man, voted in favor of giving the desired relief by *rubric,* thus postponing for three years time, the fruition of their wish; while the Bishops with a unanimity understood to have been equally striking insisted that a simple *canon,* such as could be passed on once, would suffice. And so the subject dropped.

At the late Convention of 1880 an eirenicon was discovered. The quick eye of one of the legal members of the House of Deputies detected on the fourth page of the Prayer-Book, just opposite the Preface, a loop-hole of escape, to wit, *The Ratification of the Book of Common Prayer.* Here was the very *tertium quid* whereby the common wish of both parties to the dispute might be effected without injury to sensibilities of either.

The *Ratification* certainly did not look like a Canon, neither could anybody with his eyes open call it a rubric,—why not amend that, and say no more about it? The suggestion prevailed, and by vote of both Houses, the following extraordinary document is hereafter to stand (the next General Convention consenting) in the very forefront of the Prayer-Book:—

"*The Ratification of the Book of Common Prayer. By the Bishops, the Clergy, and the Laity of the Protestant Episcopal Church in General Convention assembled.*

"The General Convention of the Church having heretofore, to wit: on the sixteenth day of October in the year A. D. 1789, set forth *a Book of Common Prayer and Administration of the Sacraments and other Rites and Ceremonies of the Church,* and thereby established the said Book and declared it to be the Liturgy of said Church, and required that it be received as such by all the members of the same and be in use from and after the first day of October, in the year of our Lord 1790; the same book is hereby ratified and confirmed, and ordered to be the use of this Church from this time forth.

"But note, however, that on days other than Sundays, Christmas Day, the Epiphany, Ash Wednesday, Good Friday and Ascension Day, it shall suffice if the Minister begins Morning or Evening Prayer at the General Confession or the Lord's Prayer preceded by one or more of the sentences appointed at the beginning of Morning and Evening Prayer, and end after the Collect for Grace, or the Collect for Aid against Perils, with 2 Cor. xxi. 14, using so much of the Lessons appointed for the day and so much of the Psalter as he shall judge to be for edification.

"And note also that on any day when Morning and Evening Prayer shall have been duly said or are to be said, and on days other than those first afore mentioned, it shall suffice when need may require, if a sermon or Lecture be preceded by at least the Lord's Prayer and one or more Collects found in this book, provided that no prayers not set forth in said book, or otherwise authorized by this Church, shall be used before or after such sermon or lecture.[51]

"And note further also that on any day the Morning Prayer, the Litany or the Order for the Administration of the Lord's Supper, may be used as a separate and independent service, provided that no one of these services shall be disused habitually."

It may seem harsh to characterize this act as the mutilation of a monument; but really it does seem to be little else. The old Ratification of 1789 is an historic landmark; it is the sign-manual of the Church of White's and Seabury's day and ought never to be disturbed or tampered with while the Prayer-Book stands. The year 1889 might very properly see a supplemental Ratification written under it; and testifying to the fact of Revision; but to write into that venerable text special directions as to what may be done on days other than Ash-Wednesday, and what must not be done without II Cor. xiii., 14, is very much as if the City Government of Cambridge should cause to be cut upon the stone under the Washington elm which now records the fact that there the commander of the American armies first drew his sword, divers and sundry additional items of information, such as the distance to Watertown, the shortest path across the common, etc. etc.

Why the Convention after having entrusted to a Joint Committee, by a decisive vote, the task of devising means for securing for the Prayer-Book "increased flexibility of use," should have thought it necessary subsequently to take up with this compromise of a compromise (for such the proposal to amend the Ratification really is) it is difficult to say. Perhaps it was with the determination to have, at any rate, something to fall back upon in case the larger and more comprehensive measure should come to naught.

The *rubric* is confessedly the proper place for directions as to how to use the services, and, but for the very natural and defensible objection on the part of some to touching the Prayer-Book at all, there never would have been any question about it.[52] This objection having been at last waived, a straight path is now open to the end desired, and it ought to be followed even at the cost of three years more of delay.

Returning to the general subject, and still following the order of the Table of Contents, we come to *Prayers and Thanksgivings upon several Occasions.*

Here it would be well to note more intelligibly than is done by the present rubric the proper places for introduction of the Prayers and

Thanksgivings, providing for the use of the former before, and of the latter after the General Thanksgiving.

As to the deficiencies in this department let the late Dr. Muhlenberg speak.

"The Prayer-Book," he says, "is not undervalued as to its treasures in asserting its wants. The latter cannot be denied. Witness the meagre amount of New Testament prayer and praise for the round of festivals and fasts; the absence of any forms suited to the peculiar circumstances of our own Church and country and to the times we live in; or for our benevolent and educational institutions. There are no prayers for the increase of Ministry, for Missions, or Missionaries, for the Christian teaching of the young; for sponsors on occasions of Baptism; for persons setting out on long journeys by land, quite as perilous as voyages by sea; for the sick desiring the prayers of the Church when there is no prospect of or desire for recovery; for the bereaved at funerals, and many other occasions for which there might as well be provision for those few for which we already have the occasional prayers."[53]

After the *Prayers and Thanksgivings* come *The Collects, Epistles and Gospels.* Here again there is some room for enrichment. Distinctive collects for the first four days of Holy Week, for Monday and Tuesday in Easter Week and for Monday and Tuesday in Whitsun Week would add very materially to our liturgical wealth, while there would seem to be no reason whatever why they should not be had. It would also serve to enhance the symmetry of the Christian Year if the old feast of the Transfiguration[54] (August 6) were to be restored to its place among the recognized holy days of the Church and given its proper collect, epistle and gospel.

There are some liturgists who desire the restoration of the introits of the first book of Edward the VI. The introit (so-called from being the Psalm sung when the priest goes within the altar rails) has been in modern usage replaced by a metrical hymn. A sufficient reason for not printing the introit for each day in full, just before the collect, as was the mode in Edward's book is that to do so would involve a costly sacrifice of room. A compromise course would be to insert between the title of each Sunday or Holy day and the collect proper to it, a simple numerical reference stating whereabouts in the Psalter the introit for the day is to be found, and adding perhaps the Latin catch-words. Any attempt to make the use of the introit obligatory in our times would meet with deserved failure; the metrical hymn has gained too firm a hold upon the affections of the Church at large ever to be willingly surrendered.

Coming, next, to the orders for the administration of the two sacraments, we find ourselves on delicate ground, where serious change of any sort is out of the question. Permission, under certain circumstances, still further to abbreviate the Office of the Communion of the Sick might, however, be sought without giving reasonable cause of alarm to any, and general consent might perhaps also be had for a provision with respect to the Exhortation "Dearly beloved in the Lord" that in "Churches where there is frequent Communion it shall suffice to read the Exhortation above written once in a month on the Lord's Day."[55]

There are three liturgical features of the Scottish Communion Office which some have thought might be advantageously transferred to our own service. They are (*a*) the inserting after Christ's summary of the law a response, *Lord, have mercy upon us and write these thy laws in our hearts we beseech thee;* (*b*) the repeating by the people, after the reading of the Gospel, of a formula of thanks corresponding to the *Glory be to thee O Lord* that precedes it; and (*c*) the saying or singing of an Offertory sentence at the presentation of the alms. Upon these suggested enrichments the present writer offers no opinion.

In the Order of Confirmation a substitution for the present preface[56] of a responsive opening, in which the Bishop should charge the Minister to present none but such as he has found by personal enquiry, "apt and meet" for the reception of the rite would be a marked improvement.

The remaining Occasional Offices would seem to demand no change either in structure or contents, although in some, perhaps in all of them, additional rubrics would be helpful to worshippers.

Some addition to the number of Occasional Offices would be a real gain. We need, for instance, a short Office for the Burial of Infants and Young children; a Day-break Office for Great Festivals; and Office for Mid-day Prayer; and Office of Prayer in behalf of Missions and Missionaries; an Office for the Setting apart of a Layman as a Reader, or as a Missionary; a Form of Prayer at the Laying of a Corner-Stone; and possibly some others. It is evident that these new formularies might give opportunity for the introduction of hitherto unused collects, anthems and benedictions of a sort that would greatly enhance the general usefulness of the Prayer-Book.

This completes the survey of the field of "liturgical enrichment." A full discussion of the allied topic, "flexibility of use," would involve the examination in detail of all the rubrics of the Prayer-Book, and for this there is no room. It is enough to say that unless the rubrics, the hinges and joints of a service book are kept well oiled, much creaking is a necessary result. There are moments in our public worship where congregations almost invariably betray an awkward embarrassment, simply because there is nothing to tell them whether they are expected to stand or to sit or to kneel. It is easy to sneer at such points as trifles and to make sport of those who call attention to them; but if it is worth our while to have ritual worship at all it is also worth our while to make the directions as to how people are to behave adequate, explicit, plain. A lofty contempt for detail is not the token of good administration either in Church or State. To the list of defective rubrics, add those that are confessedly obsolete and such as are palpably contradictory and we have a bill of particulars that would amply justify a rubrical revision of the Prayer-Book even if nothing more were to be attempted.

There is another reason. Far more rapidly than many people imagine, we are drifting away from the position of a Church that worships by liturgy to that of a Church worshipping by directory. The multiplicity of "uses" that vexed the Anglican Reformers is in our day multiplied fourfold. To those who honestly consider a directory a better thing than a liturgy this process of relaxation is most welcome, but for others who hold that, until the binding clauses of a Book of Common Prayer have been formally rescinded, they ought to be observed, the spectacle is the reverse of edifying. They would much prefer seeing the channels of liberty opened at the touch of law, and this is one of their chief reasons for advocating revision.

Two questions remain untouched, both of them of great practical importance. Could the Prayer-Book be enriched to the extent suggested in this paper without a serious and most undesirable increase in its bulk as a volume?

Even supposing this were possible, is it at all likely that the Church could be persuaded to accept the amended book?

Unless the first of these two eminently proper questions can be met, there is, or ought to be an end to all talk about revision. The advantage to a Church of being able to keep all its authoritative formularies of worship within the compass of a single volume is inestimable. Even the present enforced severance of the Hymnal from the Prayer-Book is a misfortune.[57]

Those were good days when "Bible and Prayer-Book" was the Churchman's all sufficient formula, so far as volumes were concerned.

Rome boasts a much larger ritual variety than ours, but she secures it by multiplying books. The Missal is in one volume, the Breviary in four, the Pontifical, the Ritual and the Ceremonial in one each, making eight in all.[58] This is an evil, and one from which we Anglicans have had a happy escape. It was evidently with a great groan of relief that the Church of England shook herself free from the whole host of service-books, and established her one only volume. It behooves us to be watchful how we take a single step towards becoming entangled in the old meshes.[59]

But need the enrichment of the Prayer-Book;—such enrichment as has been described, necessarily involve an unwieldiness in the volume, or, what would be still worse, an overflow into a supplement? Certainly not; for by judicious management every change advocated in this paper, and more besides, might be accomplished without transgressing by so much as a page or a paragraph the limits of the present standard book. All the space needed could be secured by the simple expedient of omitting matter that has been found by actual experience to be superfluous. Redundancy and unnecessary repetition are to the discredit of a book that enjoys such an unrivalled reputation as the Common Prayer. They are blemishes upon the face of its literary perfectness. Who has not marvelled at the strange duplication of the Litany and the Office of the Holy Communion in the Ordinal, when the special petitions proper to those services when used in that connection might easily have been printed by themselves with a direction that they be inserted in the appointed place?

Scholars, of course, know perfectly well how this came about. The Ordinal does not belong to the Prayer-Book proper, but has a separate identity of its own. When printed as a book by itself, it is all very well that it should include the Litany and the Holy Communion in full, but why allow these superfluous pages to crowd out others that are really needed?[60]

It has already been explained how the room now occupied by the "Selections" might be economized, and by the same simple device the space engrossed by divers psalms here and there in the Occasional Offices, *e.g.* Psalm li in the Visitation of Prisoners, and Psalm cxxx in the Visitation of the Sick could be made available for other use.

Again why continue to devote a quarter of a page of precious space to the "Prayer for imprisoned debtors," seeing that now, for a long time past, there has been no such thing in the United States as imprisonment for debt? By availing ourselves of only a portion of these possible methods of garnering space, all that is desired might be accomplished, without making the Prayer-Book bulkier by a single leaf than it is today.

But would a Prayer-Book thus enriched be accepted by the Church at large? Is there any reason to think that the inertia which inheres in all large bodies, and to a singularly marked degree in our own communion, could be overcome? The General Convention can give an approximate answer to these questions, it cannot settle them decisively, for it is a body which mirrors only to a certain extent the real mind and temper of the constituencies represented in it. One thing is certain, that only by allowing fullest possible play to the principle of "local option" could any wholly new piece of work on the part of revisionists, however excellent it might be in itself considered, find acceptance. To allow features introduced into the body of an existing service to be accounted optional, would indeed be impossible, without gendering the very wildest confusion. Upon such points the Church would have to decide outright, for or against, and stand by her decisions. But as respects every additional and novel Office proposed, the greatest care ought to be taken to have the indefinite *an* rather than the definite *The* prefixed to it. Before such new uses are made binding on all, they must have met and endured the test of thorough trial by some. This is only fair.

But there is a limit, it must be remembered, in the Church's case, to the binding power of precedent and prescription. The social order changes, and of these tides that ebb and flow it is our bounden duty to take note. Had mere aversion to change, dogged unwillingness to venture an experiment always carried the day, instead of having the Prayer-Book as it is, we should still be drearily debating the rival merits of Hereford and Sarum. The great question to be settled is Does an emergency exist serious enough to warrant an attempt on our part to make better, what we know already to be good? Is the Republic expecting of us, and reasonably expecting of us, greater things than with our present equipment we are quite able to accomplish? There are eyes that think they see a great future before this Church,—they are right, or is it only mirage? At any rate ours is no return trip,—we are outward bound. The ship is cutting new and untried waters with her keel at every moment. There is no occasion to question the sufficiency of either compass or helm, but in certain matters of a practical sort there is a demand upon us to use judgment, we are bound to give a place in our seamanship to present common sense as well as to respect for ancient usage, and along with it all to feel some confidence that if the ship is what we think her to be, "the winds of God" may be trusted to bring her safely into port.

---

25. The *Book of Offices* Proposed in 1889

[The contents of the book were:

1. A Short Office for Sundry Occasions, consisting of prayers for a General Ending, At Early Morning, At Noon, and at other hours, and At Late Evening.
2. A Compline Office.
3. An Office of Intercession for Unity.
4. An Office for the Fourth of July and for Special Days of Thanksgiving.
5. An Office for Special Days of Fasting.
6. An Office for Harvest-Home.
7. A Penitential Office for Lent.
8. A Commemoration of the Passion (with Collects of the Passion).
9. A Litany for Missions.
10. A Litany for the Christian Life.
11. A Litany for a Sick Person.
12. Prayers for Sundry Occasions.

The titles of all the prayers and the texts of some of them are given in the following section.]

PRAYERS.

¶ *These prayers may be used after Morning and Evening Prayer, after Sermons and Lectures, and with any Office in this Book, as occasion may require, at the discretion of the Minister.* * * *

A Morning Prayer. (2)

An Evening Prayer. (2)

A General Intercession.

For the Reunion of Christendom.

For the Increase of the Ministry. (2)

For Missions. (3)

For a Blessing on Pastor and People.

For the Clergy.

O LORD Jesus, thou great Shepherd of the flock of God, we pray thee for all whom thou hast set apart to the awful duty of caring for thy people in thy Name. Pour out a blessing, we beseech thee, and make our pastors men of faith and purity and power. Give them deep wisdom in thy Word through much reading and pondering thereof. Draw them near to thee in habits of devout prayer. Inspire them with an exceeding love of souls; make them to have a tender and careful conscience. Delight them with thy love; sober them with thy holy fear. In all their sorrows make them to enter into the patience of thy passion, and let thy joy never fail them. And as thou hast given them a high and wonderful calling to be messengers of thy grace on earth, help them to live in holy obedience, in untiring faithfulness, in care for all them that are to be heirs of thy salvation; that they may please thee and fulfil thy ministry, O blessed Saviour, who livest and reignest with the Father and the Holy Comforter, one God, world without end. *Amen.*

In the Vacancy of a Cure of Souls.

During the Building of a Church.

For Persons Preparing for Holy Baptism.

For Persons preparing for Confirmation.

O MERCIFUL Lord, we beseech thee abundantly to strengthen, with the seven-fold gift of thy Holy Spirit, thy servants who are preparing for Confirmation in this parish; that they, being admitted by thine ordinance to the fulness of Christian grace, may grow, in the exercise of the power which thou givest them, unto the perfection of Christian life; through thy Son Jesus Christ, our Mediator and Redeemer. *Amen.*

When any are about to be Admitted to the Holy Communion.

For Children. (2)

For Young Men.

O LORD Jesus Christ, grant that the young men of our country may live before thee in purity, and may use their strength and energy for thy glory, who art the source of their life and the Captain of their salvation. Reveal thyself in their hearts, that being filled with thy wisdom, they may know thee the pattern of meekness and purity, of diligence and obedience, of endurance and hope; so that they may follow without hesitation wheresoever thou shalt call them; and at length, being perfected in thee, may come to the measure of the stature of thy fulness; who art with the Father and the Holy Ghost, one God, world without end. *Amen.*

For Schools and colleges.

For a Blessing upon Special Services.

For those who serve God under Difficulties.

For those who are without the Means of Grace.

For those who are obliged to work on the Lord's Day.

O LORD, have mercy upon all those whose necessities keep them in the work of the world upon thy holy day. Draw their thoughts to thyself, and make them partakers of the benefits of the prayers and intercessions of thy holy Church. And grant to their employers grace to consider the needs of those whom thou hast made in thine image; that they who serve may fail not finally to attain to that rest which remaineth for the people of God; through Jesus Christ our Lord. *Amen.*

For those who err from the Faith.

For those who are Separated from the Church through Ignorance.

For those who live in Sin.

For Insane and Imbecile Persons.

MERCIFUL Saviour of the world, by thy hour of darkness and desolation on the Cross, we plead with thee, and entreat thee for all thy servants whom disease or infirmity of mind is separating from their brethren. Deal tenderly with them, we beseech thee, deal tenderly with them. Cherish them with guardianship of thy good angels, with compassion and gentleness of men, with kindness and wisdom in the care of them. Bring them, we pray thee, to a perfect soundness in this life, or else send in thy good time and draw forth the prisoners of hope into the light and largeness of thy Paradise. And give them all a place and name hereafter in thy joyous city new Jerusalem, where thou shalt be glorified with the Father and the Holy Ghost for ever. *Amen.*

For the Intemperate.

O GOD, we beseech thee, deliver our land from the grievous sin of drunkenness, whereby it is sorely defiled; and grant that they who indulge in whatsoever excess beclouds the mind and degrades the body, may have grace to check themselves ere they have lost the power of self-control, and finding the unsatisfying nature of all earthly excitement, may come to hunger and thirst after righteousness, and be filled with the spirit of thy love; through Jesus Christ our Mediator and Advocate. *Amen.*

Against Sensuality and Self-indulgence.

BE merciful and gracious, O Lord, unto thy servants, and pardon the infirmities of our earthly nature. Grant that all who are especially hindered in their spiritual course by the appetites of the flesh, may be quickened by the power of thy Holy Spirit, and strengthened in all holy endeavours, so that they may bring their bodies into subjection, and live in watchful observance of thy holy law, through Jesus Christ our Saviour. *Amen.*

Against Covetousness.

For the Rich.

O ALMIGHTY God, we beseech thee to send thy grace upon those whom thou hast entrusted with great possessions, that they may praise thee in their lives, honour thee with their wealth, and lead others by their example to seek for that inheritance which thy beloved Son will give to all those who have followed him. Have mercy upon such as neglect to minister to the wants of thy poor; and grant that, remembering the account of their stewardship which they must one day give, they may be faithful almoners of thy bounty, and so at last attain to thy heavenly kingdom; through Jesus Christ our Lord. *Amen.*[61]

For the Thoughtless.

O GOD and Father of all, who delightest in the happiness of thy creatures; Send down thy Holy Spirit upon all those who are drawn away to forgetfulness of thee, whether by the pleasures of youth, the opportunities of wealth, or the excitement of sin. Enlighten them, defend them, calm them, control them; make them to see the insufficiency of earthly pleasures and the joy of thy holy service; and so govern their natural energies by the power of thy love, that they, now learning to rejoice in the hope of thy glory, may hereafter attain to the fruition of thy Godhead; through Jesus Christ our Lord. *Amen.*

For Chastity.

O HOLY and immaculate Jesus, who wast born of a virgin mother, and delightest to dwell in chaste and pure hearts; With mercy behold thy servants often beset with the temptations of those fleshly lusts which war against the soul; and because we cannot stand in the day of battle and danger unless thy grace prevent and strengthen us, O let thy blessed Spirit descend upon us, the Spirit of purity and holiness, and preserve us clean and undefiled, that our bodies may be thy holy temple, and our souls thy sanctuary fit for thee to dwell in. Pardon all our past sins and self-indulgences, whether in thought, word, or deed; teach us to hate and shun all images and fellowships that corrupt the imagination and defile the body; and, O thou blessed Jesus, do thou kindle in us the fire of a divine love to burn away our dross, and make us pure in thee; that so we may not any more grieve thy Holy Spirit by any works of darkness, but being washed and cleansed in thy blood, and walking in the light as children of the light, may glorify thee in our bodies and our spirits which are thine, and at last be numbered with thy saints in glory everlasting, who livest and reignest with the Father and the Holy Ghost, one God, world without end. *Amen.*

For Reverence in Speech.

O LORD God, whose holy Name is the joy of thy creatures; Make thy Name to be so hallowed in the lives of those who have been baptized therein, and upon the lips of those who speak thereof, that its holiness may not turn to our ruin, exposing our unworthiness, but may be found to our preservation, drawing us upward in thy love; through Jesus Christ our Lord. *Amen.*

For the Spirit of Prayer.

For Defence and Discipline.

For Peace.

For the Army and Navy.

O MOST powerful and glorious Lord God, the Lord of hosts, that rulest and commandest all things; Vouchsafe, we beseech thee, to bless the officers and men of our army and navy. Grant that in the midst of the dangers and temptations which beset them, they may fight manfully against the world, the flesh, and the devil; and resisting all evil by the spirit of thy ghostly strength, may acquire true courage in the hour of danger and in the day of battle. Prosper them in the maintenance of our country's honour; keep them safe from enemies spiritual and temporal; that they may glorify thee upon the earth, until they are called to rest in the triumph of thy glory; through Jesus Christ our Lord. *Amen.*

After a Battle.

O LORD, we pray thee to have mercy upon all who are this day wounded and suffering. Let thy grace be their comfort, though kindred and friends be far away. Raise them to health again, if it be thy good pleasure; but chiefly give them such patience and faith in thee, that they, being delivered from the assaults of their spiritual enemies, may rest in peace and rise to partake of thy glory; through Jesus Christ of Lord. *Amen.*

¶ *At Anniversary or other Public Occasional Services of any Guild or Society of Christian people associated for good and lawful purposes, the Minister may use the special from of prayer of such Guild or Society;* Provided, *the same have been set forth or approved by the Bishop, and not otherwise.*

26. The Resolution of 1913

RESOLVED: That a Joint Commission consisting of seven Bishops, seven Presybters, and seven Laymen be appointed to consider and report to the next General Convention such revision and enrichment of the Prayer Book as will adapt it to present conditions, if, in their judgment, such revision be necessary; *Provided,* that no proposition involving the Faith and Doctrine of the Church shall be considered or reported upon by the Commission; and *Provided,* that no proposal to change the Title-page of the Prayer Book or the Name of the Church shall be referred to said Commission.

Notes

[1]Printed as a rubric.

[2]Beneath this address and the preceding rubric, Seabury prints the "Private Devotions for the Altar" which here follow the text of the Communion Office.

[3]This office, slightly enlarged from one compiled by William Smith the younger, survives in a fair copy in Seabury's hand, and was printed sometime in the early 1790's, but neither version bears place or date. The service was reprinted at least twice in the nineteenth century; its unofficial use in the New England states may be due to the lack of official prayers for the burial of infants until 1928. I am indebted to Prof. David Green for access to the Seabury collection at General Seminary, particularly for this text and the liturgical notebook which follows.

[4]Here and in the liturgical notebook, italics replace the red ink employed by Seabury.

[5]The large blank spaces, underlinings, strike-throughs, etc. are Seabury's.

[6]"with its sacred instruments and furniture" inserted in pencil, same hand.

[7]A number of these prayers do not have a final Amen. Here, Amen added in pencil, same hand.

[8]Amen added in pencil, same hand.

[9]Amen added in pencil, same hand.

[10]Amen added in pencil, same hand.

[11]Amen added in pencil, same hand.

[12]Seabury's heading.

[13]Seabury's heading.

[14]The hand is quite weak from this point.

[15][Muhlenberg's note.] I quote from the English Prayer Book, which keeps up the consistency of the services.

[16][Muhlenberg's note.] In its first principles and to those comparatively ignorant of them.

[17][Muhlenberg's note.] From a highly sensible corespondant of the *Evangelical Catholic.*

[18][Muhlenberg's note.] There was a proposition in the last general convention, that the Bishops be requested to prepare forms of prayer for MISSIONARIES in heath and destitute regions. But what kind of forms was it expected could be prepared? How infinite their diversity! a missionary addresses himself to hearers ignorant, if not wholly, yet to a great extent, of the Gospel, after which his prayer, for the most part, would naturally be offered in behalf of the people, that they might be inclined to receive the truths he taught, which none could make of select but himself. That a missionary is not supposed to be a perfect liberty on such occasions is a striking admission of the extreme rigidity of our system here asserted.

[19][Muhlenberg's note.] Granted that the most illiterate may be trained to it—but we must first get hold to them in order to train them, and the service does not profess to be the instrument for that. It begins with the *Dearly Beloved,* who are all ready for the Confession, absolution, and thence on to the highest acts of worship.

[20][Muhlenberg's note.] That is, prayer to which the minister is not bound by rubrical appointments—which he may use at discretion. It need not be extemporaneous. The language may have been precomposed, or selected, from inspired or other sources. If dictated by the feeling of the moment, it is not likely to be in the style of much of the extemporaneous prayers heard in places of worship where only such prayer is used. Free prayer in connection with a liturgy and in due subordination to it, will naturally borrow from it, its tone and manners. It could hardly become *preaching* prayer.

[21][Muhlenberg's note.] Custom, at present, having indeed almost the force of law, forbids this, and therefore I have not allowed for it, in what I have said elsewhere of the rigidity of our service. A clergyman, however, practising it, could defend himself on authority too high to be set aside, on any ecclesiastical trial to which it might subject him, for irregularity.

[22][Huntington's note.] The Book of Common Prayer, and Administration of the Sacraments. And other Rites and Ceremonies as revised and proposed for the use of the Protestant Episcopal Church. Philadelphia: Printed for Hall & Sellers. M.DCC.LXXXVI.

The Book of Common Prayer, and Administration of the Sacraments; and other Rites and Ceremonies of the Church, according to the use of the Protestant Episcopal Church in the United States of America: Together with the Psalter or Psalms of David. The Standard Edition of 1871.

The Memorial Papers. The Memorial with Circular and Question of the Episcopal Commission. Philadelphia: E. H. Butler & Co. 1857.

The Daily Service. A Book of Offices for Daily Use through all the Seasons of the Christian year. New York: Hurd and Houghton, 1874.

[23][Huntington's note.] Much confusion of thought and speech in connection with our ecclesiastical legislation grows out of not keeping in mind the fact that here in America the organic genetic law of Church, as well as of the State is in writing, and compacted into definite propositions. We draw, that is to say, a far sharper distinction than it is possible to do in

England between what is constitutional and what is simply statuatory. There is no function of our General Convention that answers to the "omnipotence of Parliament." This creative faculty was vacated once for all at the adoption of the Constitution.

[24][Huntington's note.] Conference, p. 461.

[25][Huntington's note.] Principles of Divine Service. Vol. I, p. 390.

[26][Huntington's note.] Church Quarterly Review. London, October, 1876.

[27][Huntington's note.] The votes of the House of Bishops are not reported numerically. In the House of Clerical and Lay Deputies the vote stood as follows:

"Of the Clergy there were 43 Dioceses represented,—Ayes, 33: nays, 9: divided, 4." Journal of Convention of 1880, p. 152. [Huntington was the author of the resolution.]

[28][Huntington's note.] Church Eclectic for Nov., 1880.

[29][Huntington's note.] Remembering the deluge of "centennial" rhetoric let loose upon the country five years ago, another critic may well feel justified in finding in the language of the resolution what he considers "an unnecessary *raison d'etre.*" But it is just possible that centennial changes rest on a basis of genuine cause and effect quite independent of the decimal system. A century covers the range of three generations, and the generation is a natural, not an arbitrary division of time. What the grandfather practices the son criticizes and the grandson amends. This at least ought to commend itself to the consideration of the lovers of mystical numbers and "periodic laws."

[30][Huntington's note.] The real argument against the "driblet method" (by which is meant the concession of improvement only as is actually conquered inch by inch) lies in the what has been already said about the undesirability of frequent changes in widely used formularies of worship.

It may be true as some allege, that a revision of the Prayer-Book would shake the Church, but it is more likely that half a dozen patchings at triennial intervals would shatter it. After twenty years of this sort of piecemeal revision, a *variorum* edition of the Prayer-Book would be a requisite of every well furnished pew.

The late Convention has been twitted with inconsistency on the score of having negatived outright the proposal for a Commission to overhaul the Constitution of the Church while consenting to send the Prayer-Book to a committee for review. Discernment would be a better word than inconsistency, for although on grounds of pure theory the Constitution and the Prayer-Book seem to stand in corresponding attitudes as respects methods of amendment, in practice the difference between the two is very wide. Triennial changes in the letter of the Constitution (and these have often been made) involve no inconvenience to anybody, for the simple reason that that document must of necessity be reprinted with every fresh issue of the Journal. Old copies do not continue in use, except as books of reference, but old Prayer Books do hold their place in parish churches and the spectacle of congregations trying to worship in unison with books some of which contained the reading of 1880, other that of 1883, and still others that of 1886 would scarcely edify. Theoretically, let it be freely granted, the "driblet method" of amendment is the proper one for both Prayer Book and Constitution but the fact that the Convention had eyes to see that this was a case to which the maxims of pure mathematics did not apply should be set down to its credit, rather than its discredit.

[31]Huntington is referring to the answer regarding the Lord's Prayer, which read, breathlessly, "I desire my Lord God, our heavenly Father, who is the giver of all goddness, to send his grace unto me, and to all people; that we may worship him, serve him, and obey him, as we ought to do. And I pray unto God, that he will send us all things that are needful both for our souls and bodies; and that he will be merciful unto us, and forgive us our sins; and that it will please him to save and defend us in all dangers both of soul and body; and that he will keep us from all sin and wickedness, and from our spiritual enemy, and from everlasting death. And this I trust he will do of his mercy and goodness, through our Lord Jesus Christ. And therefore I say, Amen, so be it.

The 1892 revisers left the catechism untouched, as Huntington predicted. In 1928 it was replaced by two "Offices of Instruction" in which there is no explication of the Lord's Prayer at all.

[32] [Huntington's note.] Reprinted together with a supplementary letter in the Journal of the Convention of 1868.

[33] This was corrected in 1892.

[34] [Huntington's note.] Dr. Coit's letter of 1868, also reprinted in Journal of that year.

[35] [Huntington's note.] See *Book of Common Prayer according to the use of King's Chapel, Boston.* Among the rhetorical crudities of this emasculated Prayer-Book (from the title page of which, by the way, the definite article has been with praiseworthy truthfulness omitted) few things are worse than the following from the form for the Burial of Children, a piece of writing which in point of style would seem to savor more of the Lodge than of the Church—"My brethren, what is our life? It is as the early dew of morning that glittereth for a short time, and then is exhaled to heaven. Where is the beauty of childhood? Where is (*sic*) the light of those eyes and the bloom of that countenance?"..."Who is young and who is old? Whither are we going and what shall we become?" And yet the author of this mawkish verbiage probably fancied that he was improving upon the stately English of the Common Prayer. It is a warning to all would-be "enrichers."

[36] [Huntington's note.] A list of the more noticeable Anglican works on Liturgics published during the period named, arranged in the order of their appearance, will serve to illustrate the accuracy of the statement made above, and may also be of value to the general reader for purposes of reference.

1832. Origines Liturgicae, William Palmer. 1833-41. Tracts for the Times. 1840. Conferences on the Book of Common Prayer, Edward Cardwell. 1843. The Choral Service of the Churches of England and Ireland, John Jebb. 1844. The Ancient Liturgy of the Church of England, William Maskell. 1845. Pickering's Reprints of the Prayer-Books of 1549, 1552, 1559, 1603, and 1662. 1846. Monumenta Ritualia, William Maskell. 1847. Reliquiae Liturgicae, Peter Hall. 1848. Fragmenta Liturgica, Peter Hall. 1849. Book of Common Prayer with Notes legal and historical, A. J. Stephens. Manuscript Book of Common Prayer for Ireland, A. J. Stephens. Tetralogia Liturgica, John Mason Neale. 1853. Two Liturgies of Edward VI., Edward Cardwell. 1855. Principles of Divine Service, Philip Freeman. History of the Book of Common Prayer, F. Proctor. 1858. History of the Book of Common Prayer, T. Lathbury. 1859. Directorium Anglicanum, J. Purchas. 1861. Ancient Collects, William Bright. 1865. History of the Book of Common Prayer, R. P. Blakeney. 1866. The Prayer-Book Interleaved, Campion and Beaumont. 1866. The Annotated Book of Common Prayer, J. H. Blunt. 1870. The Liturgy of the Church of Sarum, Translated, Charles Walker. 1870. The First Prayer-Book of Edward VI, with the Ordinal, Walton and Medd. 1872. Psalms and Litanies, Rowland Williams. 1873. Notitia Eucharistica, W. E. Scudamore. 1875-80. Dictionary of Christian Antiquities, Smith and Cheetham. 1876. First Prayer-Book of Edward VI, compared with the successive Revision, James Parker. 1877. Introduction to the History of the Successive Revision of the Book of Common Prayer, James Parker. 1878. Liturgies Eastern and Western, C. E. Hammond. 1880. The Convocation Prayer-Book.

[37] [Huntington's note.] Tract No. 3. Thoughts respectfully addressed to the Clergy on alterations in the Liturgy. [It is clear to modern students that Pusey and the others opposed revision because they believed is would go in a protestant direction, not because they believed the book incapable of improvement.]

[38] The fruits of Huntington's own researches appeared in his *Materia Ritualis*, which the reader may already have noted to be the source of new texts in the 1928 and 1979 books.

[39] [Huntington's note.] One of the most curious illustrations of the spread of Anglican ideas about worship now in progress is to be found in the upspringing in the very bosom of Scottish Presbyterianism of a Church Service Society. Two of the publications of this Society have lately fallen in the present writer's way.

They bear the imprint of Wm. Blackwood and Sons, Edinburgh, and are entitled respectively A Book of Common Order, and Home Prayer. With questionable good taste the compilers have given to the former work a Greek and to the latter a Latin sub-title (*euchologion* and *Suspiria Domestica*). Both books have many admirable points, although, in view of the facts of history, there is a ludicrous side to this attempt to commend English viands to norther palates under a thin garniture of Scottish herbs which probably has not wholly escaped the notice of the compilers themselves.

[40][Huntington's note.] See *The Guardian* (London) Feb 9th, 1881.

[41][Huntington's note.] Unless "finally to beat down Satan under our feet," be reckoned an exception.

[42][Huntington's note.] Lectures on Justification, p. 330.

[43][Huntington's note.] The rationale of this curious lapse is simple. The American revisers, instead of transferring the Commination Office *in toto* to the new book, wisely decided to engraft certain features of it upon the Morning Prayer for Ash-Wesnesday. In the process, the fifty-first Psalm, which has a recognized place in the Commination, dropped out, instead of being transferred, as it should have been, to the proper Psalms.

[44][Huntington's note.] See the convocation Prayer-Book.

[45][Huntington's note.] Prayer-Book Interleaved, p. 65.

[46]William Bright's *Ancient Collects*, which also included an appendix of prayers of his own composition, was a source for revisers of 1892, 1928, and 1979.

[47][Huntington's note.] A curious illustration of the sensitiveness of the Protestant Episcopal mind to anything that can be supposed even remotely to endanger our doctrinal settlement as afforded at the late General Convention, when the House of Deputies was thrown into something very like a panic by a most harmless suggestion with reference to the opening sentences of the Litany. A venerable and thoroughly conservative deputy from South Carolina had ventured to say that it would be doctrinally an improvement, if the tenet of the double procession of the Holy Ghost were to be removed from the third of the invocations, and a devotional improvement if the language of the fourth were to be phrased in words more literally Scriptural and less markedly theological than those at present in use. Eager defenders of the faith instantly leaped to their feet in various parts of the House persuaded that a deadly thrust had been aimed at the doctrine of the Trinity. Never was there a more gratuitous misconception. The real entrenchment of the doctrine of the Trinity, so far as the Litany is concerned, lies in the four opening words of the second and the five opening words of the third of the invocations, and these it had not been proposed to touch. In confirmation of this view of the matter, it is pertinent to instance the *Book of Family Prayers* lately put forth by a committee of the Upper House of the Convocation of Canterbury. This manual provides no less than six different Litanies, all of them opening with addresses to the three Persons of the adorable Trinity, and yet in no one instance is the principle advocated by the deputy from South Carolina unrecognized. Every one of the six Litanies begins with language similar to that which he recommended. [See also in witness of the mediaeval use, which partially bears out Mr. McCrady's thought, the ancient Litany reprinted by Maskell from *The Prymer in English.* Mon. Rit. ii, p. 95.] If the Upper House of the Convocation of Canterbury, fondly supposed by us Anglicans to be the very citadel of sound doctrine, be thus taint-ed with heresy, upon what can we depend?

Polemical considerations aside, probably even the most orthodox would allow that the invocations of the Litany might gain in devotional power, while losing nothing in august majesty, were the third to run,—*O God the Holy Ghost, Sanctifier of the faithful, have mercy upon us miserable sinners.* And the fourth as Bishop Heber's glorious hymn, *Holy, Holy, Holy, Lord God Almighty, have mercy upon us miserable sinners.* But all this is doctrinal and plainly *ultra vires.*

[48][Huntington's note.] A very natural ex-

planation, by the way, of the fact, often noticed, that there is no petition in the Litany for an increase of the ministry.

49[Huntington's note.] Here, *i.e.* in connection with Saints' Day services would be an admirable opportunity for the introduction into liturgical use of the Beatitudes. What could possible be more appropriate? And yet these much loved words of Christ have seldom been given the place in worship they deserve.

They do find recognition as an antiphon in the *Liturgy of St. Chrysostom.* To reassert a usage associated in the history of liturgics with the name of this Father of the Church and with his name only, would be to pay him better honor than we now show by three times inserting in our Prayer-Book the collect conjecturally his,—a thing the Golden-mouthed himself, when in the flesh, would not have dreamed of doing. "Once," he would have said, "is enough."

50[Huntington's note.] *The Priest's Prayer-Book* has 688 (!!) mostly juiceless.

51[Huntington's note.] In connection with this clause there sprang up an animated and interesting debate in the House of Deputies as to the wisdom of thus seeming to cut off every opportunity for extemporary prayer in our public services. Up to this time, it was alleged, a liberty had existed of using *after* sermon, if the preacher were disposed to do so, the "free"prayer which *before* the sermon it was confessedly not permitted him to have,—why thus cut off peremptorily an ancient privilege, why thus sharply annul a traditional if not a chartered right?

Atfirst sight this distinction between before and after sermon looks both arbitrary and artificial, but when examined there is found to be a reason in it. The sermon, especially in the case of emotional preachers, is a sort of bridge of transition from what we may call the liturgical to the spontaneous mood of mind, and if the speaker has carried his listeners with him they are across the bridge at the same moment with himself. The thing that would have been incongruous before, becomes natural after the Minister has been for some time speaking less in his priestly than in his personal character.

The notion that the points at issue between the advocates of liturgical and the advocates of extemporaneous worship can be settled by a promiscuous jumbling together of the two modes, is a fond conceit, as the Reformed Episcopalians will doubtless allow when they have time enough to make full trial of the following rubrics in their Prayer Book:

Then shall the Minister say the Collects and Prayer following in whole or in part, or others at his discretion.

Here may be used any of the occasional Prayers, or extemporaneous Prayer.

This is bad philosophy. It need not be said that such directions are undevotional,—for doubtless they were piously meant; but it must be said that they are inartistic (if the word may be allowed), at variance with the fitness of things and counter to the instinct of purity. Formality and informality are two things that cannot be mingled to advantage. There is place and time for each. The secret of the power of liturgical worship is wrapped up with the principle of order. A certain majesty lies in the movement which is without break. On the other hand the charm of extemporaneous devotion, and it is sometimes a very real charm, is traceable to our natural interest in whatever is irregular, fresh and spontaneous.

To suppose that we can secure at any given time the good effects of both methods by some trick of combination is an error,—as well attempt to arrange on the same plot of ground a French and English garden. If indeed Christian people could bring themselves to acknowledge frankly the legitimacy of both methods and arrange amicably for their separate use, a great step forward in the direction of Church unity would have been achieved; but for a catholicity so catholic as this, public opinion is not yet ripe and perhaps may not be ripe for centuries to come. Those who believe in the excellency of liturgies, while not believing in them as *jure divino,* would be well content in such a case to wait the working of the principle of the survival of the fittest.

52[Huntington's note.] The able and fair-minded jurist who first hit upon this ingenious scheme for patching the Ratification has lately, with characteristic frankness, said substantially this under his own signature.

"The proper place for the amendment," he writes, "is at the end of the first rubric preceding the sentences of Scripture for both Morning and Evening Prayer, after the word Scripture, as every one can see by looking." He adds, "This, however, is only a question of form, and ought not to interfere with the adoption of the amendment at the next Convention. It is to be hoped that the resolution for (Committee on?) enrichment, so called, will present a variety of additions out of which an acceptable selection can be made; and when they are finally carried that the Book of Common Prayer will be not only the standard book, but a sealed book, so to speak, for as many generations as have passed since the present book was adopted." Letter of the Hon. J. B. Howe, of Indiana, in *The Churchman* for Jan. 29, 1881.

[53][Huntington's note.] See page 578 of Evangelical Catholic Papers. A collection of Essays, Letters and Tractates from Writings of Rev. Wm. Augustus Muhlenberg, D.D., during the last forty years.

The failure of this devout and venerated man to secure certain much desired liturgical improvements (although it yet remains to be seen whether the failure has been total) was perhaps due to a certain vagueness inherent in his plans of reform. A clear vision of the very thing desired seems to have been lacking, or at least the gift of imparting it to others. But even as no man has deserved better of the American Episcopal Church than he, so it is not more than right that his deeply cherished wishes should be had in careful remembrance.

[54][Huntington's note.] Now a "black-letter day" in the English Calendar.

[55][Huntington's note.] The Convocation Prayer-Book, *in loc.*

[56][Huntington's note.] Originally only an explanatory rubric. See Procter, p. 397.

[57][Huntington's note.] Let us hope that before long there may be devised some better way of providing relief for our Widows and Orphans than that of the indirect taxation of the singers of hymns.

[58][Huntington's note.] The Greek Office Books, it is said, fill eighteen quartos.

[59][Huntington's note.] In that naive and racy bit of English (omitted in our American book) entitled *Concerning the Service of the Church*, one of the very choicest morsels is the following. "Moreover, the number and hardness of the Rules called the *Pie*, and the manifold changings of the Service, was the cause, that to turn the Book only was so hard and intricate a matter, that many times there was more business to find out what should be read than to read it when it was found out."

[60][Huntington's note.] It may be wise to buttress the position taken with a quotation out of Dr. Coit.

"We really, however, do not see any necessity for either of these Services in American Books; as with us the Ordinal always *now*, makes a part of the Prayer-Book in all editions. It would be a saving to expunge them and no change would be necessary, except the introduction of such a litanical petition and suffrage with the Services for Deacons and Priests, as already exists in the Service for Bishops. The Church of England retains the Litany in her Ordinal, for that, until lately, was printed in a separate book, and was not to be had unless ordered expressly. And yet with even such a practice she has but one Communion Service. We study cheapness and expedition in our day. They can both be consulted here, *salva fide et salva ecclesia.*" Report of 1844.

[61]This prayer is matched in its degree of outspoken social concern in the Thanksgiving Day prayer "For all Poor, Homeless, and Neglected Folk," and like it was considerably toned down before adoption in the 1928 book. Both may be examined, along with their offspring, in the "Additional Prayers" section following Family Prayers in this volume, above.